The Rise of Christian Russia

Andrzej Poppe

The Rise of Christian Russia

VARIORUM REPRINTS
London 1982

British Library CIP data   Poppe, Andrzej
                                The rise of Christian Russia. – (Collected studies
                                series; CS157)
                                1. Russia – Church history   2. Russia – History
                                to 1533
                                I. Title
                                209'.47   BR932

                                ISBN 0-86078-105-4

Copyright © 1982 by   Variorum Reprints

Published in Great Britain by   Variorum Reprints
                                     20 Pembridge Mews London W11 3EQ

Printed in Great Britain by   Galliard (Printers) Ltd
                                     Great Yarmouth Norfolk

                                     VARIORUM REPRINT CS157

CONTENTS

This volume contains a total of 346 pages

To my wife, Danuta

PREFACE

The concern of this book is with the making of Christian Russia, beginning essentially with the late tenth century and ending with the early twelfth. The period from the ninth to the eleventh centuries was a formative one in the history of the Eastern Slavs. From the late tenth, but especially during the eleventh century, Christianity became a vital creative factor in the movements and transformations which were then in progress. The acceptance of Christianity in its Byzantine attire, and of Slavonic writing with its Cyrillic alphabet, determined the course along which the spiritual culture of all three Eastern Slavic nations developed during the next thousand years.

The history of this period, of the rise of Christian Russia, has long been a fascinating topic and a seemingly endless source of stimulus and discussion. In spite of this it still abounds with enigmas and capricious interpretations. The reason for this state of affairs is to be found in the extreme paucity and the laconic nature of the primary sources. It is these sources which are the subject matter of the analytical studies published here; the purpose of the latter is to lead to a review of interpretations found in the historical literature. Only in the first article, which is an attempt to capture the historical process synthetically, did the author himself to fall into greater dependence on prevailing stereotypes and abstractions.

This collection of articles is linked by the themes and problems discussed, and could be considered chapters of a condensed study. A book on the entry of Rus' into Christendom, on its joining the Byzantine Orthodox οἰκουμένη, must also be a book on Russo-Byzantine relations, on the formation of local ecclesiastical structures, and on the reception given to the Byzantine Empire in Kievan Russia. Not included in this collection is the article on the Russo-Byzantine war of 1043.[1] This refuted the thesis of M. D. Priselkov, which has prevailed since 1913, that this conflict marked a turning-point in ecclesiastical politics in Rus'.[2] Although this critique was generally accepted, the reasons for the campaign of 1043 against Constantinople are still disputed.[3] The author will return to this question at a later date. Another article, devoted specifically to the Rus'ian titular metropolitanates,[4] has also been omitted, but in compensation information on this topic may be found in studies VII and VIII. The last study in this volume (IX), on the diocesan organization of the Kievan metropolitanate, transgresses the chronological boundaries drawn above. However this breach is justified, since it would be impossible to reconstruct the development of the ecclesiastical structures of Rus', beginning in 988, without examining its status in the twelfth century.

The studies presented here represent the fruit of the author's research during the course of nearly a quarter of a century. Their publication in Western European languages – two thirds originally appeared in Polish or Russian – has given the author the chance to improve them. The author has in fact availed himself of this opportunity; as a result the studies included here are not mere translations but improved versions or second redactions. However this also eliminates the possibility of attributing any shortcomings or errors to the passage of time. The reader's indulgence is only requested as far as the translations are concerned; these are not always perfect and not always consistent in their use of terminology and in their transliteration of Slavonic and Greek names. Thanks to the editors of Variorum Reprints it has been possible to eliminate a number of errors of spelling and improve awkwardly translated passages. The author is deeply grateful to Wladimir Vodoff, Paris, Richard Bosley, Dusseldorf, and John Smedley, London, for their assistance in this regard.

One very significant, but conscious inconsistency that remains, concerns the term Rus', which if translated as "Russia" becomes indistinct from the word Rossija. When dealing with the Middle Ages it is historically justified to use the words "Russia", "Russie" and "Russland" as direct derivatives of the medieval ethnonym Rus'. However it is impossible to deny that, given the modern meaning of the word "Russia" (= Rossija), which no longer embraces all of the Eastern Slavic nations, it is preferable for the sake of greater accuracy to use the words "Rus" and "Rus'ian" in English when talking about the medieval period. In German language literature one observes that the word "Altrussland", which has been used since the eighteenth century, is gradually being displaced by the word "Rus'", although the adjective "altrussisch" continues to be used. So far French has shown itself to be less flexible as far as this type of neologism is concerned. In sum, readers of languages which do not differentiate *Rus'* from *Rossija* will have to reckon with some uncertainty of nomenclature in the future too.

Given the multilingual nature of this collection a selected index has been compiled in English.

Finally, the author would like to express his gratitude to the original publishers of these articles for graciously consenting to their reproduction in this volume.

ANDRZEJ POPPE

Warsaw
December, 1981

NOTES

1. A. Poppe, "La dernière expédition russe contre Constantinople," *Byzantinoslavica* 32 (1971), 233-68.
2. M. D. Priselkov, *Očerki po cerkovno-političeskoj istorii Kievskoj Rusi X-XII vv.* (St Petersburg, 1913) (= Russian Reprints Series XIII, The Hague, 1966), 77-115.
3. G. G. Litavrin, "Vojna Rusi protiv Vizantii 1043 goda." *Issledovanija po istorii slavjanskich i balkanskich narodov. Epocha srednevekovaja* (Moscow, 1972), 178-222; J. Shepard, "Why did the Russians attack Byzantium in 1043?", *Byzantinisch-Neugriechischen Jahrbücher* XXII (1979), 147-212.
4. A. Poppe, "Zur Geschichte der Kirche und des Staates der Ruś im 11. Jh.: Titularmetropolen," *Das heidnische und christliche Slaventum* (Wiesbaden, 1970), 64-75.

I

Das Reich der Ruś im 10. und 11. Jahrhundert:
Wandel der Ideenwelt

Die altrussische Kultur reicht mit ihren Wurzeln bis in die urslavische Vergangenheit zurück. Deren geschichtliches Erbe bestimmte die kulturelle Grundlage des gesellschaftlichen Daseins der Ruś auch im 9. bis 11. Jahrhundert, nicht aber ihren gesamten Inhalt. Die Veränderungen, in deren Verlauf der Kiever Staat hervortrat, betrafen auch verschiedene Aspekte der altrussischen Kultur. Zu deren motorischer Kraft wurde die sich wandelnde Ideenwelt der Ruś. Der vorliegende Aufsatz versucht nicht, diese Veränderungen in ihrem systematischen Zusammenhang darzustellen, sondern konzentriert sich auf ein Problem: die ideologischen Wandlungen und ihre Rückwirkungen auf die soziale Entwicklung Altrußlands im 10. und 11. Jahrhundert[1].

Das Zentralproblem der Geschichte der geistigen Kultur der Kiever Ruś war mehr als ein Jahrhundert lang die Annahme des Christentums durch die Herrschaftsträger und die Bevölkerung. Um dieses Problem häuften sich neben vielen wertvollen Beobachtungen auch nicht wenige Mythen an, von denen sich die zeitgenössische Historiographie schrittweise befreit: Sie sucht wissenschaftliche Erklärungen der Umstände, des Ausmaßes

---

[1] Die folgenden Thesen wurden in einer ersten Fassung der 4. Internationalen Konferenz über altrussische Geschichte (Berlin, Juni 1978) vorgetragen. – Wer die Frage zu beantworten versucht, in welchem Maße und in welcher Richtung die Geschehnisse des 10. und 11. Jh. die Anschauungen der altrussischen Gesellschaft verändert haben, stößt auf schwer zu überwindende Hindernisse. Die geringe Zahl der Quellen schränkt die Möglichkeit, geistige, psychische Erscheinungen zu erkennen, bedeutend ein, und eben diese Erscheinungen widerstehen an sich schon im Vergleich zu wirtschaftlichen oder politischen sehr viel stärker der Erfassung und kritischen Beschreibung. Trotzdem wird seit längerem versucht, in den Bereich dieser verborgenen Erscheinungen vorzudringen. Unter dem Einfluß des stimulierenden philosophischen und soziologischen Schrifttums der letzten Jahrzehnte, das dem Begriff „Kultur" neue Dimensionen gab, hat Alexander Gieysztor mit souveräner Kenntnis versucht, die höchst komplizierten Erscheinungen der geistigen Kultur des sich zum Christentum wandelnden Polen durch eine Erweiterung des Fragenkatalogs und durch die Anwendung eines tiefer greifenden Begriffsapparates aufzuspüren. Von den Erfahrungen meines Lehrers, die den europäischen und slavischen Hintergrund weitgehend mitberücksichtigen, gehe ich bei dem vorliegenden Versuch aus. Ein Verzeichnis seiner zahlreichen einschlägigen Veröffentlichungen enthält die ihm gewidmete Festschrift: Cultus et cognitio. Studia z dziejów średniowiecznej kultury. Warszawa 1976, S. 16–58. Vgl. besonders: A. GIEYSZTOR Les paliers de la pénétration du christianisme en Pologne au Xe et XIe siècles, in: Studi in onore di Amintore Fanfani. Band 1, Milano 1962, S. 327–367; DERS. La strutturazione culturale dei paesi slavi nell'alto medioevo, in: Settimane di studio del Centro italiano di studi sull'alto medioevo. Band 11, Spoleto 1964, S. 371–392 (Discussione S. 425–439); DERS. Uwagi o kulturze Polski najstarszej, in: Studi slavistici in onore di Carlo Verdiani. Pisa 1979, S. 115–119. Ein zusätzliches Problem liegt in der Terminologie, die, sofern sie auch moderne Begriffe verwenden muß, die Gefahr nicht nur sprachlicher Anachronismen mit sich bringt. Da es sich nicht vermeiden läßt, solche modernen Begriffe zu gebrauchen, wenn man vielschichtige und komplizierte mittelalterliche Realitäten mitteilbar erfassen will, erscheint es zumindest angebracht, die in solchen Fällen postulierte Begriffsneutralität zu betonen. Auch ist bei Übersetzungen der jeweils eingebürgerte Sprachgebrauch zu berücksichtigen: Die Übersetzung knjaź = Fürst mag für die Kiever Zeit falsch sein, aber hätte das historisch adäquate „König" nicht zu neuen Komplikationen geführt? Zur Begriffsproblematik im altrussischen Bereich vgl. G. STÖKL Die Begriffe Reich, Herrschaft und Staat bei den orthodoxen Slawen, in: Saeculum 5 (1954) S. 104–118.

und der Qualität dieser Erscheinung². Auf methodologischer Ebene führt diese Suche zur Feststellung verschiedenartiger Aspekte des frühmittelalterlichen Denkens, die zuvor von der Wissenschaft nicht wahrgenommen wurden, da diese sich hauptsächlich mit der Religion befaßte. Diese Aspekte richten unsere Aufmerksamkeit auf ein entwickeltes politisches Denken der sozialen Oberschicht, die den Kiever Staat aufbaute und ihm ein neues Klassengefüge gab.

Der ostslavische Grundwortschatz war bereits in der älteren Epoche so reichhaltig, daß er nicht nur zur Definition äußerer Erscheinungen, darunter auch sozialer, sondern ebenso von Erscheinungen des psychischen Lebens und sogar nicht weniger abstrakter Begriffe ausreichte³. Die Erforschung der ältesten altrussischen Schriftdenkmäler hat gezeigt, wieviel Ideenintensität und politische Spannung die Geschichtsschreibung, hagiographische Erzählungen und andere Werke der kirchlichen Literatur aus der Zeit Jaroslavs des Weisen, seiner Söhne und seiner Enkel bergen⁴. Das über die Geschichte des Kiever Staates gesammelte positive Wissen entzieht heutzutage der These jegliche Grundlage, nach der allein der Taufakt den Weg zu einer qualitativ neuen sozialen Entwicklung der Ruś geöffnet habe. Was wir über die Stellung der fürstlichen Macht und die gesellschaftliche

² Die einschlägige Literatur ist aufgeführt bei A. POPPE The Political Background to the Baptism of Ruś, in: Dumbarton Oaks Papers 30 (1976) S. 195–244, hier S. 197, Anm. 2; vgl. auch S. 243–244. Ergänzend hierzu: G. G. LITAVRIN Kul'turnye svjazi drevnej Rusi i Vizantii v XI–XII vv., in: Doklady na III Meždunarodnyj s-ezd po izučeniju stran Jugovostočnoj Evropy. Moskva 1974, S. 1–19, der die Rolle des byzantinischen Erbes zutreffend einschätzt. Damit kann die einseitige, aber gelegentlich immer noch auftauchende These von der kulturellen Eigenständigkeit der Ruś wohl als überwunden gelten. Zu verweisen ist ferner auf den Sammelband: Religija i cerkoʻ v istorii Rossii (Sovetskie istoriki o pravoslavnoj cerkvi v Rossii). Moskva 1975, S. 15–62; er enthält im Kapitel „Die Annahme des Christentums in der Ruś" eine Neuausgabe der Aufsätze von S. BACHRUŠIN (1937), B. GREKOV (1953) und M. TICHOMIROV (1955, 1963), wobei bedauerlicherweise der solide Aufsatz von S. BACHRUŠIN K voprosu kreščenija Kievskoj Rusi, ursprünglich in: Istorik-Marksist (1937) Nr. 2, S. 61–76, gekürzt wurde. Im Vergleich dazu verwirrend wirkt O. M. RAPOV O nekotorych pričinach kreščenija Rusi, in: Vestnik Moskovskogo universiteta. Serija 9: Istorija 31 (1976) Nr. 4, S. 55–70. Vgl. auch die interessanten, von der Soziologie inspirierten Bemerkungen Wilinbachows über Weltanschauung und Mentalität der Heiden sowie den seiner Meinung nach destruktiven Umbruch, den die Christianisierung bewirkte: Das Christentum habe die homogene psychologische Struktur erschüttert, sei aber nicht imstande gewesen, eine neue Stabilität zu schaffen. W. B. WILINBACHOW Spoɬeczno-psychologiczny aspekt chrystjanizacji Rusi Kijowskiej, in: Kultura i Spoɬeczeństwo 18 (1974) Nr. 2, S. 13–37.

³ Vgl. P. JA. ČERNYCH Očerk russkoj istoričeskoj leksikologii. Drevnerusskij period. Moskva 1956, S. 87–93; A. GIEYSZTOR Z zagadnień historii kultury staroruskiej: Skɬadniki rodzime i obce, in: Studia historica. W 35-lecie pracy naukowej Henryka Łowmiańskiego. Warszawa 1958, S. 73–89, hier S. 78.

⁴ Darüber besteht in der Forschung grundsätzlich Einigkeit, wenn auch die Akzente verschieden gesetzt werden. Etwas zu weit ging wohl M. D. Priselkov, der in einem Chronisten vor allem einen Politiker sehen wollte. Zur umfangreichen Literatur über die altrussische Geschichtsschreibung siehe D. S. LICHAČEV Russkie letopisi i ich kul'turno-istoričeskoe značenie. Moskva 1947, S. 76–100; V. I. BUGANOV Otečestvennaja istoriografija russkogo letopisanija. Obzor sovetskoj literatury. Moskva 1975, S. 49–64, 130–151, 229–246; H.-J. GRABMÜLLER Die russischen Chroniken des 11.–18. Jahrhunderts im Spiegel der Sowjetforschung (1917–1975). II. Die „Povest' vremennych let", in: Jahrbücher für Geschichte Osteuropas. N. F. 25 (1977) S. 66–90; Sovetskoe istočnikovedenie Kievskoj Rusi. Leningrad 1979, S. 18–34. Über andere literarische Denkmäler vgl. I. U. BUDOVNIC Obščestvenno-političeskaja mysl' drevnej Rusi (XI–XIV vv.). Moskva 1960, S. 103–183; W. PHILIPP Ansätze zum geschichtlichen und politischen Denken im Kiewer Rußland. Darmstadt 1967 (reprograph. Nachdruck der Ausgabe von 1940), S. 6–33, 81–95; JA. N. ŠČAPOV Nekotorye voprosy ideologii drevnej Rusi v osveščenii buržuaznoj istoriografii, in: Kritika buržuaznych koncepcij istorii Rossii perioda feodalizma. Sbornik statej. Moskva 1962, S. 215–233.

Position des Adels in vorchristlicher Zeit wissen, widerspricht dem[5]. Heute besteht keine Möglichkeit mehr, die heidnische Ruś dadurch in das Dunkel sozialer und politischer Primitivität zu stoßen, daß man dem Christentum das ganze Verdienst an der Modernisierung der altrussischen Lebensweise zuschreibt. Die Rezeption des Christentums war das Werk einer Gesellschaftsgruppe, die sich ihrer politischen Ziele und der Mittel zu deren Durchsetzung bewußt war und den Gedanken einer politischen und kulturellen Isolierung entschieden verwarf.

Die Erbauer des altrussischen Staates fühlten die Notwendigkeit einer geschlossenen Lehre von Glauben und Anschauungen, die einmal die herrschende Schicht konsolidieren und sich gleichzeitig umfassend auf die Gesamtgesellschaft bei der Ausweitung und Vertiefung ihrer Verbindungen mit der politischen Organisation des jungen, ständig im Ausbau befindlichen Staates auswirken würde. Die Suche nach Möglichkeiten der Befriedigung dieses Bedürfnisses führte zum Ausbau und zur Politisierung heidnischer Kulte durch ihre Bindung an das Machtzentrum, was ihnen eine entsprechende religiöse Resonanz sichern sollte. In Kiev wurde schrittweise ein Pantheon heidnischer Gottheiten – nach den Namen zu urteilen – verschiedener Herkunft aufgebaut[6]. Vladimir, der die Bemühungen seiner Vorgänger um Stärkung der fürstlichen Autorität und um politisch-ideologische Geschlossenheit des Kiever Staates fortsetzte, versuchte, ehe die Stunde ihrer Abschaffung schlug, die konkurrierenden Stammes-„Bekenntnisse" zu ordnen. Doch dem Pantheon personifizierter Gottheiten war es nicht bestimmt, die lokalen Sippen- und Stammes-„Bekenntnisse" der breiten Volksmassen, die sich mit weniger entwickelten Kultformen zufriedengaben, in eine Einheit zusammenzuschließen. Die unternommenen Versuche spiegelten die Krise des archaischen Glaubenssystems wider und kündigten seinen Zerfall unter dem Einfluß einer neuen Gesellschaftsordnung an.

---

[5] Vgl. S. V. JUŠKOV Obščestvenno-političeskij stroj i pravo Kievskogo gosudarstva. Moskva 1949, S. 76ff., 90–99; H. ŁOWMIAŃSKI Początki Polski. Z dziejów Słowian w I tysiącleciu n. e. Band 3, Warszawa 1967, S. 478–482, Band 5, Warszawa 1973, S. 125–145, 177–223; V. V. MAVRODIN Obrazovanie drevnerusskogo gosudastva i formirovanie drevnerusskoj narodnosti. Leningrad 1971, S. 95–135; K. ZERNACK Fürst und Volk in der ostslavischen Frühzeit, in: Forschungen zur osteuropäischen Geschichte 18 (1973) S. 9–23; A. SOLOVIEV Byzance et la formation de l'Etat russe. Recueil d'études. London 1979, besonders die Aufsätze I, II, XIII und aus VIII (Reges Russorum paganorum) S. 145–149; CH. LOVMJAŃSKIJ [H. ŁOWMIAŃSKI] O proischoždenii russkogo bojarstva, in: Vostočnaja Evropa v drevnosti i srednevekóve. Sbornik statej. Moskva 1978, S. 93–100; H. RÜSS Adel in Altrußland, in: Lexikon des Mittelalters. Band 1, Lfg. 1. Zürich, München 1977, Sp. 133–137. Gerade die zuletzt genannte Zusammenfassung legt es nahe festzustellen, daß die ältere Geschichte des ostslavischen Adels trotz einzelner ausgezeichneten Beobachtungen noch einer grundlegenden Erforschung bedarf.

[6] Vgl. E. ANITCHKOFF [ANIČKOV] Old Russian Pagan Cults, in: Transactions of the Third International Congress for the History of Religions. Band 2, Oxford 1908, S. 244–259; DERS. Jazyčestvo i drevnjaja Ruś. S.-Peterburg 1914, S. 313–320; GIEYSZTOR Z zagadnień historii kultury staroruskiej S. 77ff. Im Gegensatz dazu vertritt Łowmiański die Ansicht, daß Vladimirs Religionsreform auf die Umwandlung des slavischen Prototheismus in einen slavischen Monotheismus (Perun) abzielte. Das Kiever Pantheon, wie es die Chronik schildert, ist seiner Meinung nach eine erst später (um 1080) in den früheren Chronikbericht interpolierte künstliche Kombination. Vgl. H. ŁOWMIAŃSKI Religia Słowian i jej upadek w VI – XII w. Warszawa 1979, S. 113–119, 400. Auch abgesehen von der Frage, ob es einen solchen früheren Bericht überhaupt gegeben hat, ist Łowmiańskis Interpretation wenig überzeugend. Zwar ist einzuräumen, daß Ilarions Erwähnungen von Götzen topischen Charakter haben (vgl. L. MÜLLER Die Werke des Metropoliten Ilarion. München 1971, S. 37, 43), aber diese literarische Ausdrucksweise entsprach um das Jahr 1050 doch wohl der Überzeugung des Verfassers und seiner herrschaftlichen Zuhörer, daß am Vorabend der Taufe in Kiev Polytheismus geherrscht hat.

Ähnlich wie andere europäische Staaten, die im 10. Jahrhundert im Verlauf oder sogar bei Beginn der Konstituierung der frühfeudalen Monarchie das Christentum annahmen, sprach sich die Ruś entschieden für diese Lösung der politischen Probleme aus, die von außen und im Innern auch auf der Kultebene zunahmen. Die herrschende Schicht der altrussischen Gesellschaft erkannte mit der Annahme des Christentums diese Lösung als nützlicher und zweckmäßiger denn andere an. Kontakte mit christlichen Ländern sowie frühere, ins 9. Jahrhundert zurückreichende und im 10. Jahrhundert zunehmende Versuche, das Christentum anzunehmen, hatten hier einen nicht zu unterschätzenden Einfluß[7].

Auch wenn man vor allem die innere Umgestaltung berücksichtigt, die sich unter dem Zeichen der Christianisierung vollzog, sowie die innere politische und intellektuelle Reife, die notwenig war, um das Christentum anzunehmen, kann man doch nicht den sehr wesentlichen internationalen Kontext der Entscheidung Vladimirs und seiner Umgebung vom Herbst 987 unbeachtet lassen. Die diplomatische Initiative des byzantinischen Kaisers eröffnete dem Kiever Fürsten nicht nur den Zutritt zur Familie der christlichen Herrscher, sondern sicherte ihm auch in ihr einen hervorragenden Platz dank der Vermählung mit einer Porphyrogenita und dank der politischen Bedeutung, die mit den Erfolgen Basilius' II. wuchs, die dieser mit Hilfe der russischen Hilfstruppen errang. Die schon früher herangereifte Wendung vollzog sich in einer politischen Situation, wie sie für die Ruś gar nicht günstiger sein konnte[8].

Der altrussische Staat entstand nicht auf Neuland; er hatte die Erfahrungen all der slavischen und nichtslavischen Herrschaftsorganisationen in sich aufgenommen, die einstmals auf den Gebieten bestanden hatten, über die er sich erstreckte[9]. Der Vielvölkercharakter des in seiner Grundlage slavischen Staates begünstigte die Rezeption des historischen Erbes und den Drang, ihm eine Form zu geben, für die als ausgezeichnetes Vorbild das multinationale byzantinische Kaiserreich und – vielleicht bescheidener, aber gleichzeitig auch viel instruktiver – das sich in statu nascendi befindende „Römische Reich" der Ottonen in Frage kam. Die regierenden Kreise in Kiev verfolgten mit Interesse die sich im Westen vollziehende – aber mit byzantinischen Säften genährte – Renovatio

---

[7] Dazu L. MÜLLER Byzantinische Mission nördlich des Schwarzen Meeres vor dem elften Jahrhundert, in: Proceedings of the XIIIth International Congress of Byzantine Studies, Oxford 1966. London 1967, S. 29–39; A. P. VLASTO The Entry of the Slavs into Christendom. An Introduction to the Medieval History of the Slavs. Cambridge 1970, S. 236–254; FR. DVORNIK Byzantine Missions Among the Slavs. SS. Constantine-Cyril and Methodius. New Brunswick, N. J. 1970, S. 262–270; G. OSTROGORSKY Byzanz und die Kiever Fürstin Olga, in: DERS. Byzanz und die Welt der Slawen. Beiträge zur Geschichte der byzantinisch-slawischen Beziehungen. Darmstadt 1974, S. 35–52. Jüngste, mit reichen Literaturangaben ausgestattete Zusammenfassung von CH. HANNICK in: Kirchengeschichte als Missionsgeschichte. Band 2: Die Kirche des früheren Mittelalters. 1. Halbband. Münster 1978, S. 232–351.
[8] Vgl. POPPE The Political Background to the Baptism of Ruś S. 197–244.
[9] Dazu grundlegend, mit eingehender Darlegung der verschiedenen Meinungen und umfangreicher Berücksichtigung der bisherigen Literatur, ŁOWMIAŃSKI Początki Polski Band 5, S. 9–223 (Kap. 1: Die Anfänge des altrussischen Staates). Zur ethnischen Vielfalt des Kiever Reiches vgl. V. T. PAŠUTO Osobennosti ėtničeskoj struktury drevnerusskogo gosudarstva, in: Acta Baltico-Slavica. Band 6, Białystok 1969, S. 159–174; englisch DERS. The Place of Ancient Rus in the History of Europe, in: The Comparative Historical Method in Soviet Mediaeval Studies. Moscow 1979, S. 40–66, hier S. 40–53; DERS. Ethnische Vielfalt und Klassenkampf in der Alten Rus', in: Quellen und Studien zur Geschichte Osteuropas. Band 23, Berlin 1977, S. 17–30. Zur Ausbreitung der Ostslaven im 9.–11. Jh. zusammenfassend B. WIDERA Zur ostslavischen Kolonisation in vormongolischer Zeit. Unter besonderer Berücksichtigung des archäologischen Materials, in: Jahrbuch für Geschichte der UdSSR und der volksdemokratischen Länder Europas 7 (1963) S. 259–317.

Imperii; nüchtern ergründeten sie die wiederbelebten universalistischen Neigungen im bescheideneren Maßstab der Welt der lateinischen kulturellen Tradition[10]. Man mag bezweifeln, ob ein ähnlicher Gedanke in Osteuropa bewußt entstand, aber es unterliegt keinem Zweifel, daß versucht wurde, ihn in die Tat umzusetzen. Die in der neuzeitlichen Geschichtsschreibung vorkommenden Bezeichnungen „Imperium der Rurikiden", „Kiever Reich" drücken diese Tatsache in einem bestimmten Grad aus[11]. Der Metropolit Ilarion, der an den „alten" Igoŕ und den „ruhmreichen" Svjatoslav erinnert, geht nicht auf die ersten Seiten der Geschichte der Ruś-Herrschaft zurück, sondern erwähnt erst ausführlich die Erbauer dieses Reiches, eines Landes, „von dem man weiß und hört an allen vier Enden der Erde"[12]. Die ideologische Begründung dieser Herrschaft läßt sich deutlich in der „Rede vom Gesetz und der Gnade" ablesen. Im Unterschied zu den westlichen Übergriffen gibt es in ihr keinen Eingriff in die Rechte des Kaisers der „Oikumene der Romäer". Geführt von dem „Wesensverwandten Konstantins des Großen" und „apostel-

[10] Die beiden bekannten russischen Gesandtschaften an den Hof Ottos I. in den Jahren 959 und 973 weisen auf das Interesse hin, das die ottonische Politik am Kiever Hof fand. Auch die Heirat Vladimirs mit der Anna Porphyrogenita muß in Kreisen des deutschen Hochadels lebhaftes Echo hervorgerufen haben. Die Erinnerungen an byzantinische Arroganz im Zusammenhang mit den erfolglosen Versuchen, eine Porphyrogenita als Gemahlin für Otto II. zu gewinnen, belebten sich. THIETMAR hat diese Mißstimmung wohl zutreffend wiedergegeben und dabei ein Porträt des wollüstigen russischen Herrschers gezeichnet, der den „renovatoribus Imperii" zuvorgekommen war (Chronicon lib. IV, 73; VII, 72; VIII, 32). Vladimirs Erfolg beeinflußte wohl auch die Bemühungen um eine porphyrgeborene Braut für Otto III. in den Jahren 995–1001. Vgl. M. HELLMANN Vladimir der Heilige in der zeitgenössischen abendländischen Überlieferung, in: Jahrbücher für Geschichte Osteuropas. N. F. 7 (1959) S. 397–412, hier S. 408–411; P. E. SCHRAMM Kaiser, Könige und Päpste. Gesammelte Aufsätze zur Geschichte des Mittelalters. Band 3, Stuttgart 1969, S. 204–208, 218–220, 235–238; POPPE The Political Background to the Baptism of Ruś S. 230–231, Anm. 114. Zusammenfassend über die deutsch-russischen Beziehungen im 10. und 11. Jh. V. T. PAŠUTO Vnešnjaja politika Drevnej Rusi. Moskva 1968, S. 119–123, 325–326 (eine neue Fassung dieses Buches in deutscher Sprache wird vorbereitet). Vgl. auch T. MANTEUFFEL Les tentatives d'ent:ainement de la Russie de Kiev dans la sphère d'influence latine, in: Acta Poloniae Historica 22 (1970) S. 36–42; M. V. SVERDLOV Političeskie otnošenija Rusi i Germanii X – pervoj poloviny XI v., in: Problemy istorii meždunarodnych otnošenij. Sbornik statej pamjati E. V. Tarle. Leningrad 1972, S. 282–297.

[11] Vgl. V. T. PAŠUTO Osobennosti struktury Drevnerusskogo gosudarstva, in: Drevnerusskoe gosudarstvo i ego meždunarodnoe značenie. Moskva 1965, S. 82–83; SOLOVIEV Byzance, Aufsatz I, S. 267–268. Die Bezeichnung „the Empire of Rurikids" geht auf das Schrifttum des 19. Jh. zurück und verdankt ihre spätere Popularität Karl Marx, der sie im Vergleich mit dem *imperium* Karls des Großen anwandte (in: „The Free Press" Nr. 26 vom 4. Februar 1857; die Popularität folgte allerdings erst dem Erscheinen der Marxschen Feuilletons in Buchform unter dem Titel: Secret Diplomatic History of the Eighteenth Century. London 1899, dort S. 76–77). Mögen auch manche Charakteristika eines Imperiums an der Kiever Ruś feststellbar sein, im ganzen paßt der Begriff schlecht zur russischen Geschichte des 10.–12. Jh.: Er ist vor allem zu statisch, um einen durch Mutabilität gekennzeichneten, gewissermaßen flüssigen Zustand zu treffen. Im Russischen klingt *imperija* geziert und wird für die Kiever Ruś selten gebraucht. Sehr viel zutreffender ist das von S. V. Bachrušin eingeführte Äquivalent „Deržava Rjurikovičej" (*deržava* in der Bedeutung von Herrschaft plus Macht). Im Gegensatz zu *imperium* scheint der deutsche Terminus „Reich" – für das alte Rußland der Kiever Zeit häufig gebraucht – der historischen Realität und deren polynomischer Struktur besser zu entsprechen. Vgl. dazu auch STÖKL Die Begriffe Reich, Herrschaft und Staat (siehe Anm. 1) und DERS. Imperium und imperiale Ideologie – Erfahrungen am Beispiel des vorpetrinischen Rußland, in: Vom Staat des Ancien Régime zum modernen Parteienstaat. Festschrift für Theodor Schieder zu seinem 70. Geburtstag. München 1978, S. 27–39, hier S. 29.

[12] Nach der ausgezeichneten deutschen Übersetzung von MÜLLER Die Werke des Metropoliten Ilarion S. 41–42; hier auch ausführliche Literaturangaben. Vgl. ferner PHILIPP Ansätze S. 6–23; A. SOLOVIEV Zur Lobrede des Metropoliten Hilarion, in: DERS. Byzance, Aufsatz III, S. 58–63.

gleichen" Vladimir und seinen Nachfolgern nimmt die Ruś, eine neue christliche Macht, ihren ihr eigenen Platz ein. Das historische Bewußtsein Ilarions, eine Frucht der byzantinisch-christlichen Kultur, erwächst aus dem heimischen Boden des politischen und historischen Denkens. Dank seiner subtilen Orientierung über den Inhalt der Titulatur der byzantinischen Kaiser bedenkt Ilarion die russischen Herrscher mit dem Titel „Kagan", der seines Erachtens dem Alleinherrscher der Ruś eher entspricht als der bereits zu verbreitete Titel „knjaź", der zudem noch bei seiner farblosen griechischen Übersetzung mit „Archon" seines Wesensinhalts beraubt wurde[13].

Der integrierenden Bedeutung der slavischen Sprache war man sich in der Ruś vermutlich schon im 10. Jahrhundert bewußt. Der Slavisierungsprozeß der Oberschicht mit der Dynastie an der Spitze hatte bereits früher eingesetzt. Der in den dreißiger Jahren des 10. Jahrhunderts geborene Svjatoslav, der Sohn Igors, trägt bereits einen slavischen Namen. Dieser Prozeß spiegelte sich auch in der zeitgenössischen slavischen Übersetzung der Verträge von 911 und 944 wider[14]. Trotz der – nach den Namen zu urteilen – skandinavischen Abstammung der Mehrheit der vertragschließenden Kiever Gesandten wurde die slavische Sprache als Staatssprache der Ruś anerkannt. Dabei spielte unzweifelhaft die sprachlich verwandte bulgarische Kultur eine Rolle. Sie drang während des ganzen 10. Jahrhunderts in das Dnjeprgebiet ein[15]. Diese Tatsache mußte nicht die Wahl des

---

[13] Unserer Meinung nach hat es Ilarion im Verständnis des geschichtlichen Zusammenhanges von Kaisertitel und Orbis Romanus ganz bewußt vermieden, Vladimir *cesař* zu nennen, weil er ihn dem *basileus* gleichstellt (vgl. L. MÜLLER [Hrsg.] Des Metropoliten Ilarion Lobrede auf Vladimir den Heiligen und Glaubensbekenntnis. Nach der Erstausgabe von 1844 neu hrsg. Wiesbaden 1962, S. 110, 117–118). Bei der Anwendung des Kagantitels ging es Ilarion offenbar darum, das Prestige des russischen Herrschers, seine Geltung in der Familie der christlichen Könige zu erhöhen. Dabei stimme ich jedoch nicht der verbreiteten Ansicht zu, daß der Gebrauch dieses Titels in direkter Verbindung mit dem Erbe des Chasarenreiches stehe, ja daß es seit dem 9. Jh. ein russisches Kaganat gegeben habe. Vgl. jüngst die kühnen Hypothesen von O. PRITSAK The Origin of Rus', in: The Russian Review 36 (1977) S. 249–273. Die Anwendung des Kagantitels auf Vladimir und Jaroslav würde ich eher mit Ilarions Gelehrsamkeit in Verbindung setzen. Über die byzantinischen Vorstellungen von den Völkerschaften des Nordens, über deren Bezeichnung als Scythen und ihrer Herrscher als Kagan durch die Byzantiner wohlunterrichtet, versuchte Ilarion vermutlich, dieses Erbe für das Ruś-Land und dessen Herrscher zu nutzen (über diese Frage bereite ich eine spezielle Untersuchung vor). Auf einem Mißverständnis beruht die Ansicht, daß die Kiever Herrscher seit Jaroslav den Kaisertitel (*cesař*, erst später, was nicht immer berücksichtigt wird, zu *car* kontrahiert) beansprucht und verwendet hätten. Das vereinzelte Vorkommen des Titels *cesař* läßt zwar gewisse Schlüsse auf das Verständnis vom Wesen der fürstlichen Macht im Hof- und Kirchenmilieu zu, aber zu einem mit der Institution verbundenen Titel ist *cesař* im Ruś-Reich nie geworden. Zu diesem Ergebnis kam letztlich auch W. VODOFF Remarques sur la valeur du terme 'tsar' appliqué aux princes russes avant le milieu du XVᵉ siècle, in: Oxford Slavonic Papers. N. S. 11 (1978) S. 1–41.
[14] Grundlegend bleibt die heute fast vergessene Untersuchung von N. A. LAVROVSKIJ O vizantijskom élemente v jazyke dogovorov russkich s grekami. S.-Peterburg 1853; 2. Aufl. Warszawa 1904. Seine These einer zeitgenössischen direkten Übersetzung bei Abschluß der Verträge wurde weiterentwickelt von S. P. OBNORSKIJ Jazyk dogovorov russkich s grekami, in: DERS. Izbrannye raboty po russkomu jazyku. Moskva 1960, S. 99–120. Eine Übersicht über den Forschungsstand bietet J. BARDACH Traktaty międzynarodowe. II. Ruś, in: Słownik Starożytności Słowiańskich. Band 1ff. Wrocław [usw.] 1961ff. (im folgenden zitiert SSS), hier Band 6 (1977) S. 130–133. Unter dem Gesichtspunkt komparatistischer Diplomatik vgl. den Beitrag von S. M. KAŠTANOV O procedure zaključenija dogovorov meždu Vizantiej i Rusju v X v., in: Feodal'naja Rossija vo vsemirno-istoričeskom processe. Sbornik statej, posvjaščennyj L'vu Vladimiroviču Čerepninu. Moskva 1972, S. 209–215.
[15] Eine Literaturübersicht bietet V. MOŠIN O periodizacii russko-južnoslavjanskich literaturnych svjazej X–XV vv., in: Trudy Otdela drevnerusskoj literatury (im folgenden zitiert TODRL) 19 (1963) S. 28–106, hier S. 50–59; E. MICHAJLOV Bǔlgaro-ruskite kulturni vzaimootnošenija ot kraja na X do

Sprachgewandes des russischen Christentums diktieren; aber sie erleichterte sie jedenfalls, obwohl Vladimir die neue Religion direkt aus Byzanz übernahm. Diese Wahl der herrschenden Kreise der Kiever Ruś bezeugt ihr Verständnis der Einschätzung der gesellschaftlichen und staatlichen Vorteile eines Lobes des „neuerkannten christlichen Gottes" in slavischer Sprache. Unzweifelhaft fand sie auch starke Unterstützung bei der Kirche – ihre griechische Hierarchie nicht ausgenommen –, die sich der Bedeutung der Sprache der Kirchenbücher und der Liturgie für die Christianisierung des Landes bewußt war.

Selbstverständlich war die internationale Lage der Ruś abhängig vom tatsächlichen Kräfteverhältnis, nicht aber von der Tatsache, die als „Taufe der Ruś" bezeichnet wird. Trotzdem fügte diese der Situation ein qualitativ neues Moment hinzu: Sie brachte auf der Stelle Vorteile in den Beziehungen zu den christlichen Staaten und versprach solche auch für die Zukunft[16]. Die herrschende Schicht des Kiever Staates gewann gleichzeitig eine mächtige ideologische Waffe gegen die heidnischen Nachbarn sowie eine Motivation zur Durchsetzung und Verstärkung ihrer Oberherrschaft an der Peripherie des Staates[17].

Die Christianisierung konnte in der Ruś ähnlich wie in anderen Ländern nicht ohne Zwangsmaßnahmen erfolgen, und das sowohl bei der Einführung der neuen Religion wie auch bei der Reaktion auf Versuche der Apostasie, die vor allem seitens der einfachen Bevölkerung vorkamen[18]. Einen Erfolg bei der Unterdrückung dieser Versuche sowie die Einführung des Christentums durch Verfügung konnte nur ein gut organisierter und stabiler Herrschaftsapparat garantieren. Über den verfügte die Kiever Ruś bereits vor der Taufe. Ein charakteristisches Merkmal für die Beständigkeit der weltanschaulichen Wandlungen im Bewußtsein der herrschenden Oberschicht der Ruś ist das Verhalten der

30te godini na XIII v. v ruskata i bŭlgarskata istoriografija, in: Godišnik na Sofijskija universitet. Filosofsko-istoričeski fakultet. Band 60 (Sofija 1966/67) kn. 3, S. 195–258; DERS. Rusi i Bŭlgari prez rannoto srednovekovije (602–964g.), ebenda, Istoričeski fakultet Band 66 (Sofija 1972; erschienen 1975), S. 79–143. Vgl. auch A. I. ROGOV Kul'turnye svjazi Kievskoj Rusi s balkanskimi stranami, in: Les cultures slaves et les Balkans. Band 1: IXe–XVIIe s. Sofia 1978, S. 42–49.

[16] T. WASILEWSKI La place de l'État russe dans le monde byzantin pendant le haut Moyen Age, in: Acta Poloniae Historica 22 (1970) S. 43–51. Vgl. auch V. T. PAŠUTO Mesto Drevnej Rusi v istorii Evropy, in: Feodal'naja Rossija vo vsemirno-istoričeskom processe S. 188–200; englisch DERS. The Place of Ancient Rus (vgl. Anm. 9) S. 53–66; W. PHILIPP Russia's Position in Medieval Europe, in: LYMAN H. LEGTERS (Ed.) Russia. Essays in History and Literature. Leiden 1972, S. 18–37. Die beiden Letztgenannten gehen auf das 10. und 11. Jh. kaum ein und scheinen in verschiedener Weise die bahnbrechende Bedeutung der Annahme des Christentums zu unterschätzen.

[17] Erkennbare Merkmale einer Christusheerfahrt hat wohl erst der Feldzug von 1111 gegen die Polovcer, aber schon in Jaroslavs Zeiten wurde der Schutz der Steppengrenze zwei Krieger-Heiligen anvertraut: Im Land Perejaslav dem *archistrategos* Erzengel Michail, rechts des Dnepr am Roś dem hl. Georg (Burg Juŕev am Roś), der dieselbe Funktion auch an der Nordwestgrenze zu erfüllen hatte (Juŕev – Tartu); der hl. Georg war der Namenspatron des Fürsten Jaroslav. Die fürstlichen Tributeinnehmer, die an Fastentagen Anspruch auf Fastenspeisen hatten, wurden an der Peripherie von Priestern begleitet, die diese Gelegenheit zur Mission und zur Bekämpfung der heidnischen Magier ausnutzten; das geht aus dem Bericht des Adligen Jań über die Ereignisse am Beloozero zwischen 1073 und 1076 hervor.

[18] Vgl. A. GIEYSZTOR Mouvements para-hérétiques en Europe centrale et orientale du IXe au XIe siècle: apostasies, in: Hérésies et sociétés dans l'Europe pré-industrielle. XI–XVIII siècles. Paris, La Haye 1968, S. 159–167. Versuche, solche Erscheinungen des heidnischen Glaubens als Auftreten der Bogomilenhäresie zu deuten, scheinen doch zu weit zu gehen. Vgl. zu dieser Frage die abwägenden Bemerkungen von E. HÖSCH Orthodoxie und Häresie im alten Rußland. Wiesbaden 1975, S. 54; DERS. Zur Frage balkanischer Hintergründe altrussischer Häresien, in: Les cultures slaves et les Balkans Band 1, S. 71–83, hier S. 73–75.

Fürsten von Polock, die angesichts des drohenden Verlustes ihres Fürstentums nicht im Heidentum das Banner des Kampfes um ihre Unabhängigkeit sahen, obwohl am Fürstenhof in Polock tätige heidnische Zauberer sich weiterhin hohen Ansehens erfreuten[19]. Ganz im Gegenteil stellte Vseslav von Polock im Kampf gegen Jaroslav und dessen Söhne der Sophia von Kiev die Sophia von Polock entgegen. Vseslav, der vier seiner sieben Söhne die Namen seiner Großonkel Boris-Roman und Gleb-David gab, trug als einer der ersten zur Verbreitung des fürstlichen Märtyrerkults bei, in dem er in christlichen Moralprinzipien die Begründung seines Widerstandsrechtes und des Rechtes seiner Linie auf den Thron von Polock fand. Diese religiös-politische Demonstration sicherte ihm die Unterstützung der Kirche[20].

Die bekannten und ohne Zweifel nicht vereinzelten spontanen Aufstände der Landbevölkerung unter Führung der Zauberer im Suzdaler Gebiet in den zwanziger und siebziger Jahren des 11. Jahrhunderts und der Abfall der Mehrheit der Stadtbevölkerung in Novgorod achtzig Jahre nach der Taufe der Stadt wurden durch die fürstliche Macht unter Berufung auf religiöse Argumente gewaltsam niedergeworfen; sie drückten den Protest gegen die neue Struktur aus, die immer konsequenter in das sozio-politische und ökonomische Gewebe des Landes eingefügt wurde, und gleichzeitig auch gegen die neue, dieses System stützende religiöse Ordnung, die durch die Autorität des Herrschenden aufgezwungen worden war[21]. Die Kirche sah – den Äußerungen ihrer Vertreter nach zu urteilen – den Taufzwang als ein völlig gerechtfertigtes Mittel an und verwies mit der Proselyten eigenen Offenheit auf die Angst vor dem Herrschaftsträger als das für die Mehrheit entscheidende Motiv bei der Annahme der neuen Religion[22]. Auf die buntscheckige städtische Masse, die nicht nur auf einer Schulter Wasser trug, wirkte das Beispiel der Fürsten- und Adelshöfe, mit denen sie durch mannigfaltige soziale und wirtschaftliche Fäden verknüpft war. Die Evangelisation bei der Hinwendung zum neuen Glauben war in der ersten Zeit nach der „Taufe der Ruś" eher die Ausnahme, ein Privileg, das nur auf die soziale Oberschicht Anwendung fand.

Einige Ansichten über die Beziehungen zwischen Herrschaft und Kirche in der Ruś im Zeitalter nach der Annahme des Christentums müssen als anachronistisch angesehen werden. Die Darstellung der Kirche, angesichts ihrer jurisdiktionellen Abhängigkeit vom Patriarchen in Konstantinopel, als einer Macht, die den Interessen von Byzanz zum Schaden vitaler Interessen des Kiever Reiches diente, fand ihren Niederschlag in

[19] Vgl. Povest' vremennych let. Čast' 1–2. Pod red. V. P. Adrianovoj-Peretc. Moskva, Leningrad 1950 (im folgenden zitiert PVL), hier Band 1, S. 104 (unter dem Jahr 1044).
[20] Nicht zufällig war er im Kiever Höhlenkloster sehr angesehen, wie aus der sog. Nestorchronik deutlich hervorgeht. Vgl. A. POPPE Państwo i kościół na Rusi w XI wieku. Warszawa 1968, S. 171–175, 220; DERS. O vremeni zaroždenija kul'ta Borisa i Gleba, in: Russia mediaevalis 1 (1973) S. 6–29, hier S. 12.
[21] Vgl. M. N. TICHOMIROV Krest'janskie i gorodskie vosstanija na Rusi XI–XIII v. v. Moskva 1955, S. 64–129; N. N. VORONIN Medvežij kul' v verchnem Povolž'i v XI veke, in: Kraevedčeskie zapiski (Jaroslavl' 1960) vyp. 4, S. 25–89; MAVRODIN Obrazovanie drevnerusskogo gosudarstva S. 90–93. Es überwiegt die Tendenz, den religiösen Widerstand als eine unbedeutende Begleiterscheinung der sozialen und politischen Konflikte anzusehen. Vgl. Anm. 18.
[22] Vladimir „gebot über sein ganzes Land hin, daß man sich taufen lasse . . . und daß alle Christen seien, die Kleinen und die Großen, die Sklaven und die Freien, die Jungen und die Alten, die Bojaren und die einfachen Leute, die Reichen und die Armen. Und da war auch nicht einer, der sich seinem frommen Befehl widersetzt hätte. Und wenn jemand sich auch nicht aus Liebe taufen ließ, so aus Furcht vor dem, der es gebot, denn seine Frömmigkeit war mit Macht verbunden". MÜLLER Die Werke des Metropoliten Ilarion S. 43; vgl. auch PVL Band 1, S. 80–81 (unter dem Jahr 988).

zahlreichen Hypothesen, die allerdings durch die Quellen nicht bestätigt werden[23]. Ohne Zweifel spielte der aus der Kaiserstadt entsandte Metropolit auch eine gewisse politische Rolle als Vertreter des Kaisers und des Patriarchen am Hof des Kiever Fürsten, aber es gibt bis ins 13. Jahrhundert keine Angaben, die den Schluß erlauben würden, sein Bemühen um Annäherung und Zusammenarbeit beider Mächte habe im Gegensatz zu Staatsinteressen der Ruś gestanden[24]. Sogar im 12. Jahrhundert, in einer Zeit, als die Streitigkeiten unter den Fürsten den Zerfall des Kiever Reiches konsequent begünstigten, die Bedeutung der Kirche aber wuchs, sprach sich Byzanz, das die Möglichkeit erhalten hatte, sich in die inneren Angelegenheiten der Ruś einzumischen, unabhängig von den Motiven, durch die es sich leiten ließ, gegen die zentrifugalen Kräfte und Bestrebungen aus[25]. Tatsache ist ebenfalls, daß nicht alle vom Bosporus stammenden Hirten der Kiever Kirche dem Metropoliten Johannes II. Prodromos oder auch dem Metropoliten Nikephoros, dem Zeitgenossen Monomachs, glichen. Aber auch die Aktivitäten der genannten Würdenträger waren durch die Möglichkeiten, Fähigkeiten und die Position der lokalen Kräfte in der Kirche begrenzt, die die russische Kirche faktisch leiteten und die tragenden Kräfte des russischen Christentums darstellten. Die Obödienz gegenüber dem Patriarchen von Konstantinopel war das Ergebnis einer politischen Übereinkunft; doch die Dauer ihres Bestehens verdankt sie den festen religiösen Bindungen. Die formalen Beziehungen, die die russische Kirche mit der byzantinischen im Verlauf der Jahrzehnte nach der Taufe verbanden, vertieften sich dank der geistigen Verbundenheit des russischen Mönchtums mit den Zentren des Klosterlebens in Byzanz. Eben diese Bande entschieden über die Treue der Kirche der Ruś gegenüber den Prinzipien der Orthodoxie in ihrer byzantinischen Interpretation. Ohne Zweifel war das Mönchtum in der Ruś mit seinem religiösen Eifer und seinem Sinn für das Staatswesen dank seiner engen Verbindung mit der sozialen Oberschicht der altrussischen Gesellschaft ein entscheidender Faktor bei der Entwicklung des Christentums und der

[23] Die „Urquelle" der Mehrheit dieser Hypothesen sind M. D. PRISELKOVs 1913 in St. Petersburg erschienene „Očerki po cerkovno-političeskoj istorii Kievskoj Rusi X–XII vv." (Reprint The Hague 1966), die beherrschenden Einfluß auf die Forschung des folgenden halben Jahrhunderts ausübten. Es sei hier nur auf die Arbeiten von Hans Koch, Eduard Winter und Bruno Widera als Beispiele in deutscher Sprache verwiesen. Vgl. H. KOCH Kleine Schriften zur Kirchen- und Geistesgeschichte Osteuropas. Wiesbaden 1962, dazu die kritische Rezension von L. MÜLLER in: Zeitschrift für slavische Philologie 31 (1964) S. 434–435; B. WIDERA Jaroslavs des Weisen Kampf um die kirchliche Unabhängigkeit von Byzanz. Dynastische Verbindungen der Rus zu Deutschland und Frankreich, in: Aus der byzantinistischen Arbeit der Deutschen Demokratischen Republik. Berlin 1957, S. 158–175 (= Berliner Byzantinistische Arbeiten Band 5). Zu E. Winter siehe L. MÜLLER Neuere Literatur zur Geschichte der russischen Kirche bis zum Jahre 1054, in: Kyrios 4 (1964) S. 48–64.
[24] Vgl. L. K. GÖTZ Staat und Kirche in Altrußland. Kiever Periode 988–1240. Berlin 1908, S. 73–110; L. MÜLLER Russen in Byzanz und Griechen im Ruś-Reich, in: Bulletin d'information et de coordination. Athènes, Paris 1971, S. 96–118; A. POPPE La tentative de réforme ecclésiastique en Russie au milieu du XIᵉ siècle, in: Acta Poloniae Historica 25 (1972) S. 5–31. Vgl. auch DERS. La dernière expédition russe contre Constantinople, in: Byzantinoslavica 32 (1971) S. 1–29 und S. 233–268, hier S. 233–239; LITAVRIN Kul'turnye svjazi S. 2–9.
[25] Das Schreiben des Patriarchen von Konstantinopel an Andrej Bogoljubskij um 1166 ist in slavischer Übersetzung erhalten: Russkaja istoričeskaja biblioteka, izd. Archeorgrafičeskoju komissieju. Band 6. S.-Peterburg 1880, 2. Aufl. 1908, Sp. 63–76. Vgl. dazu GÖTZ Staat und Kirche S. 175–195; N. N. VORONIN Andrej Bogoljubskij i Luka Chrizoverg, in: Vizantijskij vremennik 21 (1962) S. 29–50, hier S. 32–50; W. VODOFF Un „parti théocratique" dans la Russie du XIIᵉ siècle? Remarques sur la politique ecclésiastique d'André de Bogoljubovo, in: Cahiers de civilisation médiévale. Xᵉ–XIIᵉ siècles 17 (1974) S. 193–215.

Kirche in der Ruś[26]. Kirche und Staat in der Ruś können einander nicht gegenübergestellt werden. Typisch für sie war nicht nur die gegenseitige Durchdringung; man kann auch ein Übergewicht des politischen Faktors, der fürstlichen Macht, über die Kirchenorganisation feststellen. Hier reichten byzantinische und westliche Muster (vor der Gregorianischen Reform) aus. Darüber hinaus wurde die russische Kirche nur allmählich zu einer selbständigen politischen Kraft (zu einer solchen wurde sie schrittweise erst im Verlauf des 12. und insbesondere im 13. Jahrhundert). Aber die Fähigkeit, die eigenen Interessen mit denen des Staates zu identifizieren, hatte die Folge, daß die Kirche zu einem wesentlichen Bestandteil seiner Struktur wurde[27].

Die zwischen dem Herrschaftsträger und der Kirche aufkommenden Spannungen muß man im Zusammenhang mit dem Verantwortungsgefühl der altrussischen Geistlichkeit für das Schicksal des Staates sehen. Als Izjaslav sich 1068 unfähig erwies, die Ruś gegen einen Überfall der Polovcer zu verteidigen, traf ihn die scharfe Kritik des Kiever Höhlenklosters. 1073 warf der Abt des Klosters, Feodosij, Svjatoslav öffentlich vor, den „Christus liebenden" Izjaslav, „für dich Vater und ältester Bruder", ungerechtfertigt vertrieben und seinen Thron eingenommen zu haben[28]. Die Vertretung der Herrschaftsprinzipien wurde für Chronisten, Verfasser und Prediger nicht nur zur Aufgabe der politischen Gegenwart, sondern auch zur Gelegenheit, die christliche Weltanschauung ihren Leser- und Hörerkreisen gegenüber zu vertreten und zu gestalten. Der Metropolit Nikephoros lehrte Vladimir Monomach mit großem Takt, die Ausübung des Herrscheramtes mit der Sorge um das eigene Heil zu verbinden[29].

Die Bezeichnung der altrussischen Kirche als Reichskirche ist also völlig begründet. Die Kirche stärkte die Autorität der fürstlichen Macht und begründete die Ausdehung des Machtbereichs des Kiever Reiches auf neue Territorien mit dem Missionsauftrag des Christentums. Der Fürst berief Geistliche in den Staatsdienst, befriedigte ihre Bedürfnisse, ernannte hohe Geistliche (Investitur der Bischöfe, Bestimmung der Äbte autonomer Klöster, Zustimmung zur Nominierung und Teilnahme an der Inthronisation des vom Patriarchen auserwählten Metropoliten) und leitete die Bischofssynode der Kiever Metropolie, die auch zu Beratungen über Verwaltungsfragen des Landes hinzugezogen wurde. Alle diese Merkmale sind der Kirchenordnung der Ruś bereits zu Zeiten Vladimirs und Jaroslavs eigen[30].

[26] Vgl. GÖTZ Staat und Kirche S. 42–45, 127–132; A. POPPE Le prince et l'Église en Russie de Kiev depuis la fin du Xe siècle et jusqu'au début de XIIe siècle, in: Acta Poloniae Historica 20 (1969) S. 95–119, besonders S. 103, 106, 114, 118.

[27] Vgl. JA. N. ŠČAPOV Cerkóv v sisteme gosudarstvennoj vlasti drevnej Rusi, in: Drevnerusskoe gosudarstvo i ego meždunarodnoe značenie (vgl. Anm. 11) S. 279–352; DERS. Cerkóv i stanovlenie drevnerusskoj gosudarstvennosti, in: Voprosy istorii (1969) H. 11, S. 55–64; DERS. Knjažeskie ustavy i cerkóv v drevnej Rusi XI–XIV vv. Moskva 1972.

[28] So Nestor in seiner um 1085 verfaßten Vita des Feodosij, vgl. Uspenskij sbornik XII–XIII vv. Izdanie podgot. O. A. Knjazevskaja, V. G. Deḿjanov, M. V. Ljapon. Pod red. S. I. Kotkova. Moskva 1971, S. 120 (f. 58a).

[29] Siehe seinen Fastenbrief an den Fürsten in: Russkie dostopamjatnosti, izd. Obščestvom Istorii i Drevnostej Rossijskich. Čast'1, Moskva 1815, S. 61–75, hier S. 72–74; vgl. Fr. DVORNIK Byzantine Political Ideas in Kievan Russia, in: Dumbarton Oaks Papers 9/10 (1956) S. 73–121, hier S. 110–112.

[30] Eine gründliche textologische Untersuchung und Édition der ältesten Denkmäler der altrussischen Kirchenverfassung verdanken wir JA. N. ŠČAPOV: Knjažeskie ustavy i cerkóv v drevnej Rusi XI–XIV vv. Moskva 1972; DERS. Drevnerusskie knjažeskie ustavy XI–XV vv. Moskva 1976 (die Ustavy Vladimirs und Jaroslavs S. 13–139). Ščapovs Untersuchung der gesamten handschriftlichen Überlieferung (älteste Hs. aus dem 14. Jh.) bringt Klarheit in die komplizierte Geschichte der beiden

Die Christianisierung rief in Gestalt des Klerus eine neue Gesellschaftsschicht mit einer besonderen sozialen Prädestination ins Leben; sie verfügte über die alleinige Vertretung einer bestimmten religiösen Ideologie, die in sich ein bedeutendes Vereinigungspotential barg. Im Unterschied zu den Opferpriestern, Wahrsagern und anderen Vertretern des Heidentums war der gesamte christliche Klerus aufs engste mit dem Herrschaftsapparat verbunden. Seine Verwendungsfähigkeit im gesellschaftlichen Leben des Staates gab ihm eine Autorität, die das Ansehen der heidnischen Priester unverzüglich überwog.

Die Geistlichkeit insgesamt unterschied sich durch ihre Fähigkeit des Lesens und Schreibens, ihre Belesenheit, mitunter durch ihre Sprachkenntnisse, vor allem durch ihre literarische Tätigkeit; sie nahm sich der Aufgabe an, dem Ostslaventum die Werte der christlichen Kultur zu vermitteln, die einen Großteil der antiken Geistesgüter in sich aufgenommen hatte[31]. Der Beginn der von dem christlichen Weltbild inspirierten geistigen Arbeit fällt bereits ins 10. Jahrhundert; denn die schöpferische Tätigkeit Ilarions, die ein derart eindringliches Beispiel der Verbindung von byzantinischer Bildung, christlicher Weltanschauung und altrussischem geschichtsphilosophischem Denken darstellte, konnte nicht auf kulturellem Neuland entstehen. Der Klerus, eine mittelalterliche Intelligenz, förderte auch die Verbreitung der Schreib- und Lesefähigkeit sowie von Bildungselementen im weltlichen Milieu; und das nicht nur unter Fürsten, Adligen und der Gefolgschaft, sondern auch unter der Stadtbevölkerung. Bemerkenswert ist, daß alle Mitglieder der fürstlichen Dynastie – die Frauen nicht ausgenommen – schon in der auf die Taufe folgenden Generation lesen und schreiben konnten. Aus dem 11. Jahrhundert erhielten sich Spuren von vier fürstlichen Bibliotheken[32].

Texte. Die Redaktionen des 13. Jh. können nun als gesichert gelten, auch hat die Hypothese, nach der die Archetypen der beiden Statute in die zweite Hälfte des 12. Jh. zu setzen seien, viel für sich. Umstritten bleibt dagegen die weitere Annahme ŠČAPOVs, daß den erhaltenen Texten die ursprünglich von den Fürsten am Anfang und in der Mitte des 11. Jh. der Kirche verliehenen Privilegien zugrunde lägen (Knjažeskie ustavy S. 307–309). Überzeugender erscheint nach wie vor die ältere Auffassung, daß zwar einige Bestimmungen in den sogenannten Statuten von Vladimir und Jaroslav auf die Zeit dieser Fürsten zurückgehen, die älteste Fassung der Statute selbst jedoch nicht vor dem Ende des 12., Anfang des 13. Jh. datiert werden kann. Vgl. dazu GÖTZ Staat und Kirche S. 151ff.; POPPE Państwo i kościół S. 210–215. Eine Übersicht über den Forschungsstand mit ausführlichen Literaturangaben bietet J. BARDACH Statuty kościelne na Rusi, in: SSS Band 5 (1975), S. 403–408. Zur Rezeption der gemischten byzantinischen Rechtssammlungen, der sogenannten Nomokanones, in Rußland ist jetzt eine weitere gründliche Untersuchung von JA. N. ŠČAPOV heranzuziehen: Vizantijskoe i južno-slavjanskoe pravovoe nasledie na Rusi v XI–XIII vv. Moskva 1978, S. 100 ff., hier besonders S. 234–238.

[31] Zur Kenntnis der Antike im alten Rußland vgl. V. N. PERETC Svedenija ob antičnom mire v drevnej Rusi XI–XIV vv., in: Germes 21 (1917) S. 205–210, 227–229, 243–247, 259–262; Germes 23 (1918/19) S. 180–185; A. I. KLIBANOV K probleme antičnogo nasledija v pamjatnikach drevnerusskoj pis'mennosti, in: TODRL 13 (1957) S. 158–181; O. V. TVOROGOV Antičnye mify v drevnerusskoj literature XI–XVI vv., in: TODRL 33 (1979) S. 3–31. Unzugänglich war mir S. I. RADCIG Antičnoe vlijanie v drevnerusskoj kul'ture, in: Voprosy klassičeskoj filologii. Vyp. 3–4, Moskva 1971, S. 3–65. Zu den Plato- und Homerkenntnissen im besondern vgl. D. ČIŽEVSKIJ Plato im alten Rußland, in: DERS. Aus zwei Welten. Beiträge zur Geschichte der slavisch-westlichen literarischen Beziehungen, 's-Gravenhage 1956, S. 45–65; A. N. EGUNOV Gomer v russkich perevodach XVIII–XIX vv. Moskva, Leningrad 1964, S. 7–23. Zur kritischen Einschätzung des Forschungsstandes über das klassische Erbe in der Ruś vgl. D. M. BULANIN Klassičeskaja kul'tura v drevnej Rusi i problema eja izučenija, in: Russkaja i gruzinskaja srednevekovye literatury. Leningrad 1979, S. 30–39.

[32] Zur Anfangsgeschichte des altrussischen Buchwesens und zu den Wegen der Textüberlieferung siehe A. POPPE Książki, skryptoria i biblioteki. III. Ruś, in: SSS Band 2 (1964), S. 544–548; N. N. ROZOV Kniga drevnej Rusi XI–XIV vv. Moskva 1977; B. A. SAPUNOV Kniga v Rossii v XI–XIII vv. Leningrad 1978. Zur Schriftkundigkeit vgl. A. POPPE Dans la Russie médiévale, X[e]–XIIIe siècles: écriture et culture, in: Annales. Économies – Sociétés – Civilisations 16 (1961) S. 12–35.

Die Geistlichkeit, in erster Linie gelehrte Mönche, die aus Adelsfamilien stammten, trug zur Vertiefung des historischen Denkens bei, das sich bisher nur in mündlicher Tradition entwickelt hatte, und gab ihm schriftliche Gestalt durch die Übernahme verschiedener Gattungen historischen Schrifttums (annalistische Notiz, Bericht, Sage, Erzählung). Die Ausarbeitung eines eigenen Verfahrens der Geschichtschreibung, die Vereinigung aller bisherigen Gattungen zu einer neuen, der Chronikschreibung, ergab in der Ambivalenz des wohl in den Klosterzellen geformten, aber durch die Mentalität und auch von den politischen Leidenschaften dieser Welt genährten historischen Gedankens am Anfang des zweiten Jahrhunderts nach der Taufe die sog. Nestorchronik, ein Werk, dessen zentrales Thema Fürstenherrschaft und Christentum in der Ruś war: Die Ausbreitung und Behauptung der Macht wird hier in engsten Zusammenhang mit der Ausbreitung des Christentums gesetzt[33].

Bevor Grundeigentum und ständige Einkünfte zur Grundlage der materiellen Existenz der Kirche wurden, verdankte der Klerus seinen Unterhalt der fürstlichen Freigebigkeit sowie der Beteiligung – übrigens in bescheidenem Umfang – an einigen Einkünften des fürstlichen Fiskus in Gestalt des Zehnten oder eines anderen festgelegten Anteils[34]. Die Chronikmitteilung über den Abtransport des beschlagnahmten Besitzes der Kiever Zehntkirche im Jahre 1018 durch den polnischen Herzog Bolesław zeigt, daß es dem

---

[33] Vgl. A. POPPE Powieść doroczna, in: SSS Band 4 (1970), S. 258–265. Weitere bibliographische Angaben bei BUGANOV Otečestvennaja istoriografija und GRABMÜLLER Die russischen Chroniken (siehe oben Anm. 4), dazu jetzt auch heranzuziehen: Sovetskoe istočnikovedenie Kievskoj Rusi. Istoriografičeskie očerki. Leningrad 1979, S. 13–34. Die beste Ausgabe der „Povest' vremennych let" (im Deutschen nur selten korrekt als „Erzählung der vergangenen Jahre", weit öfter traditionell als „Nestorchronik" bezeichnet) in: Polnoe sobranie russkich letopisej (im folgenden PSRL). Band 1. Moskva 1926, Reprint 1962; Band 2. S.-Peterburg 1908. Einen kontaminierten Text bietet die sehr populäre Ausgabe PVL Band 1 (vgl. Anm. 19). Die deutsche Übersetzung von R. TRAUTMANN Die altrussische Nestorchronik. Povest' vremennych let (Leipzig 1931) gehört zu den besten Übersetzungen dieses Denkmals, kann aber heute begreiflicherweise nicht mehr in allem befriedigen. Ein grundlegendes Unternehmen, das eine Basis nicht nur für eine neue deutsche Übersetzung schaffen soll, wurde von L. MÜLLER in Angriff genommen. Bisher sind erschienen: Band 1: Die Nestorchronik. Der altrussische Text ... Nachdruck der zweiten Auflage des ersten Bandes der „Vollständigen Sammlung russischer Chroniken" ... Leningrad 1926–1928. München 1977; Band 2: L. SCHEFFLER Textkritischer Apparat zur Nestorchronik. München 1977; Band 3,1/Lfg. 1–2: B. GRÖBER, L. MÜLLER Vollständiges Wörterverzeichnis zur Nestorchronik. München 1977–1979 (= Forum Slavicum Band 48, 49, 50, I/1–2). Dazu die Besprechung von H. BIRNBAUM in: Die Welt der Slaven 23 (1978) S. 405–411.

[34] Über die Herkunft des Kirchenzehnten in der Ruś sind bis heute die Meinungen geteilt. Die früher dominierende Hypothese einer Übernahme aus dem lateinischen Westen (vgl. H. F. SCHMIDT Byzantinisches Zehntwesen, in: Jahrbuch der Österreichischen Byzantinischen Gesellschaft 6 [1957] S. 45–110, hier S. 91–92) hat an Überzeugungskraft verloren. ŠCAPOV (Cerkov v sisteme S. 297–325) sieht im Zehnten eine bodenständige Institution, die vor der Christianisierung zur Versorgung des heidnischen Kultes diente und dann im 11. Jh. die Hauptquelle der Kircheneinkünfte wurde. Dem entgegengesetzt ist die Auffassung POPPE (Państwo i kościół S. 215–218), der Kirchenzehnte in der Ruś, der hier nie obligatorisch war, sei unmittelbar aus dem christlichen ethischen Gebot „des zehnten Gottesteils" herzuleiten. Daß dieser Zehnte am Anfang eine außergewöhnliche Leistung in der Versorgung der Kirche darstellte, wird durch die unterscheidende Benennung der Herrscherkirche in der Umgangssprache – Desjatinnaja = Zehntkirche – bezeugt, wobei klar ist, daß Vladimir nicht die ganze neugegründete Kirchenorganisation (Metropolie) mit dem Zehnten versorgte, sondern nur seine Hofkirche, die Capella regia. Auch im 11. und 12. Jh. blieb die Bedeutung des fürstlichen Zehnten (ein anderer ist nicht bekannt) für die Versorgung der Kirche sehr bescheiden. Ob und in welcher Weise ein Einfluß der Zehntenpraxis der armenischen Kirche (der erste Kiever Metropolit Theophylaktos kam aus Sebasta, der Hauptstadt der byzantinischen Provinz Armenien II) in Betracht gezogen werden könnte, bleibt noch zu untersuchen.

Klerus der Hofkirche im Verlauf eines Vierteljahrhunderts gelungen war, bedeutende Reichtümer zu horten. Es versteht sich, daß die fürstliche Kirche und die fürstliche Freigebigkeit hier keine Ausnahme darstellten, sondern ein nachahmenswertes Beispiel. Materielle Situation, Wohlstand und sogar Reichtum von Kirche und Klerus wurden innerhalb kurzer Zeit ein zusätzlicher Faktor ihrer Autorität. In welchem Ausmaß die Kirche innerhalb der ersten Jahrzehnte ihres Bestehens zur Entwicklung des Großgrundbesitzes beitrug, darüber geben die Quellen keinen Aufschluß[35]. Daß das Höhlenkloster beinahe vom ersten Tag seines Bestehens an über Dörfer mit unfreier Bevölkerung verfügte, weist nur auf die Ausstattung und Einlagen der in die Klöster eintretenden Mitglieder adliger Familien hin. Doch unzweifelhaft muß man das Auftreten einiger Formen feudaler Abhängigkeit mit der Tätigkeit der Kirche auf diesem Gebiet in Zusammenhang bringen. „Proščenniki" [Freigelassene], „puščenniki" [Entlassene], „zadušnye ljudi" [Seelenheilleute] sind Kategorien der abhängigen Landbevölkerung, die ihren bisherigen, überwiegend unfreien Status auf den der Kirche gehörenden Besitzungen in einen neuen änderten[36]. Der Beginn dieser Erscheinung reicht in die Zeit kurz nach der Taufe der Ruś zurück. Sie muß sich im 11. Jahrhundert entwickelt haben, denn im 12. war sie bereits verbreitet. Also begünstigte der Einfluß der christlichen Moralnormen auf den Adel zusammen mit einer eigenen Wirtschaftstätigkeit der Kirche die Umgestaltung in der Sozialstruktur der Dorfbevölkerung.

Der Klerus vertrat in der Gesellschaft der frühfeudalen Zeit die religiös verinnerlichte Weltanschauung in einem ausgebauten Kult, in dem er eine deutliche Monopolstellung innehatte. Das begünstigte den Prestigezuwachs dieser Gesellschaftsgruppe und trennte sie von den anderen, was zusätzlich durch die auch außerhalb der Kirche getragene besondere

[35] Ja. N. Ščapov und I. Ja. Frojanov legen die Anfänge des kirchlichen Grundbesitzes in die zweite Hälfte des 11. Jh. und verweisen dabei auf das Kiever Höhlenkloster, ohne zu beachten, daß dieses Kloster selbst erst in den fünfziger Jahren des 11. Jh. entstanden ist. Zu anderen strittigen Fragen in diesem Zusammenhang siehe ŠČAPOV Cerkov v sisteme S. 326–338; I. JA. FROJANOV Cerkovnomonastyrskoe zemlevladenie i chozjajstvo na Rusi XI–XII vv., in: Problemy otečestvennoj i vseobščej istorii. Sbornik statej. Vyp. 2, Leningrad 1973, S. 87–95; DERS. Kievskaja Ruś. Očerki social'noèkonomičeskoj istorii. Leningrad 1974, S. 73–87. Vgl. auch A. KIJAS Własność kościelna na Rusi do początków XIII wieku, in: Słowianie w dziejach Europy. Studia historyczne ku uczczeniu 75 rocznicy urodzin i 50-lecia pracy naukowej H. Łowmiańskiego. Poznań 1974, S. 115–120.

[36] Über die Bedeutung von „proščenniki" herrscht in der Forschung keine Übereinstimmung. ŠČAPOV (Knjažeskie ustavy S. 86–91, 150) hält sie für Kirchenleute, tendiert sogar zur Bedeutung „Freigelassene", entscheidet sich dann aber doch für die alte Meinung, proščenniki seien Leute gewesen, an denen sich eine Wunderheilung vollzogen hatte und die deshalb unter das Patronat der Kirche getreten waren. FROJANOV (Kievskaja Ruś S. 147–148) meint, daß unter dieser Bezeichnung abhängige und halbfreie Leute aus dem weltlichen und kirchlichen Großgrundbesitz zu verstehen seien. Die Verwirrung geht auf ein jeweils verschiedenes Verständnis des Wortsinnes zurück, da prostiti im Altslavischen nicht nur verzeihen, vergeben bedeutet, sondern ebenso auch befreien, erlösen, liberare (Slovník jazyka staroslověnského. Lexicon linguae palaeoslovenicae. Hl. red.: Josef Kurz. Lfg. 30, Praha 1976, S. 378). Wenn man dazu berücksichtigt, daß in altrussischen Übersetzungen des 11. und 12. Jh. griech. apeleutheros durch proščennik wiedergegeben wird, so wird die Bedeutung klar. Für Freigelassene stand bei Übersetzungen außerdem auch der Terminus puščennik zur Verfügung. Daß die Wahl auf das semantisch reichere proščennik fiel, das gleichzeitig von Freilassung und Vergebung kündet, ist wohl der Kirche zuzuschreiben, die nicht nur auf die Herren im Sinne der christlichen Ethik einwirkte, sondern auch den Freigelassenen einen neuen Status unter kirchlichem Patronat versprach. Somit kann proščenie in der Ruś als manumissio per ecclesiam et pro ecclesia verstanden werden. Unter Einbeziehung dieser Ergänzungen siehe A. POPPE Proszczennicy, in: SSS Band 4 (1970), S. 363–364 Vgl. auch den jüngsten Versuch, proščenniki als Freigelassene des Fiskus zu deuten, von A. JU. DVORNIČENKO K voprosu o „proščenikach", in: Vestnik Leningradskogo universiteta 34 (1979) Nr. 14. Serija istorii, jazyka i literatury vyp. 3, S. 109–110.

Kleidung und die unterschiedliche Lebensweise hervorgehoben wurde. Die Geistlichkeit der Ruś des 11. Jahrhunderts bestand in bedeutendem Maße aus Personen örtlicher, autochthoner Herkunft. Man darf jedoch nicht die zahlenmäßig geringe, aber gewichtige Anwesenheit des griechischen Klerus vergessen, der die höheren Ränge in der Hierarchie einnahm. Er kam mit einem beträchtlichen Selbstwertgefühl in die Ruś und mit dem Bewußtsein seiner Nützlichkeit für die Kirche, aber auch für Staat und Gesellschaft; er brachte desgleichen fertige Muster der Beziehungen zwischen geistlicher und weltlicher Macht mit und förderte die Entwicklung anderer, neuer Begriffe auf dem Gebiet der Ideologie und der Technik der Machtausübung[37].

Ihre Hauptaktivität konzentrierte die Geistlichkeit natürlich auf die religiöse Ideologie und auf die mit ihr verbundenen gesellschaftlichen Erscheinungen. Die beständige und schrittweise Einwirkung auf die Denkweise der Gesellschaft, in erster Linie auf die der höheren Schichten, führte zu Mentalitätsveränderungen, die nicht allein durch den Taufakt von 988 hervorgerufen werden konnten, sich andererseits aber auch nicht auf Jahrhunderte ausdehnen lassen. Die Aneignung des christlichen Wertsystems durch die altrussische Kultur ist ein Prozeß, bei dem die Kirche auf einzelnen Gebieten ihrer Aktivität unterschiedlich erfolgreich war; doch unterliegt es keinem Zweifel, daß bereits innerhalb des ersten Jahrhunderts nach der Taufe viel erreicht wurde. Verständlicherweise muß man die ebenfalls für diese entlegene Zeit charakteristische Existenz zweier Kulturen – einer Kultur der Elite und einer Kultur der Massen – in Betracht ziehen[38]. Das geschlossene Universalsystem des christlichen Glaubens erweiterte und veränderte die Weltsicht der herrschenden Schicht, lieferte soziale Organisationsmuster und neue Arten ihrer Übertra-

[37] Vgl. DVORNIK Byzantine Political Ideas; V. VAL'DENBERG Drevnerusskija učenija o predělach carskoj vlasti. Očerki russkoj političeskoj literatury ot Vladimira Svjatogo do konca XVII věka. Petrograd 1916 (Reprint The Hague 1966), S. 82–132; POPPE Państwo i kościół S. 218– 231. Ferner auch G. G. LITAVRIN Idea verchovnoj gosudarstvennoj vlasti v Vizantii i drevnej Rusi domongol'-skogo perioda, in: Les cultures slaves et les Balkans Band 1, S. 50–56. Zur Kenntnis der „Ekthesis" des Konstantinopolitaner Diakons Agapetos aus dem 6. Jh. in der Ruś, wo dieser wahrscheinlich im 10. Jh. in Bulgarien übersetzte Fürstenspiegel schon vor 1076 fragmentarisch bekannt war, siehe den brillanten Aufsatz von I. ŠEVČENKO On Some Sources of Prince Svjatoslav's „Izbornik" of the Year 1076, in: Orbis Scriptus. D. Tschiževskij zum 70. Geburtstag. München 1966, S. 723–738. Es fällt aber schwer, Ševčenko darin zuzustimmen, daß die slavische Übersetzung der *Scheda regia* in rein moralisierender Absicht „to the upper classes in general" gerichtet war. Im Licht der bekannten Daten – es sei hier nur auf das Schreiben des Metropoliten Nikephoros an Vladimir Monomach verwiesen, in dem unter anderem die platonische Gerechtigkeitsforderung gegenüber dem Herrscher zur Sprache kommt – ist Ševčenkos Voraussetzung, daß „to exploit Agapetus for ideological purposes, for instance to apply his exhortations and fawnings to the local ruler, would be unlikely in the eleventh century" (ebenda S. 729) unzutreffend. Die „Christianisierung" der fürstlichen Macht – in den Bemühungen der Chronisten und anderen altrussischen Verfasser, das ganze die Macht betreffende Ideensystem mit den christlichen Wertvorstellungen in Zusammenhang zu bringen, deutlich erkennbar – hat an zahlreichen Beispielen M. V. ŠACHMATOV gezeigt (Opyty po istorii drevne-russkich političeskich idej. Band 1: Učenija russkich letopisej domongol'skogo perioda o gosudarstvennoj vlasti. Praha 1927 (IX, XIV, 574 S., maschinenschriftlich hektographiert).

[38] Vgl. GIEYSZTOR Uwagi o kulturze S. 119; B. A. RYBAKOV O dwuch kul'turach drevnego feodalizma, in: Leninskie idei v izučenii istorii pervobytnogo obščestva, rabovladenija i feodalizma. Sbornik statej. Moskva 1970, S. 23–33. Widerspruchsvolle Vielgestaltigkeit der altrussischen Kultur betont auch W. B. WILINBACHOW Struktura kultury staroruskiej w wiekach X–XII, in: Kwartalnik Historyczny 79 (1972) S. 832–842. Vgl. ferner die interessanten Bemerkungen über kulturelle Dichotomie unter etwas anderem Gesichtspunkt bei E. PATLAGEAN Discours écrit, discours parlé. Niveaux de culture a Byzance aux VIIIe–XIe siècles, in: Annales. Économies – Sociétés – Civilisations 34 (1979) S. 264–278.

gung und Rezeption, veränderte bisher existierende Strukturen, brachte neue Arten menschlicher Tätigkeit und führte neue Kulturrealitäten ein, die einen beträchtlichen Ideengehalt besaßen: Kunstwerke, Wand- und Staffelmalerei, Bücher, Musik, Gesang, liturgisches Drama, Architektur u. ä. Die Vermehrung dieser Werte dank einheimischer Kräfte, die sich die Innovationen schöpferisch aneigneten und sie für den eigenen Bedarf anwandten, beeinflußte die Formung eines neuen gesellschaftlichen Bewußtseins, vor allem des Selbstbewußtseins der über das Schicksal der ganzen Gesellschaft entscheidenden Oberschicht. Der Kult der Fürsten Boris und Gleb sowie die Ausdehnung des Namens Ruś auf den gesamten Herrschaftsbereich der Kiever Fürsten gestattet es, in diese neue Weltsicht Einblick zu nehmen. Die Tendenz, das „russische Land" im vollen politischen, kirchlichen wie auch ethnischen Verständnis aufzufassen, reift unzweifelhaft im Laufe des 11. Jahrhunderts; gleichwohl sind wir bereit, ihre Anfänge im 10. Jahrhundert noch vor der Taufe der Ruś wahrzunehmen. Während aus Ilarions Bezeichnung „strana russkaja" das politische und territoriale Moment herauszufühlen ist, tritt in der Auffassung des Abtes Daniel auch das – so möchte ich sagen – Moment der nationalen und religiösen Gemeinschaft zutage[39]. In den Werken der altrussischen Schriftsteller des 11. und des beginnenden 12. Jahrhunderts fand in der Sprache der tiefen geistlichen Sorge um das ganze russische Land ein bestimmtes politisches Denksystem seinen Ausdruck. Dieser Zug war der gesamten altrussischen Kirchenhierarchie eigen, die durchdrungen war von der Idee der Einheit von Staat und Kirche[40]. Diese Idee, die zur Zeit der altrussischen Monarchie gereift war, wirkte auch noch im 12. und 13. Jahrhundert fort, als die Ruś trotz ihrer politischen Zersplitterung von ihren Bewohnern wie auch in Europa als eine Einheit betrachtet wurde[41]. Man kann behaupten, daß das 10. und 11. Jahrhundert entscheidende

---

[39] Vgl. MÜLLER Die Werke des Metropoliten Ilarion S. 41–42 und Register sowie L. Müllers Kommentar zu Ilarions Bezeichnung für „Land" (zemlja, strana) ebenda S. 69–74. Der Abt Daniel stellte seine Leuchte am Heiligen Grab im Namen des „ganzen russischen Landes" auf und betete an allen heiligen Stätten des Heiligen Landes für alle russischen Fürsten und Christen. Siehe: Igumen DANIIL Choženie. Abt DANIIL Wallfahrtsbericht. Nachdruck der Ausgabe von Venevitinov 1883/85. Mit einer Einl. und bibliograph. Hinweisen von Klaus Dieter Seemann. München 1970, S. 128–129, 136, 140 (= Slavische Propyläen Band 36); dazu die Rezension von A. POPPE in: Russia mediaevalis 2 (1975) S. 166–177, hier S. 170–171.

[40] Daß diese Einheit aus der Notwendigkeit erwuchs, weil es „im Bereich des altrussischen Staates wenig gab, was einigte, und vieles, was trennte", hat mit Recht WILINBACHOW Struktura kultury staroruskiej S. 840 bemerkt.

[41] Um das Jahr 1214, also in der Zeit der weitgehenden politischen Zersplitterung des Ruś-Landes, stellten sich Gervasius von Tilbury (Otia Imperialia) und seine Berichterstatter in Rom (wahrscheinlich polnische Geistliche) Russia – Ruthenia als ein von der gens Ruthenorum bewohntes, riesiges Land vor, das sich von den Grenzen Polens, Ungarns und der Kumanen bis zum Mare Norveiae auf 100 Tagereisen erstreckte. Die Entfernungsangabe dürfte einem Bericht von Kaufleuten entstammen, da die durchschnittliche Marschgeschwindigkeit auf lange Strecken im Mittelalter etwa 20 km am Tag ausmachte. Siehe: Emendationes et supplementa Otiorum Imperialium Gervasii Tilberiensis . . ., in: Scriptorum Brunsvicensia illustrantium tomus secundus. Ed. G. W. Leibniz. Hannover 1710, S. 751–784, hier S. 765; J. STRZELCZYK Gerwazy z Tilbury. Studium z dziejów uczoności geograficznej w średniowieczu. Wrocław [usw.] 1970, S. 64–65, 158, 244 (= Monografie z dziejów nauki i techniki Band 66). Ähnlich wie die „Otia Imperialia" bestimmt die Grenzen des russischen Landes die nicht später als um 1240 entstandene Schrift „Über den Niedergang des russischen Landes". Siehe JU. K. BEGUNOV (Hrsg.) Pamjatnik russkoj literatury XIII veka. Slovo o pogibeli Russkoj zemli. Moskva, Leningrad 1965, S. 154–155. Dabei gilt, wie richtig bemerkt wurde, der Lobpreis und die Sorge des „Slovo" dem russischen Reich als ganzem im Sinne der Kiever Tradition. Vgl. W. PHILIPP Über das Verhältnis des „Slovo o pogibeli russkoj zemli" zum „Žitie Aleksandra Nevskogo", in: Forschungen zur osteuropäischen Geschichte 5 (1957) S. 7–37; A. V. SOLOVIEV Die Dichtung vom Untergang Rußlands, in: Die Welt der Slawen 9 (1964) S. 225–245.

Bedeutung für die Bildung der altrussischen *Natio* besaßen. Die Impulse, die durch die neue Ideologie verursacht wurden, spielten hierbei keineswegs eine zweitrangige Rolle[42]. Das Jahr 988 gab der Perspektive von Kontakten mit einer Welt anderer Kultur neue Ausmaße und eine neue Qualität; die Erfahrungen mit dieser Kultur ließen sich dazu verwenden, Veränderungen in der archaischen slavischen Lebensweise hervorzurufen, die die Mehrheit der Bevölkerung umfaßte. Die herrschende Klasse ließ sich bei der Rezeption der kulturellen Werte von durchdachten Auswahlkriterien leiten und scheute dabei weder Mittel noch Anstrengungen. Dieses Verhältnis der Lenker des altrussischen Staatswesens zur neuen Kultur weist darauf hin, daß man sich deren Zustrom nicht nur bewußt aneignete, sondern daß er auch bestimmt war durch die Nachfrage derer, die sich die Leistungen der byzantinisch-christlichen Welt aneigneten[43]. Die neuen Kulturwerte

[42] Dieses Moment wird am meisten unterschätzt, obwohl gerade die neue Religion auf verschiedenen Ebenen wirkte und unter anderem auch die Slavisierung der nichtslavischen Komponente der Oberschicht stark beschleunigte. Zur Bildung der altrussischen Natio, die nicht alle Stammesteilungen des Ostslaventums zu umschließen vermochte und vom 13. Jh. an sich in drei ostslavischen Völkerschaften-Nationen auseinanderzuentwickeln begann, gibt es eine sehr kontroverse Literatur. Eine außergewöhnlich umfangreiche Übersicht bringt H. Paszkiewicz The Making of the Russian Nation. London 1963, S. 176–244, mit der effektvollen, aber in jedem ihrer Bestandteile unglaubwürdigen Schlußfolgerung: „Since the Rus'ian Church and the Rus'ian State were copies of the Byzantine Church and State ... the ‚Rus'ian nation' was a copy of the Byzantine nation" (S. 243). Vgl. auch V. V. Mavrodin Proischoždenie naroda. Leningrad 1978, S. 119–147 und die Literaturübersicht in: Sovetskaja istoriografija Kievskoj Rusi. Leningrad 1978, S. 36–42. Zur Auseinandersetzung in der Frage der Schriftsprache V. V. Vinogradov Izbrannye trudy. Istorija russkogo literaturnogo jazyka. Moskva 1978, S. 65–151, 301–303, 237–253, 308; A. Issatschenko Mythen und Tatsachen über die Entstehung der russischen Literatursprache. Wien 1975, S. 8–23 (= Sitzungsberichte der Österreichischen Akademie der Wissenschaften. Phil.-Hist. Kl. Band 298, Abh. 5); D. S. Worth Was there a „Literary Language" in Kievan Ruś?, in: The Russian Review 34 (1975) S. 1–9. Vgl. auch F. P. Filin Proischoždenie russkogo, ukrainskogo i belorusskogo jazykov. Istorikodialektologičeskij očerk. Leningrad 1972, S. 30–96.

[43] Die These, daß diese Rezeption unter byzantinischer Kontrolle stand und daß Byzanz eine aktive, bewußte Kulturpolitik gegenüber der Ruś betrieb, muß zumindest als stark übertrieben gelten. Vgl. Z. V. Udal'cova Russko-vizantijskije kul'turnye svjazi, in: Proceedings of the XIIIth International Congress of Byzantine Studies, Oxford 1966. London 1967, S. 81–91. Es trifft wohl zu, daß die Rezeption in mancher Hinsicht begrenzt war (vgl. I. P. Eremin Literatura drevnej Rusi. Ètjudy i charakteristiki. Moskva, Leningrad 1966, S. 9–17, wo allerdings manches übersehen ist; ferner auch N. A. Meščerskij Istočniki i sostav drevnej slavjano-russkoj perevodnoj pis'mennosti IX–XV vekov. Leningrad 1978), aber die Aufnahme geschah *modo recipientis*, denn tätig ist – wie schon Spinoza treffend bemerkt hat – nicht der, der den Einfluß ausübt, sondern der, der beeinflußt wird. Anknüpfend an Eremins These von der thematischen Begrenztheit der Übersetzungsliteratur aus dem Griechischen hat F. J. Thomson diese als „monastic inheritance" bezeichnet und diese Charakterisierung wiederum für die Behauptung gesteigert, daß nicht die Mongolen, sondern die Kirche für die intellektuelle Isolation Rußlands verantwortlich sei. Vgl. F. J. Thomson The Nature of the Reception of Christian Byzantine Culture in Russia in the Tenth to Thirteenth Centuries and its Implications for Russian Culture, in: Slavica Gandensia 5 (1978) S. 107–139. Diese Behauptung erinnert an die Polemiken zwischen „Westlern" und „Slavophilen" im 19. Jh. Sie zu entkräften, genügt der Hinweis auf zahlreiche Lesebücher, die zu dieser Zeit übersetzt wurden und Stücke von ganz verschiedenen Verfassern, auch aus der Antike (unter anderem aus gnomischen Sammelwerken) enthielten. Des weiteren ist Rezeptivität immer vielseitig bedingt und unterliegt der Entwicklung. Während über zwei Jahrhunderten nach der Christianisierung der Ruś ist viel vollbracht worden, noch mehr aber zu tun übriggeblieben. Das 13. Jahrhundert war dann aufs Ganze gesehen vor allem eine Zeit, in der das gemeinsame Katastrophenerlebnis die Gemeinsamkeit des Bewußtseins auch in der geistigen Kultur der russischen Länder förderte. Die russische Kirche wurde mit ganz außergewöhnlichen Aufgaben konfrontiert und belastet, noch ehe sie selbst ihre eigene Reife erreicht hatte. Eine eng „eurolatinozentrische" Sicht, die alles an dem eigenen Maß mißt, erschwert das Verständnis anderer historischer Realitäten auch im Rahmen Europas.

wurden zu einem wichtigen Bundesgenossen bei der Umgestaltung der lokalen Zustände und Denkweisen. Schon allein das Erscheinen der Gotteshäuser, deren Steinmassive mit der umliegenden Bebauung aus Holzhäusern und Erdhütten kontrastierten, mußte Einfluß auf die Psyche des Christen der Ruś haben – auch dann, wenn er in Wirklichkeit noch halber Heide geblieben war. Dabei schuf der Kirchenbau als künstlerischer Komplex im Schmuck seiner Fresken und Ikonen, mit kostbaren Kultgefäßen und -geräten und als Ort des Gottesdienstes und der gesanglichen und liturgischen Aktion einen unvergleichlichen Hintergrund für emotionales und ästhetisches Erleben einschließlich der religiösen Grundstimmung und Einwirkung „in seiner allseitigen Mannigfaltigkeit des Sichtbaren und Hörbaren"[44].

Von Anfang an hatte die Kirche damit begonnen, der fürstlichen Macht sakrale Eigenschaften zuzuschreiben. Prediger und Gelehrte, Ideologen *sui generis*, propagierten die Überzeugung, daß der Fürst ähnlich wie der biblische David und der byzantinische Kaiser ein Gottgesalbter sei, daß die fürstliche Macht durch Gott errichtet und daß der Fürst als irdischer Herrscher die Ikone Christi, das irdische Abbild des Urbildes des himmlischen Herrschers sei[45]. Die Kirche schrieb dem Fürsten die Rolle des Hüters der Herde Christi, des Hüters der Rechtgläubigkeit, des Lehrers und Erziehers zu, stattete ihn mit den Eigenschaften eines Seelenhirten und Erzpriesters aus und lehrte alle seine Untertanen, daß „die Geringschätzung des Herrschers die Geringschätzung Gottes selbst sei"[46]. In den zahlreichen Epitheta des russischen Fürsten (Gottgeliebter, von Gott Bewachter, Christusgeliebter, Reingläubiger, Frömmster, Orthodoxer) fand der charismatische Charakter der Macht und der Person des Herrschers seinen Ausdruck. Den gleichen Charakter erlangte die Thronbesteigung des Fürsten, die schon im 11. Jahrhundert zur

[44] Vgl. die ästhetische Würdigung der Hofkapelle Theotokos Pharos in der zehnten Homilie des Photios, in der die Deutung der Architektur durch den Menschen des Mittelalters prägnant beschrieben wird: The Homilies of Photius, Patriarch of Constantinople. English Translation, Introduction, and Commentary by C. Mango. Cambridge, Mass. 1958, S. 184–187 (= Dumbarton Oaks Studies Band 3). Über Kirchengebäude, deren Dekoration und Bildschmuck als Sinnbild christlicher Weltanschauung und Quelle von Gefühlserlebnissen O. WULFF Das Raumerlebnis des Naos im Spiegel der Ekphrasis, in: Byzantinische Zeitschrift 30 (1929/30) S. 531–539; V. N. LAZAREV Sistema živopisnoj dekoracii vizantijskogo chrama IX–XI vekov, in: DERS. Vizantijskaja živopis. Moskva 1971, S. 96–109; in italienischer Übersetzung in: DERS. Storia della pittura bizantina. Torino 1967, S. 125–136.

[45] Am eindringlichsten deutete diese Gegenwart Christi im Herrscher der Kiever Metropolit Nikephoros in seinem Fastenschreiben an den Kiever Fürsten Vladimir Monomach kurz nach 1113, in: Russkie dostopamjatnosti č. 1, S. 61–75, hier besonders S. 75 (eine neue Ausgabe dieses wichtigen Denkmals wird vorbereitet); vgl. auch DVORNIK Byzantine Political Ideas S. 110–112; POPPE Le prince et l'Église S. 107–109.

[46] Izbornik 1076 goda. Izd. podgot. V. S. Golyšenko [u. a.]. Moskva 1965, S. 241ff. Zum altrussischen Herrscherideal vgl. PHILIPP Ansätze S. 81–95; M. HELLMANN Das Herrscherbild in der sogenannten Nestorchronik, in: Speculum Historiale. Geschichte im Spiegel von Geschichtsschreibung und Geschichtsdeutung. (Johannes Spörl aus Anlaß seines 60. Geburtstages dargebracht von Weggenossen, Freunden und Schülern.) Freiburg, München 1965, S. 224–236; G. STÖKL Der zweite Salomon. Einige Bemerkungen zur Herrschervorstellung im alten Rußland, in: Canadian-American Slavic Studies 13 (1979) Nr. 1–2, S. 23–31. Zu dem letztgenannten Beitrag wäre ergänzend zu bemerken, daß der älteste bekannte Vergleich der Ruś-Herrscher mit biblischen Königen (Vladimirs mit David, Jaroslavs mit Salomon) sich bei Ilarion findet. Vgl. MÜLLER Die Werke des Metropoliten Ilarion S. 49.

kirchlichen Zeremonie wurde[47]. Die Aufnahme der Fürsten Boris und Gleb, der Oheime
dreier damals die Ruś regierender Söhne Jaroslavs, unter die Schar der Heiligen im

[47] Trat ein Fürst die Herrschaft an, so fand das offiziellen Ausdruck in der Thronbesteigung, die
nach der Chroniküberlieferung des 12. Jh. eine religiös-kirchliche Zeremonie war, wie schon GÖTZ
(Staat und Kirche S. 30–32) zutreffend festgestellt hat. Man kann DVORNIK (Byzantine Political Ideas
S. 116–120) nicht darin zustimmen, daß diese Inthronisation ein überwiegend weltlicher Akt ohne im
einzelnen festgelegtes Zeremoniell war, bei dem die Beteiligung der Geistlichkeit zunächst den
Charakter des Zufälligen hatte und erst um die Wende vom 12. zum 13. Jh. im Fürstentum Vladimir-
Suzdal' an Bedeutung gewann. Dvorniks Konklusionen ergeben sich aus einer unzutreffenden
Beurteilung der Knappheit der Chroniküberlieferung, deren genaue Analyse jedoch nicht zu der von
Dvornik postulierten zeitlichen Abfolge führt. Die Zeremonie der Thronbesteigung läßt sich
allerdings erst auf Grund der ältesten Angaben für die erste Hälfte des 12. Jh. rekonstruieren. Die
Thronbesteigung fand in der Regel an einem Sonntag statt und bestand aus folgenden zeremoniellen
Einzelaktionen: Feierlicher Einzug des Fürsten in seine Stadt. Die Versammelten – Volk, Adelige und
Geistlichkeit im Meßgewand – akklamieren ihn „mit Ehre und Ruhm". Der Bischof (Metropolit)
spendet ihm den Segen, und wahrscheinlich unmittelbar danach leistet der Fürst den Eid, gerecht und
der Tradition gemäß zu herrschen; die Eidesleistung wird allen sichtbar im Kreuzeskuß. Danach
begibt sich der Fürst, von seinem Gefolge begleitet, mit der Geistlichkeit in die Kathedralkirche, wo
der Gottesdienst stattfindet. Nachdem der Fürst in Proskinese zu Christus und der Gottesmutter
gebetet hat – bei gleichzeitigen damit harmonierenden Invocationen (Bibelstellen über Gott als die
Urquelle jeder irdischen Macht und den Herrscher als Gotterwählten, Gottberufenen) –, kommt es
zur eigentlichen Erhebung auf den Fürstenthron, der sich stets in der Kathedrale befindet. Schließlich
nimmt der Inthronisierte die Huldigung der Anwesenden entgegen („und sie verbeugten sich vor ihm
und küßten ihn mit Ehren", PSRL Band 1, Sp. 423).
   Es bleibt die Frage, ob die Praxis dieser kirchlichen Zeremonie auch schon für das 11. Jh.
angenommen werden darf. Dafür spricht folgendes: Die Thronsetzung des Vladimir Monomach
fand am Sonntag, dem 20. April 1113 in ziemlicher Eile auf Initiative der Einwohner von Kiev statt
(PSRL Band 2, Sp. 275–276), was mittelbar darauf hinweist, daß ein festgelegtes Zeremoniell bereits
vorlag. Die Inthronisierung seines Vorgängers Svjatopolk II. fand ebenfalls an einem Sonntag, dem
24. April 1093, statt, und der Chronist berichtet vom feierlichen Einzug in die Stadt sowie von
Akklamation und Huldigung der Kiever (PSRL Band 2, Sp. 209: der sehr knappe Bericht verschweigt
die Anwesenheit der Geistlichen, die sich immerhin unter der allgemeinen Bezeichnung „Kiever"
verbergen mögen). Sehen wir die Einladung der Kiever an Vladimir, den Thron „seines Vaters und
Großvaters", das heißt Vsevolods und Jaroslavs, zu besteigen (merkwürdigerweise wird wenig später
mitgeteilt, daß sich Vladimir auf „den Thron seines Vaters und seiner Großväter" setzte, was einer
speziellen Überlegung hinsichtlich der Hss.-Tradition bedürfte) und die Chronikerwähnungen, daß
Vsevolod des Vaters (Jaroslav) und des Bruders (Izjaslav) Thron einnahm (PSRL Band 1, Sp. 204, 216,
Band 2, Sp. 195, 207), im Licht der älteren Angaben für die in der Kirche befindlichen
Fürstenthron, so liegt der Gedanke nahe, daß mit „Thron" auch schon früher durchaus der real
existierende Gegenstand, nämlich Jaroslavs Thron in der von ihm gestifteten Sophienkathedrale,
gemeint sein könnte. Direkte Hinweise auf Jaroslavs Thron kommen auch bei den Inthronisationen
der Jahre 1139 und 1169 vor (PSRL Band 1, Sp. 306, Band 2, Sp. 535). Bemerkenswert ist, daß auch
Jaroslav selbst sich im Jahre 1016 auf den „väterlichen" Thron setzte (PSRL Band 1, Sp. 142, Band 2,
Sp. 129; das nur in der Laurentius-Hs. vorkommende „großväterlichen" ist offensichtlich eine
spätere Hinzufügung); hier dürfen wir wohl an den Thron Vladimirs in der Zehntkirche-*Capella regia*
denken, der einzigen Steinkirche in Kiev zu dieser Zeit. Es ist gewiß nicht abwegig anzunehmen, daß
der Brauch, in der Kirche zu thronen, und die Idee einer beim Antritt des Herrscheramtes durch die
Kirche vermittelten Sanktion Gottes durch die Anna Porphyrogenita und den Metropoliten
Theophylaktos nach Kiev gebracht wurden. Die Kiever Herrscher und ihre Umgebung sind sich
dessen bewußt geworden, daß der christliche Charakter des Fürstenamtes einer Bestätigung bedurfte
und sie auf diese Weise fand. So wurde die Praxis des kirchlichen Zeremoniells bei der Thronbesteigung in den wesentlichen Zügen als fertige Form rezipiert, und als vom Ende des 11. Jh. an die
russischen Chronisten zu Wort kamen, war sie bereits eine altgewohnte Tradition, deren Einzelheiten
nicht mehr beschreibenswert erschienen.
   Mit einem Krönungs- und Salbungsakt ist die Inthronisation der russischen Fürsten im 12. Jh.
allerdings nicht verbunden gewesen, wie W. K. MEDLIN (Moscow and East Rome. A Political Study of

Jahr 1072 heiligte die ganze fürstliche Dynastie[48]. Die Apotheose des Fürstenhauses wurde in den vierziger Jahren des 11. Jahrhunderts programmäßig in den Wandmalereien der Sophienkathedrale in Kiev verewigt. Die Stiftungskomposition beträchtlichen Ausmaßes (25 m²) im Westteil des Hauptschiffes der Kathedrale, die Jaroslav den Weisen mit seiner Familie darstellt, korrespondiert deutlich mit dem gegenüberliegenden Mosaikfries der Eucharistie auf der gekrümmten Ebene der Apsis. Der Betrachter der beiden Kompositionen konnte sich nicht dem Eindruck entziehen, daß die zwölfköpfige fürstliche Prozession, die sich von beiden Seiten dem thronenden Christus nähert, die Prozession der Apostel in der Abendmahlszene repliziert. Dieser frappante Aufbau, deutlich ablesbar im Kontext der christologischen Thematik der übrigen Kompositionen des Haupt- und des Kreuzschiffes, stellte ein sichtbares Symbol der apostolischen Mission der herrschenden Dynastie gegenüber ihren Untertanen und gegenüber ihrem Herrschaftsgebiet, dem russischen Land, dar[49]. In diesem Plan der Zusammenstellungen bekam sogar der allgemeine Christuskult, der Kult des himmlischen Herrschers, einen zusätzlichen Sinn. Dieser Pantokrator, Erlöser und Richter, allmächtiges und dräuendes Urbild des irdischen Herrschers, überschaut aus der Höhe der Kuppeln der Sophienkathedralen in Kiev, in Novgorod und der anderen Kirchen die von ihm den Fürsten der Ruś anvertraute Erde und Gemeinde[50].

the Relations of Church and State in Muscovite Russia. Genève ˙952, S. 54–60) meint. Eine Krönung fand im Kiever Reich nicht statt, und auch die Salbung in der Form eines physischen Sakraments war der Ruś fremd; wenn von Salbung die Rede ist, so ist das wie in Byzanz metaphorisch gemeint. Jedes Mitglied des Fürstenhauses war in der Ruś *eo ipso* ein Gesalbter, wie ganz eindeutig schon aus dem Fastenbrief des Metropoliten Nikephoros an Vladimir Monomach hervorgeht: „Dich hat Gott . . . schon von Geburt geweiht und gesalbt." Vgl.: Russkie dostopamjatnosti č. 1, S. 63; POPPE Le prince et l'Église S. 112–113.

[48] Vgl. POPPE O vremeni zaroždenija kul'ta Borisa i Gleba S. 16–22; DERS. Le prince et l'Église S. 115–116.

[49] Vgl. A. POPPE Kompozycja fundacyjna Sofii Kijowskiej. W poszukiwaniu układu pierwotnego, in: Biuletyn historii sztuki 30 (1968) S. 3–29; F. KÄMPFER Das russische Herrscherbild von den Anfängen bis zu Peter dem Großen. Studien zur Entwicklung politischer Ikonographie im byzantinischen Kulturkreis. Recklinghausen 1978, S. 110–116.

[50] Hier liegt die Frage der Wahrnehmung (Rezeptivität) des heiligen Bildes durch ihrer Sinnesart nach Heiden gebliebene Neubekehrte nahe. Der Übertritt der Ruś zum Christentum geschah in einer Zeit, die den Triumph der Bilderverehrung über den Bildersturm noch frisch und lebendig empfand, als das theologische Wesen der Ikone, Programm und Wesen des Bilderdienstes sowie die Stelle der Bilderverehrung im christlich-orthodoxen Kult mit äußerster Klarheit formuliert wurden; vgl. dazu den Sammelband: Iconoclasm. Papers Given at the Ninth Spring Symposium of Byzantine Studies, University of Birmingham, March 1975. Ed. by A. Bryer and J. Herrin. Birmingham 1977, besonders die Aufsätze von L. BERNARD The Theology of Images (S. 7–13), C. MANGO The Liquidation of Iconoclasm and the Patriarch Photios (S. 133–140) und R. CORMACK Painting after Iconoclasm (S. 147–163). Mit aller Vorsicht darf man wohl behaupten, daß die Bilderverehrung von Anfang an eine zentrale Angelegenheit in der Christianisierung der Ruś war und daß hier der „Triumph der Orthodoxie" der wirklichen Evangelisation vorangíng. Nicht zufällig wurde später (um die Wende vom 12. zum 13. Jh.) der Architekt des Endsieges des Bilderdienstes, der größte Kirchenfürst der Orthodoxie zum Zeitgenossen Vladimirs und der Taufe Rußlands gemacht. Die Vermutung, daß das noch heidnische Weltbild des neubekehrten Christen die Aneignung der Bilderverehrung begünstigte, indem einfach Elemente des kultischen Verhaltens vom Götzendienst auf den Bilderdienst übertragen wurden, scheint eine Bestätigung in dem weithin bekannten, mit der Bilderverehrung verbundenen Aberglauben zu finden; man denke etwa an die „Bestrafung" der Ikone, wenn das Gebet nicht den gewünschten Erfolg brachte. In gewisser Weise konnte der Bilderdienst für einen Halbheiden-Halbchristen zunächst nur eine andere Art von Götzendienst sein. Bis ins 16. Jh. läßt sich die Gewohnheit verfolgen, Ikonen (manchmal auch Schutzamulette) ganz unabhängig vom dargestellten Inhalt als „bogi" [Götter] zu bezeichnen. Den theologischen Sinn einer Ikone zu erfassen, war gewiß

Die herrschende Schicht hatte sich für die neue Religion erklärt. Das geschah so demonstrativ, daß der Eindruck einer schnellen Christianisierung des ganzen Landes hervorgerufen wurde. Es genügt, hier auf einen so glühenden Fürsprecher der Christianisierung aller noch heidnischen Völker Europas hinzuweisen, wie es der Missionserzbischof Bruno von Querfurt war. Er kam zwanzig Jahre nach der Taufe Vladimirs nach Kiev und sah die Ruś schon als völlig christianisiertes Land an; seine ganze Sorge konzentrierte sich darauf, wie die Petschenegen auf den Weg des Heils zu führen seien[51]. Doch ist aus den Ereignissen des 11. Jahrhunderts ersichtlich, daß das Volk keineswegs so gefügig und bereit war, die neue Religion anzunehmen. In Wirklichkeit eröffnete das 10. Jahrhundert nur die Möglichkeit und schuf das 11. Jahrhundert nur die Bedingungen für das Eindringen der neuen Ideologie in – abgesehen von der Gesellschaftsspitze – breitere Volksschichten, wie es auch den Anfang machte bei der Bekämpfung der traditionellen Volksmentalität und Denkweise durch die Kirche. Das Ringen dauerte viele Jahrhunderte[52].

nur wenigen möglich, für die Mehrheit mußte die Praxis der Bilderverehrung ein Spielraum für den Doppelglauben [dvoeverie] bleiben. Es ist der Meinung zuzustimmen, daß die Kirche eine solche doppelschichtige Verehrung der Ikonen tolerierte; sie war weniger bestrebt, das vorhandene Verhältnis der Heiden zu Sakralobjekten auszurotten, als es vielmehr auf wirklich verehrungswürdige Objekte zu übertragen. Diese Toleranz würde ich aber nicht so sehr dem Bereich des bewußten Handelns, sondern mehr der Praxis zuordnen, in der wohl auch die Mehrheit des Klerus, vor allem die Pfarrgeistlichkeit, zumindest unbewußt doppelgläubig war. Zur Deutung und Symbolik der Ikone vgl. L. OUSPENSKY Symbolik des orthodoxen Kirchengebäudes und der Ikone, in: É. HAMMER-SCHMIDT, P. HAUPTMANN, P. KRÜGER, L. OUSPENSKY Symbolik des orthodoxen und orientalischen Christentums. Band 1, Stuttgart 1962, S. 54–90, hier S. 68–89; P. A. FLORENSKIJ Ikonostas, in: Bogoslovskie trudy. Band 9, Moskva 1972, S. 83–148; B. USPENSKY The Semiotics of the Russian Icon. Lisse 1976, S. 7–82; Besprechung von K. ONASCH in: Deutsche Literaturzeitung 99 (1978) S. 639–644. Vgl. auch G. K. VAGNER Problema žanrov v drevnerusskom iskusstve. Moskva 1974, S. 78–141 (zur Kiever Kunst des 10.–11. Jh.).
    [51] Siehe Brunos Brief an Heinrich II. in: Monumenta Poloniae Historica. Band 1, Lwów 1864 (Reprint Warszawa 1960), S. 224–228. Vgl. dazu HELLMANN Vladimir der Heilige S. 400–408; B. WIDERA Brun von Querfurt und Rußland. Ein Beitrag zur Geschichte der deutsch-russischen Beziehungen um das Jahr 1000, in: Jahrbuch für Geschichte der UdSSR und der volksdemokratischen Länder Europas 3 (1959) S. 365–381. Ein Wald von Kreuzen auf den Kuppeln von etwa 400 Kirchen, die es nach dem Augenzeugen von 1018 in Kiev gab (vgl. THIETMAR Chronicon lib. VIII, 32), bestimmte das Panorama der Reichshauptstadt. Diese Zahl muß nicht übertrieben sein, wie einige Forscher gemeint haben. Am 23. und 24. Juni 1124 kam es in Kiev zu einem großen Brand, dem 600 Kirchen zum Opfer fielen (PSRL Band 1, Sp. 293, Band 2, Sp. 288). Natürlich geht es in beiden Fällen überwiegend um kleinere Holzbauten, Eigenkirchen der Kiever Adeligen, deren Zahl in die Hunderte gehen mußte, wenn man nach vorsichtigen Schätzungen (P. P. Toločko) für Kiev an der Wende vom 11. zum 12. Jh. eine Einwohnerzahl von 45 000–50 000 annimmt; hundert Jahre früher können es kaum weniger als 15 000 gewesen sein. Dem Beispiel des Herrschers und dem aus Byzanz bekannten Brauch folgend, war wohl fast jeder Adelige bemüht, auf seinem Hof eine Kapelle zu errichten, anfangs vielleicht als sichtbares Zeichen des eigenen Credos und seiner Loyalität gegenüber dem Herrscher. Eine solche Kultstätte bezeugte auch die politische Position und das Ansehen der jeweiligen Adelsfamilie in der neuen christlichen Wirklichkeit. Dem Herrscher nacheifernd, waren auch die Adeligen bestrebt, auf diese Weise als Förderer und Hüter des neuen Glaubens zu gelten.
    [52] Vgl. dazu N. M. GAL'KOVSKIJ Bor'ba christianstva s ostatkami jazyčestva v drevnej Rusi. Band 1, Chaŕkov 1916, S. 101–376 (Band 2 – erschienen als Band 18 der Zapiski Imp. Moskovskago archeologičeskago instituta im. Imperatora Nikolaja II. Moskva 1913 – enthält die Quellentexte); E. V. ANIČKOV Jazyčestvo i drevnjaja Ruś. S.-Peterburg 1914, S. 105–126, 286–307. Vgl auch J. BLANKOFF À propos du „dvoeverie" et des amulettes „zmeeviki", in: Communications présentées par les slavisants de Belgique au VIIᵉ Congrès international de slavistique, Varsovie, août 1973. Bruxelles 1973, S. 67–84; B. A. RYBAKOV Jazyčeskoe mirovozzrenie russkogo srednevekov'ja, in: Voprosy istorii (1974) H. 1, S. 3–30, hier S. 18ff. Es genügt hier der Hinweis, daß – wie aus den „Kanonischen

Die Wandlungen des 10. und 11. Jahrhunderts nahmen eine Entwicklung, die nicht nur das Schicksal Altrußlands beeinflußte. Die Rezeption des östlichen Christentums und der kyrillischen Schrift legten für viele Jahrhunderte die Richtung der geistigen, religiösen und kulturellen Entwicklung der Welt aller drei ostslavischen Völker fest. Der ideologische Umbruch vollzog sich meines Erachtens in der zweiten Hälfte des 10. und in der ersten Hälfte des 11. Jahrhunderts. Die Taufe Olgas, ihre Kontakte mit Byzanz und dem Hof Ottos I. sind die spektakulären Ereignisse, die die Öffnung zum christlichen Europa verkündeten. Aber obwohl die Notwendigkeit zur Veränderung und zur Vervollständigung der Ideologie und Struktur des jungen Kiever Staates bereits stark empfunden wurde, reichten die Kräfte noch nicht aus, um endgültig mit der traditionellen Weltsicht zu brechen. Svjatoslav war nur scheinbar der Ausdruck dieser archaischen Verfassung, im Grunde genommen zerstörte er sie durch seine gesamte Tätigkeit und stellte die herrschende Schicht des Kiever Staates vor Aufgaben, die sie unmöglich ohne die Formulierung eines Programms ideologischer Wandlungen meistern konnte.

So war also der Zeitraum seit den fünfziger Jahren und über die achtziger Jahre des 10. Jahrhunderts hinaus eine Zeit der heftigen Krisis der traditionellen heidnischen Sicht- und Verstehensweise der umgebenden Welt, eine Zeit der Erschütterung des Heidentums, der archaischen Denk- und Daseinsweise und eines immer intensiveren Eindringens des Christentums in das Milieu der Machthaber und ihrer Umgebung. Mit dem Jahr 988 wurde die Epoche des Christentums für die ganze Ruś eröffnet. Den Abschnitt seit Beginn der Ereignisse dieses Jahres bis zur Mitte des 11. Jahrhunderts kann man als Zeitraum all dieser Wandlungen bezeichnen, die die Ausbreitung der neuen religiösen Ideologie in den politisch und sozial neuralgischen Zentren des Landes begünstigten. Ebenso wurden die Grundlagen zur Sicherung einer weiteren erfolgreichen Christianisierung des Landes gelegt. Sichtbarer Ausdruck der Leistungen in diesem Zeitraum wurde der in den vierziger Jahren des 11. Jahrhunderts vollendete monumentale Bau der Kathedrale der Göttlichen Weisheit in Kiev, die mit ihren 13 Kuppeln die apostolische Mission in der Ruś verkündigte[53]. Die kurz danach emporgestiegenen Repliken – die Sophien-Kathedralen in Novgorod (1050) und Polock (vor 1066) – deuteten an, daß man im Norden nicht hinter Kiev zurückbleiben wollte. Die Bedeutung der unter Vladimir und Jaroslav vollzogenen Wandlungen wurde am Dnepr bereits an der Wende vom 11. zum 12. Jahrhundert – wie aus der Kiever Geschichtsschreibung dieser Zeit herauszulesen ist – richtig eingeschätzt.

Antworten" des Kiever Metropoliten Johannes II. hervorgeht – noch ein Jahrhundert nach der Bekehrung das Sakrament der Ehe auf die Oberschicht von „Bojaren und Fürsten" beschränkt war (vgl. L. K. Götz Kirchenrechtliche und kulturgeschichtliche Denkmäler Altrußlands nebst Geschichte des russischen Kirchenrechts. Stuttgart 1905, S. 163ff.).

Das von Johannes II. unter den heidnischen Hochzeitsbräuchen des einfachen Volkes erwähnte „pleskanie" sollte nicht als Plätschern mit Wasser oder als Händeklatschen zum Zeichen des Beifalls verstanden werden, sondern als Händezusammenschlagen zur Bekräftigung des Eheabkommens. Der Brauch des Handschlages [*rukobit'e*] in der slavischen Hochzeitszeremonie – hier und da bis ins 20. Jh. – ist gut bekannt. Diese Deutung wird bestätigt durch den Novgoroder Birkenrindenbrief Nr. 9 aus dem 12. Jh., wo Ehescheidung durch Händeauseinanderschlagen bezeugt ist (A. V. Arcichovskij, M. N. Tichomirov Novgorodskie gramoty na bereste <iz raskopok 1951 g.>. Moskva 1953, S. 40–42). Die Verwendung des Wortes „pleskanie" [Klatschen] muß wohl mit der Übersetzung aus dem griechischen Original der „Antworten" des Metropoliten in Zusammenhang gebracht werden (krotēsis?).

[53] Vgl. A. Poppe The Beginning of the Church St. Sophia in Kiev, in: Journal of Medieval History 7 (1981) Nr. 1 (im Druck).

II

THE POLITICAL BACKGROUND
TO THE BAPTISM OF RUS'
BYZANTINE-RUSSIAN RELATIONS
BETWEEN 986–89

This paper is the result of studies conducted during my fellowship at the Dumbarton Oaks Center for Byzantine Studies in the academic year 1973/74. The friendly and helpful atmosphere of the Center was particularly conducive to my work. I would especially like to thank Mrs. Mary Lou Masey for her contribution to the English wording of my text.

A S the well-known Byzantinist Fjodor Uspenskij observed in his oration, "Rus' and Byzantium in the 10th Century," written for the nine-hundreth anniversary of the Russian acceptance of Christianity, everything concerning the events of the years 988–89 "still lies under the seal of mystery, which the historian, with present scientific means, is hardly in a position to break."[1] Although there has been no basic improvement in scientific methods, attempts are still being made to paint a picture of these momentous events.

I. The Conversion of Rus' to Christianity as Presented in Modern Historical Writing

I shall present a brief and slightly simplified account of the modern historian's version of the introduction of Rus' into the family of Christian nations, taken as an episode in the history of Russo-Byzantine relations.[2] In general, the story goes as follows:

In September 987, the rebellious general Bardas Phocas proclaimed himself emperor. The usurper, marching on Constantinople, was recognized by all of Asia Minor. The situation of the legitimate Emperor Basil II was desperate and he asked the Russian ruler Vladimir for help, sending an embassy which arrived in Kiev in the winter of 987/88. As Vladimir had already manifested an interest in Christianity some time before, Basil's envoys were prepared to discuss the affairs of both Church and State. The agreement which was reached

---

[1] F. I. Uspenskij, *Rus' i Vizantija v X v.* (Odessa, 1888), 35.

[2] A survey of studies and an ample bibliography are to be found in the following works: basic for the nineteenth century are the discourses by E. Golubinskij (*Istorija russkoj cerkvi* [hereafter, Golubinskij, *Istorija*], I, pt. 1 [Moscow, 1880; rep. 1901] 105–80); V. G. Vasil'evsky, *Trudy*, I (St. Petersburg, 1908), 196–210, and II (1909), 56–124 (hereafter, Vasil'evsky, *Trudy*, I and II); and V. R. Rozen (in his commentary on the History of Yaḥyā, *Imperator' Vasilij Bolgarobojca. Izvlečenija iz' lětopisi Jah'i antiohijskago* [St. Petersburg, 1883] [hereafter, Rozen, *Imperator*], 194–216). A clear and concise exposition consistent with the state of research at the beginning of the twentieth century, along with a short survey of literature and sources, is given by M. Gruševs'kij, in *Istorija Ukrajini-Rusi*, I (Kiev, 1913; rep. New York, 1954), 495–515, 572–78. Among subsequent studies and recent general works, the following should be mentioned: E. Šmurlo, "Kogda i gde krestilsja Vladimir Svjatoj," *Zapiski Russkogo Istoričeskogo Obščestva v Prage* (Prague, 1927) (hereafter, Šmurlo, "Kogda"), 120–48; S. V. Bahrušyn, "K voprosu o kreščenii Kievskoj Rusi," *Istorik-Marksist* (1937), pt. 2, pp. 40–77; G. Ostrogorskij, "Vladimir Svjatoj i Vizantija," *Vladimirskij Sbornik* (Belgrade, 1938), 31–40; M. V. Levčenko, "Vzaimootnošenija Vizantii i Rusi pri Vladimire," *VizVrem*, N.S. 7 (1953), 194–223; *idem, Očerki po istorii russko-vizantijskih otnošenij* (Moscow, 1956) (hereafter, Levčenko, *Očerki*), 340–85; I. Ševčenko, "The Christianization of Kievan Rus," *The Polish Review*, 5 (1960), 4, 29–35; G. G. Litavrin, in *Istorija Vizantii*, II (Moscow, 1967), 219, 235–36; V. T. Pašuto, *Vnešnjaja politika drevnej Rusi* (Moscow, 1968), 73–77, 316–17; G. Ostrogorsky, *History of the Byzantine State*, rev. ed. (New Brunswick, N. J., 1969), 303–5; A. P. Vlasto, *The Entry of the Slavs into Christendom* (Cambridge, 1970) (hereafter, Vlasto, *Entry*), 255–62; F. Dvornik, *Byzantine Missions Among the Slavs* (New Brunswick, N. J., 1970), 270–72; D. Obolensky, *The Byzantine Commonwealth. Eastern Europe 500–1453* (London, 1971) (hereafter, Obolensky, *Byzantine Commonwealth*), 192–201; H. Grégoire, in *CMH*, IV, pt. 1 (1966), 179–80; M. N. Tihomirov, "The Origins of Christianity in Russia," *History*, N.S., *The Quarterly Journal of the Historical Association, London*, vol. 44, no. 152 (1959), 199–211.

provided military support for Basil; in return, Vladimir was to receive the hand of the Emperor's sister Anna in marriage, on the condition that he and his people become Christians.

In the spring or summer of 988, a Russian army of six thousand men arrived in Constantinople. In the battle of Chrysopolis and that of Abydus on April 13, 989, this force tipped the scales in favor of Basil and saved his throne. These Russian mercenaries remained in the service of Byzantium, and Vladimir and the Kievan population were promptly baptized. But after the victory at Abydus, the Emperor did not hurry to fulfill his obligations to Vladimir. There was a convenient tradition against the offspring of the imperial family marrying barbarians, and the Porphyrogenite bride was unwilling to go to Kiev.

Incensed by this Greek duplicity, Vladimir decided to apply military pressure to achieve his objectives. He struck at the Byzantine possessions in the Crimea and took Cherson between April and July of 989.

After the loss of Cherson, faced with a fresh revolt on the part of Bardas Sclerus and harassed by Bulgarian enemy activity, the Emperor Basil decided to sacrifice his sister on the altar of political expediency. Anna went to Cherson, where the wedding took place. The city was then returned to the Emperor as a dowry (i.e., *veno*—the bridegroom's gift to the parents of his bride). Vladimir and his Porphyrogenite wife took with them to Russia a number of ecclesiastics to build up the Russian Church.

I have recounted here the general view which is held by the great majority of historians. However, there are some divergences that should be pointed out.

Some scholars believe that one of the terms of the agreement between the Emperor and Vladimir was the latter's demand that the Church established in Kiev have special status. The Emperor's unreliability would have confirmed Vladimir's conviction that the new Russian Church should be organized as a unit independent of the patriarch of Constantinople.[3] Many suppositions about the primary organization of the Old Russian Church[4] have their origin in just this thesis.

In an effort to reconcile the contradictory data on the time and place of Vladimir's conversion, certain scholars have suggested that his acceptance of Christianity took place in two stages: a preliminary one (catechumenate, *oglašenie, prima signatio*) when the Byzantine mission was in Kiev, and a final one, the full sacrament of baptism, in Cherson after his capture of the

---

[3] Cf. M. D. Priselkov, *Očerki po cerkovno-političeskoj istorii Kievskoj Rusi X–XII vv.* (St. Petersburg, 1913), 33 ff.; and, among many others, M. Jankovskij, "Kreščenie Rusi," *Učenye Zapiski Leningradskogo Gos. Universiteta*, no. 36 (1939), hist. ser. no. 3, pp. 55–56; N. Zernov, "Vladimir and the Origin of the Russian Church," *SIEERev*, 28 (1950), no. 71, pp. 425–32; V. Mošin, in *Byzantinoslavica*, 24 (1963), 94–96; M. Čubatij, *Istorija hristijanstva na Rusi-Ukrajini*, I (Rome-New York, 1965), 238–73.

[4] For well-grounded criticism of these theories, L. Müller, *Zum Problem des hierarchischen Status und der jurisdiktionellen Abhängigkeit der russischen Kirche vor 1039* (Cologne-Braunsfeld, 1959), 9–47; see also A. Poppe, *Państwo i Kościół na Rusi w XI wieku* (Warsaw, 1968) (hereafter, Poppe, *Państwo*), 15–39. Because this question still excites controversy, I will return to the problem in a forthcoming article about the original status of the Old Russian Church.

city.[5] This premature interpretation is dictated by an unwillingness to disregard one of the discrepant pieces of evidence.

Several scholars have emphasized that the capture of Cherson resulted chiefly in the recovery for Rus' of access to the Black Sea.[6] Carried to the extreme, such a hypothesis suggests the main reason for the ravaging of Cherson to have been the reduction of the political and economic significance of that city as a Byzantine mainstay on the Black Sea coast, and, thus, the consolidation of the position of Tmutarakan'—a Russian outpost on the Black Sea.[7]

Some scholars have tried to question the terminus ante quem (July 27) for the capture of Cherson by Vladimir. The problem with their reasoning is their use of the unreliable and contradictory chronology of events given by Old Russian sources, as well as their assumption that the Emperor would not have made peace with Bardas Sclerus in October 989 had he not been involved in a conflict with Vladimir and unable, therefore, to count on Russian support. The strength of their argument lies in the assumption that a conflict between the Emperor and Vladimir over Basil's reluctance to give Anna in marriage could have started only after the battle of Abydus (April 13, 989), from which they have concluded that the siege of Cherson began in July 989, the subsequent fall of the city taking place after October 989, most likely at the beginning of 990.[8] Others, taking into account that Cherson was captured before July 27, 989, propose that Vladimir personally commanded the Russian troops at Abydus on April 13 of that year. They further suggest that, having failed to secure his Porphyrogenite bride, Vladimir attacked Cherson on his way back to Rus'.[9] This hypothesis, however attractive, overlooks the fact that the Russian troops remained in Byzantium.

[5] So proposed by I. I. Mališevskij, in his review of Golubinskij, *Istorija*, I, pts. 1-2 (1880–81), in *Otčet o 24 prisuždenii nagrad grafa Uvarova SPb* (1882) 53, 68; Šmurlo, "Kogda," 140, 144, 148; and more recently, Obolensky, *Byzantine Commonwealth*, 195. There are no grounds for estimating the length of Vladimir's catechumenate, i.e., the gradual revealing of the truths of faith, which always preceded the final rite of baptism and was accompanied by church rites. The catechumenate could last several months, especially with the tendency to baptize at Eastertime (in Vladimir's day, the original term of three years was unknown), or only a few days (eight or forty days for adults in twelfth-century Novgorod), because, according to apostolic tradition, it was possible to baptize an eligible man directly after instruction. Also, the Byzantine *ordo* unites the function of catechumenate and baptism proper, so conversions in two stages were unknown. Cf. A. Staerk, *Der Taufritus in der griechisch-russischen Kirche. Sein apostolischer Ursprung und seine Entwickelung* (Freiburg im Breisgau, 1903), 5 ff., 22, reviewed by A. Petrovskij, in *VizVrem*, 11 (1904), 180–83, and J. Bois, in *EO*, 8 (1905), 193–200; the articles by P. de Puniet, in *Dictionnaire d'archéologie chrétienne et de liturgie* (Paris, 1910), s.v. "Baptême," II,1, cols. 285–94, and the "Catéchuménat" (according to the Byzantine rite), II,2, cols. 2619–20; Golubinskij, *Istorija*, I, pt. 2 (rep. 1904), 426.

[6] Uspenskij, *Rus'* (note 1 *supra*), 37; and, among others, B. D. Grekov, "'Povest' vremennyh let' o pohode Vladimira na Korsun'," *Izvestija Tavričeskogo obščestva istorii, arheologii i etnografii*, III (Simferopol, 1929), 99–112, rep. in *idem, Izbrannye trudy*, II (Moscow, 1959), 413–28; A. L. Jakobson, *Rannesrednevekovyj Hersones*, Materialy i Issledovanija po Arheologii SSSR, 63 (Moscow, 1959), 63–65.

[7] D. L. Talis, "Iz istorii russko-korsunskih političeskih otnošenij v IX–X vv.," *VizVrem*, N.S. 14 (1958), 108–15, in which there are many misinterpretations; for instance, the author attributes to Cedrenus and Zonaras the information that the fall of Cherson and the Russian threat aroused in Constantinople the strong fear that the Russian King would join the Bulgarians (*ibid.*, 112–13).

[8] V. Zavitnevič, "O meste i vremeni kreščenija kievljan," *Trudy Kievskoj Duhovnoj Akademii* (1888), pt. 1, pp. 135–36, 143–44; Šmurlo, "Kogda," 123–24, 143–48.

[9] Cf. N. Baumgarten, *Saint Vladimir et la conversion de la Russie* (Rome, 1932) (= *OC*, no. 79), 76–81. The author of this large but uncritical compilation was inspired in this case by the suggestions of F. Uspenskij (*ŽMNP*, 232 [April, 1884], 305, 311) and Vasil'evskij (*Trudy*, II, 90–92). However,

A number of historians have also accepted as fact the visit of papal envoys to Vladimir in Cherson after its fall.[10] However, they failed to realize that this embassy was the invention of a sixteenth-century Muscovite historian[11] who, by stressing that Vladimir's decision to be baptized according to the Greek rite was a voluntary one, gave historical basis to Moscow's claim as the third Rome.

In trying to find a motive for Vladimir's campaign against Cherson, some researchers have proposed reasons of state: Vladimir wished to enter into the orthodox Christian community—the Byzantine Commonwealth, according to today's fashion—but was too proud to ask Byzantium for the baptism of Rus', and he further wished to negotiate with the Byzantine Emperor as an equal. In demanding admission into the imperial family, Vladimir thus considered the international prestige of his country.[12] Other scholars see Vladimir's untamed sensuality: he acceded so easily to Christianization and conquered Cherson in order to win the princess "born in the purple."[13] And there are some historians who suggest that a Church independent of Byzantium was so important to Vladimir that he captured Cherson in order to have Crimean ecclesiastics to evangelize his country (with the archbishop of Cherson as a kind of supervisor for the young Russian Church).[14]

From this short review, it is easy to see that the "Cherson problem" remains the key question in the interpretation of Byzantino-Russian relations around the time of the conversion of Rus' to Christianity.

since we clearly have here a Latin mistranslation of Scylitzes and a misinterpretation of Yaḥyā's text by Ibn-al-Athīr, there are no grounds for this hypothesis; cf. Levčenko, *Očerki*, 358–59.

[10] Among others, Baumgarten, *Saint Vladimir*, 87; G. Vernadsky, *A History of Russia*. II, *Kievan Russia* (New Haven, 1948), 65; *The Russian Primary Chronicle*, ed. and trans. S. H. Cross and O. P. Sherbowitz-Wetzor (Cambridge, Mass., 1953) (hereafter, Cross, *Chronicle*), 245; B. Ja. Ramm, *Papstvo i Rus' v X–XV vekah* (Moscow, 1959), 39–40; Čubatij, *Istorija* (note 3 *supra*), 245–46; Vlasto, *Entry*, 273. F. Dvornik's suggestion (*Byzantine Missions* [note 2 *supra*], 271–72), based on a mistaken reference to the Russian Primary Chronicle, that the embassy could have come from Vladimir's wife's cousin (Empress Theophano, widow of Otto II; cf. *infra*, note 125), lacks source evidence, even if contact between them could have taken place.

[11] *Patriaršaja ili Nikonovskaja letopis'*, in PSRL, IX (St. Petersburg, 1862), col. 57; cf. cols. 64, 65, 68 for other information about Vladimir's relations with the pope in the years 991, 994, 1000/1 (with Babylon as well!). This large historiographical compilation, made during the first half of the sixteenth century and containing many interpolations even within the adopted text of the Primary Chronicle, has been considered by some modern historians as a primary source despite the fact that its author, an official historiographer, prepared his text according to the ideological and political desires of the Muscovite rulers. It is appropriate to mention here the remark of M. N. Tihomirov that the rule of Ivan III can account for the special interest toward Rome and the Roman Church in the older part of Nikon's chronicle; quoted in A. A. Zimin, *Russkie letopisi i hronografy konca XV–XVI vv.* (Moscow, 1960), 20–21; A. G. Kuz'min, "K voprosu o vremeni sozdanija i redakcijah Nikonovskoj letopisi," *ArhEž* 1962 (1963), 114.

[12] First N. Karamzin, *Istorija gosudarstva rossijskago*, I (St. Petersburg, 1816), 212; and later T. Barsov, *Konstantinopol'skij patriarh i ego vlast' nad russkoju cerkoviju* (St. Petersburg, 1878), 326–35; Golubinskij, *Istorija*, 158–63.

[13] Cf. S. Srkulj, "Drei Fragen aus der Taufe des heiligen Vladimir," *ASP*, 29 (1907), 255–67. This author went so far as to suspect a secret agreement between Basil and Vladimir: the capture of Cherson by the Rus' would help the Emperor justify his giving Anna in marriage to a barbarian (*ibid.*, 269–81).

[14] E.g., V. Zavitnevič, "Vladimir Svjatoj kak političeskij dejatel'," *Trudy Kievskoj Duhovnoj Akademii* (1888), pt. 2, p. 196; cf. G. Vernadsky, "The Status of the Russian Church during the First Half-Century following Vladimir's Conversion," *SIEERev*, 20 (1941), 298–99, 302; Čubatij, *Istorija* (note 3 *supra*), 223–29, 239; F. Dvornik, *The Slavs. Their Early History and Civilization* (Boston, 1956), 210; *idem*, *Byzantine Missions* (note 2 *supra*), 272.

POLITICAL BACKGROUND TO THE BAPTISM OF RUS'   201

II. Some Remarks about the Sources[15]

Before examining the sources, it might be worthwhile to attempt to answer a question which has vexed scholars time and again: why were both contemporary and later Byzantine writers so strangely silent on such a significant event as the conversion of Rus'? Knowing the mentality of the Byzantines, one might assume that they were so busy with their own affairs and so scornful of the barbarians that the conversion was either not noticed or not recognized as important.

In my view, however, the answer lies elsewhere. In Byzantine official opinion, as reflected in its historiography, the conversion of the Rhôs had been achieved long before—that is, about 867, as was claimed by Photius in an encyclical sent to the Eastern patriarchs. This date was also believed by the Emperor Constantine Porphyrogenitus some eighty years later, as attested in the *Life* of Basil I the Macedonian, written about 950.[16] This official point of view was no doubt useful for domestic reasons as well; it would have been embarrassing to have to admit that at Abydus, in Psellus' words, "on that day which was to determine the future of the Empire," the foremost Christian ruler was reduced to seeking help from the pagan Rhôs.

Thus, at the time of the revolt of Bardas Phocas, imperial and ecclesiastical authorities were, it seems, dealing with Rus' as a Christian country, and they saw what was happening there as nothing more than the individual, personal baptism of Vladimir along with other previously unbaptized Russians, and the organization of a Russian ecclesiastical province. In Church circles these events could have been interpreted simply as the overcoming of an apostasy.

This unrealistic attitude on the part of the Byzantines becomes more comprehensible in the light of the attitude of that zealous propagator of Christianity, Bruno of Querfurt. On his journey to the land of the Patzinaks in 1008, this missionary-bishop visited Kiev, where he established close contact with

---

[15] The idea of "source" has been rather freely interpreted by many historians: later materials (from the thirteenth to sixteenth centuries) have been evaluated on the same level as the primary sources. A critical survey of sources on the baptism of Vladimir is given by G. Laehr, *Die Anfänge des russischen Reiches* (Berlin, 1930; rep. Vaduz, 1965), 110–11 (Appendix VI); for an extensive but cursory survey, cf. M. Klimenko, *Ausbreitung des Christentums in Russland seit Vladimir dem Heiligen bis zum 17. Jahrhundert. Versuch einer Übersicht nach russischen Quellen* (Berlin-Hamburg, 1969), 31–60. A voluminous restatement of the sources can be found in F. Schlumberger, *L'Epopée byzantine à la fin du dixième siècle* (Paris, 1896–1905). The corresponding Arabic texts were published recently with a German translation and notes by P. Kawerau, in *Arabische Quellen zur Christianisierung Russlands* (Wiesbaden, 1967). I do not take into account here the Scandinavian survivals in the Icelandic sagas (mainly in the thirteenth-century saga of Olaf Truggwison) about the baptism of Vladimir. Their value has been overestimated (cf. Baumgarten, *Saint Vladimir*, 29–34, 63–68), and is justly criticized by F. Dvornik, *The Making of Central and Eastern Europe* (London, 1949), 170 ff. One can accept the theory that the circumstances of the conversion in Kiev were known in Iceland, but only indefinitely. Cf. S. H. Cross, "La tradition islandaise de saint Vladimir," *RES*, 11 (1931), 147.

[16] *Photii epistolae XIII*, 35, in PG, 102, cols. 735–38; Theophanes Continuatus, *De Basilio Macedone*, bk. V, 97, Bonn ed. (1838), 342–43 (the latter attributes this event to Patriarch Ignatius, but this divergence is not important here); cf. Golubinskij, *Istorija*, 50–52; F. Dvornik, *Les Slaves, Byzance et Rome au IXe siècle* (Paris, 1926; rep. 1970), 143–46; Obolensky, *Byzantine Commonwealth*, 182–84. See also H. Ahrweiler, "Les relations entre les Byzantins et les Russes au IXe siècle," *Bulletin d'Information et de Coordination*, 5 (1971), 44–70.

Vladimir. In his report to the German Emperor Henry II, Bruno of Querfurt evidently considered Russia a deeply Christian country. Furthermore, this future martyr and saint, so eager to spread Christianity among the pagans, accepted the form for the reality. His schoolmate, the chronicler and bishop Thietmar of Merseburg (died 1018), with all his political contacts, was apparently more interested in Vladimir's lechery than anything else. His data on Vladimir's marriage to the Byzantine princess (whom he called "Helen"!) are inaccurate and misleading. According to Thietmar, Vladimir was converted to Christianity under pressure from his Byzantine wife.[17]

What the Byzantine historians tell us about the events of 987–89 is limited to the following sources: a) Psellus' mention of the arrival of the Russian forces and their participation in the battle with the army of Bardas Phocas;[18] b) the almost identical information of Skylitzes, who also mentions Vladimir's marriage to the Emperor's sister;[19] and c) Leo the Deacon's short digression on the capture of Cherson by the Russes. The first two of these accounts belong to the second half of the eleventh century and could be considered secondhand sources. However, Leo the Deacon relates that fiery pillars (northern lights) appeared in the heavens, presaging the capture of Cherson by the Rus' and of Berrhoea by the Bulgars, and further notes that a comet gave warning of a subsequent earthquake in Constantinople.[20] This contemporary evidence is especially important since these celestial phenomena are accurately dated by the Christian Arab historian Yaḥyā of Antioch, and also, in part, by the contemporary Armenian historian Stephen of Taron, called Asoghik. Vasil'evskij and Rozen first established, in 1876 and in 1883, by comparison of these data that Cherson was taken between April 7, when the pillar of fire was seen, and July 27, 989, from which date the comet was visible for twenty days.[21]

The Armenian Stephen of Taron (Asoghik) gives more valuable data for Byzantino-Russian relations,[22] although his evidence on Russia's conversion

---

[17] Cf. Bruno's letter to Henry II, in Monumenta Poloniae Historica, I (1864), 224–25; Thietmar of Merseburg, Chronicon, ed. K. Holzmann (Berlin, 1935), IV, 73; VII, 72; VIII, 32; for one estimate of both sources, see M. Hellmann, "Vladimir der Heilige in der zeitgenössischen abendländischen Überlieferung," JbGOst, 7 (1959), 397–412; cf. Vlasto, Entry, 274–75; and infra, note 114.

[18] M. Psellus, Chronographie; ou Histoire d'un siècle de Byzance (976–1077), ed. and trans. E. Renauld (Paris, 1926) (hereafter, Chronographia), I, §§ 13–15, vol. I, p. 9; The Chronographia, trans. E. R. A. Sewter (London, 1953), 17.

[19] Ioannis Scylitzae synopsis historiarum, ed. J. Thurn, CFHB, V (Berlin-New York, 1973) (hereafter, Scylitzae synopsis), 336; cf. Georgius Cedrenus, Bonn ed., II (1839), 444.

[20] Leo Diaconus, Historia, Bonn ed. (1828), 175.

[21] V. G. Vasil'evskij, "K istorii 976–986 godov," in idem, Trudy, II, 98–106; Rozen, Imperator, 214–18; cf. Levčenko, Očerki, 360.

[22] The Armenian text was published twice (Paris, 1859, and St. Petersburg, 1885); translations: Russian, by N. Emin (Moscow, 1864); French, by E. Dulaurier and F. Macler (Paris, 1883–1917); German, by H. Gelzer and A. Burckhardt (Leipzig, 1907). A detailed introduction and commentary to the last part of this work is given by F. Macler, Histoire universelle par Etienne Asolik de Tarôn, pt. 2, bk. III (888[?]–1004[?]) (Paris, 1917) (= Publications de l'Ecole des Langues Orientales Vivantes, ser. I, vol. XVIII bis) (hereafter, Histoire universelle), pp. clxii, 209; cf. also H. Thorassian, Histoire de la littérature arménienne des origines jusqu'à nos jours (Paris, 1951), 124–25; V. Inglisian, "Die armenische Literatur," in HO, vol. 1, pt. 7, Armenisch und kaukasische Sprachen (Leiden, 1963), 187.

is unintentional. Somewhat before 1005, he tells of the incorporation of the dominions of the late Iberian ruler of Upper Tao (Tayk'), curopalates David, by Basil II in the year 1000. Among other events, he records a battle, which took place by accident at Havčič (near modern Erzurum), between the Byzantine and Georgian armies. The battle started with a fight between a Russian and a Georgian soldier over an armful of hay. When the Russian was killed, Asoghik tells us, "All the Russian folk there rose to battle—there were 6000 footsoldiers whom the Emperor Basil had received from the king of Rus' when he gave his sister in marriage to the latter, and at the time that this nation came to believe in Christ."[23] This is all that Asoghik tells us about the Russian forces, though he describes in detail the revolt of Bardas Phocas and the battles of Chrysopolis and Abydus. For an Armenian historian, not the instrument (the Russian forces) but the architect of victory (the Emperor Basil) was of greater importance. However, while assigning, with a certain amount of satisfaction, the responsibility for the bloodbath suffered by the "supercilious" Georgian princes and nobles, Asoghik felt it necessary to explain why Russian soldiers were taking part in Basil's expedition to "the Eastern countries."

I shall try to connect with Byzantino-Russian relations another account by Asoghik, a narration of the misadventure of an anonymous metropolitan of Sebaste, the capital of the Byzantine province of Armenia II. Asoghik tells us that this metropolitan persecuted Armenian priests in the year 435 (March 25, 986–March 24, 987), and soon afterward, in the same year, was sent by the Emperor to the land of the Bulgars to establish peace. The Bulgars asked the Emperor Basil to give his sister in marriage to their king. The Emperor, with the connivance of this metropolitan, betrayed the Bulgars by sending another woman in place of the promised princess, whereupon the Bulgars burned the metropolitan as a deceiver.[24]

It has been noted that this Armenian historian's treatment of Bulgarian affairs is full of errors.[25] However, although Asoghik records a legend about the well-deserved punishment of a torturer of Armenian priests, not everything in his account is fiction. A Sebastean metropolitan could have been sent on such a mission, but probably not to Bulgaria, as some scholars have been willing to believe.[26] From what is known about Byzantino-Bulgarian relations

[23] Asoghik, III, § 43 (Histoire universelle, 161–65; Des Stephanos von Taron armenische Geschichte, trans. H. Gelzer and A. Burckhardt [Leipzig, 1907] [hereafter, Des Stephanos von Taron], 209–12; Vseobščaja istorija Stepanosa Taronskogo, Asoh'ika po prozvaniju, trans. N. Emin [Moscow, 1864] [hereafter, Vseobščaja istorija], 198–201).

[24] Asoghik, III, §§ 20, 22, 24 (Histoire universelle, 74–75, 124–28; Des Stephanos von Taron, 148–49, 185–87).

[25] Ostrogorsky, History (note 2 supra), 301; cf. N. Adontz, "Samuel l'Arménien, roi des Bulgares," rep. in idem, Etudes arméno-byzantines (Lisbon, 1965), 347 ff.

[26] V. N. Zlatarski, Istorija na pŭrvoto bŭlgarsko carstvo, pt. 2 (Sofia, 1927), 665–69; G. D. Balasčev, Bŭlgariě prez' poslednitě desetgodišnini na desetija věk', pt. I (Sofia, 1929), 47–49. Adontz, who rejected Asoghik's legendary details, found such Byzantino-Bulgarian dynastic negotiations possible, reasoning that "le russe Vladimir, 'un scythe,' un païen, n'était pas plus digne d'une princesse byzantine qu'un prince bulgare chrétien" ("Samuel," 357 note 28).

ca. 986, it is improbable that such negotiations could have taken place. It is unlikely that the events described in Asoghik's account could have occurred in the period before the Byzantine defeat on August 16/17, 986; in the few months between March 25 and his mission to Bulgaria, the metropolitan of Sebaste would have had not only to persecute Armenian priests and go to Bulgaria, but to exchange polemical letters with the Armenian Katholikos Khatchik as well.[27] A historical basis for the essence of Asoghik's story can be found in the events of Russo-Byzantine contacts about this time. The large Armenian religious community in Sebaste and neighboring regions was indeed harassed by the Orthodox Church administration, and it was no coincidence that the Armenians of these parts of the Empire supported the usurpers.[28] This anonymous metropolitan of Sebaste must have been forced to leave his seat in 987 when the Armenian provinces of Byzantium fell to Sclerus and then to Phocas.[29] It would have been natural for the metropolitan to take refuge with the Emperor.

Another source gives rise to speculation about the identity and the subsequent vicissitudes of the anonymous metropolitan of Sebaste. The treatise περὶ μεταθέσεων (*De translationibus*), which is known in different versions, attests that during the reign of Basil II (976–1025) Theophylact, metropolitan of Sebaste, was transferrred to Russia.[30] In the belief that this information was taken from the history of Theodore of Sebaste, known to have been metropolitan of this city in 997, E. Honigmann concluded that this Theophylact was the predecessor of Theodore and was the first metropolitan of Russia.[31] V. Grumel has, however, questioned Honigmann's assumption that Theodore was the source of this information, pointing out that the year 997 cannot be seen as the terminus ante quem; all that can be affirmed is that Theophylact

[27] Asoghik, III, §§ 20–24; usually reliable, this historian sometimes contradicts himself in describing other contemporary events; cf. Adontz, *Etudes arméno-byzantines*, 304–5.

[28] Cf. P. Charanis, *The Armenians in the Byzantine Empire* (Lisbon, 1963), 20, 32, 37, 42, 46, 47, 52; E. Honigmann, *Die Ostgrenze des byzantinischen Reiches* (Brussels, 1935), 149–56; A. Ter-Mikelian, *Die armenische Kirche in ihren Beziehungen zur byzantinischen* (Leipzig, 1892), 77–80; H. M. Bartikian, "La conquête de l'Arménie par l'Empire byzantin," *REArm*, N.S. 8 (1971), 338–39.

[29] Bardas Sclerus crossed the Byzantine border and occupied Melitene, according to Yaḥyā, in February 987. Sebaste, situated nearby, apparently recognized the usurper without delay; in this territory no resistance was offered. In Sebaste, the Armenian population in the tenth to eleventh centuries was very large and influential. Cf. Charanis, *The Armenians*, 19, 20; D. M. Girard, "Sivas, huit siècles d'histoire," *ROChr*, 10 (1905), 80–95, 169–81, 283–88, 337–49 (the title is misleading—the author is concerned only with the eleventh century).

[30] Vladimir Archimandrite, *Sistematičeskoe opisanie rukopisej Moskovskoj Sinodal'noj biblioteki*, I. *Rukopisi grečeskie* (Moscow, 1894), 421; Nicephorus Callistus, in his *Church History*, XIV, 39 (PG, 146, col. 1196), reproduced one version of this treatise using, according to G. Gentz, the manuscript known now as *Barrocianus* 142 (fols. 265b–268b containing a list of transfers). Cf. H. O. Coxe, *Catalogi codicum manuscriptorum Bibliothecae Bodleianae*, I (Oxford, 1853), 114; G. Gentz and F. Winkelmann, *Die Kirchengeschichte des Nicephorus Callistus Xanthopulus und ihre Quellen* (Berlin, 1966), 135–36. This fragment of *Barroc.* 142, with *De translationibus*, was published in 'Επ.'Ετ.Βυζ.Σπ., 9 (1932), 179–83, 200, but Theophylact of Russia is not mentioned. The oldest manuscript in which he is mentioned is *Vaticanus* 1455, dated 1299; cf. V. Grumel, "Chronologie patriarcale au Xᵉ siècle," *REB*, 22 (1964), 53.

[31] E. Honigmann, "Studies in Slavic Church History: IV, Theophylactos, the First Metropolitan of Russia?", *Byzantion*, 17 (1944–45), 148–58.

was sent to Russia before 1025.[32] Thus, Theophylact remains the first metropolitan of Rus' to be reliably mentioned.[33] But in attempting to identify this Theophylact with the anonymous metropolitan of Sebaste mentioned by Asoghik, it is easy to imagine, following Honigmann, that Theophylact of Sebaste, since the beginning of 987 a metropolitan without a see, could have been sent by the Emperor to Kiev to seek aid, and, after concluding the agreement, could have been named the first Russian metropolitan.

The tenor of Yaḥyā of Antioch's story about the conversion of Rus'[34] is similar to that of Asoghik's. The information given in the chronicle of this contemporary historian (ca. 980–1066) about the Byzantine civil war, although second hand, has been confirmed many times in its accuracy.[35] Yaḥyā introduced the history of the revolts of Bardas Sclerus and Bardas Phocas into his chronicle after 1015 when he was settled in Antioch, where he made use of local sources (from the Melkite community?). Antioch supported the usurper, Bardas Phocas, who had been its governor in 986–87, and the city followed the progress of his army intently. Also, Antioch had seen these same Russian warriors taking part in the Emperor Basil's Syrian campaign in the 990's.[36] Yaḥyā's chronicle contains the most extensive report on the events which led to Vladimir's baptism, although this historian and his Antiochene source had no interest in it as such. They were more interested in describing how the Emperor Basil met the threat to his power, and how yesterday's enemies could be today's allies. On the basis of Yaḥyā's statement that "Basil sent an embassy to the king of the Rus', although they were his enemies," some scholars might suggest that Vladimir's army supported the Bulgars in the battle of Trajan's Gates (near Sardica, present-day Sofia) on August 17, 986, a great defeat for

---

[32] Cf. Grumel, "Chronologie," 44–71; but Grumel's other arguments in reconstructing the history of the patriarchate at the end of the tenth century, based on sixteenth-century Russian sources, are untenable. Cf. Poppe, *Państwo*, 31–32.

[33] *Ibid.*, 29–33; on the imaginary first Russian metropolitans, Leo and Michael, cf. my remarks in *Byzantion*, 35 (1965), 524–27.

[34] Yaḥyā, in Rozen, *Imperator*, 23–24; and in *Histoire de Yahya-ibn-Sa'īd d'Antioche*, ed. and trans. I. Kratchkovsky and A. Vasiliev, fasc. II, PO, 23 (Paris, 1932), p. 423; Kawerau, *Arabische Quellen* (note 15 *supra*), 14–19 (with commentary). According to J. H. Forsyth (see *infra*, note 40), who was kind enough to compare the Russian and French translations of the section on the baptism of the Rus' with the Arabic text of Yaḥyā, the Russian translation by Rozen is more literal throughout and gives a better idea of the actual grammatical constructions; the French translation by Vasiliev is only slightly looser and freer, however, and does quite accurately express what Yaḥyā says.

[35] Cf. Rozen, *Imperator*, 057–091, 194ff.; A. A. Vasiliev, *Byzance et les Arabes*, II (Brussels, 1950), 80–91; G. Graf, *Geschichte der christlichen arabischen Literatur*, II (Rome, 1947), 49–51; M. Canard, "Les sources arabes de l'histoire byzantine aux confins des Xe et XIe siècles," *REB*, 19 (1961), 300–12.

[36] Cf. Yaḥyā, in PO, 23, pp. 442–43, 457–60; and in Rozen, *Imperator*, 32–33, 40–41 note 272; Asoghik, III, §§ 42, 43. Because of the incidental burning of a church in Homs (Emise), it is known that the Rhôs took part in Basil II's Syrian campaign in autumn 999. The Emperor's detachments were quartered in Antioch and Cilicia, from which in early summer 1000 they marched to annex the dominions of David of Tayk'. Here again, because of a chance battle at Havčić, Russian soldiers are mentioned. Since Basil II appeared in person in Syria in 995, it can be supposed that he brought Russian troops with him to fight against the Fatimids. In any case, at that time it was common not only to hear about Russian soldiers, but to meet them in the streets of Antioch. Their presence reminded the local chronicler of Russian participation in the events of 988/89. Thus, it is possible that Yaḥyā's source in this regard was recorded not immediately, but some years later, perhaps around 999/1000. This could explain the sequence of events, viewed in retrospect, preserved in Yaḥyā's text.

Basil. There are no grounds for this speculation in the sources; it was inspired by a note in the Russian Primary Chronicle for 985 that "Vladimir conquered the Bulgars" and "made peace with them." This raid, however, was directed against the Bulgars on the Volga, and did not extend into Balkan Bulgaria.[37] The description of the Rus' as enemies of Byzantium seems to be connected with a prior account by Yaḥyā of the Balkan war with Svjatoslav[38] and was added here simply to emphasize the desperate situation of Basil II.

Yaḥyā's account of the conversion of Rus' reads as follows: the two sides negotiated a treaty of relationship by marriage. Vladimir married the sister of the Emperor after the latter had demanded his baptism, along with all the people of his land. And when the business of the marriage had been concluded, the Rus' forces arrived and started to fight against Phocas . . . .[39]

There is no need to repeat the entire account of Yaḥyā, especially since its three translations are easily accessible. However, it should be noted that this text, which is full of dates, stresses not a chronological but a causally consecutive sequence, although the chronological data Yaḥyā gives are of great importance for the reconstruction of the course of events.

As the rest of the Arabic sources on the baptism of Rus' are mainly derivative in nature, we can ignore them, with the exception of the account of Abū Shujāʿ, vizier of the Abbasid caliph and the continuator of the chronicle of Ibn-Miskawaih, "The Experiences of the Nation." This account has not hitherto been properly evaluated as a source for the study of Byzantino-Russian relations. Abū Shujāʿ recorded sometime between 1072 and 1092 the events of the years 979–99. His work appears to be mainly an abridgement of the missing chronicle of Hilāl B. Muḥassin b. Ibrāhīm al-Sâbî (970–1056), a contemporary of Yaḥyā.[40] "Reduced to a state of weakness," says Abū Shujāʿ, "the two emperors sent for aid to the king of the Russians; he demanded their sister's hand in marriage, but she refused to surrender herself to a bridegroom of a different religion; correspondence ensued which resulted in the Russian king adopting Christianity. The alliance was then contracted and the princess was given to him. He sent a number of his followers to assist them [the emperors], men of strength and courage. When this reinforcement reached

[37] PSRL, I, col. 84; cf. Cross's commentary to *The Russian Primary Chronicle*, 96, 294; B. D. Grekov, "Volžskie bolgary v IX–X vv.," *Istoričeskie Zapiski*, 14 (1945), 13–14; Levčenko, *Očerki*, 336.
[38] Yaḥyā, in PO, 18 (1924), 833; and in Rozen, *Imperator*, 180–81.
[39] Yaḥyā, in PO, 23, pp. 422–24; and in Rozen, *Imperator*, 23–24; Kawerau, *Arabische Quellen*, 15–18.
[40] The summarization of Abū Shujāʿ can be seen in his chronology, where several years are collected under one. Cf. H. F. Amedroz, "The Tajârib al-Umam of Abū ʿAli Miskawaih," *Der Islam*, 5 (1914), 340–41. The author concludes that both Abū Shujāʿ and Ibn al-Qalānisī based their works on Hilāl's history, but C. Cahen assumed that the question of Ibn al-Qalānisī's sources are more complex than Amedroz supposed. Cf. C. Cahen, "Note d'historiographie syrienne. La première partie de l'histoire d'Ibn al-Qalānisī," *Arabic and Islamic Studies in Honor of Hamilton A. R. Gibb* (Cambridge, Mass., 1965), 156–65. The analysis of J. H. Forsyth (in the forthcoming publication of his dissertation on Yaḥyā) leaves no doubt that Ibn al-Qalānisī has used Hilāl al-Sābī, among others, for the years 986–89. But there is no trace of a reference to Rus'. The supposition of Vasiliev (*Byzance et les Arabes*, II [note 35 *supra*], pt. 2, p. 89) and Canard ("Les sources" [note 35 supra], 297) that Yaḥyā, as well as Abū Shujāʿ, could have used the chronicle of Hilāl is unsound.

Constantinople, they crossed the strait in ships to meet Wardis [Phocas] ....
No sooner however had they reached the shore and got on the same terrain
with the enemy, than a battle commenced, wherein the Russians proved
themselves superior, and put Wardis to death."[41]
The scheme of this account is basically the same as that of Yaḥyā, except
for some differences in details, a far stronger emphasis by Abū Shūjāʿ on the
great weight carried by the Russian troops, and the fact that Yaḥyā speaks
exclusively about the Emperor Basil while Abū Shūjāʿ takes into account the
legal situation (Basil and Constantine were coemperors). The source of Abū
Shūjāʿ remains a mystery.

We must now consider to what extent the surviving Old Russian material
meets our purposes. Two such works have recorded the circumstances of
Russia's conversion: 1) the Russian Primary Chronicle, a compilation from the
second decade of the twelfth century, formerly called the "Chronicle of Nestor"
but now frequently referred to by the first sentence of the text, "The Tale of
Bygone Years";[42] and 2) the *Life* of St. Vladimir, a hagiographical work
known in several versions and redactions, of which the oldest is the so-called
"Memory and Eulogy of Vladimir."[43]
Briefly, the Primary Chronicle relates the story of the conversion as follows.
In 986, missionaries from foreign lands and of different religions came to Kiev
hoping to win over the Russian ruler. Vladimir, after questioning them,
rejected each in turn. The last to be examined was the Greek philosopher,
who seems to have completely convinced Vladimir that "the Greek faith" was
the true one. Nevertheless, Vladimir decided to "wait yet a little." In 987 he
sent his own emissaries abroad to find out still more about the religions. On
their return to Kiev, the envoys advised Vladimir to accept Greek Christianity, to which Vladimir agreed and inquired where the baptism should take
place. A year later, the Chronicle continues, in 988, Vladimir and his warriors
attacked Cherson, and the beleaguered Greek city was forced to surrender.
Then Vladimir demanded the sister of Basil and Constantine in marriage and
warned that, if this was refused, he would deal with Constantinople as he had
dealt with Cherson. The troubled Emperors replied that if Vladimir were
baptized he would be permitted to marry Anna. Vladimir told them that he
had already studied their religion and that he was willing to be baptized.
The Emperors sent to Cherson, against her will, their lamenting sister, accom-

---

[41] *The Eclipse of the 'Abassid Caliphate*. VI, *Continuation of The Experiences of the Nations by Abu
Shuja' Rudhrawari* ..., trans. D. S. Margoliouth (Oxford, 1921), 118–19; Arabic text: *The Eclipse* ...,
III, 116–17; cf. Kawerau, *Arabische Quellen*, 20–22; Russian translation by T. Kezma, with Ukrainian
introduction by A. Kryms'kyj, "Opovidannja arabs'kogo istoryka XI viku Abu-Šodži Rudravers'kogo
pro te jak oxrestilasja Rus'," in *Jubilejnyj zbirnik na pošanu D. I. Bagalěja* (Kiev, 1927), 383–87, trans.
388–95; offprint, pp. 3–7, trans. 8–15.
[42] PSRL, I, cols. 1–286; II, cols. 1–285; for an English translation with a lengthy introduction, see
Cross, *Chronicle.*
[43] Published text in Golubinskij, *Istorija*, 238–46, and A. A. Zimin, "Pamjat' i pohvala Iakova
Mniha i Žitie knjazja Vladimira po drevnejšomu spisku," *KrSoobInstSlav*, 37 (1963), 66–72 (MSS of
the fifteenth century).

panied by dignitaries and priests. By divine agency, Vladimir began to go blind from the moment of Anna's arrival, but upon her advice he was baptized and miraculously cured. Then Vladimir was taught a lengthy creed which urged him to avoid the deceit of heretics. The narrative ends with Vladimir returning Cherson to the Greeks and taking Anna and priests of Cherson to Kiev, where the mass baptism of the inhabitants then took place.[44]

Although it has long been realized that the Chronicle incorporates literary elements,[45] this story is still considered "the principle source of our knowledge of the events of Russia's conversion."[46] However, this treatment of the Chronicle as an original source in which later interpolations of marvels were inserted is not acceptable. No account of the conversion was made in Vladimir's time. This story presents a clear historiographical conception of the conversion of the Rus' according to the spirit of the age in which it was written, and one consistent with Russian reality over a hundred years after Christianization.

Some modern scholars are irritated by the chronicler's inability to provide any plausible reason for Vladimir's attack on Cherson.[47] The Crimean campaign is related without any logical sequence, and in direct contradiction, to the theological victory of the Greek philosopher. But this story has its own logic, that of Providence. The author attempted to present the Christianization of his country not as a political event but as a significant religious one. He accumulated dramatic occurrences culminating in the loss of Vladimir's eyesight, so that, after the miraculous cure by baptism, the Rus' king would say, "I have now perceived the one true God." Thus, the Chronicle's story of the conversion is a remarkable primary source for the Old Russian historical consciousness, and for literary and religious life and customs at the beginning of the twelfth century.

Yet, despite the insertion of legendary material, some reliable fragments of evidence, such as the capture of Cherson, are preserved. To the chronicler, the age of the conversion was shrouded in the mists of time, and various versions were in circulation. The author of the Chronicle, claiming that Vladimir was baptized in Cherson, remarked, "Those who do not know the truth say he was baptized in Kiev, while others assert this event took place in Vasil'ev, while still others mention other places."[48]

Scholars have noted that this Chronicle's story represents a compilation of two different versions of the conversion. The question of literary sources has been examined as well, though in many respects not thoroughly enough, and

---

[44] PSRL, I, cols. 84–121; II, cols. 71–105; Cross, *Chronicle*, 96–119.

[45] Cf. especially M. Suhomlinov, *O drevnej russkoj lětopisi kak' pamjatnikě literaturnom'* (St. Petersburg, 1856); K. Bestužev-Rjumin, *O sostavě russkih letopisej do konca XIV veka* (St. Petersburg, 1868), 31–69; and A. A. Šahmatov, *Razyskanija o drevnejšyh russkih letopisnyh svodah* (St. Petersburg, 1908), 133–61.

[46] This commonly accepted view was clearly expressed recently by Obolensky, *Byzantine Commonwealth*, 193.

[47] Cf., for instance, Zernov, "Vladimir" (note 3 *supra*), 129–30; while scholars usually describe the *Weltanschauung* of medieval chroniclers as having been providential, they often seem surprised when the chroniclers act in accordance with this interpretation.

[48] Cross, *Chronicle*, 113.

needs further clarification.[49] The first version, the "Examination of the Religions" ending with the exposition of the Eastern Orthodox doctrine, was borrowed from Old Church Slavonic writings. A polemic against the Latins, including among other things the controversy about the *azymos* (unleavened bread), allows us to date this narrative not earlier than the second half of the eleventh century, closer to the time of the chronicler who perhaps gathered and compiled the material himself.[50] The second version, the story of Vladimir's conversion at Cherson (the so-called Cherson legend), was recorded either at the Cave Monastery in Kiev or at its branch on the Black Sea near Tmutarakan' (τό Ταμάταρχα) in the seventies or eighties of the eleventh century.[51] All other expanded versions of the Cherson legend must, contrary to some opinion, derive from this version in the Primary Chronicle.[52] The local color in the legend, which has been dealt with at length by researchers,[53] gives excellent information

[49] For the sources, cf. N. K. Nikol'skij, *Materialy dlja povremennogo spiska russkih pisatelej i ih sočinenij (X–XI vv.)* (St. Petersburg, 1906), 6–43; A. A. Šahmatov, "'Povest' vremennyh let' i ee istočniki," *TrDrLit*, 4 (1940), 124ff.; Bahrušyn, "K voprosu" (note 2 *supra*), 48–50; R. V. Ždanov, "Kreščenie Rusi i Načal'naja letopis'," *Istoričeskie Zapiski*, 5 (1939), 3–30; D. S. Lihačev, *Russkie letopisi i ih kul'turno-istoričeskoe značenie* (Moscow, 1947), 72–75; Cross, *Chronicle*, notes pp. 244–49; A. S. L'vov, "Issledovanie Reči filosofa," in *Pamjatniki drevnerusskoj pis'mennosti* (Moscow, 1968), 333–96; for the inspiration of Greek literature in the account of the Russian embassies abroad, cf. R. A. Klostermann, "Eine Stelle der russischen Nestorchronik," *OCP*, 39 (1973), fasc. 2, pp. 469–80. The question of the sources is extensively examined by V. Nikolaev, *Slavjanobŭlgarskijat faktor v hristijanizacijata na Kievska Rusija* (Sofia, 1949), 4–51, whose conclusions are very often uncritical and misleading.

[50] For the beginning of the controversy about the *azymos*, cf. A. Poppe, in *Byzantion*, 35 (1965), 504–27. The chronology of the different parts of the Chronicle's story of the conversion still gives rise to conflicting opinions. Thus, for instance, L'vov ("Issledovanie," 395–96) claims that the "speech" of the Greek philosopher, East Bulgarian in origin, was adopted by Old Russian writers in the first half of the eleventh century. His only argument is that the measured tone of the "speech" is far removed from the impetuous tone of the anti-Latin tract which he attributes, after I. P. Eremin (*TrDr Lit*, 5 [1947], 158–63), to Theodosius, abbot of the Cave Monastery in Kiev, and dates to 1069 (cf. recently also Vlasto, *Entry*, 288). On the other hand, the convincing arguments for its authorship by Theodosius the Greek, abbot of the same monastery in the middle of the twelfth century, were unknown to these scholars; cf. K. Viskovatyj, in *Slavia*, 16 (1938), 535–67; N. K. Gudzij, "O sočinenijah Feodosija Pečerskogo," *Problemy obščestvenno-političeskoj istorii Rossii i slavjanskih stran* (Moscow, 1963), 62–66; Pašuto, *Vnešnjaja politika* (note 2 *supra*), 311.

[51] Nikol'skij, *Materialy*, 36–40; idem, "Slovo o tom, kako krestisia Vladimir voz'ma Korsun'," *Sbornik Otdela russkogo jazyka i slovesnosti Imperatorskij Akademij Nauk*, 82 (1907), no. 4, pp. 1–24; for the most important contribution on this problem, cf. A. A. Šahmatov ("Korsunskaja legenda o kreščenii Vladimira," *Sbornik statej posvjaščennyh ... V. I. Lamanskomu ...*, pt. 2 [St. Petersburg, 1908], 1029–1153; idem, *Razyskanija* [note 45 *supra*], 133–44), who demonstrated the legendary nature of the story about Vladimir's baptism in Cherson; Šmurlo, "Kogda," 127–31, challenges Šahmatov's thesis and concludes that the "Cherson legend is not myth invested in historical garments but quite the opposite: historical fact adorned in fabulous attire." Cf. also Lihačev, *Russkie letopisi*, 87–88.

[52] Šahmatov and many later authors considered that the Primary Chronicle has not preserved the original form of the Cherson legend, which he claims was a combination of Greek Chersonian legend about Vladimir's conversion and the Old Russian tradition of the expedition against Cherson. Šahmatov has reconstructed this nonextant form of the work ("Korsunskaja legenda," 1138–48) by making use of later chronicles and especially of different versions of the *Life* of St. Vladimir. The weakness of this attempt has been exposed by the numerous corrections of R. Ždanov ("Kreščenie Rusi" [note 49 *supra*], 15–25), who attempted to give the restored legend a more convincing form. However, in light of a close examination by Serebrjanskij of the *Lives* of St. Vladimir, Šahmatov's version of the original form of the Cherson legend is indefensible; cf. N. I. Serebrjanskij, *Drevnerusskie knjažeskie žitija (Čtenija v obščestve istorii i drevnostej rossijskih pri Moskovskom Universitete, bk. 3)* (Moscow, 1915), 43–81; A. Poppe, "Legenda Korsuńska," *Słownik Starożytności Słowiańskich*, 3 (Wrocław, 1967), 34–35.

[53] Cf. especially S. Šestakov, *Očerki po istorii Hersonesa v VI–X vekah*, Pamjatniki hristianskogo Hersonesa, III (Moscow, 1908), 83–93, 125–38; Ždanov, "Kreščenie Rusi," 25.

about the tenth- and eleventh-century topography of Cherson. Some words and expressions seem to reflect a Greek text, although the combination of legendary and historical information created some problems, such as the lack of a reason for the expedition and the question of the actual role of Cherson in the conversion of Rus'.

In the literature on the subject, many theories appear concerning the possibility of reconstructing a text of the *Life* of St. Vladimir which would precede the data preserved in the Primary Chronicle. An analysis of the versions of the life of St. Vladimir, all but one written and rewritten in the fourteenth to sixteenth century, does not permit us to share these optimistic theories. The exception, the "Memory and Eulogy of Vladimir," a triptych composed of the Eulogy itself, the *Life* of St. Olga, Vladimir's grandmother, and the *Life* of Vladimir, is attributed in toto to the monk James and dated to the second half of the eleventh century.[54] The date of its compilation should, however, be connected with the canonization of the baptizer of Rus' which occurred much later, in the second half of the thirteenth century.[55] While none of the elements of this trinomial work can be accurately dated to the eleventh century, the third part of the triptych (the oldest version of the *Life* of Vladimir) may have used an earlier source, with a chronology which conflicts with that in the Primary Chronicle. This source could have been isolated annalistic records inserted into the "Memory and Eulogy" during its compilation.[56] According to these records, Vladimir lived twenty-eight years after his baptism and took Cherson in the third year after his conversion. Since Vladimir died on July 15, 1015, the conversion of Rus' would have occurred in the year 987, and the capture of Cherson in the year 989, whereas the Primary Chronicle dates both events to the year 988. "The *Life* of SS. Boris and Gleb," written in 1072, suggests also the year 987 as the year of conversion, saying that Vladimir died twenty-eight years after his baptism.[57] Thus, the possibility of a common source for both *Lives* is not excluded. If, at the turn of the eleventh century, there was some difference of opinion about the place of Vladimir's baptism,[58] different dates for this event could also have been recorded.

This historical inheritance is not very useful for our investigation, since the material on primary sources is weak, and any additional primary evidence must be disengaged from legend and myth. We must now consider the circumstances in which this tradition was formed.

---

[54] Cf. Nikol'skij, *Materialy* (note 49 *supra*), 228–53; Šahmatov, *Razyskanija*, 13–28; Serebrjanskij, *Drevnerusskie knjažeskie žitija*, 43–51.

[55] Cf. S. A. Bugoslavskij, "K literaturnoj istorii 'Pamjati i pohvaly' knjazju Vladimiru," *Izvestija Otdelenija russkogo jazyka i slovesnosti Akademii Nauk*, 24 (1924–25), 105–41; A. Poppe, in *Słownik Starożytności Słowiańskich*, 4 (Wrocław, 1970), 16–18.

[56] Cf. A. N. Nasonov, *Istorija russkogo letopisanija XI–načala XVIII veka* (Moscow, 1969), 27–31.

[57] D. I. Abramovič, *Žitija svjatyh mučenikov Borisa i Gleba i služby im* (Petrograd, 1916), 28.

[58] Cf. Cross, *Chronicle*, 113.

III. Evidence for a Reinterpretation

Neither Leo the Deacon nor the author of the Cherson legend included in his account the reason for Vladimir's expedition to Cherson, although the latter suspected a special Providence at work. What, then, was the temporal reason for the invasion of Cherson?

Contrary to all the literature on this subject, it can be argued that Vladimir's campaign against Cherson was not directed against the Byzantine Empire, but was intended rather to support his brother-in-law, the legitimate Byzantine emperor, by suppressing an internal revolt. The starting point for this thesis is the chronology of events. The auxiliary Russian troops sent to Constantinople sometime in 988 helped the Emperor Basil to overcome the rebel Bardas Phocas on Saturday, April 13, 989. They continued to serve Basil in 989 and 990 by suppressing the prolonged revolt in Asia Minor, especially that of the Iberians; in the Bulgarian campaign at the beginning of 991; and, from 995, on the eastern borders.[59]

According to Leo the Deacon, "the columns of fire that appeared deep in the night to the north ... pointed to the capture of Cherson by the Tauroscythians, which had occurred, and to the occupation of Berrhoia by the Mysians." The "sky like a pillar of fire" was seen in Cairo on April 7, and the sun continued to change its color until April 12, 989.[60] A comet, which was visible at intervals for a certain period of time, appeared and aroused a foreboding which was confirmed, says Leo, by a devastating earthquake on the eve of St. Demetrius' day. In assessing the damage, he noted that the great dome of Haghia Sophia had collapsed. There is good dated evidence for Leo's testimony, for, according to Yaḥyā, the comet was visible in Cairo for twenty days from July 27, i.e., to August 15. The latter date is given for the presence of the comet by Asoghik, who directly connects it with an earthquake which followed soon after in "the land of the Greeks" and in Constantinople itself. The earthquake is confirmed and dated by Yaḥyā to the fourteenth year of Basil's reign, A.H. 379 (April 11, 989–March 30, 990), and is recorded in the Synaxarium of the Church of Constantinople on October 26: "In the days of

---

[59] The exact date of the battle of Abydus is given only by Yaḥyā. Scylitzes indicates the date, April, second indiction, 6497 (989). There is no indication that the Russian crack troops were used against the Bulgarians before Basil II's four-year campaign, which began in March 991. They might have been used before that in action in Asia Minor, where from the time of the agreement with Sclerus (October) until November 11, 989, Leo, the son of Bardas Phocas, held out in Antioch; and again against the Iberians led by Bardas Phocas' follower, Prince Čordvanel, who in 990 were still particularly stubborn. Cf. Asoghik, III, § 27 (*Histoire universelle*, 133–34; *Des Stephanos von Taron* [note 23 *supra*], 190–91); Yaḥyā, in PO, 23, pp. 427, 431; and in Rozen, *Imperator*, 27. Traces of the Russian–Georgian struggle in 989–90 might be seen in the events of the year 1000 described *supra*, pp. 8–9: the bloodbath at Havčić broke out as the result of a quarrel over hay between two soldiers, a Russian and a Georgian, but the explosion which followed indicates that this animosity had already been established.

[60] Leo Diaconus, 175; Yaḥyā, in PO, 23, pp. 432–33; and in Rozen, *Imperator*, 28–29. Unfortunately, the date of the fall of Berrhoia is unknown, although we do know that it was recaptured at the beginning of the campaign against the Bulgarians in the spring of 991, and afterward changed hands several times. Cf. Asoghik, III, § 33 (*Histoire universelle*, 146; *Des Stephanos von Taron*, 198); Yaḥyā, in PO, 23, pp. 430–31; and in Rozen, *Imperator*, 27–28. Cf. Adontz, *Etudes* (note 25 *supra*), 360–66; G. C. Chionides, Ἱστορία τῆς Βεροίας, II (Berrhoia, 1970), 21–22.

Basil and Constantine, in the year 6498 [989], because of many sins, there was an earthquake on this day, in the third hour of the night, when the dome of the great church of God fell and many other buildings and walls fell also." Here the earthquake is connected with the night of October 25 and the morning of October 26, St. Demetrius' day, when there were probably still earth tremors, but Leo's testimony that it started on the eve of St. Demetrius is accurate, considering the date of the earthquake in Italy on October 25, noted in *Chronica Monasterii Casinensis*, *Chronicon Romualdi Saleternitani*, *Annales Beneventani*.[61]

Thus, according to the chronology of celestial phenomena given by Leo the Deacon in connection with contemporary events, it can be concluded not only that the capture of Cherson took place after April 7 but also that the terminus ante quem, despite the doubts of some scholars, is July 27, 989. In view of the data, it is difficult to accept a situation in which Vladimir's soldiers were fighting for Basil at the same time that Vladimir was organizing an expedition against this Emperor and besieging Cherson to secure his right to the hand of the Emperor's sister. Therefore, one might conclude that the Russian ruler acted not against a city loyal to the Emperor Basil but against a rebellious one. The Crimean possessions, like some other Byzantine territories on the Black Sea, had declared themselves for the usurpers, and Vladimir, acting as the ally of Basil, attempted to establish order there for his brother-in-law. The arguments for and against this theory must be considered.

One remark of Leo the Deacon would seem to work against this thesis. After stating that the victory at Abydus had brought a halt to the chaos of the civil wars, he describes as "the next calamity" the capture (ἡ ἅλωσις) of Cherson by the Rhôs and the occupation (ἡ κατάσχεσις) of Berrhoia by the Bulgars. These words, "capture" and "occupation," were perhaps used by Leo only as a stylistic device, although one must admit that both accurately reflect the situation: in the first case, military action, and in the second, possession of the city. There is no ambiguity about military operations by the Bulgars against the Empire, and Leo sees the Russian action in the Crimea in the same way, as a severely disturbing defeat for his homeland. Rather than reject his view, one should try to understand it.

Leo the Deacon was not an official historiographer, nor was he an apologist for Basil II. While he had the good of the Empire very much at heart, he did not accept Basil's every action. He blamed the Emperor, for instance, for the defeat by the Bulgarians. Leo's deliberate omission of the marriage of the

[61] Leo Diaconus, *loc. cit.*; Yaḥyā, in PO, 23, pp. 428–29, 432–33; and in Rozen, *Imperator*, 26–27, 28–29; Asoghik, III, § 27 (*Histoire universelle*, 132; *Des Stephanos von Taron*, 190); *Synaxarium CP*, 166; MGH, *SS*, VII (Hannover, 1846), 636; Muratori, RerItalSS [N.S.], VII, pt. 1 (1914), 170 (here *calcus pisanus*, 990 = 989). Cf. Vasil'evskij, *Trudy*, II, 98–104; S. Der Nersessian, "Remarks on the Date of the Menologium and the Psalter Written for Basil II," *Byzantion*, 15 (1941), 104–6, 110–11. Skylitzes' misleading date (986) for the earthquake (cf. Cedrenus, II, 438; *Scylitzae synopsis*, 331–32) has thrown many historians into confusion. Others have uncritically repeated this date without investigating other sources, among them J. Dück, "Die Erdbeben von Konstantinopel," *Die Erdbebenwarte*, III, 10–12 (Laibach, 1904), 132; V. Grumel, *La chronologie* (Paris, 1958), 480.

Porphyrogenite Anna and the participation of the Rhôs at Chrysopolis and Abydus can be explained by his disapproval of the means by which Basil was trying to save his throne. On the other hand, Leo the Deacon's *History* is full of praise for the Emperor Nicephorus II Phocas (963–69): at the end of his history in the reign of Basil, he paints a gloomy picture of the situation, contrasting it with the prosperity of the Empire under Nicephorus Phocas and John Tzimisces (969–76).[62] The Byzantino-Russian war in Bulgaria occupies considerable space in his exposition. Giving many details of excesses in the campaign of 969–71, he portrays the Rus' as a sinister and dangerous enemy. As an example, he recalls that the Russes' king Svjatoslav, when asked to join in military action against the Bulgars in 968, turned against the Byzantines and demanded nothing less than their departure from Europe. Therefore, an appeal to the former enemy for help at the time of the civil war, an internal Byzantine affair, was shocking to Leo. He was especially outraged that Cherson, a Crimean province that was, in his opinion, a Greek city and a part of the Byzantine state, should fall prey to the barbarians whose atrocities were etched in his memory. The capture of Cherson contributed to Leo's pessimistic vision of the future of the Empire.

Leo was not alone in these views. John Geometres (Kyriotes), in his poetry written in the 970's and 980's, contrasts an idealized portrait of Nicephorus Phocas with the noble edifice of an Empire torn apart from both within and without. Anxiety about the destiny of his homeland is evident in the political, patriotic verses John Geometres wrote about events which occurred between 989–90.[63] His dismal mood is deepened by the spectacle of fratricidal war ("O bitter sight, a brother raising an axe to his brother's breast"), at a time when "noble cities are disgracefully trod under the feet of strangers." He frequently complains about the neglect of education, science, and the arts in his time; it is known from Psellus that Basil despised literary and learned men, so it is not surprising that the latter showed no sympathy or confidence in him as a ruler. Beside the restrained critical allusions to Basil II in the poetry of John Geometres, it seems possible that the "fearful Emperor and tyrant" in his paraphrase of a church song refers to Basil. The poet's continued gloomy outlook on the times is fully reflected in Εἰς τὴν ἀπόστασιν and Εἰς τὴν ἀποδημίαν, both written after the earthquake of October 25, 989, hence after Basil's April victory at Abydus and his agreement of October 11 with Sclerus. He pays no

---

[62] Cf. G. Wartenberg, "Das Geschichtswerk des Leon Diakon," *BZ*, 6 (1897), 108, 111; A. P. Každan, "Iz istorii vizantijskoj hronografii X v.," *VizVrem*, N.S. 20 (1961), 123–28; N. M. Panagiotakes, Λέων ὁ Διάκονος (Athens, 1965) (rep. from Ἐπ.Ἑτ.Βυζ.Σπ., 34 [1965], 1–138), 9–15; M. Ja. Sjuzjumov, "Mirovozzrenie L'va D'jakona," *Antičnaja Drevnost' i Srednie Veka*, 7 (= *Učenye zapiski Uralskogo gosudarstvennogo universiteta*, no. 112, hist. ser. 22) (Sverdlovsk, 1971), 136–38, 141. The latter, like Panagiotakes, identifying Leo the Deacon with Leo (metropolitan) of Karias, author of a flattering encomium addressed to Basil II, emphasizes that "judging from his *History*, Leo can on no account be recognized as a loyal follower of the Macedonian dynasty" (*ibid.*, 136). Most of the last book of Leo the Deacon's *History* consists of an enumeration of the internal and external misfortunes of the Empire during the reign of Basil II. He supports his opinion that the Rhôs are a danger to their neighbors by quoting the prophet Ezek. 38:3, 39:1; cf. Leo Diaconus, 149.

[63] Cf. Vasil'evskij, *Trudy*, II, 107–24; F. Scheidweiler, "Studien zu Johannes Geometres," *BZ*, 45 (1952), 300–19.

II

214

heed to Basil's successes, seeing only the country's calamities, plunder, drought, and earthquake, and declaring that "the East is bleeding with its own blood and the Sword is dividing kinfolk," and that the homeland is "lifeless and cast down."[64]

The question arises as to what the poet thought about those who were called upon to save the throne and the Empire. Perhaps the answer is evident in the verse Εἰς τοὺς Βουλγάρους:

Κατὰ Σκυθῶν πρὶν συμμάχους, νῦν δὲ Σκύθας
λήψοισθε, Θρᾷκες, συμμάχους πρὸς τοὺς φίλους.
σκιρτᾶτε καὶ κροτεῖτε, φῦλα Βουλγάρων,
καὶ σκῆπτρα καὶ τὸ στέμμα καὶ τὴν πορφύραν
κρατεῖτε καὶ φορεῖτε, καὶ φοινικίδας
(ζήτησον στίχον ἕνα)
μεταμφιάσει καὶ ξύλοις τοὺς αὐχένας
μακροῖς συνέξει καὶ κυφῶσι τοὺς πόδας,
ξανεῖ δὲ πολλοῖς νῶτα καὶ τὴν κοιλίαν.
ἀνθ' ὧν ἀφέντες δημιουργεῖν ⟨σχίσματα⟩
αὐτοὺς φορεῖν τολμᾶτε καὶ φρονεῖν μέγα.

About the Bulgarians

Before, Thracians, you wished to win allies against the Scythians, but now you wish to win the Scythians as allies against your friends.
Dance for joy and clap your hands, Bulgarian tribes,
take and hold scepters and the stemma and the purple, the scarlet . . .
(one line missing)
. . . he will strip off your clothes and will hold your necks and feet in long planks and pillories,
and for many of you will crush your backs and mangle your stomachs.
And so, cease to make ⟨divisions⟩ among yourselves,
and have the courage to bear yourselves as men and to be proud.[65]

[64] Cf. J. A. Cramer, *Anecdota Graeca*, IV (Oxford, 1841), 271–73, 322–35, 341ff., 347, 361; Vasil'-evskij, *Trudy*, II, 112–13, 121–23. Scheidweiler found it impossible to date both poems (about revolt and travel) after the October 25 earthquake, because the poet was traveling to Selybria ἐν μηνὶ Δύστρῳ, i.e., in March, and the revolt of Sclerus ended on October 11 ("Studien," 316–18). But the date on which he started this journey is not that on which he wrote his verse, since he described a summer drought and an earthquake, and no earthquake other than that of October 25 is known. The agreement with Sclerus did not end the revolt, so the poet could still write about the latter after October 25.

[65] The Greek text is according to Scheidweiler ("Studien," 315) after the text of Cramer (*Anecdota Graeca*, IV, 282–83), with English translation by Michael Jeffreys. Here some suppositions of Scheidweiler have been taken into account: αὐτοὺς in the last line instead of τούτους; and σχίσματα for the missing word in the penultimate line, which is out of character with the metrics but renders well the sense. I am aware of the difficulties in understanding this verse, but the revision was stimulated by existing translations and interpretations of the verse as a threat addressed to the Bulgars, rendered insolent by their success of 986, after the conclusion of the alliance between the Byzantines and the Rus'. Russian translation, cf. Vasil'evskij, *Trudy*, II, 117; Bulgarian translation by G. Cankova-

The Thracians are, of course, the Byzantines, used here perhaps ironically for Romans to underline a situation in which the entire territory of the Empire was reduced to the capital and the theme of Thrace. Since the Bulgarians are called here by their own name, "Scythians," normally used for Bulgarians, can only mean Russes, and the poet therefore intends to put them on the same level. Geometres, in speaking of "allies against the Scythians," is referring to the war of 969–71, when Thrace was menaced by Svjatoslav and the Armenians (the "allies") were fighting the Russes. Φίλοι, "friends," in this case would be accurately understood to mean "kith and kin" (φίλοι in this meaning is known), which corresponds exactly to the insurgent peoples, namely the Greeks, Armenians, and Iberians. A situation in which Russes are called upon to fight against the kith and kin of the Thracians would please only the Bulgarians, who could reach out without fear for the imperial regalia. Then, after the missing line, the poet, addressing the Thracians, warns of a dismal future and appeals to them to end the quarrels among "yourselves" (Byzantines), i.e., Thracians and φίλοι. We can only guess about the identity of the "he" from the missing line: the Bulgarian ruler who threatens Thrace with the danger of invasion; the Russian ruler who, as Svjatoslav once did, will change from ally to enemy; or Basil himself, whose policy of misalliance with the Rus' could lead "the Thracians" into slavery.

The tenor of the verse is one of concern, but it is caustic toward "the Thracians." If this interpretation is accepted, it can be assumed that the poem was written sometime in 987–88, probably with reference to the negotiations for the alliance between Basil and Vladimir. The content of this verse, as I understand it, corresponds fully with the poet's disapproval of his time, which he saw as a negation of the splendor enjoyed under Nicephorus Phocas. Did the poet's weakness for this dead Emperor extend also to the Emperor's nephew?

Another poem, probably written by John Geometres, might throw some light on the Byzantine attitude toward the Russes, if the date of its composition can be determined. This is the poem on Nicephorus Phocas, which is incorporated by Scylitzes in his *Synopsis* as an epitaph and is attributed to John, metropolitan of Melitene, who is identified chiefly with Geometres by modern scholars.[66] Until now this poem has been dated to shortly after the

Petkova, in *Fontes graeci historiae bulgaricae*, V (Sofia, 1964), 319. Very free translations and an association with the events of about 969–70 have been proposed by Balasčev, *Bŭlgariě* (note 26 *supra*), 29–30, and P. O. Karyškovskij, "K istorii balkanskih vojn Svjatoslava," *VizVrem*, N.S. 7 (1953), 228–29.

[66] *Scylitzae synopsis*, 282; Cedrenus, II, 378; the poem has been published several times: cf. I. Ševčenko, "Poems on the Deaths of Leo VI and Constantine VII in the Madrid Manuscript of Scylitzes," *DOP*, 23–24 (1969–70), 189–90; Russian translation by Vasil'evskij, *Trudy*, II, 114–15; rather free German by G. Soyter, *Byzantinische Dichtung* (Athens, 1938), 41–42. For the translation of the fragment of the poem published here I am indebted to Elizabeth Jeffreys. Recently, the authorship of the poem has been questioned: "Les rapports de Jean Géomètre avec Nicéphore sont connus, mais de là à conclure, en ne tenant compte que du style de quelques vers, à l'identité de Jean le Géomètre avec Jean de Mélitène, il y a loin. Il faudrait une preuve beaucoup plus décisive" (J. Darrouzès, "Inventaire des épistoliers byzantins du Xᵉ siècle," *REB*, 18 [1960], 120). But Scheidweiler, on the basis of his studies of the texts, remarks concerning the poems on Nicephorus Phocas that "Der Dichter ist John Geometres, daran ist kein Zweifel" ("Studien," 307–9). Ševčenko, who takes these doubts into account, tentatively ascribes the poem to John Geometres ("Poems," 191 note 16, 223). Vasil'-

death of Nicephorus Phocas (December 11, 969) and connected with Svjatoslav's campaign against Byzantium in 970. The poem is essentially an appeal to the murdered Emperor to rise from the dead and protect the city (Constantinople) against the Russes. The lines most interesting for our purposes are the following:

ὁρμᾷ καθ' ἡμῶν Ῥωσικὴ πανοπλία,
Σκυθῶν ἔθνη σφύζουσιν εἰς φονουργίας,
λεηλατοῦσι πᾶν ἔθνος* τὴν σὺν πόλιν,
οὓς ἐπτόει πρὶν καὶ γεγραμμένος τύπος
πρὸ τῶν πυλῶν σὸς ἐν πόλει Βυζαντίου.

A Russian army charges against us,
tribes of Scythians are eager for murder,
every nation* plunders your city,
(peoples) whom formerly your graven image
before the gates of the city of Byzantium terrified.

* Here the meaning seems to be "any nation," "all comers."

Poetic license alone cannot explain these verses about the presence of Russian warriors in the most holy city itself. It is true that Svjatoslav had given the Byzantines good cause for fright. He had promised, if one believes Leo the Deacon, that "he would soon be pitching his own tents beneath the walls of Constantinople"; but the Russian army came only within a hundred miles of the capital, where it was successfully halted by Arcadiopolis in the spring of 970. One of the first measures taken by John Tzimisces as emperor was to relocate the army commanded by Sclerus to winter quarters in Mysia; thus, from the beginning, the capital was well protected.[67] The poet's assertion that only Nicephorus could save the Empire would not, therefore, accord with Tzimisces' action against the Russes. The poet's gloomy presentation might be explained by his strong antipathy toward the new Emperor and his mistress, Theophano (widow of Nicephorus and mother of Basil II), but the false accusation about Russian plunder in the city would only weaken the political trend of the poem. Scheidweiler, finding that such a literary production would have been very risky, supposed that John Geometres could not have released the epitaph to Nicephorus during Tzimisces' lifetime, and that perhaps he made it public after becoming metropolitan of Melitene.[67a] More

evskij, who dated this epitaph to 970–72 (*Trudy*, II, 115), noted that only two lines of the poem, if they were to be interpreted literally, seem to contradict this dating (cf. *Scylitzae synopsis*, 282, lines 70–71):

ὁ μηδὲ νυξὶ μικρὸν ὑπνώττειν θέλων   He who was unwilling to sleep briefly even at night
ἐν τῷ τάφῳ νῦν μακρὸν ὑπνώττει χρόνον.   Now sleeps for a long time in the grave.

But the phrase "for a long time" can be interpreted in many different ways; so I reject this poet's observation as an argument for my later dating of the poem.

[67] Cf. Leo Diaconus, 105–11; *Scylitzae synopsis*, 287–91; Cedrenus, II, 383–88. P. Karyškovskij, "O hronologii russko-vizantijskih vojn pri Svjatoslave," *VizVrem*, N.S. 5 (1952), 135–38; A. D. Stokes, "The Balkan Campaigns of Svjatoslav Igorevich," *SIEERev*, 40 (1962), 491–94.

[67a] "Studien," 307–9 and note 4 on p. 309.

simply, it can be suggested that this poem was written nearly twenty years after Nicephorus Phocas' death. What are the arguments in support of this thesis ?

First and foremost is the poem's statement about the presence of the Russian army in the capital, which actually occurred after 988/89, as a result of the agreement between Basil and Vladimir. What, then, are the Russes doing in the capital, according to the poet ? They are plundering the imperial city, but though "eager for murder," they only plunder. This situation corresponds to the presence of the Russian contingent in Constantinople before the battles of Chrysopolis and Abydus. The behavior of foreign allied troops is always troublesome for the host country, and the visiting Russian warriors were no exception. The poet simply exaggerated the existing situation, either reflecting rumor or indulging his own prejudices, which, of course, is not exceptional.

Finally, all of Asia Minor was rife with rumors hostile to Basil and his policy, and the pretender and his followers were vitally interested in them. Stories such as those told by Leo about the impalement by Russes of 20,000 inhabitants of Philippopolis in 970 were surely revived, and incited the imagination of the Byzantines. The poet, if not directly involved in the rivalry between Basil and Bardas Phocas, was no doubt kindly disposed toward the nephew of his hero.

Such an appeal to this hero could be expressed in verse at any time after his death, but political poetry, addressed to contemporaries and seeking an echo in society, contains a certain reality which can result even from the poet's own interpretation. During the reign of Tzimisces, the circumstances for such an appeal were unfavorable, but they were fitting for the time of Basil, especially in the eighties. In the political verse Εἰς τὸν κομιτόπολον, John Geometres appeals to Nicephorus to "come for a little from the grave" to teach the Bulgarians a lesson. Recently, this verse was dated convincingly to about 986/87.[68] Further, the verse written by John Geometres concerning the reasons for the Byzantine defeat of August 16–17, 986, contains an unmistakable allusion to Nicephorus Phocas.[69] Even if John Geometres did not compose the epitaph to Nicephorus, this would only strengthen the conviction that at that time, i.e., the last two decades of the tenth century, John Geometres and Leo the Deacon were not alone in their nostalgia for the days of Nicephorus, the very symbol of the Empire's prosperity.

There is one more piece of evidence of the prejudice against the Rhôs during the reign of Basil II which better reflects public sentiment than the personal feelings of a historian and deacon at the court, and of a poet and metropolitan.

---

[68] A. Leroy-Molinghen, "Les fils de Pierre de Bulgarie et les Cométopoules," *Byzantion*, 42 (1972), 405–19; and P. Orgels, "Les deux Comètes de Jean Geomètre," *ibid.*, 420–22. Earlier, the verse "On the Comet" was connected with the comet of 975, and dated to a time shortly after its appearance; cf. Vasil'evskij, *Trudy*, II, 116. Scheidweiler accepted this date, but noted that the content of the verse "ist geschichtlich falsch und ungerecht gegen Tzimiskes" ("Studien," 313). The later dating adds a new dimension to this matter.

[69] Cf. Cramer, *Anecdota Graeca*, IV, 296; Vasil'evskij, *Trudy*, II, 117; Scheidweiler, "Studien," 313–14; *Fontes graeci* (note 65 *supra*), 320.

218

This mention of Russes in a topographical guidebook to the curiosities of Constantinople, the so-called Πάτρια Κωνσταντινουπόλεως, has attracted the attention of historians. Among the descriptions of many monuments of the capital is one of an equestrian statue in the Forum of Taurus which, according to tradition, was brought from Antioch. On the pedestal of this statue were bas-reliefs depicting "the last days of the City, when the Rhôs should destroy it."[70] The prediction that the Russes would destroy Constantinople testifies to the fear of the Rhôs which had ignited the popular imagination more deeply than fear of the Arabs or the Bulgarians. This odd belief probably had its origin in the completely unexpected attack by the Rhôs on Constantinople in 860. For our purposes it is important that this conviction existed when the above-mentioned *Patria* was compiled after 989, around the year 995; the date was established by Th. Preger.[71] Thus, despite the new relationship between Basil and Vladimir a few years after Abydus and the continuing participation of Russian crack troops in battles on the Bulgarian and Syrian fronts, popular sentiment had not changed. A newcomer, visiting the Forum of Taurus at the turn of the tenth century, would have heard the same commentary on the bas-reliefs of the monument. Perhaps the presence of Russian allied troops in the capital in 988–89 was so distressing that it inspired an apocalyptic vision of the end of the city with the complicity of the Rhôs.

Surely this obsession with "the end of the city and the end of history" were connected with the rise of millenarian beliefs, but it is significant that the inhabitants of the center of the Empire saw the Russes as the future destroyers of their city and the precursors of the end. There is no doubt that Basil's new policy toward Kiev was greeted by many with misgivings and anxiety about the future of the Empire, and in popular circles this fear was translated into the language of eschatological prophecy.

A second argument against the thesis formulated here is supported by the matrimonial tradition of the Byzantine emperors. The prohibition against marrying barbarians—that is, foreigners and infidels—was frequently repeated, although, for reasons of political expediency, the emperors did occasionally enter into such misalliances. Constantine Porphyrogenitus firmly upheld the

---

[70] *Scriptores originum Constantinopolitanarum*, ed. Th. Preger, II (Leipzig, 1907), 176. Some historians, in references to the *Patria Constantinopoleos*, are misleading in their reports of the inscription. It seems more likely from the text that the anonymous author of the *Patria* recorded an oral interpretation of the sculptured scenes.

[71] Th. Preger, *Beiträge zur Textgeschichte der* Πάτρια Κωνσταντινουπόλεως (Munich, 1895), 4–6. As far as I know, this date has never been questioned, but scholars generally prefer to use a less precise dating, "from the end of the tenth century" or "at the close of the tenth century." Cf. also C. Diehl, "De quelques croyances byzantines sur la fin de Constantinople," *BZ*, 30 (1930), 192, 194–95; A. A. Vasiliev, "Medieval Ideas of the End of the World: West and East," *Byzantion*, 16 (1942–43), 462, 470–71, 478f., 487–95; *idem*, *The Russian Attack on Constantinople in 860* (Cambridge, Mass., 1946), 242; P. J. Alexander, "Historiens byzantins et croyances eschatologiques," *XIIe Congrès International des Etudes Byzantines. Résumés des Communications* (Belgrade-Ochrid, 1961), 2; D. A. Miller, *Imperial Constantinople* (New York, 1969), 159–62. Miller makes an interesting remark that the unknown writer of the *Patria* "may have been responding to the campaigns of Svjatoslav . . . or even to the presence of the Varangian guard in the city" (*ibid.*, 162).

strict injunction against the emperor's family marrying any other *ethnos*, especially "any of these shifty and dishonorable tribes of the north," and warned that "he who dared to do it was to be condemned as an alien from the ranks of the Christians and subject to the anathema, as a transgressor of ancestral laws and imperial ordinances." When Liutprand of Cremona came to Constantinople in 968 as the ambassador of Otto I to negotiate a marriage for the German Emperor's son, he was told: "It is an unheard of thing that a daughter born in the purple of an emperor born in the purple should marry a foreigner."[72]

Thus, the conviction has grown, as if there were direct source evidence for it, that Vladimir could not have been accorded this honor without extreme pressure on his part, which the capture of Cherson could have provided. However, while this honor had twenty years earlier been denied the German Emperor, who far outranked the Russian King in international status and power, the Byzantine Emperor Nicephorus Phocas was not in such desperate straits as was Basil II. This disparity was not lost on contemporaries of both Emperors. Hence, one must take into account not the imperial doctrine but the political reality.

The situation of the legitimate dynasty was critical. The year 987 left Basil an emperor without an empire. All the Asian provinces had fallen to the rebellious Bardas Phocas, and in most of the European provinces the Bulgars were dominant.[73] Most important was the fact that the Armenians and the Iberians supported Phocas; these crack troops, especially the Iberians, had been the Empire's strongest military force.[74] Basil could not rely upon the Greeks either. Psellus wrote: "In opposition to Basil, the greater part of the army ranged beside Bardas Phocas, who had won over the leading and most powerful families .... The Emperor Basil was well aware of disloyalty among the Romans .... It was no longer in imagination, but in very truth, that Bardas Phocas put on the imperial robes, with the emperor's crown and the royal insignia of purple."[75] In order to save his crown, Basil had to take radical action.

On April 4, 988, Basil finally repealed for domestic reasons Nicephorus Phocas' law of 964 against monastic and ecclesiastical possessions. Some

---

[72] *Constantine Porphyrogenitus, De Administrando Imperio*, § 13, ed. Gy. Moravcsik, trans. R. J. H. Jenkins (Budapest, 1949), 70–73; *Liudprandi Legatio*, Bonn ed. (1828), 350. Cf. Ostrogorsky, "Vladimir" (note 2 *supra*), 34–36; Obolensky, *Byzantine Commonwealth*, 196–97; references to bibliography: *De Administrando Imperio* (hereafter, *DAI*), II, *Commentary*, ed. R. J. H. Jenkins (London, 1962), 67–68.

[73] Cf. Yaḥyā, in Rozen, *Imperator*, 27; and in PO, 23, p. 430; Zlatarski, *Istorija* (note 26 *supra*), II, 675–87; I. Dujčev, "Napadenija na car Samuel v oblasta na Lariso prez 987–989," *Sbornik na Bŭlgarskata AN*, 41 (1945), 20–24.

[74] The Armenians supporting Bardas Sclerus had taken part in the revolt from its beginning, whereas the Iberians had been an important part of the Byzantine army commanded by Bardas Phocas. When the latter revolted, he also received military aid from the ruler of Upper Tao, David. Cf. Asoghik, III, §§ 24, 25; Yaḥyā, in Rozen, *Imperator*, 22, 24, 26, 27; and in PO, 23, pp. 421–24, 427–29; Psellus, *Chronographia*, I, § 10. The Iberians had upon the revolt of Bardas Sclerus in 979. Cf. M. Tarchnišvili, "Die Anfänge der schriftstellerischen Tätigkeit des hl. Euthymius und der Aufstand von Bardas Skleros," *OrChr*, 38 (1954), 123–24; N. Lomouri, "K istorii vosstanija Vardy Sklira," *Trudy Tbilisskogo gosud. universiteta*, 67 (1957), 29–46.

[75] Psellus, *Chronographia*, I, §§ 10, 13; trans. Sewter, 15, 17.

scholars doubt that the chrysobull is genuine because this decree had already been repealed by Tzimisces. In addition, the pro-monastic emphasis of this document contradicts the subsequent edict of 996, in which Basil tried to restrict the extension of ecclesiastical property, in apparent disregard of his repeal of 988.[76] But since textual tradition supports the reliability of the novel of 988,[77] the contradiction seems to lie, not in the documents, but in the circumstances of the times. In 988 Basil needed the support of the Church. Even if the novel of Nicephorus had been revoked, or unenforced after 969, Basil's disassociation from it was well timed; he writes in his chrysobull, "... a law whose issuance was unjust and insolent not only to the churches and the pious institutions but to God Himself, has been the cause and source of the present evils and of the general upheaval and disturbance ...."[78] This explicit declaration of his Church policy put an end to rumors fanned by his enemies.[79] By 996 the crisis was over, and Basil could take some measures against lay and ecclesiastical land magnates. But he avoided any allusion to the more radical and extensive edict of Nicephorus Phocas.

In the arena of international politics, between September 987 and April 988 Basil negotiated an accord with the Fatimid Caliphate of Egypt. It was no coincidence that at a time when the eastern part of the Empire was under the rule of Phocas, Basil sent an embassy to Cairo and accepted, according to Arab historians, "distressing terms."[80] This was a diplomatic strike at the usurper, but for a military action a strong army, such as that of the Rus', was needed. Byzantine emperors had called upon this army before, but because of the loss of his Armenian and Iberian troops, Basil needed a reliable force.

---

[76] F. Dölger, *Regesten der Kaiserurkunden des oströmischen Reiches*, I (Munich, 1924), nos. 772, 783; Ostrogorsky, *History* (note 2 *supra*), 293 note 2, 306–7.

[77] Cf. N. Svoronos, *La Synopsis Major des Basiliques et ses appendices* (Paris, 1964), 22, 39, 61, 85, 97, 155, 157, 168.

[78] *Jus Graeco-Romanum*, ed. C. E. Zachariae von Lingenthal, III (Leipzig, 1856), 303–4; English trans. in P. Charanis, "Monastic Properties and the State in the Byzantine Empire," *DOP*, 4 (1948), 62.

[79] Cf. Charanis, "Monastic Properties," 60–64; A. P. Každan, *Derevnja i gorod v Vizantii IX–X vv.* (Moscow, 1960), 74. Charanis, arguing for the authenticity of the novel of April 988, thinks that Phocas' novel against the monasteries was not repealed until the reign of Basil II (cf. *ibid.*, 61 note 23). But the assumption that it could not have been cancelled twice is only legally correct. In December 969, the new Emperor John Tzimisces probably repealed Nicephorus Phocas' novel by damaging it or returning it to the Synod (cf. Dölger, *Regesten*, 726), although no written statement was submitted to the Church until 988. Because of the pessimistic tone of this novel, its date of April 4, 988, is commonly seen as the terminus post quem of the arrival of Russian troops in the imperial city. This inference results from an oversimplification, that Russian help was the crucial remedy, and from a failure to see the different aspects of Basil's action. The date of the novel is not important here.

[80] Dölger, *Regesten*, no. 770 (end of 987); Rozen, *Imperator*, 202–5; M. Canard, *Histoire de la Dynastie des H'amdanides de Jazîra et de Syrie*, I (Algiers, 1951), 853–55. The embassy is dated by Abu'l Mahasin and al-'Ainī to A.H. 377 (May 3, 987–April 20, 988), and its necessity arose sometime after Bardas Phocas' treason (September 14, 987).

It was a shaky peace; hostilities were resumed in 991. But it is not true that "Basil II was obliged to sign this treaty" (M. Canard, in *CMH*, IV, pt. 1 [1966], 724), because the presence of the Fatimid army on the southeast border of the Empire, at that time under Bardas Phocas' rule, served Basil's purposes. Perhaps he merely wanted to prevent an agreement between Phocas and Egypt. It is also possible that "Emperor" Bardas Phocas himself negotiated with the Fatimid Caliph; the information given by both fourteenth-century Arab historians, who used a common source, is too general and does not give the Emperor's name. A clause in this treaty, which requests the mention of the Caliph's name in prayers at the mosque in Constantinople, might point to the actual rather than the potential master of the capital.

The question was whether he could be sure of the Rus'. The Russian King Svjatoslav had taught the Byzantines a bitter lesson: although he had been paid handsomely in the finest gold, Svjatoslav, when called upon to repress the Bulgars, had demonstrated political ambitions of his own. It is true that in a Byzantino-Russian treaty concluded in July 971 Svjatoslav had declared: "If any foe plans to attack your [Byzantine] realm, I shall resist him and go to war against him." But the promise of a Russian king killed by Patzinaks at Byzantine instigation could hardly carry much weight.[81]

The idea of a new appeal to the Rus' must have filled the Emperor and his entourage with some misgivings, but Basil had no choice. He had to protect himself against surprises and assure himself of continued armed support, and the best possible solution appeared to be a matrimonial relationship between the two dynasties. Since for some time Kiev had been ready and willing to adopt Christianity, this alliance could be established as a religious partnership.

Of course, for Vladimir the alliance was an exceptional honor, but Basil was vitally interested in such a connection. Not long before, Basil's grandfather Constantine Porphyrogenitus had admitted with distaste that his father-in-law Romanus Lecapenus had given his granddaughter to the tsar of Bulgaria. Romanus was "a common, illiterate fellow ... not from among those who ... followed the Roman national customs ... [and was] of a temper arrogant and self-willed ...."[82] The same criticisms were surely leveled against Basil, but in a short time it became clear that he was following Roman national interests. Thus I conclude that the real initiator of Vladimir and Anna's marriage was the Emperor Basil himself, and in this case, the Cherson legend shows more knowledge of imperial matrimonial customs than of historical realities.

The foregoing analysis of possible counter-arguments neither proves nor disproves my thesis, although the acquired insight into the historical context makes it more convincing. But what support is there for the theory that Cherson was in revolt against Basil?

The history of Cherson reveals that this once autonomous Greek city never gave up its separatist tendencies, even during the tenth and eleventh centuries, which led to a compromise: the dual power of a military governor and a primate of the Chersonite municipality.[83] The situation was so special and so important for the Empire that Constantine Porphyrogenitus gave much attention to the history of, and imperial policy toward, the city in his *De Administrando Imperio*. Recommending that local authority not be trusted, he repeated the advice given to Emperor Theophilus: "If you wish complete mastery and dominion

[81] Cf. PSRL, I, cols. 71–74; Cross, *Chronicle*, 88–90; *Scylitzae synopsis*, 309–10; Cedrenus, II, 412–13. In the light of both sources, there is no doubt of Byzantine involvement in the final defeat of Svjatoslav's army on the rapids of the Dnieper. For Byzantine-Russian relations under Svjatoslav, cf. Levčenko, *Očerki*, 252–90; Stokes, "Balkan Campaigns" (note 67 *supra*), 466–96; Pašuto, *Vnešnjaja politika* (note 2 *supra*), 69–73.
[82] Constantine Porphyrogenitus, *DAI*, § 13, p. 73.
[83] Cf. Šestakov, *Očerki* (note 53 *supra*), 57–94; A. A. Vasiliev, *The Goths in the Crimea* (Cambridge, Mass., 1936), 87–135; Jakobson, *Rannesrednevekovyj Hersones* (note 6 *supra*), 35–66; A. F. Višnjakova, "Svincovye pečati vizantijskogo Hersonesa," *VestDrIst*, 1(6) (1939), 121–33.

over the city of Cherson and of the places in Cherson, and that they should not slip out of your hand, appoint your own military governor and do not trust in their primates and nobles." Most instructive is the passage about the vigorous reprisals ordered against Chersonite men and property in the event of a revolt. In particular, the Emperor ordered that all Chersonite ships with cargo along the coast of the provinces of the Armeniakoi, of Paphlagonia, and of Boukellarian must be confiscated. Then the "imperial agents must forbid the Paphlagonian and Boukellarian merchant ships and coastal vessels of the Pontus to cross to Cherson with grain or wine or any other necessary commodity or merchandise." The Emperor's conclusion is also worth quoting: "If the Chersonites do not journey to Romania and sell the hides and wax that they get by trade from the Patzinaks, they cannot live. If grain does not pass across from Amisos and from Paphlagonia and the Boukellarioi and the flanks of the Armeniakoi, the Chersonites cannot live."[84] Thus, the Byzantine Emperor clarifies the economic basis of Cherson's political orientation, i.e., that whoever had control of the above-mentioned provinces on the Black Sea had the key to Cherson. Since 987 this had been the usurper Bardas Phocas, who occupied all the ports and coastal cities in Asia Minor excluding Abydus.[85] Economic reasons alone, therefore, were sufficient for Cherson's recognition of the real ruler of Asia Minor.

However, there do seem to be some political reasons as well behind Chersonian support of Bardas Phocas, from whom the city could look forward to more autonomy. Traces of political tension between Byzantium and Cherson are discernible at the end of the sixties, when Cherson played an important role in Byzantino-Russian relations. Kalokyros, son of the Chersonian primate (and very likely a primate himself), who was made *patricius* by Nicephorus Phocas, recruited Svjatoslav for the expedition against the Bulgars, and then, according to Leo the Deacon, with the help of the Russian ruler, made a bid for the imperial crown itself.[86] We don't know what eventually happened to Kalokyros because, unfortunately, little is known of the history of Cherson at this time. Thanks to the entanglement, which was favorable for Cherson, of Byzantine, Khazar, Russian, and finally Patzinak political and economic affairs in the Crimea, the city apparently still enjoyed some autonomy.[87] It is too risky to

[84] Constantine Porphyrogenitus, *DAI*, §§ 42, 53, pp. 185, 259–87; cf. *Commentary*, II, 209.
[85] Leo Diaconus, 173.
[86] *Ibid.*, 63, 77, 79, 134; *Scylitzae synopsis*, 277, 288, 295; Cedrenus, II, 372, 383–84, 394; N. D. Znojko, "O posol'stvĕ Kalokira v' Kiev'," *ŽMNP*, N.S., pt. 8 (April, 1907), 229–72. In the Dumbarton Oaks Collection there are a few seals of Spatharocandidatus Kalokyros, dated to the tenth century (D.O. 58.106:1029, 2258, 3866, 3848).
[87] The treaty of 971 concluded between Svjatoslav and Tzimisces seems to accentuate the special status of Cherson, to whom Svjatoslav undertook an obligation:
"... jako nikoliže pomyšlu na stranu [ἡ χώρα?] vašju ni sbiraju voi (ljudii) ni jazyka [τὸ ἔθνως?] ni inogo privedu na stranu vašju i eliko est' pod' vlast'ju [ἡ ἐξουσία or ἡ ἀρχή?] greč'skoju: ni na vlast' [ἡ ἀρχή or ἡ χώρα?] Korsun'skuju i eliko est' gorodov'ih'ni na stranu Bolgar'sku...."
"... never to be ill-intentioned toward your country nor to collect warriors (people) or to lead other nations against your country and those which are under Greek rule: neither against the Khersonian dominion and those cities which belong to it, nor against the Bulgarian land...."
This treaty was translated from the Greek, and hypothetical words of the original text are given in brackets. The Old Russian text is published in PSRL, I, col. 73, and II, cols. 60–61, with one se-

attempt to identify the Chersonian Kalokyros with the *patricius* Kalokyros "Delphinas," who was governor of Byzantine Italy in the early eighties[88] and in 988 commanded the usurper's troops at Chrysopolis. Taken prisoner, he was impaled by order of Basil.[89]

There was probably a distressing political situation in Cherson before 989 at the time of the civil war, since even during the stable time of Constantine Porphyrogenitus, in the fifties, the court had to contend constantly with insubordination and revolt in the city. Its return, plundered and partially ruined, to imperial authority in 989 did not end this ferment, which later led to open revolt, suppressed in 1016, with the help of the Rus', by the Emperor Basil's navy.[90]

Returning to the so-called Cherson legend, it is easier now to understand its failure to offer an explanation for the Cherson expedition. While the citizens had no desire to recall their disloyalty to the legal emperors, they were anxious to connect events in Cherson with the Russian conversion and to emphasize the usefulness of their city for imperial policy in the north. The most accurate part of the legend concerns the ecclesiastical equipment and treasures which were taken from Cherson as booty for the new churches in Kiev.[91] The legend contains few realistic details regarding the siege, but the suggestion that the city was subjected to a naval blockade permits us to conclude that the siege began before the winter of 988.[92] Because of secret information given to Vladi-

---

mantic difference—*voi* (warriors) in the Laurentian MS and *ljudii* (people) in the Hypatian MS. The translation by Cross, *Chronicle*, 89–90, is inaccurate. On the position of Cherson in the treaty of 944, see *infra*, notes 144, 145.

[88] Cf. V. von Falkenhausen, *Untersuchungen über die byzantinische Herrschaft in Süditalien vom 9. bis ins 11. Jahrhundert* (Wiesbaden, 1967), 84, 168–70.

[89] Leo Diaconus, 173–74; *Scylitzae synopsis*, 336. There can be no doubt that Kalokyros, katepan of Italy (982–84), was also the follower of Bardas Phocas. The absence of "Delphinas" as a nickname for Kalokyros about 970 can be easily understood, but it would be harder to explain if "Delphinas" were a patronymic, which would lead us in the eleventh century to Thessalia (cf. *Sovety i rasskazy Kekavmena*, ed. and commentary G. G. Litavrin [Moscow, 1972], 256–57, 527–28). But most at variance with this identification is the account of Leo the Deacon, for whom the Kalokyros of around 970 and the Kalokyros of 988 are two different people. Reference to the complicated sources of Leo's *History* (cf. Každan, "Iz istorii" [note 61 *supra*], 106–28, and P. Karyškovskij, "Balkanskie vojny Svjatoslava v Vizantijskoj istoričeskoj literature," *VizVrem*, N.S. 6 [1953], 54–56) does nothing to clarify these matters. The fact is that Leo was a contemporary of these people and events; he was in the capital in 967, at age eighteen or nineteen (cf. Panagiotakes, Λέων [note 62 *supra*], 4–5), when Nicephorus Phocas sent Kalokyros to Kiev, and he would surely have identified two well-known personages who figured prominently in important events of the time if in fact they had been one and the same person. A dignitary named Kalokyros is known from the end of the tenth century, but the supposition that all the Kalokyroi originated in Cherson (cf. J. Darrouzès, *Epistoliers byzantins du Xe siècle* [Paris, 1960], 169–70, 355–56) seems doubtful.

[90] *Scylitzae synopsis*, 354–55; Cedrenus, II, 464. Cf. I. V. Sokolova, "Pečati Georgija Culy i sobytija 1016 g. v Hersone," *Palestinskij Sbornik*, 23/86 (1971), 68–74. Cf. A. P. Každan, in *Byzantinoslavica*, 33 (1972), 298.

[91] The most impressive trophy, the captured quadriga, was still on public display at the beginning of the twelfth century. Cf. Cross, *Chronicle*, 116: "Vladimir also found and appropriated two bronze statues and four bronze horses, which now stand behind the Church of the Holy Virgin, and which the ignorant think are made of marble."

[92] For arguments in support of a very long siege, cf. A. Berthier-Delagarde, "Kak Vladimir osaždal Korsun'," *Izvestija Otdelenija russhago jazyka i slovestnosti AN*, vol. 14, bk. 1 (1909), 252–57; N.V. Pjatyševa, "'Zemljanoj put',' rasskaza o pohode Vladimira na Korsun'," *SovArh* (1964), pt. 3, pp. 104–14.

mir by a Chersonite called Anastasius, the water supply was cut off and the city surrendered. Anastasius of Cherson was a real person who played a role in the events of the year 1018 in Kiev.[93] Consequently, it is possible to determine the reasons for the city's capture shortly after April 13. When the news of Basil's victory at Abydus reached Cherson, the partisans of the Emperor took heart. They were too weak to change the policy of the city, which was counting on the new revolt of Bardas Sclerus, but they were able to help the Emperor by contributing toward its surrender to Vladimir.

IV. Byzantium and Rus': an Attempt to Reconstruct the Course of Events between 986–89

From the foregoing discussion we can attempt to reconstruct the events that on one hand led the Byzantine Empire out of the morass of civil war and on the other brought Kievan Russia into the sphere of Christian civilization. Essential to a reconstruction of the chronology of events are the date of the agreement between Emperor Basil II and King Vladimir I and the date of its fulfillment by both parties.

The severe military defeat and more painful loss of prestige in a battle with the Bulgars on August 17, 986, caused Basil II to revise the Byzantine policy toward the Bulgars, which had been formulated by Tzimisces.[94] By that time, the young Emperor must have already realized that the Byzantine defeat in the battle of Trajan's Gates was due not only to the success of the Bulgar troops but also to the scheming of the higher military aristocracy, whose influence had diminished or whose position was imperiled, and who thought that this Emperor, suspicious, independent, and inexperienced in military affairs, should be taught a lesson.[95] The Emperor, seeking revenge, but not at the price of concessions to this aristocracy against whom his suspicions appeared to be justified, was forced to look for an ally who would be able to suppress the rebellious Bulgars. The conquest of the Bulgars by Svjatoslav suggested the idea of renewing the agreements of the treaties of 945 and 971 that provided for Russian military aid against the enemies of Byzantium. It is

[93] Cf. PSRL, I, cols. 109, 116, 121, 124, 144; Cross, Chronicle, 112, 116, 119, 121, 132; but the identification of Anastasius with the archbishop of Kiev mentioned by Thietmar, Bishop of Merseberg, Chronici libri VIII, ed. F. Kurze (Hannover, 1889), IX, 32, p. 258, is wrong (cf. Cross, Chronicle, note 140 on p. 254). For Anastasius' position in Kiev, cf. Müller, Zum Problem (note 4 supra), 42–47, and Poppe, Państwo, 46–48.

[94] Cf. Ostrogorsky, History, 295–96, 300–3; R. Browning, Byzantium and Bulgaria (London, 1975), 71–75.

[95] Leo Diaconus, 171, speaks of the incompetence of commanders. John Scylitzes' report implies a climate of suspicion and charges of treason, which were probably unjust, but there is no doubt that high-ranking army officers did not like Emperor Basil. See Scylitzae synopsis, 331–32; Cedrenus, II, 436–38; Psellus, Chronographia, I, § 30, vol. I, pp. 18–19; cf. Rozen, Imperator, 20, 172–74; Vasil'-evskij, Trudy, II, 85–87; Ostrogorsky, History, 305–6, and idem, "Observations on the Aristocracy in Byzantium," DOP, 25 (1971), 7; cf. also A. Každan, Social'nyj sostav gospodstvujuščego klassa Vizantii XI–XII vv. (Moscow, 1974), 206–9, 255–56.

most probably with this end in view that contacts with Kiev were made, shortly after the painful retreat from Bulgaria.[96] A few months later, when the Byzantine aristocracy, encouraged by the Emperor's lack of success, openly declared themselves against the Macedonian dynasty, Basil had no choice but to smash their political ambitions.

The news of the crushing defeat of Basil's armies by the Bulgars resulted in a new revolt by Bardas Sclerus in December 986. Aided in Baghdad by the emir of Buwayhid Samsam al-daulah, he reached Melitene early in February 987 and proclaimed himself emperor.[97] With the help of troops recruited from Arab nomads and Kurds, and especially with the support of the Armenian population in the eastern provinces of Byzantium, Sclerus extended his rule within the month as far as Sebaste. The metropolitan of Sebaste, Theophylact, fearing reprisals by the local Armenian population, fled to the capital.[98] Basil II sought the help of the talented commander and ambitious politician, Bardas Phocas, though the latter was suspected of having taken part in the *paracoemomenus* plot in 985. Phocas had defeated Sclerus once before, in 979.[99] Basil distrusted Phocas from the beginning, but he had no other choice and probably counted on the animosity that still existed between the two old rivals. In April 987 he restored the title of *domesticus* of the East to Bardas Phocas and appointed him commander-in-chief of the army, which consisted of Greek and Iberian units, against Sclerus. Though he had sworn allegiance to the Emperor on everything holy, Phocas did not keep his oath. Without delay, probably as early as April or May, he began negotiations through Constantine, his brother-in-law and the brother of Bardas Sclerus.[100] After agreeing to the division of the Empire, the two claimants to the throne met twice. The first meeting was held on the Djeyhan River, halfway between Antioch and Melitene, not later than the beginning of July and perhaps as

[96] Abū Shujā' Rudhrawari's mention of the exchange of correspondence between the two Emperors and the Russian King (see *supra*, pp. 206–7 and note 41) indicates that the negotiations were in progress in autumn 986, if we assume that the alliance itself was contracted in late summer or early autumn 987.

[97] Sclerus and his men were released in the month of Shâban 376 (December 6, 986–January 3, 987) and left Baghdad in that same month, arriving in Melitene in February 987 (Yaḥyā, in PO, 23, p. 420; and in Rozen, *Imperator*, 22). Asoghik, III, § 24, who dates these events toward the end of the year 435 of the Armenian cycle (March 25, 986–March 24, 987), says that Arab nomads "conducted Sclerus hurriedly to Melitene, situated thirty-one days from Baghdad" (*Des Stephanos von Taron*, 187; *Histoire universelle*, 128; *Vseobščaja istorija*, 177). The journey could not have lasted longer, so Sclerus reached Melitene in the beginning of February 987.

[98] Asoghik, III, §§ 20, 22, connects with the year 435 of the Armenian cycle Theophylact's conflict with Armenian priests and the Emperor's calling him to diplomatic tasks in Bulgaria; thus, Theophylact must have left Sebaste before March 24, 987. The real reason for the departure was not the summons of the Emperor (for more detail, see *supra*, pp. 204–5) but the rebellion of Bardas Sclerus. Sebaste, populated mostly by Armenians and situated 120 miles from Melitene, could have declared itself for the usurper several days after the fall of Melitene.

[99] See Leo Diaconus, 170; *Scylitzae synopsis*, 324–27; Yaḥyā, in PO, 23, p. 399; and in Rozen, *Imperator*, 3, 12, 20; Asoghik, III, § 15 (*Des Stephanos von Taron*, 141–42; *Vseobščaja istorija*, 135); Psellus, *Chronographia*, I, §§ 5, 9, vol. I, pp. 4–6; cf. Vasil'evskij, *Trudy*, II, 59–60.

[100] Yaḥyā, in PO, 23, pp. 419, 421–22; and in Rozen, *Imperator*, 20, 22–23: "Basil felt the necessity of returning to Bardas Phocas the title of *domesticus* in the month of Dul Hijja 376 [April 3–May 2, 987]," but Phocas, who was at that time (from the end of 985) "the governor of Antioch and all districts of the East" could have contacted Sclerus even before his nomination.

early as June.[101] The negotiations and the agreement, mediated by Constantine Sclerus, might have taken place in April or May or, at the very latest, in June. It was about this time that Basil II learned of the treason of Bardas Phocas. He received reliable information about the secret agreement between the two usurpers from Roman, son of Sclerus, who did not trust Phocas, and who, suspecting some plot against his father, had departed for Constantinople.[102]

At the second meeting, Bardas Phocas imprisoned Bardas Sclerus through a clever ruse and openly proclaimed himself emperor, according to Scylitzes on August 15 and according to Yaḥyā on Holy Cross Day, Wednesday September 14, 987.[103] Since the information given by Scylitzes is not as accurate as that of Yaḥyā, the earlier date may refer to the confinement of Sclerus, since between the dates of the imprisonment of the latter in the Tyropoion fortress (Jérôs)[104] and the proclamation of Phocas as emperor at the court of the Cappadocian magnate Eustathius Maleinus, some time must have elapsed.

The crack troops of the Byzantine army—the Armenians, who supported Sclerus, and the Iberians, who backed Phocas—were now among the adversaries of Basil II. With the unfavorable attitude of the military and the landed aristocracy, the opposition within the Church, and the hostility of the population of the Empire, Basil must have realized that the alliance against him by the two Bardases meant the beginning of the end of his reign. He tried to prevent the cooperation of these forces, but in order to save the throne it was necessary to oppose the armies of the usurpers with some superior force. It seems likely that Basil had begun negotiations with the Russian ruler before the new rebellion, since the issues were settled and help was forthcoming in

---

[101] Djeyhan (Ǧaihan) is the Arabic name for the river Pyramos in Cilicia. The suggestion of Honigmann (*Die Ostgrenze* [note 28 *supra*], 103, 153) that this meeting took place at the beginning of September is unacceptable, because there would have been no time for a second meeting of the two Bardases. I share his opinion that they met on the Djeyhan river, but Yaḥyā's text and the mention in Asoghik, III, § 14, allow us to conclude that there was a district of the same name situated in the area of the river basin in the vicinity of Melitene; cf. Rozen, *Imperator*, 2, 23, 85, 193. According to W. Tomaschek, *Zur historischen Topographie von Kleinasien im Mittelalter*, SBWien, Phil.-hist. Kl., 124 (1891), Abh. VIII, p. 68, the Arab geographers meant by "Djeyhan" only the important crossing of this river at al-Massisa (Mamistra).

[102] According to the record of Yaḥyā (in PO, 23, pp. 421–22; and in Rozen, *Imperator*, 23), Roman Sclerus defected to the Emperor Basil after the conclusion of the conspiracy, but before his father's first meeting with Phocas. From *Scylitzae synopsis*, 335, we know that Sclerus himself inspired his son's departure to secure the family interests in the event of defeat. Among Scylitzes' sources was the chronicle of the house of Phocades, wherein Roman's act was thus interpreted; cf. Každan, *Iz istorii* (note 62 *supra*), 106–23.

[103] *Scylitzae synopsis*, 332; Yaḥyā, in PO, 23, p. 421; and in Rozen, *Imperator*, 23. The accurate record of the Arab historian, who gives both a Moslem and a Seleucidian date pointing out the feast day and the day of the week, indicates a source from Antioch, where this event was well known (see *supra*, p. 12ff.). Holy Cross day was exceptionally suited to the proclamation of an emperor. The reliability of Yaḥyā's date is attested in the manuscript tradition of his chronicle, as witnessed by his own statement that "the revolt [of Phocas] lasted one year and seven months," exactly the time between September 14, 987 and April 13, 989 (Yaḥyā, in PO, 23, p. 426; and in Rozen, *Imperator*, 25). In Vasil'evskij's opinion (*Trudy*, II, 81), the proclamation of Bardas Phocas as emperor on August 15, 987, at the court of the Maleini was "at first the secret deed of conspirators."

[104] *Scylitzae synopsis*, 336; Asoghik, III, § 25. Tyropoion is identified with Tyriaïon in Byzantine Pisidia near Iconium (present-day Ilghin, near Konya); see W. M. Ramsay, *The Historical Geography of Asia Minor* (London, 1890), 141–42, 355–56, and map facing p. 197. According to Schlumberger (*L'Epopée byzantine* [note 15 *supra*], I, 694), the fortress Jeròs mentioned by Asoghik could be a corruption of the name Tyraïon (Tyriaïos, Teraos).

such a short time. After Basil received the news of the agreement between the two pretenders to the throne, these earlier contacts with Kiev assumed major importance. He sent envoys to Kiev invested with full powers to ensure success not only in procuring military aid but also in winning over Vladimir to the cause of the Macedonian dynasty. This mission must have set out, at the latest, after the Emperor received the news of the betrayal of Bardas Phocas, that is, in May or June 987. At this time, the most favorable for crossing the Black Sea, it would have taken no more than four to six days at a moderate speed of four or five knots to cover approximately 500 nautical miles. The 900-kilometer route up the river Dnieper to Kiev, at a speed of about twenty-five kilometers a day, could be traversed in about forty days. Counting possible delays, the journey could have lasted fifty days, or less if the Russes, informed of the envoys' approach, had sent a convoy to the rapids on the Dnieper, 500 kilometers below Kiev, to provide protection against the Patzinaks. For the rest of the journey the important members of the embassy could have gone by horseback, which would have shortened their journey by at least ten days. Thus, the Byzantine envoys probably traveled from Constantinople to Kiev in not less than thirty and not more than fifty days,[105] arriving in Kiev in July or August. A later arrival in autumn is possible, but information, mentioned below, convinces me that the envoys who contracted the treaty of alliance arrived in Kiev sometime during the summer months of 987. At any rate, we can no longer accept the popular view, based on a literal interpretation of the chronological sequence of events according to Yaḥyā, that envoys were sent to Kiev after the armies of Bardas Phocas reached the waters separating Asia from Europe.[106]

Earlier attempts to gain military aid from the Rus' could have been made in connection with a campaign against Bulgaria which would at least have ensured peace in the European area during the action against Sclerus, but in

---

[105] On travel conditions between Constantinople and Kiev, see Constantine Porphyrogenitus, *DAI*, II, *Commentary*, 31–32, 37–40, 48, 54–55 (rep. D. Obolensky, *Byzantium and the Slavs: Collected Studies* [London, 1971], V, same page nos.); A. Poppe, "La dernière expédition russe contre Constantinople," *Byzantinoslavica*, 32 (1971), 239–45. I assumed less favorable sailing conditions for my estimate for crossing the Black Sea. In summer, in good weather, such a voyage took two to three days and nights, and, at the narrowest point (144 miles), eighteen to twenty hours. Cf. D. Berenbejm, "O puti Grekov čerez Černoe more," *SovArh* (1958), pt. 3, pp. 201–3. In June 1389, Pimen, Metropolitan of Moscow, crossed the Black Sea between Caffa and Sinope (*ca.* 200 miles) in five days because of adverse winds (PSRL, XI [1897], 97). For the average speed of inland and sea navigation, cf. P. Ludwig, *Untersuchungen über die Reise und Marschgeschwindigkeit im XII. nud XIII. Jahrhundert* (Berlin, 1897), 21, 122, 131–32, 144, 155–59, 163, 184–85.

[106] Rozen, *Imperator*, 197–98; and, for instance, Šmurlo, "Kogda," 136, who states that Yaḥyā testifies categorically that the Emperor Basil had sent the envoys to Kiev only when Bardas Phocas reached Chrysopolis, which could have happened no sooner than the end of the year 987. Cf. Ostrogorskij, "Vladimir" (note 2 *supra*), 33; Vernadsky, *Kievan Russia* (note 10 *supra*), 63. There is no discrepancy between Yaḥyā and Psellus, who state that not long before the rebel army had reached the Propontis and made their entrenchment secure, "a picked band of Scythians had come to help him [Basil] from the Taurus" (Psellus, *Chronographia*, I, §§ 12, 13: ed. Renauld, vol. I, p. 9; trans. Sewter, p. 17). Yaḥyā's record (in PO, 23, pp. 423–25; and in Rozen, *Imperator*, 25–26) on the alliance of Basil and Vladimir is his own interpolation. At the point in the narrative where the army of Bardas Phocas reached Chrysopolis, Yaḥyā, before giving the account of Basil's victory at Chrysopolis, saw fit to clear up this unexpected turn of events. It is implicit from Yaḥyā's record that to prepare such a coup would have taken a great deal of time.

the summer of 987 much more was expected and much more was offered. Hence, the embassy's rank had to be in accordance with the importance of the affairs that were to be discussed. Theophylact, the metropolitan of Sebaste, known for his above-mentioned conflicts with the Armenian clergy, was probably at the head of the deputation. In the spring of 987 after the uprising of Sclerus, who sympathized with the Armenians, he had taken refuge in the capital and thereby linked his fate with that of the Macedonian dynasty. Asoghik's statement that the metropolitan of Sebaste acted as envoy in the matrimonial negotiations of Basil's sister, combined with the happenings of 987 and 988, the establishment of the metropolitanate of Rus' between 970–97, and the transfer of the metropolitan Theophylact from Sebaste to the see of 'Ρωσίας during the reign of Basil Porphyrogenitus,[107] indicates that this Church dignitary, devoted to the Emperor, was eminently suited to diplomatic as well as missionary activities. The success he achieved made him the first ambassador of the Empire to the court of the Kievan ruler, and the first leader of the Old Russian Church.

In the agreement between Basil and Vladimir, three essential problems, the acceptance of Christianity by the Rus' and their ruler, his marriage to Anna Porphyrogenita, and effective military aid for the Empire, were discussed and decisions binding on both parties were made as follows:

1. Vladimir declared in his own name as well as in the name of his subjects, "the boyars and all the people in the Russian land," his willingness to be baptized. To propagate and to strengthen the Christian faith it was decided to establish a separate Russian eparchy, a metropolitanate subordinate to the Patriarchate of Constantinople. The Byzantine party offered to organize it, and the Russian ruler gave assurances of his protection and promised to provide and maintain conditions necessary for its activity.

2. Through the mediation of their envoys, the two Emperors, Basil and his brother Constantine, expressed their readiness to become kinsmen of the ruler of the Rus' by giving him their sister Anna in marriage upon his acceptance of the Christian faith.

3. Vladimir undertook an obligation to give military aid against any enemies of the Empire, and to send to the Bosphorus, as soon as possible, several thousand warriors to fight the army of the usurpers.[108] It was also agreed that

---

[107] See note 30 *supra*, and Honigmann, "Studies" (note 31 *supra*), 142–58; Poppe, *Państwo*, 25–33.

[108] The information of Asoghik, III, § 43 (see *supra*, p. 203), about 6,000 warriors has usually been accepted as reliable, although given this historian's predilection for the numbers 3, 6, 12, and their multiples, this figure 6,000 should be considered more as an approximate than as an exact number. It is of interest that the 6,000 warriors were associated by the Armenian historian with the crack troops. Cf. Asoghik, II, § 3; III, §§ 41, 43 (*Vseobščaja istorija*, 85, 194, 200; *Histoire universelle*, 156, 164; *Des Stephanos von Taron*, 84, 205, 211). Although I have reservations about the accuracy of Asoghik's account, I am not inclined to believe that he exaggerated the size of the Russian detachment. The *Tactica* of Leo VI, concerned with the art of war, estimated the Byzantine forces from all the themes to be 40,000, but recommended that operations be conducted with two or three basic units, each 4,000 strong. In the tenth–eleventh centuries, operational units were 4,000–6,000 each and the whole Byzantine operational force was a combination of several such units. Cf. H. Delbrueck, *Geschichte der Kriegskunst*, 2nd ed., III (Berlin, 1923), 197, 208–9; F. Lot, *L'Art militaire et les armées*

Russes would subsequently undertake military action in the Crimea against Cherson because of its declaration for the usurpers.

Beside the basics of the alliance there were other less urgent items, essential to ordinary Byzantino-Russian contacts, which can also be seen in the treaties preserved from the tenth century: commercial terms and privileges, the status of Russian and Byzantine newcomers in both countries, etc.

It was of utmost importance to fix the dates for the implementation of the agreements reached. The speedy arrival in Constantinople of a strong battle contingent of Rus' was essential to the Byzantine party. If the alliance was presumably contracted in September, it would have been quite possible to send a detachment of several hundred in the autumn before navigation ceased, but it would have taken several months to prepare and send an armada of several thousand warriors. This must have been the size of Vladimir's military forces, which were scattered over his large territory. Bearing in mind the security of his own country, Vladimir could not have put at Byzantine disposal all of his armed forces.[109] He would have had to raise additional troops, drawing them from various parts of his state and probably hiring Varangians from Scandinavia as well. A lot of time would have been required to equip properly such an expeditionary force, to float shipping timber, and to build and outfit 120 to 150 ships for inland and sea navigation each with forty to sixty warriors on board.[110] The agreement must have been reached not later than September in order to give Vladimir enough time to raise a corps to start south as soon as conditions were favorable, that is, at the end of April or in May, when the high water level allowed easier navigation of the rapids by heavy warships. A voyage down the Dnieper would last twenty to thirty days, the cabotage on the Black

---

au Moyen Âge en Europe et dans le Proche Orient, I (Paris, 1946), 62–73; V. V. Kučma, "'Taktika L'va' kak istoričeskij istočnik," *VizVrem*, N.S. 33 (1972), 84. Cf. also Aristakes of Lastivert, *infra*, note 141. The striking force of Basil II in the conquest of Bulgaria was surely about 15,000 strong, and judging from the distribution of spoils in 1016 the Russes must have comprised half of the troops. Cf. *Scylitzae synopsis*, 355; Cedrenus, II, 465; A. Dain, "Le partage du butin de guerre d'après les traités juridiques et militaires," *Actes du VIe Congrès International d'Etudes Byzantines, Paris, 27 juillet-2 août, 1948*, I (Paris, 1950), 347–54. To bring about the collapse of the rebellion, the confederate Rhōs contingent in 988 was probably as large as that which fought a quarter of a century later.

[109] The mobilization potential of the Kievan state about the year 1000, with an estimate of one warrior for every ten families and a population of five million, was about 80,000 soldiers, but actually it took considerable effort to put 20,000 in the field. The Russian striking force at the beginning of Svjatoslav's Balkan campaign in 968 consisted of about 12,000 warriors, as did the armada of the last Russian raid in 1043 against Constantinople. In the civil war between Vladimir's sons, Iaroslav of Novgorod started against Svjatopolk of Kiev with 4,000 troops; among them were 1,000 mercenary Varangians. On the social structure and size of the Old Russian armed forces, see B. D. Grekov, *Kievskaja Rus'* (Moscow, 1953), 320–53; T. Wasilewski, "Studia nad składem społecznym wczesnośredniowiecznych sił zbrojnych na Rusi," *Studia Wczesnośredniowieczne*, IV (Wrocław, 1958), 301–87, reviewed by H. Łowmiański, in *Kwartalnik Historyczny*, 67 (Warsaw, 1960), 436–47; *idem*, *Początki Polski Z dziejów Słowian w I tysiącleciu n.e.*, III (Warsaw, 1967), 458–62.

[110] For the annual making and equipping of boats (*monoxyla*) for Kievan trade with Constantinople, see Constantine Porphyrogenitus, *DAI*, § 9, pp. 56–57, and *Commentary*, pp. 23–25, 35–37. Cf. Vernadsky, *Kievan Russia* (note 10 *supra*), 28–31. The Emperor–bookman in his *De cerimoniis, lib. II, cap.* 44 (Bonn ed. [1829], I, 660), describes seven 'Ρως καράβια with a crew of 415 men, sixty to a boat; the Primary Chronicle speaks of forty-man boats in a naval raid on Byzantium in 907 (Cross, *Chronicle*, 68). Psellus (*Chronographia*, VI, § 91) writes that for the naval expedition of 1043 the Russes "made boats large and small." Cf. Poppe, "La dernière expédition" (note 105 *supra*), 244 note 115, 249 and note 129.

Sea six days. A swift warfleet could thus make the voyage from Kiev to Constantinople in twenty-six to thirty days and even at a slower pace would have arrived in the Bosphorus in June.[111] There are grounds, therefore, for the opinion expressed in the literature that the Rus' troops arrived in Constantinople in the summer (not in the spring) of the year 988, but the suggestion that the troops were sent by land across Bulgaria[112] is not probable. First of all, such a march would have taken additional time; furthermore, there would have been no sense in draining the strength of the Rus' troops by forcing them to fight their way across the fields and gorges of Bulgaria when Basil needed them desperately on the outskirts of the capital.

There was no difficulty in deciding on a date for the baptism of Vladimir and his subjects, the aristocracy, the knights, and other inhabitants of Kiev. It should be remembered that a substantial number of the upper class and their households and many tradespeople were already Christians.[113] Some of the Byzantine envoys remained in Kiev to prepare the catechumens and to perform the rite of baptism that was to take place at a convenient time before the date, determined during the negotiations, of the arrival of Anna Porphyrogenita in Kiev. At the earliest, it could have been the summer of 988.

The giving of a Porphyrogenite in marriage within less than a year of the agreement may seem unlikely if compared with similar endeavors by the Ottonians: for three years Otto I carried on unsuccessful negotiations with Nicephorus Phocas for a Porphyrogenite for his son, whereas the negotiations for a Porphyrogenite for Otto III (995–1001) lasted more than six years.[114]

---

[111] According to Constantine Porphyrogenitus, *DAI*, § 9, pp. 58–59, the Kievan trade flotilla went to Constantinople in June of every year. Military expeditions reached the Bosphorus in 860 on June 18, in 941 on June 8, and in 1043 in June or July. Cf. H. Grégoire and P. Orgels, "Les invasions russes dans le Synaxaire de Constantinople," *Byzantion*, 24 (1954), 141–45; *Scylitzae synopsis*, 430; *DAI*, *Commentary*, II, 37; G. G. Litavrin, "Ešče raz o pohode russkih na Vizantiju v ijule 1043 g.," *VizVrem*, N.S. 29 (1969), 105–7; Poppe, "La dernière expédition," 240–45.

[112] Cf. Vasil'evskij, *Trudy*, II, 118.

[113] On evangelization in Kievan Russia before 988, see N. Polonskaja, "K voprosu o hristianstve na Rusi do Vladimira," *ŽMNP*, 71 (1917), 33–80; Dvornik, *Byzantine Missions* (note 2 *supra*), 259ff.; Vlasto, *Entry*, 247–54. Cf. G. Ostrogorsky, "Vizantija i kievskaja knjaginja Ol'ga," in *To Honor Roman Jakobson*, II (The Hague, 1967), 1458–73.

[114] Cf. P. E. Schramm, *Kaiser, Könige und Päpste*, III (Stuttgart, 1969), 204–8, 218–20, 235–38; W. Ohnsorge, "Die Heirat Kaiser Ottos II mit der Byzantinerin Theophano (972)," *Braunschweigisches Jahrbuch*, 54 (1973), 25–34. They expressed the view that Otto I had been negotiating since 967 for the four-year-old Porphyrogenite Anna to be the bride of Otto II (cf. Schramm, *op. cit.*, 204; Ohnsorge, *op. cit.*, 32). Anna, the last child of the Emperor Romanus II, was not his only daughter, as Fr. Dölger believed (*BZ*, 45 [1952], 467–68), although he demonstrated correctly that Theophano could not have been the sister of Anna. G. Ostrogorsky (*Byzantion*, 7 [1932], 198) called attention to the testimony of *De ceremoniis*, lib. II, *cap.* 15 (Bonn ed., p. 597), that at least one child of Romanus and Theophano attended a palace reception on September 9, 957. Because their sons Basil II and Constantine VIII were born in 958 and 961 respectively, the child seated at the dessert table in 957 must have been a girl, at least three years old. (Cf. A. A. Vasiliev, "Hugh Capet of France and Byzantium," *DOP*, 6 [1951], 244.) It seems that Thietmar mentions her name in his chronicle (VII, 72): "from Greece Vladimir brought himself a wife named Helene, who was destined for Otto III and hereafter denied him." While he confuses facts, persons, and time, he did not invent them (cf. Thietmar von Merseburg, *Die Chronik*, eds. R. Holzmann and W. Trillmilch [Berlin, 1957], 432). It is likely that the elder daughter of Romanus II and Theophano was named for her paternal grandmother, the Empress Helena Lecapena, wife of Constantine VII Porphyrogenitus. So this Porphyrogenite Helena born about 954/55 could have been "the desired girl" requested in 967/68 by Otto for his son Otto II (cf. note 127 *infra*).

POLITICAL BACKGROUND TO THE BAPTISM OF RUS'   231

When the initiative was taken by an Emperor himself, matters proceeded more quickly. The marriage of Otto II and Theophano took place within a year and a half, although the bride was not a Porphyrogenite but only a relative of John I Tzimisces. Faced with the need to concentrate his whole military might in Bulgaria against Svjatoslav, the Emperor decided it was not advisable to continue military action against the Western Empire in Italy. In September 970 he began to negotiate with Otto I, and Byzantine envoys, equipped with full power to act, not only managed to negotiate a cessation of hostilities but also concluded a marriage contract. At the end of 971 Theophano left for the West, and on April 14, 972, she was married to Otto II in Rome.[115]

Tzimisces' temporary difficulties, which caused him to revise the policy of his predecessor toward the Ottos, were minimal compared to the sad plight of Basil II. Realizing his danger and the perilous situation of the Macedonian dynasty, Basil decided to break with tradition, and to give a legitimate daughter of an Emperor in marriage to a ruler from outside the borders of the Empire. Having contracted the marriage agreement of Anna and Vladimir, he was anxious to have it fulfilled without delay; with his sister in Kiev, he would be sure of his brother-in-law's effective support and could rely on the assistance of the Rus' troops in putting down the rebellion.

It was especially important to Vladimir that the marriage take place as soon as possible. This pagan King, ambitious architect of an extensive and dynamic state, yet to the heirs of the Roman Empire still a barbarian, had achieved an alliance that other Christian rulers could not. The court in Kiev did not avoid contacts with other countries, and the endeavors of the Ottos, as well as their meager success with the non-Porphyrogenite Theophano, who was received with discontent by many in the higher ranks of the Ottonian state, were known there. The periodic news of conversions of several Slav and Scandinavian dynasties had created a feeling of isolation, and contributed to a readiness, encouraged by some of the entourage of the Kievan ruler who were already converted, to incorporate Rus' in the family of Christian nations. The decision to convert, in the light of prospective relations with the Emperor of the Romans, was especially attractive. The Rus' King, on becoming a Christian, not only joined the European family of rulers, but at once gained a position of honor in this hierarchy[116] because of his marriage to a Porphyrogenite. The union of the Macedonian and Rjurikid houses, which contemporaries considered important, helped to lead to a historic turning-point in the Christianization of Rus'.

[115] Ohnsorge, "Die Heirat," 35–60.
[116] Cf. G. Ostrogorsky, "The Byzantine Emperor and the Hierarchical World Order," *SlEERev*, 35 (1956), 5–14; F. Dölger, "Die Familie der Könige im Mittelalter," in *idem, Byzanz und die europäische Staatenwelt* (Darmstadt, 1969), 34–69; A. Grabar, "God and the 'Family of Princes' Presided over by the Byzantine Emperor," *HSlSt*, 2 (1954), 117–23; J. Shepard, "Some Problems of Russo-Byzantine Relations c. 860–c. 1050," *SlEERev*, 52, no. 126 (Jan., 1974), 26–30. However, in the light of the *princeps editio* of John Scylitzes, I must revise my interpretation that Vladimir was called the brother of the Emperor in the meaning of πνευματικὸς ἀδελφός, a member of the family of rulers (cf. A. Poppe, "Le prince et l'église en Russie de Kiev depuis la fin du Xe siècle jusqu'au début de XIIe siècle," *Acta Poloniae Historica*, 20 [1969], 110). As it now appears, the original reading was Βλαδιμηροῦ, τοῦ γαμβροῦ τοῦ βασιλέως (*Scylitzae synopsis*, 354⁹²), and Cedrenus replaced γαμβροῦ with ἀδελφοῦ (cf. Bonn ed., II, 464).

Since both parties were anxious to conclude the agreement without delay, the Rus' wedding party must have been sent to Constantinople that autumn. The treaty was to be ratified in the presence of Russian envoys by the Emperor himself.[117] Part of the Byzantine embassy, most of whom were ecclesiastics, remained in Kiev to make preparations and to baptize the Rus' ruler and his pagan attendants. The rest, together with the Rus' envoys and probably, as mentioned above, a detachment of several hundred troops, set out for Constantinople by the water route while it was still accessible to navigation.[118] Their arrival in the capital of the Empire in October, or at the latest at the beginning of November, can be determined by the fact that news of Vladimir's successful matrimonial negotiations reached the courts of western Europe in January 988.

In my opinion, some light is thrown on the chronology of the Russo-Byzantine negotiations by the abandonment by the King of France, Hugh Capet, of his attempt to obtain a Porphyrogenite bride for his son Robert. In a letter addressed to the Byzantine Emperors Basil II and Constantine, written just after the coronation of Robert on Christmas day 987, the king of the Franks offered friendship and an alliance and asked for the hand of *filiae sancti imperii* for his son.[119] The chronological arrangement of this letter, written *ex persona*, in the collection of correspondence of Gerbert of Aurillac, trusted secretary of the archbishop of Reims, also indicates the very end of the year 987 or very beginning of 988. Since shortly after that, probably even before the first of April 988, Robert married Suzanna, the widow of Arnulf II, count of Flanders, some researchers think that the letter was never sent to Constantinople,[120] that it was written by Gerbert of his own accord without the King's knowledge;[121] but this is not confirmed by any of the remaining eighty political letters written by Gerbert at the request of others, among them Hugh Capet.

[117] I assume that the procedure was similar to that in the treaty between Tzimisces and Otto I. Cf. Ohnsorge, "Die Heirat," 35, 37.

[118] Navigation on the Dnieper was no longer possible toward the end of November; Black Sea navigation was suspended between December and March. In Caffa, due to much risk, sailing was forbidden from December 1 until March 15. Cf. Berenbejm, "O puti" (note 105 *supra*), 203. In November, severe weather conditions made navigation very difficult; for example, in 1419 a voyage from the mouth of the Dniester to the Bosphorus (*ca.* 400 miles) took three weeks. But in October, travel by the Black Sea route would be normal: the Kievan sovereign Olga left Constantinople after the imperial reception on October 18, 957, and the Russian metropolitan Cyprian set out from Constantinople for home on October 1, 1389. Cf. M. N. Tihomirov, "Puti iz Rossii v Vizantiju v XIV–XV vv.," in *idem, Istoričeskie svjazi Rossii so slavjanskimi stranami i Vizantiej* (Moscow, 1969), 71–72; Poppe, "La dernière expédition" (note 105 *supra*), 29.

[119] Cf. the most recent critical edition with a short survey of opinions, ed. F. Weigle, *Die Briefsammlung Gerberts von Reims*, MGH, *Briefe*, II (Berlin, 1966), no. 111, pp. 139–40; English trans. and commentary in H. P. Lattin, *The Letters of Gerbert, with his Papal Privileges as Sylvester II* (New York, 1961), 151–52. For a more detailed interpretation, see D. and A. Poppe, "Dziewosłęby o pofirogenetkę Annę," in *Cultus et Cognitio: In Honorem A. Gieysztor* (Warsaw, 1976), 451–68.

[120] Ch. Pfister, *Etudes sur le règne de Robert le Pieux* (Paris, 1885), 42–46; F. Lot, *Les derniers Carolingiens* (Paris, 1891), 218–19. Cf. K. Leyser, "The Tenth Century in Byzantine-Western Relationships," in *Relations Between East and West in the Middle Ages*, ed. D. Baker (Edinburgh, 1973), 41–42.

[121] J. Havet, *Lettres de Gerbert (983–997)* (Paris, 1889), 102; Cf. F. Lot, *Etudes sur le règne de Hugues Capet et la fin du Xe siècle* (Paris, 1903), 4 note 2.

Other scholars think that the letter was not sent because of the changed political situation.[122] Vasiliev, who devoted a special study to the contents of the letter, came to the conclusion that "if the authors of the message were well acquainted with the political situation of the Byzantine Empire in 988, they may have realized that this year was not appropriate for matrimonial negotiations and therefore abandoned their project."[123]

The complex manuscript tradition is reflected in two versions of Gerbert's collection of letters, essentially different in form, content, and purpose. Many controversial opinions have been expressed concerning the date and circumstances of the origin of both versions. Upon closer scrutiny, one can conclude from the common elements that one of the versions (the so-called copy P), which contains our letter, was a private one, not intended for publication, that Gerbert kept in the years 982–96; the other (codex L), in which thirty letters found in copy P are omitted, is a collection of Gerbert's writings and letters, intended for wider circulation, which were compiled either by him or shortly after his death in 1003.[124] The fact that the political contents of these thirty letters betray the too far-reaching efforts of the archbishop of Reims and his secretary on behalf of Hugh Capet and Theophano in their political game against the last Carolingians seems to show that they were not meant for wider distribution. The omission of the letter with which we are concerned from the collection intended for a wider circle of readers, whether it was removed during the reign of Capet himself or that of Robert the Pious, is for reasons of simple discretion quite understandable; indeed, a reminder of the ambitious but unsuccessful attempt of Capet and his son to enter the arena of European politics might have been considered an open affront to the sovereign, the more so if the letter had never been sent and was known to only a narrow circle of persons.

The initiative taken by Hugh was quite consistent with his far-reaching ambitions and his high opinion of his own royal status. He did not abandon it because of an unfavorable political situation in Byzantium, since, in fact, it was his understanding of the situation, which was extremely favorable for Capet's plans, which prompted the idea. The Byzantine matrimonial customs were too well known in the European courts for the King of the Franks, who had at his disposal such excellent and well-informed advisers as Gerbert, to risk ridicule under normal conditions. Gerbert obtained his information about the situation in the Eastern Empire from his correspondents in Rome. He was

[122] Weigle, *Die Briefsammlung*, 6, and *idem*, *Studien* (note 124 *infra*), in *DA*, 14 (1958), 202–3.
[123] Vasiliev, "Hugh Capet" (note 114 *supra*), 245; cf. also p. 233.
[124] Codex L = MS of the eleventh century: *Cod. Vossianus lat.* Q 54 from the Library of Leiden University. Copy P is the generally accepted designation of another MS of the eleventh century, which was owned by Pithoei in the sixteenth-seventeenth century and was lost after 1636. The contents of this MS are reconstituted on the basis of *cod. Vallicellanus* G 94 (*ca.* 1602) and the editions of J. Masson (1611) and A. Duchesne (1636), which have all used the perished copy P. Among numerous studies of the P and L tradition of Gerbert's letters are the basic works by N. Bubnov, *Sbornik' pisem' Gerberta kak' istoričeskij istočnik'*, pt. I: *O rukopisiah i redakcijah sbornika pisem' Gerberta* (St. Petersburg, 1888); F. Lot, *Etude sur les receuils des lettres de Gerbert*, BECh, 100 (1939), 8–62; and Fr. Weigle, "Studien zu Überlieferung der Briefsammlung Gerberts von Reims," *DA*, 10 (1953), 19–70; 11 (1955) 393–421; 14 (1958), 149–220; 17 (1961), 385–419.

also in regular contact with the Empress Theophano, who was related through Tzimisces to Bardas Sclerus and Bardas Phocas and therefore had reason to be interested in the development of the situation in her native land.[125] Dux Hugh, who, on July 3, 987, had just begun to wear the crown, felt that the royal title of the newly founded dynasty needed additional validation. His intention to ennoble the family tree of the Capetians must have arisen in the last months of the year 987, during the preparations, forced upon the archbishop and the nobility, for the coronation of his son.[126] Hugh was hoping that the legitimate Emperors would be desperate enough to give away the Porphyrogenite for a guarantee of the security of Byzantine possessions in southern Italy. The wording filia sancti imperii came from the pen of that consummate diplomat, Gerbert. Although, according to custom, he did not mention the name of the bride,[127] it was clear that he had in mind Anna, who was related equally to both Emperors and was the only nubilis virgo at that time who had been born in the purple (March 13, 963). Hugh could not have planned the engagement of his son to one of Constantine's daughters, Eudocia or Zoe, born about 978/79.[128]

Since word of his projected marriage did not get beyond the discreet circle of those directly concerned, and since attempts were undertaken at once to marry Robert to the widow of Arnulf II, to form a stronger union between Flanders and the Frankish kingdom, news of the betrothal of Anna and the Rus' ruler must have reached France shortly after the letter had been written, that is, at the beginning of or during January 988.[129] In order to have reached

[125] Her uncle, John Tzimisces, was related through his mother to the Phocades, and his first wife Maria was a sister of Bardas and Constantine Sclerus. The second daughter of Otto II and Theophano was named Sophia, apparently after her maternal grandmother. According to A. Rauch's likely supposition, Theophano was the daughter of Constantine Sclerus and Sophia who was a sister of Bardas Phocas; quoted in Schramm, Kaiser (note 114 supra), 240–41; P. Charanis, "The Armenians in the Byzantine Empire," Byzantinoslavica, 22, 2 (1961), 220, 223–25. For a detailed survey of opinions regarding the lineage of Theophano, see W. H. Rüdt von Collenberg, "Wer war Theophano ?," Genealogisches Jahrbuch, 4 (1964), 49–71.

[126] Richeri Historiarum libri IIII, ed. G. Weitz (Hannover, 1877), 133–34 (lib. IV, 12, 13). Cf. Weigle, Die Briefsammlung (note 119 supra), 140–41; Lattin, The Letters (note 119 supra), 153.

[127] Perhaps this custom explains why Liutprand of Cremona, head of the matrimonial embassy of 968, in his speech to Nicephorus Phocas (Legatio, VII) asking for "a daughter of Emperor Romanus and Empress Theophano" to marry Otto II, did not mention her name.

[128] Of his three daughters, the eldest, Eudocia, born in 977/78 and pock-marked from the age of six, was sent to a convent. Neither Zoë, born about 979, nor Theodora, a few years younger (cf. Psellus, Chronographia, II, §§ 4, 5; VI, § 160; N. Skabalanovič, Vizantijskoe gosudarstvo i cerkov' v' XI věkě [St. Petersburg, 1884], 10–11), was at that time of marriageable age. If Hugh Capet had Zoë in mind, the sudden abandonment of his intentions without waiting for an answer would be incomprehensible. That Anna must have been considered as a possible bride for Robert shows also that Hugh was asking not for filia Constantinini imperatoris, but for filia sancti imperii. Cf. Vasiliev, "Hugh Capet" (note 114 supra), 245.

[129] I assume that the letter was not sent because an answer was not expected. Legations from Western Europe to Byzantium in the ninth and tenth centuries lasted about one year. Embassies going and returning within six to eight months were an exception. Cf. V. Menzel, Deutsches Gesandschaftswesen im Mittelalter (Hannover, 1892), 199–204. All data appear to connect King Robert's marriage to Rosala-Suzanna of Flanders with the year 988, although the terminus ante quem accepted so far for this marriage, April 1, 988, is not reliable because the document bearing that date is a forgery. Cf. Diplomata Belgica ante annum millesimum centesimum scripta, eds. M. Gysseling and A. C. Koch, I, Textes (Brussels, 1950), no. 71, pp. 175–77; and, in detail, Poppe, "Dziewosłęby" (note 119 supra), 456–62.

Reims or the court in Compiègne by then, the news must have left Constantinople not later than October or the beginning of November, since a messenger traveling at an average speed of about fifty kilometers a day would have required fifty-five to sixty days, or a little more, to cover (via the court of Theophano?) the distance of about 2650 kilometers.[130] If the French project was abandoned because of the news, this would provide additional proof that the Russo-Byzantine agreement in Kiev was reached not later than September, since the Rus' wedding embassy needed thirty to thirty-five days for the journey to Constantinople.

Elsewhere in this study I have discussed the time necessary to prepare an expeditionary force in Kiev and have shown that it could not have arrived in Byzantium before June 988. The date of the battle of Chrysopolis in the summer of 988, in which the Rus' troops took part, has been accepted as the terminus ante quem for their arrival, but the precise date of the battle still remains to be determined. In examining this question, I wish to point out that there is another possibility for fixing the approximate time of arrival of the Rus' troops in the capital.

After Bardas Phocas proclaimed himself emperor in Cappadocia in September 987, his armies occupied the whole of Asia Minor and reached the straits separating it from Europe. The occupation of the vast Asiatic provinces of the Empire must have taken several months, especially since the adherents of the imprisoned Bardas Sclerus had to be won over, or at least neutralized. It would seem, therefore, that most of Phocas' forces must have reached the straits in the summer of 988 and prepared to cross in two groups. One group pitched camp directly across from the capital, on the hills surrounding Chrysopolis (Skutari), and the other laid seige to Abydus on the Hellespont, the only bridge-head of Basil II in Asia.[131] After Phocas' troops had arrived in the suburbs of Constantinople, Basil sent one of his few loyal commanders, the magister Gregory the Taronite, by sea to Trebizond, from which he increased his detachment and set off in the direction of the Euphrates, that is, through territories densely populated by Armenians. This was a diversionary tactic intended to raise a revolt in the area occupied by Phocas. The fact that he chose Gregory the Taronite, an aristocrat of Armenian descent, and sent him through a province with a large Armenian population indicates that Basil II wanted to take advantage of the Armenians' discontent and distrust

---

[130] Cf. Ludwig, *Untersuchungen* (note 105 *supra*), 115–17, 179–93; Schramm, *Kaiser* (note 114 *supra*), 252–53.

[131] That the occupation of Asia Minor was carried out in stages is reflected in one of Yaḥyā's Antiochan sources, which recorded the arrival of Phocas' army at Dorylaion, about eighty miles southeast of Nicaea and over 200 miles east of Abydus. I conclude that the siege of Abydus by Phocas, emphasized in Leo Diaconus, p. 173, and in *Scylitzae synopsis*, pp. 336–37, was unknown to Yaḥyā or omitted in a summary of his sources. Nevertheless, from his record that Phocas "dominated the land of the Greeks to Dorylaion and to the sea, and his army reached as far as Chrysopolis "(Yaḥyā, in PO, 23, p. 422; and in Rozen, *Imperator*, 23), it seems clear that only after the seizure of Dorylaion was it possible to reach and besiege "the key to the Byzantine capital"—Abydus. On the importance of Abydus, cf. Tomaschek, *Zur historischen Topographie* (note 101 *supra*), 15–16.

of Phocas after the imprisonment of Sclerus.[132] Phocas sent his son Nicephorus at the head of the Iberian troops to eliminate this diversion from the
rear. With the help of the Iberian ruler David of Tayk', a friend of Phocas,
Gregory the Taronite's detachment was defeated. Shortly afterward, the
Iberian troops, still concentrated in the region of the battlefields, received
news of Basil's success at Chrysopolis.[133] Gregory's operation must have
lasted several months if one considers the time Phocas needed to organize a
counterattack, and it ceased approximately when Basil II had his first success in the West.

So, when did the battle of Chrysopolis take place? Asoghik mentions the
year 437 of the Armenian cycle, that is, between March 24, 988, and March 23,
989. According to his account of the event, it appears that the battle was
fought at the end of the year 437, but that at the beginning of the next year
(after March 23, 989)[134] the decisive engagement against Phocas took place in
the correctly dated battle of Abydus on April 13, 989. It appears from the
account of Leo the Deacon, and somewhat less clearly from the description
of Scylitzes, that there was only a short interval between the two battles.[135]
This interpretation of the text of both historians is fully confirmed in the
letter, quoted by Yaḥyā, which Bardas Phocas sent to his son Leo, his governor
in Antioch, asking him to remove Patriarch Agapetus from the town to stop
his scheming. On Saturday March 2, 989, Leo managed to entice the patriarch, together with a large group of local dignitaries, from the city and to
prevent their return.[136] It took special messengers from fifteen to eighteen days
to travel 900 kilometers to deliver the letter, and it took Leo several days to
arrange favorable circumstances for the execution of his plot. Phocas, therefore, must have dispatched his letter to Antioch at the beginning of February,
shortly after receiving the news of the defeat of his army at Chrysopolis and

[132] It is not without significance that in 976–79 Gregory the Taronite took part in Sclerus' revolt.
Cf. N. Adontz, "Les Taronites en Arménie et à Byzance," Byzantion, 10 (1935), 541–43; ibid., 11
(1936), 21–22; Charanis, "The Armenians" (note 125 supra), 229.

[133] Yaḥyā, in PO, 23, pp. 424–25; and in Rozen, Imperator, 24, 207–8. Asoghik, III, § 26, after his
record of the battle at Chrysopolis (III, § 25) tells us that Phocas dismissed the Iberian troops and
himself moved with the Greek army to the sea, that is, to Abydus. This enigmatic information and the
time of the dismissal becomes clear in the light of Yaḥyā's record. The Iberian unit was sent under the
command of Nicephorus Phocas to fight against Gregory the Taronite, but far from all the Iberians
were dismissed to the east: we know from Psellus, Chronographia, I, §§ 15, 17, that the best Iberian
units fought at Abydus. No doubt Asoghik's record reflects the contemporary opinion that the absence
of those Iberians who were sent to the east tipped the scales at Abydus.

[134] Asoghik, III, §§ 25, 26 (Histoire universelle, 130; Vseobščaja istorija, 179; Des Stephanos von
Taron, 189). I accept the long forgotten interpretation of the Armenian historian by Vasil'evskij, who
dated the battle at Chrysopolis to February or the very beginning of March 989 (cf. Trudy, II, 197),
while at the same time trying to contribute some new arguments. Schlumberger was the first to adopt
Vasil'evskij's opinion in his exposition of the events, but also wrote: "La victoire de Chrysopolis eut
peut-être lieu dès l'été de l'an 988 et précéda ainsi de plusieurs mois celle d'Abydos" (L'Epopée byzantine [note 15 supra], I [1896], 733–34, 745; 2nd ed. [1925], 655, 663).

[135] Cf. Leo Diaconus, 173–74, whose record seems more precise than Scylitzae synopsis, 336–38.
Psellus, Chronographia, I, §§ 13–15, presented the first combat at Chrysopolis as a direct prelude to the
main battle at Abydus, but knowing his predisposition to generalize, it would be risky to draw any
conclusions.

[136] Yaḥyā, in PO, 23, p. 425; and in Rozen, Imperator, 24–25, 209. The report that Leo Phocas was
in rebellion in Antioch until November 1, 989, is of local origin.

after becoming aware of the new situation and the changes in public opinion. So it can be assumed that the battle of Chrysopolis took place in the second half of January or at the very beginning of February 989.

At this time, or at the most two weeks later, Gregory the Taronite was defeated. But he had accomplished his task, drawing away some of the Iberian troops from the western front and depriving Phocas of them in the decisive battle of Abydus. His expedition from Constantinople was inspired by the arrival of several thousand Rus' warriors in Constantinople, when the Emperor launched an offensive. After the approaching Rus' armada broke through the blockaded passage of the Bosphorus to the Black Sea, it was possible to send Gregory the Taronite by sea to Trebizond with a small detachment. It was not until then that the Emperor could spare such a detachment without weakening the defense of the capital. As his campaign had to last at least several months, but no longer than six or seven, it can be assumed that Gregory the Taronite set out at the Emperor's order in the summer of 988 after the arrival of the Rus' troops.

From this time until the battle of Chrysopolis was about half a year, which proves that Basil II was a good commander, having learned well the lesson taught by the Bulgars. Psellus stressed the effort put into the preparation of the Rus' troops and the other detachments for the offensive.[137] The newly arrived Russes were not immediately sent into battle, but were given time to get accustomed to the new conditions and, by joining with the rest of the Emperors' armies, to form one operating force. Individual detachments were drilled and maneuvers in groups were carried out, stressing the cooperation of the different units. From the description given by Asoghik of the battle at Chrysopolis, it is apparent that the whole operation had been well drilled, and its success was due to attacking the enemy unawares. At night, under cover of darkness, a very large unit had crossed the Bosphorus. Taking advantage of the hilliness of the area and of not being recognized, they approached the rear of the enemy's fortified camp at daybreak in order to attack when the usurper's army was distracted by a sham attack of battleships and Greek flamethrowers.[138]

In choosing winter to open the attack, the resistance of the northern allies to cold was taken into consideration.[139] The small, agile, and silent Rus' war boats were, in comparison to the Byzantine ships, very well suited to capitalizing on the element of surprise, hence the idea of a secret landing operation. In taking his time to prepare for the operation, Basil was aware of the signif-

---

[137] Psellus, *Chronographia*, I, § 13; cf. also his estimation of the Emperor Basil as a commander-in-chief (I, §§ 32–33, vol. I, pp. 20–21). It seems that the experience of his first successes at Chrysopolis and Abydus influenced his military thought and actions.

[138] See Asoghik, III, § 25 (*Histoire universelle*, 130; *Des Stephanos von Taron*, 188–89; *Vseobščaja istorija*, 178–79). Cf. Leo Diaconus, 173–74. For the classes of Byzantine warships, see H. Ahrweiler, *Byzance et la mer* (Paris, 1966), 408–18; E. Eickhoff, *Seekrieg und Seepolitik zwischen Islam und Abendland* (Berlin, 1966), 135–50.

[139] The winter is usually mild on the Bosphorus. In January the temperature is from 0^0 to $+ 4^0$ C, rarely -5^0 C. Cf. Psellus' remark (I, § 32) that Basil II waged campaigns against custom, disregarding the season, whether it was hot or cold.

icance for morale of an initial success. Upon hearing the news of Chrysopolis, the allies began to desert Phocas.[140] Since both parties needed time to collect their forces on the Hellespont, the battle on April 13 took place ten to twelve weeks after Chrysopolis. Basil intended to eliminate the concentration of enemy forces and to open a water route for freight ships. After achieving this, he intended to measure his strength against Phocas himself. The latter, aware that after the defeat of his army at Chrysopolis time was working against him, quickly directed his forces by land and by sea toward Abydus. A surprise attack from the sea and the burning of the usurper's fleet, which was moored on the coast, shows that here, too, the advantages of the Rus' boats were exploited. The death of the hitherto invincible commander, Phocas, on the battlefield sealed Basil's victory.[141]

At the time the Empire was torn by civil war, three events of differing importance were taking place in the north: the conversion of Rus', the marriage of Vladimir and Anna, and the siege and conquest of Cherson by the Russes. The questionable credibility of the so-called Cherson legend as a historical source for the conversion of Rus' applies also to the time sequence and the place of the events that it suggests. Not only does our entire argument weigh against the theory that the baptism of the Russes and Vladimir's marriage to the Porphyrogenite took place in Cherson, but, as we shall see below, an analysis of other Old Russian records also testifies against it. The Cherson legend omitted the real reason for Rus' action against Cherson, and presented the city as a glamorous place in which important ceremonies were held. But in reconstructing the history of these years, the legend recorded details of the siege and conquest of the city, still fresh in the memory of the eleventh century, and its part in the Christianization of Rus'. The spoils of war, holy relics, church objects, and icons urgently needed for the newly erected temples in Kiev, were sent north, as were numerous priests of Cherson, most likely not of their own accord.[142]

But of all these events, only the date of the conquest of Cherson, between April 7 and July 27, 989 (6497), is certified by the sources. The collapse of the

---

[140] David of Tayk' and two sons of Bagrat, princes of Armenian origin occupying the theme of Chaldia, had withdrawn 2,000 riders on the pretext that they had fulfilled their task, which was to defeat Gregory the Taronite. The Iberian warriors commanded by Nicephorus Phocas had fallen as well. See Yaḥyā, in PO, 23, pp. 424–25; and in Rozen, *Imperator*, 24, 79–80. Cf. Honigmann, *Die Ostgrenze* (note 28 *supra*), 149–55.

[141] The information that Basil shared his forces with two armies and that the battle of Abydus consisted of two operations follows from the accounts of Leo the Deacon and Asoghik. In the first stage, the troops annihilated Phocas' navy, defeated a number of his units, and threatened an encircling maneuver. Then began the battle between the main body of Phocas' army and Basil's forces, which had crossed the Hellespont some time before and were camped at Abydus. See Leo Diaconus, 174; Asoghik, III, §§ 15–17; *Scylitzae synopsis*, 337–38. The Armenian historian Aristakes of Lastivert wrote shortly after 1072 that Basil won the victory over Bardas Phocas when, with "only four thousand men, he crossed the sea at night and attacked the innumerable army of the usurper." Cf. *Povestvovanie Vardapeta Aristakesa Lastivertci*, trans. K. N. Juzbašjan (Moscow, 1968), 64. Beneath this legend there is, it seems, an actual figure, not of the number of Basil's army at Abydus but of all his forces before the Russes came to his aid (cf. note 108 *supra*).

[142] Cross, *Chronicle*, 111–13, 116, and note 94 on pp. 247–48. Cf. *supra*, p. 207 ff. and notes 51, 52.

defense was probably due to the news of the defeat and death of Phocas at Abydus on April 13, 989. Because the Rus' troops reached the walls of the city by sea, it can be assumed that the siege began not later than the autumn of 988.[143] The Rus' operation against Cherson was based on an agreement of 987, probably confirmed in detail in the summer of 988, which reflected the intent of an article of the treaty of 944 providing that if the theme of Cherson broke loose from the sovereignty of the Empire the Rus' prince could wage war on it and could depend on Byzantine support.[144] This paragraph was in character with the general policy of the Emperors toward the rebellious city.[145] New treason made it timely once again, and Basil II decided to crush the political ambitions of Cherson. To punish the city severely, he allowed it to be sacked and virtually destroyed. We can deduce from the traces of ruin and fire that this was done by the conquerors after the city had already surrendered and opened its gates. Although it did not fall completely into decay, it never regained its former splendor, its economic significance, or its population.[146]

---

[143] Navigation on the Dnieper began about halfway through April, so in 989 the Russes could not get through before May. It is generally agreed that they reached Cherson by sea. Cf. Berthier-Delagarde, "Kak Vladimir" (note 92 *supra*), 244–50; B. D. Grekov, "'Povest' vremennyh let' o pohode Vladimira na Korsun'," in *idem, Izbrannye Trudy*, II (Moscow, 1959), 423–24; Vasiliev, *The Goths* (note 83 *supra*), 132–34.

[144] The obscure wording of this article gave rise to many different interpretations. Cf. N. Lavrovskij, *O vizantijskom elemente v jazyke dogovorov Russkih s Grekami*, 2nd ed. (Warsaw, 1904), 141–43; G. Vernadsky, "The Rus' in the Crimea and the Russo-Byzantine Treaty of 945," *Byzantina-Metabyzantina*, I (1946), 257–58 (cf. also English trans. in Cross, *Chronicle*, 76); A. Zimin, in *Pamjatniki prava Kievskogo gosudarstva*, I (Moscow, 1952), 33, 38, 47; I. Sorlin, "Traités de Byzance avec la Russie au Xe siècle," *Cahiers du monde russe et soviétique*, II (1961), 450, 460. They are not all convincing. The key to understanding this article of the treaty is in the phrase "i ta strana ne pokorjaetsja vam"—"if that country does not submit itself to you [i.e., the Russes]." I agree with the emendation proposed by A. A. Šahmatov: nam/to us, i.e., the Greeks, instead of vam/to you. See his reconstruction in *Povest' vremennyh let*, I (Petrograd, 1916), 57, 379. Frequent confusions of personal and possessive pronouns in the text of the treaties and the circumstances of their redaction in two Greek versions (the first was written in the name of the Byzantine party; the second formulated the articles of the treaty in the name of Rus', and therefore the pronouns of the first person were replaced by those of the second, and vice versa) and subsequent translation into Slavonic speaks for the possibility of error. See Šahmatov, "'Povest' vremennyh let'" (note 49 *supra*) 112, 115–17; 120; cf. Sorlin, *op. cit.*, 326–28. Then the correct sense of this article is as follows: "And concerning the country of Cherson and all the towns in that region the Russian prince does not have the right to wage war against them. But if that country does not submit itself to us (i.e., the Greek emperors), then if the Russian prince asks us for soldiers to wage war, we shall give him as many as he needs" (PSRL, I [1926], 50–51, II [1908], 39).

[145] With the emendation proposed in note 144, the contents of this article of the treaty of 944 will become clear and can be seen to correspond strictly to the Byzantine policy toward Cherson as formulated by Constantine Porphyrogenitus, in *DAI*, §§ 42, 53 (cf. *supra*, p. 38 ff.), an emperor concluding the treaty with the Russes in 944. An example of this article in operation is the combined Russo-Byzantine action against Cherson in 1016 (cf. *Scylitzae synopsis*, 354, with commentary by E. Č. Skržinskaja, in *VizVrem*, N.S. 6 [1953], 266–67).

[146] The decline in population is estimated at nearly half. Some quarters of the city were left deserted in the eleventh century. Cf. A. L. Jakobson, *Srednevekovyj Herson v XI–XIV vv.* (Moscow, 1950), 12–15; *idem, Rannesrednevekovyj Hersones* (note 6 *supra*), 42 (cf. *supra*), 297, 361; *idem*, "O čislennosti naselenija srednevekogo Hersonesa," *VizVrem*, N.S. 19 (1962), 160–61; Talis, *Iz istorii* (note 7 *supra*), 114 note 54; *idem*, "Voprosy periodizacii istorii Hersona v èpohu rannego sredenvekov'ja," *VizVrem*, N.S. 18 (1961), 67–73. The decline of Cherson after 989 was believed to have been due to the aspiration of Kiev to weaken Byzantine positions on the north coast of the Black Sea. That Cherson ceased to mint its own money indicates not only the economic collapse of the city but also the fact that the Emperor deprived Cherson of this right.

Reconstructing the succession of events connected with the conversion of Rus', it is impossible to overlook some concurrence with the record of the "Memory and Eulogy of Vladimir," in which it is said: "After his holy baptism the blessed King Vladimir lived twenty-eight years. In the second year after baptism he went toward the rapids, in the third he captured the city of Cherson."[147] The difference in the succession and chronology of events in comparison with the Primary Chronicle presumes that the annalistic records of the "Memory and Eulogy," compiled in the thirteenth century, originated from another tradition. This tradition was still alive in Kiev in the second half of the eleventh century, as evidenced in both Lives of SS. Boris and Gleb.[148] If those twenty-eight years are subtracted from the date of Vladimir's death 6523 (1015), the date of his conversion is 6495 (March 987–February 988). That same year is indicated, too, from the record that Cherson was captured in the third year after Vladimir's baptism. Numbering from 6495, that would be the year 6497, the correctly attested date of the fall of this city. There is another record from the "Memory and Eulogy" indicating the year 6495 as the date of Vladimir's conversion: "Prince Vladimir was baptized in the tenth year after murdering his brother Yaropolk." The latter's death is dated therein to the year 6486 (978).[149]

The year 6495 for Vladimir's baptism appears to be a reliable tradition. The mission that remained in Kiev after the agreement had been concluded in September 6495 (987) had enough time to convert the Rus' ruler. Only a bishop could administer the sacraments of baptism and confirmation; so there must have been at least one of this rank at the head of the mission. As there was no need to hurry, the probable intention of the mission was to give the ceremony a solemn character. The day chosen for baptism was most likely Epiphany, the closest canonically approved day and the most suitable for the baptism of the ruler. So Vladimir's catechumenate would have been during Advent, and at

---

[147] Zimin, "Pamjat'" (note 43 supra), 72; Golubinskij, Istorija, 245. Views have repeatedly been expressed in favor of the chronological testimony of the "Memory and Eulogy" and against the dating in the Primary Chronicle (beginning with Golubinskij; cf., for instance, L. V. Čerepnin, "'Povest' vremennyh let,' ee redakcii i predšestvujuščie ej letoposnye svody," Istoričeskie Zapiski, 25 [1948], 332; Pašuto, Vnešnjaja politika [note 2 supra], 74; Vlasto, Entry, 257–58); but although critical verification of those dates has been lacking, it is becoming possible with the reconstruction of events on the basis of other sources.

[148] The anonymous Skazanie ("The Tale and Passion and Encomium of the Holy Martyrs Boris and Gleb"), written about 1072, says that "Vladimir, when already 28 years had passed after the Holy Baptism, fell into a heavy illness" and soon died. The second hagiographer, the monk Nestor of the Kiev Monastery of the Caves, in his Chtenie ("Reading concerning the Life and Murder of the Blessed Martyrs Boris and Gleb"), written about 1080, named the year of the baptism but unfortunately an error appeared in sixteen MSS. The year 6490 (982) is given instead of 6495 (987), noted by only three MSS which, however, go back to the common, unpreserved archetype of the Chtenie, according to Bugoslavs'kij, the best judge of the manuscript tradition of the Lives of Boris and Gleb. Paleographically, this is just the error (omission of ε=5) which is most likely. See S. Bugoslavs'kij, Ukrajino-rus'ki pamjatky XI–XVIII vv. pro knjaziv Borisa ta Gliba (Kiev, 1928), 117, 139, 179–80, 183; and his unpublished study, Drevnerusskie proizvedenija o Borisa i Glebe (Moscow Institute of World Literature of the Academy of Sciences, 1939), 200–9. For an ample treatment of both Lives, see J. Fennell and A. Stokes, Early Russian Literature (London, 1974), 11–32.

[149] Zimin, "Pamjat'" (note 43 supra), 72. According to the Primary Chronicle, Yaropolk died in 6488 (980) and Vladimir was baptized nine years later.

Christmas the preliminary solemn ceremonies, such as the reciting of the Creed by the convert, could have begun. During the ritual of conversion, Vladimir was given a new Christian name,[150] Basil—the name of the Emperor of the Romans, his brother-in-law, and the elder brother in the family of rulers. The Byzantine Emperor patronized the ceremony of the conversion of the Rus' ruler and was, it can be said, *per procura*, his godfather. The day of the patron of both rulers, St. Basil the Great, which was at the same time a holiday, *Circumcisio Domini* (i.e., Sunday January 1, 988), could have been chosen to christen Vladimir after his godfather. On Epiphany the sacraments were fulfilled, and at the same time the Rus' ruler's still unconverted entourage was baptized.

It remains to solve the enigmatic note on Vladimir's voyage toward the Dnieper rapids in the year between two important events in his life, the baptism in the year 6495 and the capture of Cherson in 6497. Has this note been preserved in its original reading? If so, its brevity would suggest that the record was made at a time when the reason for the King's voyage toward the rapids was obvious.

What could have induced Vladimir to undertake this voyage, which definitely took place in the first half of 6496, the period of navigability on the Dnieper, that is, from spring to autumn 988? Conjectures have been made that he set out to protect the corps en route to aid Basil from the Patzinaks while it crossed the rapids.[151] This should not be rejected *a limine*, though it seems that a battle contingent of several thousand would scarcely have needed such protection, much less the personal escort of the ruler. But there could have been another reason: the Rus' King could well have set out to greet his bride and to assure her entourage of safety during the dangerous crossing of the rapids. There are some grounds for this interpretation of the brief reference: there was from the mid-twelfth century on a custom for the Rus' princes to proceed to the rapids or even to the mouth of the river Dnieper to meet a bride and her attendants.[152] While Vladimir was awaiting the arrival of Anna at the rapids, guarded by his warriors, a fleet of Russian boats must have sailed down the Dnieper nearer to the mouth in order to take on board the Porphyrogenite and her suite. The interpretation of the record in the "Memory and Eulogy" that Anna arrived in the year following Vladimir's baptism, that is, in the summer of 988, is entirely in accordance with the argument proving both rulers' eagerness to consolidate their mutual obligations. It would not have been in the interests of the Macedonian dynasty to delay the union that was to cement the alliance.

---

[150] Cf. Staerk, *Der Taufritus*, Puniet, in *Dictionnaire*, and Golubinskij, *Istorija* (note 5 *supra*); E. Herman, "Baptême en Orient," in *DDC*, II (1937), 174–91; J. A. Jungmann, "Kathechumenat," in *LThK*, VI (1961), 51–54.

[151] Cf. Zavitnevič, "O meste" (note 8 *supra*), 142; Šmurlo, "Kogda," 123, 145.

[152] Cf. The Laurentian Chronicle for the years 1153 and 1154, in PSRL, I, 340, 341. It has been suggested that this record from the "Memory and Eulogy" indicates that Vladimir was expecting the arrival of Anna at the rapids, but that "she did not come," and "incensed by Greek duplicity," Vladimir attacked Cherson. Cf. Levčenko, *Očerki*, 359–60; Vlasto, *Entry*, 259.

242

To fulfill the condition of conversion before the arrival of and the marriage to Anna, Vladimir could have had a choice of two other canonically approved days suitable for the baptism of adult neophytes: Easter and Pentecost. In the year 988 these holidays fell on April 8 and May 27 respectively. This possibility cannot be completely eliminated, but its acceptance contradicts the date of the "Memory and Eulogy," which has been shown to be reliable. It would also be difficult to explain the delay of Vladimir's catechumenate and the exclusion by the mission of such a date as the Epiphany, which was exceptionally suitable, because of its symbolism, to the baptism of a ruler. If all arguments accept the year 6495 for Vladimir's baptism, January 6 (988) appears to be the most likely day for that sacrament.

On either Easter or Pentecost in 6496 (988) the mass baptism of Kievans assembled in the waters of the Dnieper could have taken place. The Primary Chronicle has recorded a description of this event: "Then Vladimir sent his heralds throughout the whole city, proclaiming: 'If anyone does not come tomorrow to the river, be he rich or poor, pauper or slave, my adversary he will be.' Hearing this, people gladly went, saying joyfully: 'If this were not good, the king and the boyars would not have accepted it.'"[153] The metropolitan of Kiev, Ilarion, of equally ardent faith, appraised the event more soberly: "And no one dared to oppose his [Vladimir's] pious order. Even if someone were baptized not for love, he was baptized for fear of him who gave the order, because his piety was linked with authority."[154]

The question arises as to why the Cherson legend, which contained the events discussed here, was placed in the Primary Chronicle in the year 6496 (March 988-February 989). The legend itself, consistent with its character, did not mention any dates. For the author-compiler of the Primary Chronicle, the Cherson version was most reliable because it presented the most providential view of the conversion of Rus'. But as the author-compiler himself acknowledged, he was acquainted with other versions which were probably as brief and prosaic as the records in the "Memory and Eulogy" quoted above. He might have had at his disposal the date of at least one of these events, and on this basis placed the Cherson legend in the chronological scheme of the Chronicle. It might have been the year of Anna's arrival, or perhaps the start of the expedition to Cherson, but most probably it was the year of the baptism of crowds of Kievans. About the year 1060 there were people living in Kiev who still remembered "the baptism of the Russian land."[155] That memorable day in the year 6496 lived on in the memory of the next two or three generations. On that day on the banks of the Dnieper "a countless multitude assembled, stepped into the water, and stood there: some up to their necks, others to their chests in the water, the younger ones nearer the bank and others,

---

[153] PSRL, I, 117, II, 102; cf. Cross, *Chronicle*, 116.

[154] *Des Metropoliten Ilarion Lobrede auf Vladimir den Heiligen und Glaubensbekenntnis*, ed. L. Mueller (Wiesbaden, 1962), 105.

[155] "There was likewise another brother [i.e., monk] named Jeremy, who remembered the baptism of the Russian land," PSRL, I, 189, II, 180; Cross, *Chronicle*, 159–60.

adults holding children, waded, while the priests standing to the front said prayers."[156]

Historiography, so abundant in controversy, has inspired my attempt to reinterpret the tradition based on the sources, as well as to reconsider some widely-held opinions. If this attempt withstands critical examination, the possibility may arise for a new outlook on Russo-Byzantine relations and on different aspects of the history of both states at the end of the tenth century. Though the process of Christianization itself is not the subject of this study, it must be considered here for a moment, lest this analysis of the political circumstances of the baptism of Rus' be construed as support for the widespread, but to my mind erroneous, view that the conversion of Rus' was the act of the Byzantines.[157] The acceptance of Christianity was not imposed by chance and was not instigated by the Byzantine ruler. The date and the conditions of the baptism of the Rus' ruler and his entourage were the result of a concrete political situation. But the entry of the Kievan state into Christendom was preceded by more than a hundred years of penetration of Christianity into the area of the middle Dnieper and by its growing influence at the Kievan court, especially after the baptism of Vladimir's grandmother, Olga-Helena, the sovereign of Kiev.

The diplomatic initiative of Basil II was taken for political and military reasons resulting from the struggle with the usurpers. In the years 986–89 the Emperor was far from contemplating a real conversion of Rus'. The Macedonian dynasty, the Emperor's court, was most certainly eager to justify breaking the tradition, but at the time all this was being decided it was enough that the new relative and ally not be pagan, in name at least. If the idea of the conversion of Rus' had originated on the Bosphorus, a return to paganism would have been inevitable; this had happened shortly after the premature initiative of Photius in 867 and in the time of Olga's son Svjatoslav, when the need for a change was felt but the fear of a break with tradition was still very strong. This fear decreased in the following decades, and the circumstances created by Basil II made it much easier to put Vladimir's decision in an international context based on the alignment of real political power. The ruling class of the Kievan state was ripe politically for conversion and, thus, the permanence of that conversion was assured.

The conversion evoked no response on the part of Byzantine society. Basil's Rus' allies were looked upon as an apocalyptic force, threatening the Empire and its capital with extermination.[158] Byzantine historians maintained aston-

---

[156] PSRL, I, 117–18, II, 102–3; cf. Cross, *Chronicle*, 116–17.
[157] Cf., for instance, Dvornik, *Byzantine Missions* (note 2 *supra*), 270; Obolensky, *Byzantine Commonwealth*, 201.
[158] See *supra*, p. 212ff.; cf. Shepard, "Some Problems" (note 116 *supra*), 12–13. After finishing this paper, I became acquainted with the new and attractive hypothesis of A. Markopoulos on the much interpreted, enigmatic passage about the Rôs-Dromitai in Pseudo-Symeon. By plain emendation (ἀπ' ἠχήματος instead of ἀπηχήματος), and by assigning its text to the time of Basil II, the author sees in the crucial sentence of the passage a reference to the participation of the Russes in the events of

ishing reserve, even when the Emperor was victorious in battle thanks to the support of the Russes, thus proving the correctness of his choice. Psellus, in his history written in the middle of the eleventh century, treats the Tauro-scythian barbarians as if Rus' were still a pagan country.[159] In the eleventh century, Byzantine political thought still did not include Rus' in its ideal Οἰκου-μένη τῶν 'Ρωμαίων.[160]

The initiative for Christianization developed in the ruling class of the Kievan state. The new religious ideology owed its further successes and its permanence to the upper class of Old Russian society. So the conversion of Rus' resulted not from the energy of the expansion of Byzantine civilization itself, but from effective attempts of the leading strata of Old Russian society to find stimuli in the Christian framework of values which would help to provide the answers to their own questions. It was a combination of ripe circumstances and correct decisions that achieved the epochal events of the years 987-88.

988/89 and thereafter. This sentence, with a proposed translation, reads as follows: 'Ρῶς ... διαδραμόν-τες ἀπ' ἠχήματος τῶν χρησαμένων ἐξ ὑποθηκης ἢ θεοκλυτίας τινὸς καὶ ὑπερσχόντων αὐτοὺς ἐπικέκληνται (Ρôs ... sont accourrus à l'appel de ceux qui les ont employés à la suite d'un conseil ou d'une prémunition divine et qui les ont retenus sous leur emprise). See Markopoulos, "Encore les Rôs-Dromitai et le Pseudo-Symeon," *JÖB*, 23 (1974), 90–99, esp. 97. Attention is called to the motivation behind the appeal for Russian aid, which was evidently such a shock to public opinion that the need arose to refer to θεοκλυτία—God's inspiration. Has Pseudo-Symeon retained a trace of the imperial propaganda of the time?

[159] Psellus, *Chronographia*, VI, §§ 90, 91, 96: ed. Renauld, vol. II, pp. 8–10; trans. Sewter, pp. 147–48, 150.

[160] After 988, the membership of Kievan Russia in the Byzantine Christian *oikoumene* became a fact, but its recognition by the Byzantine upper classes was long delayed, indicating once more how unpopular the Emperor Basil's close relationship (again referring to Psellus) was with "the barbarian world."

On the place of Kievan Russia in Europe and within the orbit of the Byzantine world, cf. the writings of recent years: Pašuto, *Vnešnjaja politika* (note 2 *supra*), 19–136; Obolensky, *Byzantine Common-wealth*; *idem*, *Byzantium and the Slavs* (note 105 *supra*), I, 52–60, II, 20–35; T. Wasilewski, *La place de l'Etat russe dans le monde Byzantine pendant le haut Moyen-Âge*, Acta Poloniae Historica, 22 (1970), 43–51; Shepard, "Some Problems" (note 116 *supra*), 27–33; I. P. Medvedev, "Imperia i suverenitet v srednie veka," in *Problemy istorii meždunarodnych otnošenij* (Leningrad, 1972), 421–22. About the contradictions in the Byzantine attitude toward Rus', cf. *supra*, p. 201 ff.

III

THE ORIGINAL STATUS OF THE OLD-RUSSIAN CHURCH

At the turn of 987, the over one-hundred-year old penetration of Christianity in its Byzantine form and Slavonic language variety into the Old-Russian upper social strata, i.e. the prince's court, the knights and merchants, was crowned by an act of the ruler carried out in an exceptionally favourable political situation.[1] Vladimir I gave up his effort to expand the pagan cult and decided to adopt the Christian system of beliefs and ideas of an incomparably stronger impact. It was a mature decision, dictated by the understanding of the growing need to modernise the country and the society through an ideological consolidation of its ruling class, and to acquire the ideological means of influencing the entire population. So Christianisation became law, the state was to watch over it but the Church had its own hierarchy to carry it out. What then was the church organization at its very inception, whose duty it became to consolidate the prestige of the state and the ruling dynasty, and to lay the foundations for the evangelisation of the people of the vast expenses of Kievan Rus'?

---

[1] A. Poppe, *The Political Background to the Baptism of Rus'. Byzantine-Russian Relations between 986—989*, "Dumbarton Oaks Papers," vol. XXX, 1976, pp. 197—244.

6

INVESTIGATIONS AND SPECULATIONS

The paucity of source information which, to make it worse, has been hitherto partly neglected or erroneously interpreted, made the reconstruction of the early history of the Rus'sian Church a genuinely difficult task. At the same time, the intricacy and obscurity of the problem have been further compounded by conclusions both biased and *a priori*, often formed under the pressure of a confessional orientation and other prejudices. The 19th-century Russian historiography professed the idea, strongly entrenched for centuries, of the Byzantine origin of Christianity and the Church in Rus'. More importance was attached to the conviction about the pure orthodoxy of the East Slavic Church than to finding answers in source material. On the other hand, Catholic historiography, based on facts both true and invented during the age-long confrontation of the two Churches (particularly in the struggle for the adherence of the Orthodox to the Greek-Catholic uniate Church), proclaimed the contribution of the Roman Church to the evangelisation of the Eastern Slavs.

The first scientific investigations date back to the last quarter of the 19th century and they have to be credited to E. E. Golubinskij, author of the fundamental *History of the Russian Church*. Many are the scholars who had worked in order to pave the way for the answer to the question about the original status of the Rus'sian Church. Today it should be particularly emphasized that the hypotheses and queries which have not stood the test of time and confrontation with the few but credible source data, have played the role of negative catalysts beneficial to the prospects of research. The main credit for supplying documentary evidence for the assertion about the jurisdictional dependence of the Rus'sian Church on the patriarch of Constantinople from the times of Vladimir I, goes, in our opinion, to V. Laurent and E. Honigmann who drew attention to some unappreciated Greek records, and to L. Müller who also examined Old-Russian records and made a thorough and convincing criticism of the various attempts at a solution.[2] It is their work that laid the foundations

---

[2] V. L a u r e n t, *Aux origines de l'Eglise Russe. L'établissement de la hiérarchie byzantine*, "Echos d'Orient," vol. XXXVIII, 1939, pp. 279—295;

for the attempt at the verification of all the known source information and the documentation of the fact that the Rus'sian Church not only came under Constantinople but that it was from the very beginning an ordinary (with suffragans) metropolis i.e. a church province of the Constantinople patriarchate.[3] But this assertion, propounded over a period of thirty years (1939—1968), although it gained many supporters among the scholars, is still being questioned, directly and indirectly. To some extent this can be explained by ignorance of those works and a tendency towards the traditional ideas of local schools of history. But this does not explain the main opposition which stems, in the first place, from the conviction of the crucial importance of the year 1037 in the history of the Rus'sian Church, and secondly, from the conviction about the complete silence of Old-Russian sources on the subject of Rus'sian church hierarchy and organisation. But both these statements are difficult to substantiate. The second con-

E. Honigmann, *Studies in Slavic Church History. A. The Foundation of the Rus'sian Metropolitan Church according to Greek Sources*, "Byzantion," vol. XVII (American Series III), 1944/45, pp. 128—162; L. Müller, *Zum Problem des hierarchischen Status und der jurisdictionellen Abhängigkeit der russischen Kirche vor 1039*, Köln — Braunsfeld, 1959, p. 84. Honigmann's opinion was shared by M. V. Levčenko, *Očerki po istorii vizantijsko-russkih otnošenij*, Moskva 1956, pp. 373—377. The opinion that from the time of Vladimir's conversion the new Rus'sian Church was subordinated to the Patriarchate of Constantinople was consistently supported in all his works by D. Obolensky. Cf. idem, *Byzantium, Kiev and Moscow: A Study in Ecclesiastical Relations*, "Dumbarton Oaks Papers," vol. XI, 1957, pp. 23—24; idem, *The Byzantine Commonwealth. Eastern Europe 500—1453*, London 1974, pp. 258—259. This scholar also drew attention to the passage in Nicephorus Gregoras (*Historia*, lib. 36, cap. 22—23) that since the baptism of Rus' the Rus'sian Church had formed one single ecclesiastical province, the metropolitanate, whose primate was subordinated to the jurisdiction of Constantinople (idem, *Byzantium, Kiev...*, p. 24). But we would rather not treat as source evidence this accurate statement of a Byzantine historian writing around 1355, since his opinion had a current political overtone, though it confirms our own opinion and was probably based on patriarchal archives then in existence.
    [3] A. Poppe, *Państwo i Kościół na Rusi w XI wieku* [State and Church in Rus' in the 11th Century], Warszawa 1968, pp. 15—39. A. P. Vlasto has devoted a subchapter of his book (*The Entry of the Slavs in the Christendom*, Cambridge 1970, pp. 268—281) to the original status of the Rus'sian Church. He relates the various opinions on the matter and gives priority to the assertions about the subordination to Constantinople. But his nescience of some vital works (e.g. those quoted in Note 2) and his sometimes insufficiently critical attitude towards sources of doubtful credibility, particularly when of Russian provenance, have weakened the importance of his cogent argument.

viction might be justified if there existed some set of Rus'sian sources from that period i.e. from the years 987—1037. But even if some information has been preserved, it is dispersed in fragments over later works, mostly in the well-known *Primary Chronicle* from the opening years of the 12th century. On the other hand, hypotheses about the existence of earlier chronicles from the first half of the 11th century or even the end of the 10th century are in themselves subjects for discussion and cannot constitute a convincing basis for further hypotheses. Moreover, it is clear, though the inference is indirect, from the extant specimens of ancient Old-Russian literature, beginning with the oldest *Sermon on Law and Grace* by Ilarion and dating back to the mid-11th century, that the status of the Rus'sian Church had remained unchanged. As concerns the crucial meaning of the year 1037, the exposition of the premises and the erroneous interpretation of sources, from which this conviction has grown of fundamental importance for it, has also stimulated all those ideas which, without doubting the Byzantine jurisdiction, assumed that up to 1037, Rus' did not have the status of a metropolitanate but some sort of temporary arrangement.[4]

The year 1037 owes its assumed crucial importance to the research carried out by A. A. Šahmatov into the most ancient Rus'sian chronicles. They strongly stimulated investigations and various guesses as to the original organisation of the Rus'sian Church. The hypothesis put forward by that scholar that the most ancient chronicle compilation came into being in 1039, in the metropolitan curia in Kiev, was supported by the statement about

---

[4] Not only Fr. D v o r n i k, A. S t o k e s and A. V l a s t o but even L a u r e n t, *Aux origines...*, p. 295, and M ü l l e r, *Zum Problem...*, pp. 74—75, have bowed to this "evidence." Laurent acknowledged the events of 1037 as an act of demotion of an autonomous archbishopric (like Ochrida and Cyprus) to the rank of a simple metropolitanate; Müller saw there the possibility of a promotion of a titular archbishopric to the rank of metropolitanate. Cf. also H. G. B e c k, *Kirche u. theologische Literatur im Byzantischen Reich*, München 1959, pp. 68, 187; P. D e v o s, in: "Analecta Bollandiana," vol. LXXIII, 1955, p. 244; W. T. P a š u t o, (*Vnešnjaja politika Drevnej Rusi*, Moskva, 1968, pp. 75, 317) hesitated, admitting the possibility of the metropolitan organisation having been formed only around 1037, but ultimately inclined to the Byzantine thesis. Cf. i d e m, in: "Sovetskoje Slavjanovedenie", 1969, No. 6, p. 78.

the founding in 1037—39 of a metropolitanate in Kiev.[5] This assertion was supposedly proved in the chronicle under the year 1037 that *"Yaroslav [...] založi že i cerkov' svjatyja Sofija mitropol'ju"* [Yaroslav [...] founded also the church of St Sophia the metropolis], which referred, apparently, to the foundation of a metropolis. Yet, even from the language point of view, this passage should be understood as information about the building of the stone metropolitan cathedral of St Sophia, founded by the prince.[6] The word *"mitropol'ju"*, (metropolis, metropolitan) whether treated as a noun or an adjective, remains an apposition in relation to the preceding *"cerkov' svjatyja Sofija."* The author simply indicates that it is a metropolitan church, a cathedral, and it is in this sense that it is used in Old-Russian writings. A few lines higher up, under the year 1036, the same chronicler noted that the battle with the Pechenegs was fought *"na mjestje idje že nynje stoit' svjataja Sofija mitropol'ja rus'skaja"* [on the spot where the Rus'sian metropolitan church of St Sophia now stands].[7] Thus the record mentions only the construction of the metropolitan cathedral, the first of brick and stone, as we know, but not the first altogether, for there had been previously a wooden St Sophia in Kiev erected in the time of Vladimir and rebuilt, according to Thietmar, after the fire of 1017.[8] The conviction that the 1037 entry concerned the foundation of a metropolitanate, was expressed earlier but was unreservedly accepted by historians only after it had been propounded by the prominent philologist.

[5] A. A. Š a h m a t o v, *Razyskanija o drevniejšyh russkih letopisnyh svodah*, SPb. 1908, pp. 398—420; for a concise exposition of Šahmatov's hypothesis see M. D. P r i s e l k o v, *Istorija Russkogo letopisanija XI—XV vv.*, Leningrad 1940, pp. 26—29.

[6] *Povest vremennyh let* (hereafter PVL), vol. I, Moskva 1950, p. 102; *The Russian Primary Chronicle*, Laurentian Text, translated and edited by S. H. Cross and O. P. Sherbowitz-Wetzor. Cambridge, Mss., 1953, p. 137: "[Yaroslav] founded also the metropolitan Church of St. Sophia." Cf. M ü l l e r, *Zum Problem...*, p. 66; J. F e n n e l l and A. S t o k e s, *Early Russian Literature*, London 1974, p. 56.

[7] PVL, I, p. 102. see also Laurentian chronicle under the year 1203: *"i mitropol'ju svjatuju Sofiju rozgrabiša i Desjatinnuju svjatuju Bogorodicu rozgrabiša"*, in: *Polnoe Sobranie Russkih Letopisej* (hereafter PSRL), vol. I, Leningrad 1928, col. 418.

[8] See A. P o p p e, Russkije mitropolii konstantinopolskoj patriarhii v XI veke, "Vizantijskij Vremennik", vol. XXVIII, 1968, pp. 86—96; i d e m, *Zasnuvannja Sofiji Kyivskoj*, "Ukrajins'kyj Istoričnyj Žurnal," 1965, No. 9, pp. 97—104.

The scientific prestige of A. A. Šahmatov was such that the assertions and hypotheses of that outstanding scholar were propagated as certainties and used as starting points for hypotheses by other scholars, M. D. Priselkov in particular.[9] Once the idea about the metropolitan chronicle of 1039 was accepted, the conclusions were far-reaching because this compilation said absolutely nothing about the Rus'sian ecclesiastical hierarchy and organisation. On this basis Priselkov contended that the Greek metropolitan purposely ignored the earlier history of the Rus'sian Church as not worthy of attention, because only the establishment of Constantinople's authority in 1037—1039 was the beginning of the true Church and of Christianity.[10] This assertion was later frequently repeated in the writings on the subject.

Critics have so effectively undermined the premises of the hypothesis about the chronicle of 1039 that it can now be safely shelved. Also the very idea to link the chronicle-writing with the metropolitan curia is indefensible.[11] Let us add that the entire series of records included by Šahmatov in the 1039 text of the chronicle, for instance, those which tell about the conversion of Vladimir to Christianity, about the murder of Boris and Gleb, and particularly the record under the year 1037 containing information about the building activity of Yaroslav, date back to the second half of the 11th century.[12] L. Müller is right when he says

---

[9] Even Šahmatov cut himself off from such research process. See A. A. Š a h m a t o v, *Zametki k drevnejšej istorii russkoj cerkovnoj žizni,* "Naučnyj Istoričeskij Žurnal," 1914, No. 4, pp. 30 sq. Cf. also I. U. B u - d o v n i c, *Ob istoričeskih postrojenijah M. D. Priselkova,* "Istoričeskie Zapiski," vol. XXXV, 1950, pp. 199 sqq.

[10] M. D. P r i s e l k o v, *Očerki po cerkovno-političeskoj istorii Kievskoj Rusi X—XII vv.,* SPb, 1913, pp. 82—87. The opinion about the Byzantine censoring of the Old-Russian chronicle still lingers on. In 1965, it was repeated by M. Čubaty (see Note 32 below).

[11] D. S. L i h a č e v, *Russkie letopisi,* Moskva—Leningrad, 1947, p. 62 sqq. M. N. T i h o m i r o v, *Istočnikovedenie istorii SSSR,* vol. I, Moskva 1962, pp. 61—63. M. K. K a r g e r, *K harakteristike drevnerusskogo letopisca,* "Trudy otdela drevnerusskoj literatury" (hereafter TODRL), vol. XI, 1955, pp. 70—72. N. N. I l'i n, *Letopisnaja statja 6523 goda i eë istočnik,* Moskva, 1957, pp. 3—20. U. I. B u d o v n i c, *Obščestvenno-političeskaja mysl' drevnej Rusi,* Moskva 1960, pp. 28—34. A. P o p p e, *Latopisarstwo staroruskie,* in: *Słownik starożytności słowiańskich [Lexicon Antiquitatum Slavicarum]* (Hereafter SSS), vol. III, Poznań 1968, p. 22 sq. H. Ł o w m i a ń s k i, *Początki Polski [Poland's Beginnings],* vol. V, Warszawa 1973, p. 111.

[12] M ü l l e r, *Zum Problem...,* pp. 55—60. A. P o p p e, *Powieść doroczna,* in: SSS, vol. IV, 1970, pp. 259—265.

that the objection concerning the text of the chronicle up to 1039, can be applied to the whole *Primary Chronicle* which is not at all interested in church hierarchy and, particularly, in matters concerning the metropolitanate. Literally only a few extant texts, except the one about the appointment of metropolitan Ilarion, mention metropolitans casually, in connection with events in which they took part (mainly religious ceremonies). The mentions are later; it is only beginning with the eighties that, though similarly rare, they become almost contemporary with the events they describe.[13] So the silence of the chronicler about the main centre of ecclesiastic authority does not mean that it did not exist. It simply did not attract the interest of chroniclers who only by the close of the 11th century became sophisticated enough to try and write a comprehensive history of Rus'; this was attempted in the princely monastery of the Caves, independent of the metropolitan jurisdiction, and the monk who wrote it was mainly interested in the State and Christianity in Rus'. He lauded the deeds of the princes, the asceticism of the monks of the Caves, but had nothing or practically nothing to say about the men at the helm of the Church.

Proving the erroneousness of the opinion that the years 1037—1039 were of a crucial nature to the church affairs in Rus' has deprived of fundamental motivation all the substitute theories on the status of the Rus'sian Church in 988—1037. In those years it was exactly the same as after 1037. But since not everybody has been convinced[14] and different ideas on the beginnings of the Rus'sian Church linger on, some mention should be made of the

---

[13] M ü l l e r, *Zum Problem...*, pp. 52—55. A. P o p p e, *Uwagi o najstarszych dziejach kościoła na Rusi* [*Remarks about the oldest history of the church in Rus'*], "Przegląd Historyczny," vol. LV, 1964, pp. 372—373.

[14] Anyway, some historians remain under the spell of opinions formed on the grounds of A. Šahmatov's hypothesis. Cf. e.g. B u d o v n i c, *Obsčestvenno-političeskaja mysl...*, pp. 88, 91. H. P a s z k i e w i c z (The Making of the Russian Nation, London 1963, pp. 95—97) remarks that "Although much has been written on this subject, it still remains insufficiently clear," and thinks that the jurisdictional position of the Russian Church up to 1037 was fluid. Similarly, K. R o s e, *Byzanz und die Autonomiebestrebungen der russischer Kirche in der Zeit von X bis XVJh.*, in: *Byzantinistische Beiträge*, Berlin 1964, pp. 304—308, and the authors of the collective work, *Cerkov v istorii Rossji*, Moskva, 1967, pp. 43, 47, who think that the all-Russian church organisation was founded by metropolitan Theopemptos who came only in 1039. Cf. also Note 4 supra, and Notes 15, 29 below.

works that have appeared after the publication of the studies by Laurent, Honigmann and Müller. Then we shall proceed to an analysis of the sources.

The opinion that up to 1037, Perejaslav was the original see of the Rus'sian metropolitanate has lately found advocates in G. Stokes and V. Mošin.[15] This variant of the Byzantine thesis has become indefensible after it had been proved that all the sources about the Perejaslav metropolitanate refer to the second half of the 11th century, when the bishopric in Perejaslav ranked temporarily as a titular metropolitanate.[16]

After the critics have had their say from 1913 onwards, after the works of J. Snegarov and L. Müller, there would be no need to return to the baseless opinion of M. D. Priselkov about the jurisdiction of the archbishopric-patriarchate of Ochrida over the Russian Church before 1037, if it had not been for its amazing vitality. This opinion has been uncritically repeated not only before the publication of V. Laurent's and E. Honigmann's studies but also in works written in the past decades.[17] Having read all these outworn expositions one feels inclined to share Šahmatov's opinion:

---

[15] A. D. S t o k e s, *The Status of the Rus'sian Church 988—1037*, "The Slavonic and East European Review", vol. XXXVII, 1959, pp. 430—442. V. M o š i n, *Poslanie russkogo mitropolita Lva ob opresnokah v Ohridskoj rukopisi*, "Byzantinoslavica," vol. XXIV, 1963, pp. 87—105. V l a s t o (*The Entry...*, pp. 280 sqq) is willing to suppose that the *Primary Chronicle* marked under the years 1037 and 1039 the return of the Metropolitanate to Kiev after a period of "exile" at Perejaslav which temporarily (1026—1037/9) became the acting centre of the Old-Russian Church.

[16] A. P o p p e, *Le traité des azymes Leontos metropolitou tēs en Rōsia Presthlabas; Quand, où et par qui a-t-il été écrit?*, "Byzantion," vol. XXXV, 1965, pp. 504—527. I d e m, *Zur Geschichte der Kirche der Rus im 11 Jh.: Titularmetropolen*, in: *Das heidnische und christliche Slaventum*, vol. I. Wiesbaden 1970, pp. 64—74.

[17] Cf. e.g. I. N a z a r k o, *Svjaty Volodimir Veliky, Volodar i Hrestytel Rusi-Ukrainy*, Roma 1954, pp. 108 sq. P. K o v a l e v s k i, *L'Eglise russe en 1054*, in: *L'Eglise et les Eglises"*, vol. I, Chevetogne, 1954, p. 475 sqq. A. V. K a r t a š e v, *Očerki po istorii russkoj cerkvi*, vol. I, Paris 1959, pp. 157—181, cf. review by L. M ü l l e r in: "Kyrios," vol. III, 1963, No. 4, pp. 243—253. M o š i n, *Poslanie...*, pp. 94—96, who modernises the Bulgarian thesis arguing that the jurisdiction of Ochrida over Kiev existed only in 988—991, when the patriarch of Ochrida supposedly sent Metropolitan Michael to Rus'. H. K o c h's article, *Byzanz, Ochrid und Kiev 987—1037*, first published in "Kyrios," vol. III, 1938, pp. 253—292, which defended the Bulgarian assertion, was reprinted in: H. K o c h, *Kleine Schriften zur Kirchen- und Geistesgeschichte Osteuropas*, Wiesbaden, 1962. L. Müller was right when he pointed to the purely jubilee value of this reprint in: "Zeitschrift für Slavische Philologie," vol. XXXI, 1964, p. 434 sqq.

"In the end, it seems that the whole hypothesis propounded by M. D. Priselkov rests on the common name of the hierarchs of Kiev and Ochrida who lived in the twenties of the 11th century."[18] There is no need to go too far in arguing with a notion that has already been abolished[19] but it would be instructive to illustrate the feebleness of M. Priselkov's construction with one example: He says, for instance, that the "*archiepiscopus civitatis illius*" in Thietmar's narrative who welcomed the Russian prince Svjatopolk and the Polish Duke Boleslaw at the gates of Kiev, was the archbishop-patriarch John of Bulgaria, who at the time was supposedly visiting the Rus'sian church province subordinated to him. So, in 1018, when Basil the Bulgar-Slayer was putting an end to the existence of the West-Bulgarian state, the head of the Bulgar Church was to visit Kiev and be the same archbishop *predictae sedis* who in August 1018, went to Novgorod as a mediator in the negotiations between Bolesław and Svjatopolk, on the one hand, and Yaroslav on the other. John of Ochrida could not have been that archbishop if only for the simple reason that he assumed the see only in the summer of 1018.[20] Priselkov's and his epigones' ignorance of Bulgarian events is all the more glaring in that, according to their own opinion, Yaroslav's recognition of Ochrida's church jurisdiction was to be an expression of the anti-Byzantine policy of that prince. So it would be consistent to presume that Yaroslav gained archbishop John of Ochrida for his policies; yet, the archbishop, though canonically not under the authority of the patriarch in Constantinople, was nevertheless entirely dependent on the Emperor, for he acceded to the archbishop's see by the imperial will alone.[21]

---

[18] S a h m a t o v, *Zametki...*, p. 56. For a critique of the Bulgarian thesis as treated by Priselkov's other epigones, see E. M i h a j l o v, *Bylgarsko-russkite vzaimootnošenija ot kraja na X do 30-te godiny na XIII v. v russkite i bylgarskite istoriografija*, "Godišnik na Sofijskija universitet. Istorič. fak.," vol. LIX, 1966, book 3, pp. 171-175.

[19] M ü l l e r, *Zum Problem...*, pp. 12—17. P o p p e, *Uwagi...*, pp. 375—377.

[20] V. Z l a t a r s k i, *Istoria na Bylgarskata država prez srednite vekove*, vol. I—II, Sofia 1927, pp. 775 sqq., vol. II, Sofia 1934, p. 17 sqq. F. G r a n i č, *Kirchengeschichtliche Glossen zu den vom Kaiser Basileios II dem autokephalen Erzbistum von Achrida verliehenen Privilegien*, "Byzantion," vol. XII, 1937, p. 395 sqq.

[21] G r a n i č, *Kirchengeschichtliche Glossen...*, p. 398 sqq. A. M i c h e l, *Die Kaisermacht in der Ostkirche (843—1204)*, Darmstadt, 1959, p. 46.

14

Let us also remark that supporting the assertion about the church supremacy of Ochrida over Kiev by pointing to the vast cultural and religious contacts, does not explain anything, because long before its conversion to Christianity as well as after the 987/9 events Rus' benefited immensely from the achievements of Southern Slavs. Bulgaria made a considerable contribution to the spreading of Christian culture among Eastern Slavs and to the evangelisation of Rus'.[22]

It is from the critical attitude towards M. Priselkov's Bulgarian thesis and from the assertion about the crucial importance of the year 1037, that have sprung the Tmutorokan and Cherson theses. The first, formulated by G. Vernadsky, supposes that Vladimir gave authority over the Rus'ian Church to the archbishop|of Tamatarkha (Matrakha)-Zikhia because of the role that bishopric, situated on the territory of the Rus'sian Tmutorokan kaganate, was supposed to play in spreading Christianity among the Russes in the 9th—10th centuries.[23] But this guess has not even circumstantial evidence to support it, although it is obvious that the contacts of the Russes who arrived in the Taman peninsula with the local Christian population had exerted an impact on the Christianisation of the knights and merchants who formed the

G. G. L i t a v r i n, *Bolgaria i Vizantija v XI—XII vv.*, Moskva, 1960, p. 356 sqq. G. O s t r o g o r s k y, *History of the Byzantine State*, New Brunswick, N. J. 1969, p. 311.

[22] Cf. M. S p e r a n s k i j, *Otkuda idut starejsie pamjatniki russkoj pismennosti i literatury*, "Slavia," vol. VIII 1928; I. S n e g a r e v, *Duhovno-kulturni wrzki meždu Bulgaria i Rusija prez srednite vekove*, Sofia 1950. For an extensive review of the state of research in Bulgarian with French résumé, see E. M i h a j l o v, *Relations culturelles Bulgaro-russes de la fin du Xme siècle jusqu'aux trente années du XIIIme siècle dans l'historiographie russe et bulgare*, "Godišnik na Sofijskija Universitet, Istorič. fak.", vol. LX, 1967, book 3, pp. 193—260; i d e m, *Les Russes et les Bulgares au cours du haut Moyen Age, ibidem*, vol. LXVI, 1975, pp. 77—143. In publications on this subject it happens, unfortunately, that unreliable texts have been used like that of the *Joachimian Chronicle* which is an early 18th century compilation of various legends culled from 16th—17th century works. Cf. e.g. B. S t. A n g e l o v, *K voprosu o načale russko-bolgarskih literaturnyh svjazej*, TODRL, vol. XIV, 1958, pp. 132—138.

[23] G. V e r n a d s k y, *The Status of the Russian Church during the first Half-Century Following Vladimir's Conversion*, "The Slavonic and East European Review," vol. XX (The Slavonic Yearbook, Amer. ser. I), 1941, pp. 294—314. For concise treatment of this opinion see i d e m, *Kievan Russia*, New Haven 1948, p. 67 sqq. (where polemics with E. Honigmann announced), repeated unaltered in the last edition during its author's lifetime of Kievan Russia, New Haven and London 1973, pp. 66—69.

majority of the new-comers. But two vital factors speak against the supposed ecclesiastical role of Tmutorokan. First, the extension of Tmutorokan's jurisdiction over the whole of Rus' would require the decision of the patriarch and the emperor, and would also mean the recognition of the right of Rus' to the lands which Byzantium considered its own. Secondly, if it did happen, Tmutorokan would have to advance to the rank of an ordinary metropolitanate; yet, both in the 10th and in the 11th century it remained a titular archbishopric, that is a bishopric directly under the authority of the patriarch but without the right of having its own suffragans.[24] So the Rus'sian bishops before 1037 could not be the suffragans of the archbishop of Tmutorokan (Zikhia). Neither could the titular archbishop of Cherson have suffragans; F.Dvornik was quite ready to attribute to him the supervision over the Rus'sian church up to 1037, on the grounds that the town, captured by Vladimir, was supposed to have become the place of his baptism; he took the Chersonian priests and Anastasius the Chersonite from there to Kiev. Anastasius was to have been the first Kievan bishop, suffragan of Cherson.[25] The share of Cherson in the Christianisation of Rus' is indubitable[26] but this does not mean that it had rights to church jurisdiction.

---

[24] G. P a r t h e y (ed.), *Hieroclis synecdemus et notitiae graecae episcopatuum*, Berolini 1866, p. 100. H. G e l z e r, *Ungedrückte und ungenügend veröffentlichte Texte der Notitiae episcopatuum*, "Abhandlungen der philosophisch-philologischen Classe der königl. Bayerischen Akademie der Wissenschaften," vol. XXI, München 1901, p. 575; C. de B o o r, *Nachträge zu den Notitiae episcopatuum*, "Zeitschrift für Kirchengeschichte," vol. XII, 1891, pp. 319, 531. B e c k, *Kirche...*, p. 176. H o n i g m a n n, *Studies...*, pp. 130—142, where he convincingly demolishes G. V e r n a d s k y's thesis. The critique was rounded up by M ü l l e r, *Zum Problem...*, pp. 17—18. Cf. also P o p p e, *Państwo...*, pp. 192—196.

[25] Fr. D v o r n i k, *The Making of Central and Eastern Europe*, London 1949, p. 177 sqq., repeated in: i d e m, *The Slavs, Their Early History and Civilisation*, Boston 1956, p. 210. For critique of the Chersonian thesis see M ü l l e r, *Zum Problem...*, pp. 19—22. In his last work he seems to tone down his earlier statements. In the text he speaks of the establishment of "the archbishop of Cherson as a kind of supervisor of the young Russian Church," while in the notes he emphasizes the Byzantine origins of Christianity in Kiev and refers readers to D. Obolensky's work (see Note 2 *supra*). See Fr. D v o r n i k, *Byzantine Missions among the Slavs*, New Brunswick, N. J. 1970, pp. 272, 417, Note 32.

[26] But more modest than usually thought. About the role of Cherson in the events of 986—989 see P o p p e, *The Political Background...*, pp. 198—200, 221—224.

The concept linking the original church organisation in Rus' with the Apostolic See has lost its advocates;[27] in the face of unquestionable evidence it has been reduced to the thesis about the missionary activity of bishops without determining their outside legal status.[28] This assertion is supported by unquestionable but modest influences in ecclesiastical writings and terminology, and in diplomatic and missionary contacts. At the time Rus' was not a backwater and did not isolate itself from the rest of Europe, subtle dogmatic disputes were alien to it, the two Churches, notwithstanding differences, did not fight each other as they were to do beginning with the second half of the 11th century. No wonder then that the influence of the Latin Church reached Rus', although it was not strong enough to vie in Kiev for the place occupied by the representative of Hagia Sophia.

After the critical remarks by L. Müller who effectively undermined the thesis about the missionary bishoprics, A. Amman tried to defend his stand,[29] but his main argument: the silence of Bruno of Querfurt on the subject of the status of the church in Rus' in the letter he sent in 1008 to King Henry II, if it does prove anything, it is the wrongness of his conception. Church relations must have been settled in Rus' at the time and been known in the West since they required no commentary. Bruno, who went abroad to convert the Pechenegs, wrote primarily about his own mission. He mentioned the Rus'sian ruler, because he was his host but he did not call him by name nor did he mention Kiev where he stayed twice. Bruno was not interested in Christian, as he sup-

---

[27] Among the best known in the 1920s and 1930s were N. Baumgarten and M. Jugie. For criticism of their theories see M ü l l e r, *Zum Problem...*, pp. 26—36.

[28] A. M. A m m a n n, *Die Anfänge der Hierarchie im Kiewer Rus'-Reich*, "Ostkirliche Studien," vol. II, 1953, pp. 59—64; i d e m, *Untersuchungen zur Geschichte der kirchlichen Kultur und des religioses Lebens bei den Ostslaven*, Würzburg 1955, p. 35 sqq.

[29] M ü l l e r, *Zum Problem...*, pp. 36—42, and A. A m m a n n's reply, *Gedanken zu einigen neueren Veröffentlichungen aus der frührussischen Kirchengeschichte*, "Ostkirchliche Studien, vol. IX, 1960, No 2/3, p. 104 sq. An opinion akin to Ammann's was voiced by E. W i n t e r, *R u s s l a n d und das Papstum*, B. I, Berlin 1960, pp. 27—34, who makes even Theophylact of Sebaste a missionary bishop, and describes the period up to 1037 as a time of Byzantine—Roman rivalry and wavering on the part of the Russes.

posed, Rus', but in the conversion of the Pechenegs.[30] After all, if we have learned from Thietmar that Kiev had its archbishop, it is only because he took part in the political events of 1018, related by the German chronicler.

The missionary thesis is close to the assertion about the autonomous status of the Rus'sian Church up to 1037, as the result of the interaction of the influences of various church centres (Byzantium, Ochrida, Rome). Its fullest exponent was N. Zernov, who saw an independent bishop of Kiev in Anastasius the Chersonite; but it was refuted convincingly by L. Müller.[31] A new version of it has been put forward by M. Čubaty. It is really just a conglomerate of all the theses which question the jurisdiction of the Constantinople patriarch over the Rus'sian Church until 1037. Čubaty argues that there was no need in Vladimir's time to found a metropolitanate and bring its head from abroad, because for a long time on the territory of the Rus'sian state there existed two centres of church authority: the Tmutorokan archbishopric and the bishopric in Peremyšl in the Slav rite belonging to the Moravian church province.[32] The supposition about the alleged foundation of a bishopric in Peremyšl in early 10th century is pure fantasy, and the reference to post-war archaeological investigations does not help it in the least. It is easy to see through

[30] *Monumenta Poloniae Historica*, vol. I, 1864 (re-ed. 1960), pp. 224—228; let us note that when writing about his visit to Poland, Bruno does not mention at all the Polish Church hierarchy; the only clear point is the Roman sovereignty because, when speaking about St Peter as the country's defender, he adds that Duke Boleslaw calls himself his tributary. Cf. also M. H e l l m a n n, *Vladimir der Heilige in der zeitgenössischen abendländischen Überlieferung*, "Jahrbücher für Geschichte Osteuropas," vol. VII, 1959, p. 397 sq.

[31] Cf. N. Z e r n o v, *Vladimir and the Origin of the Russian Church*, "The Slavonic and East European Review," vol. XXVIII, No. 70, 1049, pp. 123—138, No. 71, pp. 425—438. Similar opinion on the independent status of the Russian Church was expressed by N. L a v r o v in: *Istoria Kultury Drevnej Rusi*, vol. I, Moskva 1950, p. 90, and smatteringly by O. M. R a p o v, *O nekotoryh pričinach kresčenija Rusi*, "Vestnik Moskovskogo Universiteta," istoria, 1976, No. 4, p. 68 sq. For criticism of this opinion see M ü l l e r, *Zum Problem...*, pp. 42—47.

[32] M. Č u b a t y, *Istoria xristianstva na Rusi—Ukraini*, vol. I ("Opera Graeco-Catolicae Academiae Theologicae," vol. XXIV—XXV), Roma—New York, 1965, pp. 101 sqq., 122—134, 257 sqq., 274 sqq., 297 sqq. Very critical reviews by: L. M ü l l e r in "Jahrbücher für Geschichte Osteuropas," vol. XVII, 1969, pp. 271—273, and O. B a c h u s, H. S t a m m l e r in "Slavic Revue," vol. XXX, 1971, pp. 361—365.

the author's intentions; he wants to show the age-long links between Rus'-Ukraine and the Apostolic See dating back to the very beginnings of Christianity. M. Čubaty thinks that two hierarchs, of Tmutorokan and Peremyšl, with the help of Anastasius the Chersonite, who was probably the bishop of Kiev, and the Cherson and Bulgarian clergy laid the foundations of the Russian church organisation by founding new bishoprics and ordaining bishops. The head of the Rus'sian Church was supposedly the archbishop of Tmutorokan, freed, seemingly at Vladimir's request, from the jurisdiction of the patriarch. Čubaty has even managed to reconcile his vision with the Perejaslav thesis: the Tmutorokan archibishop was to have his temporary residence in Perejaslav when he visited Rus'. In more than 100 pages devoted to the years 989—1054, M. Čubaty has passed over in silence the evidence illuminating the status of the Russian church prior to 1037. Although his extensive bibliography includes the works by V. Laurent and E. Honigmann, he has not deemed it apposite to quote their arguments. He has ignored L. Müller's thorough study and mentioned only that its author had not been able to explain the silence of all the Rus'sian and other sources on Byzantine Church supremacy.[33] After Čubaty's work had been severely criticised, its author tried to defend his views but he has considered neither the main sources of the disputed subject nor the studies which had pointed to the lameness of the arguments referred to by himself and his predecessors.[34] Let us concentrate on Čubaty's main argument in favour of the existence in 989—1037 of an independent archbishopric of Rus' "outside of the boundaries of the traditional patriarchates," because it affords a good opportunity to get to know his way of working. The fundamental sources consist here of the accounts of the events of about 1020, in the two hagiographic works on Boris and Gleb. Čubaty is right when he says that their authors, Anonymous and Nestor, give John, then the head of the Rus'sian Church, the title of archbishop. But why does he forget to add that they also call him metropolitan and that they use these titles alternately also with

---

[33] Č u b a t y, *Istoria...*, p. 241.
[34] N. D. Č u b a t y, *Kievan Christianity Misinterpreted. Response to Reviewers*, "The Ukrainian Historian," vol. IX, 1972, Nos 3/4, pp. 5—15.

regard to George, metropolitan of Kiev in the seventies of the 11th century? Next, Čubaty suggests that "both authors call the residential archiepiscopal church "Catholicane Ecclesia" which supposedly proves that the Church in Rus' had the same autocephalous status as the national churches such as the Armenian, Georgian, Bulgarian.[35] First, it should be noted that Nestor solely used that term when talking about the dedication of a church to SS Boris and Gleb in Vyšgorod near Kiev; he says that after the ceremony had ended Archbishop John, who officiated, "returned to his *kafolikani iklisia*."[36] This Greek note (καθολική ἐκκλεσία) in Cyrillic transliteration means, as is known also to Old-Russian sources, the main church in the town, in this case, a cathedral one.[37] This meaning is clear from its very context, and though the semantics of the term may give ground to some other interpretations in Christian terminology, here a reference to them, considering the context, would be devoid of any grounds.[38] Nestor did not use a translation, although he had the Slavonic equivalent (*zbornaja cerky*), not perhaps because of his own literary style, but probably because he repeated the term applied to St Sophia's cathedral in Kiev by the metropolitan's entourage. Unfortunately, Čubaty has not even as much as mentioned such a simple interpretation of the text. He has preferred an artificial one, best serving the hypothesis to which Nestor's text gives no ground at all.

There is no doubt that in this case we have a question exceptionally poor in sources and hence extremely complex, from

---

[35] *Ibidem*, pp. 10—11.

[36] *Die altrussischen Hagiographischen Erzählungen und liturgischen Dichtungen über die Heiligen Boris und Gleb*. Nach der Ausgabe von D. Abramovič herausgegeben von L. Müller, München 1964, p. 19; for an interpretation of this text identical with Čubaty's see K a r t a š e v, *Očerki*, vol. I, p. 163, with the difference that according to the latter it was John, archbishop of Ochrida, to the former — the archbishop-katholikos of Tmutorokan (Tamatarkha).

[37] D u C a n g e, *Glos. graecitatis*, p. 537; i d e m, *Glos. latinitatis*, vol. III, p. 224; I. I. S r e z n e v s k i j, *Materialy dla slovarja drevnerusskogo jazyka*, vol. I, col. 1201, vol. III, col. 650—651. The -an- inserted into *kafolikani* seems to be a Slavic adjective-formative suffix, which has to "slavonise" the Greek form.

[38] Cf. in the dogmatic sense, in Ilarion's Creed: "K Kafolikii i Apostolstej Cerkvi pritekaju." *Des Metropoliten Ilarion Lobrede auf Vladimir den Heiligen und Glaubensbekenntnis*. Nach der Erstausgabe von 1844 neu herausgegebenn, eingeleitet u. erläutert von L. Müller, Wiesbaden 1962, p. 143. Cf. *ibidem* p. 192 the relevant Greek text from the Creed of Michael synkellos.

the source point of view. A proper picture of the situation may be created only through the comprehensive checking of all texts which, treated singly, could seem enigmatic. The data which we now have at our disposal thanks to our predecessors makes it possible to defend the thesis that the Rus'sian Church had from its inception been a metropolitan diocese of the Byzantine Church. So it is worthwhile to put them in order again together, and to add new details.

ORDO THRONORUM

In *Notitia episcopatuum* of the Constantinople partriarchate, drawn up and promulgated under Alexius Comnenus around 1087, among the eighty listed metropolitan sees, the sixtieth place is occupied by the metropolitanate ἡ ʽΡωσία. In a similar official register drawn up under emperor Leo the Wise and the patriarch Nicholas Mystikos in 901—902, among the fifty-one listed metropolitanates and as many autocephalous archbishoprics there is no mention of Rus'.[39] In his analysis of the time when twenty-nine metropolitanates were founded, H. Gelzer concluded that their order on the list of around 1087 reflected the order in the time of their creation in the years 902—1084. This meant that the establishment of the dates of foundation of metropolitanates prior to and following that of Rus' would determine the time limits of its emergence. But the eminent scholar made a mistake which casts a doubt on the proposed criterion: lacking information about the time of the foundation of many Greek metropolitanates, he took over from Russian ecclesiastical historiography the mistaken opinion that linked the emergence of the metropolitanate with the year 1037 and made this date (or 1035) the chronological determinant of the *terminus ante quem* and *post quem* of the

---

[39] P a r t h e y..., (*Notitia* II), pp. 96—98; *Patrologia Graeca*, vol. CXIX, cols 819—820; G e l z e r, *Ungedrückte* [...] *Texte*..., pp. 550—559; i d e m, *Zur Zeitbestimmung der Notitia episcopatuum*, "Jahrbücher für protestantische Theologie," vol. XII, 1886, pp. 540—541; Cf. H o n i g m a n n, *Studies*..., p. 143. B e c k, *Kirche*..., p. 151 sq.; F. D ö l g e r, *Regesten der Kaiserurkunden des oströmischen Reiches*, th. I. München 1924, No. 1140; V. G r u m e l, *Les Regestes des Actes du Patriarchat de Constantinople*, vol. I, Kadiköy—Paris 1932—1947, Nos 598, 943.

creation of other Greek metropolitan sees.[40] Later, the discovery of other source texts made it possible to correct some of H. Gelzer's statements. So it came out that the metropolitanate of Alania, listed 61st, whose creation that scholar put in the years 1035—1084, existed as early as 997. Also, as pointed out by C. de Boor, the metropolitanate of Keltzene, listed 55th, was founded before the year 1000, not after 1022, as Gelzer thought. On this basis, V. Laurent and E. Honigmann, taking into account also other sources, questioned the date 1035—1037 as that of the creation of the metropolitanate of Rus', and said that it must have been founded before the promotion of the archbishopric of Alania to the rank of a metropolitanate.

The corrections brought by the advances in the knowledge of Byzantine Church geography to H. Gelzer's time-table, have questioned the very usefulness of the date criterion proposed by that scholar. So it is no wonder that G. Konidaris, while emphasizing that the order in drawing up the *Notitiae* or in signing documents at synods was determined by the dignity (τὸ αἰδέσιμον) of the see,   does not say what relation it bears to the date of the foundation of the given see.[41] It seems that the order on the lists followed that of the foundations. This order determined their αἰδέσιμον   and only later political criteria may have had their impact on certain shifts. In an indirect way, these doubts as to the chronological criterion of order were reflected in H. G. Beck's compendium, published in 1959, which to some metropolitan sees applies the newly established dates, to others those established by Gelzer. For instance, for the metropolitanates of Colonea, Thebes and Serres, listed 56th, 57th and 58th, he adopts Gelzer's dates of 1022—1035 as those of their foundation; for the 59th metropolitanate of Pompeiupolis the first half of the 11th century, for Rus', in the 60th place, the year 1037, for Alania (61st) end of the 10th century; Ainos, listed 63d, is dated by him to the years 1035—1054.[42]

---

[40] G e l z e r, *Zur Zeitbestimmung*, pp. 538—540.
[41] Cf. G. I. K o n i d a r i s, *Die neue in parallelen Tabelen Ausgabe der Notitia episcopatuum und die Echtheit der Notitia D*, Cod. Paris 1555 A, in: *Haristerion eis A. K. Orlandou*, vol. 4, Athinai 1967—1968, pp. 248, 250—252.
[42] B e c k, *Kirche...*, pp. 166, 168, 170, 174, 177, 180, 187.

22

In order to obtain a sure answer to the question whether the order in which a see is listed in *Notitiae* can constitute a date criterion, we have to check the whole list of the metropolitan sees founded in the 10th—11th centuries.

Below is a list of the metropolitanates created in 902—1084 after the Ordo thronorum of c. 1087 (Parthey, *Notitia* II) taking into account the known data about the time of their foundation:

52. Amastris 53. Khonai	prior to 940, for the two sees are mentioned in *Nea Taktika*, written in that year at the latest.[43]
54. Hydrus/Otranto	in 968, as witnessed by Liutprand of Cremona, *Legatio* § 62.[44]
55. Keltzene	969—972, appears in *Notitia* (*Cod. Athen.* 1372) dated to the first period of the reign of Tzimiskes.[45]
56. Koloneia	972—976; mentioned as the last of the metropolitan sees in the original version of *Notitia* III drawn up in the second period of the reign of Tzimiskes.[46]
57. Thebai	from a note by Nicethas of Amasea it follows that Thebes was a metropolis as early as the end of the 10th century.[47]

---

[43] G e l z e r, *Ungedrückte* [...] *Texte...*, pp. 565, 570; H o n i g m a n n, *Studies...*, p. 144; B e c k, *Kirche...*, pp. 168, 169. The letter of 945 was addressed to the metropolitan of Chones Procopius. See J. D a r r o u z è s, *Epistoliers byzantins du X° siècle*, Paris 1960, pp. 63, 82.

[44] MGH SS vol. III, p. 361; G r u m e l, *Les Regestes...*, No. 792; B e c k, *Kirche...*, p. 183; V. L a u r e n t, *Le Corpus des Sceaux de L'Empire Byzantin*, vol. V-1-A. Paris 1963, p. 728; V. v. F a l k e n h a u s e n, *Untersuchungen über die byzantinische Herrschaft in Süd-Italien vom 9 bis ins 11 Jh*, Wiesbaden 1967, p. 148.

[45] G e l z e r, *Ungedrückte* [...] *Texte...*, p. 572; C. d e B o o r, *Nachträge...*, pp. 321—322; H o n i g m a n n, *Studies...*, pp. 144—145; R. J a n i n, in: *Dictionnaire d'Histoire et de Géographie Ecclesiastiques* (hereafter DHGE), vol. XII, col. 130—131; B e c k, *Kirche...*, p. 168; L a u r e n t, *Le Corpus...*, p. 627. G. I. K o n i d a r i s narrowed the accepted dating of 969—976, by pointing to the year 972 as terminus ante quem, in his *Zur Frage der Entstehung der Diozese des Erzbistums von Ochrida und der Notitiae No. 3 bei Parthey*, "Theologia," vol. XXX, Athinai 1959, p. 10 sq.

[46] P a r t h e y.., p. 128; K o n i d a r i s, *Zur Frage...*, pp. 1—19. Before, *Notitia* III was dated to the years 980—985; see G e l z e r, *Ungedrückte* [...] *Texte...*, p. 572; L a u r e n t, *Le Corpus...*, p. 630.

[47] J. D a r r o u z è s, *Documents inédits d'ecclesiologie byzantine*, Paris 1966, pp. 170—171; L a u r e n t, *Le Corpus...*, p. 591. The metropolitan of Thebes, present at the synod in December 1079, signed his name in the order in accordance with his rank in *Notitia* II, after Koloneia and before Pompeiupolis. See J. G o u i l l a r d, *Un Chrysobulle de Nicephore Botaneiates à subscription synodale*, "Byzantion," vol. XXIX/XXX, 1960, p. 31.

58. Serrhai 59. Pompeiupolis	976—997; *Notitia* from Tzimiskes' time mentions them both as archbishoprics. The signatures of the two metropolitans are on the synodal document of February 21, 997.[48]
60. Rhōsia	?
61. Alania	prior to 997; confirmed in the synodal document of May 1024, referring to a privilege granted to the metropolitan of Alania, Nicholas, in the year 6506 /997/8/.[49]
62. Ainos	prior to 1032, as evidenced by the signature on a synodal document of 1032.[50]
63. Tiberiupolis	no data, localisation uncertain.
64. Eukhaneia	prior to 1054, as witnessed by the signature of metropolitan Nicholas on a synodal document of July 24, 1054. In the note on one of the MSS the metropolitan of Eukhaneia Nicholas was called "the man of Theodora Porphyrogenite." This note may date to the time before 1042, when Theodora became empress.[51]
65. Kerasus	1024—1058; in 1024 it was not yet a metropolitanate; a metropolitan of this see, a contemporary of Michael Cerularius (1043—1058), is known.[52]
66. Nakoleia	prior to 1066; a signature on a synodal document of April 21, 1066.[53]
67. Germia	no precise data; a synodal document of December 1079 was signed by the metropolitan of Germia as the last of those present (after Kerasus). In the synodal minutes of April 11, 1062, Germia is listed among those present between Tiberiupolis (63) and

---

[48] G e l z e r, *Ungedrückte... Texte...*, p. 571; *Patrologia graeca*, vol. 119, col. 741ᵃ; G r u m e l, *Les Regestes...*, No. 804; L a u r e n t, *Le Corpus...*, pp. 595, 598.

[49] Published by G. F i c k e r in "Byzantinisch-Neugrichische Jahrbücher," vol. III, 1922, pp. 93—95. See G r u m e l, *Les Regestes...*, No. 806, No. 827; H o n i g m a n n, *Studies...*, p. 146; L a u r e n t, *Le Corpus...*, p. 613; C l e m e n t, metropolitan of Alania, was listed before Ainos in a document of the year 1032. (Cf. F i c k e r, Note 50 below).

[50] G. F i c k e r, *Erlasse des Patriarchen von Konstantinopel Alexios Studites*, Kiel 1911, p. 26; G r u m e l, *Les Regestes...*, No. 840; L a u r e n t, *Le Corpus...*, pp. 614—615. Cf. V. G r u m e l, *Les Metropolites sincelles*, "Etudes Byzantines," vol. III, 1945, p. 110.

[51] G r u m e l, *Les Regestes...*, No. 869; R. J a n i n, in: DHGE, vol. XV, col. 1313 sq.

[52] N. S k a b a l a n o v i č, *Vizantijskoje gosudarstvo i cerkov v XI veke*, SPb 1884, p. 416; B e c k, *Kirche...*, p. 170.

[53] *Patrologia graeca*, vol. CXIX, col. 756; G r u m e l, *Les Regestes...*, No. 896; B e c k, *Kirche...*, pp. 172.

Abydos (74); also mentioned in *Notitia Cod Coislin.* 211, f. 261v, of c. 1082/4.[54]

68. Madyta   1059—1067, promoted to the rank of titular metropolitanate by Constantine Ducas.[55]

69. Apameia   date of foundation unknown, mentioned among the present metropolitans between Kerasus (65) and Dristra (71) in the synodal minutes of March 21, 1082, and in *Notitia, Cod. Coislin.* 211.[56]

70. Basileion   1059—1067, promoted by Constantine Ducas.[57]

71. Dristra   belonged to the patriarchate of Ochrida, separated from it and subordinated to Constantinople probably after the Bulgarian rising in 1040/1. It obtained the rank of metropolitanate before 1071, as witnessed by the signatures of Dristra metropolitan Leo on the synodal documents of November 6, 1071 and March 14, 1072.[58]

72. Nazianzos   1068—1071, status of metropolitanate obtained from Romanus Diogenes.[59]

73. Kerkyra   1072—1082; nearer to the latter date, because in *Notitia Cod. Coislin.* 211. f. 261v—262, it is both on the list of metropolitanates and that of autocephalous archbishoprics where there is also a note about its promotion.[60]

---

[54] F. I. U s p e n s k i j, *Deloproizvodstvo po obvineniju Ioanna Itala v eresi,* "Izvestija russkogo arheologičeskogo instituta v Konstantinopole," vol. II, Odessa 1897, p. 62; G o u i l l a r d, *Un Chrysobulle...,* p. 31. Cf. L a u r e n t, *Le Corpus...,* p. 638. About Notitia in Cod. Coislinianus see A. P o p p e, *Russkije mitropolii Konstantinopolskoj patriarhii v XI stuletii,* "Vizantijskij Vremennik," vol. XXVIII, 1968, pp. 98—101, where also a photograph of the folio with the texts of the taxis.

[55] G r u m e l, *Les Regestes...,* No. 938; L a u r e n t, *Le Corpus...,* p. 552.

[56] U s p e n s k i j, *Deloproizvodstvo...,* p. 36. P o p p e, *Russkie mitropolii...,* p. 99.

[57] *Patrologia graeca,* Vol. CXIX, col. 877. D ö l g e r, *Regesten...,* Nos 964, 1011, 1140; G r u m e l, *Les Regestes...,* Nos 904, 934, 943; B e c k, *Kirche...,* p. 162; L a u r e n t, *Le Corpus...,* p. 617.

[58] N. O i k o n o m i d e s, *Un decret synodal inédit du Patriarche Jean VIII Xiphilin,* "Revue des Etudes Byzantines," vol. XVIII, 1960, p. 57. Cf. H o n i g m a n n, *Studies...,* p. 159; G. G. L i t a v r i n, *Bolgaria i Vizantija v XI—XII vv.,* Moskva 1960, pp. 332—354. Judging from its place in *Notitia Cod. Coislin.* 211, it was promoted in the 1060s. Cf. P o p p e, *Russkie mitropolii...,* pp. 101—104.

[59] *Scylitzes-Kedrenos,* vol. II (Bonnae, 1839), p. 705; D ö l g e r, *Regesten...,* No. 974; G r u m e l, *Les Regestes...,* No. 899; H o n i g m a n n, *Studies...,* p. 162; B e c k, *Kirche...,* p. 159. On the list of the metropolitans present on March 14, 1072, Gregory, metropolitan of Nazianzos, is the last. See O i k o n o m i d e s, *Un decret synodal...,* p. 67—68.

[60] B e c k, *Kirche...,* p. 182; L a u r e n t, *Le Corpus...,* p. 618; P o p p e, *Russkie mitropolii...,* pp. 99—100; G r u m e l, *Metropolites sincelles...,* p. 110.

74. Abydos	c. 1081/2, all three figure also in *Notitia Cod.*
75. Methymna	*Coislin.* 211 as metropolitan sees; in the synodal
76. Christianupolis	edict of March 14, 1072, Methymna is confirmed as an archbishopric. Christianopolis confirmed as a metropolitanate in the synodal minutes (*Cod. Athos.* 120. f. 711) of March 20 and 21, 1082, Abydos in those of April 11, 1082.[61]
77. Rhusion	In 1082; after March 24, 1082 (*Cod. Athos.* 120 f. 711) when it is still an archbishopric. Like Kerkyra, it figures twice in *Notitia Cod. Coislin.,* 211 /1082/4/ with note about promotion.[62]
78. Lakedaimon	around January 1, 1083, promoted by Alexius Comnenus.[63]
79. Naxia	in May 1083.[64]
80. Attaleia	between September 1, 1083 and August 31, 1084 (6592); promoted metropolitanate by Alexius Comnenus.[65]

The survey of the dates on which the particular metropolitan sees were created in the 10th and 11th centuries, although it intro-duced vital corrections into the concrete dates proposed by H. Gel-zer, wholly confirmed his assertion that the metropolitanates were listed in the *Notitiae* in order of their foundation. The figures listed above show that the dates of the promotion of this or that see are not known in all cases, but wherever they can be credibly though unfortunately only approximately established, their pattern

---

[61] U s p e n s k i j, *Deloproizvodstvo...,* pp. 30, 36, 62; B e c k, *Kirche...,* pp. 162, 175, 179; L a u r e n t, *Le Corpus...,* pp. 622—624; O i k o n o m i d e s, un decret synodal..., pp. 57—68. In the inscription 6594 of the year 1085/86, Methymnoi figures as a metropolis.

[62] U s p e n s k i j, *Deloproizvodstvo...,* pp. 31, 36; G r u m e l, *Les Re-gestes...,* No. 897; B e c k, *Kirche...,* p. 174; L a u r e n t, *Le Corpus...,* p. 719; P o p p e, *Russkie mitropolii...,* pp. 99—100. In the synodal papers of March 14, 1072 and December 1079, it figures as a titular archbishopric. See O i k o-n o m i d e s, *Un decret synodal...,* p. 68.

[63] P a r t h e y..., (*Notitia* III, scholion), p. 119, cf. pp. 216, 259; D ö l g e r, *Regesten...,* No. 1086; G r u m e l, *Les Regestes...,* No. 928; L a u r e n t, *Le Corpus...,* p. 624; i d e m, *La date de l'érection des métropoles Patros et de Lacédémon,* "Revue des Etudes Byzantines," vol. XXI, 1963, pp. 136—139.

[64] P a r t h e y..., (*Notitia* III, scholion), p. 123; D ö l g e r, *Regesten...,* No. 1088; G r u m e l, *Les Regestes...,* No. 929; B e c k, *Kirche...,* p. 174.

[65] P a r t h e y..., (*Notitia* III, scholion), p. 116; D ö l g e r, *Regesten...,* No. 1112; G r u m e l, *Les Regestes...,* No. 930; B e c k, *Kirche...,* p. 166.

is evidently chronological.[66] Thus the conclusion that the metropolitan see of Rus' was founded prior to 997 has been confirmed. As follows from the *Notitiae*, it was founded after the promotion of Serres and Pompeiupolis between the years 976 and 997. It is precisely the time of the events which created the conditions for the establishment of the metropolitan see in Rus'. This act could not have been promulgated earlier than in 987/8, but close to that date, if one considers that Alania obtained a metropolitanate after Rus' but prior to 997.

TRANSLATION OF METROPOLITAN THEOPHYLACT

Another evidence of the sovereignty of Constantinople over the Russian church during the reign of Basil Porphyrogenitus, that is before 1025, has been preserved in the *Church History* by Nicephorus Callistus Xanthopulus, completed around 1317, and in some unpublished versions of the treatise *peri metatheseon (de translationibus episcoporum)*. One of them in the *Vatican codex*, No. 1455, of 1299, was referred to by V. Laurent,[67] another, from the Jerusalem collection in a 1687 copy, has for long been signalled to scholars[68] without, unfortunately, arousing due interest.

---

[66] It is worth noting that the documentation of this fourth successive attempt (1st — Gelzer, 2nd — Honigmann, 3rd — Poppe) has more details also in comparison with the third (cf. Poppe, *Państwo...*, pp. 26—28). In the 11th century, the metropolitans-synkelloi tried to revise the accepted *ordo praesidentiae metropolitanum (taxis prokathedrias)* based, as it is right to assume, on the principle of the seniority of a see. But these attempts failed, when in May 1065, the Emperor backed the old ranking order. See D ö l g e r, *Regesten...*, No. 961; G r u m e l, *Les métropolites syncelles...*, p. 92 sq. Beginning with the 12th century the changes in the rank of particular sees basically disturbed and later destroyed its chronological order. Cf. D a r r o u z è s, *Listes synodales et Notitiae*, "Revue des Etudes Byzantines," vol. XXVIII, 1970, pp. 57—94.

[67] L a u r e n t, *Aux origines...*, p. 293, following him, V. G r u m e l, *Chronologie patriarcale au X⁰ siècle*, "Revues des Etudes Byzantines," vol. XXII, 1964, p. 53.

[68] A. P a v l o v, *Zamiečatelnyje rukopisi kanoničeskogo soderžanija v Moskovskoj Sinodalnoj (byvšej patriaršej) biblioteke*, "Zapiski Imp. Novorossijskogo Universiteta," vol. XIII, Odessa, 1874, p. 170; V l a d i m i r a r h i m a n d r i t, *Sistematiceskoje opisanije rukopisej Moskovskoj sinodalnoj biblioteki*, part 1, *Rukopisi grečeskije*, Moskva 1894, p. 491. The Canonical Codex of Synodal Library (now in the State Historical Museum, Moscow), No. 336, containing part of the treatise *peri metatheseon*, was copied in 1687 in Jerusalem on the instruction of Dositheos, the patriarch of Jerusalem, for the library of the Moscow patriarch where it arrived in 1693.

Xanthopulus in his account of the promotion of Proklos, metropolitan of Cyzicus, to the patriarchal throne in 434, makes a lengthy digression quoting examples of bishops being moved from one see to another over the centuries. Among such examples which took place during the reign of Basil II Porphyrogenitus, there is the mention that "during his rule, Theophylact was promoted from this see of Sebaste to the see of Rhōsia."[69] E. Honigmann, who understood the importance of this unexplored text, tried to find out the source of Xanthopulus's information about the translation of Theophylact. In comparing the account of the transfers of bishops with the anonymous treatise *peri metatheseon* in which there is, unfortunately, no mention of the case of interest to us, he noticed that the two works on that subject have only one point in common: the information about the transfer of Agapetos from Seleucia to Antioch. As the anonymous author quotes Theodore of Sebaste[70] but at the same time commits errors which Xanthopulus does not, Honigmann decided that the latter drew his information about the translations of Agapetos and Theophylact directly from the chronicle of Theodore of Sebaste. The latter, a metropolitan and author of a lost monograph on the reign of Basil II, upon which later Byzantine chroniclers drew, particularly John Scylitzes, was confirmed in his see in 997.[71] From this the obvious conclusion was that Theodore must have succeeded Theophylact in the see; so the latter must have

---

[69] N i k e p h o r o s K a l l i s t o s X a n t h o p u l o s, *Ekklesiastike isto-ria*, 1b, XIV, 39 (*Patrologia graeca*, vol. CXLVI, col. 1196ᶜ). This historian was a member of the clergy of Hagia Sofia and had access to its rich library. See about him Gy. M o r a v c s i k, *Byzantinoturcica*, vol. I, Berlin, 1958, pp. 459—560; B e c k, *Kirche...*, pp. 705—706. Attention was drawn to Kall-isto's information by V. G. Vasiljevskij (Trudy, vol. II—1, SPb., 1909, p. 67) who, bearing in mind the mention under the year 1039 in the Primary Chronicle (PVL), remarked that "if one was to read Theopemptos, it would indicate that it referred to the metropolitan of Rus'."

[70] *Patrologia Graeca*, vol. CXIX, col. 905, 908. Cf. H o n i g m a n n, *Studies...*, p. 150. I. S y k o u t r e s, *Synodikos tomos tes ekloges tou patriarh-ou Germanou tou III* (1265—1266), "Epetēris Hetaireias Byzantinōn Spou-dōn," vol. IX, 1932, p. 200, note 5. The author of this anonymous treatise was Balsamon who composed it on the occasion of the transfer in 1189 of the Jerusalem patriarch Dositheos to the throne of Constantinople. See G r u-m e l, Le *Peri metatheseon et le Patriarche de Constantinople Dosithee*, "Etu-des Byzantines," vol. I, 1943, pp. 239—248.

[71] M o r a v c s i k, *Byzantinoturcica*, vol. I, pp. 336, 345, 426; G r u m e l, *Les Regestes...*, No. 805; H o n i g m a n n, *Studies...*, p. 156.

been transferred to Rus' before 997. As in 992—996 the throne of the patriarch was vacant, Honigmann concluded that the translation of Theophylact must have occurred under the pontificate of the patriarch Nicholas Chrysoberges, that is before December 16, 991, so that Theophylact of Sebaste was the first metropolitan of Rus'.[72]

This conclusion was questioned by V. Grumel who argued that Nicephorus Callistus Xanthopulus did not consult the chronicle of Theodore of Sebaste but one of its numerous versions *peri metatheseon.* The only passage in common, the mention of the transfer of Agapetos which in the published treatise on translations contains a clear reference to Theodore of Sebaste, resembling it also from the stylistic point of view, is so different from the passage in Xanthopulus that the latter compiler's direct knowledge of the chronicle of Theodore of Sebaste must be excluded. Another argument against the information about Theophylact having been drawn from that source was the fact that in the version of *peri metatheseon* in the *Codex Vatican.* of 1299, where both the examples of translations are quoted, they are separated by twenty others. In conclusion Grumel wants to show that the information about Theophylact did not have to come from Theodore of Sebaste but from some other of the lost chronicles (e.g. that of Demetrius of Cyzicus); but then Theophylact might just as well have occupied the Sebaste see after Theodore and the year 997 would then lose its feature of *terminus ante quem,* and there remains only the certainty that the transfer took place in the period up to 1025.[73]

Grumel's noticing that the passage about translations in Xanthopulus did not contain Theodore of Sebaste among its sources seems convincing, but the argument that since the two entries do not, in one of the versions of *peri metatheseon,* figure next to each other and so do not come from the same source, may turn out to be misleading. Grumel himself remarks that, according to V. Laurent, more than one-hundred unpublished manuscripts of *peri metatheseon* have survived in various versions, prepared

---

[72] H o n i g m a n n, *Studies...,* pp. 148—158.
[73] G r u m e l, *Chronologie patriarcale...,* pp. 51, 57.

probably as historical motivation in the fairly frequent cases of transfers from one see to another which was contrary to canons.[74] So records from one source could find their way to two different texts and later meet again in some new compilation. During such peregrinations they underwent stylistic changes, and this is well brought out by the comparison of the passage under discussion as treated by:

Nicephorus Callistus Xanthopulus:

ἐπὶ δὲ τῆς αὐτῆς ἡγεμονίας Θεοφύλακτος ἐκ τῆς Σεβαστηνῶν εἰς ῾Ρωσίαν ἀνάγεται.[75]

Peri metatheseon in Cod. Vat. 1455 of 1299, and in Cod. Sinod. 336 of 1687 (copy of Jerusalem Cod.)

ἐπὶ τῆς βασιλείας (βασιλείου) τοῦ πορφυρογεννήτου Θεοφύλακτος ὁ Σεβαστείας μετετέθη εἰς τὴν῾Ρωσσίαν (εἰς ῾Ρωσίαν).[76]

---

[74] This contradiction was resolved by forbidding *metabasis* that is transfer at the request of the interested person, but not *metathesis* — transfer for the good and need of the Church, and always an exception. Cf. G r u m e l, *Chronologie patriarcale...*, p. 53; B e c k, *Kirche...*, pp. 72 sq., 593. A. P. L'H u i l l i e r, *Les translations épiscopales*, "Messager de l'Exarchate russe en Europe occidentale," vol. XV/57, Paris, 1967, pp. 24—38. About the filling of vacant sees and translations of bishops in Byzantium in the 4th—14th centuries, see also M. M. P e t r o v i č, *Nomokanonski propisi i popunjavanju upražnjenih eparhia i promistaju arhijereja*, "Pravoslavna misao," vol. XXII, Beograd 1975, pp. 13—22.

[75] *Patrologia graeca*, vol. CXLVI, col. 1196[c], it follows from the preceding sentence that it concerns the times of the reign of Basil Porphyrogenitus. Some light is thrown on the data about the transfers in X a n t h o p u l o s's *Church History* by the *Codex Barrocianus*, No. 142, of the Oxford Bodleian — a collection of source extracts drawn up by himself. (Cf. G. G e n z, F. W i n k e l m a n n, *Die Kirchengeschichte des Nicephorus Callistus Xanthopulos und ihre Quellen*, Berlin 1966, pp. 135—136). The text on translations, contained in it and written in 1265 (*Baroc.* f. 266v—268v), was published by S y k u t r i s, *Syndikos tomos...*, pp. 179—183. It contains no information about the transfer of Theophylact to Rus', but the information about the translation of Agapetos to Antioch (*ibidem*, p. 181) differs in form from that in *Church History* where the text is closer to that in the anonymous treatise *peri metatheseon* (cf. their comparison in Honigmann, Studies, p. 150). It follows that although Xanthopulos had Cod. Barrocianus at hand and used it, he drew the information about the translation of Agapetos from another source (another version of *peri metatheseon*?) which may also have contained the information about Theophylact.

[76] V l a d i m i r, *Sistematičeskoje opisanie...*, p. 140; L a u r e n t, *Aux origines...*, p. 293; in brackets readings from Cod. *Vatic,*; F r. D v o r n i k, *The Making...*, p. 179, Note 131, preferred to see in Theophylact the bishop of Sebaste under the metropolis of Laodicea (Phrygia) transferred to an episcopal see in Rus'. Doubts as to such an interpretation were raised by O b o l e n s k y, *Byzantium, Kiev...*, p. 58. In his later works Fr. Dvornik no longer referred to this opinion but it should be noted that although the doubt about which Sebaste was involved might have some justification (although we have presented arguments in this article which definitely

The two passages express exactly the same thing, the syntax also shows that they come from the same original text, but at the same time there are differences which mark the separate lives of the two items.

Although Honigmann's arguments in favour of Theodore of Sebaste have been weakened, his chronicle still seems the most probable original source of the mention   of   the translation of Theophylact. We do not know how long Theodore occupied the see of Sebaste, which fact is confirmed in 997, while the next reference to a   metropolitan of Sebaste dates only to 1030 and 1032, when the see was occupied by George.[77] There is enough time between these two dates for Theophylact to hold the see of Sebaste and then to accede to the metropolitanate of Rus'. But if one considers that Theodore was the chronicler of an emperor who was his contemporary and thus wrote probably in the second half of the long reign (from 976, but in fact from 985 to 1025) of Basil II, and that a translation after 1018 seems unlikely because the Kievan see was then occupied by metropolitan John I, then the period from before 997 suits best the transfer of Theophylact to Rus'.

Let us note that Grumel's critical yet controversial remarks about Theophylact's transfer are not "disinterested." For the case of Theophylact attracted the attention of Byzantinists   who wanted to resolve a chronological puzzle in the light of contradicting evidence: when did the four-year long vacancy in the patriarchal see occur, before or after the patriarchate of Nicholas Chrysoberges? But these investigations were marred by trust in later Russian texts about the first metropolitans Michael and Leo, which are really only the product of the inquisitiveness of Old-Russian bookmen in the 13th—14th centuries, who tried to fill in the gap in knowledge about the beginnings of church hierarchy

---

speak in favour of Sebaste in the theme Armenia II), nevertheless it follows from the two items that, in accordance with established ecclesiastical nomenclature, they speak not about an (episcopal) see in Rus' but exclusively about the see of Rus' which, as we know from *Notitiae*, was a metropolitan one. After all, the transfers noted down always concern promotions to a metropolitan or a patriarchal see; in our case, the participation of the Emperor also points to this.

[77] F i c k e r, *Erlasse...*, pp. 19, 26; Cf. G r u m e l, *Les Regestes...*, No. 839, No. 840.

III

THE ORIGINAL STATUS OF THE OLD-RUSSIAN CHURCH 31

in Rus'.[78] G. Grégoire and P. Orgels, trusting the data contained in the 16th century *Nikon Chronicle* and *Book of Degrees* about the appointment of Leo to the metropolitan see in 991—992, and accepting Honigmann's assertion that Theophylact preceded Theodore of Sebaste, cast a doubt on the possibility of a vacancy on the patriarchal throne in the years 992—996; they assumed that the appointment of Theophylact to the Rus'sian metropolitanate, which could have occurred some time after 992 and before 997, required the participation of the patriarch.[79] Though he admits the account of Yahya of Antioch about the four-year vacancy after the death of Nicholas Chrysoberges, Grumel also uses the Rus'sian data about the ordination of Leo in 922, as an argument for shifting the date of this patriarch's death from December 16, 991 to 992. He also excludes the possibility of Theophylact's having been translated during the vacancy, that is between December 16, 992 to April 12, 996.[80]

The involvement of Michael and Leo, the supposed metropolitans of Rus', in the study of the chronology of the patriarchate at the close of the 10th century, has confused even more the already sufficiently vague situation. But, Grumel is right that the case of Theophylact cannot constitute an argument in considering the time of the patriarchate of Nicholas Chrysoberges. In the light of well-known fact of the intervention of emperors into ecclesiasti-

---

[78] Cf. P o p p e, *Le traité...*, pp. 524—527; i d e m, in: SSS, vol. III, pp. 43—44 (Leo), pp. 241—243 (Michael). Let us add here an interesting re-adaptation of the legend about Michael and Leo. The *Nikon Chronicle* in the early forties of the 16th century lists them in the following order: the first metropolitan — Michael, the second — Leo, but repeats the older version that both had been sent by patriarch Photius (cf. PSRL, vol. IX, pp. 57, 64). Twenty years later, the author of the *Book of Degrees* (an excellent example of a historian writing on commission; he was concerned with illustrating the unbreakable bonds between the ruling dynasty and the Church in Rus'), took another step: he still makes Photius send Michael, but for Leo, having observed the glaring anachronism, he replaces Photius by Nicholas Chrysoberges (cf. PSRL, vol. XXIII, pp. 102—113).
[79] G. G r é g o i r e, P. O r g e l s, *La chronologie de Nicolas II Chrysoberges*, "Byzantion," vol. XXIV, 1954, pp. 161—172.
[80] G r u m e l, *Chronologie patriarcale...*, pp. 54—56, 69—70. This opinion was uncritically repeated by V l a s t o, *The Entry...*, pp. 227—278, who thought that the transfer of Theophylact during the vacancy was technically impossible because "there was no patriarch to consecrate." The fact that Theophylact had already been bishop and that consecration was unrepeatable has been forgotten.

cal affairs, it is true that among the imperial rights was the right to translate bishops. The agreement of the patriarch and his synod, the so-called *synodos endemousa*, was not necessary in this act, which was not quite consistent with the canons. The emperor, on the other hand, as commented by Theodore Balsamon, a 12th-century Byzantine canon lawyer, was not bound by canons in undertaking measures serving the common good, he was above them.[81] So the emperor's decision about translations may have been the result of his wish to by-pass the regular procedure of appointing bishops. Though the emperor could exert his influence on it, yet the patriarchal synod was also involved; the candidate, in order to obtain consecration from the patriarch, had to fulfil certain conditions, and the entire procedure lasted several weeks, sometimes even two to three months.[82] When choosing a candidate from among consecrated officiating hierarchs, the emperor avoided the formalities in the competence of the patriarchal synod and gained time. It is clear that he used this right primarily during a patriarchal vacancy when the appointment to a see could not be carried out in the regular way, even if there was a suitable candidate on hand but not a consecrated bishop. Thus, the translation of the metropolitan of Sebaste did not have to, but could have taken place precisely at the time of the vacancy in Hagia Sofia. Anyway, the need to create a new church province and the appointment of its head emerged during the civil war and the undoubtedly tense relations between Basil II and at least part of the higher church hierarchy. Only the emperor's intervention into church affairs could have satisfied that need without much delay. Perhaps the time factor was also

---

[81] Cf. M i c h e l, *Die Kaisermacht...*, p. 27 sqq, particularly pp. 37—39; B e c k, *Kirche...*, pp. 72—73; J. M. P e t r i t a k i s, *Interventions dynamiques de l'empereur de Byzance dans les affaires ecclesiastiques*, "Byzantina," vol. III, 1971, pp. 137—146. Many interesting opinions on the Emperor's interventions into ecclesiastical affairs are contained in the works of various authors, recently collected and published by H. H u n g e r in: *Das Byzantinische Herrscherbild*, Darmstadt 1975. There is no information to indicate that translations had to be put on the agenda of the patriarchal synodos endemousa, cf. J. H a j j a r, *Le synode permanent dans l'église byzantine des origines au XI⁰ siècle*, Roma 1962, pp. 142—143.

[82] B e c k, *Kirche...*, pp. 70—71; H a j j a r, *Le synode...*, pp. 140—142. E. H e r m a n, *Appunti sul diritto metropolitico nella chiesa bizantina*, "Orientalia Christiana Periodica", vol. XIII, 1947, p. 522 sqq.

of importance should Theophylact have been the metropolitan sent to Rus' together with the emperor's sister Anna Porphyrogenita.

In line with Honigmann's hypothesis, Theophylact was the first metropolitan of Rus', but it should be emphasized that the text about his transfer from Sebaste to Rus' justifies only the assertion that Theophylact was the first credibly confirmed metropolitan of Rus'.

There exists, however, a source which, despite some vagueness it contains, gives better grounds for arguments in favour of Honigmann's opinion. It is the information supplied by the Armenian historian, Stephen of Taron (Asoghik) which, it seems, fits well with the   account of   the transfer of the metropolitan of Sebaste Theophylact to the metropolitanate of Rus'. We learn from it that the Sebaste metropolitan persecuted and tortured the clergy of the Armenian rite, and together with "his other numerous colleagues" wrote polemical letters to the katholikos of Armenia, Khatchik; in that same year 435, he was sent by the emperor to the land of the Bulgars with his sister who was to be the bride of the Bulgarian ruler. When the Bulgars learned that they had been deceived, for the princess turned out to be a simple court servant, they tortured the metropolitan and burnt him at the stake as a cheat.[83]

Considering other misinterpretations about Bulgarian affairs handed down by Asoghik, this relation could be taken as a moralising story about the punishment deservedly meted out to a persecutor of the Armenian Christians in Sebaste; but it contains some elements which are not fiction. The main reason for which Asoghik became interested in the fate of a metropolitan, whose name he did not divulge, was the insertion in his *History* of the extensive reply of katholikos Katchik I (972—992) to his polemical letter.[84] This argument did really take place and Asoghik's information about one of its participants and addressees of the katholikos' theological expositions, that is the metropolitan of

---

[83] A s o g h i k, 1b. III, §§ 20, 22, 24; for French translation see F. M a c - l e r, *Histoire universelle par Etienne Asolik de Taron*, II partie, Paris 1917, pp. 74—75, 124—125, 127—128.
[84] A s o g h i k, 1b. III, § 21; M a c l e r, *Histoire universelle*, pp. 76—123.

Sebaste, was not completely fictitious.[85] In Chapter 43, book III, there is a hint about the time the historian obtained this information. In relating Basil II's expedition to Armenia in the summer of 1000, in order to incorporate Upper Tao into the Empire after the death of its ruler curopalates David, Asoghik mentions that on the road near Melitene the Emperor received a delegation of the Armenian clergy of Sebaste which solicited the confirmation of their religious freedoms infringed sometime before by the metropolitan described by him.[86] So this would constitute *terminus post quem* the story was related to Asoghik (probably by some member of the Sebaste Armenian clergy) who wrote it down before the year 1005.

It is also true that in the year 435 of the Armenian era (March 25, 986 — March 24, 987) the metropolitan of Sebaste had to leave the town occupied in February 987 by the usurper Bardas Sclerus, immensely popular with the Armenian population. He could find shelter only in the capital under the Emperor's protection. While everything speaks against any possible negotiations between Basil II and the Bulgars, we know that such negotiations were undertaken in the summer-autumn of 987 with Rus', and that they were concerned with the marriage of the emperor's sister with the ruler of Rus'.[87]

A church dignitary, as devoted to the emperor as was the Sebaste metropolitan Theophylact, was eminently qualified to lead a mission going to Kiev and then to become the first head of the Rus'sian Church. This reconstruction of the life of the first metropolitan of Kiev is supported by the fact, contained also in Asoghik's account, that anyway he did not return to his see after Basil's victory, in 990/91, when the Armenian themes were restored to the emperor's authority. It was not in Basil's interest,

---

[85] Mathias of Edessa lb. I, XXV in telling about this argument drew from another source; among its Greek participants he mentions the patriarch and the metropolitan of Melitene, a locality neighbouring on Sebaste. Cf. M a c l e r, *Histoire universelle*, p. 75, Note 6. A. T e r - M i k e l i a n, *Die armenische Kirche, in ihren Beziehungen zur byzantinischen*, Leipzig 1892, pp. 77—80. P. C h a r a n i s, *The Armenians in the Byzantine Empire*, Lisboa 1963, pp. 20, 23, 27, 33, 52, 200.

[86] A s o g h i k, lb. III, § 43; M a c l e r, *Histoire universelle*, p. 163. Cf. H. M. B a r t i k i a n, *La conquête de l'Arménie par l'Empire byzantin*, "Revue des Études Arméniennes," n.s, vol. VIII, 1971, pp. 332 sq.

[87] P o p p e, *The Political Background...*, pp. 202—204, 224—225, 228 sqq.

who even during the wars with the usurpers, tried to win over the Armenian population, and in the year 1000 confirmed the religious freedoms of the Armenians of Sebaste, to return the Sebaste see to a prelate who had fallen foul of them.[88] A new appointment resolved the whole matter, and the Sebaste see soon went to another supporter of the emperor and later his historian, Theodore who, as we know, held it in 997.

Admittedly, the source material with which we are trying to reconstruct the curriculum vitae of the first Rus'sian metropolitan is somewhat shaky. But too many factors speak in favour of the identity of the two metropolitans of Sebaste, Anonymous and Theophylact, Emperor Basil II's contemporaries, for the assertion to be abandoned outright.

ACCOUNT OF YAHYA OF ANTIOCH

That Byzantine high church hierarchs were sent to Rus' immediately upon the decision of Vladimir to be baptised can be concluded from the writings of Yahya ibn Said al-Antaki, i.e. of Antioch, a Christian historian of Egyptian origin, and writing in Arabic (c. 980—1066). He wrote that, when the rebel Bardas Phocas, on September 14, 987, put on the royal purple and proclaimed himself emperor: "*La situation était devenue grave et l'empereur Basile en était préoccupé à cause de la force de ses troupes et de l'avantage qu'il avait sur lui. Les caisses étaient vides. Dans ce besoin pressant [Basile] fut contraint de demander secour au roi des Russes, qui étaient ses ennemis. Le [Russe] y acquiesça; après ils firent une alliance de parenté, et le roi des Russes épousa la soeur de l'empereur Basile à la condition qu'il se ferait baptiser avec tout le peuple de son pays. Le grand peuple des Russes n'avaient à cette époque aucune loi ni aucune foi religieuse. Par après, l'empereur Basile lui envoya des metropolites et des éveques qui baptisèrent le roi et tout le peuple de son pays; en même temps il lui envoya sa soeur qui fit bâtir plusieures*

---

[88] Cf. P o p p e, *The Political Background...*, pp. 235—236. For the ethnic situation in the region of Sebaste see N. Ó i k o n o m i d e s, *L'organisation de la frontière orientale de Byzance aux Xe—XIe siècles et le Taktikon de l'Escorial*, in: *Actes du XIVe Congrès International des Etudes Byzantines*, Sept. 6—12, 1971, vol. I, Bucuresti 1974, pp. 296—298.

églises dans le pays des Russes."[89]   Then follows an account of the arrival of the Russian troops and the victorious battles at Chrysopolis and Abydus.

From the last quoted sentence it follows that Yahya's text is not contemporary with the events. We learn from his own preface to his chronicle that even before his moving over to Antioch in 1014—1015, he had time not only to write his work (c. 1006—1007) but also to supplement it with fresh material and revise it as well as the work of his predecessor. Later, after he had settled in Byzantine Antioch, he wrote "I revised it again, and I found other chronicles from which I took what (I deemed useful) to add to it and supplement it, and I changed part of it and left the whole work in this form."[90]

Yahya devoted much room to the events in the Christian church and world for he was the continuator of the chronicle of Eutychios, patriarch of Alexandria (933—940), and his relative. It would seem that such an event as the accession to the Christian world of "a big people" did not pass unobserved by the Christian community in Egypt. But this supposition lacks confirmation, if we analyse Yahya's text about the baptism of Rus' in the wider context of his account entirely devoted to the events occurring within the Byzantine empire, and to the revolt of Bardas Sclerus and Bardas Phocas, in particular.   The account of these events required the introduction of Rus'sian troops which were instrumental in the defeat of the usurper. The appearance of the Rus'sian forces in the Empire had to be explained: hence the information about the agreement, the baptism of Rus' and the marriage of the Russian ruler with a Porphyrogenita. It explains the circumstances and the conditions in which the alliance between two hostile states was concluded.[91]

---

[89] *Histoire de Yahya-Ibn-Sa'id d'Antioche*, editée et traduite en français par I. Kratchkovsky et A. Vasiliev, vol. II, in: *Patrologia Orientalia* (hereafter PO), vol. XXIII/3, Paris 1932, p. 423. See also Russian translation by V. N. R o z e n, *Imperator Vasilij Bolgarobojca. Izvlecenija iz letopisi Jahii Antiobijskogo*, SPb, 1883, pp. 23—24, and commentary p. 194 sqq. (Reprint 1972 by "Variorum")

[90] *Histoire de Yahya...*, fasc. I in: Po, vol. XVIII, 1924, p. 708. R o z e n, *Imperator...*, pp. 013—016.

[91] Speaking of hostility Yahya thought about Svjatoslav's struggles with the Empire, of which he wrote earlier. Cf. *Histoire de Yahya...*, in PO, vol. XVIII, 1924, p. 833; R o s e n, *Imperator...*, pp. 177—181, 195.

We think that Yahya began to take particular interest in the internal events in Byzantium when he settled for good within the borders of the Empire and when, as he himself says, he came upon fresh chronicles. The matter of his sources has not been satisfactorily studied so far, but V. Rozen's findings have made it possible to establish that Yahya had Greek chronicles at his disposal (such as the Continuation of Theophanes or Symeon Logothetes) and the local chronicle with good knowledge of events in Antioch in the second half of the 10th century, including the fighting against pretenders in 987—989. Yahya's Antiochian source may also have been reminded of it by the presence of Russian troops taking part in the Syrian campaign, who were several times quartered in Antioch in the years 995—1001.[92]

So most probably the information about the revolt of Sclerus and Phocas as well as about Rus' was introduced by Yahya into his chronicle after his arrival in Antioch, i.e. after 1014, when he gained access to new material. The revised chronicle was completed before 1027. The detailed information about the internecine struggles in the Empire must have been taken from a chronicle compiled in Antioch. The credibility of Yahya's text about the Byzantine-Russian agreement of 987 and the Byzantine church hierarchs having been sent to Rus' following this accord, the text being an integral part of the account of the rebellion, is of first-rate quality.

Yet A. Ammann tried to undermine it: Yahya's statement that "Emperor Basil sent metropolitans and bishops (matārinat wa asaqifat) who baptised the King (Vladimir) and the whole people of his country" was supposedly of no value to the matter of the status of the Russian Church because the metropolitans are mentioned in the plural.[93] There is an inaccuracy here but it does not

---

[92] P o p p e, The Political Background..., pp. 205—206, where Yahya's data are discussed in detail.

[93] A m m a n n, Untersuchungen..., pp. 38—39; for criticism of such an attitude see M ü l l e r, Zum Problem..., pp. 41—42, cf. also p. 23, Note 9a. Let us add that Ammann's sceptic attitude towards Yahya's information is due to reading Koch (see Note 17 supra) who repeated Priselkov's opinion, while the latter emphasized that "metropolitans and bishops figure exclusively as baptizers, not as members of church hierarchy in Rus'." He described the paragraph about baptism as interpolation and referred to V. Rozen who, however, spoke about digression not insertion. Cf. P r i s e l - k o v, Očerki..., pp. 30—33. R o z e n, Imperator..., p. 197.

discredit Yahya's text. Arabists would be more competent in explaining it but certain suggestions could be advanced. The possibility of an error — the change of the singular into plural — is inherent in the fact that Yahya's chronicle has come to us in later MSS, the oldest of which dates back to the turn of the 14th century.[94] If the plural (*matārinat* instead of *matran*) was present in the original text — which is more probable — then the inaccuracy may be explained by the specific character of the source upon which the Arabian historian drew in Antioch. The Greek equivalent of the two ecclesiastical titles, turned by Yahya into Arabic, *matārinat wa asaqifat*, could have been one term *archiereis* used in Byzantine church nomenclature as a collective term for bishops of all degrees but not assimilated by the Arabic. If so, the original text would only relate about the sending to Rus' of some number of *archiereis*. It is only when compared with the known principles of the organisation of a church province under the jurisdiction of the patriarch in Constantinople and the source information about the Rus'sian Church, that is becomes obvious that the group of church prelates which went to Kiev must have been capable of founding such a province, i.e. was composed of suffragan bishops with a superior (*proedros*) bishop i.e. metropolitan. Finally, the fact that Yahya or the copyist of his chronicle, mentioned metropolitans in the plural is not surprising in view of the church relations in Asia Minor, particularly in the area under the jurisdiction of the patriarchate of Antioch where there were more metropolitans among the hierarchy than plain bishops.[95]

So we cannot dismiss Yahya's passage about the original church hierarchy in Rus' on the grounds of a small and easily explained inaccuracy, all the more so as his text is fully supported in the Byzantine sources, discussed above, and in Ilarion's text about Vladimir: "You, together with our new fathers, the bishops, often

---

[94] *Histoire de Yahya...*, in PO, vol. XVIII, p. 702 (introduction to the edition); R o z e n, *Imperator...*, p. 091 sqq.: H o n i g m a n n, *Studies...*, p. 152, Note 102.
[95] For church geography of the patriarchate of Antioch see B e c k, *Kirche...*, pp. 190—196.

congregated conferring with great humbleness about how to consolidate the divine laws in those newly converted people."[96]

THIETMAR AND ILARION

Much light is thrown on the legal status of the Russian church in 1018 by the eminently credible writings of Thietmar, bishop of Merseburg, from which it follows that Kiev had its own archbishop, residing at the time in the still wooden cathedral of St Sophia.[97] The early history of the Kievan cathedral church, which has been treated separately,[98] supplies yet another convincing proof to support the assertion that Kiev had been from the very beginning the seat of the head of the Rus'sian Church subordinated to the patriarch of Constantinople. Here it is worth adding that the dedication of the Kievan cathedral to the Divine Wisdom points to the model: the Hagia Sofia of Constantinople. The geographical pale of the spread of this dedication, reserved exclusively to cathedrals, determines not only the scope of the Empire's influence but, first and foremost, of the Byzantine ecclesiastical jurisdiction. Thietmar's relation proves that in 1018, Kiev was within its pale.

Many writers on the subject have tried to interpret Thietmar's mention of the Kiev archbishop as information about the different organisation of the Rus'sian Church prior to 1037. Yet, to Thietmar the title of archbishop was the most adequate equivalent, adopted in the Western Church, of the Greek metropolitan — a hierarch at the head of a church province.[99] In Byzantium, hence also in Rus', the two terms were used alternately, not only in writing, as al-

---

[96] *Des Metropoliten Ilarion Lobrede auf Vladimir den Heiligen und Glaubenbekenntniss*, nach der Erstausgabe von 1844 neu herausgegeben, eingeleitet und erläutert von Ludolf Müller, Wiesbaden 1962, pp. 117—118. Cf. also the remark of the author of the *Primary Chronicle* about the bishops taking part in the prince's council under Vladimir, PVL, vol. I, p. 86 sq. *The Russian primary Chronicle...*, p. 122.
[97] T h i e t m a r, lib. VIII, c. 32.
[98] Cf. Note 8 supra.
[99] See D u C a n g e, *Glos. latinitatis*, vol. I, p. 366, vol. V, p. 371. I d e m, *Glos. graecitatis*, pp. 129—130, 931. Cf. V. L a u r e n t, *La succession épiscopale de métropole de Thessalonique*, "Byzantinische Zeitschrift", vol. LVI, 1963, p. 289.

ready mentioned,[100] but also in the official church nomenclature as evidenced in the recently published collection of seals of Byzantine bishops. The title of archbishop was used not only by the metropolitans of the western provinces of the Empire like Thessalonica, Corinth or Dyrrachion which inherited this title from the time of Roman jurisdiction, but also by heads of the oldest metropolitan sees of Caesarea, Ephesus and Heraclea. It also figures on the seals of the metropolitans of Mitylene, Euchaite and Ancyra.[101] It is significant that by the end of the 11th century the title of archbishop disappeared from the seals of the metropolitans under the patriarch of Constantinople; this is due to the putting in order of ecclesiastical matters at the patriarchal synod with the participation of Alexius Comnenus. The title of archbishop was reserved for the patriarch and the heads of the autonomous churches of Bulgaria and Cyprus and to titular archbishops i.e. autocephalous bishops subordinated directly to the patriarch.[102]

Some writers on the subject contended erroneously that Rus' could have originally obtained an archbishopric of the same rank as did Cyprus and Bulgaria, which only in 1037 was demoted to the rank of an ordinary metropolitanate.[103] This contention contradicts the texts, mentioned above; L. Müller has used some very apposite arguments against it.[104] It is also worth noting that this supposed promotion would have been of a doubtful nature because the Churches of Cyprus and Bulgaria (after 1018), although they did not come under the patriarch, were entirely dependent on the emperor. It is no accident that Nilus Doxopatres in his treatise of 1143, on church geography, says that since the time of Basil II "and up till now Cyprus and Bulgaria have received their bishops from the emperor, and their own bishops consecrate them," and

---

[100] M ü l l e r, Zum Problem..., pp. 64—65; P o p p e, Uwagi..., p. 374 sq. Cf. A. V. S o l o v i e v, Metropolitensiegel der Kiever Russland, "Byzantinische Zeitschrift," vol. LVI, 1963, p. 320.

[101] L a u r e n t, Le Corpus..., Nos 246, 247, 254, 262, 301, 338, 447, 449—454, 456, 554—560, 670—672, 735, 751, 764.

[102] L a u r e n t, Le Corpus..., pp. XXVIII—XXXI; Cf. G r u m e l, Les Regestes..., Nos 940, 942, 943.

[103] So still B e c k, Kirche..., pp. 68, 187. V. L a u r e n t who earlier assumed this possibility, in his review of M ü l l e r's Zum Problem... came out in favour of the precedence of the metropolis ("Byzantinische Zeitschrift," vol. LIII, 1960, p. 401).

[104] M ü l l e r, Zum Problem..., pp. 68—70.

remarks that "the patriarch of Constantinople sends a metropolitan to great Rhōsia." He does not list Rus' among the Byzantine metropolitanates, and thus emphasizes, in the formal and legal sense, the purely ecclesiastical character of the bonds between Constantinople and Rus'.[105]

In the light of the foregoing it is impossible to admit that originally there was in Rus' an autocephalous archbishopric of a lower rank, that is a titular one,[106] for the Rus'sian Church had four or five suffragans as early as during Vladimir's and Yaroslav's reigns before 1037.[107] Such an opinion is also contradicted by the alternate calling of Rus'sian hierarchs metropolitans and archbishops in two old texts: *The Anonymous Tale of the Holy Martyrs Boris and Gleb*, of about 1072, and *Reading Concerning the Life and Murder of the Blessed Martyrs Boris and Gleb*, of c. 1080, by Nestor. It is certainly a manner proper to hagiography but it is also possible that the 11th century Rus'sian metropolitans used the archbishop title in imitation of the chief Byzantine metropolitanates. Although in the *ordo thronorum* Rhōsia was listed 60th, they were aware of their exceptional mission. V. Laurent, trying to explain the archiepiscopal title on the seal (mid-10th century) of the metropolitan of second rank Euchaite, supposes that the metropolitan used that title in connection with his court office of synkellos.[108] Let us note that among the Rus'sian metropolitans called by the alternate title of archbishop, Georg (he held Kiev before and after 1072) also held the honorary office of

---

[105] P a r t h e y..., pp. 285—286, 297. Considering that Doxopatres wrote his treatise at the court of Roger II in Sicily, whom he wanted to gain for the idea of the church supremacy of New Rome (cf. B e c k, *Kirche...,* pp. 152, 619—620), his drawing attention to the ecclesiastical status of politically sovereign Rus' may not have been accidental.

[106] M ü l l e r, *Zum Problem...,* pp. 71—75. But he formulated this opinion as an alternative (favouring also the precedence of the metropolis) and later abandoned it. See i d e m, *Staat u. Kirche in der Rus' im XI Jh. Bemerkungen zu einem Buch von Andrzej Poppe*, "Jahrbücher für Geschichte Osteuropas," vol. XX, 1972, pp. 241—246. About the origins of the institution of autocephalous titular archbishops and titular metropolitans see E. C h r y - s o s, *Zur Entstehung der Institution der autokephalen Erzbistümer*, "Byzantinische Zeitschrift," vol. LXII, 1969, pp. 263—286.

[107] By the end of the 11th century Kiev had nine suffragans. See A. P o p p e, *L'organisation diocésaine de la Russie aux XI*ᵉ*—XII*ᵉ *siècles,* "Byzantion," vol. XL, 1970, pp. 165—217.

[108] Cf. L a u r e n t, *Le Corpus...,* No. 764, p. 585 sq.

synkellos.[109] But in our case of greater importance are the two old hagiographic texts which say that in the first years after the accession of Yaroslav the Wise to the throne of Kiev (1019) the Rus'sian Church was ruled by archbishop-metropolitan John.[110] Although the doubts as to the chronology of the steps taken for the canonisation and the canonisation itself of Boris and Gleb which, according to the two hagiographers, took place soon after 1019, are justified, this does not mean that their works do not mention a real hierarch. The name of the Kiev hierarch of the second and third decade of the 11th century should have been well known in Kiev around the year 1070. The hagiographical evidence has gained fresh support from the seal of John "mētropolitē Rhōsias" which V. Laurent has dated to the turn of the 10th century on the basis of its engraving and epigraphy; he excludes all possibility of ascribing it to John II, of the eighties of the 11th century.[111] So John I would be the second thoroughly confirmed metropolitan of Rus'.[112] He could also be the archbishop who in 1018 welcomed Bolesław and Svjatopolk to Kiev. The third head

---

[109] Die altrussischen hagiographischen Erzählungen..., (see Note 36 supra), pp. 21, 55—56; S o l o v i e v, Metropolitensiegel..., "Byzantinische Zeitschrift," vol. LV, 1962, p. 294; L a u r e n t, Le Corpus..., Nos 784, 785.

[110] The two hagiographers, Anonymous and Nestor, use both titles alternately in respect of John. See Die altrussischen hagiographischen Erzählungen..., pp. 17—19, 53—59. This may be the result of literary influences but it is more probable that the custom when addressing a metropolitan was then to call him archbishop. Cf. e.g. what Nestor says: "John [...] archbishop, when he learned about it [...] said to Christ-loving [Yaroslav]: it would be a good thing, orthodox Emperor, if we built a church in their [Boris and Gleb] name. Hearing these words from the metropolitan, the Christ-loving prince said to him [...]" (ibidem, p. 17). For the two old texts see J. F e n n e l l, A. S t o k e s, Early Russian Literature, London 1974, pp. 11—31. Cf. S t. M a c z k o, Boris and Gleb: Saintly Princes or Princely Saints?, "Russian History," vol. II, fasc. 1, Pittsburgh 1975, pp. 68—76.

[111] L a u r e n t, Le Corpus..., No. 781, p. 600. But the scholar unnecessarily refers to information about John I dating to the 15th-16th centuries. The officium in worship of SS Boris and Gleb is ascribed to John I, but it could not have originated earlier than in the second half of the 11th century. See A. P o p p e, O vremeni zaroždenia kulta Borisa i Gleba, "Russia Mediaevalis," vol. I, 1973, pp. 6—29.

[112] When speaking about the seal ascribed by Laurent to John I, which is in the Dumbarton Oaks collection, V. Janin emphasized that "the opinion of such a prominent expert in Byzantine sfragistics is of great import" but inclined towards linking it with the metropolitan John IV (1164—1166) solely on the grounds that he considered open the question of the status of the Rus'sian Church prior to 1037. See V. J a n i n, Aktovyje piečati drevnej Rusi X—XV vv., vol. I, Moskva 1970, No. 50, pp. 51, 175.

of the Rus'sian Church known by his name is metropolitan Theopemptos, well confirmed by three independent sources.[113]
Among the texts which support the Byzantine origins of the
Rus'sian Church is also the discourse *Sermon on Law and Grace*
which Ilarion delivered around 1049. The orator, soon to be the
metropolitan of Rus', probably of the same age as Yaroslav i.e.
born around the date of the baptism of Rus', in his eulogy of the
work of Vladimir, speaks thus about the path of that ruler to the
awareness of one God: "The most he heard about was the ever
orthodox land of Greece, Christ-loving and strong in faith," then
goes on to compare the Rus'sian prince with Constantine the
Great: "He, together with his mother Helena, brought the cross
from Jerusalem and having spread the faith throughout the world
consolidated it: you, with your grandmother Olga, have brought
the cross from the new Jerusalem, from the city of Constantine,
and placing it on your land have consolidated the faith."[114] The
cross, as L. Müller has remarked, is used here metaphorically. It
expressed not only the triumph of Christianity in Rus' but also
disclosed its origins and the institutional bonds. Yaroslav continued
his father's work: "he does not infringe on your decisions but
consolidates them," while the whole family of the prince "watches
over the orthodoxy in accordance with your will."[115] Ilarion clearly
emphasized the continuity between Vladimir's and Yaroslav's
ecclesiastical policies; it is yet another evidence that the status of
the Rus'sian Church had been determined under the rule of the
baptizer of Rus'.

All these arguments suffice to leave aside indirect evidence.
But one thing should be mentioned: the preserved foundations and
details of the interior decoration of the first stone church built in

---

[113] It is mentioned in Primary Chronicle (PVL, vol. I, p. 103; C r o s s,
The Russian Primary Chronicle..., p. 138), in September 1039, he was present at the synod in Constantinople (F i c k e r, *Erlasse...*, p. 42). For his seal
see L a u r e n t, *Le Corpus...*, No. 782; S o l o v i e v, *Metropolitensiegel...*,
p. 293; J a n i n, *Aktovyje pečati...*, No. 41.
[114] *Des Metropoliten Ilarion Lobrede...*, pp. 102, 118—119, 169. For *Sermon*
and its dating see A. V. S o l o v i e v, *Zur Lobrede des Metropoliten Ilarion*,
in: *Das heidnische und christliche Slaventum*, Wiesbaden 1970, pp. 58—63.
L. M ü l l e r, *Ilarion Werke* (Forum slavicum 37), München 1971, pp. 7—18;
J. Fennell, and A. Stokes, *Early Russian Literature*, London 1974, pp. 41—60.
[115] *Des Metropoliten Ilarion Lobrede...*, pp. 121, 125. Cf. M ü l l e r, *Zum
Problem...*, p. 76 sq.

Rus' at the close of the 10th century, the Church of the Holy Virgin of the Tithe (the *Desyatinnaya*) not only emphatically confirm the text of the *Primary Chronicle* about the masters brought over from Greece but also indicate the direct links with the art and architecture of Constantinople itself.[116]

So the Rus'sian Church was from its very beginnings a metropolitanate that is a church province of the Constantinople patriarchate. From this followed certain rights of the patriarch in administration, justice and legislation.[117] The most important was the right to appoint the holders of metropolitan sees. In the 10th—11th century this right was within the competence of the patriarchal synod which presented to the patriarch three candidates who fulfilled the conditions determined by canons. The bishop elect was consecrated by the patriarch. If the candidate was chosen in advance (often the emperor's will had to be considered), then at least the valid procedure was observed.[118] The path to the Kievan see was the same and that is why the Russian metropolitans were members of the standing patriarchal synod: the first known participant of the synodos endemousa was metropolitan Theopemptos in September 1039. The difference in comparison with the metropolitans within the Empire consisted only in that the enthronement was an ecclesiastical act as well as an act of political accreditation. It was held in the Kiev cathedral. The

---

[116] PVL, vol. I, p. 83; C r o s s, *The Russian Primary Chronicle...*, p. 119; M. K. K a r g e r, *Drevnij Kiev*, vol. II, Moskva—Leningrad 1961, pp. 27—58; N. P. S y č e v, *Drevnejšij fragment russko-vizantijskoj živopisi*, "Seminarium Kondakovianum," vol. II, 1928, pp. 90—104, table XIII; V. L a z a r e v, *Regard sur l'art de la Russie prémongole*, "Cahiers de civilisation mediévale," vol. XIII, 1970, No. 3, pp. 195—200; H. S c h ä f e r, *Architekturhistorische Beziehungen zwischen Byzanz und der Kiever Rus' im X und XI Jh.*, "Istambuler Mitteilungen," vol. XXIII/XXIV, 1974, pp. 199, 202—205, 218.

[117] About these rights see E. E. G o l u b i n s k i j, *Istoria russkoj cerkvi*, vol. I, Part 1, Moskva 1901, p. 269 sqq; Pl. S o k o l o v, *Russkij arhierej iz Vizantii i pravo jego naznacenia do nacala XV v.*, Kiev 1913, p. 6 sqq; L. K. G ö t z, *Staat und Kirche in Altrussland, Kiever Periode 988—1240*, Berlin 1908, p. 8 sqq.

[118] Cf. B e c k, *Kirche...*, p. 63 sqq; H e r m a n n, *Appunti...*, p. 255 sqq; H a j j a r, *Le synode...*, p. 140 sqq; M i c h e l, *Kaisermacht...*, p. 36 sqq., 56 sqq; R. P o t z, *Patriarch und Synode in Konstantinopel. Das Verfassungsrecht des Ökumenischen Patriarchates*, Wien 1971, pp. 27—31, 41—46.

reception of the newcomer, the permission to hold the enthronement ceremony and the participation in it of the prince and his court meant the *de facto* confirmation of the proceedings that had taken place in Constantinople.[119]

(Translated by Krystyna Kęplicz)

---

[119] This custom was confirmed only under the year 1104 in the *Primary Chronicle*, but it was nothing new. Metropolitan Nicephorus arrived in Rus' on December 6, 1104. His enthronization was held on the second Sunday after his arrival, December 18. See PVL, vol. I, p. 185; C r o s s, *The Russian Primary Chronicle...*, p. 202. On the role of Kievan metropolitans in church and state of Rus' see L. M ü l l e r, *Russen in Byzanz und Griechen in Rus'-Reich*, in: *Bulletin d'Information et de Coordination*, Association internationale des Études Byzantines, No. 5, Athinai—Paris 1971, pp. 96—116.

IV

The building of the church of St Sophia in Kiev

Figure 1. Church of St Sophia, Kiev, modern view from the east.

The subject of this study is the much-debated question of when and under what circumstances the cathedral of St Sophia in Kiev was built. After an analysis of the primary sources and a critical review of the arguments in favour of a date of construction between 1017 and 1031, the author substantiates the view that the entire church, including towers and external ambulatories, was built and decorated between 1037 and 1046, and not, as some think, over a period of nearly a century.

Because of the complexity of the sources, the construction of St Sophia is seen against the background of the cultural, political and ecclesiastical history of Kievan Rus' in the late tenth and eleventh centuries, including the building of the cathedrals of Cernigov and Novgorod, and the church of the Tithe and the katholikon of the Caves monastery in Kiev.

The study sheds new light on the early history of Kievan stone architecture which, as some reasonably assert, was closely linked with the architectural school of Constantinople. The construction of the capella regia, *known as the church of the Tithe in the 990s, by Greek masters, who followed the Porphyrogenite princess Anna to Kiev, was an isolated episode which was followed by a hiatus of forty years. The extensive building programme begun by Jaroslav the Wise after 1036, which continued after his death in 1054, was completed by Byzantine masters with local help, permitting the formation of native cadres of masons, artists and other specialists. It was the project of Jaroslav which laid the groundwork for an indigenous stone architecture in Rus'.* *

©North-Holland Publishing Company

The early history of the cathedral church of Kiev is at the same time so enigmatic and yet so fascinating because it is inextricably linked to the larger issues of the ecclesiastical and political status of Rus' shortly after its conversion. Among the numerous studies of the cathedral, the article published by S. H. Cross and K. J. Conant (1936:490-8) over forty years ago is significant.[1] Another well-known scholar of medieval Kiev (Karger 1961:98ff,) was compelled to admit, after having reviewed previous scholarly research on the cathedral and reached some new conclusions, that many questions still remained unanswered.

My own attempt (Poppe 1965a; 1968a; 1968b:86-96; 1968c:40-59) to solve some of these questions was not entirely accepted. In particular, I tried to prove that the stone church of the Holy Virgin erected by Vladimir I, known as the church of the Tithe, was not, as was widely believed, the cathedral church of Kiev before the construction of the stone church of St Sophia. I sought to prove, instead, that the church of the Tithe was, from the outset, a palace church, and that the stone cathedral church dedicated to Holy Wisdom was preceded by a wooden structure.

This view is opposed by those who date the beginning of the construction of the stone church of St Sophia to an earlier period, usually to 1017 (Toločko 1969; 1972:93-104: Vysoc'kyj 1975; 1976:240-52; Logvin 1977). Consequently, one must also answer a number of difficult questions concerning the construction of the church, in particular whether it was completed before the death of Jaroslav the Wise in 1054 or whether the construction continued during the greater part of the century.[2] The answers to these

interrelated questions are of vital importance, not only for the history of the cathedral church, but also for the ecclesiastical cultural and political history of Rus' during the first century after its entry into Christendom.

The task of solving these problems is made even more difficult by the number o' interpretations which are unsupported by facts; many of these date back to the nineteenth century and are accepted and repeated uncritically by modern scholars Consequently, the present study will avoid secondary works as much as possible and wil concentrate on a critical analysis of the sources.

1. The wooden cathedral church

Thietmar of Merseburg (8.32) relates that on 14 August 1018 Kiev opened its gates to the Polish prince Bolesław and to *seniori su* Svjatopolk. He described the event in the following manner: *archiepiscopus civitatis illiu cum reliquis sanctorum et ceteris ornatibus diversi hos advenientes honoravit in sancte monasteri Sophiae, quod in priori anno miserabiliter cas accidente combustum est* (Trillmich 1957:474) Contrary to the generally accepted view, the word *monasterium* in this context should not be translated literally as monastery (Vysoc'ky 1975:177; 1976:248-9)[3] but as cathedra church.

Thietmar's account is based on eye witness information supplied by a Ger man (Saxon) knight who participated in Bolesław's campaign and who was in Kiev in 1018. The knight left the city in September of that year and would have returned to Merseburg by October or November and talked to Thietmar before the latter's death on 1 December. Both the knight and Thietmar would have called the cathedral a *monasterium* because *in Germania cathedralis ecclesia dicuntur muenster* (Du Cange 5:457; Blatt 1963:765f.; Grimm 6:2698). In fact, the word *monasterium* could either be applied to the *ecclesia maior* itself, or to the entire complex of buildings around and including the *ecclesia maior*/cathedral church.[4]

Examples of this usage are found in Thietmar's chronicle. He uses *monasterium* and *ecclesia maior* (3.12, 15; 6.18) interchangeably to refer to the cathedral of Magdeburg and adjacent buildings (Trillmich 1957:98, 102, 262) as a single complex,[5] but in one instance (7.35) he uses *monasterium* to refer to the church itself.[6] In another place, Thietmar (6:17) mentions a fire in the cathedral of Paderborn[7] which, according to other ninth- to eleventh-century sources, was usually called a *monasterium*.[8]

A close reading of Thietmar's entry concerning the events in Kiev provides further proof that the *monasterium sanctae Sophiae* was the cathedral church of Kiev. Firstly the name of the *monasterium* – Holy Wisdom – would in all likelihood have only been given to a cathedral church in Rus'. Secondly, there is the presence of the archbishop/metropolitan of Kiev, who welcomed both rulers to his *kafolikani ikklisia*.[9]

One must ask, nevertheless, why a German knight would have applied a term common in his native land to a church in Kiev. The answer is that he undoubtedly identified the cathedral ensemble of Kiev with the episcopal minsters which he had seen elsewhere in Germany. To a knight from Saxony the church, the court of the metropolitan and the buildings for the *kliros*

(a body of cathedral priests and monks) in Kiev would have seemed very similar to a *monasterium episcopale* or *monasterium cathedralis ecclesiae* consisting of the cathedral church, the bishop's house, dormitory, refectory and other buildings for the cathedral chapter. The Saxon knight was not the only person to make such an association: Foucher of Chartres (1.5[3], 9[1]), author of a chronicle of the First Crusade, called St Peter's in Rome a *monasterium* and, summarizing the churches of Constantinople, called them *monasteria* (Hagenmayer 1913:147, 176). Geoffroy de Villehardouin and Henri de Valenciennes, participants in the Fourth Crusade, called Hagia Sophia in Constantinople and metropolitan churches in Nikomedia, Thessalonika and Thebes *moustier* (Wailly 1874: 154, 230, 272, 274, 290, 364, 408).[10]

In view of Thietmar's account of the official welcoming of Bolesław and Svjatopolk, it appears that St Sophia had already been reconstructed after the fire in 1017, which in itself proves that the church was made of wood. The construction of such a church within a year would have been relatively easy, since builders in ancient Rus' were accustomed to building wooden structures during one season.

Scholars who have not considered the possibility that a wooden church of St Sophia preceded the stone construction of Prince Jaroslav, assumed that the church of the Holy Virgin, known as the church of the Tithe, must have been originally dedicated to Holy Wisdom and that this name was transferred to the new metropolitan cathedral built in the 1030s (Golubinskij 1904: 100). However, this hypothesis is opposed by evidence in the Rus'ian sources (PSRL 1: 121, 124, 130, 153; Cross 1953:119, 120–1,

124, 138; Müller 1962:120–1; Abramovič 1967:5), which specifically state that Vladimir founded a church dedicated to the Holy Virgin. Moreover in Thietmar's (7.14) chronicle we find the statement of an eyewitness that Vladimir was buried *in ecclesia Christi martiris et papae Clementis iuxta predictam coniugem suam, sarcofagis eorundem in medio templi palam stantibus* (Trillmich 1957:436).[11]

Reliable Rus'ian sources (Müller 1962: 121; Abramovič 1967:29; PSRL 1:130) state that Vladimir was buried in the church of the Virgin, known as the church of the Tithe. Some scholars explain Thietmar's statement that Vladimir was buried in the church of Christ's martyr Pope Clement by saying that he was actually buried in a side chapel or aisle of the church of the Tithe where there was an altar dedicated to this bishop of Rome. The main problem with this interpretation is that Thietmar's source specifically says that the sarcophagi of Vladimir and his wife stood *in medio templi*, that is, in the middle of the building.[12]

According to the *Primary chronicle* (PSRL 1:116; 2:101; Cross 1953:116; Ajnalov 1918:25–6), some of the remains of Pope St Clement were brought from Cherson and placed in the church of the Tithe.[13] What probably happened was that the German knight participating in Bolesław's campaign remembered two significant details: the sarcophagi of Vladimir and Anna and, since he was a Roman Catholic, the relics of Clement, bishop of Rome. Either the knight or Thietmar combined the two, thereby recording the name of Vladimir's church erroneously.

Summing up the evidence found in Thietmar's chronicle it seems clear that, at least in the eyes of a German mercenary soldier, there were two important churches in Kiev in 1018: the cathedral of St Sophia and the church in which the sarcophagi of Vladimir and Anna were placed, that is, the church of the Tithe. Consequently the church of the Tithe could not have served as the cathedral church in 1018. Given that the church dedicated to Holy Wisdom was burned in 1017 and rebuilt the following year, it would appear that it was built of wood. Furthermore, from the account it appears that the church of St Sophia with adjacent buildings served as the residence of the metropolitan of Rus' prior to 1017, that is, apparently in the time of Vladimir. The evidence provided by Thietmar's chronicle must be used as a basis for any solution to the problem under discussion.

Attempts to analyze the Rus'ian chronicle entries which concern the cathedral of St Sophia have caused many scholars to conclude that these sources are hopelessly confused. This scepticism, however, is itself the result of a number of errors and misinterpretations. The Rus'ian chronicles can, in fact, provide reliable information when used with care. It is first of all necessary to review the chronicles involved.

The *Primary chronicle*, Laurentian MS (PSRL 1:142), states that in 1017 a church burned in Kiev: *pogore cerkvi*. Other basic MSS. of the same chronicle, the Radziwiłł, Academy, Hypatian and Xlebnikov MSS (PSRL 2:130) use the plural: "the churches burned"/*pogoreša cerkvi*. The text in both cases is corrupt, indicating that the confusion occurred before the *Primary chronicle* was finally completed, since it was transmitted to all MSS. The original entry undoubtedly named the edifice or edifices which were burned.[14] If we accept the singular verb the

the text must refer to St Sophia which, according to Thietmar, was burned in 1017. The lacuna may be explained in the following manner: a chronicler, copying the entry "In the year 6525/1017 Jaroslav went to Kiev and the church of St Sophia burned", at the end of the eleventh century, was confused because the entry for 1037 relates in great detail that Jaroslav *founded* the church of St Sophia. As a result he simply dropped the words "St Sophia" in the 1017 entry.

This lacuna was noticed by A. A. Šaxmatov, who believed (1908:576) that the correct reading of the 1017 entry was " . . . the church of the Holy Virgin [that is, of the Tithe] burned."[15] But this interpretation is difficult to reconcile with Thietmar's account: one can hardly imagine a German knight admiring the sarcophagi of Vladimir and Anna in the middle of a burned-down church!

It is possible that the plural verb is the primary reading, although it is likelier that the plural verb arose as an attempt to correct an already corrupt text. Some proof of this is seen in the Vladimir and Trinity MSS. of the *Primary chronicle* (see note 14) which, together with the Laurentian MS. are derived from the chronicle compilation of 1305 (Lur'e 1976:17–36).

In the final analysis, this is a minor problem since the entry in the *Primary chronicle* – whether with a singular or plural verb – is confirmed by Thietmar (8.32), who says that in addition to St Sophia, other parts of Kiev burned, following the attacks of the Pechenegs allied with Prince Boleslav.[16]

Important information is also found in the *Novgorod first chronicle* (Nasonov 1950:15). Under the year 6525 (March 1017–February 1018) we read: "Jaroslav went to

Brest, and St Sophia was founded (*založena byst'*) in Kiev."[17] This passage has also been the source of considerable debate. Some scholars (Ajnalov 1917:34ff.; Alpatov 1932: 10) have maintained that this entry preserves the real date of the founding of the church of St Sophia and that the entries of 1036 and 1037 in the *Primary chronicle* are unreliable.[18] Others disqualify this entry in the *Novgorod first chronicle* on the grounds that all the information on Kiev contained therein is derived from the *Primary chronicle*; consequently, the reference to the founding of St Sophia in 1017 must be a scribal error.[19] They believe that "all attempts to determine the credibility of this entry meet with insurmountable obstacles" (Šaxmatov 1908: 228)[20].

This problem is indeed insoluble, if one assumes that the entries of both 1017 and 1037 refer to the stone church of St Sophia. A solution is possible only if one assumes that the entry of 1017 refers to a wooden church.

Let us return to Thietmar's chronicle. We have seen that St Sophia seems to have been a working church in August 1018, although it had been destroyed by fire the previous year.[21] This could only have been possible if the church had been made of wood and rebuilt in one season. As for the *Novgorod chronicle*, there is some evidence that the text in question is based on contemporaneous annals and is independent of the Kievan account of 1037.[22] The *Novgorod chronicle* says: "Jaroslav went to Brest, and St Sophia was founded in Kiev". The account does not ascribe the foundation to Jaroslav at all, although the foundation is obviously linked in some way with Jaroslav's going to Brest.

We know for certain (Łowmiański 1970: 231–4, 236–7, 243–4) that Jaroslav did in fact go to Brest in 1017.[23] Thietmar (7.65) tells us that in October 1017 the Emperor Henry II was staying in Merseburg and heard that the *Ruszorum rex* had attacked Prince Bolesław. (Trillmich 1957:426). It is clear from the context that the *Ruszorum rex* is Jaroslav; Thietmar adds that Jaroslav failed to capture a certain town which he had besieged.[24] N. Karamzin was the first to state that this besieged town was, in fact, Brest. If the news of this attack reached Merseburg in October 1017, then Jaroslav's campaign must have taken place that summer, which was when St Sophia was founded in Kiev. This would explain the use of the impersonal verb in the Novgorod chronicle account of 1017: "was founded" /*založena byst'*, since Jaroslav was on campaign at the time.

The verb *založiti* requires additional explanation. Toločko (1969:198; 1972:96) thought that this word was only used in connection with stone buildings.[25] But an examination of the sources proves that such a conclusion is untenable. *Založiti* has several meanings: sometimes it was applied to the earlier stages of construction, especially to laying the corner stone; at other times, however, it was applied to the construction of the building itself.[26]

The chronicles usually use *založiti* in connection with stone buildings, but there are two important reasons for this which have nothing to do with the lexical meaning of the word. First of all, as noticed by Voronin (1962:15), since there were many more wooden buildings than stone buildings in Kievan Rus', the chronicles rarely record the construction of the former. The second reason is connected with the realities of building in stone and wood. The construc-

tion of a stone church lasted several years consequently *založiti* was used by chroniclers to mean "begin" or "found". A wooden church, on the other hand, would already have been completed by the time the chronicler recorded the event, and so the verbs *srubiti* and *postaviti* with the primary meanings of "to chop" and "to establish" were usually used.

The best source of information on this question is the *Novgorod first chronicle*, which usually specifies if a church was built of stone.[27] Other chronicles are not so specific, and additional information must be obtained in order to determine the nature of the building.

A good example of this is the chronicle account of the building of a church in the monastery of the Caves in Kiev. In the *Primary chronicle* (PSRL 1:159; Cross 1953: 141) we read that about 1060 "the prior and the brethren founded (*založiša*) a great church there and fenced in the monastery with a palisade". Later, under the year 1073, we read that a stone church was begun in the monastery (PSRL 1:183; Cross 1953:156, 164). On the basis of this information alone we would not know whether the first church was of wood or of stone, nor whether the second was intended to replace the first. These questions can only be answered by referring to the *vita* of Theodosij by the monk Nestor, who states that Theodosij was divinely inspired "to build a large church of stone because the previous wooden church was too small for all the brothers" (Knjazevskaja 1971:124–5, and also 89, 133).

The situation is much worse for wooden churches, since the foundation of these is almost never reported in the chronicles.[28] However, there are frequent references to the foundation of town ramparts; these are usually phrased "the walls were founded"/ *založen byst' grad*. From archaeological excavations we know that fortifications were usually made of earth and wood.[29]

Summing up the foregoing discussion, we may conclude that the account of 1017 in the *Novgorod first chronicle* refers to the construction of a wooden church of St Sophia but we cannot determine from the phrase *založena byst'* if the entry records the foundation or completion of the church.[30]

The hypothesis that the stone church of St Sophia was preceded by a wooden one is not entirely new (Maksimović 1877:132–40; Lebedincev 1878:53–8), but it is the result of a completely new line of reasoning.[31] Moreover it found support in the observed tendency in Rus'ian ecclesiastical architecture for a wooden church to be replaced by a stone one of the same name. Sometimes the stone church was built on the very spot where the wooden church had stood. Toločko (1969:197; 1972:96) and Vysockij (1976:247) transformed this observation into an obligatory principle and concluded that the stone St Sophia was founded in 1017 on the very spot where the wooden church had stood before being destroyed by fire. But the entire argument is unsubstantiated. Churches were frequently rebuilt on the same site after a fire; in the case of stone structures, the same foundations were often used (Poppe 1962:46–7, 85). However, specific conditions determined the course of action in each case. A stone church, by its very nature, required the careful selection of a construction site. Three examples will serve to illustrate this fact.

The stone church of the monastery of the Caves, mentioned above, was built between 1073 and 1076 on a hill several hundred meters away from the wooden church which it was intended to replace. From the *vita* of Theodosij we learn that the choice of a site was the subject of considerable discussion and that the matter was resolved when Prince Svjatoslav granted the brothers a tract of land adjacent to the monastery (Knjazevskaja 1971:125).[32]

Another example is the church of SS Boris and Gleb in Vyšgorod. The earliest church, where the sarcophagi of the brothers were located, was made of wood. About 1071 another wooden church was erected nearby; this church was still being used in 1115. In 1074 yet another church dedicated to the brothers was begun – this time made of stone. It was intended to replace the wooden church but was built on a different site. Owing to a number of circumstances the stone church was not completed until 1112. When it was finally finished Svjatopolk, prince of Kiev, did not want to transfer the sarcophagi to the new church because it had been founded by his cousin Oleg, prince of Černigov. Svjatopolk intended to build his own stone church on the site of the oldest wooden church, around the sarcophagi of the saints, saying "I dare not transport them from place to place" (see Abramovič 1967: 21, 55, 60, 62, 64, 65; PSRL 2:280–1).

Yet another example which is particularly pertinent to this question is seen in the church of St Sophia in Novgorod. The wooden church of St Sophia with thirteen domes was burnt on 4 March 1049. However, a stone church dedicated to Holy Wisdom had been founded by Vladimir, son of Jaroslav the Wise, in 1045, that is, while the wooden church was still standing. Vladimir's structure was completed in 1050 and was not located anywhere near the original church. Proof of this is found in a chronicle entry from the 1160s which says that the wooden church of St Sophia had stood "at the end of Bishop's Street, where not long ago Satko built the stone church of SS Boris and Gleb, on the bank of the River Volxov" (Nasonov 1950:16, 181, 219).[33]

These examples suggest that the stone church of St Sophia in Kiev was not necessarily built on the same spot as the wooden structure. The wooden cathedral church – both the one which was destroyed by fire in 1017 and the one which replaced it – were situated within the walls of Vladimir's fortified town. The stone St Sophia could only have been located in the fortified part of Kiev, but these very fortifications were enlarged to make room for a number of new buildings constructed by Jaroslav. In other words, the construction of the stone church of St Sophia was part of an entire building programme which cannot be attributed to the years 1015–1019 when the sons of Vladimir were warring for the throne of Kiev (see Karger 1958:247–62; 1961:98ff., Plate 81; Cross 1936:490ff.)[34].

With this in mind we can re-examine the entry in the *Primary chronicle* under the year 1036, describing the battle between Jaroslav and the Pechenegs "where the church of St Sophia, the Rus'ian metropolis, now stands; at that time there were fields outside the town" (PSRL 1:151; 2:138; Cross 1953: 136–7). This passage, which is a stumbling block to those who maintain that St Sophia was built in 1017, is obviously completely straightforward. Clearly, the author of the *Primary chronicle*, writing around the year 1100, had a good knowledge of the topography of Kiev. This passage suggests that

Jaroslav may have chosen to build the new cathedral on the site of his victory (Lazarev 1960:22ff.)

Another important source which must be considered is Ilarion's *Sermon on law and grace* which praises the building activities of Vladimir and Jaroslav in the following terms (Müller 1962:121–2):[35]

. . . a very good and true witness [is] thy son George [Jaroslav] whom the Lord made heir to the sovereignty after thee, not breaking the injunctions but confirming them, not belittling the creations of thy piety but adding to them, not distorting but perfecting. He finished thy unfinished works, as was done for David by Solomon. He built a great house of God, of His Holy Wisdom, for the holiness and enlightenment of thy city and adorned it with every beauty.

On the basis of Ilarion's eulogy, Ajnalov (1917:35–6; 1932:12) and Vysockij (1976: 245–6) concluded that Vladimir actually began the construction of the stone church of St Sophia.[36] They maintained that the preparations were so advanced that neither the death of Vladimir on 15 July 1015, nor the fratricidal wars for the throne of Kiev which followed, could stop the foundation of the church in 1017. However, one cannot draw such a conclusion from Ilarion's speech: in comparing Vladimir and Jaroslav to David and Solomon, Ilarion was drawing on the Books of Kings and Chronicles in which we read that David only intended to build the temple and that the actual construction was both begun and completed by Solomon.[37]

This is not to say that Ilarion's comparison of Vladimir and Jaroslav to the anointed David and Solomon as the planner and the builder, was pure allegory.[38] It is entirely possible that Vladimir dreamed of building a stone metropolitan cathedral worthy of the name, and that the wooden church was only an interim solution. It is worth noting that Ilarion, in discussing the proof of Vladimir's orthodoxy, only mentions Vladimir's foundation "the Holy Church of the Holy Mother of God" (Müller 1962:120) that is, the church of the Tithe, clearly indicating that wooden churches were of secondary importance.[39] Perhaps Vladimir began the tradition in Rus' according to which someone who had promised to build a church could first build it in wood in the expectation that he or his successors would be able to replace it with a stone structure at a later time.

We conclude, therefore, that when St Sophia was destroyed by fire in 1017, circumstances dictated that it be rebuilt immediately in wood.[40] The stone church was begun two decades later under completely different conditions and must, therefore, be considered Jaroslav's foundation.

The preceding discussion has attempted to prove the existence of a wooden church of St Sophia. In connection with this, we must discuss the problem of when the church was built. This question must be approached in a very roundabout way. According to the later *Novgorod third chronicle* (Byčkov 1879: 173) the oak cathedral of St Sophia in Novgorod was built in 989 (6497) and stood for sixty years.[41] The year 989 is probably unreliable: it is the year of the baptism of Rus' and the chronicler probably assumed that the bishopric of Novgorod and the cathedral church were founded in the same year. In fact, the bishopric of Novgorod was established together with the metropolitanate of Rus' in Kiev and with the first suffragan bishopric in Belgorod (Poppe 1971a:174–6). Consequently, the wooden St Sophia in Novgorod was probably built in the last decade of the tenth century and was

destroyed by fire in 1049, a period of some fifty, not sixty, years.

An unusual note in the Novgorod chronicle states that the wooden St Sophia in Novgorod had thirteen domes, as did the stone St Sophia in Kiev, begun much later. Although some would like to believe that the architecture of the church in Novgorod influenced the design of the church in Kiev,[42] it is likelier that the earliest wooden St Sophia in Kiev served as a model for both.[43]

The use of thirteen domes was previously considered an original feature of old Rus'ian architecture (Zabelin 1900:80–91; Golubinskij 1904:104–5; Voronin 1952:277–8). Although the use of a great number of domes must be seen as an answer to architectural necessities, the use of exactly thirteen domes can only have resulted from the influence of Christian symbolism (Cross 1949:11).[44] As far as architectural necessities are concerned, it appears that the construction of thirteen cupolas placed atop drums was dictated by practical considerations of lighting, rather than by some hypothetical tradition of wooden architecture. In particular, the architect needed to bring sufficient light into the galleries built for the prince and his court, to transform them into lofty, spacious halls suitable for worship. This, at least, has been convincingly demonstrated for the stone church of St Sophia. Moreover, the style is not unusual in Byzantine architecture (Komeč 1972:50–64).

On the other hand, there is no doubt that the exact number and arrangement of the cupolas were chosen for the visual effect on the observer outside the cathedral (Komeč 1968:232–8). This can only be understood within the context of Christian symbolism.[45] Twelve domes represented the twelve

23

apostles, the Church itself, while the thirteenth dome in the very centre stood for the Supreme Being.[46] Together, they emphasized the concept of the "one universal and apostolic Church" and provided a visual demonstration to those who had just converted to Christianity.

2. The church of the Tithe as capella regia

Thus, weighty arguments lead us to the conclusion that the wooden cathedral of St Sophia in Kiev was built in connection with the establishment of the Church of Rus' shortly after 988. Moreover, the architecture of both the wooden and stone churches of St Sophia in Kiev influenced the architecture of the wooden and stone churches of St Sophia in Novgorod rather than vice-versa. In view of this, we must reject the widely-held belief that the church of the Holy Virgin (the church of the Tithe), which was built by Vladimir, was the first cathedral of the head of the Church of Rus' until it was replaced by Jaroslav's construction.

The stone church of the Tithe was built by Byzantine architects in the years 989-996 and was furnished with icons and liturgical vessels brought from Cherson. After this, Vladimir "entrusted the church to Anastasius of Cherson, and he appointed Chersonian priests to serve in it". Furthermore, Vladimir "gave the tithe to Anastasius of Cherson" (PSRL 1:121–2, 124; 2:106, 109; Cross 1953:119, 121).[47]

Anastasius is mentioned again in the *Primary chronicle* under the year 1018, in connection with the departure of the Polish prince Bolesław from Kiev. Bolesław, who was laden with booty, "made Anastasius of the church of the Tithe the steward of the property, for the latter had won his confidence by his flattery" (PSRL 1:144; 2:131; Cross 1953:132). It is noteworthy that Anastasius is referred to as being *desjatinnyj*, that is, "of the church of the Tithe", indicating that he performed the same duties in 1018 as he had twenty years before under Vladimir. Since the wooden cathedral of St Sophia had been built before 1017, Anastasius could not have been, as some have proposed, a member of the cathedral chapter (*kliros*) in charge of the treasury (*oekonomos*). He was, as the text clearly states, attached to the church founded by the monarch of Rus'.

The church of the Tithe was not just a princely foundation; it was the royal church, the *ekklésia basiliká, capella regia, capella palatina*, known equally well in the East as in the West, an institution which was of tremendous significance as a representation of kingship and in the symbolism of the medieval state (see Grass 1967:61–96). Anastasius of Cherson was in all likelihood the provost or *oekonomos* of the church of the Tithe.[48] If he was, in fact, the *oekonomos* he may well have been a layman, since laymen frequently held this and other high ecclesiastical positions in the Byzantine Church.[49] Nor would this have been surprising, viewed within the context of Byzantine custom: as founder and sponsor of the church of the Tithe, Prince Vladimir enjoyed very clearly defined administrative, property and liturgical rights (*ta ktitoriká dikaia*) and it was expected that he would have named his own candidate to be provost or *oekonomos* of his church (Zhíshman 1888; Troicki 1935:81–132). Moreover, when we remember that Vladimir had a Porphyrogenite wife, we can understand that he would have been well informed about Byzantine ecclesiastical matters, especially about the emperors' rights *vis-à-vis* their own churches and their right to nominate candidates to ecclesiastical offices (Beck 1959:100–1; Michel 1959:34–5). The princes of Rus', like the Byzantine emperors, maintained their own clergy independent of the local bishop.[50]

As provost/*oekonomos* of the palatine church, Anastasius of Cherson was a court figure and could not have avoided becoming involved in the struggle for power after Vladimir's death. While the metropolitan was undoubtedly mediating between Boleslaw and Svjatopolk in Kiev and Jaroslav in Novgorod, Anastasius must have decided that there was little future for him in Kiev and that this was an opportune time to leave Rus' for good.

The foregoing permits us to re-interpret Vladimir's granting of a tithe to the church of the Holy Virgin. The tithe was not intended for the whole Church of Rus' or even for the metropolitan cathedral, but exclusively for the maintenance of the royal chapel. The metropolitan church undoubtedly had some endowment or source of revenue, but the *Primary chronicle* tells us nothing about it. However, the popular name of the prince's church, "church of the Tithe", indicates that this sort of endowment was the exception rather than the rule.[51] Moreover, the fact that the palace church was built of stone and that its clergy were independent of the metropolitan, whose church was built of wood, indicates that for many years the wooden cathedral of St Sophia was overshadowed by the palatine church of the Holy Virgin.

The very location of the church of the Holy Virgin near Vladimir's palace (Karger 1961: 60–75; Korzuxina 1966:228–9; Toločko 1972:76–81) confirms its role as a palatine church. The church was dedicated to the Holy Virgin probably on the insistence of Anna Porphyrogenita, not because of the popularity of the cult of the Theotokos in Byzantium but because of the important role played by two basilicas dedicated to the Virgin in the court life of Constantinople: the churches at Chalkopratei and Blachernae. In addition, the church of the Virgin at Pharos, near the throne hall (*aula*), was considered the *capella imperatoris*. The emperor's church was, however, first and foremost the church complex of the Virgin at Blachernae, where official ecclesiastical ceremonies which included the emperor and his court were held. (Schneider 1951:82ff; Janin 1953:169–79; 241–9; Beck 1959:157).

The question has been raised whether or not the church of the Tithe was dedicated only to the Virgin or to one of her holidays (Il'in 1965:266–8). It has been generally assumed that it was dedicated to the Virgin alone (Poppe 1968b:91, note 27), since there is no proof in the sources that it was dedicated to the Dormition (*koimesis, uspenie*). Strictly speaking, however, we can only say with certainty that the sources refer to the church as the "church of the Mother of God", which does not really prove anything. We know without any doubt that the principal church of the monastery of the Caves was dedicated to the Dormition of the Virgin, though as a rule it was simply called "The church of the Mother of God". Nevertheless, there are circumstances in which one would expect to find the entire dedicatory name of the church of the Tithe with no omissions. Let us examine the two such references.

In the *Primary chronicle*, under the year 996, we find a prayer supposedly spoken by Vladimir as he entered the church for the first time: "Lord God . . . look upon this thy church which I, thine unworthy servant, have built in the name of the Ever-Virgin Mother of God who bore thee" (PSRL 1:124; Cross 1953:120). In another source, Ilarion's eulogy of Prince Vladimir, the author says: "a good testimony to your piety, o blessed one, is the Holy Church of Mary, the Holy Mother of God." This is fairly clear, as far as evidence *ex silentio* goes, because shortly after this passage, Ilarion says of Jaroslav's church of the Holy Virgin built above the Golden Gate: "You placed your people and the city under the protection of the glorious Holy Mother of God, who is ever-ready to help Christians, and you built a church over the main gate in the name of the first holy day of the Lord, the holy Annunciation" (Müller 1962:120–1, 123–4).

Since Ilarion is so specific about Jaroslav's church above the Golden Gate, we can conclude with reasonable certainty that the church of the Tithe was dedicated to the Virgin as patroness of Kiev, not to her Dormition. This, too, would correspond to Byzantine custom: the Virgin, particularly the Virgin of Blachernae, was the protectress of the holy city on the Bosphorus. There are, however, other analogies between the two churches: the Rus'ians spoke of the "indestructible wall" (*nerušimaja stena*) in connection with the Maria Orans, and it is supposed that such a fresco or mosaic adorned the apse of the church of the Tithe. This would correspond to the Byzantine epithet of *apoliorketon teichos* applied to the Virgin of Blachernae (Lazarev 1960:29–30, 99–102; Averincev 1972:46–9; Belting-Ihm 1976:

38–50). There is yet another parallel between the churches in Constantinople and Kiev. The Virgin's veil was kept in the church at Blachernae in Constantinople, while a study of the azimuth of the axis of the church of the Tithe in Kiev indicates that it was founded on or very near 2 July, the feast of the Finding of the Virgin's robe (Rappoport 1974:47–8).

In view of this, it does not seem likely that the custom of building cathedral churches in many towns of Rus' dedicated to the Dormition of the Virgin was an indication of the importance of the church of the Tithe (Il'in 1965:268). It is much more likely that these churches were named after the main church of the monastery of the Caves in Kiev, founded in the 1050s. The idea of dedicating the church to the Dormition of the Virgin seems to have been borrowed by the monks of the Caves monastery from the Rus'ian monastery on Mount Athos. Be that as it may, the first cathedral churches dedicated to the Dormition of the Virgin were, to the best of our knowledge, in Rostov, Turov and Vladimir-in-Volhynia. They were built when bishoprics were established in these cities in the 1070s and 1080s, and in each case the Kievan Caves monastery played an important role (Poppe 1971a:189–201).

3. Could the stone church of St Sophia have been built before 1036?

The date of the erection of the stone church of St Sophia remains the subject of considerable controversy. This has resulted from the erroneous juxtaposition of the entry in the *Novgorod chronicle* under the year 1017 with the entry in the *Primary chronicle* under the year 1037. The juxtaposition is erroneous since, as was discussed above, the two entries discuss different buildings. The first, of 1017, concerns the completion of the wooden cathedral mentioned by Thietmar in 1018, while the second, of 1037, concerns the stone foundation of Jaroslav the Wise. Although the previous discussion of these two entries proved that the stone church of St Sophia was not built in 1017, it did not *ipso facto* prove the reverse, namely that the cathedral was completed in 1037 as stated in the *Primary chronicle*.

The chronicle entry of 1037 in the *Primary chronicle* is actually a much later eulogy of Jaroslav the Wise, praising his whole building programme and his activities as a Christian ruler (Lixačev 1950:374–5; Müller 1959:57–8). If we read the entry carefully, we see that the eulogy was not necessarily inserted under the year 1037 because of the church of St Sophia, since four other foundations are mentioned (PSRL 1:151; 2:139; Cross 1953:137)[52]:

In the year 6545 Jaroslav founded the great town wall which has the Golden Gate. He also founded the metropolitan church of St Sophia, the church of the Annunciation over the Golden Gate, and then the monastery of St George and the convent of St Irene.

We see that the chronicler mentions the citadel, that is, the fortified ramparts, of Kiev first and the cathedral church in second place. Consequently, we should consider the possibility that the eulogy was included under the year 1037 in connection with the most grandiose of the projects mentioned: the construction of the town walls. In fact, the original entry was probably very brief: "In 6545 Jaroslav founded (*založi*) the great ramparts." The other

structures were added later. Given the fact that *založi* refers to a number of structures built at different times, one should translate it broadly, as *founded* or *erected*.

It seems likely that the town walls were, in fact, begun in 1037, if we consider the historical background of the events of the previous year. In 1036, Mstislav, prince of Černigov, died, leaving Jaroslav the sole ruler of Rus'. Consequently, after Mstislav's death, Jaroslav would have been more willing to rule permanently in Kiev. Of greater importance, however, is the fact that the Pechenegs attacked in force in 1036, making it necessary to fortify the capital. We know that the cathedral of St Sophia was within the new ramparts known as Jaroslav's town, and that the church must therefore have been founded at the same time or even later than the ramparts, namely 1037 or later.

The year 1036 as the *terminus ante quem non* for the foundation of the stone St Sophia has been questioned on the following grounds:

1) The battle with the Pechenegs did not take place in 1036, as is stated in the *Primary chronicle*, but in 1017. The information about the battle was misplaced under the year 1036 during later revisions of the chronicle. Consequently, the statement that the battle took place "on the spot where the metropolitan church of St Sophia now stands, since at that time there were fields outside the town walls" loses its value as a chronological indicator (Toločko 1969:198–9; 1972:96–100; Logvin 1977:173–4).

2) The eulogy of 1037 accurately sums up all Jaroslav's building activities up to that year, and he could not have found the money and manpower to build everything mentioned during the last seventeen years of his

life, 1037–1054. Those who argue along this line also point out that it is highly unlikely that Jaroslav would not have erected a single building worthy of the chronicler's attention during the first twenty years of his reign, and that he was suddenly seized with a fit of building activity in 1037. They also reject the theory that the rivalry between Jaroslav and his brother Mstislav caused the former to refrain from building anything in Kiev, pointing out that Mstislav began to build the cathedral of the Saviour in his capital Černigov before 1036, and that Jaroslav would have been compelled to answer this undertaking in kind. In short, these scholars believe that both the city walls ("Jaroslav's town") and St Sophia were built in the two decades between 1017 and 1037, and would agree with Šaxmatov's interpretation that the chronicle entries of 1037 and 1039 refer to the completion of St Sophia (Toločko 1969:200–1, 100–2).[53]

3) One of the most conclusive arguments put forward by those who believe that St Sophia was built before 1037 is to be found in the inscriptions scratched into the plaster on the walls covered with frescoes. These graffiti date from the years 1030, 1032, 1042, 1052 and 1054 (Vysoc'kyj 1975:171–81; 1976:240–57 Toločko 1972: 102–3; Logvin 1971:8; 1977:174).

Let us return to the first objection to the 1036 date, based on the date of the battle with the Pechenegs. This is the weakest objection, since it is essentially circular. The only substantive reason for redating the battle with the Pechenegs to 1017 is the existence of references to the construction of the church of St Sophia in the *Novgorod chronicle* and in Thietmar of Merseburg, and the assumption that they refer to the stone

church (Il'in 1957:120–3).[54] This argument is groundless since, as we have seen, these references refer to the reconstruction of the wooden church damaged by fire.

There are, however, other reasons against redating the battle with the Pechenegs to 1017. One is the remark made by the chronicler that the battle of 1036 near Kiev was the last pitched battle between Pechenegs and the warriors of Rus'. It is difficult to maintain that this really occurred in 1017 because Thietmar (8.32) informs us that the Pechenegs made frequent inroads against Kiev in 1017 and 1018 (Trillmich 1957:474). The battles with the Pechenegs which took place between 1015 and 1019 were unusual inasmuch as the Pechenegs fought as allies of one prince of Rus' (Svjatopolk) against another prince of Rus', thereby influencing the struggle for succession to the throne of Kiev. Svjatopolk's defeat in 1019 on the river Al'ta ended the civil wars and deprived the Pechenegs of any further chance of interfering in the affairs of Rus'. It is noteworthy that they were not involved in the battle between Jaroslav and Mstislav in 1024.

The peace treaty which Jaroslav and Mstislav concluded in 1026 made it possible for the brothers to commit more energy to the defence of the southern steppes. The danger of Pecheneg attacks must have been great, since Jaroslav extended the fortified, defensive zone intended to protect the Kievan lands from the nomads by building fortresses along the river Ros', a tributary of the Dniepr, in 1031 and 1032, and by peopling the land with settlers (PSRL 1:150; 2:137; Cross 1953:136; Dovženok 1968:37–41; Łowmiański 1970b:553–4).

In view of all this, it is difficult to claim

that the last great battle with the Pechenegs mentioned by the chronicler occurred in 1017. On the contrary, the traditional date of 1036 is very acceptable, in view of the international situation as reflected in the accounts of the period. We know, from John Scylitzes, that the Pechenegs plundered Byzantine territories near Thessalonika in 1034, and that they crossed the frozen Danube during the winter of 1035–36 and plundered Moesia, Thrace and Macedonia. During the spring of 1036, they again attacked in three waves, inflicting heavy losses on Byzantine troops protecting the Danubian provinces (Thurn 1973: 373, 385, 397–99; compare the commentary in Ferluga 1966:162–3; Diaconu 1970:39–49). Then, suddenly, the nomads withdrew, despite the lack of effective defense on the Byzantine side, and a period of relative peace ensued along the Danubian frontier. This sudden turn of events can be explained in terms of the *Primary chronicle* entry of 1036 (Rasovskij 1933:7).

It is conceivable that the news of the death of Prince Mstislav of Černigov reached the Pechenegs during the spring of 1036. The nomads could well have expected another outbreak of fratricidal warfare such as that which had occured after the death of Vladimir in 1015. As a result, they withdrew from the Danube to attack the lands south of Kiev, which they expected to be easy prey. Jaroslav, however, "assumed the entire sovereignty and became autocrat of the Rus'ian land" (PSRL 1:150–1; 2:138–9; Cross 1953:136–7).[55] Mstislav died leaving no offspring, and Jaroslav's last surviving brother, Sudislav, was charged with conspiracy and treason and imprisoned in a dungeon. Jaroslav was in Novgorod when the Pechenegs attacked Kiev; he assembled, as he had done before, an army of Novgorodians and Varangian mercenaries and, having joined forces with men from Kiev, inflicted a crushing defeat on the Pechenegs on the outskirts of Kiev. The extent of Jaroslav's victory can be seen from the fact that the nomads undertook no military actions until 1046 when, having been pushed westwards by other nomads, they again attacked the Byzantine provinces along the Danube.

The events outlined above took place during the year 6544, that is, between March 1036 and February 1037. Mstislav probably died in the spring or early summer of 1036, and the news of his death reached the Pechenegs shortly thereafter. Jaroslav seems to have had enough time to secure Mstislav's realm, which consisted of Černigov and the right bank of the Dniepr, and to journey to Novgorod to install his son Vladimir as governor of the city. The Pechenegs almost certainly attacked at the end of the summer of 1036 while Jaroslav was in Novgorod. Jaroslav seems, nevertheless, to have had sufficient time to assemble his forces, since Norsemen were among their number. The actual battle with the nomads would, therefore, have taken place near Kiev in the late autumn of 1036.

This reconstruction lends credence to the account of 1036, at least as far as the chronology is concerned. Although the chronicler who wrote the final account of the event years later may have exaggerated when he said that the battle occurred on the site of the stone church of St Sophia, there is no doubt that the battle did take place outside the town walls of that time. In view of this, we may confidently conclude that 1036 is indeed the *terminus ante quem non* for the construction of both the enlarged town walls and of the stone cathedral church.

Scholars who reject the year 1036 as the starting point for the building programme mentioned in the chronicle under the year 1037 argue that construction of the five structures mentioned in the account would have lasted at least twenty to twenty five years (Toločko 1972:101–3; Logvin 1977: 172–3).[56] We must, therefore, determine whether or not everything could have been built during the last seventeen years of Jaroslav's life, from 1037 until February 1054.

One could, theoretically, explain the speed of construction by arguing that so many architects and masters came from Byzantium that several buildings were built simultaneously. It is likelier, however, that only one relatively small team of Byzantine masters was assembled to work on all the churches, one after another, by being shifted from site to site according to a well-conceived plan. Local Kievan labourers would have been working constantly to produce and supply the necessary building materials. Consequently, the periods of construction of the churches would have overlapped. Seen in this light, seventeen years does not seem too short a time for constructing the cathedral of St Sophia, the Golden Gate with the church of the Annunciation, and the churches of St George and St Irene. So far, the fifth structure, the fortifications known as "Jaroslav's town" has been omitted, since it was fundamentally different in nature from the four churches. The latter were architecturally difficult structures made of stone, whereas the ramparts were made of earth and timber and could have

been built by local workmen at the same time as the churches. Nevertheless, P. Toločko (1972:82–3, 101) has emphasized the extensive nature of the ramparts, which required a tremendous amount of digging, the transportation of timber and earth, the construction of wooden structures inside and atop the ramparts and three gates, including the stone Golden Gate. Toločko's point is that the ramparts would have required so much time, material and manpower that they could not have been built at the same time as the other four structures.

However, Toločko does not discuss the exact details of the ramparts. They had an estimated length of 3.5 kilometers, were 20 meters thick at the bottom and 12 meters high. Near the Golden Gate, they were 30 meters thick at the bottom and 11 meters high, with a wooden superstructure which made the entire height 16 meters. The walls would have required an estimated 630,000 cubic meters of earth and 50,000 cubic meters of oak timber. On the basis of these estimates, the ramparts could have been built by 1,000 men working steadily 300 days a year for 4 years (Rappoport 1956: 92–7; 1969:43–7; Karger 1958:247–62).

Let us examine the question of the work force more closely. P. Toločko has estimated that the population of Kiev in about 1037 was, judging conservatively, 25,000–30,000 people. In addition, the ruler of Rus' would certainly have been able to require *corvée* from the inhabitants of the surrounding villages. It would seem that there could well have been 1,000 labourers working simultaneouly on the ramparts, and perhaps even more. Even if we decrease the number of work days to 250 per year and increase the amount of soil needed for construction by venty percent, the walls could still have been completed within five or six years. Moreover, it is likely that, when Jaroslav became the sole ruler of all Rus' after the death of Mstislav, he would have wanted to build the ramparts as quickly as possible, not only to protect those who had been living until then in the *suburbs*, but also to give the capital a new image associated with his reign.[57] Thus, it does not seem unreasonable to suppose that Jaroslav mobilized an army of 2,000 or even 3,000 labourers.

These estimates are confirmed by entries in the Rus'ian chronicles. We frequently read, for example, that earth and wood fortifications known as the *grad* or *gorod* were constructed in the course of one year. Although in the majority of cases we know little or nothing about the length and size of the ramparts, we do know quite a bit about several of them. In Perejaslavl' Zalesskij, for example, a wooden stockade three to four meters high was built during the course of several months in 1195. The ramparts themselves were 2.5 kilometers long and were ten to sixteen meters high.[58] In Suzdal' a similar type of wooden stockade atop an earthen wall three kilometers long was built during a similar period of time in 1192 (PSRL 1:409).[59] The oak fortifications of the Moscow Kremlin, about 1.5 kilometers long, were built in four months during the winter of 1339–40. Lastly, we know that the fortifications of Vladimir on the Kljazma, which consisted of a wooden stockade atop huge earthworks almost six kilometers in length, were rebuilt at tremendous speed – a total of two months – in 1492 after they had been destroyed by fire the previous year (PSRL 25:172, 332–3).[60]

These examples indicate that Jaroslav

could well have completed the fortifications of Kiev within a few years and then shifted the labourers to help in the construction of the churches, so that all could have been completed within the seventeen years allotted by the *Primary chronicle*. As we shall see below, Jaroslav's main foundations were actually completed within a considerably shorter span of time.

One must, nevertheless, address the question of why Jaroslav only began his massive building programme after 1036, and why he built nothing worthy of mention prior to that year. We know from the *Primary chronicle* (PSRL 1:140-9; Cross 1953:124–36) that Kiev changed hands several times during the period of civil strife between 1015 and 1019. Even after Jaroslav had emerged victorious and become the ruler of Kiev, he was in Novgorod for most of the time until 1026 (Tixomirov 1955:72; Il'in 1957:118–9).[61] Even after Jaroslav concluded a peace treaty with his brother Mstislav in 1026, after which "they . . . began to live in peace and fraternal love", we cannot determine from the laconic chronicle entries whether he really took up residence in Kiev and used it permanently as his capital. Some assert that Jaroslav did not feel secure in the middle Dnieper region and did not settle permanently in Kiev until after the death of Mstislav and his own tremendous victory over the Pechenegs in 1036. (Cross 1936:492; Lazarev 1960:9).[62]

Because there is almost no information in the chronicles on the period in question, the preceding hypothesis is based almost entirely on Jaroslav's close ties with Novgorod, a centre of strong political separatism, and on the events of 1024–1026, when Jaroslav "did not dare to return to Kiev" despite Mstislav's offers of peace. Only after he had marshalled a sizeable army in Novgorod did Jaroslav journey to Kiev to conclude a peace treaty with his brother (PSRL 1:149; Cross 1953: 135). It is possible that Jaroslav doubted the sincerity of this treaty and so would have maintained a strong army and would have been afraid to settle for good in Kiev.

There is, of course, some indication that Jaroslav was not always in the north between 1026 and 1036. We read (PSRL 1:149) that he fought and subdued the Čud tribe in the northwest and built a castle which he named Jur'ev (which later became the town known as Tartu or Dorpat) to secure his hold on the region.[63] However, we also know that between 1030 and 1032 Jaroslav and Mstislav undertook a joint campaign against the Poles, and that Jaroslav settled captives from this campaign in the frontier areas along the River Ros'. He also built a string of forts in the territory along the right bank of the Dniepr to protect the Kievan lands from inroads by the nomads. Lastly, it appears that when Mstislav died in 1036, Jaroslav was indeed in the south.

Nevertheless, it appears from the same chronicle account of 1036 that Jaroslav had personally ruled in Novgorod until that year. The *Primary chronicle* (PSRL 1:150) relates that, after securing Mstislav's lands, Jaroslav went to Novgorod to establish his eldest son Vladimir as prince and governor of the city.[64] This act was accompanied by the granting of privileges which were intended to secure the loyalty of the upper social strata of Novgorod towards the monarch (Šaxmatov 1908:513, 623; Zimin 1954:176–8; Čerepnin 1965:158–63). Taken together, these acts are incomprehensible unless we assume that Jaroslav made Kiev his permanent

residence and capital only from 1036 on

There is no doubt that Novgorod's mil tary and financial support aided Jaroslav o more than one occasion between 1015 an 1026, and that without Novgorod Jarosla would probably not have become the ruler o Rus'. Even after the two brothers signed peace treaty in 1026, Jaroslav would prob ably not have felt very secure in Kiev, whic is geographically very close to Mstislav capital of Černigov. Moreover, Jaroslav defeat at Listven in 1024 would hav remained in his memory and made hi suspicious of his brother. There is thus ever reason to believe that Jaroslav would no have handed over Novgorod to his son a this time since his power in the city seems t have been personal in nature, and he woul have been threatened without Novgorod support. We may conclude, therefore, tha Jaroslav ruled his domain between 1026 an 1036 by travelling throughout his vast realm and not by remaining in Novgorod, yet tha he only felt himself lord of the entire Dniepr and of Rus', and heir to the heritage o Vladimir, on the death of Mstislav.[65] Onl after 1036 did he decide to glorify his reig and his capital through the construction o monumental buildings in Kiev.

As has been noted before, this is a hypo thetical reconstruction of the situation be tween 1026 and 1036. Nevertheless, th hypothesis is supported by the few har facts at our disposal and by the genera historical background. Together, they con firm the year 1036 as the *terminus ante quem no* of the extension of Kiev's fortifications, development which ushered in a new perio in the urban and architectural history o Kiev.

In view of the fact that Jaroslav began h

tensive building programme after 1036, ere is no indication that it was a response to stislav's construction of the cathedral of e Savior (strictly speaking the cathedral of e Transfiguration of Christ) in Černigov. hen Mstislav died in 1036, this church was built as high as a man on horseback uld reach with his hand "(PSRL 1:149).[66] would not have taken too long to build the alls, which were somewhat over three eters high. Consequently, the cathedral as probably started in 1035, a year before stislav's death.[67]

The basic ground plan of the cathedral of e Savior was quite similar to that of the urch of the Tithe in Kiev.[68] Both were uciform-shaped, domed churches with ree aisles and a narthex. Stylistically, erefore, they were related to the churches Constantinople built in the tenth and eventh centuries (Cross 1949:15–16; Lazarev 1970a:196–8; Komeč 1975:25–6). stislav probably told the architects from onstantinople to model his new cathedral, e first church built of stone in Černigov, ter the church in which his father was uried. Proof that the founder's wish was ecisive in determining the architecture of e church is seen in the fact that the urches of St Sophia both in Kiev and ovgorod are typologically completely ifferent from the cathedral of Černigov, though all were built by the same masters.

Despite these fundamental differences, e cathedrals of Černigov, Kiev and Novorod do have certain similarities: wide side ambulatories, identical brick ornaentation, cruciform-shaped pillars, roundd and triangular projections, composite ilasters on the façades, drum-shaped structres (tambours) supporting the cupolas and

identical masonry of the 'recessed' technique. All these characteristics were typical of architecture in Constantinople in the eleventh century (see Lazarev 1970a:198–9; 1972:180–1; Karger 1961:157; Štender 1974:204; Schäfer 1974:198–9, 202, 210, 214, 218–9; Mango 1976:325, 328). Consequently, the widely held opinion that the same group of architects worked on all three churches appears to be well founded. At the very least, one can say that the architects of all three churches were trained in the same architectural school of the Byzantine capital.[69]

We can see that the architects were true masters from the way they varied traditional architectural styles to incorporate individual traits in each building. One specialist on the cathedrals of Kiev and Černigov has rightly observed that all the primary architectural traits of these churches are common to the architecture of Constantinople in the tenth and eleventh centuries (and earlier), so that the element of innovation resulted from altering these established norms to meet the requirements and desires of the specific time and place, including the wishes of the princely donor (Komeč 1972:50–64; 1975:9–24; compare Schäfer 1974:211–3; Mango 1976:325–6). It is apparent, therefore, that the cathedral of the Savior in Černigov was begun before St Sophia in Kiev, but it is not evident which of the two was completed first. We do not know, for example, if the building continued without interruption, despite the death of its founder, Mstislav.[70] However, we must take into account the fact that the interior construction, dimensions and arrangement of internal space were all fixed when the foundation was laid in 1035.

At the outset Mstislav wanted, as was noted above, his cathedral to resemble his father's church of the Tithe in Kiev. This was natural, since at that time the latter was the only stone church in Kiev. This, in turn, is another indication that St Sophia was begun after 1036: it is difficult to imagine that St Sophia was already completed, dominating the skyline of Kiev, and that Mstislav and his architects chose to ignore it and model the new cathedral of Černigov after an older church. On the contrary, the scope of the undertaking represented by St Sophia, the solutions to the complex problems of space, all appear to be the result of Jaroslav's desire to surpass the cathedral of Černigov then under construction (for dimensions, see Afanasjev 1961:52–61 and note 108 below). In short, there are no indications that Mstislav's church was begun after the stone St Sophia had been built and that it was a reply to the architectural challenge made by Jaroslav.

We have demonstrated above that the church mentioned in the chronicles under the year 1017 was the reconstructed wooden church of St Sophia, and that some of the arguments of those who believe that the stone St Sophia was built before 1036 have serious defects. But we still have to show that all other arguments in favour of the construction of the stone St Sophia prior to 1036 are groundless.

Among the evidence most often cited by those who claim that St Sophia was built before 1036 are the graffiti scratched into the stone walls of the cathedral. Indeed, these grafitti have been called "a very important and credible source which offers a solution to the lengthy controversies surrounding the date of construction" (Logvin 1977:174).

The grafitti should indeed provide chrono logical information of great significance since they were scratched into the plaste when it had already been painted wit frescoes. As a result, they should not only tel us the date of construction of the cathedral but when the decoration was completed. Le us examine whether or not the grafitti reall do provide fresh information for this debate

Graffito No. 99, which was found in th main aisle on the second cruciform-shape pillar from the altar, supposedly mentior the birth of Vsevolod, son of Jaroslav th Wise, mentioned in the *Primary chronicl* under the year 6538/1030.[71] Vysockij attrib utes this graffito to Vsevolod, son c Jaroslav, for the following reasons: 1) th extant portion of the name appears to b part of the name Vsevolod in the genitiv case . . . *voloda*; 2) the archaic paleograph and the use of the large *jus* in the inscriptio points to the eleventh century, when ther was only one Vsevolod, namely, the son o Jaroslav; 3) graffito No. 99 is located nea graffito No. 4, which concerns Vsevolod" death. Vysockij (1966b:104–5; 1976:9–11 250–1) assumes that the author of the las graffito wanted to record the death of hi favourite prince close to the note of his birth

There is no doubt that the paleography i archaic, but it is impossible to limit th inscription to the first half of the eleventl century, since the same forms of letters ar found throughout the twelfth century, eve in inscriptions in St Sophia. The large *ju* which is used twice in graffito No. 99, is als found in the graffito recording the death c Jaroslav the Wise in 1054, as well as in Nos 42 and 120 which Vysockij (1966a:89, tab XLI; 1976:42, 187–8, tabl. XXV XXVII)[72] dates to the twelfth century!

gure 2. St Sophia, Graffito No. 99: (a) photograph
d (b) photostat.

The large *jus* is sometimes used in the
onuments written during the Kievan
·riod to indicate the sound *u*, but it is much
ore frequently used in texts copied from
iginals written by south Slavs.[73] The
ppearance of the large *jus* in inscription No.
) only proves that the writer was familiar
ith old Slavonic ecclesiastical texts. Conse-
uently, the Vsevolod mentioned in graffito
o. 99, assuming that . . . *voloda* should be
·ad as the genitive of Vsevolod, could be any
rince of this name from the eleventh or
velfth centuries.[74]

Near graffito No. 99 is another which
ppposedly records the death of Prince
sevolod: it mentions the burial of the
Rus'ian prince Andrew" on Maundy
hursday, 14 April. Since Andrew was in

fact Vsevolod's Christian name and Maundy
Thursday did fall on 14 April in 1093, the
year of Vsevolod's death as given in the
Primary chronicle, we are tempted to agree
that the inscriptions refer to one and the same
person, as Vysockij (1966a:18–24; tabl. V,
VI) suggested. However, we must examine
graffito No. 99 completely by itself; if we do,
we discover several readings other than the
one given by Vysockij.

Graffito No. 99 consists of four lines. The
left side of the inscription has been damaged
and is illegible, while the right side is still
intact. Vysockij (1976:266–7, tabl. I-II)
concentrated on the second line, which he
interpreted as [*vse*] *voloda rodi*, that is,
". . . gave birth to Vsevolod". However,
rodi need not be taken as a third person
singular verb with a genitive/accusative
object. It could equally well be the nomin-
ative plural of the noun with a genitive,
meaning "the kinsmen of Vsevolod".[75] *Rodi*
could also be the first part of the reflexive
verb *rodisja*, assuming that *-sja* was carried
over to the third line and is now illegible. We
would then have: "[*u vse*] *voloda rodi* [*sja*]",
meaning "to Vsevolod was born". In other
words, the inscription could have recorded
the birth of Vsevolod's son, not Vsevolod's
birth. This reading is to be favoured for
stylistic reasons, since the reflexive construction is found much more frequently
than Vysockij's direct object construction.
The chronicles almost always use the reflexive construction with the father's name
"to Jaroslav was born a son"/*rodisja u
jaroslava syn* or *u vsevoloda rodisja syn* (see **PSRL**
1:146, 149, 160, 174, 280, 408, 410, 412, 441,
444, 470, 475, 477, 486).[76] Vysockij (1976:
11, 251) considered these grammatical alter-
natives but rejected them because their

acceptance "impairs the logical and semantic association between these two graffiti inscribed alongside one another, one recording the prince's birth, the other, his burial". There is, in other words, no scholarly reason for Vysockij's interpretation other than his desire that it be so. Consequently, we cannot accept Graffito No. 99 as a basis for dating the beginning of St Sophia.[77]

Vysockij (1966a:15–16, tabl. I–II) discovered two other inscriptions, Nos. 1 and 2, on the south pillar of the second, north, aisle in the chapel of St George, which he dates to 1031/1032 and 1042. Inscription No. 2 has letters used as numbers ЅФМІД which he interpreted as "in the year 6540, of the indiction 14."[78] This, he connected with another badly preserved graffito of which only the word *ho hagios* is legible (1972:283–6; 1976:198–201, Fig. 10). He concludes that the grafitti were made by a Greek master who signed his fresco with his patron saint's name, and the date of the fresco's completion.

Vysockij's argument raises a number of problems. The two inscriptions cannot be shown to be by the same hand, on the basis of their paleography. Furthermore, there are many graffiiti in St Sophia which are unrelated although they are found near one another. Nevertheless, let us assume that we really do have the date 6540, the fourteenth year of the indiction. If the inscription were really made by a Byzantine, it would be according to the September calendar, that is, 1 September 1031–31 August 1032, which would be the fifteenth year of the indiction, an error. Vysockij explains (1976:200–1) that the graffito was made according to the ultra-March system, 1 March 1031–28 Feb-

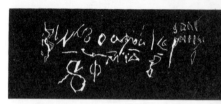

Figure 3. St Sophia, Graffito No. 2 with Greek in scription: (a) photograph and (b) photostat.

ruary 1032, the first half of which (until 31 August) would have been the fourteenth year of the indiction.

Unfortunately the use of the ultra-March system is not documented in Rus' until the second decade of the twelfth century (Berezkov 1963:28–36, 41–7).[79] Vysockij does not bother to discuss how a Greek artist should have learned of a calendar system unknown in Byzantium and not used in Rus' until, as far as we can tell, the twelfth century, nor why he should have used it. It is possible that this graffito recorded some bygone event as of the time of its writing, but it is too unreliable to be used as evidence for the construction and decoration of the cathedral about the year 1031. We are confronted with numbers completely out of context, an exercise in aritmetic, and are left to divine how and why the date was recorded in a peculiar calendar system, and why we should use the result to contradict all the evidence marshalled so far.

Vysockij devotes a great deal of attention

the previous graffito, No. 2, which is ppposedly from 1031/1032 and which he lls "particularly important for the subject der consideration". However, he devotes tle attention to graffito No. 1; apparently is supposed to be self-evident that this dates om the year 1042 (Vysoc'kyj 1975:178; 76:250–2; compare Logvin 1977:174).[80] et us examine this inscription more closely. ysockij, without lengthy argumentation, ads it as въ ͞лто N ͞SФлое, in other words n the year 50 and 6500" ЛОЕ is taken, erefore, to be the accusative neuter suffix the ordinal number 500, пятисотлое. t least Vysockij recognizes that it is tremely peculiar to find the number ritten in this manner. Normally one would pect "6500 and 50". The only parallel ysockij can find is a colophon in a fifteenth-ntury Bible (Vysoc'kyj 1966:104). There, owever, the irregularity is not so surprising: n the first year after 7000", emphasizing, course, the year after the turn of the illenium.

Graffito No. 1 deserves a much more norough paleographic study. Firstly the tter H is not N (= 50) at all but И (Latin I). he horizontal stroke in the letter H was the roper way of writing И (= 8) in the leventh-thirteenth centuries: the diagonal ppeared only later. Vysockij foresaw this rgument and conceded (Vysoc'kyj 1966b: 04, note 2) that it should actually be И (8) ut then ЛОЕ would no longer be a com-lete adjectival ending but Л used as the umber 30 plus the ending OE, producing 538/1030.

Although the ending -OE or -HOE contrary to the unusual лое) for ordinals is noroughly acceptable, even this interpre-ation is unreliable, since it is hard to accept

Figure 4. St Sophia, Graffito No. 1.

the reading Л. It is much more likely that this is, in fact, the letter П poorly written. П written with sloping lines and a longish "roof", is found frequently in other in-scriptions in St Sophia, whereas Л is found elsewhere in grafitto No. 1 without a hori-zontal stroke above it.[81] It is strange that Vysockij did not include this Л from graffito No. 1 in his review of the paleography of Л in the eleventh-thirteenth centuries, since the graffiti of St Sophia very seldom contain examples of the letter Л written like the letter П.[82]

Consequently, we could choose to read this inscription as въ лето ͞И ͞SФПое, that is, "in the year 8 and 6580". Even here the problem of inversion arises, since the date begins with the smallest number, 8. The best solution is that the letter И is not a number at all but the conjunction "and", and means "that is" or "namely", or is used to avoid the repetition of the preposition "въ" meaning "in". The graffito could be read "In the year, that is, 6580". In either case the in-scription refers to 1072 or 1080, much too late to provide information on the construc-tion of the cathedral.

In contrast to graffiti Nos. 1, 2, and 99 which are illegible and refer to indeterminate events, we should point to inscriptions Nos. 3

37

Figure 5. St Sophia, Graffito No. 3 dated 3 March 1052.

and 8, engraved on the fresco of St Panteleon on the third pillar from the apse of the main aisle on the south side. No. 3 mentions a storm (Vysockij 1966a: 16–18, tabl. III), and is a model of chronological precision: "In the year 6560 (1052) on 3 March, it thundered at 9.00 in the daytime, and on that [day] was the feast of St Eutropius".[83] No. 8 is the much discussed inscription concerning the death of Jaroslav the Wise on 20 March 6562 (1054) (Vysockij 1966a: 39–41, table IX; Rybakov 1964: 13–16, nos. 1, 2). These inscriptions give us substantial proof that at least the main aisle of the cathedral was built and decorated by 1052.

4. The stone cathedral church of St Sophia: period of construction

The graffiti dated 3 March 1052 and 20 February 1054 are reliable proofs of the date by which the interior decoration of St Sophia was completed. Other information permits us to date the time of construction even more precisely.

In 6559 (1051) the presbyter Ilarion w chosen, consecrated and enthroned as metr politan of Kiev in St Sophia (Müller 196! 143: PSRL 1:155–6; 2:143–4). In h *Sermon on law and grace*, Ilarion, who had n yet become metropolitan, described th foundation of Jaroslav the Wise in th following terms: "... he who has built great House of God's Holy Wisdom for th holiness and enlightenment of thy [Vlad mir's] city and adorned it with every beaut with gold and silver and splendid stones ar sacred vessels. The church is wondrous ar glorious to those in countries round abou and another like it will not be found in all th land of the north from east to west" (Müll 1962: 122–3).[84] From this we may conclud that, at the time Ilarion delivered th eulogy at the tomb of Vladimir in the churc of the Tithe, the cathedral of St Sophia wa already completed and decorated with slat marble, mosaics and frescoes. It also appea from this speech that at that time th Kievan landmark had already becom famous far and wide.[85] We should also no that Ilarion limits his comparison of S Sophia to the churches of northern Europ which attests to Ilarion's sober realism ar adequate knowledge of the Byzantine- Eur pean world.[86]

Clearly, we may establish a *terminus an quem* for the construction of St Sophia b means of the date of composition of Ilarion *Sermon on law and grace*: as a result of indepen dent research by several scholars over th last few years, we have considerable eviden pointing to 1049–1050. The most convincin argument in favour of this date is the fact tha Jaroslav's princess, Irina/Ingigerd, is ad dressed directly in the eulogy. Irina died o 10 February 1051. On the other hand, th

dress also mentions the grandchildren of
oslav and Irina as present. Unfortun-
ly, it is not known exactly which grand-
ldren were present and how old they were,
t they must have been at least two or three
rs old to be present at a ceremony in a
urch. They were undoubtedly the children
Jaroslav's eldest sons, Vladimir and
aslav, who were married in 1043 and 1044
ozov 1963:147–8; Poppe 1968c:56–7;
loviev 1979:3 59–60).[87]
Although the *Sermon on law and grace* was
parently written and read in 1049 or 1050
does not necessarily follow that the
hedral was completed at this time since
Sermon says that St Sophia was already
nous in other countries. This statement is
bably not just a figure of speech: the
hedral was undoubtedly seen in 1048 or
9 by the French envoys who had come to
v to take Jaroslav's daughter to wed their
g.[88]
There is yet another piece of evidence
ich indicates that at least the masonry, if
the interior decoration, of St Sophia was
npleted by 1045: in that year, a new
hedral church of the same name was
gun in Novgorod which incorporated all
basic architectural traits found in the
evan cathedral (Afanasjev 1961:38, 41,
6, 215–35; Lazarev 1970a:201–2). All
scholars who have considered the two
urches agree that a single group of masters
rked on both structures using the same
hitectural style, technical solutions and
sonry and brick decorations. More recent
earch (Stender 1974:206–11; 1977:37;
meč 1976:147–50) has confirmed the
se link between the two churches of St
phia even more emphatically, not only in
ms of the floor plan and structure but also

in a number of technical aspects and decoration.

V. N. Lazarev (1960:55–7; 1971:238)
was among those to assert that the nucleus of
St Sophia of Kiev was completed by 1046,
although not all his arguments are still
acceptable. One reason for accepting this
date is, in Lazarev's opinion, the fact that
11 May, the day on which St Sophia of Kiev
was consecrated, fell on a Sunday in 1046.
But the assumption made by this great art
historian that churches were consecrated
only on Sundays is neither supported by
canon law nor by ancient Rus'ian practice
(Poppe 1968b:93). On the other hand, his
assumption that the cathedral was consecrated on 11 May is very likely correct. That
date may have been chosen to coincide with
Byzantine practice, according to which 11
May was celebrated in St Sophia in Constantinople as the day of the foundation of the
city (Janin 1953:484). The date is found in
several old Rus'ian liturgical calendars. But
the fact that the metropolitan and prince of
Kiev chose 11 May reflects more than just
the desire to imitate Byzantine customs. The
construction of St Sophia of Kiev was only a
part of a monumental building programme
which included new city walls; the latter
enlarged the fortified area of Kiev by almost
ten times, amounting to a virtual refounding
of the city of Kiev. Ultimately, of course
Kiev was following the example set by the
capital of the Empire.[89] Although there is no
proof that St Sophia of Kiev was consecrated
exactly in 1046, this could not have occurred
much before or after that time.

Lazarev also erred when he said that St
Sophia was completed by 1046 because the
fresco of Jaroslav and his family depicts the
daughters of Jaroslav, who became the

queens of Norway, Hungary and France shortly afterwards, without crowns. This is a fallacious argument, since the crowns worn by Jaroslav and Irina are a later addition. On the other hand, Lazarev's observation (1960:56–7; 1970b:37–48; 1971:236) concerning the age of the children depicted in the fresco of the founder and his family is extremely valuable, although we must reject his attempt to identify the children with specific members of Jaroslav's family (Poppe 1968d:1–29).

There is no need to discuss in this study the original composition of this important fresco and the number of offspring portrayed in (for the state of research, see Kämpfer 197 111–6). It is sufficient to note that, on basis of the extant portion of the fresco a the sketch of it made by A. Westerfeld in mid-seventeenth century, it depicted eig male and female figures, the children Jaroslav; the youngest were about eight ten years old and the oldest about twenty As far as the age of the three daught mentioned previously is concerned, we kn only that they were given in marria between 1043 and 1049. On the other hand we know the precise dates of five of Jaroslav

Figure 6. The founder, Prince Jaroslav, with his family. A. von Westerfeld's 1651 drawing of a fresco in St Sop

ns: Vladimir, the eldest, was born in 1020;
e fifth, Vjačeslav, was born in 1036; Igor',
e sixth and youngest, was born not long
ter Vjačeslav (PSRL 1:146, 149, 150,
1–2; 2:133, 136,–7, 151: Cross 1953:
4–6, 142–3). Consequently, it would seem
asonable to postulate that the fresco was
inted about 1045 when the interior
coration of St Sophia was completed. The
act date may vary by two or three years
ound 1045, but given the ages of the
ildren portrayed, the fresco could not have
en painted in the 1030s. Those who favour
ch an early date (even 1030 or 1031) do not
ke the ages of the children into account.[91]
We conclude, therefore, that the construc-
n of the cathedral continued between 1043
d 1046, a period of tension involving a
eak in the relations between Byzantium
d Rus'. Peace was restored with the treaty
1046 (Poppe 1971b:262–8). Neverthe-
ss, this period of hostility apparently did
t slow or stop the construction and decora-
n of the Kievan cathedral. It appears,
erefore, that not only were the Greek
chitects and artists already in Kiev but

gure 7. The uncovered fragment of a fresco of
roslav' family depicting his two youngest sons, St
phia.

that all the materials necessary for the
decoration of the cathedral – including
marble for the cornices, columns, capitals,
slabs, thresholds and altar rails from the
islands of the Sea of Marmora and the smalt,
dyes and other materials for the mosaics and
frescoes – were delivered by the end of the
sailing season of 1042, since the Rus'ian
attack on Constantinople in July 1043 cut
off sea traffic between Kiev and the Byzantine capital. All this indicates very strongly
that the construction of St Sophia was
nearing completion at the time of the last
Rus'ian attack on Constantinople.

This is not to say, however, that absolutely
all the building materials were delivered by
1043. Although the amount of marble used
in St Sophia is by no means insignificant, it
was noted long ago that there was less of it
than in the church of the Tithe or the
cathedral of the Savior in Černigov (Ajnalov
1905:5–11; Cross 1949:12, 15–16).[92] The
decoration of St Sophia consists, to a
significant degree, of cut schist sheets from
local quarries. The use of schist from pyro-
phylite shale for architectural details may
have been planned from the beginning, of
course, but a lack of marble would certainly
have influenced the extent of its use.

For a long time, specialists have noticed
one aspect which distinguishes St Sophia and
other churches of Kievan Rus' from churches
in Byzantium proper. The interiors of
Byzantine churches were usually decorated
with mosaics in the upper registers, and
faced with marble in the lower zones (Demus
1947:61ff.; Lazarev 1960:63).[93] The walls
of St Sophia are covered with frescoes
down to the floor, and display a general ab-
undance of ornamentation. However, in the
twelfth century there were Byzantine

41

'churches in which the walls below the cornice were not revetted but decorated with fresco.[94] Therefore, one could say that St Sophia in Kiev is the oldest known example demonstrating the prevalence of fresco decoration. This style, which was found un-Byzantine in nature, might have resulted from the need to use imported marble and mosaic, which were much more expensive than fresco, sparingly. The departure from the norm might also have been made for consideration of time – in the case of Kievan St Sophia because of a disruption of deliveries.[95] In connection with this, we should examine the limits of the monumental mosaic picture which extends to the conche and walls of the apse, the vault and walls of the altar arch, the concave portion of the main cupola, piers of the drum, pendentives and the arches of the central square (the four bows supporting the drum of the cupola). The positioning of the mosaic is not accidental: it marks out the nucleus of the church, in which the liturgy takes place, from the rest of the structure.

It is known that finished sheets of smalt mosaic were sent to Kiev from Byzantium in the second half of the eleventh century. Furthermore, archaeological excavations have uncovered workshops in Kiev in which smalt for mosaics was produced; these too have been dated to the end of the eleventh century. Apparently, the quality of the products of these local ateliers left something to be desired: part of the mosaic of the katholikon of the monastery of the Caves separated as it aged, and lost its appearance and texture.[96]

Chemical, spectrographic and petrographic analyses of the mosaic smalt in St Sophia permit us to divide the mosaics into two categories: 1) alkaline-lime-silica, and 2) lead-silica. On the basis of these findings, t conclusion has been reached that the sm was made in Kiev and that local mast participated in its production (Levitsk 1963:146–9, 155–6). However, the existen of two types of smalt can be better explain if we assume that the production of lea silica smalt required imported lead and t and that these would already have be refined before being added to the char The lead-silica smalt was probably import in finished sheets, whereas the technolo cally simpler alkaline-lime-silica smalt w produced in Kiev by Greek specialis Whether the masters used two types of sm to produce different optical effects, whether they were forced to switch to t simpler, locally produced variety becau shipments were interrupted cannot now ascertained.

The production of smalt for mosa required considerable skill and experien The technology was enshrined in u changing traditions passed down from gen ation to generation in particular centres production. The mosaics of St Sophia made with a palette of 177 shades of colour the colour green alone has thirty-four shac (Levitskaja 1963:105–63; Lazarev 196 138–42). Thus, the smalt produced in Ki could have been made only by masters p sessing great experience from one of t main centers of production in Byzantiu Local artisans could have worked only assistants in the production, not just becau of the complexity of the process, but becau they could not have had any experience Kievan Rus' prior to that time, since alm forty years had elapsed since the constructi of the stone church of the Tithe.[97] T monumental projects commissioned by Ja av required the labour of local craftsmen ı auxiliary roles, gradually producing ıdres of Rus'ian masters. To learn the fine rt of making mosaic smalt would have ːquired not only a long apprenticeship but ɔnditions under which the Byzantine artists ˈould have been willing to reveal the secrets f production.[98]

In the light of the remarks made above, it possible that the conflict between Byzanıum and Rus' in 1043, despite the disruption f communications, did not produce signifiınt difficulties in the construction of Jaroav's foundation. However, the conflict ıight have caused certain changes in the riginal plan of the cathedral, especially as ır as the decoration was concerned. We can ˈell imagine that the builders found themˈlves running low on the imported materials ːcessary for decorating the cathedral. The ːmporary impossibility of obtaining more ıpplies could have resulted in certain hanges which have long been regarded as ˈon-Byzantine stylistic traits. Such imˈrovised solutions made under pressure in ıe midst of construction could only have een made by very experienced masters.

We have seen that the dating of the conːruction of St Sophia is complicated enough, ut is made even more complex by the ːdditional problem of the original form of ˈe cathedral: was the entire mass, which as survived up until our time, built all at nce or did the building continue for several ˌecades? Over ten years ago the author ˈPoppe 1968d:2ff.; 1972:28–31) defended ˈe first view at a time when it was believed ˈhat St Sophia was built in stages.[99] Accordˌng to the latter theory, the cathedral was ˌlanned and built as a five-nave, crossˌupola structure with an open, single-story ambulatory. Twenty or thirty years later, a second level was added to the inner ambulatories and then, in order to prevent damage to the structural support of the church, external arcaded ambulatories and a system of flying buttresses were built. The southern tower was built to provide access to the galleries; the northern tower, however, was built only at the end of the eleventh or beginning of the twelfth century (Cross 1936:494ff.; Karger 1961:140–75; Lazarev 1970a:199–200).[100]

This theory of construction in instalments is very weak in a number of ways, and has produced a good deal of confusion. It has also given rise to a good deal of criticism and clever, but ultimately unconvincing, defences. The supporters of the 'instalment' theory were unable to explain satisfactorily, for example, how the faithful entered the galleries before the south tower was built. They also resorted to extremely artificial and arcane interpretations concerning the ambulatories and tower which belonged to the original structure of the cathedral of St Sophia in Novgorod. The outside ambulatories of the two churches are similar, but the intrusion of chronology led to the conclusion that "the Novgorodians shared their experience with the Kievans who, at an earlier stage, had been the source of knowledge" (Lazarev 1968:13).[101]

Studies over the past few years involving the architecture, archaeology, art-history and even chemistry of St Sophia have produced convincing evidence that the metropolitan cathedral was planned and built from the very beginning with two-story internal ambulatories, a one-story outside ambulatory and two towers with staircases (Logvin 1974:154–60; 1977:178–80). The dimensions of the plastered walls, their surface, which was painted at one time, the nature of their seams, the direction in which the plaster overlaps, show that the outside ambulatories were not only painted at the same time as the inside ambulatories, but at the same time as the core of the five-nave church (Toc'ka 1975:182–94; Toc'ka and Jerko 1976:119–30). Moreover, a chemical analysis of the plaster solutions used in construction and in the frescoes (primer and ground) throughout the entire church – the inside and outside ambulatories the two towers, the side and central nave of the choir – shows that the mixtures were identical in composition and in the presence of albuminous additions of animal and vegetable material. The plaster used as a ground for the frescoes was made with a crushed, glassy material as an additive, apparently the slag or waste from the production of smalt (Strilenko 1975:195–201).

These observations provide the basis for a reconsideration of the date at which the outside ambulatories were painted. The conclusion confirms the view of André Grabar (1918:98–106) and V. K. Mjasoedov (1918:1–6) expressed over sixty years ago. Basing their opinion on the style, manner, and technique of the painting in the south and north outside ambulatories, these two scholars stated that the inside and outside ambulatories and the core of the cathedral were painted at the same time.[102] Grabar also (1935:103–17) attributed the famous frescoes of a secular nature in the stairwells of both towers to the same period.[103]

Moreover, an examination of the masonry technique, of the colour and composition of the lime compounds, and of the dimensions of the plinths from which the main five-nave

structure and the ambulatories and tow‹ were constructed, indicates that all parts the cathedral were constructed simi taneously. The identical structure of bo towers, the fact that the four spirals of sta‹ (two in each tower) have identical positio within the geometry of the towers and th the arches of the stairs all have ninete‹ segments, points to the craftsmanship of single master. The fact that the two towe‹ are asymmetrically set against each other the result of their entrances being in d‹ ferent places: the northern tower was us‹ only to ascend to the second story from insi‹ the church.

The absence of windows in the walls of t‹ choir of the five-nave church would ‹ incomprehensible if the ambulatories we‹ originally only one story high, as som suppose. Moreover, the absence of plaster c the joints of the walls of the tower an‹ ambulatories also indicates that the enti‹ church was built and plastered at one tim We also see this in the fact that there are n‹ signs of weathering or accumulation of di‹ and fungi on the masonry and brickwor‹ which would have occurred if they had bee‹ exposed to the open air. Similarly, the lack ‹ bonds between the towers and galleries ‹ proof of a coherent construction plan whic‹ took into account the tendency of structur‹ of different heights to settle unequall (Logvin 1974:154–8; 1977:176, 178, 180).[1‹

These studies conducted on St Sophi‹ open the way to more detailed analyse‹ Nevertheless, they provide enough har‹ information for us to conclude that th‹ strongest arguments favour the thesis tha‹ the entire structure of St Sophia was built a‹ one time.

How long could it have taken to build th‹

thedral, consisting of a five-nave church, a o-story ambulatory, a external single-ried ambulatory and two towers – 23,290 bic meters in all – and decorated according a particular plan? V. N. Lazarev (1960:) calculated that it took seven or eight ars, but this estimate was linked with the pothesis that the church was built in ges. G. Logvin (1974:159–60; 1977:178) s on firmer ground when he suggested a ilding time of nine or ten years, allowing e seasons for building the church, one or o for finishing the details and allowing the ucture to settle and dry and for preparing e surfaces for decoration, and three seasons r the frescoes and mosaics.[105]

This estimate is reasonable in view of the rely historical calculations made earlier, at the construction was begun after Mstis-v's death and finished about 1046. Never-eless, the only convincing way of verifying is estimate is by comparing it with the cts known about similar churches built in ievan Rus' at roughly the same time, and nder roughly similar conditions.

One such church is the katholikon of the onastery of the Caves in Kiev. It was built four years but only three building seasons, nce it was founded on 15 August 1073, hen the building season was already rawing to a close, and finished on 11 July 076.[106] It was decorated under Abbot ikon in the 1080s and consecrated for the cond time on 14 August 1089 (PSRL :207).[107] Consequently, the main church of he monastery of the Caves in Kiev, of oughly the same size as the church of the ransfiguration in Černigov, was built with-ut decoration in three to four years.[108]

The stone cathedral of St Sophia in Novgorod, which has been mentioned sever-

al times so far, is roughly the same size at St Sophia in Kiev without the external ambu-latories. It was founded in 1045, probably on 21 May, and completed and consecrated on 14 September, 1050 (Nasonov 1950:181). Therefore, the construction lasted six build-ing seasons, seasons which were shorter than those in Kiev, further to the south. [109] It is unclear how long it took to complete the decoration of St Sophia of Novgorod: according to current scholarly opinion, it was decorated at the beginning of the twelfth century. V. N. Lazarev (1968:20, 55–8) believes that St Sophia of Novgorod was not completely painted with frescoes in the eleventh century, but admits that certain frescoes of an "icon type", such as that of Constantine and Helen, may have adorned the church by this time. Moreover, he notes that the frescoes in the drum supporting the dome are closer to Byzantine art of the eleventh century than of the twelfth, but explains this as the result of the persistence of "archaic tendencies" in this local school of artists working in the early twelfth century.

However, according to Brjusova (1968: 103–14), the oldest mural painting, which dates from about 1050, was originally not as small as it is at present. At the beginning, it covered a portion of the central area of the church and the vestibules with ornamental-decorative motifs, despite the presence of a few frescoes of an "icon type". According to this view, the central dome and drum supporting it were also painted at this time.[110]

This theory is much more convincing since, if there were frescoes in the vestibules (that of Constantine and Helen is in the south gallery), one would also expect to find them in the central portion of the church, that is, the nave and the concave surface under the main dome, where the liturgy was performed. However, it is extremely hard to judge what the original frescoes of St Sophia of Novgorod were like, since this church was repainted more than once during the course of several centuries.

It is interesting to note that the picture of Constantine and Helen is not a fresco in the normal sense but a 'fresco-secco', that is, a painting on a thin lime ground spread on dried plaster (Brjusova 1968:104–5; Lazarev 1968:20–2). It would be interesting to know why this method was used; it required speed of execution and a firm hand, accustomed to and unerring in the drawing of figures (Dmitriev 1954:271–6). Perhaps the artists were simply making use of Novgorod's humid climate; perhaps they were just in a rush, since the decoration can be completed more quickly with this technique.

Although a number of problems concerning the mural painting of St Sophia of Novgorod remain unanswered, it seems clear that it was more modest in scope than that of its Kievan counterpart, and that there was no single, harmonious plan for all of the paintings. There are other signs of this difference: the altar rail in St Sophia in Kiev is made of marble; in Novgorod it is made of wood. Furthermore, parts of the architectural decoration on the inside of the cathedral of Novgorod – the synthronus with mosaic slabs, fragments of wall mosaics and slate with mosaic incrustations used on the floor – which were long considered part of the original church, have recently been dated to the middle of the twelfth century (Štender 1968:83–107).[111]

According to Štender (1968:104–6), the original mid-eleventh century interior of St Sophia of Novgorod had, when compared its subsequent decoration, "an unusual simple and severe appearance. The co⟨n⟩tinuous tapestry of frescoes, the floors mosaics, were lacking".[112] Although th⟨e⟩ description is perhaps too extreme, there ⟨is⟩ no doubt that the interior architecture an⟨d⟩ decoration were considerably more mode⟨st⟩ and economical when compared with th⟨e⟩ Kievan foundations of Jaroslav (Cross 194⟨9:⟩ 30–2; Vagner 1964:8–9). This thrift on th⟨e⟩ part of a prince who generously spent hug⟨e⟩ sums on church construction, was probabl⟨y⟩ the result of a desire to concentrate th⟨e⟩ resources available on the Kievan churche⟨s.⟩ By 1054 the churches of St George and S⟨t⟩ Irene were built; judging from their archaeo⟨-⟩ logical remains both were of considerabl⟨e⟩ size and richly decorated (Karger 196⟨1:⟩ 216–26, 232–7).

It appears that either the church of S⟨t⟩ George or St Irene was begun by 1049/105⟨0⟩ by the architects and builders who had jus⟨t⟩ completed St Sophia in Novgorod. Perhap⟨s⟩ the seventy-year-old Jaroslav decided t⟨o⟩ limit the decoration of the Novgorodia⟨n⟩ cathedral to a minimum in order to procee⟨d⟩ as quickly as possible with the decoration ⟨of⟩ the churches dedicated to his patron sain⟨t⟩ and the patron saint of his wife.

If the foregoing theory be true, it woul⟨d⟩ indicate that the Kievan monarch had only ⟨a⟩ limited number of masters and artists at hi⟨s⟩ disposal, men who could work rapidly an⟨d⟩ well, moving from one church of Kiev t⟨o⟩ another, but who were too few in number t⟨o⟩ work in Kiev and another city simul⟨-⟩ taneously. If we recall that St Sophia o⟨f⟩ Novgorod was built in four or five years, an⟨d⟩ that only one season was probably devote⟨d⟩ to the interior decoration, we can wel⟨l⟩

imagine that the adornment would have been modest or even minimal.

Unlike the cathedral of St Sophia in Novgorod, the decoration of the church of St Michael of the Golden Dome was almost as sumptuous as St Sophia of Kiev, although St Michael is rather smaller than the core of the metropolitan cathedral.[113] St Michael was founded by Prince Svjatopolk II of Kiev for the glory of his guardian angel on 11 July 1108. The church was already completed when Svjatopolk died on 16 April 1113. In all likelihood, it was finished in the previous season, in time to be dedicated on 8 November 1112, the feast of the Archangel Michael (PSRL 1:283: 2:259, 275; Lazarev 1966: 25–31; Rappoport 1974:46).

Consequently, five building seasons were sufficient to build this church with three naves, one domed cupola and towers, similar in dimensions to the church of the Dormition in the Caves monastery, and to decorate it with frescoes and mosaics. There were, however, fewer mosaics in St Michael than in St Sophia: they were limited to the altar area and probably covered the surfaces beneath the cupola and the arches of the central square. Otherwise, the walls were decorated with frescoes; the altar rail was of marble and the floor of red schist sheets encrusted with mosaics (Ajnalov 1926: 201–16; Cross 1947:55–61; 1949:18–20; Lazarev 1966:31–7).

The information on the construction of the three churches mentioned above – the church of the Dormition in the Caves monastery, St Sophia in Novgorod and St Michael of the Golden Dome – permits us to conclude that St Sophia of Kiev could have been built and fully decorated within seven to ten years. We assume, of course, that a

not great but sufficient number of very experienced master architects and artists from Constantinople were present in Kiev and that they were aided by as many local labourers as was necessary. St Sophia of Kiev was the largest and grandest church of ancient Rus' and it is clear that Jaroslav, having become the sole monarch in 1036, was able to direct a considerable portion of his resources towards its completion.

Let us review the events leading up to the construction of the most magnificent cathedral in the Eastern European plain.

The events of 1036 were of great importance for subsequent developments. Jaroslav, having become the sole ruler of all of Rus' in the summer of 1036, inflicted a crushing defeat on the Pechenegs in the late fall of that year, thereby freeing the lands of southern Rus' from the menace of the steppes for many years. Kiev again became the undisputed center of Rus', and Jaroslav decide to give his city the appearance worthy of the capital of his realm. It was decided to build a large, new city which would include within its walls a significant portion of the populated territory hitherto undefended.

The oak logs needed for the walls were probably cut and prepared during the winter of 1036–1037 and floated down the Dniepr to Kiev after the high waters of spring 1037. In the spring, workmen from Kiev and the surrounding regions began work on the massive earthworks; within two or three years – or at the very most four – they had completed fortifications 3.5 kilometers in length consisting of a ditch, a rampart of earth and wood topped with a solid wall of logs.

Another facet of this grandiose plan began

to take shape at the same time as the ramparts were being built. The foundation of the new, stone cathedral may have been laid as early as 1037, although the actual construction could only have begun in 1038, since building materials had to be obtained and prepared at the building site.[114] It is less likely that the cathedral was begun as late as 1039. Master builders and artisans were transferred from the site of the cathedral of Černigov to work on St Sophia only when they had finished their former task; Jaroslav could have requested more specialists from Constantinople, but they could not have reached Kiev before the late summer or fall of 1037. There are insufficient grounds for assuming that the death of Mstislav would have halted the construction of the cathedral of the Savior in Černigov. Jaroslav, having just seized power, would not have risked tension with the bishop and élite of Černigov by withdrawing the architects.

In view of the previous calculations of the tempo of construction, we may justifiably suppose that the construction of the cathedral church of Černigov which was begun in 1035 continued into 1036 and 1037 when the masonry was finished. By the fall of 1037 or in 1038 at the latest the architects would have been transferred to Kiev. Only the artists involved in the interior decoration of the church remained in Černigov. Even if more architects and artists arrived in Kiev from Byzantium at this time, they would have been of the same architectural school of Constantinople as those who had been working in Černigov and would have only been used to increase the number of specialists.

Thanks to the concentration of manpower and resources, St Sophia was built rapidly.

The entire core, that is the five-naved central structure, the cupolas, two-level inside ambulatories, and one-level outside ambulatories, was completed in four building seasons (compare Logvin 1974:160), 1038–41. The vaults of the outside ambulatory and some secondary masonry could have been completed in the fifth building season, 1042, when the architects had already been transferred to the main gates of the new ramparts, later known as the 'Golden Gate', and the church of the Annunciation built atop them.

At this time, artists would have spent two or three seasons preparing the interior decoration of the cathedral, dressing the marble and schist details, making the schist and mosaic floor slabs and so on, while the structure settled and dried. The necessary materials were either brought from distant Byzantium or from local quarries. By 1042 all the artists and artisans needed for the interior decoration of the new cathedral were ready to start: some had come from Černigov after completing the decoration of that cathedral, while others had come from Constantinople.

The two towers were apparently built as soon as the nucleus of the cathedral was completed, that is, 1042–1044, since, judging by the seams between them and the pillars and flying buttresses of the ambulatories, the ambulatories were built before the towers, but both were plastered at the same time. In 1044 or 1045 all of the work on St Sophia and the Golden Gate with the church of the Annunciation above it was completed, and the team of builders was sent to Novgorod to build the second stone St Sophia in Rus'.

In 1043 or 1044 the cathedral of Kiev was

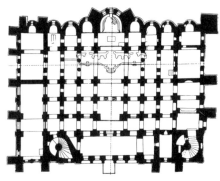

Figure 8. St Sophia, present ground plan.

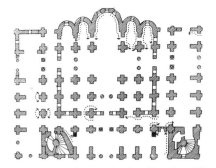

Figure 9. St Sophia, ground plan. The dotted lines with arrows indicate the direction in which the walls were plastered for fresco.

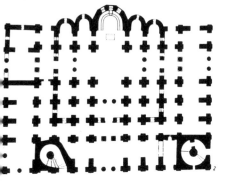

Figure 10. St Sophia, reconstructed ground plan.

plastered and work began on the frescoes and mosaics. Evidence of the speed of the work is seen in the fact that the main and four side aisles were painted at the same time: this can be seen from the overlaps of the plaster in the embrasures separating them (Logvin 1974: 154–6). This tempo permits us to say that all of the frescoes and mosaics of St Sophia were finished in three seasons, 1044–1046. Given the climate of the region, work on the interior decoration would have been carried out from the early spring to the late fall – and perhaps even in the winter when the temperature was a few degrees above freezing.

The towers were painted last of all, in late 1046 or 1047. The stairways leading to the choir of the cathedral itself were decorated with secular scenes from the life at the Byzantine imperial court (Grabar 1935: 103–117; 1936:51, 71–4). Their profane subject matter distinguishes them from the rest of the mural paintings in the church (see Logvin 1971: Plates 249–260; Lazarev 1973: ills. 107–121). It is clear that these motifs of life at the imperial court would have been totally familiar to the artists working in St Sophia, but the decision to use them on the staircases of the towers must have been a decision of the princely founder.

The fact that Jaroslav agreed to motifs depicting the entertainment of the court in Constantinople reminds us that these frescoes must have been painted no earlier than the summer of 1046, when peaceful relations had already been established between Kiev and the Byzantine Empire (Poppe 1971b: 262ff.; Každan 1977:65–77, 327f.). It is most likely that the towers were decorated in the late summer or autumn of 1046, but no later than 1047. St Sophia was consecrated, in all likelihood, on 11 May 1046, when the decoration of the towers was not yet completed, or on the same day in 1047, and became the new cathedral of the metropolitans of Rus'.

The church of the Annunciation atop the Golden Gate, and in all likelihood the prince's new residence, were also decorated with frescoes between 1046 and 1048.[115] At the very end of the decade, the team of architects and builders returned from Novgorod and began constructing in turn the churches of St George and of St Irene, founded by Jaroslav and his wife for their patron saints. It appears that the decoration of one of them was begun in 1050 or 1051; in any event, both were decorated and consecrated before Jaroslav's death in 1054.

The extensive stone church construction in Kiev begun by Jaroslav and continued by his sons and grandsons required the assistance of a significant amount of local manpower and caused the formation of cadres of native Rus'ian masons and artists in the capital of Rus' (Compare Mango 1976:328ff.) This continuity permits us to say that, although St Sophia was built by foreigners, it marks the beginning of stone Rus'ian architecutre. In this sense the stone cathedral of Kiev is fundamentally different from the *capella regia*, the stone church of the Tithe.

The stone church of the Tithe and adjoining stone palace were built in the 990s by Byzantine masters from Constantinople who had followed Anna Porphyrogenita to Kiev.[116] By nature this remained an isolated, unique monument for decades, artificially set down upon Kievan landscape from without. The forty-year hiatus between the building of the church of the Tithe and the stone St Sophia proves that stone construction did not immediately take root in the

Figure 11. West view of St Sophia as reconstructed by K. J. Conant.

Figure 12. East view of St Sophia as reconstructed by K. J. Conant.

newly-converted land.

On the other hand, the range of wooden church construction was very wide, if we are to judge by Thietmar who, at the beginning of the eleventh century, attested the existence of hundreds of wooden churches in Kiev; these were apparently, for the most part, chapels built by the élite who demonstrated their conversion to Christianity in this manner. But the enigmatic thirteen-domed wooden cathedrals of St Sophia in Kiev and Novgorod were undoubtedly both in plan and in form complex structures.[117]

The early history of Novgorod's stone architecture was similar to that of Kiev: the cathedral of St Sophia of Novgorod, built in stone by foreign masters, remained a unique monument in the city throughout the entire eleventh century. The next stone churches appear in Novgorod only in the first decades of the twelfth century. They were built by masters from Kiev who also followed the model of St Sophia of Novgorod (Komeč 1978:45–62).

The same may be said of stone architecture in other areas of Rus': it came into being gradually throughout the twelfth century, under the influence of Kievan architecture. The latter transcended the confines of the capital to fill specific orders (Vyšgorod, Perejaslavl', Černigov), but, on the whole, developed in isolation throughout the second half of the eleventh and the first quarter of the twelfth century. This explains the architectonic unity of stone church building in Rus' before the Mongol invasion (Il'in 1968:87–94). One can speak of the germination of a few regional schools of architecture in the second half of the twelfth century but, apart from these, stone architecture continued to develop within the mainstream of Kievan tradition and attained its full flowering in the varied church structures of the late twelfth century and the first four decades of the thirteenth (Rappoport 1970:3–25; 1977: 12–29).

Notes

* For the English translation of this paper I am indebted to Dr Richard Bosley, Stanford, California.
1 For a lengthier monograph on St Sophia in Kiev in English (with 336 illustrations) see Powstenko 1954: 9–162. On the question of the foundation of the cathedral, Powstenko limits himself to short summaries of the various points of view.
2 Lazarev 1971:238; 1973:22, outlines three periods in the construction and decoration of St Sophia. The cathedral was built between 1037 and 1046, the decoration of the side naves was completed by 1061–67, and the two towers, baptistry and outside ambulatories were built and decorated during the first quarter of the twelfth century. See also Mango 1976:324–5.
3 This extreme viewpoint is frequently countered with the argument that Thietmar was indeed referring to the cathedral church of Kiev, and that his use of the term *monasterium* was due to his limited knowledge and experience.
4 *Monasterium* in the sense of cathedral church is also attested in France and England. A document written in 1269 in'Tournai says: *Ce fu fait et moustier Nostre Dame à Tournai* (Guesnon 1910:27). See also Murray 1903:479 (Minster).
5 See also the document of Henry IV from 1071 in which the cathedral church of Magdeburg is called the *monasterium sancti Maurici* (MGH DD 6/1, 1953: No. 238). This usage is encountered frequently in this period (see MGH DD 6/3:1051). Another indication that *münster* meant "cathedral church" in everyday German in the early medieval period is seen in the *Niebelungenlied*, where the cathedral church of Worms is twice called a *münster* (strophes 812–3). See Honselmann 1959:12.
6 Thietmar added with his own hand that Reding, provost of the cathedral of Madgeburg, died and was buried in porticu australia iuxta monasterium (Trillmich 1957:392).
7 In Pathelbrunnun monasterium et omnis eiusdem apparatus, flamma nostrae iniquitatis ultrix consumens. The same usage is seen (4.9) in the note

recording that after the death of Otwin, bishop of Hildesheim, Osgadus eiusdem monasterii prepositus successit (Trillmich 1957:260, 124).

[8]   See Mariani Scotti, *Chronicon*, a. 1080: Badaebrunna civitas cum duobus monasteriis id est episcopatus et monachorum . . . igne consumitur (MGH SS 5:558). For further proof that the monasterium Padebrunnensis is the cathedral church, see Honselmann 1959:5–8.

[9]   This term, untranslated, is applied by Nestor the hagiographer (Abramovič 1967:19) to the cathedral of the pastor of the Church of Rus'. The slavonic translation of $\kappa\alpha\theta o\lambda\iota\kappa\acute{\eta}\ \grave{\epsilon}\kappa\kappa\lambda\eta\sigma\acute{\iota}\alpha$, *sobornaja cerky* was used as the Greek term to mean the main church of a town or a monastery, and not just the church of a bishop. Consequently, it is incorrect to always translate *sobor* as *cathedral*, as many historians do.

[10]   Their chronicle contains a passage which is analogous to Thietmar's description of the events of 14 August 1018 in Kiev: Li emp'erères est entrés en Thèbes, me avant k'il entrast en le ville, il descendi si ke li archevêques et li clergies le menèrent au moustier Nostre Dame (Wailly 1874:408).

[11]   This is an addition to 7.73, which also mentions the death of Vladimir, made by Thietmar himself apparently in October 1018.

[12]   It is impossible to expect archaeology to confirm this because of the destruction of the church of the Tithe. The original site of two sarcophagi made of local red schist (Grabar 1976:86, Plates 56, 57) cannot be determined. The fragments of a marble sarcophagus were found during excavations in 1939 (Karger 1940b: 76–80; Powstenko 1954:108–10). However, the discovery of a wooden sarcophagus in the central nave of the church (Karger 1940a:12–20) indicates that it was a place of burial for princes. In connection with this, one should note the debate between the princes (PSRL 2:281) about placing the sarcophagi of SS Boris and Gleb in the centre of their church or in the side aisle, beneath the arches of the choir.

[13]   Compare Ajnalov 1918:25–6. It appears from the Psalter of Odalric (f. 214v) that the French knew of the transference of the remains of Pope St Clement from Cherson to Kiev before the middle of the eleventh century; the presence of these relics in Kiev was confirmed by the French royal delegation (1050). See Loriquet 1904:23; Gaiffier 1974:318.

[14]   This was noticed by chroniclers copying this entry into their compilations. The Vladimir chronicler, for example, added: *i pogore cerkvei mnogo* (PSRL 30:42). The compilation of 1408, which is derived from the same protograf as the *Vladimir chronicle*, added even more: *pogore cerkvei mnogo v Kieve* (Priselkov 1950:128).

The entry is expanded even further in the *Nikon chronicle* (PSRL 9:75) of the sixteenth century, which states that 700 churches were burned.

[15]   Šaxmatov 1908:483, 576, believed that the entry was made from memory at the beginning of the 1040s, when the chronicle compilation of 1039 was written. However, in order to harmonize the conflicting entries, Šaxmatov supposed that the words "of the Holy Virgin" were already omitted in the chronicle compilation of 1095. In his reconstruction of the *Primary chronicle* Šaxmatov (1916:181) already took into account the chronicles with a plural verb. Cross 1953:132 and note 133, bases his translation on Šaxmatov's reconstruction, despite his announced purpose of translating the Laurentian MS. This is not the only such instance in the book.

[16]   *Urbs autem Kitava nimis valida ab hostibus Pedeneis ortatu Bolizlavi crebra inpugnatione concutitur et incendio gravi minoratur* (Trillmich 1957:474).

[17]   The juxtaposition of this entry with the entry in the chronicles about the foundation of St Sophia in 1037 caused uneasiness in the fifteenth century and produced attempts to harmonize these apparently contradictory entries. The oldest (Sinodal) MS. retains the original reading without emendations, but in the later MSS. of the *Novgorod first chronicle* and in the *Novgorod fourth* and *Sofia first chronicles* the entry of 1037 is emended with the word *sveršena/*"completed". The reader of the chronicle now had a completed text: it appeared that St Sophia of Kiev was begun in 1017 and finished in 1037. Consequently, modern scholars were not the first to think that St Sophia might have been built before 1037. The proponents of this theory in the middle ages, however, could resolve the problem by emending a text which they did not understand to agree with their interpretation. See Nasonov 1950: 180; PSRL 4/1/1:108, 114; 5:136–7. Proxorov (1977: 176), noting the change of sense which happened to the 1037 entry in its transference from the *Laurentian chronicle* to the *Sofia first chronicle*, is prone to see here a sloppy copyist at work. Some of the copyists were indeed slipshod, but here we have to do with a deliberate re-interpretation.

[18]   Il'in (1957:118–21) tried to demonstrate on the basis of textology that St Sophia was founded in 1017 and that the reference was transferred to 1036/1037. See also Aleškovskij 1969:29–30. The most comprehensive defence of this theory in recent years was made by Toločko 1969:196–202; 1972:93–100. See also Vysockij 1976:240–57; Schäfer 1974:206–7.

[19]   Šaxmatov (1908:228–30, 620) found a textological basis for this argument. This theory has been repeated by many scholars, such as Karger 1961:98–

101; Cross 1936:490–1.

[20] Šaxmatov 1908:414–6, 583, weakened his view considerably by advancing a hypothesis from which it followed that St Sophia was already consecrated in 1039.

[21] Vysoc'kyj (1975:177) attempts to contradict this evidence by reinterpreting Thietmar's statement. He asserted that the metropolitan of Kiev met Bolesław and Svjatopolk at the gates of the monastery which served as his residence, and that the stone church of St Sophia was already being built there to replace the wooden structure which had been burned.

[22] H. Łowmiański (1970:229–41) has convincingly demonstrated the existence of such annals made up of short notes.

[23] Łowmiański's point of departure is the accurate observation that the town of Brest on the border with Poland is mentioned among Svjatopolk's personal domains in 1017. It is not surprising, then, that Brest served as Svjatopolk's last stronghold, and that it was defended by troops of the Polish prince Bolesław who had come to the aid of his son-in-law.

[24] One gets the impression from the context in which this information is found that the news was brought by an emissary of the Polish prince, who arrived in Merseburg about that time.

[25] This confirmation was recognized by a recent reviewer who had not purposely intended to verify it. See Kaiser 1976:7–8.

[26] For an article on the word *założiti* with supplementary references, see Poppe 1962:22. The reader will find there forty-six quotations from primary sources in which this word is used.

[27] Where it is not otherwise specified, one may rightly suppose that the entry refers to a wooden structure, for example: "In the year 1335 Archbishop Vasilij founded (*założi*) the church of the Holy Mother of God in Zverinec, while [ex-] Archbishop Moisej founded the stone church of the Holy Resurrection . . . In that year Archbishop Vasilij completed the church of the Holy Mother of God in Zverinec, and Moisej the other, the stone one of the Holy Resurrection" (Nasonov 1950:346–7). From this we realize that it was the stone church at Zverinec which was first founded in 1399 (Nasonov 1950:91, 394).

[28] Very seldom it is mentioned indirectly. For example, when the main church of Ustjug was built in 1491, the architect Aleksius of Vologda did not found the church on the "old manner"/*ne po starine krešćatu i srubil do šti rjadov*. See Serbina 1950:98. Compare *ibidem*:99, and Poppe 1962:45 (*oklad*), 63 (*rublenik*). See also the reference from 1383: "They founded (*założiša*) the church: three layers of the frame (*tri*

vency)", PSRL 8:48.

[29] Only occasionally can we tell from the text itself if a structure was of wood; one instance is in the *Laurentian chronicle* under the year 1192: "in that year the fortifications (*grad*) of Suzdal' were founded (*založen*), and were built (*srublen*) in the same year" (PSRL 1:409, see also 412). In 1339 "the fortifications of Moscow were founded (*založen*), and they were built (*srublen*) that winter", while in 1374 "the prince founded (*založi*) the fortifications of Serpuxov . . . and ordered them to be built (*srubit'*) only of oak" (PSRL 25:172, 189). See also the references in the Pskov chronicles: "the citizens of Pskov built (*založiša*) a wooden wall . . ." and "they founded (*založiša*) new fortifications . . . half of the wall was of wood, half of stone" (Nasonov 1941:39, 40).

[30] *Založiti* is used in the completed sense of "built" in the *Primary chronicle* in the previously mentioned entry of 1037 in which the chronicler lists the foundations of Jaroslav, and again in 1089 where the chronicler lists the foundations of Efrem, metropolitan of Perejaslavl'; see PSRL 1:151, 209; Cross 1953:137, 170. The entry for 1086 was also written with this sense in mind: "Vsevolod founded (*založi*) the church of St Andrew during the tenure of the holy metropolitan John. Beside this church he also built a convent"; PSRL 2:209. See also PSRL 1:205 and Cross 1953: 168. Note also the alternating use of the words *založiti* and *postaviti* in the *Novgorod first chronicle* under the year 1192: "Varlam the monk founded (*postavi*) a church below at Xutyn" and dedicated it to the Saviour", Nasonov 1950:40. This same text was altered as follows when it was copied in the later *Pskov chronicle*: "Abbot Varlam founded (*založi*) the church of the Savior at Xutyn'", Nasonov 1955:77.

[31] Both believed that St Sophia was built by Olga, the tenth-century princess of Rus'. Their only sources were a dubious reference in the *Ioakim chronicle*, compiled at the end of the seventeenth or early eighteenth century, and a calendar from an MS., *Acts of the Apostles*, written in 1307 which mentions the consecration of St Sophia on 11 May 6460/952. The year 952 is undoubtedly the result of scribal error. See Lazarev 1960:55, note 8 and Poppe 1968b:94–5, note 44.

[32] The old, wooden church was still used in the 1080s but was burnt during the Polovcian attack on the monastery in June 1096. See Knjazevskaja 1971:125, 133; PSRL 1:156, 157, 232–3; Poppe 1974:176–8.

[33] Both recensions of the *Novgorod first chronicle* confirm the existence of a wooden church of St Sophia in Novgorod, but the earlier and more chronologically exact entry is, in this case, preserved in the "Commission" MS. See Šaxmatov 1908:191–4, 202–4, 218, 523,

and the reconstructed text *ibidem*:625. See also Lixačev 1950:382; Berežkov 1963:221. Janin (1974:88; 1977: 123–4), however, believes that the Sinodal MS. preserves the older entry, from which it follows that the stone St Sophia was begun only when the wooden church had been destroyed by fire. To support his thesis, Janin asserts that the chronicle was written according to an ultra-March chronology and that the construction of the cathedral church must be redated to 1046. Some criticism of this theory is found in Berežkov 1963:342, note 21. Janin (1974:89–90; 1977:125–8) also doubted that the wooden St Sophia was located on the spot where the church of SS Boris and Gleb was later built, since this site was outside the fortifications of Novgorod until 1116. We agree with Aleškovskij (1962:3–26) that the fortifications around the centre of the town were only extended during the construction of 1116. However, we should note the chronicle entry for the year 1113, which relates that the fire destroyed the *gorod kromnyj*, that is, the "inner burg". If we agree that this was term given to the inner fortification (*detinec*), then the chronicle entry implies that the city also had outward fortifications (the *okolnyj grad* or *okolotok*). It is possible that the first cathedral church was not built within the inner burg; it was enough that it was built in the fortified area of the "outer burg". Further proof that the chronicler's information about the location of the wooden St Sophia is reliable is found in one topographical detail which he could not have invented: he states that the cathedral church was located "at the end of Bishop's Street" (Nasnov 1950:181).

[34] Although Toločko (1969:198–202) asserted that the construction of the stone St Sophia began in 1017, he admits that the construction of "Jaroslav's town" was begun later, while the stone church was built outside the fortifications of the city in a "fortified monastery". Vysockij (1976:249), who shares Toločko's opinion, believes that the fragments of the stone wall of the metropolitan's court, uncovered during archaeological excavations (to a total length of 213 meters) were the previously mentioned fortifications. However, the exact date of their construction in the eleventh century is uncertain; see below note 56. ·From Vysockij's method of argumentation, it follows that this wall for defence already existed in 1017, and that it protected the wooden St Sophia which was located outside the centre of the city. However, those who believe that the stone St Sophia was built in 1017 ignore the fact (Rappoport 1956:117) that the wall uncovered during excavations can hardly be considered part of a system of fortifications: the wall was, instead, representational in nature, as is seen by

the use of decorative pilasters, and by the fact that it was not placed atop an earthen rampart, and that there are no traces of a moat in front of it.

[35] Cross' translation (1936:491) cannot be used because it is incorrect in a number of places. An accurate German translation is in Müller 1971:49. See also the interesting comments on the 'Sophialogical' symbolism of this text in Averincev 1972:44–5.

[36] Ajnalov believed that Vladimir not only intended to build the stone St Sophia, but that he had "blueprints" and building materials prepared, and had hired the architects and builders who had constructed the church of the Tithe to build St Sophia. Cross (1936:490–2) argued against this view, but Cross in turn explained Ilarion's statement as a reference to the church of the Tithe which was built by Vladimir and presumably rebuilt by Jaroslav. L. Müller (1962:171) accurately observed in his commentary on Ilarion that Ajnalov "overinterprets Ilarion's text". Ajnalov's theory was again set forth by Vysockij (1976:245–6), who interpreted the comparison between Vladimir and Jaroslav and David and Solomon as one of the most important arguments in Ilarion's work, proving that the construction of St Sophia was already begun in 1017.

[37] See 2 Chronicles 6:7–10. Now it was in the heart of David my father to build an house for the name of the LORD God of Israel. 8. But the LORD said to David my father, Forasmuch as it was in thine heart to build an house for my name, thou didst well in that it was in thine heart: 9. Notwithstanding thou shalt not build the house; but thy son which shall come forth out of thy loins, he shall build the house for my name. 10. The LORD therefore hath performed his word that he hath spoken: for I am risen up in the room of David my father, and am set on the throne of Israel, as the LORD promised, and have built the house for the name of the LORD God of Israel. See also 1 Kings 5:3, 5; 6:1, 14, 37, 38; 8:17–20, 24, and 1 Chronicles 17:25; 22:2–19; 28:3–6, and 2 Chronicles 2:1–9; 3:1–2.

Vysockij (1976:246) apparently had not read the biblical texts carefully when he said that Ilarion recorded that St Sophia of Kiev was built during the course of twenty years, as was the Temple of Jerusalem. for the Temple was built during seven years (1 Kings 6:38), and so this argument in favour of a period of construction from 1017 to 1037 is fallacious.

[38] Taking into account the fact that the approach to the Temple of Solomon as a prefiguration of the Temple of God, the Church of the New Law established by Christ, was well known to Ilarion, one can understand his attempt to present Vladimir and Jaroslav as establishers of the Church in Rus'. On the

dissemination of the comparison of the building with the Temple of Solomon and of the builders with Solomon, see the papers of S. Ferber and W. Cahn (Gutmann 1976:21ff., 56ff.) where also the earlier literature is mentioned.

[39] Prior to this, Ilarion states that Vladimir "established the faith in all his realm and erected churches of Christ".

[40] In 1399 carpenters from Novgorod rebuilt a church which had been destroyed by fire in the town of Ustjug. The church, of considerable size and 28.5 meters high – almost as high as St Sophia of Kiev – was built during the summer months (Serbina 1950:67; Voronin 1962:219–21).

[41] The *Novgorod second chronicle* (PSRL 30:177) mentions the period of four years. This, however, was undoubtedly the result of the erroneous combination of the entries in the *Novgorod first chronicle* about the foundation of (the stone) St Sophia in 1045 and the burning of (the wooden) St Sophia in 1049, owing to the assumption that they referred to the same church. This was noticed by Šaxmatov 1908:218.

[42] This was the view of Cross and Conant (1936: 489, 496), who said: "the thirteen *verxi* of the wooden cathedral of St Sophia in Novgorod has supplied the motive for the same number of domes on Jaroslav's St Sophia in Kiev". One must remember, however, that the authors did not take the existence of the wooden St Sophia of Kiev into account.

[43] From this it would follow logically that the wooden church of St Sophia of Kiev, rebuilt in 1017 after the fire, maintained the same number of domes as its predecessor, which had served as a model to the builders of the wooden St Sophia of Novgorod.

[44] On the other hand C. Delvoye (1966:57) said of the architecture of St Sophia: *les treize cupoles se rattacheraient à la vieille tradition* [sic!] *des églises russes en bois*. Mokeev 1978:49ff. even envisions the influence of some imaginary tradition of pagan wooden temples which, as a reflection of the Slavic polytheistic religion, were supposedly many-domed.

[45] For an explanation of the profound symbolism of a single mosaic inscription in St Sophia of Kiev, see Averincev 1972:25–49. Krasovskij (1916:286, 289–93, 370–2) said of the multi-domed churches that the theological interpretation of the number of domes came after the fact, and that the architectural reason for the composition predominated, since "carpenters were not versed in theology". But Krasovskij ignores the fact that ecclesiastics would have sought to inspire the architect and supervise the construction. On the other hand, it is true that certain architectural forms, such as numerical combinations, would have been

repeated by craftsmen who had no understanding of their symbolism because they were considered traditional.

[46] For Christian numerical symbols, especially 12 and 13 (12 + 1) see Hopper 1938:61, 70–4; Grossmann 1964:19–54. The numbers 12 and 13 were also important in the philosophy of the Manichaeans. Their meaning was both derived from orthodox Christianity and then influenced it in turn. The number 13 symbolized the divinity of light, supreme wisdom, the thirteen-number Supreme Being, the divine. See Troje 1925:3ff., 99ff.

[47] For a detailed criticism of the theory that Anastasius was the first bishop of Kiev, see Müller 1959:42–7; Poppe 1968c:46–7.

[48] Proof that Anastasius of Cherson managed the prince's *capella regia* is seen not only in the chronicle entries quoted above but in the use of the technical term *poručiti*, "to entrust" or "to commission". In other words, Vladimir authorized and empowered Anastasius to manage the affairs and property of his princely foundation.

[49] The fact that the chronicler twice mentions Anastasius in connection with the priests of Cherson, and yet distinguishes him from them, seems to indicate that Anastasius was not a priest. See Cross 1953:116, 119. Golubinskij 1901:519 considered Anastasius a layman who fulfiled the duties, having analogy with *advocatus ecclesiae* in the Catholic Church. Romanos Argyros was the great oeconomos of Hagia Sophia before he became emperor (Hussey 1963:122–3).

[50] Strictly speaking the first proof of this is from the year 1136 (Nasonov 1950:24), but from the context it appears that it was not a new institution in Rus', but one which almost certainly dated from the time of Vladimir and Anna.

[51] The first direct reference to the church of the Virgin as the church of the Tithe is in the *Primary chronicle* under the year 1093 (Cross 1953:179). But the fact that Anastasius of Cherson was called "of the Tithe" indicates that this name was used much earlier. For a discussion of unresolved problems connected with the reception and spread of the church tithe in Rus', see Poppe 1968c:216–8; Ščapov 1972:122–7. Murjanov 1978:171–5 has suggested that the name "church of the Tithe" indicates that the church was built as a liturgical offering (?). It has been known for a long time that the church of the Tithe was built on a cemetery. Murjanov believes that it was a Christian rather than a pagan cemetery, and that the site was chosen because of its sacred nature.

[52] Vysockij 1976:242, correctly believes that the name "Golden gate" appeared later, since Ilarion only

refers to it as the "main gate".

[53]   Toločko attempts to explain Šaxmatov's views by playing on supposed inconsistencies. In reality, Šaxmatov clearly stated that the chronicle entries of 1036 and 1037 were reliable and that the Novgorod information was secondary in nature and based on an erroneous chronology. On the other hand he conjectured that the entry of 1039 referred to the consecration of the newly-built St Sophia, not the church of the Tithe, and he (1908:228–9, 414–6) apparently believed, although he did not state *expressis verbis*, that St Sophia was built in the course of three years. Toločko believes that a period of construction of only three years was too short; his solution therefore, is to "accept" Šaxmatov's conjecture about the 1039 entry while rejecting the corresponding statements about 1036/1037. He is thus forced to ignore all the criticism of such a conjecture about the 1039 entry.

[54]   Il'in's (1957:120–3) justification for this chronology of events is based on the sixteenth-century *Nikon chronicle* and the *Saga of Eimund*. However, the former, which is a compilation and which combines and confuses the chronicle entries of 1017 and 1037 in the *Primary chronicle* and later redactions of the *Novgorod chronicles*, cannot be considered a primary source for the case in hand. Moreover, even if we agree that the information in the *Saga of Eimund* is correctly interpreted and in fact concerns the Pecheneg siege of Kiev in 1017, this cannot be used to cast doubt on the reliability of the account in the *Primary chronicle* about the battle with the Pechenegs at the walls of Kiev in 1036. It is curious to see that Aleškovskij (1969:29–30) refers to the saga which supposedly mentions the construction of the rampart of the new "town of Jaroslav" in 1017, and states that the Pechenegs broke into this town. The text of the saga, *Eymund þáttr Hringsonnar* is contained in the *Flateyjarbok* from the late fourteenth century and has been published many times. A Russian translation was made by E. Rydzevskaja 1978:89–104. See also the comment of Džakson 1978:128–43 on the use of sagas as a source for Rus'ian history.

[55]   The connection between the Pecheneg attack on Kiev and the events of 1036 in Rus' is derived indirectly from the distorted account of Scylitzes. Immediately after mentioning the three attacks of the Pechenegs in 1036, he mentions the death of the archontes of Rus' Nesisthlabos and Hierosthlabos, and states that Zinisthlabos took power (Thurn 1973:399). The juxtaposition of these two entries caused Shepard to theorize (1975:211–5) that Scylitzes was referring to three Rus'ian princes who were in command of mercenaries serving under the Byzantines, two of whom

fell in battle when the Pechenegs renewed their attack on the Empire, while the third took their command. However, this theory is insupportable in view of the information in the chronicles about the events of 1036 in Rus' in which princes with those names – Mstislav, Jaroslav, and Sudislav – took part. Although the Rus'ian information on this problem is meager, it is still extremely unlikely that three princes of Rus' with the same names and from the same dynasty as the well-known sons of Vladimir could have been in Byzantium at that time. It is much more likely that the familiar story about the death of Mstislav, Jaroslav's accession to power, and Sudislav's incarceration was distorted in transmission or that Scylitzes himself confused things when abridging from his source.

[56]   Toločko also believes that Jaroslav constructed the wall around the metropolitan's court and the large church near St Sophia; only the foundations of the latter have been found and it is not known to whom it was dedicated. Karger (1961:206–16, 226–32) stated that the church was contemporary with the constructions of Jaroslav, but his archaeological explanation for doing so is groundless since, from a technical standpoint, the foundations laid in the eleventh and even early twelfth centuries are identical. Consequently there is no reason to expand the list of Jaroslav's foundations. On the other hand, there is no reason to exclude the possibility that the stone wall of the metropolitan's court was built as soon as the cathedral was completed, since its construction was a simple matter and would have been completed by local workmen within a few months.

[57]   Although the walls of "Jaroslav's town" enclosed an area of about 70 hectares, a significant portion of Kiev remained outside the fortifications. Archaeological excavations show that at least part of the territory newly enclosed by Jaroslav's ramparts was already inhabited (Toločko 1972:87; Borovskyj 1976:86–107). Logvin (1977:169) unjustifiably criticizes the reliability of the *Primary chronicle*, because it supposedly says that Jaroslav wanted to enclose vacant land within the rampart. However, the chronicler's reference to the "field outside the town" simply refers to an open area, settled or not, outside the town walls.

[58]   The construction was begun on 29 July 6703, and completed in the same year, consequently not later than February 1196 (PSRL 1:412). The wooden fortifications of Perejaslavl' were rebuilt in 1396 in a similar period of time (Voronin 1961:101–3, 180).

[59]   From archaeological excavations, which were, however, limited to the inner town, we may conclude that the height of the earthen rampart was increased by about 1.5 meters. See Rappoport 1961:99ff. 112–3;

Sedov 1974:61-3.

[60]   In one building season in 1367 about 2,000 workmen, according to Voronin's (1962:229-33) calculation, built walls for the Moscow Kremlin about two kilometers long, about two meters thick and eight meters high, with nine towers. For the fortifications of the city of Vladimir, see Voronin 1961:128-31; Rappoport 1961:212-5.

[61]   Even Vysockij (1976:251), who thinks that the stone St Sophia was founded in 1017, admits that the construction of the cathedral only began in earnest after 1026.

[62]   G. Vernadsky (1948:7) has said of the period 1026-36: "in this period of cooperation between the brother princes the city of Kiev seems temporarily to have lost its predominance in Russian politics. Novgorod and Chernigov now emerged as the two leading political centres". The sources do not give even indirect support to Parxomenko's thesis (1930:142-3) that from 1026 to 1036 Kiev was under the hegemony of the Pechenegs and that it was retaken by Jaroslav with the help of Varangians in 1036.

[63]   It is possible that at this time Jaroslav consolidated his power in ·the Rostov-Suzdal region and founded Jaroslavl' on the Volga. See Janin 1962:49, note 17; Kučkin 1969:65.

[64]   Novgorod chronicles from the mid-fifteenth century mention a certain Il'ja, the son of Jaroslav, who supposedly ruled in Novgorod before Jaroslav's son Vladimir. Even if we disregard the strangeness of the name for a prince, we must conclude that Il'ja is a legendary figure in view of the exact information in the *Primary chronicle* on the order of birth of the sons of Jaroslav. Vladimir is named as the eldest, which is seen in his very name – Vladimir, the name of Jaroslav's father. It is, of course, possible that Il'ja was Vladimir's Christian name, and that by the fifteenth century the Novgorod chronicler had no way of identifying the two figures.

[65]   See the panegyric to Jaroslav in Ilarion's *Sermon on law and grace* which focusses exclusively on the period in which Jaroslav ruled alone, that is, after 1036 (Müller 1962:121-5).

[66]   Cross 1953:136, erroneously translated *vzvyše* as "higher than" instead of "as high as".

[67]   In view of the fact that the cathedral was dedicated to the Transfiguration, the feast of its foundation was probably on 6 August 1035, the Church's feast of the Transfiguration of Christ. The view that it was begun in 1031, frequently repeated in scholarly literature on the subject, is an arbitrary conclusion which assumes unusual delays during construction; see, for example, G. N. Logvin 1969:193.

Our conclusion that the cathedral of Černigov was begun in 1035 is the result of a comparative approach, especially with the facts known about the katholikon of the monastery of the Caves which was of roughly the same size as the cathedral of Černigov. The corner stone of the church in the monastery of the Caves was laid on the feast of the Dormition of the Virgin, 15 August 1073. When Abbot Theodosij died on 3 May 1074, the foundations were already laid; given the length of the building season, the foundations were probably almost completed by the end of 1073, since not much work could have been done in the following season before 3 May. The new abbot continued the work, and the construction (the masonry alone, without frescoes) was completed on 11 July 1076, that is, in less than three full seasons. See PSRL 1:183, 188, 198; Rappoport 1974:46-7. An analysis, made after the destruction of the church in 1941, of the height of the masonry laid each season, shows that it varied by as much as four or five meters; see G. Logvin 1974:160. For the study of the daily output of masons in the twelfth century see Černyšev 1966:289-93.

[68]   Komeč 1975:11, found additional support for this connection in the typological similarity of the church of the Saviour in Černigov and the church of the Virgin at Pharos. He pointed to the possibility that a continuous architectural tradition linked the church at Pharos, the church of the Tithe and the cathedral of Černigov. Attempts to reconstruct the floor plan of the church of the Tithe have given rise to a number of disputed questions, some of which may be clarified by the information in about 500 recently discovered and so far unused photographs made during the excavations of 1908-09; see Tomes 1974:240-1. However, one's expectations should not be too great, because these excavations uncovered only fragments of the walls of the ambulatories. These ambulatories are generally dated to the late 1030s, but this question should be considered completely open.

[69]   Since the view of the Constantinopolitan affiliation of early Rus'ian architecture has found widespread acceptance among experts, the opinion that Armenian art influenced the architecture and decoration of St Sophia of Kiev must be considered unfounded. For a moderately critical examination see Dachkévytch 1974:328-36. Moreover, the marble sarcophagus considered to be Jaroslav's sepulchre (Powstenko 1954:105-6, 109; Logvin 1971: Figs. 273-4) is not a work of Armenian but of Constantinopolitan masters (Grabar 1976:87-90).

[70]   One frequently encounters the opinion, in the older literature on the subject, that the death of Mstislav caused a pause in construction. This view

seems, at first glance, to be confirmed by the traces of a joint, noticed not long ago during an inspection of the apse (Schäfer 1974:214). However, this joint could simply mark the end of a building season. The question requires full documentation and publication since, in the opinion of Morgilevskyj (1928:169), who made a complete examination of the church, there were no traces of a hiatus in the construction of the building.

[71] "To Jaroslav was born (*rodisja Jaroslavu* . . .) his fourth son and he named him Vsevolod" (PSRL 1:149; Cross 1953:136).

[72] Large *jus* also appears in graffiti Nos. 14, 102, 107, which Vysockij (1966: tabl. XIX; 1976: tabl. VI, VII, XIV) dates to the eleventh century. However, on the basis of their paleography, the chronological limits should be expanded and the graffiti dated to the eleventh-twelfth centuries.

[73] The large *jus* is a common trait of Old Rus'ian monuments of the eleventh and first half of the twelfth centuries. It is rarely found in the second half of the twelfth century and disappears entirely during the thirteenth. It only reappears during the "second South Slavic influence" at the end of the fourteenth century. See Karinskij 1905:12; Ščepkin 1967:114, 130; Borkovskij 1965:66–7.

[74] For example, Vsevolod the son of Mstislav, the grandson of Vsevolod Jaroslavič; Vsevolod, the son of Igor' Jaroslavič; or Vsevolod Olgovič, prince of Kiev in 1139–46 (Baumgarten 1927: tables V–1, VI–8–12).

[75] See the twelfth-century letter on birch bark No. 9: ježe mi otec dajal i rodi sdajali/"which my father and my blood relatives gave to me," Arcixovskij 1953:40–1. See also the letter of Vladimir Monomach to Oleg, PSRL 1:254; Cross 1953:217, translates *rodi* as "family."

[76] Cross 1953:142, 150, translates "a son was born to Vsevolod" (1053, 1070). Only as an exception do the sources mention the mother. See, for example, the legend about the quarrel between the princes of Polock and Kiev in the *Laurentian chronicle* under the year 1128: i narekoša jei imja Gorislava i rodi Izjaslava/ "and they named her Gorislava, and she gave birth to Izjaslav"; PSRL 1:300. See also the entry: "In the year 1053 a son was born to Vsevolod (and he named him Vladimir) by the Greek princess", PSRL 1:160; Cross 1953:142.

[77] As a result of this author's criticism (Poppe 1968a:95–6) even Vysoc'kyj (1975) was inclined to change his opinion and failed to mention graffito No. 99. However, one year later in a new publication of graffiti, he returned to his original hypothesis (1976: 9–11). It is noteworthy that Logvin (1977) also ignored graffito No. 99, although he accepted Vysockij's

interpretation of the supposed dates 1031/1032 and 1042.

[78] Vysockij (1966a:16) originally read this inscription as referring to the year 1046/6554/, suggesting an unusual way of writing 54 as 40 + 10 + 4. This supposedly arose as a result of the ignorance or carelessness of the person who inscribed the date. Subsequently Vysockij (1975:179–80) abandoned this hypothesis as a result of Poppe's (1968a:94) criticism.

[79] Kuźmin first attempted in 1969 and continues to attempt (1977:227–39) to demonstrate that the ultra-March system was used in Rus' in the second half of the eleventh century. For criticism of this unsubstantiated theory see Poppe 1974:175–8. In connection with Kuz'min's rebuttal (1978:230–2) we should point out that we do not reject the *possibility* that the ultra-March style was used in Rus' even in the eleventh century, but insist that there is no proof, not even circumstantial evidence, which permits us to say that it was used.

[80] Vysockij omitted the arguments which he had advanced at an earlier date (1966a:15–16). He also failed to respond to the critical remarks made by Poppe 1968a:93–4.

[81] For examples, see Vysockij 1966a: No. 4/ tabl. V, No. 8/tabl. IX, No 18/tabl. XXIII, No. 59/tabl. LVII, No. 80/tabl. LXXI, and Vysockij 1976: No. 99/tabl. I, No 123/tabl. XXX, No 156/tabl. LXI, No. 170/tabl. LXIX, No. 192/tabl. LXXXVI. Vysockij 1976:167, also noticed the presence of the letter П among the graffiti with the horizontal line extended beyond the vertical lines. The letter П written in exactly the same manner is found in the inscription recording the death of Prince Vsevolod-Andrew in 1093 (graffito No. 4, tabl. V) and four times in graffito No. 239 (tabl. CXXVII).

[82] See the graffito from the late twelfth century (Vysockij 1966a: No. 46 (tabl. XLIII), in which the letters Л and П are similar, and like the letter П in graffito No. 1.

[83] On the question of the correct reading of this text, see also Strumins'kyj 1976:15–16.

[84] The translation by Cross (1936:491) is in need of corrections. I translate the phrase *kamenje dragoje* as "splendid" and not as "precious stones" or "jewels" as one frequently finds. The phrase is used in the broad sense of "expensive" or "sumptuous", rather than "precious, noble", since it refers to the interior decoration of the cathedral with marble, schist and mosaics made of little smalt and natural stones.

[85] An indirect confirmation that St Sophia had been completed for some time may be seen in Ilarion's reference to the church of the Annunciation atop the

Golden Gates; according to the entry of 1037 in the *Primary chronicle*, the church of the Annunciation was built after the cathedral. However, it would be wrong to see a strict chronology in Ilarion's list of Jaroslav's foundations, since the guiding principle was probably the importance of the various structures.

[86] Ilarion's knowledge of Greek and his good theological education indicate, at least indirectly, that he was in touch with Byzantium. It would also seem probable that he formed part of the royal delegation accompanying Anna, the daughter of Jaroslav, to France to marry Henry II; see Müller 1971:80–6.

[87] Ignoring the argument based on the age of Jaroslav's grandchildren, J. Fennell (1974:58) concluded that "certainly there is nothing to help us date the work more precisely than between 1037 and 1051".

[88] The embassy included several ecclesiastics; judging by the interest which they displayed towards the relics of Pope St Clement, they must have visited the church of the Tithe, although they did not mention it. See Gaiffier 1974:318.

[89] Adam of Bremen (2.22), who wrote between 1072 and 1076, testified that this architectural and urban plan was successfully realized. Based on the accounts of those who had seen it, he described Kiev, the capital of Rus' as *aemula sceptri Constantinopolitani, clarissimum decus Graciae* "the largest city of Russia is Kiev, emulator of the sceptre of Constantinople, the brightest ornament of Greece" (Trillmich 1961:254). Although *aemula* usually is translated as "rival" (as in the English translation by Tschan 1959:67) it is much more likely that it is used in its second, broader meaning of one who emulates or imitates.

[90] Illustrations of the frescoes and reproductions of Westerfeld's drawings are in Lazarev 1970b:29–31, 39, 41, 43, 45 and the supplement between 48 and 49; Poppe 1968d: ills. 2, 3a, b, c, d, 4, 9, 10; Lazarev 1973: ills. 102–6; Powstenko 1954: ills. 149, 153–60 and pp. 138–9.

[91] G. Logvin (1977:174–6) avoided the crux of this question. Although his remarks about a number of Lazarev's interpretations are reasonable, he categorically declared that, as a result of restoration in the eighteenth-twentieth centuries, the fresco-portrait of Jaroslav the Wise and his family "has lost all its strength as an authentic source and cannot be used as an argument either in dating the portrait, or in the attribution of the various figures, or to justify the date of the construction of the cathedral of St Sophia". This extreme scepticism is unfounded, although the portrait shows clear traces of disfiguration. He avoids discussing the portrait of two young princes, which are in poor condition but which are in their original,

unrestored, state. See Powstenko 1954: ill. 115; Lazarev 1970b: ills. between pp. 48 and 49; Poppe 1968d: ill. 3c. There is no need to debate Logvin's arguments, since we still have two essential facts at our disposal: 1) when the fresco was painted, Jaroslav had at least eight sons and daughters; 2) the stature of the children in the fresco and in Westerfeld's drawing (and the stature remained unchanged) roughly indicates their age. However, Logvin makes no effort to juxtapose these facts with the circumstances in Jaroslav's family in 1030–1031, when he believes the portrait was painted. At that time, Jaroslav had only three sons (Vladimir, Izjaslav, Svjatoslav) 11, 7, and 4 years old. The fourth, Vsevolod was still in a cradle. Each source must be examined to determine its degree of credibility; one cannot lightly remove one or the other from the list of those which bear upon a particular question.

[92] For a discussion of the fragments of the architectural decoration of the church of the Tithe and St Sophia which have been found, see Karger 1961:56–9, 182–205; Powstenko 1954:85–99. For instances of sculpted pieces with commentary see, Grabar 1976: 83–91; see also Karger 1947:15–50. We still do not know from which quarries the marble used to decorate St Sophia came. Judging by its colour – almost white with bluish-gray veins – it could have come from the island of Prokonnesos in the Sea of Marmora. It could also have been marble 'recycled' from buildings which had collapsed, perhaps in the Crimea.

[93] The quantity of marble fragments of the type used for revetment found during excavation of the church of the Tithe, and the use of the attribute "marble" applied to the church in the pre-Mongol period, permit us to assume that the lower parts of the walls of the *capella regia* were covered with marble. The floor of the church of the Tithe was *opus sectile* like a Byzantine church, whereas the mosaic floor of St Sophia of Kiev, made of schist sheets with mosaic incrustations made of smalt of various colors, only imitated this style. See Karger 1961: tabl. XIII, XXIII–XXV; Schäfer 1974:210, table 87. The floor of the church of the Saviour in Černigov, laid in all probability originally in the early 1040s, was also of red schist with mosaic incrustations.

[94] According to Professor Ernest J. W. Hawkins, fragments of decoration from about 1125 in the church of the Saviour in the Chora (Kariye Camii) testify to the use of frescoes below mosaics. Professor D. Oates and Dr B. Ousterhout are continuing their work on this monument. Another example is the Kosmosotira, the church at Ferrai, founded in 1115, where the walls were also not revetted but decorated with frescoes. Mosaics were reserved for the upper levels. I am

indebted to Professor Hawkins and Dr Judith Herrin for this information.

[95] That must have been the case with the supports which held up the vaults of the choir enclosing the cross-shaped portion of the church from the south, north and west. The architects had only two marble columns at their disposal. They probably decided even before the conflict of 1043 to dispense with the difficult transportation of heavy marble pillars by water up the Dniepr and around the rapids. The two marble columns were placed in the central nave, while the north and south choirs of the transept rest on eight-sided pillars. Schäfer is right when he remarks: *Dass für die übrigen Emporenstützen keine Marmorsäulen standen, hat man offenbar als Mangel empfunden, denn man entschloss sich nicht, die Emporstützen im "Querschiff" als rechteckige Pfeiler zu bauen, sondern ahmte die runde Säulenform nach, indem man ihnen durch die Verwendung vom Formziegeln einen – in Byzanz unbekannten – achteckigen Grundriss gab,* Schäfer 1974:215. See also Karger 1961:130–2, 140–1, table XXXIV.

[96] Ščapova 1975:209–22, believes that the disintegration of the smalt resulted from the fact that the Byzantine masters kept part of their techniques secret. It is simpler to postulate that, as in the case of any product, some of the smalt was always defective, but that this became apparent only after some time had elapsed.

[97] Ajnalov (1917:35, 39) advanced the hypothesis that the Greek masters who worked on the construction and decoration of the church of the Tithe were employed by Jaroslav in St Sophia. After sixty years, this hypothesis has been taken up again by Logvin 1977:181. Even if we assume, as Logvin does, that St Sophia was built with interruptions between 1017 and 1031, it is impossible to believe that the Greek masters who had built the court ensemble, the centre of which was the church of the Tithe/*capella palatina*, in the 990s sat in Kiev twiddling their thumbs for the next twenty years, waiting for another job.

[98] In the opinion of most specialists, glass was already produced in Rus' at the beginning of the eleventh century. It is likelier, however, that the Rus'ian masters only mastered the technology of producing smalt in the twelfth century. Certainly the numerous construction projects of the time of Jaroslav and his sons, on which foreign masters were employed, aided the development of a local glass industry. See Ščapova 1972:181–91; 1978:208–12.

[99] Lazarev (1971:238, note 25) characterized my opinion as: *une conclusion hative* which ignores *la différence de style qui existe entre les différents groupes de fresques*.

[100] Although K. Conant shared Cross's view he noted (1936:498) that "The main lines and the details of this work [the construction in *opus mixtum*] are hardly different from the oldest parts of the cathedral". Kresalnyj (1972:65–79) continues to defend his point of view, presented in the first version in 1968, with some modifications. He is willing to admit the possibility that the external ambulatory, the second level of the inner ambulatory and the south tower were built during Jaroslav's life, that is, before 1054, but he insists that the north tower was built at the end of the eleventh century.

[101] Lazarev and other scholars who believed that St Sophia at Kiev was built in stages, refer to the fact that the metropolitan Efrem consecrated the cathedral for the second time in the 1050s or 1060s. But the reason for the second consecration could be completely unconnected with the history of the construction of the church; see Poppe 1968b:94–6; 1972:28–30. This observation is also applicable to the wide-spread hypothesis that the church of the Tithe, burned in 1017, was renovated and even enlarged simply because it was reconsecrated in 1039 (Karger 1961:48–9; Cross 1936:482, 485, 494; Schäfer 1974:201). Compare note 68 above.

[102] Logvin 1977:181, asserts in a peculiar manner that "the style of the frescoes and mosaics [of St Sophia], which all specialists believe are closely analogous to the paintings of Hosios Lukas, Vatopedi and Nea Moni" speaks for an early date of the construction of the cathedral, namely about 1030. But Logvin forgets to mention when these churches were built, and on what basis he is able to date the frescoes and mosaics of St Sophia so accurately to 1030 instead of 1046. The katholika of Hosios Lukas and Vatopedi cannot be precisely dated within the eleventh century. However, the church of Nea Moni on the island of Chios was built in the years 1042–1045 by architects from Constantinople. See Mango 1975:219, 222, 224, 354 note 25.

[103] Grabar apparently considered it so obvious that the frescoes of the tower were painted at the same time as those of the church itself that he did not discuss the question of their date in this article.

[104] Kresalnyj 1972:73–5, notes the remains of a mosaic composition on some of the steps of the north tower similar in design to the mosaic floor in the central part of the cathedral and in the drum beneath the main dome, but does not draw the necessary conclusion. Having discovered a ceramic floor slab in the northern tower identical to floor slabs in the northern ambulatory, he advances the hypothesis that the latter structure was rebuilt towards the end of the eleventh century. For a critique of this theory, see Toc'ka and

Jerko. 1976: 119–30.

[105] According to Levitskaja 1959:169ff. all the mosaics of St Sophia of Kiev could have been completed by twenty artists working for three or four seasons. See also Lazarev's remarks 1960:152–3. As a general rule, it took anywhere from two to twelve years to build a church in the Byzantine Empire. Even the grandiose Hagia Sophia in Constantinople was built in five or six years (532–537). Byzantine churches constructed at about the same time as St Sophia of Kiev were usually built and decorated within a few years, for example those of Maria Perileptos, 1028–34, SS Kosmas and Damian, 1034–41, St George in Mangana during the 1040s; see Mango 1975 [1976]: 28, 214, 215, 231, 235, 354; see also *Synoptische Übersicht* in appendix: 366–71. We know that in the fourteenth century the frescoes of churches in Moscow were painted within one or two years, although, of course, these cannot compare with the decoration of St Sophia in Kiev; see PSRL 25:152, 175, 222, 229, Mango 1972: 256.

[106] See above, note 67. One frequently encounters the year 1077, the "third year" from 1075, under which there is an entry in the *Primary chronicle* about the construction of the church. However, if we follow the sense of the chronicle entry, we should count from 1074, the year of Theodosij's death and the beginning of Stefan's abbacy; see PSRL 1:198; Cross 1953:164.

[107] It is generally believed that this was the first consecration of the church, but this view is incorrect. From the *vita* of Theodosij, written before 1088, we learn that the new church was functioning immediately after it was completed under Abbot Stefan, or at least before he resigned from the abbacy at the end of 1077. See Knajzevskaja 1971:125, 133; Poppe 1965b: 292–6. Consequently, the consecration of 1089 was the second (the great?) consecration, while the first (the lesser?) probably occurred immediately after the completion of the church on 14 or 15 August 1076.

[108] The church of the Saviour, including the apses, was 35.25 meters long and 22.4 meters wide. The church of the Dormition was 35.25 meters by 23.5 meters. St Sophia of Kiev is 34.25 meters long, including the apses, 39.2 meters wide without external ambulatories (41.75 meters long and 54.6 meters wide including them), and 28.5 meters high to the keystone of the dome. The corresponding proportions of St Sophia of Novgorod are: 39.35 meters, 34.5 meters, 30.8 meters; see Afanasjev 1961:250–1.

[109] Brjusova 1974:111–13, advances the theory that the church was consecrated twice, the second time in 1052, after "the completion of the first stage of decoration with paintings". The idea of two conse-

crations is, as we have seen, plausible, but in this case the basis for such an assertion is weak. The sources indicate not that the church was consecrated a second time, but that the fifteenth- and sixteenth-century chroniclers and scribes were confused.

[110] Brjusova claims that work on the frescoes was stopped because of the death of Vladimir, the son of Jaroslav, on 4 October 1052. But this argument is unconvincing, since the co-founder, Jaroslav the Wise, was still alive and well. It was Jaroslav who sent the fresco painters from Kiev, and they would have remained there until he ordered them to return.

[111] Since the fragments of the schist-mosaic floor of St Sophia of Novgorod are similar to the floor of St Sophia of Kiev and to those of several churches in southern Rus' from the period 1050–1150, Štender (1968:102) is prepared to doubt that the schist-mosaic floor of St Sophia of Kiev was made first. He writes: "so far there is no consensus of opinion on the date of the mosaic floor of St Sophia of Kiev". However, no one has yet offered any arguments against the generally accepted view which are worthy of serious consideration.

[112] Štender (1974:202–12) has discussed the decorative motifs on stone and brick masonry which supposedly made up for the lack of frescoes. He (1968: 94–5) makes the startling remark that the traces of the letter A inscribed in the damp mortar is proof that the cathedral was built by Rus'iañ masters. Without discussing the details of this confused argument, it is worth noting that the author is apparently unaware of the fact that more than sixty years separated the construction of St Sophia of Novgorod from the next stone churches in the city.

[113] The dimensions of the church of St Michael of the Golden Dome are: 18.75 meters wide, 28.6 meters long including the apses, and 26.5 meters, to the keystone of the dome. The corresponding dimensions of St Sophia without the ambulatories are: 29.3 meters wide, 29.55 meters long, 28.5 meters high (Afanasjev 1961:69–72, 251). By Karger 1961:281–2, the church is erroneously dated to about 1060. See Lazarev 1966:31–7.

[114] The ceremony of laying the corner stone could have taken place on 4 November, on the anniversary of the victory over the Pechenegs, as the following considerations suggest. As is well known, the second consecration of St Sophia took place on 4 November. From the purely ecclesiastical point of view, the choice of this date is incomprehensible, but, nevertheless, might not have been arbitrary. In the 1050s and 1060s people would have remembered the date of the victory and of the foundation of the church, which occurred on

the anniversary of the victory. The choice of this date for the consecration of the church would have been natural.

[115] The ruins of five stone palace buildings have been examined archaeologically and all dated to the tenth or early eleventh centuries (Karger 1961:59–87). The idea of five stone structures built in this period raises serious doubts, and the date of one of them, alongside the church of St Irene, is unacceptable since it implies that a palace would have been built outside the fortifications! The chronology of the palace buildings within 'Vladimir's town' requires further study. For a review of the data gathered so far, see Kilievič 1976:189–92.

[116] One or two buildings which undoubtedly served as the prince's residence were built at that time near the church of the Tithe (Karger 1961:23, 59ff.), but they were not large and could have been built by the same masters during the course of one, or at most two, seasons.

[117] For the ancient wooden architecture of Rus', see Krasovskij 1916; Voronin 1952; Logvin 1976: 151–9.

Literature

Abramovič, D. I. (ed.). 1967. Die altrussischen hagiographischen Erzählungen und liturgische Dichtungen über die Heiligen Boris und Gleb. Nach der Ausgabe von Abramovič in Auswahl neu herausgegeben und eingeleitet von L. Müller. Slavische Propyläen B. 14. München.

Afanasjev, K. N. 1961. Postroenie arxitekturnoj formy drevnerusskimi zodčimi. Moskva.

Ajnalov, D. V. 1905. Mramory i inkrustacji Kievo-Sofijskogo sobora i Desjatinnoj cerkvi. Trudy XII Arxeologičeskogo S'ezda v Xarkove 3:5–11. Moskva.

Ajnalov, D. V. 1917. K voprosu o stroitel'noj dejatelnosti sv. Vladimira. In: Sbornik v pamjat' sv. ravnoapostolnogo knjazja Vladimira, 21–39. Petrograd.

Ajnalov, D. V. 1918. Sud'by kievskogo xudožestvennogo nasledija. Zapiski otdelenija russkoj i slavjanskoj arxeologii 12:23–39.

Ajnaloff, D. (Ajnalov). 1926. Die Mosaiken des Michaelklosters in Kiev. Belvedere 9/10:201–16.

Ajnalov, D. V. 1932. Geschichte der russischen Monumentalkunst der vormoskovitischen Zeit. Berlin.

Aleškovskij, M. 1962. Novgorodskij detinec 1044–1430gg. Arxitekturnoe nasledstvo 14:3–26.

Aleškovskij, M. 1969. Pervaja redakcija "Povesti Vremennyx Let". Arxeografičeskij ežegodnik za 1967:13–40.

Alpatov, M. and Brunov, N. 1932. Geschichte der altrussischen Kunst. 2 vols. Augsburg.

Arcixovskij, A. V. and M. N. Tixomirov. 1953. Novgorodskie gramoty na bereste iz raskopok 1951 goda. Moskva.

Averincev, S. S. 1972. K ujasneniju smysla nadpisi nad konxoj centralnoj apsidy Sofii Kievskoj. In: Drevnerusskoe iskusstvo; xudožestvennaja kultura domongolskoj Rusi, 25–49. Moskva.

Baumgarten, N. 1927. Généalogies et mariages occidentaux des Rurikides russes du Xe au XIIIe siècle. Roma.

Beck, H. G. 1959. Kirche und theologische Literatur im Byzantinischen Reich. München.

Belting-Ihm, Ch. 1976. "Sub matris tutela". Untersuchungen zur Vorgeschichte der Schutzmantelmadonna. Heidelberg.

Berežkov, N. G. 1963. Xronologia russkogo letopisanija. Moskva.

Blatt, Fr. (ed.). 1963. Novum glossarium mediae latinitatis ab anno DCCC usque ad annum MCC. Fasc. Miles-Mozytia. Hafnae.

Borkovskij, V. A. and P. S. Kuznecov. 1965. Grammatika russkogo jazyka. Moskva.

Borovskij, Ja. E. 1976. Arxeologični doslidžennja v "gorodi" Jaroslava. In: Arxeologični doslidžennja starodavnjogo Kyjeva, 86–107. Kiev.

Brjusova, V. G. 1968. O datirovke drevnejšix fresok Sofijskogo sobora v Novgorode XI-načala XII v. Sovetskaja arxeologija 1:103–14.

Brjusova, V. G. 1974. O vremeni osvjaščenija Novgorodskoj Sofii. In: Kultura srednevekovoj Rusi, 111–13.

Byčkov, A. F. (ed.). 1879. Novgorodskije letopisi. St Petersburg.

Čerepnin, L. V. 1965. Obščestvenno-političeskie otnošenija v drevnej Rusi i Russkaja Pravda. In: Drevnerusskoe gosudarstvo i ego meždunarodnoe značenie, 128–278. Moskva.

Cross, S. H. and K. J. Conant. 1936. The earliest mediaeval churches of Kiev (in collaboration with H. V. Morgilevskij). Speculum 11:477–99 + 9 plates.

Cross, S. H. 1947. The mosaic Eucharist of St Michael's Kiev. The American Slavic and East European review 6:55–61.

Cross, S. H. 1949. Mediaeval Russian churches, ed. by K. J. Conant. Cambridge, Mass.

Cross, S. H. (ed.). 1953. The Russian primary chronicle. Laurentian text. Translated and edited by S. H. Cross and O. P. Sherbovitz-Wetzor. Cambridge, Mass.

Černyšev, M. B. 1966. O proizvoditelnosti truda kamenščikov v drevnej Rusi. In: Kultura drevnej Rusi, 289–93. Moskva.

Dachkévytch, Ya. 1974. Les Arméniens à Kiev (jusqu'à 1240). Revue des études Arméniennes 10:305–58.

Delvoye, C. 1966. L'architecture byzantine au XIe siècle. In: Thirteenth International Congress of Byzantine Studies. Supplementary Papers. Summaries, 53–8. Oxford.

Demus, O. 1947. Byzantine mosaic decoration. London.

Diaconu, P. 1970. Les Petchénègues au Bas-Danube. Bucarest.

Dmitriev, Ju. N. 1954. Zametki po texnike russkix stennyx rospisej XI–XII vv. In: Eżegodnik Instituta Istorii Iskusstv ANSSSR, 238–78. Moskva.

Dovżenok, V. 1968. Storoževyje goroda na juge Kievskoj Rusi. In: Slavjane i Rus', 37–41. Moskva.

Du Cange, Glossarium mediae et infimae latinitatis 5.

Dżakson, T. N. 1978. K metodike analiza russkix izvestij islandskix korolevskix sag. In: Metodika izučenija drevnejšix istočnikov po istorii narodov SSSR, 128–43. Moskva.

Fennell, J. and A. Stokes. 1974. Early Russian literature. London.

Ferluga, J. (ed.). 1966. Vizantijski izvori za istoriju naroda Jugoslavije 3. Beograd.

Gaiffier, de B. 1974. Odalric de Reims, ses manuscrits et les reliques de Saint Clément à Cherson. In: Etudes de civilisation médiévale, IXe-XIIe siècles. Mélanges offerts à Edmond René Labande, 315–20. Poitiers.

Golubinskij, E. 1901 and 1904. Istorija russkoj cerkvi. 1 vol. in 2 parts). Second edition. Moskva

Grabar, A. 1918. Freski apostolskijo pridela Kievo-Sofijskogo sobora. Zapiski otdelenia russkoj i slavjanskoj arxeologii 12:98–106.

Grabar, A. 1935. Les fresques des escaliers à Sainte-Sophie de Kiev et l'iconographie impériale byzantine. Seminarium Kondakovianum 7:103–17. Praha.

Grabar, A. 1936. L'empéreur dans l'art byzantin. Reprinted 1971. Strasbourg.

Grabar, A. 1976. Sculptures byzantines du moyen age, 2. Paris.

Grass, N. 1967. Königskirche und Staatssymbolik. Beegnungen zwischen Griechischem Osten und Lateinischem Westen im Bereich von Staatsrepresentation und Sakralkultur. In: Gedächtnisschrift Hans Peters, 61–96. Berlin.

Grimm, J. and W. 1877. Deutsches Wörterbuch, 6.

Grossmann, U. 1964. Studien zur Zahlensymbolik des Frühmittelalters. Zeitschrift für katholischeTheologie 76/4:19–54.

Guesnon, A. (ed.). 1910. In: Mélanges M. Wilmotte, 27. Paris.

Gutmann, J. (ed.). 1976. The Temple of Solomon. Archeological fact and medieval tradition in Christian, Islamic and Jewish art. Missoula, Montana.

Hagenmayer, H. (ed.). 1913. Fulcheri Carnotensis Historia Hierosolymitana. Heidelberg.

Honselmann, K. 1959. Münster und Dom. Sprachgeschichtliches in westfälischen Urkunden. Westfalen 37:2–16.

Hopper, V. F. 1938. Mediaeval number symbolism; a study in the history of ideas. New York.

Hussey, J. M. 1963. Church and learning in the Byzantine Empire, 867–1185. Second edition. New York.

Il'in, N. N. 1957. Letopisnaja stat'ja 6523 goda i jeje istočnik. Moskva.

Il'in, M. A. 1965. O naimenovanii Desjatinnoj cerkvi. Sovetskaja arxeologija 2:266–8.

Il'in, M. A. 1968. O edinstve domongolskogo russkogo zodčestva. Sovetskaja arxeologija 4:87–94.

Janin, R.1953. Les églises et monastères de Constantinople. Paris.

Janin, V. L. 1962. Novgorodskije posadniki. Moskva.

Janin, V. L. 1974. Cerkov' Borisa i Gleba v Novgorodskom detince. In: Kultura srednevekovoj Rusi, 88–93. Leningrad.

Janin, V. L. 1977. Očerki kompleksnogo istočnikovedenija. Moskva.

Kaiser, D. H. 1976. In search of old Kiev: a review of the literature. Recenzija 7/1:1–13. Cambridge. Mass.

Kämpfer, F. 1978. Das russische Herrscherbild. Recklinghausen.

Karger, M. K. 1940a. Knjažeskoe pogrebenie XI v. v Desjatinnoj cerkvi. Kratkie Soobščenija Instituta Istorii Materialnoj Kultury 4:12–20.

Karger, M. K. 1940b. K voprosu o sarkofagax kn. Vladimira i Anny. Kratkie Soobščenija Instituta Istorii Materialnoj Kultury 7:76–80.

Karger, M. K. 1947. K voprosu ob ubranstve inter'era v russkom zodčestve domongolskogo perioda. Trudy Vserossijskoj Akademii Xudožestv 1:15–50 + 27 ill.

Karger, M. K. 1958 and 1961. Drevnij Kiev. 2 vols. Leningrad.

Karinskij, N. M. 1905. Slavjanskaja paleografija. Warszawa.

Każdan, A. 1977. Once more about the "alleged" Russo-Byzantine treaty and the Pechenegs crossing of the Danube. Jahrbuch der österreichischen Byzantinistik 26:65–77 (see also H. Hunger, 327f.).

Kilievič, S. R. 1976. Arxeologična karta Kyivs'kogo ditinca. In: Arxeologični doslidžennja starodavnogo Kyjeva, 179–213.

Knjazevskaja, O. A. and other (eds.). 1971. Uspenskij sbornik XII–XIII vv. Moskva.

Komeč, A. I. 1968. Postroenie vertikalnoj kompozicii Sofijskogo sobora v Kieve. Sovetskaja arxeologija 3:232–8.

Komeč, A. I. 1972. Rol knjažeskogo zakaza v postroenii Sofijskogo sobora v Kieve. In: Drevnerusskoe iskusstvo; xudožestvennaja kultura domongolskoj Rusi, 50–64. Moskva.

Komeč, A. I. 1975. Spaso-Preobraženskij sobor v Černigove. In: Drevnerusskoe iskusstvo; zarubežnye svjazi, 9–26. Moskva.

Komeč, A. I. 1976. Rol pridelov v formirovanii obščej kompozicii Sofijskogo sobora v Novgorode. In: Srednevekovaja Rus', 147–150. Moskva.

Komeč, A. I. 1978. Dva napravlenija Novgorodskoj arxitektury načala XII v. In: Srednevekovoe iskusstvo, Rus' i Gruzija, 45–62. Moskva.

Korzuxina, G. F. and P. A. Rappoport. 1966. Review of the work by V. Petrov, 1964, on the historical topography of Kiev. Sovetskaja arxeologija 4:228–9.

Krasovskij, M. 1916. Kurs istorii ruskoj arxitektury, 1: Derevjannoe zodčestvo. Petrograd.

Kresalnyj, N. I. 1972. Novye issledovanija severozapadnoj bašni Sofii Kievskoj. In: Drevnerusskoe iskusstvo; Xudožestvennaja kultura domongolskoj Rusi, 65–79. Moskva. The first version of this article was published 1968 in Vizantijskij Vremennik 19:211–31.

Kučkin, V. A. 1969. Rostovo-suzdalskaja zemlja v X-pervoj treti XIII v. Istorija SSSR 2:62–94.

Kuz'min, A. G. 1977. Načalnye etapy drevnerusskogo letopisanija. Moskva.

Kuz'min, A. G. 1978. Nado li menjat' "A" na "B"? (Po povodu zametki A. V. Poppe.) Istorija SSSR 4:230–2.

Lazarev, V. N. 1960. Mozaiki Sofii Kievskoj. Moskva.

Lazarev, V. N. 1966. Mixailovskie mozaiki. Moskva.

Lazarev, V. N. 1968. O rospisi Sofii Novgorodskoj. In: Drevnerusskoe iskusstvo; xudožestvennaja kultura Novgoroda, 7–62. Moskva.

Lazarev, V. N. 1970a. Regard sur l'art de la Russie prémongole. Cahiers de civilisation médiévale 13/3: 195–208.

Lazarev, V. N. 1970b. Russkaja srednevekovaja živopis'. Moskva.

Lazarev, V. 1971. Le système de la décoration murale de Sainte Sophie de Kiev. Cahiers de civilisation médiévale 14/3:221–38.

Lazarev, V. 1972. Byzanz und die altrussische Kunst.

Jahrbuch der österreichischen Byzantinistik 21: 179–88.

Lazarev, V. N. 1973. Drevnerusskie mozaiki i freski XI–XV vv. Moskva.

Lebedincev, P. G. 1878. O Sofii Kievskoj. In: Trudy 3 Arxeologičeskogo S'ezda 1:53–8. Kiev.

Levitskaja, V. L. 1959. O nekotoryx voprosax proizvodstva nabora mozaik Sofii Kievskoj. Vizantijskij Vremennik 15:169–83.

Levitskaja, V. L. 1963. Materialy issledovanija palitry mozaik Sofii Kievskoj. Vizantijskij Vremennik 23:105–57.

Lixačev, D. S. 1950. Povest' vremennyx let 2: statji i kommentarii. Moskva.

Logvin, G. N. 1969. Spasskij sobor v Černigove. Istorija SSSR 6:193–8.

Logvin, G. N. 1971. Sofia Kievskaja. Kiev.

Logvin, G. N. 1974. Novye nabludenija v Sofii Kievskoj. In: Kultura srednevekovoj Rusi, 154–60. Leningrad.

Logvin, G. N. 1976. O derevjannom zodčestve domongolskoj Rusi. In: Srednevekovaja Rus', 151–9. Moskva.

Logvin, G. N. 1977. K istorii sooruženija Sofijskogo sobora v Kieve. In: Pamjatniki kultury. Novye otkrytija. Ežegodnik 1977:169–86. Moskva.

Loriquet, H. 1904. Catalogue général des manuscrits des bibliothèques publiques de France. Départements. Vol. 38: Reims vol. 1. Paris.

Łowmiański, H. 1970a. Świetopełk w Brześciu w 1019 r. In: Europa-Słoiańszczyzna-Polska; Festschrift K. Tymieniecki, 229–41. Poznań.

Łowmiański, H. 1970b. Roś. In: Słownik Starozytności Słowiańskich 4:553–4.

Lur'e, Ja. S. 1976. Obščerusskie letopisi XIV–XV vv Leningrad.

Maksimovič, M. A. 1877. Sobranie sočinenij 2:132–40 Kiev.

Mango, C. (ed.). 1972. The art of the Byzantine Empire; sources and documents. Englewood Cliffs N. J.

Mango, C. 1976. Byzantine architecture (German transl. Byzantinische Architektur Stuttgart 1975. New York.

Michel, A. 1959. Die Kaisermacht in der Ostkirche 843–1204. Darmstadt.

Mjasoedov, V. 1918. Freski severnogo pritvora Sofijskogo sobora v Kieve. Zapiski otdelenij russkoj i slavjanskoj arxeologii 12:1–6.

Mokeev, G. E. 1978. Mnogoglavye xramy drevne Rusi. Arxitekturnoe nasledstvo 26:41–52.

Morgilevskyj, I. 1928. Spas'kyj sobor v Černigovi za novymi doslidami. In: Černigiv i pivnicne Livo bereżžja, 169–83 + 10 ills. Kiev.

Müller, L. 1959. Zum Problem des hierarchischen Status und der jurisdiktionellen Abhängigkeit der russischen Kirche vor 1039. Köln.

Müller, L. (ed.). 1962. Des Metropoliten Ilarion Lobrede auf Vladimir den Heiligen und Glaubensbekenntnis. Wiesbaden.

Müller, L. (ed.). 1971. Die Werke des Metropoliten Ilarion. München.

Murjanov, M. F. 1978. O Desjatinnoj cerkvi knjazja Vladimira. In: Vostočnaja Evropa v drevnosti i srednevekov'e, 171–5. Moskva.

Murray, J. A. H. (ed.). 1903. A new English dictionary on historical principles, 6. Oxford.

Nasonov, A. N. (ed.). 1941 and 1955. Pskovskie letopisi. 2 vols. Moskva.

Nasonov, A. N. (ed.). 1950. Novgorodskaja pervaja letopis' staršego i mladšego izvodov. Moskva.

Parxomenko, V. 1930. Rus' i Pečenegi. Slavia 8:138–44.

Poppe, A. 1962. Materiały do słownika terminów budownictwa staroruskiego X–XV w. Wrocław.

Poppe, A. 1965a. Zasnuvannja Sofii Kyivskoi. Ukrainskyj Istoryčnyj Žurnal 9:97–104.

Poppe, A. 1965b. Chronologia utworów Nestora hagiografa. Slavia Orientalis 14:287–305.

Poppe, A. 1968a. Graffiti y data spodrudżennja Sofiji Kyjivs'koji. Ukrainskyj Istoryčnyj Žurnal 9:93–7.

Poppe, A. 1968b. Russkije mitropolii Konstantinopolskoj patriarxii. v XI v. Vizantijskij Vremennik 28:85–108.

Poppe, A. 1968c. Państwo i kościół na Rusi w XI wieku. Warszawa.

Poppe, A. 1968d. Kompozycja fundacyjna Sofii Kijowskiej. W poszukiwaniu układu pierwotnego. Biuletyn historii sztuki 30:1–29 + ills.

Poppe, A. 1971a. L'organisation diocésaine de la Russie aux XIe–XIIe siècles. Byzantion 40:165–217.

Poppe, A. 1971b. La dernière expédition russe contre Constantinople. Byzantinoslavica 32:1–29, 233–68.

Poppe, A. 1972. La tentative de la réforme ecclésiastique en Russie au milieu du XIe siècle. Acta poloniae historica 25:5–31.

Poppe, A. 1974. K voprosu ob ultramartovskom stile v Povesti Vremennyx Let'. Istorija SSSR 4:175–8.

Powstenko, O. 1954. The cathedral of St Sophia in Kiev. Annals of the Ukrainian Academy of Arts and Sciences in the U.S. 3–4. New York. English text pp., 9–162, Ukrainian text pp. 167–242.

Priselkov, M. (ed.). 1950. Troickaja letopis'. Rekonstrukcija teksta. Moskva.

Proxorov, G. M. 1977. Letopisnyje podborki rukopisi

GPB, F. IV. 603 i problema svodnogo obščersuskogo letopisanija. Trudy otdela drevnerusskoj literatury 32:165–98.

PSRL = Polnoe sobranie Russkix letopisej, 1, 2, 4, 5, 8, 9, 25, 30.
  Vol. 1: Lavrentjevskaja letopis'. Second edition. Leningrad 1926–28, reprinted 1962.
  Vol. 2: Ipat'evskaja letopis'. Second edition. Sankt-Petersburg 1908, reprinted 1962.
  Vol. 4/1/1: Novgorodskaja četvertaja letopiś. Petrograd 1915.
  Vol. 5: Pskovškie i Sofijske letopisi. Sankt-Petersburg 1851.
  Vol. 8: Voskresenskaja letopis' 2. Sankt-Petersburg 1859.
  Vol. 9: Nikonovskaja letopis'. Sankt-Petersburg 1862, reprinted 1965.
  Vol. 25: Moskovskij letopisnyj svod konca XV v. Moskva 1949.
  Vol. 30: Vladimirskij letopisec. Novgorodskaja vtoraja/arxivskaja/letopis'. Moskva 1965.

Rappoport, P. A. 1956. Očerki po istorii russkogo voennogo zodčestva X–XII vv. Moskva.

Rappoport, P. A. 1961. Očerki po istorii voennogo zodčestva severovostočnoj i severo-zapadnoj Rusi X–XV vv. Moskva.

Rappoport, P. A. 1969. Russian mediaeval military architecture. Gladius 8:39–62.

Rappoport, P. A. 1970. O vzaimosvjazi russkix arxitekturnyx škol v XII v. Trudy Instituta Živopisi, Skulptury i Arxitektury im. Repina 3:3–25.

Rappoport, P. A. 1974. Orientacija drevnerusskix cerkvej. Kratkie Soobščenija Instituta Arxeologii 139:43–8.

Rappoport, P. A. 1977. Russkaja arxitektura na rubeže XII i XIII vekov. In: Drevnerusskoe iskusstvo; problemy i atribucii, 12–29. Moskva.

Rasovskij, D. A. 1933. Pečenegi, torki i berendei na Rusi i v Ugrii. Seminarium Kondakovianum 6:1–66.

Rozov, N. N. (ed.). 1963. Sinodalnyj spisok sočinenij Ilariona, russkogo pisatela XI v. Slavia 32:141–75.

Rybakov, B. A. 1964. Russkie datirovannye nadpisi XI–XIV vv. Moskva.

Rydzevskaja, E. 1978. Drevnjaja Rus' i Skandinavija IX–XIV vv. Moskva.

Šaxmatov, A. A. 1908. Razyskanija o drevnejšix russkix letopisnyx svodax. Sankt-Petersburg.

Šaxmatov, A. A. 1916. "Povest'" Vremennyx Let' 1: Vvodnaja čast ,tekst, primečanija. Petrograd.

Ščapov, Ja. N. 1972. Knjažeskie ustavy i cerkov' v drevnej Rusi. Moskva.

Ščapova, Ju. L. 1972. Steklo Kievskoj Rusi. Moskva.

Ščapova, Ju. L. 1975. Novye materialy k istorii mozaik Uspenskogo sobora v Kieve. Sovetskaja arxeologija 4:209–22.

Ščapova, Ju. L. 1978. O drevnerusskom steklovarenii. In: Drevnjaja Rus' i slavjane, 206–12. Moskva.

Ščepkin, V. N. 1967. Russkaja paleografija. Second edition. Moskva.

Schäfer, H. 1974. Architekturhistorische Beziehungen zwischen Byzanz und der Kiever Rus' im 10 und 11 Jahrhundert. Istanbuler Mitteilungen 23/24:197–224, Tafel 87–101.

Schneidér, A. M. 1951. Die Blachernen. Oriens 4:82–120.

Sedov, V. V. 1974. Dve zametki po arxeologii Suzdala. In: Kultura srednevekovoj Rusi, 61–64. Leningrad.

Serbina, K. N. (ed.). 1950. Ustjužskij letopisnyj svod. Moskva.

Shepard, J. 1975. Byzantinorussica. Revue des études Byzantines 33:211–25.

Soloviev, A. 1979. Byzance et la formation de l'État russe. Recueil d'études. Variorum reprints. London.

Štender, G. M. 1968. K voprosu ob arxitekture malyx form Sofii Novgorodskoj. In: Drevnerusskoe iskusstvo; xudožestvennaja kultura Novgoroda, 83–107. Moskva.

Štender, G. M. 1974. K voprosu o dekorativnyx osobennostjax stroitelnoj texniki Novgorodskoj Sofii. In: Kultura srednevekovoj Rusi, 202–12.

Štender, G. M. 1977. Pervičnyj zamysel i posledujuščye izmenenija galerej i lestničnoj bašni Novgorodskoj Sofii. In: Drevnerusskoe iskusstvo. Problemy i atribucii, 30–54. Moskva.

Strilenko, Ju. M. 1975. Analiz zrzkiv freskovyx ta budivelnyx rozčiniv Sofii Kyivs'koi. In: Starodavnyj Kyiv, 195–201. Kiev.

Strumins'kyj, B. O. 1976. Review of Vysockij 1966 and 1976. Recenzija 7/1:14–33. Cambridge, Mass.

Thurn, J. (ed.). 1973. Ioannis Scylitzae synopsis historiarum. Berlin.

Tixomirov, M. N. 1955. Krestjanskie i gorodskie vosstanija na Rusi XI-XIII vv. Moskva.

Toc'ka, I. F. 1975. Pro čas vykonannja rospisiv galerej Sofii Kyivskoj. In: Starodavnyj Kyiv, 182–94. Kiev.

Toc'ka I. F. and O. F. Jerko. 1976. Do istorii pivničnoi galerei Sofii Kyivs'koi. In: Arxeologični doslidžennja starodavn'ogo Kyjeva, 119–30. Kiev.

Toločko, P. P. 1969. Do istoriji budovnictva "goroda Jaroslava" ta Sofiji Kyjivs'koji. Arxeolohia 22:196–202.

Toločko, P. P. 1972. Istoryčna topografija starodavn'-ogo Kyjeva. Second edition. Kiev.

Tomes, T. E. 1974. Zametki arxivista. Sovetskaja arxeologija 1:240–1.

Trillmich, W. (ed.). 1957. Thietmari Merseburgensis episcopi Chronicon. Ausgewählte Quellen zur deutschen Geschichte des Mittelalters, 9. Reprinted 1962. Berlin.

Trillmich, W. (ed.). 1961. Adam Bremensis Gesta Hammaburgensis ecclesiae pontificum. In: Quellen des 9. und 11. Jhm. zur Geschichte der Hamburgischen Kirche und des Reiches, 137–499. Berlin.

Troicki, S. 1935. Ktitorsko pravo u Vizantiji i u Nemanickoj Srbiji. In: Srpska Kraljevska Akademija, Glas 168, 2 razred, 86/3:81–132.

Troje, L. 1925. Die Dreizehn und die Zwölf im Traktat Pelliot. Dogmen in Zahlenformeln. Ein Beitrag zu den Grundlagen des Manicheismus. Leipzig.

Tschan, F. J. (ed.). 1959. Adam of Bremen's History. New York.

Vagner, G. K. 1964. Dekorativnoe iskusstvo v arxitekture Rusi X-XIII vv. Moskva.

Vernadsky, G. 1948. Kievan Russia. Seventh printing 1973 New Haven.

Voronin, N. N. 1952. U istokov russkogo nacionalnogo zodčestva. In: Ežegodnik Instituta Istorii Iskusstv, 257–316. Moskva.

Voronin, N. N. 1961 and 1962. Zodčestvo severovestočnoj Rusi XII-XV vv. 2 vols. Moskva.

Vysockij, S. A. (ed.). 1966a. Drevnerusskie nadpisi Sofii Kievskoj XI-XIV vv. Kiev.

Vysoc'kyj, S. O. (Vysockij, S. A.). 1966b. Grafiti ta sporudžennja Kyivs'koi Sofii. Ukrains'kyj istoričnyj žurnal 7:103–6.

Vysoc'kyj, S. O. (Vysockij' S. A.). 1975. Grafiti ta čas pobudovi Sofijs'kogo soboru v Kyjevi. In: Starodavnyj Kyiv, 171–81. Kiev.

Vysockij, S. A. (ed.). 1976. Srednevekovye nadpisi Sofii Kievskoj. Kiev.

Wailly, de N. (ed.) 1874. Geoffroi de Villehardouin: Conquête de Constantinople avec la continuation de Henri de Valenciennes. Paris.

Zabelin, K. E. 1900. Čerty samobytnosti v drevnerusskom zodčestve. Moskva.

Zhishmann, J. 1888. Das Stifterrecht in der morgenländischen Kirche. Wien.

Zimin, A. A. 1954. K istorii teksta kratkoj redakcii Russkoj Pravdy. Trudy Moskovskogo Gosudarstvennogo Istoriko-Arxeografičeskogo Instituta 7:155–208.

V

LA TENTATIVE DE RÉFORME ECCLÉSIASTIQUE EN RUSSIE AU MILIEU DU XIe SIÈCLE

La métropole de Kiev, fondée à la fin du Xe siècle, a constitué dès sa création une province ecclésiastique du patriarcat de Constantinople. C'est dans la situation intérieure de l'Empire et dans la politique extérieure de la Russie soutenant Georges Maniakès, le chef des troupes byzantines en Italie qui convoitait le stemma de l'empereur des Romains, que résident les raisons du conflit russo-byzantin de 1043. Elles ne concernaient pas la question de la juridiction ecclésiastique, c'est pourquoi le traité de paix de 1046 rétablissant les relations amicales entre les deux États ne pouvait que confirmer la position juridique de l'Église russe [1]. En 1039, et probablement au cours de la cinquième décennie, le métropolite de Russie était Théopemptos, et il n'y a aucune raison de croire, comme le suggère la littérature concernant cette question, que le siège de Kiev vaquait durant de longues années. Celui-ci était vacant avant 1051 ou peut-être même cette année-là lorsque se posa la question de l'ordination d'un nouveau métropolite [2]. C'est la procédure exceptionnelle et les circonstances de l'accession du moine russe Hilarion à la dignité de métropolite qui constituent le canevas du présent article.

Les ouvrages qui abordent « l'affaire Hilarion » abondent en suppositions, mais les matériaux de source qui la concernent sont particulièrement indigents. Le *Récit des temps passés* nous apprend, pour l'année 6559 (mars 1051 - février 1052), que: « Jaroslav, ayant réuni les évêques, nomma Larion, un Russe, métropolite de Sainte-Sophie ». On peut penser

---

[1] A. Poppe, *Państwo i Kościół na Rusi w XI w.* [*L'État et l'Église en Russie au XIe siècle*], Warszawa 1968, pp. 15 - 39, 82 - 130; idem, *La dernière expédition russe contre Constantinople*, « Byzantinoslavica », vol. XXXII, 1971, n°1, pp. 1 - 29, n° 2, pp. 233 - 268.

[2] Idem, *Państwo...*, pp. 101 - 104, 131 - 132.

que cette brève notice a été rédigée peu de temps après cet événement. Le récit *Du début du couvent des Cryptes*, inséré dans la même année et rédigé dans la dernière décennie du XIe siècle, au plus tard au cours des dix premières années du XIIe siècle, témoigne en faveur de cette thèse. L'auteur, qui entra au couvent vers 1070 à l'âge de 17 ans, en expliquant l'origine du nom du couvent, déclare dans l'introduction qu' Hilarion, prêtre de l'église des saints Apôtres de Berestovo, « homme juste, savant et ascète », qui avait coutume de se rendre dans un bois sur la rive escarpée du Dniépr, y creusa une crypte où il priait dans la solitude. Peu de temps après, lorsqu'il fut nommé métropolite sur l'intervention du prince, la crypte, délaissée, fut occupée par le moine Antoine qui venait du Mont Athos. Devenu un ermite célèbre, celui-ci réunit autour de lui, peu après 1054, douze novices, agrandit avec leur aide les cryptes et fonda le couvent [3]. L'introduction du récit sur le début du couvent fait nettement apparaître la raison pour laquelle ce récit a été placé dans l'anneé 1051: la notice sur l'élévation d' Hilarion au rang de métropolite était un point de départ chronologique commode pour présenter la préhistoire du couvent. Cette notice a pu être insérée dans la chronique compilée au couvent sur la base d'annales antérieures, elles-mêmes rédigées, peut-être, aussi au couvent, à partir de la septième décennie du XIe siècle. On ne peut pas cependant exclure qu'elle soit de la même origine et de la même date que le récit sur le début du couvent, mais, dans ce cas également, nous avons affaire à une information fournie par les contemporains d'un événement insolite dans la vie de l'Église: il y avait au début du XIIe siècle au couvent des Cryptes des moines vénérables qui se souvenaient des événements de la première moitié du siècle précédent. Le premier récit sur les débuts du couvent des Cryptes vient compléter d'une façon essentielle la brève note exprimant l'approbation par le couvent de la nomination d' Hilarion: « Puis Dieu inspira le coeur du prince et [celui-ci] nomma [Hilarion] métropolite de Sainte-Sophie ». Il est caractéristique que l'auteur du récit souligne la pertinence du choix, quant à la nomination du métropolite par le prince, il la présente comme un fait évident, n'exigeant aucun commentaire.

Le *Credo* qu'Hilarion exprima au moment où il revêtit la dignité épiscopale constitue le second témoignage des sources. Celui-ci se termine par la formule de présentation suivante: « Moi, par la grâce de Dieu miséricordieux, Hilarion, moine et prêtre, de par Sa volonté ai été consacré et intronisé par les pieux évêques à Kiev, ville grande et protégée de Dieu, afin d'y être métropolite, pasteur et maître. Ceci s'est produit

---

[3] *Povest' vremennyh let* [par la suite *PVL*], vol. I, Moskva 1950, pp. 104 - 106.

en l'an 6559 sous le règne du kagan orthodoxe Jaroslav, fils de Vladimir. Amen » [4].

Conformément à la coutume, le candidat rédigeait de sa main sa profession de foi, la lisait à haute voix le jour de la consécration et la signait immédiatement dans l'église [5]. La formule, que nous venons de citer, représente sans aucun doute la signature élargie apposée par Hilarion dans l'archicathédrale Sainte-Sophie le jour du sacre épiscopal, d'où son caractère purement ecclésiastique et le fait que la nomination par le prince soit passée sous silence.

En rapprochant les deux témoignages qui se complètent, on voit nettement apparaître leur indépendance réciproque. Alors que le *Récit des temps passés*, mettant l'accent sur le rôle de Jaroslav, n'évoque que les opérations préalables, le choix et la nomination d' Hilarion par le souverain et par l'assemblée des évêques, le *Credo* fait état des autres cérémonies de l'ordination: la cérémonie de la consécration et de l'intronisation célébrée par les évêques, sur place, à Kiev.

L'élévation d'un candidat local au rang de métropolite sans la participation de Constantinople constituait un événement exceptionnel, vu la procédure appliquée à l'époque dans ce domaine. C'est pourquoi l'historiographie a cherché à éclaircir les raisons de cette mesure, les premiers essais ayant été ceux de l'auteur de la *Chronique nikonienne* au XVIe siècle. Pour la plupart des chercheurs, ce fut là la suite du conflit byzantino-russe de 1043, une nouvelle tentative de libérer l'Église russe de la domination byzantine [6]. Indépendamment de ces divergences, ou d'autres encore, ce point de vue devrait mener logiquement à la conclusion qu'il

---

[4] Pour la publication du *Credo* voir: *Pamjatniki drevnerusskogo kanoničeskogo prava*, IIe partie, Petrograd 1920, pp. 102 - 103; L. M ü l l e r, *Des Metropoliten Ilarion Lobrede auf Vladimir den Heiligen und Glaubenbekenntnis*, Wiesbaden 1962, pp. 141 - 143; N. R o z o v dans « Slavia », vol. XXXII, 1963, pp. 174 - 175.

[5] Cf. I. S o k o l o v, *Izbranie arhiereev v Vizantii IX—XV vv.*, « Vizantijskij Vremennik », vol. XXII, 1915 - 1916, pp. 241 - 242; N. M i l a š, *Pravoslavno cerkovno pravo*, Mostar 1902, pp. 387 - 388.

[6] Cela a été formulé avec force par M. P r i s e l k o v, *Očerki po cerkovno-političeskoj istorii Rusi X—XII vv.*, St. Petersburg 1913, p. 92 et suiv. De nombreux historiens l'ont suivi, tel par exemple B. W i d e r a, *Jaroslavs des Weisen Kampf um die kirchliche Unabhängigkeit von Byzanz*, « Berliner Byzantinistische Arbeiten », vol. V, Berlin 1957, pp. 158, 175; K. R o s e, *Byzanz und die Autonomiebestrebungen der russischen Kirche in der Zeit vom 10. bis 15. Jahrhundert*, dans: *Byzantinistische Beiträge*, Berlin 1964, pp. 308 - 310; M. Č u b a t y j, *Istorija christianstva na Rusi-Ukraine [De historia christianitatis in antiqua Rus'-Ukraina a primis exordiis usque ad a. 1353*, Roma - New-York 1965, p. 315 et suiv. Une juste critique de cet ouvrage a été donnée par L. Müller, cf. « Jahrbücher für Geschichte Osteuropas », vol. XVII, 1969, n° 2, pp. 271 - 273.

s'agissait de la dépendance, non seulement ecclésiastique, mais aussi politique de la Russie envers Byzance.

Le raisonnement d'autres chercheurs qui se sont penchés sur le problème des relations byzantino-russes au XIe siècle a suivi une autre voie. Ils sont d'accord pour négliger ou même nier tout rapport entre le conflit de 1043 et la nomination d'Hilarion en 1051. En partant de ce principe, E. Golubinskij a supposé que l'acte de 1051 exprimait le mécontentement de Jaroslav du procédé appliqué pour la nomination du métropolite et son intention d'introduire de nouveaux principes. Il faisait remarquer en même temps judicieusement que, si Jaroslav avait tendu réellement à modifier la procédure en vigueur, il aurait dû avoir des imitateurs parmi ses successeurs. C'est pourquoi, en fin de compte, cet érudit considérait la nomination d'Hilarion comme étant un fait isolé, dénué de toute signification politique. Elle n'aurait été que l'expression de la sympathie et de l'admiration du souverain pour les qualités d'esprit et d'âme du prêtre Hilarion. En considérant qu'il était difficile de trouver un candidat plus digne, Jaroslav ordonna aux évêques de le consacrer, sans avoir le moins du monde l'intention de créer un précédent ou de rompre les liens ecclésiastiques avec Constantinople [7].

P. Sokolov, lui, niait carrément qu'il y ait eu un rapport entre l'acte de 1051 et les événements de 1043. Il considérait que la nomination d'Hilarion était le résultat de l'application par Jaroslav et par le clergé du Nomocanon en XIV titres. Ce Nomocanon, parallèlement aux décisions des conciles relatives à l'élection et à la consécration des évêques (et des métropolites) par le synode des évêques de la province, contenait les Novelles 123 et 127 de Justinien d'après lesquelles le choix de l'évêque dépendait du clergé et des notables de la cité. Du point de vue du Nomocanon, l'acte de Jaroslav aurait été parfaitement légal, et on ne peut que lui reprocher d'avoir pris sa décision sans s'être entendu avec le patriarche. Mais, même dans ce cas, Jaroslav est justifié par l'imprécision de ces Novelles qui stipulent que le meilleur parmi les élus soit ordonné par le jugement ou la conviction de celui qui ordonne [8]. Sokolov était donc d'avis que l'initiative de Jaroslav découlait d'une connaissance insuffisante des règles ecclésiastiques et qu'en particulier il n'avait pas

---

[7] E. Golubinskij, *Istorija russkoj cerkvi*, vol. I², 1, Moskva 1901, pp. 297 - 299, repris par L. K. Götz, *Staat und Kirche in Altrussland. Kiever Periode 988 - 1240*, Berlin 1908, pp. 82 - 84; M. Hruševskyj penchait également en faveur de la thèse de Golubinskij (cf. Hruševskyj, *Istorija Ukrainy-Rusi*, vol. III, Lviv 1905, pp. 261 - 262), en soulignant en même temps qu'il est impossible de trancher ce dilemme.

[8] On traduit par « ordonner » le vieux-slave *postaviti*, expression qui signifiait aussi bien « établir », « nommer » quelqu'un, que « ordonner » dans le sens du sacrement de l'ordination.

su faire la différence entre deux moments, le moment juridique, c'est-à-dire la confirmation de la candidature, dans ce cas particulier, par le patriarche lui même, et d'autre part le moment sacramentel que constitue la consécration par le collège des évêques. L'érudit concluait que l'élection d' Hilarion était un acte de piété allié à l'ignorance. Pour Constantinople c'était là une atteinte aux prérogatives du patriarche. Mais l'affaire pouvait être réglée à l'amiable puisqu'il n'était pas dans l'intention de Jaroslav de procéder à l'émancipation de l'Église de Russie [9]. Il est difficile d'être entièrement d'accord avec P. Sokolov, car il attache trop d'importance à la piété candide de Jaroslav qui pourtant n'explique pas l'attitude du synode des évêques. Ajoutons qu'il est vain, dans la nomination de l'évêque, de différencier le juridique du sacramental, car, à cette époque, en ce qui concerne les métropolites, ces deux éléments constituaient un privilège du patriarche et de son synode. D'ailleurs Jaroslav pouvait connaitre ou non les règles du droit ecclésiastique, mais, par contre, aussi bien lui que son entourage, étaient parfaitement au courant de la coutume en vigueur: le métropolite arrivait en Russie, ayant été élu ou nommé et consacré sur les bords du Bosphore, et l'archicathédrale de Kiev n'était que le cadre de son intronisation.

G. G. Litavrin explique l'acte de 1051 par les divergences dans la politique européenne des deux États. La tentative entreprise par Cérulaire, au seuil du schisme de 1054, d'exercer une influence sur la politique étrangère de la Russie, amicale envers les pays occidentaux et la papauté, aurait provoqué le mécontentement de Jaroslav et la nomination d'Hilarion en dépit du patriarche [10]. Remarquons en passant que les

---

[9] P. S o k o l o v, Russkij arhierej iz Vizantii i pravo ego naznačenija do načala XV veka, Kiev 1913, pp. 42 - 52.

[10] G. G. L i t a v r i n, Psellos sur les causes de la dernière expédition russe contre Constantinople en 1043 (en russe), «Vizantijskij Vremennik», vol. XXVII, 1967, pp. 80, 85, et du même auteur Istorija Vizantii, vol. II, Moskva 1967, p. 351. Dans les ouvrages qui se réfèrent au texte de Nicéphore Grégoras (livre 36, c. 22 - 23), on suggère qu'il y avait peut-être dès le début un accord qui prévoyait alternativement l'élévation à la métropole de Kiev de prélats d'origine grecque et russe. Cette assertion est contredite par le procédé de promotion à la chaire de Kiev, que l'on peut observer jusqu'au milieu du XIII⁰ siècle. C'est pourquoi D. O b o - l e n s k y (Byzantium, Kiev and Moscow: a Study in Ecclesiastical Relations, «Dumbarton Oaks Papers» vol. XI, 1957, pp. 30 et suiv., 70) incline vers un jugement plus nuancé selon lequel la concession byzantine a eu lieu au XIII⁰ siècle, lorsque le patriarche fut obligé de résider à Nicée. Le témoignage de Grégoras du milieu du XIV⁰ siècle, équivoque d'ailleurs, doit être examiné dans le contexte des disputes de l'époque portant sur l'organisation ecclésiastique de la Russie. Cf. P. S o k o l o v, Russkij arhierej..., pp. 36 et suiv.; J. M e y e n d o r f f, Alexis and Roman: a Study in Byzantino-Russian Relations (1352 - 1354), «Byzantinoslavica», vol. XXVIII, 1967, pp. 278 - 288.

événements de 1054, que l'on désigne traditionnellement et incorrectement du terme de schisme, n'avaient pas le poids et les conséquences qu'on leur accorde en général. Au milieu du XIᵉ siècle, la papauté n'avait pas d'influence sur la politique des pays d'Europe orientale envers Byzance. Politiquement affaiblie, elle comptait à l'époque sur le soutien de Byzance pour faire front à l'agression normande. Quant à Byzance, après son alliance avec la papauté, elle escomptait également que la défense de ses possessions en Italie lui serait facilitée [11]. Même si l'on fait abstraction du fait que rien ne prouve que des liens quelconques aient uni la Russie à la papauté, il est difficile d'admettre que Jaroslav aurait en 1051 assujetti sa politique à des événements dont leurs responsables eux-mêmes n'étaient pas conscients.

De l'avis de L. Müller, l'acte de 1051 n'était pas l'expression d'un conflit. Les témoignages qui nous sont parvenus n'autorisent pas à interpréter l'élévation d'Hilarion comme une manifestation de l'autocéphalie de l'Église de Russie, car le seul critère qui d'après lui serait valable, à savoir la position, vis-à-vis de cet acte, du patriarche détenant le droit de confirmation, nous est inconnu. Mais, en même temps, ce savant présente son hypothèse selon laquelle l'élévation d'Hilarion fut le résultat d'un accord avec Byzance: le choix et la nomination du candidat du prince russe se seraient effectués, selon les usages établis, à Constantinople où l'on aurait également été d'accord pour que la cérémonie du sacre épiscopale d'Hilarion se déroulât à Kiev [12]. Ces suppositions quant à la réalisation de cet accord sont en contradiction avec le témoignage du *Récit des temps passés* dont nous ne pouvons rejeter la véracité. Il découle nettement du *Récit* que le choix et la nomination ont eu lieu à Kiev. Si nous approuvons L. Müller lorsqu'il soutient que l'acte de 1051 ne saurait être interpreté comme une tendance à l'autocéphalie, nous sommes cependant enclins à y voir le reflet d'un conflit au sein de l'Église, puisque cet acte d'élévation au trône de la métropole présente une façon de procéder tout à fait inconnue à cette époque dans le patriarcat de l'oikouménĕ des Romains.

---

[11] Cf. J. Gay, *L'Italie méridionale et l'Empire byzantin (867 - 1071)*, Paris 1904, pp. 440 et suiv.; A. Michel, *Schisma und der Kaiserhof im Jahre 1054*, dans: *L'Église et les Églises 1054 - 1956*, vol. I, Chevetogne 1954, pp. 351 et suiv.; P. Lemerle, *L'orthodoxie byzantine et l'oecuménisme médieval: les origines du « schisme » des Églises*, «Bulletin de l'Association Guillaume Budé», ser. IV, 1965, n° 2, pp. 240 - 242; V. v. Falkenhausen, *Untersuchungen über die byzantinische Herrschaft in Süditalien vom IX. bis ins XI. Jahrhundert*, Wiesbaden 1967, pp. 59 et suiv., 189 et suiv.

[12] L. Müller, *Des Metropoliten Ilarion Lobrede...*, pp. 1 - 11, où l'on trouve aussi une critique pertinente des thèses de M. Priselkov et de ses adeptes; idem, *Ilarion u. Nestorchronik*, «Russia Mediaevalis», I, 1972 (à paraître).

L'hypothèse de l'accord serait acceptable, si la prise en considération par l'empereur et le patriarche du voeu de Jaroslav quant à la personne du candidat était seule entrée en considération. Mais, en adoptant cette hypothèse, à la lumière du témoignage des sources, il faut admettre que le patriarche a renoncé au droit de consécration, qui n'appartenait qu'à lui, en faveur des évêques de la province russe.

Cet accord aurait été en fait une reconnaissance par Constantinople du caractère autonome de l'Église russe. La centralisation du système de direction de l'Église byzantine qui, dépassant ses compétences, s'arrogeait le droit de nommer en commun avec le pouvoir impérial les patriarches occidentaux, ainsi que l'attitude autoritaire du patriarche Michel Cérulaire, font que ce renoncement est plus qu'improbable.

Il est évident que le processus de l'élévation d' Hilarion était en contradiction absolue avec le procédé en vigueur, car le droit de promotion revenait au synode du patriarche et au patriarche. Mais on peut demander ce que représentait cet acte du synode des évêques de la métropole russe par rapport au droit canon?

L'élection du métropolite s'effectuait auparavant en vertu des mêmes principes que celle des évêques ordinaires, c'est-à-dire qu'elle relevait du clergé de la cathédrale, des fidèles et des évêques de la province qui procédaient également au sacre épiscopal de l'élu [13]. Le canon 28 du IVᵉ concile oecuménique de Chalcédoine de 451 annonçait déjà des modifications. Ce canon, sanctionnant la supériorité du patriarcat de Constantinople, postulait la consécration du métropolite par l'archevêque de Constantinople après une élection et une présentation appropriée, avec la participation donc du synode des évêques de la province comme le formulaient le canon 6 du synode de Sardique de l'an 343 et la lettre canonique du IIIᵉ concile oecuménique adressée au synode de la province de Pamphylie [14]. La coutume de la consécration du métropolite par le patriarche n'était pas encore généralisée cent ans plus tard, comme le prouve la législation de Justinien reflétant, dans les rédactions successives de certaines résolutions, le processus croissant de la centralisation également de

---

[13] Cf. A. L e b e d e v, *Ob izbranii v episkopskij san v drevnej vselenskoj i russkoj cerkvi*, « Russkij Vestnik », vol. CVII, 1873, n° 9, pp. 53 - 66; F. X. F u n k, *Die Bischofswahl im christlichen Altertum und im Anfang des Mittelalters*, « Kirchengeschichtliche Abhandlungen », Bd. I, Paderborn 1897, pp. 23 - 39.

[14] J. B. P i t r a, *Juris ecclesiastici Graecorum historia et monumenta*, vol. I, Romae 1864, pp. 472, 532 - 533; V. N. B e n e š e v i č, *Syntagma XIV titulorum sine scholliis secundum versionem paleoslovenicam adjecto textu graeco*, vol. I (1 - 3), St.-Petersburg 1906 - 1907, pp. 125, 284. Cf. I. S o k o l o v, *Izbranie arhiereev...*, pp. 201, et suiv.; E. H e r m a n, *Appunti sul diritto metropolitico nella Chiesa byzantina*, « Orientalia Christiana Periodica », vol. XIII, 1947, pp. 528 et suiv., 533 et suiv., 539 et suiv.

l'administration ecclésiastique. Dans la *Novelle* 123, c. 3, la question du sacre des évêques de différents rangs est soulevée lorsqu'est évoqué le problème des dons ordinaires. Il est également question des métropolites « consacrés par leur propre synode ou par les patriarches bénis ». Il en résulterait que l'on constate simplement l'existence de deux coutumes parallèles. Mais déjà vingt ans après, un nouveau pas est réalisé par la *Novelle* 137, éditée le 25 mars 565. Il devient obligatoire de présenter au moins trois candidats « dont le meilleur sera élevé par le choix et le jugement de celui qui consacre ». Le droit de nommer les métropolites devenait en fait une prérogative du patriarche, et la nomination des évêques relevait de la compétence du métropolite. En même temps, cette *Novelle* maintenait la juridiction des synodes, mais la restreignait considérablement dans la pratique en créant une juridiction concurrente des métropolites et des patriarches à l'égard des évêques qui leur étaient soumis [15]. Jean le Scolastique, connu pour ses travaux de codification de la législation ecclésiastique entamés avant qu'il n'occupe le trône patriarcal en 565, omit, il est vrai, dans son recueil d'extraits des *Novelles de Justinien*, compilé vers 570 (appelé en général *Collectio 87 capitulorum*), la *Novelle* 137, mais il apportait, sous l'influence de cette *Novelle*, une importante modification à la *Novelle* 123, supprimant la possibilité, évoquée ci-dessus, pour les métropolites d'être élévés au siège par leur propre synode [16]. La *Novelle* 123 avait été ensuite remaniée de nouveau et élargie sous l'influence de la *Novelle* 137. Il est cependant remarquable de constater que, bien que dans les *Basiliques*, compilation législative datant de l'an 890 environ, le texte de la *Novelle* 123 ait été refondu dans l'esprit des décisions de la *Novelle* 137, on a maintenu en même temps la remarque de la *Novelle* 123, c. 3 sur la consécration du métropolite par son propre synode. Il n'apparaît pas clairement pourquoi les *Basiliques* mentionnent un usage qui n'était plus observé. Peut-être n'étaient-ils pas un code admis dans le droit byzantin, mais une simple compilation destinée à la formation des juristes [17].

[15] P. S o k o l o v, *Russkij arhierej*..., pp. 3 - 6; E. H e r m a n, *Appunti*..., pp. 529, 546 et suiv.

[16] *Collectio 87*..., c. 32; G. H e i m b a c h, *Anekdota*, vol. II, Lipsiae 1840, pp. 221; cf. P. S o k o l o v, *Russkij arhierej*..., pp. 6 - 7.

[17] *Basiliques*, III, 1, 10; voir G. H e i m b a c h, *Basilicorum Libri LX*, vol. I, Lipsiae 1833, pp. 94 - 95. Cf. G. O s t r o g o r s k y, *Histoire de l'État byzantin*, Paris 1956, pp. 245, 267, 270 - 271, et A. K a ž d a n, *Vasiliki kak istoričeskij istočnik*, « Vizantijskij Vremennik », vol. XIV, 1958, pp. 56 - 66. P. S o k o l o v (*Russkij arhierej*..., pp. 8, 22) était d'avis que cette résolution a été maintenue dans les *Basiliques* en considération des archevêchés indépendants de Constantinople, comme celui de Chypre par exemple.

Bien que l'évolution des rapports entre la hiérarchie locale et la hiérarchie centrale de l'Église ne soit pas discernable dans les sources, en
particulier les étapes au cours desquelles le synode permanent (endémuse)
s'est approprié les prérogatives des synodes provinciaux, il faut constater
qu'au IX° siècle déjà nous ne connaissons pas de cas d'élection du métropolite par son synode. Le synode de la capitale, de son côté, veillait
jalousement au droit qu'il avait acquis de présenter au choix du patriarche
trois candidats ayant subi les épreuves avec succès et élus à l'issue d'un
scrutin secret. Telle était la procédure habituelle de la promotion d'un
métropolite aux X° et XI° siècles d'après les oeuvres des écrivains et des
dignitaires de l'Église, Euphémien de Sardes et Nicétas d'Amasée. Ce
dernier soulignait avec insistance que le droit de décider en dernier ressort
revenait au patriarche [18].

Ajoutons que celui-ci ne faisait souvent qu'exprimer la volonté de
l'empereur. Le canoniste byzantin Théodore Balsamon confirmait, à la fin
du XII° siècle, dans son commentaire du Nomocanon en XIV titres, cette
procédure d'élévation au trône de la métropole comme étant une règle
constamment en vigueur depuis le concile de Chalcédoine, et il faisait
remarquer « qu'avant ce canon (c'est-à-dire le 28ème de Chalcédoine),
ce n'était pas les patriarches qui consacraient les métropolites, mais les
évêques de chaque éparchie » [19].

On ne peut donc rien discerner dans l'action des évêques de la province
russe qui soit contraire aux canons puisqu'ils renouaient avec la pratique
canonique initiale, vivante encore au VI° siècle et dont les vestiges s'étaient
peut-être maintenus jusqu'au IX° siècle. Il est évident que le rappel par
le synode métropolitain de ses anciennes prérogatives canoniques était
une querelle de compétence, mais elle ne mettait pas en doute la supériorité du patriarcat de Constantinople. Ce procédé ne sapait pas le droit
du patriarche de confirmer l'élection et la consécration du prélat, droit
qui découlait d'une interprétation conforme du canon 4 du concile de
Nicée I. Mais alors le rôle du patriarche se réduisait à constater que les
actions du synode des évêques avaient été conformes ou non aux canons,
et le patriarche ne pouvait les annuler que s'il y avait eu vice de forme.

Qu'est-ce qui avait donc incité les évêques de la métropole russe à
entreprendre une action qui visait nettement à priver le synode endémuse
et le patriarche du droit de disposer du siège de Kiev?

[18] J. D a r r o u z è s, *Documents inédits d'ecclésiologie byzantine*, Paris 1966,
pp. 108 - 115, 160 - 175; cf. I. S o k o l o v, *Izbranie arhiereev...*, p. 251; E. H e r m a n,
Appunti..., pp. 523 et suiv.; 539 et suiv.; J. H a j j a r, *Le synode permanent dans
l'Église byzantine des origines au XI° siècle*, Roma 1962, pp. 140 - 142; H. G. B e c k,
Kirche und theologische Literatur im Byzantinischen Reich, München 1959, p. 70.

[19] Cf. « Patrologia graeca », vol. CXXXVII, col. 1446.

Cette action était menée avant tout contre le patriarche. Michel Cérulaire était l'un de ces archevêques de la Nouvelle Rome qui menait sa
propre politique, débordant le cadre des questions strictement ecclésiastiques. Son programme ambitieux qui s'exprime même dans l'iconographie [20] ne visait pas seulement à mettre un terme à l'ingérence de
l'autorité séculière dans les problèmes de l'Église. Il s'inspirait également
de l'idée, formulée déjà dans l'*Épanagogé*, de la primauté du sacerdoce sur
l'empire. Constantin Monomaque, souverain influençable, bien qu'il se
soit heurté au patriarche autoritaire, lui accordait sa confiance même
lorsque celui-ci, à l'encontre des plans politiques de l'empereur concernant
l'Italie, aggrava la querelle avec l'Ancienne Rome. Après la mort de
Monomaque, l'intervention de Cérulaire dans les affaires de l'État dété-
riora gravement ses relations avec l'impératrice Théodora. L'ambition
exagérée du patriarche devait entraîner sa chute un an après que l'éner-
gique et non moins ambitieux Isaac Comnène se fut emparé, avec sa participation, du trône impériale [21]. L'attitude impérieuse de Cérulaire, ne
supportant aucune opposition, se faisait sentir en premier lieu dans les
questions internes de l'Église; sa personne et sa politique devaient susciter
le mécontentement du clergé grec, en particulier dans les milieux
monastiques. Qu'un patriarche monte sur le trône d'une manière non
canonique et en ignorant l'endémuse n'était pas exceptionnel. Mais le
fait pouvait être exploité contre lui en cas de conflit, d'autant plus que
Cérulaire avait été nommé par un empereur marié pour la troisième fois
en violation flagrante des canons.

Le réquisitoire contre Cérulaire, préparé à la demande de l'assemblée
réunie au Palais avec la participation des prélats, par Psellos pour être prononcé au synode qui devait déposer le patriarche, présente son patriarcat
comme une suite d'incessantes violations des canons [22]. Il s'agit là d'un
pamphlet écrit par un habile manoeuvrier, c'est pourquoi on ne peut atta-
cher d'importance à ses reproches d'hérésie et de profanation. Néanmoins,
le pamphlet traduit très bien l'atmosphère malveillante envers le patriarche autoritaire qui régnait à la cour et aussi parmi la hiérarchie ecclésias-

---

[20] Cf. B. J. H. J e n k i n s, *A Cross of the Patriarch Michael Cerularius*, « Dumbarton Oaks Papers », vol. XXI, 1967, pp. 232 - 249. Cf. les objections de Ch. W a l-
t e r dans son compte rendu dans la « Revue des Études Byzantines », vol. XXVI,
1968, pp. 407 - 408.

[21] N. S u v o r o v, *Vizantijskij papa*, Moskva 1902, pp. 79 - 158; V. S. R u n c i-
m a n, *The Eastern Schism*, Oxford 1955, pp. 39 et suiv.; G. O s t r o g o r s k y,
Histoire..., pp. 360 - 363.

[22] *Michaelis Pselli scripta minora*, éd. S. E. K u r t z, F. D r e x e l, vol. I, Milano
1936, pp. 232 - 328.

:ique siégeant au synode, sur l'appui duquel on comptait en le convoquant hors de la capitale, loin de la pression de la population de Constantinople favorable à Cérulaire [23]. Il mourut avant de comparaître devant ses juges.

Le mécontentement qu'entraînait le gouvernement du patriarche avait cru très tôt, comme le prouve le violent conflit qui opposa le patriarche aux moines au cours des années quarante du XIe siècle. L'affrontement avec Cérulaire devait avoir des bases profondes, puisque c'est le fameux couvent de Stoudios qui prit la tête de l'opposition, couvent qui à partir du IXe siècle, suivant en cela l'enseignement de son maître Théodore Stoudite, se fit le gardien de l'orthodoxie et qui, plus d'une fois, s'engagea aux IXe et Xe siècles dans des disputes avec les patriarches, les admonestant et exigeant d'eux la fidélité aux dogmes et aux canons de l'Église [24]. Nous ignorons les raisons de la tension existant entre les stoudites et Cérulaire, mais nous connaissons deux mesures prises contre le couvent. Le patriarche mettait en doute le droit, pour les diacres de Stoudios, de porter des ceintures spéciales durant les cérémonies liturgiques. Les stoudites répliquèrent par un traité écrit par Nicétas Stéthatos, *Des ceintures des diacres stoudites*. La querelle a dû se prolonger, car, en 1054, le patriarche Pierre d'Antioche, dans une lettre à Cérulaire, lui faisait remarquer que celui-ci n'avait pu, en dépit de ses nombreux efforts, supprimer cette coutume [25].

Cet incident, insignifiant semblerait-il, illustre incontestablement l'épreuve qui opposa le couvent, juridiquement indépendant du patriarche [26], à Cérulaire qui cherchait à concentrer la plénitude du pouvoir sur toutes les institutions ecclésiastiques de l'Empire Le Stoudios, dans sa

---

[23] *Attaleiates* (éd. Bonnae 1853), pp. 64 - 65. N. S k a b a l a n o v i č, *Vizantijskoe gosudarstvo i Cerkov' v XI v.*, St.-Petersburg 1884, pp. 388 - 390; N. S u v o-r o v, *Vizantijskij papa*, pp. 111 - 112, 118 - 125; A. Michel, *Schisma...*, pp. 430 - 434.

[24] Cf. I. S o k o l o v, *Sostojanie monašestva v vizantijskoj cerkvi s poloviny IX do načala XIII v.*, Kazan' 1894, pp. 504 et suiv. Sur Théodore Stoudite v. H. G. B e c k, *Kirche...*, p. 491 et l'index. Sur les influences politiques du monachisme byzantin v. H. H u n g e r, *Reich der neuen Mitte*, Graz 1965, pp. 266 et suiv.

[25] Lettre de juillet 1054 dans «Patrologia graeca» vol. CXX, col. 809. Cf. N. S k a b a l a n o v i č, *op. cit.*, p. 382; A. M i c h e l, *Schisma...*, p. 376. Cette ceinture (zoné) faisait partie des habits liturgiques de l'évêque et du prêtre. Cf. T. P a p a s, *Studien zur Geschichte der Messgewänder im byzantinischen Ritus*, München 1965, pp. 131 - 134.

[26] Stoudios était du nombre des couvents indépendants placés sous le patronage de l'empereur (*monasteria autodespota kai auteksousia*). Les couvents de cette catégorie bénéficiaient du privilège d'être indépendant non seulement de l'autorité diocésaine, mais aussi patriarcale, du point de vue administratif et parfois même de celui de la juridiction. Cf. I. S o k o l o v, *Sostojanie monašestva...*, pp. 353 - 355, 367 - 370; H. G. B e c k, *Kirche...*, p. 130.

défense, a dû trouver appui parmi les autres couvents indépendants qui avaient parfaitement compris que leurs propres privilèges étaient également menacés. Le conflit entre Stoudios et Cérulaire portait sur une question plus importante que la volonté du patriarche d'étendre son contrôle sur le couvent. La glose du texte de *Skylitzès-Kedrenos* prouve que Cérulaire avait recommandé de radier le nom de saint Théodore Stoudite du « nombre de ceux qui sont cités dans les prières de l'Église », c'est-à-dire des diptyques, et il n'annula sa décision que sous la pression de l'empereur [27]. Le conflit avait donc dû avoir des raisons profondes et les stoudites s'opposant au patriarche invoquaient visiblement les oeuvres de leur maître spirituel. Sans multiplier les suppositions, nous pouvons constater que Cérulaire a dû avoir contre lui la plupart des moines de l'Empire tout le temps que dura sa dispute avec les Stoudites, pendant laquelle il avait osé mettre en doute la sainteté de la plus grande autorité du mouvement monastique orthodoxe, car c'est ainsi qu'il convient d'interpréter la radiation du nom de Théodore du synodikon [28].

Le Mont-Athos, également indépendant et jouissant de la protection de l'empereur, était avec Stoudios l'un des hauts-lieux de la vie monastique. En 1046, Constantin Monomaque avait confirmé le statut d'indépendance que Jean Tzimiskès avait accordé en 972 à la congrégation des couvents de la Sainte-Montagne [29]. Il est possible qu'Athos ait cherché une confirmation de ses privilèges menacés par les prétentions du patriarche. Les réformes menées durant les années quarante renforcèrent la position du Mont-Athos en tant que centre de l'ascèse et de la vie religieuse et contemplative. Il était également à cette époque le lieu de contacts et d'influences réciproques du monachisme d'Orient et d'Occident

---

[27] *Skylitzès-Kedrenos* (éd. Bonnae 1839), vol. II, p. 555. Cf. A. M i c h e l, *Die Kaisermacht in der Ostkirche (843 - 1204)*, Darmstadt 1959, p. 94.

[28] On a dû cependant parvenir à un accord avant 1054, puisque durant la polémique avec les légats du pape ce même Nicétas Stethatos, moine stoudite, soutenait activement Cérulaire de sa plume. Pour ses traités contre les Latins v. B e c k, *Kirche...*, pp. 535 - 536; A. M i c h e l, *Schisma...*, pp. 35 et suiv. Le rapprochement a dû probablement intervenir face au visées de Constantin Monomaque, dans la dernière partie de son règne (1052 - 1054), tendait à s'approprier une partie des biens ecclésiastiques et en particulier ceux des couvents au bénéfice de la trésorerie. Cérulaire se fit le défenseur véhément de la propriété de l'Église, tout comme en 1057 lorsque Isaac Comnène en revint aux plans de sécularisation de Monomaque; v. N. S k a b a l a n o v i č, *op. cit.*, pp. 288 - 291; I. S o k o l o v, *Sostojanie monašestva...*, pp. 143 - 145.

[29] F. D ö l g e r, *Regesten der Kaiserkunden des oströmischen Reichen*, Teil 1: *565 - 1025*; Teil 2: *1025 - 1204*, München — Berlin 1924 - 1925, Reg. 745, 879; H. H u n - g e r, *Johannes V Paleologos und der Heilige Berg*, « Bizantinische Zeitschrift », Bd. XLV, 1952, p. 367; A. M i c h e l, *Die Kaisermacht...*, p. 52.

dominé alors par l'esprit de Cluny.[30]On devait sans doute s'y interroger sur les questions concernant la hiérarchie ecclésiastique et le mode de promotion aux sièges épiscopaux. L'attitude de l'higoumène géorgien Georges Mtasmideli (mort le 29 VI 1065) du couvent Iberon du Mont Athos telle qu'elle est présentée dans sa *Vie* rédigée par son disciple vers l'an 1068, reflétait ces idées [31]. Georges Mtasmideli, arrivé en 1060 en Géorgie venant d'Athos, propageait l'idée d'une réforme de l'Église géorgienne. Il condamnait la vente des dignités épiscopales à des gens indignes et ignorants et demandait que le souverain choisisse des candidats dignes parmi les moines qui auraient obtenu l'appui « des maîtres inspirés de Dieu », c'est-à-dire du synode des évêques [32]. La critique de l'higoumène géorgien du Mont-Athos, bien qu'elle ne visât que la situation régnant au sein de l'Église de Géorgie, était dirigée contre les plaies et les abus qui accablaient l'Église toute entière. La simonie sous différentes formes était générale. La question se pose de savoir si la tendance aux réformes engendrée dans le milieu monastique byzantin et réclamant l'assainissement et la démocratisation du système de promotion aux sièges épiscopaux n'aurait pas, dans des conditions propices, atteint également la Russie?

A Athos il y avait, outre le couvent georgien d'Iberon et d'autres couvents nationaux, un couvent russe, celui du Xylourgou, dédié à la Dormition de la Vierge et fondé avant 1016 [33]. Déjà avant 1051 des moines de ce couvent rentraient en Russie; c'est d'Athos que vint Antoine de Lioubetch, fondateur du couvent des Cryptes, c'est de là aussi que vinrent les moines qui, avant 1064, fondèrent le couvent de la Sainte-Montagne près de Vladimir en Volhynie. Il n'est pas exclu non plus qu' Hilarion ait vécu dans le couvent du Xylourgou ou dans un couvent

[30] Cf. I. S o k o l o v, *Sostojanie monašestva...*, pp. 237 et suiv., 378 - 380; O. R o u s s e a u, *L'ancien monastère bénédictin du Mont Athos*, « Revue liturgique et monastique », vol. XIV, 1929, pp. 530 - 547; H. G. B e c k, *Die Benediktinerregel auf dem Athos*, « Byzantinische Zeitschrift », vol. XLIV, 1951, pp. 21 - 24; J. L e c l e r q, *Les relations entre le monachisme oriental et le monachisme occidental dans le haut Moyen Age*, dans: *Le Millénaire du Mont Athos, 963 - 1963. Études et Mélanges*, vol. II, Chevetogne 1964, pp. 49 - 80.

[31] Cf. l'introduction de P. P e e t e r s à sa traduction latine de la *Vie de Saint Georges l'Hagiorite* du texte vieux-géorgien d'un manuscrit de 1074, dans: *Analecta Bollandiana*, vol. XXXVI/XXXVII, 1917 - 1919 (publié en 1922), pp. 8 - 9, 69 - 74; cf. B e c k, *Kirche...*, pp. 580 - 581.

[32] *Vie de Saint Georges l'Hagiorite*, c. 60, 61; *ibidem*, pp. 124, 125; cf. I. D ž a v a h o v, *K istorii cerkovnyh reform v drevnej Gruzii* « Žurnal Ministerstva Narodnogo Prosveščenia », vol. CCCLI, 1904, n° 2, pp. 358 - 372.

[33] V. A. M o š i n, *Russkie na Afone i russko-vizantijskie otnošenija v XI - XII vv.*, « Byzantinoslavica », vol. IX, 1947 - 1948, pp. 55 et suiv.

byzantin, car il connaissait vraisemblablement le grec [34]. Comme on l'a démontré récemment, Hilarion n'ignorait pas non plus la tradition liturgique et les écrits occidentaux qu'il avait pu étudier dans des traductions effectuées à Kiev et pendant son voyage à la cour du roi Henri de France [35], qui eut lieu peut être vers l'an 1049, ou, ce qui est également probable, grâce aux contacts avec les bénédictins au Mont-Athos.

Les relations des moines russes avec Stoudios nous sont confirmées à partir des années soixante du XIe siècle. C'est à cette époque qu' Ephrème, moine des Cryptes et futur métropolite de Perejaslav, séjourna dans l'un des couvents de Constantinople. Étant donné qu'à la demande de Théodose, higoumène du couvent des Cryptes, il lui envoya la règle de Stoudios [36], on peut penser qu'il a vécu justement à Stoudios. L'influence de ce couvent sur le monachisme russe a pu se faire sentir bien avant la date du premier témoignage que nous possédons. Des contacts précoces avec Stoudios auraient pu être établis notamment par l'intermédiaire du métropolite Théopemptos, évoqué plus haut, qui, si nous en croyons l'image de saint Jean Prodrome figurant sur son sceau, sortait du couvent qui avait ce saint pour patron [37]. On ne peut pas non plus sous-estimer la présence en Russie de moines grecs et slaves originaires des provinces balkaniques de l'Empire. Avec le même zèle que les moines russes, ils se dévouaient à l'évangélisation du pays et à l'édification de l'Église russe qu'ils auraient voulu voir exempte des plaies qu'ils dénonçaient chez eux et proche des idéaux que proclamaient les apôtres et les pères de l'Église.

Ces considérations vont nous permettre de comprendre l'acte de l'élévation d' Hilarion au trône métropolitain de Kiev, comme étant une manifestation de ce mouvement de renouveau au sein du monachisme

---

[34] L'auteur du *Discours sur la loi et sur la grâce* a dû lire dans le texte les ouvrages qu'il a consultés. Cf. le commentaire linguistique de L. M ü l l e r, *Des Metropoliten Ilarion Lobrede...*, pp. 57 et suiv.

[35] V. L. M ü l l e r, *Eine Westliche liturgische Formel in Ilarions Lobpreis auf Vladimir den Heiligen*, « L'Annuaire de l'Institut de Philologie et d'Histoire Orientales et Slaves », vol. XVIII, 1966 - 1967 (publié en 1968), pp. 299 - 305; N. N. R o z o v, *Iz istorii russko-českih literaturnyh svjazej*, « Trudy Otdela Drevnerusskoj Literatury », vol. XXIII, 1968, pp. 71 - 85.

[36] Cf. *La vie de Théodose des Cryptes* dans: *Sbornik XII veka Moskovskogo Uspenskogo Sobora*, éd. A. Š a h m a t o v et P. L a v r o v, Moskva 1899 (édition photomécanique de D. Čiževskij, s-Gravenhage 1957), pp. 54 - 57.

[37] V. L a u r e n t, *Le corpus des sceaux de l'Empire byzantin*, vol. V: *L'Église*, 1, Paris 1963 - 1965, n° 782, planche 107. L'image de Jean Baptiste figure également sur les sceaux (*ibidem*, n°s 13, 14) du patriarche Alexis III Stoudite (1025 - 1043) et sur 8 autres sceaux de métropolites et d'évêques datés des Xe - XIe siècles (n°s 616, 659, 683, 690, 694, 704, 753, 950), dont ni les noms ni les vocables de leurs cathédrales n'expliquent le choix du patron. Ne venaient-ils pas de Stoudios tout comme le patriarche Alexis?

byzantin qui cherchait à rétablir les hiérarques ecclésiastiques dans l'
autorité morale qu'ils se devaient de posséder comme pasteurs.

L'acte de 1051 n'était donc pas né de l'intention d'arracher l'Église
russe à la communauté spirituelle byzantine; c'était un rappel des droits
incombant au synode des évêques d'une province. Le mécontentement
des évêques et des moines russes pouvait également découler du fait que
les hiérarques qu'envoyait Constantinople étaient dépourvus, de l'avis
de ces néophytes brûlants de foi, des qualités qui devaient marquer un
véritable timonier de l'Église. Les demandes de « dons » venant de Constantinople pour les promotions ne pouvaient pas non plus être bien ac-
cueillies. Elles plaçaient la jeune Église, vivant de la générosité du prince,
dans une situation malaisée, en nécessitant non seulement des sommes
appropriées, mais mettant également à jour ce péché honteux qu'était la
simonie [38]. Il n'aurait pas été étonnant que des moines s'opposant à ces
pratiques à Byzance aient voulu les étouffer dans l'oeuf en Russie.

La procédure d'accession aux plus hautes dignités épiscopales in-
quiétait les milieux monastiques et elle intéressait aussi directement, sous
un autre aspect, la hiérarchie supérieure de l'Église. Deux traités polémiques sont éloquents à cet égard: le premier, anonyme, *Sur les prérogatives des métropolites,* le second *Sur le droit de vote du patriarche* de
Nicétas d'Amasée. Les deux traités ont été écrits au cours d'une période
qui couvre une centaine d'années et qui va du dernier quart du Xe siècle
à la septième décennie du XIe. Indépendamment de la date exacte de ces
ouvrages, un fait demeure indiscutable: les différents points de vue qu'on
y trouve quant au choix des métropolites sont demeurés vivaces tout au
long du XIe siècle. C'est ce que prouvent avec force les prises de position
de Nicétas, métropolite d'Ancyre, dont les lettres, datées de 1084 à 1086,
défendant les prérogatives des métropolites s'inspirent entre autres du
traité de l'Anonyme [39].

---

[38] Cf. E. H e r m a n, *Zum kirchlichen Benefizialwesen im byzantinische Reich*,
« Studi Bizantini e Neoellenici », V, Rome 1939, pp. 663 - 665; d u m ê m e a u t e u r,
Die bischofliche' Abgabewesen im Patriarchat v. Konstantinopel, « Orientalia Christiana Periodica », vol. V, 1939, pp. 455 - 460. En Russie au début du XIIIe siècle la
redevance pour une consécration épiscopale s'élevait à 1000 *grivny* d'argent (5 kg)
soit environ 80 à 100 *nomismata*. E. G o l u b i n s k i j (*op. cit.*, vol. I-1, p. 531) était
d'avis que cette somme équivalait au revenu annuel d'un diocèse.

[39] J. D a r r o u z è s, *op. cit.*, pp. 23 - 53; avec les textes de l'Anonyme (pp. 116 -
159), de Nicétas d'Amasée (pp. 160 - 175), de Nicétas d'Ancyre (pp. 176 - 265). L'éditeur, dans sa savante introduction, penche en faveur d'une date plus ancienne pour
les oeuvres de Nicétas d'Amasée et de l'Anonyme, en soulignant la discorde au
sein de l'Église, de 963 à 969, sous le patriarche Polyeucte (*ibidem*, pp. 24 - 27, 31 - 33).
Mais les conflits entre les métropolites et le patriarche, comme ceux qui auraient
pu déclencher ce genre de polémique, ont eu lieu aussi plus tard, en 1037 par

Nicétas d'Amasée argumente que le droit péremptoire d'élir à la dignité de métropolite l'un des trois candidats qui lui sont présentés par le synode permanent revient uniquement au patriarche. Il défend donc la pratique en vigueur. L'Anonyme, lui, se fait le représentant des intérêts du haut clergé qui participe au synode permanent, en se déclarant en faveur du droit péremptoire de ce corps de pourvoir aux chaires vacantes, ne laissant au patriarche que le rôle de président du synode et la consécration de l'élu. L'Anonyme essaie, dans ses propositions de réforme tendant à assurer la prédominance du principe de collégialité de l'autorité ecclésiastique, de démontrer le caractère restreint des droits du patriarche qui, à son avis, contrairement aux autres patriarches, n'était pas au début à la tête de l'éparchie et ne disposait pas de suffragants, et c'est pourquoi les métropolites du patriarcat de Constantinople demeurent souverains dans leur action . D'après lui, le patriarche, en tant qu'évêque de la capitale de l'Empire, n'a droit qu'au rôle honorifique de primat et qu'au droit de juridiction de l'exarque — gardien de l'orthodoxie et arbitre. L'Anonyme rejette donc le principe généralement admis selon lequel les rapports entre le patriarche et les métropolites étaient assimilés au rapport de subordination des évêques ordinaires diocésains envers le premier d'entre eux, placé à la tête de l'union métropolitaine. Il est remarquable que le réformateur anonyme ne propose pas d'en revenir au principe de la collégialité d'avant le concile de Chalcédoine, mais donne une interprétation des résolutions du concile en faveur des prérogatives du synode permanent de la capitale, se refusant en même temps à reconnaître les droits de l'archevêque de la Nouvelle Rome, qui justement en découlent.

Assurément l'autorité du patriarche pesait beaucoup trop aux métropolites du X* et du XI* siècles, partisans des idées de l'Anonyme, surtout lorsque la nef de l'Église byzantine était guidée par des personnalités aussi autoritaires que Polyeucte ou Cérulaire. En même temps, et conformément aux intérêts de leur corporation, désireuse de décider des affaires de l'Église avec la participation du patriarche tenant le rôle de président honorifique, ils n'étaient pas enclins à réclamer le retour aux principes d'avant le concile de Chalcédoine et de faire relever l'élection des métro-

---

exemple, lorsqu'un groupe de métropolites tenta, à l'initiative de Jean l'Orphanotrophe, frère de l'empereur Michel IV, de déposer Alexis Stoudite, ainsi qu'à l'époque du pontificat de Cérulaire, ce que nous avons évoqué ci-dessus. Nous nous permettons aussi de remarquer que l'on peut avoir quelques doutes au sujet de l'attribution du texte en question à Nicétas d'Ancyre, vu la glose du manuscrit ambrosien qui désigne Démétrius, métropolite de Cysique (les années 30 - 50 du XI* siècle), comme l'auteur du texte. La critique du pouvoir patriarcal et l'idée de l'égalité et de l'unité des évêques, que l'on trouve dans le traité (*ibidem*, p. 37, 200 et suiv., 230), correspondaient fort bien à la situation en Russie.

polites de la compétence des évêques suffragants qui leur étaient soumis. Mais l'idée même du caractère souverain de l'autorité du timonier de l'union métropolitaine et celle surtout de l'autonomie de l'éparchie-métropole, qui remontait à une période reculée de la vie de l'Église, correspondaient bien aux tendances réformatrices du mouvement monastique.

L'élection, par le synode des évêques de la province russe, d'un métropolite en la personne d'un moine-prêtre, ascète, savant et théologien, correspondait bien aux postulats qu'avait formulés Georges d'Athos à l'encontre du corps des électeurs et des candidats. Jaroslav le Sage avait également participé à l'élévation d' Hilarion. Georges d'Athos, critiquant le mode de promotion aux sièges épiscopaux en Géorgie, ne rejetait pas du tout le droit du souverain de procéder à des nominations. Bien au contraire, il le reconnaissait, en lui délimitant cependant un cadre stricte qui devait empêcher les abus de la part de l'autorité séculière. Le monarque avait le droit d'élire un évêque parmi les candidats répondant à des conditions déterminées et considérés comme dignes par le synode des évêques. Nous ne savons pas si ces conditions ont été soumises à Jaroslav; ce qui est sûr, c'est que le monarque russe s'y était conformé d'une manière idéale. Les évêques et les moines de l'Église russe reconnaissaient donc à Jaroslav les mêmes prérogatives qui, dans l'esprit des moines byzantins, revenaient au basileus, et, d'après Georges d'Athos, au monarque de Géorgie. Théodore Stoudite lui-même défenseur de la substance spirituelle et matérielle de l'Église, étant pour le monde entier la plus grande autorité en matière d'orthodoxie, reconnaissait que la participation de l'empereur à l'élection d'un évêque était légale. Interrogé par Nicéphore Ier sur la question de savoir qui il considérait comme étant digne de monter sur le trône patriarcal, il répondit que l'empereur peut se charger de l'élection avec les évêques, les moines et les stylites qui descendront des montagnes, et trancher en tant qu'arbitre en présentant le plus digne [40]. Les droits de l'empereur portant sur la nomination ou la confirmation des higoumènes des couvents autonomes et impériaux, qui tendaient à être le plus possible indépendants de la surveillance du patriarche, étaient unanimement respectés par les moines byzantins. Le prote de la congrégation des couvents du Mont-Athos était personnellement confirmé dans son élection par l'empereur. Il en était de même pour l'higoumène de Stoudios [41]. La participation de Jaroslav à l'élévation d' Hilarion n'était donc pas due à sa piété candide.

---

[40] Cf. la lettre de Théodore à l'empereur, « Patrologia graeca », vol. XCIX, col. 960; F. D ö l g e r, *Regesten der Kaiserkunden...*, n° 367.
[41] A. M i c h e l *Die Kaisermacht...*, 9, 28, 52 - 53.

Concluant son *Credo* Hilarion s'adresse aussi à ceux qui, sur cette terre, ont contribué à son élévation, attendant d'eux qu'ils l'appuient dans sa nouvelle mission: « Gloire à Toi, Seigneur, pour tout ce que Tu me prédestines au-dessus de mes forces. Priez donc pour moi honorables maîtres et *vladyki* de la terre russe ». Les « maîtres » ce sont évidemment les évêques, quant au terme de *vladyki* il faut sans conteste le traduire par souverains, seigneurs, c'est, en effet, dans ce sens qu' Hilarion l'emploie à plusieurs reprises [42]. On pourrait penser qu' Hilarion lisant son *Credo* dans l'archicathédrale de Kiev en présence de toute la famille du prince Jaroslav, y compris ses fils âgés, seigneurs dans leurs apanages, a sciemment employé le pluriel [43]. Ainsi donc Hilarion lui-même, qui le fait indirectement, et pas seulement le *Récit de temps passés*, confirme la part prise par l'autorité princière à sa promotion au siège de Kiev. C'est de la même façon que s'est déroulée en 1036 la nomination par Jaroslav de Lucas à l'évêché de Novgorod. Il avait été élu par le synode des évêques conformément au voeu de Jaroslav et consacré par le métropolite. Ici d'ailleurs les droits du patriarche et du synode endémuse n'avaient pas été enfreints. Le droit du prince de procéder à l'investiture des suffragants de la métropole remonte sans conteste à l'époque de Vladimir. Limité tout d'abord formellement à la confirmation des candidats venus de l'extérieur et proposés par le métropolite et son synode, il devint de plus en plus effectif au fur et à mesure que se présentaient des candidats locaux dignes d'être élus. Lucas Jidiata fut justement l'un des premiers.

Les milieux monastiques russes reconnaissaient pleinement le droit du prince de participer aux affaires de l'Église. Telle était la position nette du couvent autonome des Cryptes, dont la situation juridique peut être comparée au statut des couvents byzantins placés sous la protection de l'empereur, comme Stoudios et Athos. C'est pourquoi le chroniqueur-moine des Cryptes considère la participation de Jaroslav à l'acte de 1051 comme étant une chose naturelle, conçue par inspiration divine. En 1108 Théoctiste, higoumène du couvent des Cryptes, désireux de répandre le

---

[42] Cf. L. M ü l l e r, *Ilarion Lobrede...*, pp. 101, 107, 121, 126, 128, 139, 143.

[43] L. M ü l l e r (*Die Werke des Metropoliten Ilarion*, München 1971, pp. 59 - 60) en critiquant mon interpretation pense que nous avons ici le premier exemple de l'emploi du titre « seigneurs » pour les évêques. En effet, en Russie à partir du XIIe s., on décernait le titre de *vladyka* (correspondant au *despotes* grec) aux princes de l'Église, mais il est vrai, que dans les autres neuf cas, Hilarion a employé ce terme pour designer les pouvoirs laïques et deux fois pour Dieu. L. Müller considère avec raison qu'il est superflu d'émender au singulier ce titre général en le rapportant seulement à Jaroslav.

culte de saint Théodose dans toute la Russie, intercéda auprès du prince
de Kiev Svjatopolk II qui, faisant suite à sa demande „ordonna au métropolite de l'inscrire dans le synodikon". De même, la consécration par
le métropolite de l'higoumène, élu par le couvent des Cryptes, se faisait
sur recommandation du prince [44]. Le prince de Kiev jouissait donc de
prérogatives identiques à celles de l'empereur byzantin, car l'inscription
au synodikon pouvait se faire sur ordre du basileus, et il était également
de sa compétence de confirmer et d'investir les higoumènes des couvents
impériaux et autonomes placés sous la protection impériale [45].

     A la lumière de ces considérations, le rôle joué par Jaroslav dans
l'acte de 1051 apparaît comme étant le fruit d'une collaboration entre le
prince russe et la hiérarchie ecclesiastique de la Russie, collaboration
dont on trouve un témoignage dans le *Récit des temps passés*: « [...] et
Jaroslav aimait les rites ecclésiastiques, il aimait beaucoup les prêtres.
et en particulier les moines [...]» [46]. L'idée de renouveau était née incontestablement dans le milieu ecclésiastique, qui avait su y gagner le
monarque. Il est, en effet, évident que Jaroslav, malgré toute son autorité,
n'aurait pu, en dépit des évêques et du clergé, en particulier du clergé
régulier, confier la métropole à Hilarion sans déclencher une crise. La
période de la scission ecclésiastique de 1147 - 1155 au cours de laquelle
le prince de Kiev, sans égard pour le patriarche, avait tenté de confier
la chaire métropolitaine à Clément, son candidat, est assez éloquente à cet
égard [47]. En 1051 d'ailleurs les motifs politiques, dont se sont inspirés
les princes du milieu du XIIe siècle dans leur querelle au sujet du mode
de promotion et de la personne du métropolite, ne surgissaient point. S'il
avait importé uniquement à Jaroslav d'élever son candidat désigné, il
aurait été plus simple de chercher à obtenir à Constantinople une promotion appropriée. C'est bien de cette façon que le prince Vsevolod, fils
de Jaroslav, avait obtenu la dignité de métropolite titulaire de Perejaslav
pour le moine russe Éphrème.

     Tout mène à la conclusion qu'à l'origine de l'acte de 1051 se trouvent
les moines de l'entourage de Jaroslav et le synode des évêques se com-
posant des six suffragants de la métropole.   On y rallia, en lui présentant des résolutions canoniques appropriées, connues à cette époque
dans leur traduction slave, le monarque qui « s'adonnait aux livres et les

---

[44] Cf. *PVL*, vol. I, pp. 187, 195.
[45] A. M i c h e l, *Die Kaisermacht...*, pp. 53, 94 - 96.
[46] *PVL*, vol. I, p. 102.
[47] Cf. E. G o l u b i n s k i j, *op. cit.*, vol. I-1, pp. 300 et suiv.; P. S o k o l o v,
Russkij arhierej..., pp. 55 - 95.

lisait souvent » [48]. Nous ne connaissons qu'un seul évêque Lucas Jidiata de Novgorod. Nous ne savons pas quelle était la nationalité des autres mais ce fait n'a pas une grande importance, si l'on prend en considération l'état d'esprit du milieu monastique byzantin, celui d'Athos en particulier. Ceux qui voulaient arriver et toucher de gros revenus n'étaient guère pressés de monter sur le trône épiscopal dans un pays fraichement converti où il était aisé de conquérir la palme du martyr. Les premiers évêques étaient incontestablement d'une haute tenue morale, profondément et sincèrement devoués à la mission qui leur avait été confiée. L'acte de 1051 était né non pas de l'opposition au byzantinisme et de l'intention d'édifier une Église nationale russe, mais d'un besoin de renouveau de la vie ecclésiastique en général, besoin qui était peut-être ressenti le plus vivement dans les couvents, et exprimé là où le monachisme de l'Europe orientale était parvenu à exercer une certaine influence sur l'autorité séculière et sur la hiérarchie ecclésiastique, comme c'était le cas en Géorgie et, visiblement, en Russie également.

L'acte de 1051 n'était pas la conséquence du conflit byzantino-russe de 1043 - 1046, mais l'atmosphère de cette période, défavorable non pas à Byzance en général, mais au parti de Monomaque et de Cérulaire, se faisait encore sentir. Les accusations de conduite immorale adressées au premier, et celles d'élevation non canonique au trône patriarcal adressées au second [49] ne pouvaient être oubliées facilement par les moines de Kiev d'autant plus que la querelle entre Cérulaire et Stoudios, et peut être aussi Athos, se prolongeait.

C'est évidemment d'une façon différente qu'on jugeait à la cour de

---

[48] Cf. V. N. Beneševič, Syntagma..., pp. 62, 84 - 85, 112, 123 - 124, 284, 334, 740, 741, 765, 800 - 801. A Kiev on connaissait alors deux versions du Nomokanon: Synagogè de Jean le Scolastique dans la traduction et la rédaction de Méthode (donc avant 867) et le Nomokanon en XIV titres (la traduction bulgare datant de la fin IXᵉ - début Xᵉ siècle?). En 1051 on s'inspirait surtout du recueil du Scolastique comme étant « plus orthodoxe », d'autant plus que le milieu monastique de Byzance (Athos) encore à la fin du XIᵉ siècle ne se laissait pas guider par le Nomokanon en XIV titres. Cf. I. Žužek, Kormčaja kniga, dans: Studies on the Chief Code of Russian Canon Law, Rome 1964 (OrChrAn 168), pp. 14 et suiv. et W. Swoboda Nomokanon, Lexicon Antiquitarum Slavicarum III, Wrocław 1967, pp. 408 - 409 où la bibliographie du sujet; J. N. Ščapov, O sostave drevneslavjanskoj kormčej Efremovskoj redakcii, dans: Istočniki i istoriografija slavjanskogo srednevekovija, Moskva 1967, pp. 207 - 215; S. Troicki, Nomokanon sv. Mefodija, dans: Macedonian Academy of Sciences and Arts. Symposium: The 1100th Anniversary of the Death of Cyril of Thessalonica, 1. Skopje 1970, pp. 261 - 273.

[49] Le pape Léon IX reprochait en 1054 à Cérulaire Ordinatio per saltum sine canonico intervale (« Patrologia latina », vol. CXLIII, col. 764, 771). On ne peut faire confiance à Psellos lorsqu'il parle de corruption. Cérulaire jouissait, en effet, de l'appui de l'empereur. Cf. N. Suvorov, Vizantijskij papa..., pp. 10 - 11.

Kiev les relations avec Byzance et les questions ecclésiastiques envisagées dans ce contexte. Les motifs qui incitèrent Jaroslav à soutenir l'initiative de ses moines et de ses évêques ne pouvaient être de nature politique. Après 1046, les contacts avec l'Empire, renforcés par des liens matrimoniaux [50], reprirent leur cours normal; rien ne vient donc soutenir la thèse qui voit en Jaroslav un vassal indocile cherchant coup sur coup, et sans succés d'ailleurs, à rejeter la suzeraineté de l'Empire. On peut donc penser que Jaroslav, vu la vacance du siège métropolitain (Constantinople tardant peut-être à y pourvoir), avait penché pour une nouvelle solution. Le clergé russe la désirait, convaincu que l'Église avait besoin d'un véritable timonier. Un prélat venant du Bosphore, ignorant la langue du pays dont il devait diriger l'évangélisation—la vocation lui faisait peut-être défaut pour cette mission—aurait été avant tout un ambassadeur byzantin dans la capitale du monarque russe. Ce n'est pas par hasard que le *Récit des temps passés*, dont le sujet principal est l'histoire de l'État et de la chrétienté russe, n'accorde aucune place à ceux qui, de part de leur office, auraient dû propager la nouvelle foi. Parmi les prélats grecs du XIᵉ siècle, seul le métropolite Jean II Prodromos (vers 1077 - 1089) a mérité des louanges pour son érudition et sa moralité. Le moine-chroniqueur écrivait au début du XIIᵉ siècle: « [...] il n'y en a pas eu de semblables auparavant en Russie, et il n'y en aura pas de semblables après lui » [51]. Le mérite de la diffusion du christianisme et de l'édification de l'organisation ecclésiastique revenait, dès le XIᵉ siècle, au clergé slave avant tout. Le monachisme russe, dans la première moitié du XIᵉ siècle, s'était affermi au point d'engendrer des personnalités telles que Lucas Jidiata, Hilarion, Antoine des Cryptes. Dans la 2ᵉ moitié du XIᵉ siècle, le couvent princier des Cryptes avait acquis une grande importance: à la fin de ce siècle, la majorité des évêques russes en sortaient.

Mais les maîtres kiéviens, malgré leur respect pour les questions religieuses et pour l'Église, étaient absorbés par les affaires politiques, et c'est de ce point de vue qu'était analysée la présence à Kiev du représentant de Hagia Sophia et de la cour impériale. Ce n'est pas par hasard que les métropolites, sur lesquels nous sommes un peu mieux renseignés grâce aux données de la sigillographie, étaient également revêtus de la dignité sénatoriale, celle de syncelle et de protoproèdre. Et

[50] A. S o l o v i e v, *Marie, fille de Constantin IX Monomaque*, « Byzantion », vol. XXXIII, 1963, pp. 241 - 248; A. P o p p e, *Expédition...*, « Byzantinoslavica », XXXII, 1971, pp. 262 - 268.

[51] *PVL*, vol. I, p. 137. A. P. K a ž d a n a mis en doute l'identité de Jean II métropolite avec l'oncle du poète bizantin Théodore Prodromos, mais il n'a pas résolu, lui non plus, ce problème d'une mánière convaincante (*Prodrom i jego stihi na roždenije Alekseja Komnina*, « Vizantijskij Vremennik », XXIV, 1964, pp. 66 - 67.

V

c'est pourquoi peut-être l'expérience faite avec Hilarion, ayant buté sur la résistance de Constantinople, tourna court. Le milieu ecclésiastique russe, privé d'appui politique, a dû revenir à l'ordre établi.

On est réduit aux suppositions quant au sort du métropolite élu et consacré par son synode. Nous savons seulement que après son élévation au siège métropolitain, il exerça son ministère pendant un certain temps, c'est lui qui dédia, entre 1051 et 1053, l'église Saint-Georges fondée par Jaroslav [52]. En connaissant Cérulaire, il est difficile de supposer qu'il ait consenti à confirmer un métropolite qu'il n'avait pas consacré lui-même. D'autre part, face à la poussée des nomades d'au-delà du Danube, la cour byzantine tenait à entretenir de bons rapports avec Kiev et ne voulait pas s'aliéner Jaroslav par une réaction violente. Probablement, conformément à la coutume byzantine, on fit trainer l'affaire en longueur. Une chose est certaine, c'est qu'on obtint l'assurance, soit de Jaroslav (avant février 1054), soit de son successeur Izjaslav, qu'on en reviendrait à la procédure habituelle de promotion à la métropole. En 1055 Éphrem, métropolite et protoproèdre, en était déjà à la tête [53]. La haute dignité aulique d'Éphrem attire notre attention: protoproèdre des protosyncelles. C'est la première fois qu'apparaît ce titre, qui a peut-être été créé à Constantinople spécialement à cette occasion. Sous le règne de Michel VIII (1071 - 1078), ce titre était porté par le premier ministre, Jean, métropolite de Side. L'archevêque bulgare Léon d'Ochride, contemporain d'Éphrem, était protosyncelle [54].

---

[52] N. Nikolskij, *Materialy dlja povremennogo spiska russkih pisatelej i ih sočinenij, X - XI vv.*, St.-Petersburg 1906, pp. 122 - 126.

[53] *Novgorodskaja pervaja letopis' staršego i mladšego izvodov*, éd. par A. Nasonov, Moskva 1950, p. 183; le sceau connu d' «Éphrem protoproèdre et métropolite de Russie» (cf. A. Soloviev, «Byzantinische Zeitschrift», vol. LV, 1962, pp. 294 - 295, tabl. IV - 1) doit être rattaché sans conteste à la personne du prélat portant ce nom et qui siégea sur le trône métropolitain de Kiev approximativement de 1055 à 1065. V. Laurent (*Le corpus des sceaux...*, n° 783), induit en erreur par la littérature du sujet sur l'existence de deux Éphrem métropolites de Russie au XI° siècle, hésitait pour l'attribution. Celle-ci cependant sûre, car le second Éphrem n'a jamais été métropolite de Russie, mais uniquement métropolite titulaire de Perejaslav (vers 1078 - vers 1100). Cf. A. Poppe, *Russkie mitropolii Konstantinopolskoj patriarhii*, «Vizantijskij Vremennik», vol. XXVIII, 1968, pp. 94, 105 - 108.

[54] Cf. V. Grumel, *Titulature des métropolites byzantins, I: Les métropolites sincelles*, «Études Byzantines», vol. III, 1945, pp. 94 - 97, 102 - 107, 110 - 113; V. Laurent, *Le corpus des sceaux...*, XXXIII, n°s 407, 418, 541, 783. Comme l'ont constaté les deux érudits que nous venons de citer, le titre de *protoproedros ton protosynkellon* apparaît également sur les sceaux sous la forme abrégée de *protoproedros*. V. Laurent doute que ce fut précisément le métropolite de Russie qui ait été justement le premier à porter un titre qui n'apparaît qu'au début du règne de Michel VII Doukas. Étant donné que les hauts dignitaires de l'Église n'avaient

Nous avons le droit de penser que les mesures de rétorsion d'Éphrem envers Lucas Jidiata (trois ans d'emprisonnement) se rattachent à l'attitude de l'évêque de Novgorod s'en tenant au droit du synode d'élir et de consacrer le métropolite de sa province. Mais le parti des tenants de la réforme a dû renoncer, ayant perdu l'appui de la cour de Kiev. Ce renoncement a, peut-être, été facilité par le rapprochement qui, dans la dernière période du règne de Constantin Monomaque (1052 - 1054), s'esquissa entre le patriarche et les moines.

M. Čubatyj a récemment introduit une grande confusion dans l'affaire Hilarion. Cet auteur prétend que l'absence du métropolite russe au synode de 1054, auquel s'étaient rendus tous les métropolites du patriarcat de Constantinople, prouve qu' Hilarion exerçait encore son office et que Kiev n'était toujours pas soumise à la juridiction de Constantinople. C'est ce que prouverait également le passage à Kiev des légats du pape, de retour de Constantinople, afin d'obtenir le soutien du timonier de l'Église russe pour le point de vue de Rome, et afin de soutenir l'autocéphalie de cette Église pour l'isoler de Constantinople [55].

En réalité 16 métropolites, sur près de 70 soumis au patriarche, assistèrent au synode du 24 juillet 1054 qui excommunia le cardinal Humbert et ses compagnons [56]. M. Čubatyj déduit la présence des légats à Kiev du texte *Brevis et succinta commemoratio* d' Humbert où est citée la « *civitas Russorum* » d'où ceux-ci, après avoir quitté Constantinople, envoyèrent à l'empereur sur sa demande le texte certifié de la bulle d'excommunication de Cérulaire et de ses adhérents. L'historiographie a cependant établi depuis longtemps qu'il ne peut être question du retour des légats à Rome *via* la Russie, car l'empereur, par le truchement d'un courrier, a consulté par deux fois en dix jours les légats sur le chemin du retour, entre le 18 et le 27 juillet. La tradition manuscrite de la *Commemoratio* (le plus ancien manuscrit *Cod. Bernensis lat. 292, XI s.*) tend à exclure une erreur du copiste dans les mots *civitas Russorum*, nous avons donc à faire à une association du nom grec de la ville (Rhusion) avec celle des Russes [57]. De même, l'hypotèse de M. Priselkov selon

---

obtenu, dans les années 50 et 60, que le titre de « sincelle » et un titre nouveau, celui de « protosincelle », on peut aussi penser que l'empereur décernait simplement aussi aux prélats le titre de protoproèdre, qui ensuite, à partir de 1071, prit la forme étendue de protoproèdre des protosincelles.

[55] M. Č u b a t y j, *op. cit.*, pp. 338 et suiv., 353 et suiv.

[56] V. G r u m e l, *Les regestes des actes du Patriarcat et de Constantinople*, vol. I, Kadiköy, Paris 1932 - 1947, nᵒˢ 867, 868, 969.

[57] Une interprétation juste en principe des événements qui se déroulèrent après le départ des légats de Constantinople a déjà été donnée par W. S z c z e ś n i a k, *Rzekoma bytność legatów papieża Leona IX na Rusi w roku 1054* [*La prétendue présence des légats du pape Léon IX en Russie en 1054*], « *Przegląd Historyczny* »,

laquelle Hilarion, forcé de renoncer à ses fonctions, se retira au couvent des Cryptes, où il prit le nom de Nikon, est à ranger parmi les malentendus que reprennent malheureusement certains historiens [58]. La supposition que Nikon (mort en 1088), moine et prêtre, puis higoumène du couventdesCryptes,et l'ancien métropolite Hilarion auraient été la même personne est inacceptable. Déchoir de la dignité épiscopale équivalait à déchoir de la prêtrise, car ramener un évêque au rang de prêtre aurait été, en vertu du canon 29 de Chalcédoine, un sacrilège. Si Hilarion avait été privé de sa dignité épiscopale, il aurait pu rentrer dans les ordres, mais il ne pouvait devenir prêtre de nouveau, car c'eût été contraire aux canons et aurait contredit l'idée même du sacrement de la prêtrise [59].

Par contre, on ne peut pas ne pas prêter attention à l'événement qui se produisit sous le successeur d'Hilarion. Une notice véridique du calendrier de l'Evangéliaire de Mstislav, daté environ de l'an 1117, évoque la dédicace de l'archicathédrale Sainte-Sophie de Kiev par le métropolite Éphrem un 4 novembre. Il est impossible de déterminer l'année, car la cérémonie ne s'est pas déroulée forcément un dimanche comme on le pensait il n'y a pas longtemps encore. Quoiqu'il en soit, elle a dû avoir lieu au plus tard dans la première moitié de la septième décennie, car le nouveau métropolite et syncelle Georges arriva en Russie vers 1065. Il ne fait pas de doute qu'il s'agit là d'une nouvelle consécration de Sainte-Sophie, la première ayant eu lieu avant 1049 [60].

On a tenté de rattacher la seconde consécration à l'adjonction d'une suite de galeries extérieures ou à l'achèvement de leur peinture [61]. Mais la thèse de la construction ultérieure des galeries extérieures entourant Sainte-Sophie ne repose sur aucun argument convaincant. L'analyse du décor murale des galeries extérieures sud et nord, ainsi que celle des

---

vol. III, 1906, pp. 162 - 165, 169 - 176. La question a été définitivement tranchée par I. Š e v č e n k o, The Civitas Russorum and the Alleged Falsification of the Latin Excommunication Bull by Kerularios, dans: Actes du XIIᵉ Congrès international d'études byzantines, Ochride 10 - 16 IX 1961, vol. II, Belgrad 1964, pp. 203 - 207.

[58] M. P r i s e l k o v, Očerki..., pp. 172 - 184. En dépit des critiques, celui-ci reprit ses thèses dans son ouvrage: Nestor-letopisec, Petrograd 1923. Cette thèse a été reprise dernièrement par A. K a r t a š e v, Očerki po istorii russkoj cerkvi, vol. I, Paris 1959, p. 170.

[59] Cf. J. B. P i t r a, Juris..., vol. I, p. 533: V. N. B e n e š e v i č, Syntagma..., p. 127; A. K o r o l e v (compte rendu de l'ouvrage de Priselkov) dans « Žurnal Ministerstva Narodnogo Prosveščenija », vol. LIII, 1914, n° 10, pp. 397 - 398.

[60] Cf. A. P o p p e, Russkie mitropolii..., pp. 92 - 96.

[61] M. K. K a r g e r, Drevnij Kiev, vol. II, Moskva — Leningrad 1961, pp. 103, 166 - 167; V. N. L a z a r e v, Mozaiki Sofii Kievskoj, Moskva 1960, pp. 56 - 57. Dernièrement N. K r e s a l n y j (dans « Vizantijskij Vremennik », vol. XXIX, 1968, pp. 211 - 233) a conclu que les galeries encadrant les nefs ont déjà été ajoutées du vivant de Jaroslav le Sage, soit avant 1054.

fresques de la nef principale et des nefs latérales, non seulement n'a pas fait apparaître de différences prouvant un échelonnement chronologique, mais, bien au contraire, elle suggère que l'ensemble de la peinture à fresque de l'archicathédrale a été réalisée dans le même temps [62]. V. N. Lazarev, du fait de la seconde consécration, envisageant la possibilité que les travaux picturaux aient pu se poursuivre jusqu'après les années soixante, déclare cependant que « la décoration picturale de Sainte-Sophie de Kiev est marquée par une unité déterminée de style » et « qu'il ne fait aucun doute que les fresques de la galerie s'inspirent du même programme qui avait été tracé du vivant de Jaroslav » [63]. Nous ne pensons pas cependant que l'exécution du décor pictural de la Sagesse Divine se serait étendue sur des dizaines d'années, car celle des parties principales de l'archicathédrale a été achevée avant 1046. Il est difficile d'admettre que Jaroslav n'ait pas fait achever ces travaux, puisque,après celle de Sainte-Sophie, il a procédé à trois autres fondations: celle de l'église de l'Annonciation sur la Porte d'Or et celle des couvents de Saint-Georges et de Sainte-Irène.

On ne peut donc pas rattacher la nouvelle consécration de l'archicathédrale à l'achèvement des fresques des galeries extérieures, d'autant plus que la consécration par Éphrem était une grande dédication, célébrée par la suite dans des fêtes annuelles [64]. Analysant cette question par ailleurs nous sommes parvenus à la conclusion que la nouvelle consécration a été provoquée par l'annulation, par le patriarche, de l'élection d' Hilarion, ce qui conduisait à reconnaître comme sacrilège ses fonctions dans l'archicathédrale en tant que métropolite [65]. Bien qu' aujourd'hui encore nous ne rejetions pas cette possibilité, nous nous rendons pleinement compte de la fragilité de ses prémisses. Même si Hilarion avait été réellement forcé à renoncer à ses fonctions, le nouveau métropolite, arrivant à Kiev, a dû faire preuve de beaucoup de tact pour ne pas heurter les sentiments du clergé et de la cour princière. D'ailleurs, il y avait un nombre suffisant de raisons supplémentaires pour que l'on procèdât à une nouvelle consécration de l'archicathédrale. Il suffisait qu'elle eût été le théâtre d'un crime ou qu'elle fût profanée par la présence d'animaux. L'église de la Vierge appelée Diesjatinnaja (église de la Dîme) avait été dédiée à deux reprises: en 966 et, une seconde fois, par Théo-

---

[62] Cf. V. M j a s o e d o v, *Freski severnogo pritvora Sofijskogo sobora v Kieve*, « Zapiski otdelenija russkoj i slavjanskoj arheologii Russkogo Arheologičeskogo Obščestva », vol. XII, 1918, pp. 1 - 6, tabl. 1 - II; A. G r a b a r, *Freski apostolskogo pridela Kievo-Sofijskogo Sobora, ibidem*, pp. 98 - 103.

[63] V. N. L a z a r e v, *Mozaiki...*, pp. 57, 74.

[64] N. N i k o l s k i j, *op. cit.*, pp. 143 - 144.

[65] Cf. A. P o p p e, *Russkie mitropolii...*, p. 96.

pemptos en 1039. Le problème demeure entier. Cependant, cherchant une explication, il convient de prendre en considération la possibilité suivante: puisque la première dédicace de Sainte-Sophie de Kiev (par Théopemptos?) a eu lieu tout de suite après sa construction, donc vers 1045/46, soit pendant la période de conflit avec Byzance, elle s'est déroulée sans l'autorisation conforme (sans l'envoi de reliques) du patriarche. Dans tous les cas suscitant des doutes, il était recommandé de procéder à une nouvelle consécration [66]. Vu les circonstances il n'y a qu'Éphrem, venu en Russie en 1054/55, qui put obtenir mandat du patriarche pour procéder à la dédicace de l'archicathédrale de Kiev.

*

La recherche d'une explication des circonstances de l'élévation d'Hilarion au siège métropolitain nous a amené à rejeter l'idée prédominant dans l'historiographie, selon laquelle Jaroslav le Sage aurait pris cette initiative afin de rendre l'Église russe indépendante de la suprématie byzantine. Cette thèse implique que la Russie a dû, avant 1051, et puis juste après cette année-là, tolérer la juridiction byzantine c'est-à-dire qu'elle était de facto et de iure un État dépendant du basileus, astreint à la soumission en dépit de ses ambitions et de son programme politique. Vu sous cet angle, le retour, après 1051, de l'Église russe sous la juridiction de Constantinople équivalait à une défaite politique ramenant sans équivoque la Russie au rang du vassal de l'Empire. La situation politique d'alors et la position internationale de la Russie ne permettent pas d'étayer ces suppositions. Ailleurs, nous avons également prouvé que le conflit de 1043 n'a pas été une tentative des barbares révoltés visant à se soustraire à l'hégémonie des Romains. L'analyse des rapports byzantino-russes à la fin du Xe et pendant tout le XIe siècle ne permet pas de formuler la thèse de la suprématie politique de l'Empire.

Les liens ecclésiastiques rattachant la province ecclésiastique russe au patriarcat de Constantinople ont été, dès le début, le résultat d'un choix effectué de plein gré. Des contacts s'étendant sur plusieurs dizaines d'années ont fait que ces liens, instaurés autrefois par une décision du souverain russe, s'approfondirent et contribuèrent à engendrer une couche peu nombreuse, il est vrai, mais imbue des idéaux chrétiens et consciente de sa vocation d'évangéliser son peuple. En moins d'un demi-siècle, sous la puissante influence des idées et des principes du mona-

---

[66] Cf. D. S t i e f e n h o f e r, *Die Geschichte der Kirchweihe vom 1. bis 7. Jh.*, München 1909, pp. 45 et suiv., 69 - 71, 88 et suiv. Cf. P. d e P u m e t, *Dédication des églises*, dans: *Dictionnaire d'archéologie chrétienne et de liturgie*, Paris 1920, vol. IV, 1, pp. 374 - 405.

chisme byzantin, en particulier de la congrégation d'Athos, un mouvement monastique était né en Russie, sensible au courant du renouveau ecclésiastique.

Il faut donc envisager l'acte de 1051 comme une tentative de réforme ecclésiastique dirigée contre la machine centralisée et exagérément étendue de l'Église, et tendant à rendre au principe de la collégialité le rang que lui avaient déterminé les Pères de l'Église. Les initiateurs de la réforme avaient également compris qu'afin d'atteindre leur but ils devaient gagner le souverain aux principes de la réforme. Ils y parvinrent au début, mais pas pour longtemps. Jaroslav malgré sa piété et en dépit du fait qu'il prêtait l'oreille aux réformateurs était, avant tout, un politique; l'organisation ecclésiastique avait encore trop peu d'importance et elle était trop fortement associée à l'appareil de l'État pour qu'il puisse considérer que le droit de présenter un candidat au siège de la métropole fût une prérogative souhaitable. Il exprimait de toute façon sa volonté en accréditant à Kiev un prélat envoyé par Byzance. Le procédé d'élévation à la métropole russe, approuvé par son père, était bénéfique, en assurant la continuité des contacts avec l'Empire, et il ouvrait des perspectives dépassant largement le cadre des questions purement ecclésiastiques.

Il faut souligner tout particulièrement que l'élévation d'Hilarion au siège métropolitain par le prince et par le synode des évêques n'équivalait, ni dans son principe, ni du point de vue canonique à une rupture, ou même à une remise en question des liens de juridiction, mais bien à une tentative visant à restreindre les compétences du patriarche et de l'endémuse. C'est pourquoi l'acte de 1051 n'impliquait pas un conflit politique entre la Russie et l'Empire, et le retour rapide au *status quo ante* a été possible grâce justement à la coopération politique des deux États. *

(Traduit par Jan Stodolniak)

---

* Récemment, V. N. Lazarev (*Le système de la décoration murale de Sainte-Sophie de Kiev*, « Cahiers de Civilisation Médiévale », vol. XIV, 1971, n° 3, p. 238) s'est opposé à mon opinion que toute la décoration murale de l'archicathédrale de Kiev a été exécutée sous Jaroslav (voir supra p. 29). Mais, en reprenant l'idée que les fresques des quatre collatéraux ont été faites vers les années 60 du XIe siècle et celles de la galerie extérieure et des tours au XIIe siècle, l'éminent savant ne soumet pas à la critique des arguments tendant, entre autres, à prouver l'unité de style qui existerait selon V. Mjasoedov et A. Grabar (voir note 62) entre les fresques de la croix centrale et celles de la galerie extérieure. Le problème reste ouvert.

La naissance du culte de Boris et Gleb*

15 juillet 1015 s'éteignit le souverain de la Russie, celui qui avait introduit le christianisme ns le pays, le prince Vladimir Ier. Conformément au droit successoral, l'héritier du trône it l'aîné de ses fils vivants, Svjatopolk. Cependant, aussitôt après la mort de Vladimir, s rivalités éclatèrent entre ses fils au sujet de Kiev. Les luttes des prétendants, qui durèrent qu'en 1019, aboutirent à la défaite de Svjatopolk et à la victoire de Jaroslav, celui-là même i est entré dans l'histoire avec le surnom de « Sage », et dont la fille Anne épousa, vers 1050, oi de France Henri Ier. Parmi les victimes de ces troubles se trouvaient deux des fils cadets Vladimir, Boris et Gleb. La tradition, telle qu'elle est conservée, souligne leur soumission onditionnelle à leur frère aîné, le souverain légitime de Kiev, Svjatopolk, rend ce dernier ponsable de leur meurtre, et fait de Jaroslav le vengeur de ses deux frères innocents assinés. Toutefois l'histoire de cette période, qui nous est rapportée sous un vêtement giographique, soulève plus d'une question. La mère de Boris et Gleb aurait été bulgare, dis que leurs prénoms chrétiens Romain et David justifient l'opinion selon laquelle ils raient été les fils d'Anne, la princesse byzantine que Vladimir avait épousée en 988, fille rphyrogénète de l'empereur Romain II et sœur de Basile II. Il ressort d'un passage de la ronique de l'évêque Thietmar de Mersebourg, achevée en 1018, que Vladimir en mourant ıfia son héritage à deux fils, alors que Svjatopolk, inculpé de complot contre son père, était dé en prison (lib. VII, 72-73). Puisque Jaroslav, qui détenait alors Novgorod, s'était lui ssi brouillé avec son père pour avoir refusé en 1014 de payer le tribut coutumier à Kiev, st sûr qu'il n'était pas l'un des deux fils que Vladimir avait choisis comme successeurs. ssi peut-on, en principe, supposer qu'il s'agit de Boris et Gleb. Cela expliquerait leur sort finalement leur mort lors des troubles dynastiques que suscita le décès de Vladimir. Ces ıx rejetons, peut-être de sang impérial, même s'ils ne tentèrent pas d'obtenir par les armes droits que la volonté de leur père leur conférait, ont pu être considérés par leurs autres frères nme de dangereux prétendants au trône. Bien que la tradition attribue sans ambiguïté Svjatopolk leur mise à mort, dans les travaux récents on soupçonne de ce meurtre le ınqueur final de la lutte, Jaroslav. Quoi qu'il en soit, l'histoire de ces dramatiques conflits tour du trône de Kiev n'a pas encore reçu, jusqu'à présent, d'explication claire et satisfante. La raison de cet état de choses réside dans les résultats, hautement controversés, nplis de contradictions et s'excluant réciproquement, auxquels a abouti la critique historique des sources existantes.

* Je tiens à exprimer mes chaleureux remerciements à mes savants collègues et amis MM. Christian Hannick nster) et Wladimir Vodoff (Paris) qui ont bien voulu assumer la charge de la traduction de cet article.

I

Au cours des cent années qui suivirent ces conflits, plusieurs œuvres furent consacrées a princes-martyrs *(strastoterpcy)* Boris-Romain et Gleb-David[1] ; ceux-ci furent reconnus com saints et entourés d'un culte qui joue un rôle essentiel dans la vie religieuse et politique de Russie kiévienne. Mais à quelle date et dans quel ordre ces différentes œuvres furent-e créées, quand et dans quels milieux le culte des deux princes commença-t-il à prendre vie quand parvint-il à leur faire attribuer l'auréole de la sainteté? Toutes ces questions n' pas reçu de réponse unanime. Avant de définir les objectifs propres de notre étude, examin l'état actuel des recherches sur les plus anciens textes consacrés à Boris et Gleb.

Le *Dit des martyrs Boris et Gleb (Skazanie... mučeniku Borisa i Gleba)* qui, avec le *Dit miracles (Skazanie čudes)* des frères martyrs, apparaît comme un texte hagiographic indépendant[2], est une œuvre du genre des *passiones* appartenant au type byzantin b connu de l'ἄθλησις - *martyrium*. Si l'on y reconnaît une œuvre homogène, due à la plume d' seul auteur, on peut la situer à une date légèrement postérieure aux cérémonies de la tra lation du 2 mai 1115 par lesquelles se clôt la narration[3]. Toutefois l'opinion prévaut que *Dit des martyrs* a d'abord constitué une œuvre séparée, rédigée dans les années 1020[4] ou b seulement vers 1050[5] ou bien encore plus tard, lors de la préparation des cérémonies de

---

1. Les œuvres consacrées à ce thème ont été éditées plusieurs fois. Une anthologie des différents textes consa à Boris et Gleb a été donnée par D. I. ABRAMOVIČ, *Žitija svjatych mučenikov Borisa i Gleba i služby im*, Petrograd, 1 xxiii-205 pp. Rééd. des principaux textes augmentée d'une introduction substantielle par L. MÜLLER, *Die altrussis hagiographischen Erzählungen und liturgischen Dichtungen über die heiligen Boris und Gleb*, Munich, 1967 (D. I. ABRAMO p. 1-66, 95-97, 115-121, 136-150, 201-205). Les origines byzantines de l'hagiographie russe ont été démontrées de f convaincante sur l'exemple des plus anciennes œuvres consacrées à Boris et Gleb par F. VON LILIENFELD, dans *ältesten russischen Heiligenlegenden. Studien zu den Anfängen der russischen Hagiographie und ihr Verhältnis zum by tinischen Beispiel*, « Berlin. Byzantin. Arbeiten », V, 1957, p. 237-271 et dans les travaux de L. MÜLLER cités *infra*.

2. Il est conservé dans six rédactions, attestées par 175 manuscrits datés du xiiᵉ au xviiᵉ s., parmi lesquels les présentent le texte complet, d'autres un résumé, d'autres enfin se limitent soit au *Dit des martyrs*, soit au *Dit des mira* Le texte complet le plus ancien du *Dit* dont on dispose est celui qui est conservé dans un recueil hagiograph homilétique, l'*Uspenskij sbornik XII-XIII vv.*, édité sous la dir. de S. I. KOTKOV, Moscou, 1971, p. 42-71. La meill éd. critique, avec un essai de reconstitution du texte original du *Dit des martyrs*, a été publiée par S. A. BUHOSLAV' *Ukrajins'ko-rus'ki pam'jatky XI-XVIII vv. pro knjaziv Borysa ta Hliba. Rozvidka i teksti*, Kiev, 1928, 178 p. Dans l'in duction à cette éd., p. XIX-XXXIII, S. A. Buhoslav'kyj présente les résultats de ses recherches sur les trois œuvres les anciennes. Une étude philologique complète due à cet auteur, *Drevnerusskie literaturnye proizvedenija o Borise i G* achevée en 1939, est restée inédite. Le texte dactylographié original (10+xvi+355 pp.) en est conservé à l'Institu littérature mondiale de l'Académie des Sciences d'U.R.S.S., la bibliothèque de l'Institut d'Histoire de l'Universit Varsovie en possède un microfilm. On trouvera une présentation de la tradition manuscrite du *Dit des martyrs* es tiellement, ainsi que d'importantes considérations sur l'histoire ultérieure de cette œuvre, dans : N. I. SEREBRJANS *Drevnerusskie knjažeskie žitija. Obzor redakcij i teksty*, « Čtenija v. Imp. Obščestve istorii i drevnostej rossijskich Moskovskom Universite », 1915, 3, p. 20-21, 81-107 (textes : p. 27-47, 163-164).

3. La thèse selon laquelle le texte complet est l'œuvre d'un seul auteur avait déjà été formulée au xixᵉ s. L'ex le plus complet en a été donné par N. N. VORONIN, *Anonimnoe skazanie o Borise i Glebe, ego vremja, stil'i avtor*, « Tr otdela Drevnerusskoj literatury » (référence abrégée : TODRL), XIII, 1957, p. 11-56. Selon l'hypothèse exposée dan travail, l'auteur du *Dit* serait l'évêque Lazare de Perejaslavl' (mort le 6 novembre 1117), ancien supérieur (jusqu'en 1 de l'église de Boris et Gleb à Vyšgorod. Jusqu'au début du xxᵉ s. on avait identifié l'auteur tant du *Dit des martyrs* même que du texte complet avec le moine Jacques. Des doutes de plus en plus nombreux amenèrent cependant l'aban de cette attribution. C'est alors que se répandit le point de vue selon lequel l'œuvre serait anonyme. Un exposé clair résultats acquis au cours du xixᵉ s. a été donné par N. K. NIKOL'SKIJ, *Materialy dlja povremennogo spiska russ pisatelej i ich sočinenij (X-XI vv.)*, Saint-Pétersbourg, 1906, p. 253-257.

4. En tout cas — comme le pense L. MÜLLER — sous la métropole Jean Iᵉʳ, auquel succéda sur le trône mé politain, peu avant 1039, Théopemte. Le même auteur a fourni des arguments détaillés en faveur de l'apparition à c époque de la « prélégende » *(Urlegende)* qui serait le *Martyrium* (« ersten greifbaren hagiographischen Darstellung Todes der heiligen Brüder »), L. MÜLLER, *Studien zur altrussischen Legende der Heiligen Boris und Gleb*, « Zeitschr. f. s Philol. », XXV, 1956, p. 350-363 ; le même, *Einleitung*, dans *Die altrussischen hagiographischen Erzählungen*, p. Une critique de cette thèse situant aussi tôt le début du culte a été formulée par A. POPPE, *O vremeni zaroždenija k Borisa i Gleba*, « Russia Mediaevalis », I, 1973, p. 6-29.

5. S. A. BUHOSLAV'SKYJ, *Ukrajins'ko-rus'ki pam'jatky*, p. xxi-xxii ; le même, *Žitija*, dans *Istorija russkoj literat* I, Moscou/Leningrad, 1941, p. 319-321.

onisation et de la translation le 20 mai 1072[6]. Dans ce cas, le *Dit des miracles*, qui lui fait
e, aurait été composé progressivement entre 1072 et 1115 par plusieurs auteurs : d'après
tains, par trois, qui se seraient succédé en 1089-1105, en 1108-1113 et aussitôt après 1115[7],
près d'autres, par deux dont l'un aurait été à l'œuvre en 1073, après la canonisation de
2, tandis que l'autre aurait complété le *Dit des miracles* peu après la translation des reliques
saints princes dans le sanctuaire nouvellement construit (1115)[8].

st au genre des *vitae* reproduisant fidèlement le modèle métaphrastique de l'hagiographie
antine qu'appartient la *Lectio (čtenie)* sur « la vie et la mise à mort des bienheureux
rtyrs Boris et Gleb » dont l'auteur est le moine Nestor du monastère des Grottes[9]. On doit
lement à sa plume la *Vie* de saint Théodose, abbé de ce même monastère. L'identification
Nestor l'hagiographe avec Nestor le chroniqueur a cependant, plus d'une fois, soulevé
 critique justifiée[10]. La date de la rédaction de la *Vie* de saint Théodose définit le *terminus*
e *quem* de la composition de la *Lectio* de Boris et Gleb. Des recherches complexes ont établi
latation des deux *Vies* dans les années quatre-vingt du XIe s. et la *Lectio* de Boris et Gleb
écrite, plus précisément, entre 1079 et 1085[11]. Bien que cette datation ait recueilli de larges
frages, elle n'a pas éliminé cependant le point de vue qui situe la rédaction de ces œuvres
commencement du XIIe s. après 1108[12]. L'argument central en faveur de cette datation
dait dans la conviction que la description du miracle de la libération des prisonniers dans
Lectio de Boris et Gleb dépendait d'un récit semblable dans une rédaction du *Dit des miracles*

6. N. N. Il'in, *Letopisnaja stat'ja 6523 goda i ee istočnik (Opyt analiza)*, Moscou, 1957, p. 170-183 ; A. Poppe, *Opowieść*
eczeństwie i cudach. Okoliczności i czas powstania utworu*, « Slavia orientalis », XVIII, 1969, p. 267-292, 359-382. La
truction de N. N. Il'in pêche par le fait que, voulant mettre en doute l'authenticité historique du *Dit* considéré comme
œuvre hagiographique, il a eu recours à la *Eymundar-saga*, en utilisant, pour la reconstitution des événements des
ées 1015-1019, d'une façon non critique les données fournies par ce texte. Sous une forme extrême, qui enfreint les
es de l'exploitation critique des sources, ce point de vue est présenté par A. M. Členov, *Zur Frage der Schuld an der
ordung des Fürsten Boris*, « Jahrb. f. Gesch. Osteuropas », XIX, 1971, p. 321-346.
7. Ce point de vue avait déjà été formulé par S. A. Bugoslavskij, *K voprosu o charaktere i ob''eme literaturnoj
el'nosti prepodobnogo Nestora*, « Isvestija otdelenija russkogo jazyka i slovesnosti Imp. Akademii nauk » (référence
gée : IORJaS), XIX, 1914, no 1, p. 131 et ss. Devant les critiques exprimées par A. A. Šachmatov, *Povest' vremennych
I : Vvodnaja čast', Tekst, Primečanija*, Pétrograd, 1916, p. LXII-LXXVII, S. A. Bugoslavskij changea quelque peu ses
tions dans *Ukrajins'ko-rus'ki pam'jatky*, p. XIV-XV, XXV et ss, et dans *Istorija russkoj literatury*, I, p. 324 et ss.
8. A. Poppe, *Opowieść*, p. 271-292 ; l'auteur accepte ici en partie l'hypothèse de N. N. Voronin (cf. n. 3) selon laquelle
que Lazare serait l'auteur de la seconde partie du *Dit des miracles* qui se termine par la description inachevée de la
slation du 2 mai 1115. Sur la dépendance où se trouve la relation de la Chronique sur la translation de 1072 par rapport
donnée dans le *Dit des miracles*, voir A. Poppe, *Uwagi o najstarszych dziejach kościoła na Rusi*, III,
zegląd Historyczny », LVI, 1965, p. 560-563.
9. Elle est conservée dans vingt manuscrits dont six présentent le texte complet. Le plus ancien témoin remonte
nilieu du XIVe s. (manuscrit de Sylvestre). D. I. Abramovič, dans l'éd. citée *supra* (n. 1), a retenu neuf manuscrits,
s c'est sur dix-neuf manuscrits alors connus que S. A. Buhoslavs'kyj a fondé son édition de la *Lectio* de Nestor,
ajins'ko-rus'ki pam'jatky*, p. 179-206.
10. L'identité de Nestor l'hagiographe avec Nestor le chroniqueur a été défendue plusieurs fois par A.A. Šachmatov
tre les critiques, *Povest'*, p. XVIII-XXI. Ce point de vue est partagé et repris par D. S. Lichačev, *Russkie letopisi*,
cou/Leningrad, 1947, p. 147-168 ; le même, *Velikoe nasledie. Klassičeskie proizvedenija literatury Drevnej Rusi*, Moscou,
5, p. 89-92, 103 et ss. Les défenseurs de la thèse opposée se prononcent pour l'existence de deux auteurs différents
s homonymes ou bien ne voient un personnage historique qu'en Nestor l'hagiographe. Nestor le chroniqueur serait
s le produit d'une tradition née de la parenté thématique entre certains passages de la Chronique et les *Vies* dues à la
ne de Nestor. Voir les arguments complets à ce sujet chez E. Ščepkin, *Zur Nestorfrage*, « Arch. f. slav. Philol. », XIX,
7, p. 498-554 ; S. A. Bugoslavskij, *K voprosu*, « IORJaS », XIX, 1914, 1, p. 131-186, 1914, 3, p. 153-191 ; A. Poppe,
onologia utworów Nestora hagiografa*, « Slavia Orientalis », XIV, 1965, p. 287-292.
11. A. A. Šachmatov, *Razyskanija o drevnejšich russkich letopisnych svodach*, Saint-Pétersbourg, 1908, p. 55-57 ;
ême, *Povest'*, p. LXVIII-LXXII ; A. Poppe, *Chronologia utworów*, p. 292-305.
12. S. A. Bugoslavskij, *K voprosu*, « IORJaS », XIX, 1914, 1, p. 165-175 ; le même, *Žitija*, p. 326 et ss. Le point de
et les arguments de S. A. Bugoslavskij sont acceptés par A. G. Kuz'min, *Načal'nye etapy drevnerusskogo letopisanija*,
cou, 1977, p. 143, 148-155. L'auteur de ce livre n'a pas critiqué l'argumentation opposée que nous avons présentée.
s reviendrons sur ce sujet dans un article particulier.

antérieure à 1115[13]. Mais le défaut de cette thèse a été démontré par la possibilité d'» dépendance inverse[14].

La troisième œuvre consacrée à Boris et Gleb est la relation de la *Chronique* conservée, s« l'année 1015, dans le *Récit des temps passés (Povest' vremennych let)*[15]. Le fait qu'un te analogue, dans une relation légèrement différente, apparaisse également dans la *Chroni« de Novgorod* rend hautement vraisemblable la thèse selon laquelle la relation du meurtre Boris et Gleb dans la *Chronique* faisait déjà partie de la compilation rédigée, vers 1095, monastère des Grottes, et intégrée dans la seconde décennie du xiie s. au *Récit des ten passés*. Selon une opinion largement répandue cette relation faisait déjà partie, dans sa premi rédaction, de textes hypothétiques, comme la *Chronique de Kiev* de 1039 ou les différents ré« sur les débuts de la diffusion du christianisme en Russie, composés dans les années quara du xie s.[16]. Tel qu'il nous est conservé, et bien qu'il se présente sous la forme d'une relat d'annales, le texte rapporté par la *Chronique* peut difficilement être considéré comme un tén gnage plus ou moins digne de foi des événements. C'est ce que prouve d'emblée la prése1 d'éléments hagiographiques : acathiste, prières, laudes, extraits de psaumes, nombreuses exp1 sions stylistiques propres à la littérature hagiographique et hymnographique traduite du g1

La présence d'éléments hagiographiques dans la relation de la *Chronique* a suscité deux ex] cations. Selon les uns, la relation de la *Chronique* est une passion laïcisée, par conséquen1 résultat d'un remaniement adéquat du *Dit des martyrs Boris et Gleb*[17]. Selon les autres, «

13. S. A. Bugoslavskij, *K voprosu*, « IORJaS », XIX, 1914, 1, p. 165-168 ; le même, *Ukrajins'ko-rus'ki pam'jc* p. xxvi-xxviii.

14. L. Müller, *Studien zur altrussischen Legende der Heiligen Boris und Gleb: Die wunderbare Gefangenenbefreï nach dem Bericht des Skazanije und des Čtenije*, « Zeitschr. f. slav. Philol. », XXIII, 1954, p. 60-77. L. Müller ne va jusqu'à proposer une dépendance inverse, mais se contente de remarquer que le texte de Nestor, dans le cas donné, plus proche de la source commune et que Nestor ne pouvait pas connaître la version du miracle de la libération prisonniers que donne le *Dit*. Les recherches de N. W. Ingham sur l'influence de la *Vie* de saint Václav sur les d descriptions russes du miracle ont confirmé l'antériorité de la version de Nestor. Ce dernier savant arrive à la conclu« que cette influence apparaît de façon plus nette dans la version de Nestor, à laquelle par conséquent la version du mir de la libération des prisonniers dans le *Dit* n'avait pas pu servir de modèle, N. W. Ingham, *Czech Hagiography in K The Prisoner Miracles of Boris and Gleb*, « Die Welt der Slaven », X, 1965, p. 166-182. Ajoutons que la version rus également été influencée par le thème analogue dans les Miracles de saint Nicolas, A. Poppe, *Chronologia*, p. 303 ; le mê *Opowieść*, p. 281-283.

15. *Chronique laurentienne*, « Polnoe sobranie russkich letopisej » (référence abrégée : *PSRL*), I, Léningrad, ì (réimpr. anast. 1962), p. 132-141 ; *Chronique hypatienne*, *PSRL*, II, *ibid.*, 1908 (réimpr. anast. 1962), col. 118-Voir la recension novgorodienne dans *Novgorodskaja pervaja letopis'*, éd. A. N. Nasonov, 1950 (référence abrégée : Nov let), p. 169-174. Édition amendée dans : *Povest' vremennych let*, I, éd. D. S. Lichačev, Moscou/Leningrad, 1950 (référe abrégée : PVL), p. 90-96

16. A. A. Šachmatov, *Razyskanija*, p. 473-476, 485 ; D. S. Lichačev, *Russkie letopisi*, p. 66 et ss ; le même, *Viš nasledie*, p. 62 et ss.

17. Ce point de vue, défendu par les savants tels que I. I. Sreznevskij (1853) et K. N. Bestužev-Rjumin (18 domina jusqu'à l'apparition du livre déjà cité d'A. A. Šachmatov (1908). N. N. Il'in, *Letopisnaja stat'ja*, p. 189-s'en fit de nouveau le défenseur dans sa polémique avec A. A. Šachmatov. Mais cette thèse a perdu de sa crédibilité suite de l'insuffisance de la critique des sources de travail de N. N. Il'in, cf. *supra* n. 6. De même la tentative d'ét< une dépendance directe et génétique entre le *Dit des martyrs* et les légendes tchèques des saints Václav et Ludmila pas reçu l'approbation même du critique le plus favorable à la thèse fondamentale de N. N. Il'in : O. Králík, *Nove p o Povesti vremennych let*, « Československá Rusistika », VI, 1961, p. 173-179. Sans nous arrêter sur la diffusion légendes en vieux slave de saint Václav en Russie (après 1050 ?), nous pouvons, sur un plan plus large, reconnaître phénomène probablement semblable, celui du culte des souverains-martyrs dans toute l'Europe du haut moyen « comme l'a montré N. W. Ingham, *The Sovereign as Martyr, East and West*, « Slavic a. East Europ. Journ. », XVII, 1 p. 1-17 ; voir aussi R. Jakobson, *Russkie otgoloski drevnečešskich pamjatnikov o Ljudmile*, dans *Kul'turnoe nas« Drevnej Rusi* (Mélanges D. S. Lichačev), Moscou, 1976, p. 46-49, et B. N. Florja, *Václavská legenda a borisovsko« bovský kult (shody a rozdily)*, « Československý Časopis Historický », XXVI, 1978, p. 82-90. C'est peut-être dans c même perspective que l'on peut considérer le thème de la non-résistance et de la mort volontaire, dont la présence « la *Vie* de Boris et Gleb et dans la *Quête du Saint Graal* de la fin du xiie s. a permis une conclusion prématurée et err« selon laquelle l'auteur de la Quête, un moine cistercien, aurait eu à sa disposition une traduction latine de la légen« de Boris et Gleb ou tout au moins son « historical core », G. Krugovoj, *A Motif from Old Russian « Vita Sanctorum Arthurian Romance*, « Canadian Slavonic Papers », XV, 1973, p. 351-374. La possibilité d'une diffusion de la légend« Boris et Gleb en Europe Occidentale ne manque pas d'intérêt, surtout en ce qui concerne les rapports dynastiques e les cours princières ; toutefois nous ne disposons d'aucun élément qui nous autorise à affirmer qu'il en existait une tradu« latine.

LA NAISSANCE DU CULTE DE BORIS ET GLEB

stitue la plus ancienne œuvre conservée sur Boris et Gleb, c'est-à-dire un récit historique
té d'éléments hagiographiques. La conviction que la version originale de celui-ci, dépourvue
léments hagiographiques, n'est pas conservée, a conduit à formuler diverses hypothèses
mi lesquelles l'explication la plus érudite s'avéra être la thèse selon laquelle les deux
vres composées avant 1039 reposent sur la relation de la *Chronique* : tant la relation séculière
elée *saga*, que le récit hagiographique appelé *Récit primitif (Urlegende)*. Ce dernier servit
lement de source au *Dit des martyrs Boris et Gleb*[18].

recours à cette solution invérifiable qui permet d'attribuer l'origine de toutes les obscurités
es œuvres hypothétiques et perdues est apparu en liaison avec la conviction que la cano-
ation de Boris et Gleb se situait très tôt (dans les années 1020-1030) et que le *Dit des martyrs*
endait de la relation de la *Chronique*. Deux arguments sont proposés à cet effet comme
versibles : le premier est que la liste des fils de Vladimir dans le *Dit des martyrs* devait
ulter d'une combinaison de deux listes semblables dans le *Récit des temps passés* ; le second
que la citation dans la même chronique, sous l'année 1019, de la traduction slave de la
onique de Georges Hamartole apparaît probablement dans le *Dit des martyrs* sous une forme
à très remaniée[19]. Cependant on a mis en doute ces deux arguments en démontrant que les
nnées généalogiques sur les fils de Vladimir dans le *Récit des temps passés* sont de seconde
in et que l'expression composée de trois mots sur « le châtiment pernicieux » *(pagubnaja*
a) qui frappa Svjatopolk n'était pas due au texte d'Hamartole cité dans la *Chronique*[20].
a étant accepté, il faut ajouter que la citation sous l'année 1019 doit être analysée globale-
nt avec les vingt-cinq autres citations d'Hamartole dans le *Récit des temps passés*. On voit
si que la citation sous l'année 1019 qui prête à Svjatopolk, à propos d'Hérode, une expres-
n prise chez Hamartole, a pu avoir été empruntée par l'auteur de la *Chronique de Kiev*
plus tôt dans la dernière décennie du XIe s. ou même vingt ans plus tard par l'auteur du
it des temps passés*[21].

ns les recherches consacrées aux textes perdus concernant Boris et Gleb, on a tenté d'utiliser
lement les sources iconographiques. Pour cela on fit appel aux manuscrits enluminés des

---

8. Le caractère secondaire du *Dit des martyrs* par rapport à la relation de la *Chronique* a été prouvé par A. A. ŠACH-
ov, *Razyskanija*, p. 33-37 et par S. A. BUHOSLAVS′KYJ, *Ukrajins′ko-rus′ki pam′jatky*, p. XIX-XXIII. Mais, tandis que
ernier supposait une dépendance immédiate, en montrant que le *Dit des martyrs* ne contenait aucun fait historique
nnu de la *Chronique*, A. A. ŠACHMATOV, corrigeant son point de vue antérieur, formula l'hypothèse de l'existence
e source supplémentaire, commune aux trois œuvres, dans laquelle il faudrait reconnaître « la forme primitive du
des martyrs, son noyau fondamental », A. A. ŠACHMATOV, *Povest′*, p. LXXV. Ce qui n'était à proprement parler qu'une
othèse de travail reçut, à la suite des recherches fouillées de L. Müller, le caractère d'une hypothèse scientifique. Cet
lit voulut y voir une « prélégende » (un *martyrium*) perdue. Il consacra à ses recherches sur les *Vies* de Boris et Gleb
, études dont il a résumé les résultats dans l'article *Neuere Forschungen über das Leben und die kultische Verehrung
heiligen Boris und Gleb*, dans *Slawist. Stud. z. V. Internat. Slawistenkongr. in Sofia* (« Opera slavica », 5), Göttingen,
3, p. 295-317 ; voir aussi son introduction à *Die altrussischen hagiographischen Erzählungen*, p. XI-XVII.
19. L. MÜLLER, *Studien zur altrussischen Legende der Heiligen Boris und Gleb*, « Zeitschr. f. Slav. Philol. », XXV,1956,
-338 ; le même, *Neuere Forschungen*, p. 300-301.
20. O. KRÁLÍK, *Vztah Povesti vremennych let k legendě o Borisu a Glebovi*, « Československá Rusistika », XII, 1967,
)-102. Remarquons en outre que ni A. A. Šachmatov ni S. A. Bugoslavskij n'ont relevé, dans la relation de la *Chronique*,
races du texte d'Hamartole ; ils estimaient au contraire que le texte primitif de la *Chronique* a été défiguré par
erpolation postérieure d'un emprunt à Hamartole et que c'est le *Dit des martyrs* qui a conservé le texte primitif,
A. ŠACHMATOV, *Razyskanija*, p. 50 ; S. A. BUHOSLAVS′KYJ, *Ukrajins′ko-rus′ki pam′jatky*, p. XX.
21. A. A. ŠACHMATOV, *Povest′ vremennych let i ee istočniki*, « TODRL », IV, 1940, p. 41-61, sur la citation de l'année
9, voir p. 57-58 ; O. V. TVOROGOV, *Povest′ vremennych let i Chronograf po velikomu izloženiju*, « TODRL », XXVIII,
4, p. 107, 113. Comme il ressort des considérations d'O. V. Tvorogov, cette citation a pu être empruntée aussi bien
traduction de la chronique d'Hamartole directement qu'à une compilation chronographique concernant ce fragment.
tout cas l'opinion antérieure de P. V. Golubovskij et de A. A. Šachmatov, selon laquelle cette citation dans la *Povest′*
nennych let était due à une lecture liturgique (παροιμία) pour la fête de Boris et Gleb *(Die altrussischen hagiographischen
ihlungen*, p. 120*)*, ne résiste pas à cette démonstration. Le texte complet a été composé sur la base de matériaux
runtés à la *Chronique*.

VI

xive-xvie s. du *Dit des martyrs* et au cycle des miniatures de la fin du xve s. qui illustre
relation de la *Chronique* dans le manuscrit de Königsberg (Radziwill) ou bien à des icôn
sur bois des xive-xviie s. représentant les saints frères entourés de scènes hagiographiqu
(v žitijach). En partant du fait que les différentes scènes correspondent tantôt à l'une, tant
à l'autre œuvre consacrée à Boris et Gleb, on a tenté de prouver qu'il existait une version pl
ancienne dont se seraient servis les auteurs des trois œuvres conservées[22]. L'analyse
l'iconographie du culte de Boris et Gleb a cependant révélé que les miniatures exécutées a
xive-xvie s. ne reflétaient déjà plus la phase initiale de l'apparition et de la formation
l'iconographie de Boris et Gleb. Bien que les cycles primitifs fussent thématiquement l
aux œuvres qu'ils illustraient, ils n'échappèrent pas, au cours des siècles, à l'influence qu
exerçaient les uns sur les autres. La peinture d'icônes puisait, en effet, depuis le début, po
les différentes compositions, son inspiration non pas dans la consultation d'une seule œuv
mais dans une lecture globale de la littérature consacrée aux saints princes. Il découle de c
que ces œuvres iconographiques ne constituent aucune base pour affirmer l'existence d'u
version perdue d'une *Vie* de Boris et Gleb ; elles n'autorisent pas davantage la reconstructi
d'une hypothétique version primitive de l'une ou l'autre œuvre consacrée à Boris et Gle
elles ne projettent, enfin, aucune lumière sur les rapports réciproques entre les œuv
existantes[23].

Cependant le rapport entre les différentes œuvres appartient aux questions controvers
non seulement dans le cas du *Dit des martyrs* et de la relation de la *Chronique* mais aussi da
celui de ces deux œuvres et de la *Lectio* de Nestor. Le point de vue selon lequel la relation de
Chronique serait le témoin le plus ancien est habituellement lié à la conviction que le *Dit*
martyrs dépend lui aussi de la *Lectio* de Nestor[24]. Mais une argumentation envisagée sous tc
les angles conduit à admettre que la *Lectio* est un remaniement hagiographique et littéra

22. D. A. AJNALOV, *Miniatjury Skazanija o svjatych Borise i Glebe Sil'vestrovskogo sbornika*, « IORJaS », XV, 191(
p. 1-128 (41 ill.) ; E. S. SMIRNOVA, *Otraženie literaturnych proizvedenij o Borise i Glebe v drevnerusskoj živop
« TODRL », XV, 1958, p. 312-327. En s'appuyant sur les représentations de Boris et Gleb sur des croix-*enkolpia* et sur
effigies en cuivre, V. I. LESJUČEVSKIJ a essayé de prouver l'antériorité de la *Lectio* de Nestor par rapport au *Dit*
martyrs : V. I. LESJUČEVSKIJ, *Vyšgorodskij kul't Borisa i Gleba v pamjatnikach iskusstva*, « Sovetskaja Archeologi
VIII, 1946, p. 225-247.
23. A. POPPE, *O roli ikonografičeskich izobraženij v izučenii literaturnych proizvedenij o Borise i Glebe*, « TODR
XXII, 1966, p. 24-25. On trouve une critique indirecte des opinions de D. A. Ajnalov et de E. S. Smirnova dan
considérations de M. V. Alpatov sur l'attitude des artistes de la Russie ancienne envers les sources littéraires et sur
participation à la formation des légendes, considérations fondées sur une analyse de l'iconographie du dernier épisod
la *Vie* de Boris et Gleb, la mort de Svjatopolk. L'auteur remarque avec raison qu'« il est faux de se figurer que les ic
graphes étaient toujours des illustrateurs fidèles des textes », M. V. ALPATOV, *Gibel' Svjatopolka v legende i v ikono*
« TODRL », XXII, 1966, p. 18-23. A la lumière des observations de M. Ch. ALEŠKOVSKIJ, une opinion que j'avais éno
(« TODRL », XXII, 1966, p. 41-42) appelle une correction : un nouvel examen des représentations des *enkol*
convaincante que les saints frères ne portent pas dans leur main le modèle de l'église qui leur avait été consacrée r
plutôt la couronne des martyrs. La ressemblance des formes due à la dimension très réduite de l'objet tenu dans la n
de chaque saint avait favorisé cette interprétation erronée des représentations, M. Ch. ALEŠKOVSKIJ, *Russkie gl
borisovskie enkolpiony*, dans *Drevnerusskoe iskusstvo. Chudožestvennaja kul'tura domongol'skoj Rusi*, Moscou, 1972, p.
125. En revanche, la reprise de la thèse de V. I. Lesjučevskij, qui avait tenté, sur la base des représentations des *enkol*
de distinguer les étapes du culte de Boris et Gleb, d'abord comme saints thaumaturges, puis à partir du commencen
du xiie s., comme saints guerriers défenseurs de la Russie et patrons de ses princes, ne trouve sa confirmation ni c
les sources écrites, ni dans les sources iconographiques. Sur ce point nos remarques de 1966 n'ont rien perdu de
actualité.
24. Ce point de vue formulé d'abord sur un ton très catégorique par A. A. ŠACHMATOV, *Razyskanija*, p. 38 et ss, le
ensuite de façon plus atténuée. Devant les critiques de S. A. Bugoslavskij, A. A. Šachmatov (*Povest'*, p. LXXIV e
accepta de reconnaître une source commune mais rejeta une dépendance inverse à cause de ses présuppositions chr
logiques. La question a été présentée quelque peu différemment par N. N. VORONIN, *Anonimnoe skazanie*, p. 48 e
53, selon lequel l'auteur du *Dit des martyrs* connaissait la *Lectio* rédigée par Nestor mais ne l'a pas utilisée, se laissant gu
par d'autres motifs idéologiques et artistiques.

34

Dit des martyrs[25]. En face de ces positions contradictoires ainsi que de l'échec des tentatives
ne analyse comparée des textes, on a cherché à découvrir des sources communes perdues.
is la ligne de ces hypothèses, qui se différencient dans les détails tout en se ressemblant
fond, le *Dit des martyrs* et la *Lectio* de Nestor se seraient inspirés de la version primitive
premier ainsi que des notices provenant du sanctuaire de Vyšgorod où étaient conservées
tombes des saints Boris et Gleb[26]. Ce n'est que récemment que l'on a essayé de définir
rement en quoi avait consisté la forme primitive du *Dit des martyrs*[27]. L'hypothèse sur
istence des notices de Vyšgorod ou bien de récits de miracles apparus sur les tombes des
its et d'une description de leur translation était indispensable dès que l'on supposait
tout le *Dit des miracles* avait été composé après la *Lectio* de Nestor[28]. Si l'on adopte en
anche la thèse selon laquelle le *Dit des miracles* serait l'œuvre de deux auteurs, une telle
othèse devient inutile. En effet les liens entre le *Dit des miracles* et la description des
acles dans la *Lectio* de Nestor s'expliquent sans le recours à une source commune perdue,
'on admet que Nestor a utilisé le *Dit des miracles* d'après la rédaction du premier auteur.
int au deuxième auteur du *Dit*, celui qui a complété le texte après la translation de 1115,
utilisé le récit de Nestor sur le miracle de la libération des prisonniers. La démonstration
établit une telle relation entre les deux œuvres hagiographiques repose sur la hase de
nées vérifiées et sans recourir à des œuvres hypothétiques perdues[29].

plus des trois œuvres dont il a été question, il faut citer l'office (ἀκολουθία - *služba*) en
nneur de Boris et Gleb[30], dont la paternité est généralement attribuée au métropolite
n Ier qui gouverna l'Église russe dans les premières années du règne de Jaroslav le Sage,
plus tard jusqu'au début des années trente du XIe s. C'est à cet office que se réfèrent les
tisans de la naissance du culte de Boris et Gleb et de leur canonisation à une date précoce[31].
endant la dépendance que l'on a constatée de cette plus ancienne œuvre hymnographique
sacrée aux premiers saints russes par rapport au *Dit des miracles*, plus exactement à la
tie due au premier auteur, ainsi que par rapport à la *Lectio* de Nestor prouve que cette
vre n'a pas pu être composée avant les années quatre-vingt du XIe s.[32]. L'information sur

---

5. S. A. BUGOSLAVSKIJ, *K voprosu*, « IORJaS », XIX, 1914, 1, p. 131-186 ; 1914, 3, p. 153-191 ; le même, *Ukrajins' ko-
'ci pam'jatky*, p. XXV-XXXI. L'antériorité du *Dit* par rapport à la *Lectio* ressort des considérations de S. Maczko, selon
el ces deux œuvres représentent des étapes successives du culte de Boris et Gleb, c'est-à-dire leur transformation de
ncely saints » en « saintly princes », S. MACZKO, *Boris and Gleb : Saintly Princes or Princely Saints*, « Russian History »,
1975, 1, p. 68-80. On regrettera que dans cet article, riche en idées, une interprétation excessive aille de pair avec
sous-estimation de la critique des sources. Entre autres mauvaises interprétations, on y retrouve le point de vue périmé
n lequel le *Dit* ne correspond pas aux modèles byzantins.
6. L'hypothèse sur l'existence des notices de Vyšgorod a été formulée par P. V. GOLUBOVSKIJ, *Služba svjatym
enikam Borisu i Glebu v Ivaniceskoj minee 1547-1579 g.*, « Čtenija v obščestve Nestora letopisca », XIV, 1900, 3,
31 et ss. Grâce à A. A. Šachmatov, cette hypothèse se répandit largement, bien qu'il subsistât des divergences quant
mpleur de ces notices. Le point de vue selon lequel elles ne concernaient pas uniquement l'activité des saints comme
amaturges, mais aussi le meurtre des deux frères, a été exprimé par N. N. VORONIN, *Anonimnoe skazanie*, p. 47 et ss.
7. Il s'agit de l'article de L. Müller, cf. *supra*, n. 18.
8. Le principal représentant de ce point de vue, N. N. Voronin, remarque en même temps que ces notices sont
stées de façon plus précise, plus fidèle et plus complète dans le *Dit des martyrs* que dans la *Lectio* de Nestor (*Anonimnoe
anie*, p. 20 et ss, 31 et ss, 41 et ss).
9. Cf. A. POPPE, *Opowieść*, p. 271-292, 359-367.
0. *Die altrussischen hagiographischen Erzählungen*, p. 136-143.
1. P. V. GOLUBOVSKIJ, *Služba*, p. 127 et ss ; N. K. NIKOL'SKIJ, *Materialy*, p. 48 et ss ; L. MÜLLER, *Neuere Forschungen*,
14 et ss ; le même, *Einleitung*, dans *Die altrussischen hagiographischen Erzählungen*, p. XIII, XXII. Il est impossible de
prendre le point de vue de N. N. Il'in (*Letopisnaja stat'ja*, p. 165-167), qui, d'une part se prononce pour la canonisation
Boris et Gleb en 1072 et, d'autre part, situe la composition de l'office qui leur a été consacré entre 1021 et 1035 et
pte l'opinion selon laquelle l'auteur en aurait été le métropolite Jean Ier.
2. Nous consacrons à cet office un article spécial, déjà prêt pour l'impression. Remarquons seulement ici que la
tion qui figure dans le titre de l'office, « œuvre de Jean, métropolite de Russie, en l'honneur des saints martyrs Boris
leb », a dû être rédigée quelque temps après le texte lui-même, car, à l'opposé du titre, le texte de l'office lui-même
ifie toujours Romain et David.

l'auteur que donne le titre de l'œuvre peut se rapporter aussi bien au métropolite de Rus Jean II Prodromos (1076-1089), d'autant plus que l'auteur de ce premier office en l'honn des princes-martyrs était un Grec ou, en tout cas, savait le grec, puisqu'il traduisit et ada pour glorifier ces saints russes, des hymnes grecques composées en l'honneur d'autres sai comme cela apparaît dans le *prooimion* et dans l'*oikos* du *kondakion*[33].

Le point de vue que nous présentons, qui s'appuie sur certains résultats obtenus à la suite recherches antérieures et sur nos thèses personnelles, suggère l'image suivante de l'hist des débuts de la littérature consacrée aux saints princes[34].

L'œuvre la plus ancienne, le *Dit des martyrs Boris et Gleb*, fut composée lors de la préparat de leur canonisation qui eut lieu le 20 mai 1072. C'était une œuvre appartenant au genre *passiones*, mais avec en plus un net accent politique dicté par le rapport des forces qui exis à cette époque entre les princes membres de la même dynastie. L'idée de la soumission incor tionnelle à l'aîné, le droit des cadets à la résistance en cas d'abus de pouvoir de la part celui-ci, définissaient le contenu politico-social du culte nouvellement instauré. Peu ap la canonisation (avant 1076) c'est le rôle de thaumaturges des princes-martyrs qui, à tour, reçut une forme littéraire. Le nouveau texte fut ajouté au *Dit des martyrs* comme continuation et c'est sous cette forme que cette œuvre fut accessible, au début des ann 1080, à Nestor l'hagiographe, devenant en tant que canevas biographique la source princip et unique de sa *Lectio* de Boris et Gleb. Peu après fut composée la première œuvre hym

---

33. F. KELLER, *Das Kontakion aus der ersten Služba für Boris und Gleb*, dans *Schweizer. Beitr. z. VII. Inter Slavistenkongr. in Warschau* (« Slavica Helvetica », VII), Lucerne, 1973, p. 65-74.

34. Le point de vue exposé ici repose sur nos études citées plus haut, ainsi que sur un mémoire inédit *Legenda o Bor i Glebie w piśmiennictwie staroruskim XI w.* (1960). Les principaux résultats figurent également dans les travaux prése au Vᵉ Congrès International des Slavistes à Sofia en 1963 et la notice *Legenda o Borysie i Glebie* dans *Lexicon antiqu slavicarum*, III, Wrocław/Varsovie/Cracovie, 1967, p. 33 et ss. Dans des publications précédentes (A. POPPE, *Opou* p. 281-282, 292 ; le même, *O vremeni*, p. 21, 28) nous avons soulevé la question de la traduction de la *Vie* des sa Romain-Boris et David-Gleb dans les synaxaires arméniens, dont la rédaction la plus ancienne, dite de Ter Israël, rem à la première moitié du XIIIᵉ s. (éd. avec trad. franç. par G. Bayan, *Patrologia Orientalis*, XXI, Paris, 1930, fasc. 3, p. 403, d'après un manuscrit de 1316, ainsi que fasc. 6, p. 772-779, d'après une rédaction du XVᵉ s., J. MÉCÉRIAN, *Bul arménologique, II : Introduction à l'étude des synaxaires arméniens*, « Mélanges de l'Univers. Saint Joseph », XXX, 1 nᵒ 4, p. 120 et ss). En comparant les textes, nous sommes arrivé à la conclusion que le texte arménien dépendait exclus ment du *Dit des martyrs et des miracles de Boris et Gleb* dans sa rédaction complète, c'est-à-dire celle qui est apparue après 1115 ; mais il fut probablement déformé par le traducteur pour permettre l'adaptation d'un texte trop long exigences d'un synaxaire. Cette conclusion a été accueillie favorablement, mais en même temps ma thèse, selon laq le texte arménien serait une traduction du grec, fut contestée par Ya. DACHKÉVYTCH, *Les Arméniens à Kiev (jus 1240)* : 13. *La Vie de Borys et Hlib en arménien*, « Rev. des ét. arméniennes », n.s., XI, 1975-1976, —. 346-375. N conviction qu'il a existé une traduction grecque du *Dit des martyrs* découle des recherches antérieures de V. N.Beneš (1914) et L. Melikset-Bek (1946), mais surtout du fait que les anthroponymes russes dans le texte arménien ont les suff flexionnels des noms propres grecs : Romanos, Bladimos (Vladimir), Meroneos (Mironeg), Stapolkas (Svjatopolk). Dac vytch explique ce phénomène par le fait que, « possédant indubitablement certaines connaissances de la langue gree — la *lingua franca* de l'époque — surtout dans le domaine ecclésiastique, le traducteur arménien, pour faciliter l'assin tion des noms slaves étrangers au lecteur arménien de ce temps (qui se trouvait lui aussi partiellement sous l'influ de la culture byzantine), avait ajouté les terminaisons *-os*, *-as* aux noms slaves et scandinaves », *ibid.*, p. 360. C explication peut être acceptée, compte tenu du fait que la traduction est apparue vraisemblablement en Crimée, cor l'une des possibilités. En revanche, parmi les arguments de nature philologique en faveur d'une traduction direct arménien, il en est un qui sans aucun doute est d'un poids considérable : c'est la graphie arménienne du prénom de (sous la forme *Hlep/Hleb*, où g est rendu par le graphème arménien Հ = *ho*, c'est-à-dire conformément à l'articula fricative (ukraino-russe) de g en [h]. Une telle transcription n'aurait pas été possible dans le cas d'un intermédiaire Selon Ya. Dachkévytch, la présence de quelques autres phénomènes phonétiques dans la transcription arménienne an à la conclusion « que le traducteur arménien connaissait non seulement la langue ruthène écrite, mais aussi sa vari parlée méridionale (ancien ukrainien) » (*ibid.*, p. 362-367). Par conséquent, il faut reconnaître que cet argument ainsi certains autres de Ya. Dachkévitch mettent en doute l'existence d'un texte grec du *Dit des martyrs*, bien que toute affirmations catégoriques de cet auteur (*ibid.*, p. 375) puissent être considérées comme prématurées tant que nou disposons pas d'une édition critique des *Vies* arméniennes de Boris et Gleb établies d'après les nombreuses copies conser et alors que même la copie la plus ancienne, dans le synaxaire de Venise de 1269, est encore inédite. On ne peut m pas exclure l'hypothèse que les faits phonétiques observés ont un caractère secondaire, ce qui revient à les attribuer pas au traducteur, mais au copiste du manuscrit de Crimée de 1316, ce dernier pouvant fort bien connaître la lar parlée dans le bassin du Dnepr ou du Dnestr.

phique consacrée aux saints (quarante-quatre hymnes) ; elle fut augmentée de vingt et une
nnes à l'occasion de la translation de 1115. Quand fut composée, autour de 1095, au
nastère des Grottes, la *Chronique de Kiev (Načal'nyj svod)*, on utilisa comme matériaux
ir les notations des années 1015, 1019, 1072, le *Dit des martyrs* et le *Dit des miracles* de
ʾis et Gleb. Ainsi la relation de la *Chronique* sur le meurtre de Boris et Gleb est un réma-
nent du *Dit des martyrs* destiné à conférer à l'œuvre hagiographique l'aspect d'une relation
ʾorique. L'auteur de la version de la *Chronique* connaissait également la *Lectio* de Nestor.
ı après les cérémonies de 1115, l'un des rédacteurs du *Récit des temps passés* compléta
ʾelation de la *Chronique* par un éloge en s'inspirant de la nouvelle œuvre hymnographique
ʾétait l'office en l'honneur de Boris et Gleb. Les cérémonies de la translation du 2 mai 1115
ıstituèrent également une incitation à compléter le *Dit des miracles* par une relation sur la
ʾration merveilleuse des prisonniers innocents (adaptation d'un épisode pris à la *Vie* de
ıtor), ainsi que par une description (inachevée) de la translation elle-même.

te thèse, bien qu'elle n'ait pas été jusqu'à présent critiquée directement, fut accueillie
c réserve[35]. Indépendamment cependant de la solution que l'on peut apporter à notre
position ou à d'autres, tous les efforts de recherche accomplis jusqu'à maintenant dans ce
s ont fait apparaître des divergences de nature fondamentale. Elles concernent les voies
es méthodes de la démarche scientifique : il s'agit, ou bien de recherches fondées sur la
lition manuscrite des textes concrets jusqu'à l'épuisement des hypothèses contrôlables,
bien d'une reproduction de constructions qui s'appuient sur des textes perdus et dont
istence est hypothétique, ce qui facilite la tâche mais conduit les recherches sur le terrain
solutions incontrôlables. Une autre divergence réside dans la question de savoir ce qui a eu
d'abord : les récits sur Boris et Gleb reçurent-ils leur première forme littéraire à partir
a tradition historique ou à partir de la tradition hagiographique, c'est-à-dire est-ce que la
rce fut la relation sur les événements dramatiques des années 1015-1019, ou bien le chro-
ueur a-t-il été inspiré par une œuvre hagiographique consacrée aux princes déjà canonisés?
ır comprendre les problèmes très enchevêtrés de l'histoire de la Russie au XIᵉ s. et entre
res la genèse et le développement de la littérature vieux-russe en général et de l'historio-
phie en particulier, la réponse que l'on peut donner à ces questions a une importance
lamentale.

5. L. MÜLLER, dans « Russia Mediaevalis », III, 1977, p. 192 ; S. MACZKO, *Boris and Gleb*, p. 69, 75 ;
h. ALEŠKOVSKIJ, *op. cit.*, et A. G. KUZ'MIN, *op. cit.*, tout en traitant de ce thème, n'ont pas pris position sur mes
ications, ce qui peut fort bien résulter des difficultés linguistiques. Un éditeur et traducteur récent du *Dit des martyrs*,
ʾessant un inventaire général des travaux consacrés à Boris et Gleb, passe sous silence les publications des dernières
nnies : L. A. DMITRIEV, dans *Pamjatniki literatury drevnej Rusi XI — načala XII veka*, Moscou, 1978, p. 452 et ss.
ʾormation qu'on trouve là n'est pas toujours exacte, par exemple l'affirmation que « le point de vue de
, Šachmatov a été soutenu et développé par N. I. Serebrjanskij ... ». Ce dernier, dans son livre par ailleurs excellent,
ıst pas occupé de la question des rapports entre les trois œuvres principales sur Boris et Gleb et a simplement affirmé
partageait entièrement le point de vue de A. A. Šachmatov. Par conséquent, il n'a pas développé les positions de
ʾrudit, mais des questions qu'il soulève il ressort qu'il avait des doutes à leur sujet. Il prend une position nettement
critique à l'égard de l'hypothèse de A. A. Šachmatov sur l'existence d'une première version, perdue, du *Dit des*
yrs, en affirmant que, ni dans les chroniques, ni dans la littérature ecclésiastique sur Boris et Gleb, il n'y a de trace,
nême une allusion à l'existence d'une telle œuvre, N. I. SEREBRJANSKIJ, *Drevnerusskie knjažeskie žitija*, p. 103-106.
éritable continuateur de l'orientation et des conceptions que représentait dans les recherches sur *Boris et Gleb*
, Šachmatov est L. Müller, dont les travaux ne sont même pas mentionnés par L. A. Dmitriev.

II

A la lumière de ce qui vient d'être dit, on peut considérer comme ouverte la question
l'origine et des relations réciproques entre les différentes œuvres consacrées aux fils canon
de Vladimir Ier ainsi que celle de leur chronologie. L'extrême contradiction des conclusi
qui règne dans la littérature scientifique atteste avec évidence la complexité exceptionn
de l'analyse critique des œuvres connues. A l'époque actuelle, afin de sortir de l'impass
laquelle l'étude de cette question a abouti, il faut, à notre avis, changer quelque peu le m
d'investigation. Tout d'abord, sans chercher à préciser les rapports réciproques entre les di
rentes œuvres et surtout ceux qui auraient eu lieu entre leurs sources communes suppos
il faut établir avec toute la précision possible le moment et les circonstances où furent comp
les différents textes existants, et avant tout le moment de l'apparition du culte même de B
et Gleb. L'essai de solution que nous nous efforçons d'apporter ici permettra de proposer
limite chronologique avant laquelle aucune œuvre consacrée à Boris et Gleb (tant celles
sont connues que celles dont l'existence est hypothétiquement reconstituée) n'a pu
composée.

L'apparition même du culte devança sans aucun doute sa reconnaissance officielle
l'Église : aussi les données hagiographiques sur lesquelles repose l'opinion, assez répan
selon laquelle la canonisation de Boris et Gleb se situerait peu après leur mort en 1015 doiv
elles être soumises à un examen critique. L'attention de l'hagiographe ne se portait pas t
sur la véracité historique de la narration que sur l'exposé des vertus et des mérites dignes
l'auréole de sainteté ; c'est pourquoi, pour déterminer le moment de l'apparition du cu
une œuvre telle que le *Discours* d'Hilarion, ou l'anthroponymie princière, en particulier le de
des prénoms Boris-Romain, Gleb-David et Svjatopolk, revêtent une plus grande importa
que les *Vies* elles-mêmes.

Le *Discours sur la Loi et la Grâce et éloge de notre kagan Vladimir (Slovo o zakone i blago
i pochvala kaganu našemu Vladimiru...)* — une œuvre oratoire du prêtre de l'église princ
de Berestovo, premier Russe à avoir occupé la chaire métropolitaine de Kiev en 1051
a été rédigé, comme l'ont prouvé les recherches de ces dernières années, dans la seco
moitié des années quarante du XIe s., après 1046, cette date étant la plus vraisemblable p
l'achèvement des principales constructions dues à l'initiative de Jaroslav et dont il est ques
dans le texte (fortifications de Kiev, cathédrale Sainte-Sophie et église de l'Annoncia
de la Porte d'Or), et avant le 10 février 1051, date de la mort de l'épouse de Jaros
Ingigerd-Irène, qu'Hilarion mentionne encore parmi les vivants. D'autres considérati
comme par exemple la présence dans l'assistance, lors du sermon solennel, des petits-enf
de Jaroslav amènent à considérer les années 1049-1050 comme la date la plus vrais
blable[36]. Le *Discours*, qui fut prononcé dans la chapelle palatine de la Mère de Dieu, l'é

---

36. L. MÜLLER, *Des Metropoliten Ilarion Lobrede auf Vladimir den Heiligen und Glaubensbekenntnis*, Wiesb
1962, p. 16-32 (on y trouvera, avec la réimpression de l'éd. donnée par A. V. Gorskij en 1844, un commentaire exempl
N. N. Rozov, *Sinodal'nyj spisok sočinenij Ilariona — russkogo pisatelja XI v.*, « Slavia », XXXII, 1963, p. 141-175
la datation, voir les remarques substantielles d'A. V. Soloviev dans son compte rendu du livre de L. Müller,
« Internat. Journ. of Slavic Linguistics a. Poetics » XI, 1968, p. 188-191 ; A. POPPE, *Państwo i kościół na Rusi
wieku*, Varsovie, 1968, p. 56-57 ; voir aussi l'introduction de L. Müller à la trad. des œuvres d'Hilarion : *Die Wer
Metropoliten Ilarion. Eingeleitet, übersetzt und erläutert*, Munich, 1971, p. 10-18 (« Forum Slavicum », XXXVII).
possible de faire coïncider le « Discours » avec l'anniversaire de la mort de Vladimir, le dimanche 15 juillet 1050, cc
le propose L. Müller, ou bien selon N. N. Rozov avec le jour de Pâques qui tombait le lendemain de la fête de l'Ann
tion, le 26 mars 1049.

LA NAISSANCE DU CULTE DE BORIS ET GLEB

la Dîme *(Desjatinnaja cerkov')* près de la tombe du père de la Russie chrétienne, se divise
˙ sa forme et par son contenu en trois parties : la première développe l'idée de la suprématie
la Grâce universelle sur la Loi de Moïse limitée à un seul peuple, de la supériorité du Nouveau
stament sur l'Ancien, la seconde, historique, donne le récit de la diffusion de la Grâce sur
te la terre jusqu'au moment où la source évangélique a coulé sur « notre peuple russe ».
puisque l'initiative de l'intégration de la Russie à la « foi de la Grâce » revient à Vladimir,
troisième partie est précisément consacrée à la glorification du grand kagan, « apôtre parmi
princes », tout en constituant en même temps un panégyrique en l'honneur de son conti-
ateur dans la vraie foi, son fils Jaroslav. Cette troisième partie, « l'éloge de Vladimir », doit
e assurément considérée comme le noyau idéologique et le principal thème du *Discours*.
n que les éloges et les panégyriques ne fussent pas uniquement destinés à la glorification
, saints ou des candidats à la canonisation[37], mais aussi à celle des souverains et des hommes
itiques défunts et vivants — Hilarion continue ici le genre littéraire bien connu de la rhéto-
ue antique et byzantine de l'ἐγκώμιον — on est forcé d'admettre à ce propos qu'Hilarion
ılait prouver que Vladimir était digne d'éloges en tant que « notre docteur et notre maître
ıs la vraie foi », c'est-à-dire qu'il voulait créer une atmosphère favorable à la canonisation
l'apôtre de la Russie[38].

ıs vouloir approfondir ici la problématique, si riche en idées, de ce triptyque littéraire,
se demandera pourquoi, dans une œuvre consacrée à l'adhésion de la Russie au christianisme
ıs Vladimir et à l'affermissement de celui-ci sous Jaroslav, il n'est fait nulle mention de
ris et Gleb — qui à cette époque auraient été déjà canonisés. On aurait été en droit d'attendre
celui qui glorifiait les mérites de « l'imitateur du grand Constantin » qu'il fît référence à
saints fils. Il est difficile d'imaginer qu'Hilarion, en louant les descendants de Vladimir
ır avoir « conservé la vraie foi selon la tradition que tu leur as transmise » et particulièrement
˙oslav, sous lequel « les églises s'épanouissent et le christianisme grandit », pouvait totale-
nt ignorer un événement aussi essentiel pour la jeune église russe que le culte de ses propres
nts, martyrs et thaumaturges, canonisés grâce au zèle de leur pieux frère.

Müller essaie d'expliquer l'absence de toute mention de Boris et Gleb par le fait qu'Hilarion,
cherchant à faire admettre au nombre des saints le père de deux fils déjà canonisés, ne
ırait pas susciter d'impression défavorable, ni exciter la méfiance du métropolite (un
ɔc) à l'endroit d'une telle politique de canonisation dynastique. Il est toutefois bien étrange,
culte qu'il fallait dissimuler ! Dans cette explication on perçoit un écho des opinions
endant la tendance antibyzantine du *Discours*, opinions que L. Müller a lui-même réfutées
manière si convaincante. En rédigeant son sermon, Hilarion ne redoutait aucunement
tre suspecté de vouloir implanter un culte dynastique. C'est ce que montre bien sa prière
ır Jaroslav, suivie du vœu formulé à l'adresse de « notre pieux kagan », quand il accostera
havre de la céleste sécurité..., de se tenir avec toi [= Vladimir] sans honte devant le
ne du Dieu tout-puissant et de recueillir de Lui, pour son labeur en tant que pasteur de
troupeau, la couronne de gloire incorruptible avec tous les justes qui ont peiné pour Lui »[39].

37. K. Ziegler, *Panegyricus*, « Pauly-Wissowa », XVIII, 3, p. 559-570 ; Th. Payr, *Enkomion*, dans *Reallexikon für
ıke und Christentum*, V, 1964, p. 332-343. La nouvelle manière, avec une conception expressément ecclésiastique
ge d'un souverain chrétien), est représentée par la *Vie* de Constantin due à Eusèbe de Césarée que probablement
rion connaissait directement. Pour des rapprochements avec des œuvres grecques qui auraient pu avoir inspiré
ırion, voir le commentaire de L. Müller.
38. L. Müller, *Des Metropoliten Ilarion Lobrede*, p. 20 et ss.
39. N. N. Rozov, *Sinodal'nyj spisok*, p. 170 ; L. Müller, *Des Metropoliten Ilarion Lobrede*, p. 129, n'a malheureusement
commenté ce passage. Voir *PVL*, I, p. 91 : le bienheureux Boris trépassa et reçut la couronne du Christ Dieu et fut
pté parmi les justes. Voir L. Müller, *Die altrussischen hagiographischen Erzählungen*, p. 33, 37, 43.

Hilarion, de surcroît, n'introduisait aucune nouveauté : il était de coutume de compter souverains au nombre des saints pour leurs mérites envers l'Église et, à Byzance mêm on connaît toute une catégorie de saints empereurs et impératrices.

L. Müller explique le silence du *Discours* également par l'argument qu'Hilarion aurait à dess évité de mentionner Boris et Gleb, parce que les deux frères glorifiés par le don des mirac ne s'avéraient pas être un précédent heureux en vue de la canonisation de Vladimir duq on attendait vainement la manifestation d'un tel don[40]. Müller fonde sa supposition sur paroles de l'éloge de Vladimir inclus sous l'année 6523 (1015) dans le *Récit des temps passe* le chroniqueur y regrette que celui qui a baptisé le pays russe ne soit pas l'objet d'un cu correspondant à ses mérites et appelle à prier Dieu afin « qu'il le glorifie ». Or N. K. Nikol's et A. A. Šachmatov considéraient ce fragment comme un ajout postérieur, placé lors de rédaction du *Récit des temps passés*, c'est-à-dire dans la deuxième décennie du XIIe s.[41]. faut remarquer que tout le texte de l'éloge de Vladimir dans la chronique ne fut pas comp avant la fin du XIe s., soit plusieurs générations après la conversion de la Russie, si l'on en cr le texte lui-même : « s'il ne nous avait pas baptisés, nous serions encore maintenant abu par le diable tout comme nos ancêtres ont péri ». De même la comparaison avec Constan le Grand a été incontestablement formulée sous l'influence du *Discours* d'Hilarion[42]. En ou il faut rapprocher l'éloge de la *Chronique* des autres informations sur Vladimir dans les passa de la *Chronique* correspondant aux années 6494-6496 (986-988) qu'on ne peut, en aucun c dater avant la seconde moitié du XIe s.[43]. Si Hilarion s'efforçait de créer le culte de l'apô de la Russie, on comprend qu'un demi-siècle plus tard, l'auteur de l'éloge de la *Chroni* se soit affligé de ce que Vladimir ne fût pas encore agrégé au chœur des saints[44]. Mais l'afflict exprimée ici à propos de l'absence, pour Vladimir, de « l'honneur qui lui est dû pour ce q a donné » ne peut pas justifier le silence apparent d'Hilarion.

40. L. Müller, *Des Metropoliten Ilarion Lobrede*, p. 23-24 ; le même, *Neuere Forschungen*, p. 316 ; le même, *Problem des hierarchischen Status und der jurisdiktionellen Abhängigkeit der russischen Kirche vor 1039*, Cologne/Brauns 1959, p. 39-40. C'est dans le même esprit quant au fond, mais *a contrario*, que S. Maczko tente d'expliquer le sil d'Hilarion. Selon lui, l'éducation byzantine et la conception du monde d'Hilarion « make him unwilling to acknowl the sanctity of Boris and Gleb on the basis of the blatantly political circumstances surrounding their deaths », *Boris Gleb*, p. 75. Mais une telle explication de la conduite du plus proche collaborateur du souverain de la Russie aurait ét quelque manière opportune, si l'on présupposait une tentative avortée de canoniser Boris et Gleb en 1051-1053 sou métropolite Hilarion. Du reste cette affirmation s'accorde mal avec l'opinion du même S. Maczko qui, continuant la pe de S. A. Bugoslavskij, estime que le *Dit des martyrs* aurait été composé comme une apologie de Jaroslav et une légitima de ses droits au trône de Kiev pendant la dernière période de son gouvernement, c'est-à-dire dans les années où le cons le plus proche du prince en matière ecclésiastique était Hilarion. Mais en l'occurrence l'essentiel de cette controve dans laquelle on fait appel au silence d'Hilarion, porte sur la question de savoir si Boris et Gleb ont été ou non cano avant Hilarion et avant 1035. S'ils avaient été comptés au nombre des saints déjà sous Jean Ier, Hilarion n'aurait pa ignorer un tel fait, en heurtant ainsi de surcroît Jaroslav, dans lequel le même Hilarion voyait déjà le son vivan saint. Sur Hilarion, voir aussi notre article, *infra*, n. 83.
41. *PVL*, I, p. 89-90. Voir N. K. Nikol'skij, *Materialy*, p. 278 ; A. A. Šachmatov, *Razyskanija*, p. 42, 571 ; le mê *Povest'*, p. 165-167.
42. *PVL*, I, p. 89 ; L. Müller, *Des Metropoliten Ilarion Lobrede*, p. 117-118 (44, 6 ; 44, 12-16).
43. C'est ce qu'indiquent les accents anti-latins, en particulier la mention des azymes, qu'il n'y a aucune raiso considérer comme une adjonction postérieure, comme le propose M. Ch. Aleškovskij, *Pervaja redakcija Povesti vremen let*, « Archeografičeskij ežegodnik », 1967, p. 34.
44. Vladimir ne fut canonisé qu'à la fin du XIIIe s., E. E. Golubinskij, *Istorija kanonizacii svjatych v russkoj ce* Moscou, 1903, p. 56-57 ; G. P. Fedotov, *Kanonizacija svjatogo Vladimira*, dans *Vladimirskij sbornik*, Belgrade, 1 p. 188-196 ; Ju. K. Begunov, *Pamjatnik russkoj literatury XIII v., Slovo o pogibeli russkoj zemli*, Moscou/Leningrad, 1 p. 49. Dans la *Chronique hypatienne*, sous l'année 1254, Vladimir est mentionné comme saint (*PSRL*, II, col. 821) question de la datation de cette note reste cependant ouverte, si l'on prend en considération les rédactions ultérie successives entre 1269 et le début du XIVe s. A. I. Hens'ors'kyj, *Halyc'ko-Volyns'kyj litopys (Proces skladannja, red i redaktory)*, Kiev, 1958. Même si l'on considère cette notice comme contemporaine, elle peut tout aussi bien témoi d'un culte non encore reconnu par l'Église. Le fait que Vladimir n'était pas encore canonisé vers 1250 est attesté l'attribution au prince de Volynie, Vladimir Vasil'kovič, né autour de cette année, d'un prénom de baptême, (*PSRL* II, col. 920).

conséquent, si nous ne trouvons pas dans le panégyrique en l'honneur de Vladimir la **ti**on de Boris et Gleb, nous en tirerons la conclusion qu'à l'époque de la rédaction du *cours*, en 1049-1050, la question de leur canonisation ne se posait pas encore. Tout en **1**ant conscience des risques qui résultent des conclusions *ex silentio*, nous pensons que, **s** le cas présent, le silence éloquent d'une œuvre telle que le *Discours* d'Hilarion mérite **t** à fait d'être pris en considération.

naissance et le développement du culte de Boris et Gleb sont liés fatalement aux destinées **n**om de Svjatopolk. Le premier détenteur de ce nom qui nous soit connu est précisément **s** de Vladimir, gendre du duc de Pologne Bolesław le Vaillant et prince de Kiev en 1015- **9**. Svjatopolk — fils de deux pères (il aurait été fils de Jaropolk adopté par Vladimir) **n**eurtrier de trois de ses frères — est entré dans l'histoire à travers l'hagiographie et reçut **u**rnom de « maudit » *(okajan'nyj)*. Ce prénom apparaît en Russie, tout comme dans la **a**stie polonaise des Piastes, par suite des liens familiaux avec les Mojmiroviči de Moravie[45]. plus de Svjatopolk Ier nous connaissons encore trois princes russes porteurs de ce nom, semble ainsi appartenir au répertoire onomastique de la lignée princière[46].

atopolk II Michel était le fils d'Izjaslav Jaroslavič, né peut-être du mariage conclu en **3**-1044 avec Gertrude, la sœur du duc de Pologne Casimir le Rénovateur. Sa date de **s**sance en 1050, signalée dans la copie synodale de la *Chronique de Novgorod*, ne suscite **u**n doute[47]. Quand Izjaslav, en 1050, alors qu'il occupait le trône de Turov, donna au **v**eau-né le nom princier de son oncle, cela ne devait pas évoquer des réminiscences néfastes, **u**me celles qu'inspire la lecture des œuvres consacrées à Boris et Gleb. Dans le cas contraire, **h**oix par Izjaslav pour son fils du nom de Svjatopolk aurait été un défi lancé à son propre **t** en sa qualité à la fois de vengeur de ses frères tués innocemment, d'initiateur et de

5. Peut-être par l'intermédiaire de la cour princière tchèque ou polonaise. Świętopełk, le fils de Mieszko Ier et d'Oda, **é** vers 980, c'est-à-dire à la même époque que son homonyme russe. Les Přemyslides non plus ne répugnaient pas à se **o**rmer aux traditions grand-moraves, mais nous ne rencontrons la le prénom de Svjatopolk qu'au XIIe s. L'une des **n**es de Vladimir Ier était tchèque et peut-être était-ce la mère de Svjatopolk. Ce prénom est fréquent dans les dynasties **s** laquelle le péché engendre le crime, mais ne peut pas être retenue comme le témoignage d'une source digne de foi. **i**ev, G. LABUDA, *Dynastie pomorskie*, dans *Słownik Starożytności słowiańskich*, I, Wrocław, 1961, p. 429-430, pl. III, **S**t. KETRZYŃSKI, *O imionach piastowskich do końca XI w.*, dans le recueil de l'auteur, *Polska X-XI wieku*, Varsovie, **,** p. 625-627. La légende des deux pères de Svjatopolk et de sa mère, la belle Grecque, défroquée et pécheresse *(Die* **s**sischen hagiographischen Erzählungen*, p. 27-28 : *PVL* I, p. 56) illustre de façon imagée la thèse de l'hagiographe **6**. Svjatopolk, mentionné dans la *Chronique hypatienne* sous l'année 1173 *(PSRL* II, col. 564) est le prince **o**polk IV, et non un grand *(bojarin)* de Galicie comme l'indique de façon erronée l'index de *PSRL* I-VIII (Saint- **r**sbourg, 1898) et celui de la *Chronique hypatienne* qu'a publié l'Institut d'histoire de l'U.R.S.S. (Moscou, 1975, p. 58). **7**. *Novg. I let.*, p. 16 ; *PVL* I, p. 116 ; cf. S. A. VYSOCKIJ, *Drevnerusskie nadpisi Sofii Kievskoj*, Kiev, 1960, p. 73-80, **,** ; V. L. JANIN, *Russkaja knjaginja Olisava-Gertruda i ee syn Jaropolk*, « Numismatika i Epigrafika », V, 1963, p. 142- **C**ependant l'identification de la mère de Svjatopolk II avec la princesse Olisava (Elisabeth), morte à Kiev le 4 janvier **,** est peu sûre. Contre cette possibilité (la coutume de donner un nouveau prénom à l'épouse conformément à sa **e**lle règle est bien connue à cette époque en Europe) on peut citer les propres paroles de Gertrude notées au début **m**éranie, mais le plus ancien témoignage, situé à la limite du XIe et du XIIe s., semble indiquer un lien avec la cour **n**nées quatre-vingts du XIe s. : Gertrude prie *pro unico filio meo Petro*, qualifiant deux fois dans ses prières son fils **e**-Jaropolk (tué le 12 novembre 1086) d'« unique », *Codex Gertrudianus Manuscriptum Gertrudae filiae Mesconis II Poloniae*, éd. V. MEYSZTOWICZ, « Antemurale », II, 1955, p. 151, 152, 156. Tout aussi vain s'avère l'essai d'attribuer **p**rincesse Gertrude-Olisava un sceau avec les représentations de sainte Elisabeth et de l'archange Gabriel au revers, **,** laquelle selon laquelle Gabriel serait le prénom orthodoxe du prince. Au monastère des Grottes **e**v, on n'avait pas le moindre doute ni sur l'orthodoxie du prince lui-même ni sur celle de l'église dédiée à saint Pierre avait fait édifier. L'impossibilité de l'hypothèse d'une conversion au catholicisme de Jaropolk et de sa mère a été **,**rée par J.-P. ARRIGNON, *A propos de la lettre du pape Grégoire VII au prince de Kiev Izjaslav*, « Russia Mediaevalis », **1**977, p. 13-17. La question de l'identité de Gertrude — Olisava requiert des recherches ultérieures. Peut-être Izjaslav conclu un second mariage déjà en 1050, ou la mère de Svjatopolk est-elle devenue princesse plus tard ? Remarquons ment ici que, dans les recherches généalogiques sur les fils des princes, on a coutume de considérer la légitimité de l'**a**nce selon la conception actuelle du mariage, alors qu'en Russie, les fils de princes nés de concubines n'étaient **n**ement limités dans leurs droits de succession, S. V. JUŠKOV, *Obščestvenno-političeskij stroj i pravo Kievskogo gosu-* **v**a, Moscou, 1949, p. 450-451.

protecteur de leur culte. La loyauté d'Izjaslav envers son père-autocrate ne permet pas
le soupçonner d'un tel sentiment. Le choix du nom n'était par ailleurs nullement fortu
la principauté de Turov-Pinsk représentait, en effet, le territoire *(udel)* que Svjatopolk
avait reçu du vivant de son père. Izjaslav, que son père Jaroslav avait installé là, se souve
de ce qu'il était l'héritier de l'ancien territoire de son oncle et il le marqua en donnant le n
de Svjatopolk à son fils.

Le meurtre de ses frères, que l'on attribue à Svjatopolk, ne suscita pas en soi une réprobat
exceptionnelle de la part des contemporains, si bien qu'en 1050 les querelles entre les fils
Vladimir étaient déjà à demi oubliées. Le temps avait effacé le souvenir des détails
événements mouvementés et leurs témoins avaient disparu à tout jamais, ou bien, reconn
sant la fragilité de leur mémoire personnelle, accordaient leur préférence à la version offici
en cours dans le palais princier du vainqueur. Par ailleurs, la mort de son propre frère, Jarop
pesait sur la conscience de Vladimir, le père de Svjatopolk et de Jaroslav, et malgré c
Hilarion désirait le voir ceint d'une auréole de sainteté. Ce n'est que sous la plume de l'ha
graphe que la personnalité du prince reconnu coupable de la mort de Boris et Gleb rev
des traits apocalyptiques[48]. Et néanmoins le nom de Svjatopolk se rencontre encore deux
au XIIe s. dans les milieux princiers. Que ce nom ne disparût pas aussitôt peut s'expliq
uniquement par le fait que, de 1093 à 1113, à Kiev régna Svjatopolk II-Michel. Svjatopolk
était le fils du prince de Novgorod Mstislav et le petit-fils de Vladimir Monomaque. L'an
de sa naissance n'est pas connue, mais il semble être le fils de la première femme de Mstis
(morte avant 1122), puisqu'il prit part en 1134 à des actions militaires[49] ; il doit donc être
avant 1113, et son père lui donna un nom princier en l'honneur de son grand-oncle qui av
occupé le trône de Kiev. Bien que les relations entre Monomaque et son fils Mstislav a
Svjatopolk II aient connu des hauts et des bas, un tel geste envers l'aîné des princes, le sou
rain de Kiev, bénéficia de circonstances particulièrement favorables au moment du mari
entre Jaroslav Svjatopolkovič et la fille de Mstislav, célébré le 12 mai 1112[50]. Il est très proba
que le troisième fils de Mstislav, Svjatopolk, naquit à un moment proche de cet événeme

Svjatopolk IV-Michel, prince de Turov, fils de Georges (Jurij) et petit-fils de Jaros
Svjatopolkovič, né après 1144, reçut son nom en l'honneur de son arrière-grand-père, con
le souligne le chroniqueur. Il fut enterré en 1189 dans l'église Saint-Michel-l'Archange-
Toit-d'Or à Kiev, une fondation de son arrière-grand-père[51].

Ainsi l'attribution de ce nom à deux reprises dans la première moitié du XIIe s. se ratta
à Michel-Svjatopolk II qui, lui, fut nommé ainsi apparemment avant la canonisation des fr
de son grand-père Jaroslav. Dans la seconde moitié du XIIe s. l'atmosphère religieuse et ec

---

48. *Die altrussischen hagiographischen Erzählungen*, p. 7, 8, 9, 14, 32, 38, 39, 47 ; *PVL* I, p. 98. L'amalgame ent
prénom Svjatopolk et l'épithète *okajannyj* ne se réalisa pas tout de suite, d'autant plus que ce surnom n'était pas
voque ; à l'origine il signifiait « malheureux, pitoyable, pécheur ». Dans un premier temps le surnom attribué à Svjatc
signifiait « malheureux », dans le sens « celui qui apporte le malheur », et ce n'est que peu à peu qu'il devint l'équiv;
de « maudit », I. I. SREZNEVSKIJ, *Materialy dlja slovarja drevne-russkogo jazyka*, II, Saint-Pétersbourg, 1895, col. 639
Dans un synaxaire grec du XIIe s., l'épithète de Svjatopolk est traduite par τάλας — « malheureux, malencontreux, fa
« *Zametki XII-XV vv. otnosjaščiesja k Krymskomu gorodu Sugdee (Sudaku), pripisannye na grečeskom sinaksare »*
par l'archimandrite ANTONIN, « Zapiski Imp. Odesskogo obščestva istorii i drevnostej », V, 1863, p. 620 ; *Thesa*
Graecae linguae, VII, p. 1790.
49. *PSRL* II, col. 286-295 ; N. DE BAUMGARTEN, *Généalogies et mariages occidentaux des Rurikides russes du X*
XIIIe s., Rome, 1927, tabl. V, no 25 (« Orientalia christiana », IX).
50. *PVL* I, p. 195. Dans *Novg. 1 let.* le mariage est situé par erreur en 6621 (1113).
51. *PSRL* II, col. 665 ; N. DE BAUMGARTEN, *Généalogies*, tabl. II, no 22 ; N. G. BEREŽKOV, *Chronologija russ*
letopisanija, Moscou, 1963, p. 205.

tique s'avéra plus forte. Ce nom, blâmé du haut de l'ambon et dans la littérature hagio-
ohique, cessa d'être un nom usuel. Accolé à l'épithète « maudit », il devenait synonyme
'ratricide - sacrilège. Le développement du culte de Boris et Gleb fit disparaître le nom
Svjatopolk dans l'usage de la dynastie princière.

qui éclaire le mieux la naissance du culte de Boris-Romain et Gleb-David, c'est le sort de
s propres noms. Si Jaroslav, comme on l'admet en général à la suite des hagiographes,
tribua de façon décisive à la canonisation de ses frères dès le début de son règne, pourquoi
un de ses six fils, nés entre 1020 et 1040, ne reçut-il le nom de l'un de ses saints oncles[52]?
revanche, cinq de ses quinze petits-fils qui nous sont connus furent appelés de ces noms.
cinq fils de Svjatoslav Jaroslavič (né en 1027) trois furent nommés respectivement Gleb,
'id et Romain. Des indications indirectes, en particulier un portrait en groupe de la famille
Svjatoslav dans une miniature de l'*Izbornik* de 1073[53] où ils sont représentés vers l'âge
iviron 18 à 25 ans, permettent de situer la date de leur naissance vers 1045-1055. L'aîné
t Gleb, que nous rencontrons en 1064 à Tmutarakan' comme « prince délégué » *(područnyj*
iz') de son père ; à partir de 1073, il régna à Novgorod et périt en 1078. David était un
plus âgé que Romain qui mourut encore jeune en 1079. Nestor parle dans la *Lectio* des
inces cadets » qui payèrent de leur vie « l'insoumission aux aînés » ; il a en vue non seulement
nain, mais aussi Boris Vjačeslavič qui tomba au champ Nežatina le 3 octobre 1078[54]. Boris,
du prince de Smolensk Vjačeslav Jaroslavič (né en 1036 et mort en 1056), naquit aux
irons de cette dernière date. C'est également à Smolensk que dut naître vers 1058-1060
'id Igorevič, fils du plus jeune des fils de Jaroslav (mort en 1060).

s peut-on voir dans la vogue de ces noms dans le milieu princier un témoignage de la
ssance du culte des deux frères de Jaroslav assassinés? Nous sommes là, sans aucun doute,
présence d'un éveil de l'intérêt porté à leur mémoire. Nous trouvons une analogie signi-
tive dans le texte du *Récit des temps passés* sous l'année 1044 : « On déterra les deux princes
opolk et Oleg, fils de Svjatoslav et on baptisa leurs os et on les déposa dans l'église de
ainte Mère de Dieu ». Peu après, les noms de ces princes furent donnés aux petits-fils de
oslav : Jaropolk-Pierre, fils premier-né d'Izjaslav et Gertrude, qui dut voir le jour peu
ès 1044, et Oleg-Michel, fils de Svjatoslav, qui était un peu plus âgé que Vladimir
iomaque, né en 1053. Apparemment ce fut vers cette époque qu'eut lieu la translation
restes de Gleb de Smjadyn' à Vyšgorod. Et ce ne fut pas par hasard que ce nom fut attribué
fils de Svjatoslav né dans la seconde moitié des années quarante.

ious n'avons pas osé jusqu'à présent reconnaître dans cette popularité des noms de Boris-
nain et de Gleb-David la manifestation d'un culte, la situation dans la maison princière
Polock dissipe dans une large mesure nos doutes. En effet, le prince de Polock Vseslav
rt en 1101), fils de Brjačeslav (mort en 1044), petit-neveu de Jaroslav mais de la même

---

2. *PVL* II, p. 99, 100, 101, 108, 109. Le plus jeune fils, Igor, est né après Vjačeslav, venu au monde en 1036-1037.
rtir d'Izjaslav, né en 1024, tous étaient les fils de la même mère, Ingigerd-Irène (*PVL* I, p. 108). Était-elle la mère de
limir né en 1020 ? Une tentative récente de reconnaître comme authentique une tradition novgorodienne tardive sur
use (la première ?) de Jaroslav, Anne, a démontré la nécessité d'une étude attentive de cette question, voir
Dryhalkin, *Do biografiji knjazja Jaroslava Mudroho*, « Ukrajins'kyj istoryčnyj žurnal », 1970, n° 2, p. 93-96. Trois
fils de Jaroslav portèrent les mêmes prénoms que leurs oncles Izjaslav, Svjatoslav et Vsevolod, N. de Baumgarten,
ialogies, table I, n°s 2, 5, 6, 23, 25, 26.
3. A. N. Svirin, *Iskusstvo knigi Drevnej Rusi*, Moscou, 1964, p. 176.
4. A. Poppe, *Chronologia utworów Nestora hagiografa*, p. 301-305. L'importance du sort des prénoms princiers pour
de du culte de Boris et Gleb a été soulignée par M. Ch. Aleškovskij, *Povest' vremennych let*, Moscou, 1971, p. 86 et ss.
considérations font écho à mes observations, A. Poppe, *Opowieść o męczeństwie i cudach*, « Slavia Orientalis », XVIII,
, p. 369-372.

génération que les fils de Jaroslav, donna à quatre de ses sept fils les noms suivants : B
(mort en 1128), Gleb (mort en 1118), David (mort après 1129), Romain (mort en 11
L'énumération dans cet ordre des fils de Vseslav n'offre aucune garantie en ce qui conce
l'aînesse ; il en est de même pour les trois autres fils, probablement plus jeunes, Rogvc
Svjatoslav, Rostislav. On peut supposer que tous sont nés dans les années soixante-dix
XIᵉ s. On aimerait donner des conclusions plus précises sur un point aussi essentiel, mais
bases de celles-ci font défaut. De toute façon, en 1067-1068, deux des fils de Vseslav ava
déjà au moins 13-14 ans, puisqu'ils accompagnèrent leur père et se trouvèrent en pr
à Kiev. Les quatre noms choisis par le prince de Polock pour ses fils témoignent certes s
aucun doute du culte que Vseslav portait à la mémoire de ses grands-oncles, mais il s'
avant tout d'une manifestation politique. Précisément Vseslav, contraint de défendre
indépendance à l'égard de Kiev et les droits de sa lignée au trône de Polock, trouvait dan
culte de Boris et Gleb une base religieuse et morale pour avoir le droit de s'opposer à l'injus
et à la tyrannie d'un plus puissant, droit qui lui garantissait le soutien de l'Église[55]. On p
supposer que ce furent les mêmes motifs qui amenèrent Vjačeslav et Igor à donner en 1(
1059 à leurs fils les noms de Boris et David. Ce sont les plus jeunes fils de Jaroslav qui res
taient le plus particulièrement leur dépendance vis-à-vis de leurs frères aînés.

Le choix des noms de Boris et Gleb, qui appartenaient au répertoire onomastique princ
est totalement compréhensible sur l'arrière-fond de la tradition dynastique. En revan
l'apparition dans le milieu princier des premiers noms chrétiens adoptés non comme n
de baptême mais comme premiers prénoms, utilisés dans la vie courante, présuppose une a
raison. Dès l'adoption du christianisme en Russie, on prit l'habitude de donner deux préno
l'un ecclésiastique, l'autre séculier. Les princes, en plus de leur prénom princier hérité
leur lignée et utilisé dans la vie quotidienne, recevaient à leur baptême le nom d'un s
patron dont il était fait mention rarement et occasionnellement, surtout dans les notices
leur naissance et leur trépas. Le plus souvent on ne peut que deviner avec plus ou moins
certitude le nom de baptême des princes d'après les dénominations des églises édifiées
leur initiative et à leurs frais ou d'après les matériaux sigillographiques. C'est pourquoi t
les princes sont connus d'après leur nom princier et seulement quelques-uns également d'ap
leur nom de baptême. La tendance de donner le prénom chrétien en tant que nom prin
apparaît dans la seconde moitié du XIᵉ s., puis se développe dans le courant du XIIᵉ s. ; à
fin du XIIIᵉ s. la coutume de nommer les princes d'après leur nom séculier dispara
Primitivement ne devenaient noms princiers que les noms chrétiens qui revêtaient une nouv
nuance, sacrale et dynastique, exprimant l'appartenance princière dans la mesure où ils ava
été employés comme noms de baptême pour des princes-oints. Les princes se contentèr
alors progressivement d'un seul nom de ce type qui présentait le double caractère de sacra
chrétienne et dynastique. On citera ici l'exemple des deux fils de Monomaque : Geor
(Jurij Dolgorukij) né vers 1090, fut appelé ainsi en l'honneur de son arrière-grand-p
Georges-Jaroslav le Sage ; André, né en 1102, le fut en l'honneur de son grand-père And
Vsevolod. On est moins certain à propos de Vasil'ko Rostislavič, né vers 1067 et appelé d'ap
le diminutif du nom de baptême de son grand-père Vladimir (dont le nom chrétien n'est

55. A. POPPE, Państwo i kościół, p. 172-174, 220, 232-234.
56. Nous n'abordons pas ici le problème de l'utilisation en Russie de deux prénoms chrétiens. Cette coutume, atte
à partir du XIVᵉ-XVᵉ s., est peut-être apparue pour remplacer la tradition onomastique « semi-païenne ». Les indica
des chroniques plus détaillées montrent que, en plus du prénom donné lors du baptême, on conférait un second pré
chrétien d'après le calendrier, c'est-à-dire en prenant le saint dont la fête tombait le jour de la naissance,
N. P. LICHAČEV, Materialy dlja istorii vizantijskoj i russkoj sfragistiki, I, Leningrad, 1928, p. 86-89.

LA NAISSANCE DU CULTE DE BORIS ET GLEB

r) ou de son arrière-grand-père Vladimir-Basile qui baptisa la Russie. En tout cas il est discutable que les premiers noms de baptême qui apparaissent comme noms princiers dans dynastie dès les années cinquante du XIe s. sont les noms de Romain et David. Et puisqu'ils rencontrent indépendamment de ceux de Boris et Gleb, il n'y a pas de doute que l'usage ns le milieu princier de ces quatre noms correspond à une vénération des ancêtres Boris-)main et Gleb-David, qui revêtit bientôt tous les aspects d'un culte religieux (ce qui n'équi-ut pas obligatoirement à la canonisation). La signification qui se rattachait à ces noms)uve un témoignage éloquent dans la liste des princes russes pour lesquels pria l'abbé ıniel devant le Saint-Sépulcre en 1106-1107. Ce n'est pas nu hasard si tous les princes entionnés là portent deux noms à l'exception de trois d'entre eux : David Svjatoslavič, ʻris Vseslavič et Gleb Vseslavič[57]. Pour ceux qui portaient les noms de Boris et Gleb, déjà mis au rang de saints, un second nom chrétien s'avérait superflu. On peut admettre qu'une le coutume fut adoptée dans les milieux princiers dès les débuts du culte avant que la sainteté s deux frères fût officiellement reconnue par l'Église[58].

s remarques que nous venons d'exposer sur le sort des noms de Boris, Romain, Gleb et ıvid contredisent les conclusions proposées par V. L. Janin dans son ouvrage capital sur sceaux vieux-russes : « D'après les nombreux matériaux de l'époque pré-mongole, l'identité ınstante des noms Boris et Romain d'une part, Gleb et David d'autre part, peut être ıilement relevée »[59].

ı analysant les données des sources primaires et en prêtant particulièrement attention aux rsonnes que Janin identifie sous ces doubles noms lors de l'attribution des sceaux repré-ıtant Boris et Gleb, nous n'avons pas trouvé jusqu'au XIIIe s. une seule preuve confirmant ypothèse de la synonymie des noms Boris-Romain et Gleb-David dans l'anthroponymie ıncière. L'observation juste de V. L. Janin selon laquelle les représentations de Boris ou eb reconnaissables surtout d'après leurs bonnets princiers correspondent aux bulles portant noms de Romain ou David, ne prouve aucunement que ces noms avaient fusionné dans vie quotidienne des princes. Ils étaient synonymes uniquement lorsqu'ils concernaient saints qui, de fait, étaient vénérés sous leurs deux noms, ce qui s'explique, comme nous ıayons de le montrer plus bas, dans le contexte de la période primitive de leur culte, quand ̣glise reconnaissait comme saints les princes-martyrs Romain et David. C'est pourquoi, r la suite, lors de l'attribution de ces noms à des princes, il ne s'agissait pas des saints

57. IGUMEN DANIIL, *Choženie* (réimpr. de l'éd. de M. A. VENEVITINOV, 1883/85), Munich, 1970, p. 140, 210-211 ıavische Propyläen », XXXVI) ; trad. franç. par B. DE KHITROWO, *Itinéraires russes en Orient*, I/1, Genève, 1889, 2 et ss ; (une nouvelle trad. franç. est en préparation à Paris), V. L. JANIN, *Mežduknjažeskie otnošenija v epochu Mono-:ha i « Choždenie igumena Daniila »*, « TODRL », XVI, 1960, p. 122-130. Le nom royal du psalmiste David, qui joua un considérable dans l'idéologie et la symbolique du pouvoir, aurait pu devenir un prénom princier indépendamment du ̣e de Boris et Gleb, mais étant donné qu'il apparut en même temps que celui de Romain, le lien avec le nouveau culte indubitable. Les noms de Boris et Gleb, une fois devenus chrétiens, apparurent à partir du XIIe s. hors du milieu ıcier. La plus ancienne mention se trouve dans *Novg. 1 let.* sous l'année 1120 où il est question du gouverneur de ̣vgorod, Boris.
58. Il arrivait que dans les familles princières, conformément à la tradition, on ne se contentât pas d'un seul prénom, is ou Gleb, mais dans ce cas, ces derniers assument déjà leur nouvelle fonction de prénom chrétien. Ainsi, par exemple, 167 Oleg Svjatoslavič eut un fils « qu'il nomma lors du baptême Boris et dans le siècle Svjatoslav » (*PSRL*, II, col.526). ıtefois, d'après les indications de l'abbé Daniel, il est difficile de considérer comme une seule et même personne Boris ̣gvol'd, fils de Vseslav de Polock ; voir L. V. ALEKSEEV, *Polockaja zemlja*, Moscou, 1966, p. 252, et le compte rendu de ̣ASILEWSKI dans « Kwartalnik Kultury Materialnej », XVI, 1968, p. 376. Contrairement à V. L. JANIN, *Mežduknja-ie otnošenija*, p. 130, une identification des fils de Vseslav, Boris et Romain, est impossible, puisqu'il est clair qu'il ̣it de deux personnes distinctes, *PSRL*, II, col. 284, 293.
59. V. L. JANIN, *Aktovye pečati drevnej Rusi X-XV vv.* I : *Pečati X-načala XIII v.*, Moscou, 1970, p. 31-32, 92-98.

patrons de Boris et de Gleb[60] mais bien d'eux-mêmes sous leurs noms chrétiens, ce qui reflète dans l'iconographie des sceaux des princes qui portaient les noms de Romain ou David[61]. La constatation que les princes (et plus tard pas seulement eux) ne recevaient qu' seul des quatre noms des deux saints ancêtres, à moins que l'on ne démontre le contrai implique la reconsidération de l'attribution de tous les sceaux des princes Boris et Roma Gleb et David, qui reposent sur la présomption de la synonymie de ces prénoms.

Le fait que, depuis le début des années quarante jusqu'aux années soixante-dix du xie neuf princes que nous connaissons reçurent les noms des princes-martyrs témoigne de naissance et du développement de leur vénération religieuse dans la dynastie. Le culte Boris et Gleb fut d'ailleurs, tant à son origine que dans son développement ultérieur, dura la période kiévienne, avant tout un culte princier. Son origine ne remonte pas à une célébrati de leur mémoire par l'Église. L'apparition du culte en milieu princier, la reconnaissance (ancêtres en tant que saints protecteurs de la dynastie et de ses possessions précédèrent canonisation et créèrent les conditions favorables à l'entrée officielle de Boris et Gleb da l'assemblée des saints.

On notera aisément que, dans cette première période, les traces de la vénération de Bo et Gleb n'apparaissent pas dans toutes les familles princières. En dehors des trois princes plus faibles, « inégaux en droit », Vseslav de Polock et les deux fils cadets de Jaroslav, s Svjatoslav vénérait la mémoire de ses oncles. Il est significatif qu'il a donné à son fils a le nom de Gleb, tandis que les puinés reçurent comme noms princiers les noms de baptê de leurs grands-oncles[62]. Ne faut-il pas voir ici l'indice de ce que c'est précisément Svjatosl — lui qui avait régné à Vyšgorod jusqu'à la mort de Jaroslav en 1054 —, qui devint, ap le transfert des reliques de Gleb de Smjadyn', l'initiateur ou le co-instigateur de ce cul Il suffit de rappeler avec quel zèle, utilisant les droits de souverain de Kiev qu'il venait s'attribuer, il se hâta dès 1073 d'édifier en l'honneur des saints une église en pierre de dimensi grandiose[63] au lieu du sanctuaire en bois qu'Izjaslav venait d'ériger.

D'après l'opinion couramment admise, Boris et Gleb furent canonisés sous le métropol Jean Ier, donc au plus tard dans les années trente du xie s. Ce point de vue a pour base

---

60. La question de savoir lequel des quatre saints Romains a été le patron de Boris doit être résolue en suivant indications, indirectes mais claires, de Nestor l'hagiographe, selon lesquelles il s'agirait de Romain le Mélode. Le text Nestor est encore plus explicite pour nous permettre d'affirmer que Gleb avait reçu lors de son baptême le prénom du biblique *Die altrussischen hagiographischen Erzählungen*, p. 5-6 ; V. L. JANIN, *Aktovye pečati*, p. 31, 36.
61. Toutefois ce n'est pas toujours le cas. Sur les sceaux de David Igorevič découverts à Sutejsk on trouve représ le roi David, V. L. JANIN, *Aktovye pečati*, n°s 26-28. Le sceau de Peremyšl', découvert en 1962, ne manque pas d'inté l'inscription grecque y est semblable aux inscriptions des sceaux de David Igorevič, mais sur l'avers est représenté s Démétrios en pied portant un glaive et un bouclier avec l'inscription Ο ΑΓΙΟΣ ΔΑΒΙΔ. N'a-t-on pas affaire ici à essais de représentations iconographiques de saint Gleb-David ? Une représentation analogue du martyr de Thessaloni sur un sceau byzantin de la fin du xie ou du début du xiie s. appartenant au curopalate Michael Kontostephanos m'a aimablement indiquée par Mme V. S. Šandrovskaja (Collection de l'Ermitage, M. 2980).
62. M. P. POGODIN, *Drevnjaja russkaja istorija do mongol'skogo iga*, III-2, Moscou, 1871, p. 10, avait attiré l'atten des historiens sur un Boris, nommé dans la liste des princes de la *Chronique* du monastère de la Résurrection (*Voskresen letopis'*, *PSRL*, VII, Saint-Pétersbourg, 1859, p. 232), mais il s'agit ici d'une fausse identification avec Boris Vjačesla mentionné plusieurs fois dans la *PVL* sans patronyme. Sur la préférence du culte de Gleb dans la famille de Svjato et de celui de Boris-Romain dans la famille de Vladimir Monomaque, voir les considérations intéressantes M. Ch. ALEŠKOVSKIJ, *Povest' vremennych let*, p. 87-92, et du même, *Russkie glebo-borisovskie enkolpiony*, p. 111 e Cependant l'hypothèse proposée là d'une transformation du culte, d'abord « populaire », de Boris et Gleb thaumatu en un culte « féodal » des saints soldats n'est pas très convaincante : deux ou trois mentions de Gleb en première p avant Boris, ne constituent pas une preuve dans ce sens.
63. M. K. KARGER, *Drevnij Kiev II*, Moscou/Léningrad, 1961, p. 318-336 ; A. POPPE, *Opowieść*, p. 285, 287. La « li de Svjatoslav » témoigne d'un intérêt particulier pour le culte de ses saints ancêtres même au xiie s. ; par exemple, pre au même moment où était achevée (1112) et consacrée (1115) par Oleg Svjatoslavič l'église de Vyšgorod, David Svjatosl construisit à Černigov une église dédiée à Boris et Gleb, N. V. CHOLOSTENKO, *Issledovanie Boriso-glebskogo sobo Černigove*, « Sovetskaja Archeologija », 1967, n° 2, p. 188-210.

nseignements fournis par le *Dit des miracles* et la *Lectio* de Nestor sur le transfert des corps corruptibles des martyrs et l'instauration de leur fête annuelle le 24 juillet à l'initiative ı métropolite Jean et de Jaroslav. Il est possible en effet que Jean Ier ait gouverné l'Église sse dans les deuxième et troisième décennies du xie s. Probablement immédiatement après ı et pas plus tard que vers 1035, la métropole était dirigée par Théopempte[64]. De sorte que ıroslav et Jean Ier pouvaient agir ensemble entre 1019 et 1035. A. A. Šachmatov, prêtant édit à cette information et supposant que la canonisation eut lieu un dimanche, proposa ımme dates 1020 ou 1026, années où le 24 juillet tomba un dimanche[65]. Cette possibilité est fïrmée par le fait que pendant ces années, et jusqu'à la conclusion d'un traité de paix avec ıtislav en 1026, Jaroslav ne se sentait pas pleinement maître à Kiev et résidait principalement Novgorod. Ce n'est qu'après la mort de Mstislav qu'il se crut en pleine possession du pouvoir ns le Sud. Les initiatives les plus importantes que nous pouvons attribuer à ce prince en ıtière de construction à Kiev remontent toutes à l'époque postérieure à 1036, quand il ıit devenu, selon les termes de la *Chronique*, « autocrate du pays russe ». De même le *Dit* ı *martyrs* rapporte que le transfert des restes de Gleb de Smjadyn' (près de Smolensk) Vyšgorod (près de Kiev) où était enterré Boris, eut lieu alors que Jaroslav « avait pris tout pouvoir en Russie » *(preja v'sju volost' rus'kuju)*, c'est-à-dire après 1036[66].

ır ailleurs la description même des événements avec la participation de Jean Ier fait surgir ı doutes sérieux : on y observe trop de lieux communs propres à l'hagiographie. Dans la ıscription de la cérémonie de l'ouverture des cercueils exhumés de Boris et Gleb en présence ı métropolite Jean Ier, l'auteur du *Dit des miracles* écrit : « Ils virent un miracle très glorieux : ı corps des deux saints ne portant aucune altération mais parfaitement intègres et leurs ıages resplendissants comme ceux de deux anges ». Un peu plus loin dans la description de translation des saints dans la nouvelle église (1072), il rapporte que l'on découvrit dans les âsses ouvertes les reliques, c'est-à-dire les ossements de Boris et Gleb, ce que confirme ılement le récit ultérieur. Mais c'est Nestor qui décrit l'aspect des reliques de la façon plus imagée. En rapportant que le métropolite Georges prit le bras de Boris, il explique : arce que celui-ci reposait en os »[67]. En comparant les descriptions des deux translations, remarque que les cercueils de Boris et Gleb furent ouverts d'abord pour la reconnaissance ı reliques lors de la solennité qui eut lieu à Vyšgorod le 20 mai 1072. La première description noigne uniquement de la familiarité de son auteur avec la littérature hagiographique d'après ıuelle l'incorruptibilité des corps et le parfum qui s'en dégageait étaient retenus comme des ınes de sainteté. C'était un cas idéal, souhaité, un miracle « supplémentaire » mais non lispensable pour l'admission au nombre des saints[68]. Lors de la véritable ouverture des

---

64 A Poppe, *Państwo i kościół*, p. 38, 101-104.
65. A. A. Šachmatov, *Razyskanija*, p. 58 ; M. D. Priselkov, *Očerki po cerkovno-političeskoj istorii Kievskoj Rusi X-I vv.*, Saint-Pétersbourg, 1913, p. 71. Voir les corrections apportées par L. Müller, *Neuere Forschungen*, p. 314, qui pose de reculer les dates jusqu'à 1026-1039, ce qui ne change rien au fond du problème. Aucune preuve en faveur d'une onisation précoce ne peut être apportée par la tradition selon laquelle le monastère de Boris et Gleb près de Toržok ıit été fondé par un acteur des événements de 1015, Ephrème, le frère de Georges, le domestique de Boris ; cf. A. Šachmatov, *Razyskanija*, p. 75-76, 87 ; *PVL*, II, p. 358. Cette légende est consignée dans la *Vie* d'Ephrème de ıotoržok, texte embrouillé du milieu du xviie s. à peine plus ancien que la vénération locale de ce saint en 1584-1587, O. Ključevskij, *Drevnerusskie žitija svjatych kak istoričeskij istočnik*, Moscou, 1871, p. 335 ; E. E. Golubinskij, ırija kanonizacii, p. 117.
66. *PVL*, I, p. 99-101 ; *Die altrussischen hagiographischen Erzählungen*, p. 48. Sur la position de Jaroslav avant et ès 1026 voir N. N. Il'in, *Letopisnaja stat'ja 6523 goda i ee istočnik*, Moscou, 1957, p. 118-119 ; M. N. Tichomirov, ıv, « Journal of Medieval History », VII, 1981, n° 1, p. 27-29, 31-32.
67. *Die altrussischen hagiographischen Erzählungen*, p. 22, 54.
68. E. E. Golubinskij, *Istorija kanonizacii*, p. 34-35, 301.

châsses en 1072, on constata l'état de conservation réel des restes de Boris et Gleb, ce qu conformément à la tradition et à la pratique ecclésiastiques, n'apportait nul préjudice à le sainteté.

L'essentiel de la fête de Vyšgorod en 1072 consista non pas dans la translation des sain dans une nouvelle église, mais, comme il ressort indirectement du *Dit des miracles*, da l'admission de Boris et Gleb au nombre des saints. A la différence de l'Église catholiqu romaine qui, aux XIe-XIIe s., réserva le droit de canonisation au seul pape, l'Église byzanti demeurait plus proche de la pratique de l'Église primitive. Chaque évêque possédait le dr de porter un défunt au nombre des saints locaux vénérés dans les limites de son diocès ainsi, à l'intérieur des frontières de la Russie, le chef de l'Église russe disposait de ce dro Un culte de caractère local n'avait pas besoin de la sanction de Constantinople. La procédu de canonisation consistait dans la présentation des preuves de sainteté parmi lesquelles principale et la seule indispensable était la glorification par le don de thaumaturgie. I canonisation elle-même consistait en la fixation d'un jour déterminé pour la fête annue en l'honneur du glorifié. La reconnaissance officielle était précédée habituellement, ma pas obligatoirement, par l'«invention» des reliques du canonisé — ouverture du tombea translation des reliques dans une nouvelle châsse et installation de celle-ci à un emplaceme approprié dans l'église — ; elle culminait par une liturgie solennelle célébrée par l'évêq le jour désigné comme fête annuelle de la mémoire du saint. De préférence, pour le jour de glorification officielle, on composait une *Vie*, un éloge et des notes ou des témoignages ora sur les miracles accomplis ; au même moment, ou peu après, on rédigeait un office en l'honne du saint[69].

Le *Dit* attestait pour Boris et Gleb le fait de la mort en martyrs, mais il ne s'agissait pas d' martyre pour la foi, de sorte que Boris et Gleb ne pouvaient pas être *eo ipso* considérés comr saints. Il fallait absolument prouver que des miracles avaient été opérés par leur médiatio selon les conditions bien connues en Russie : « Si l'on trouve quelque part dans la terre d reliques, qu'elles opèrent trois miracles : qu'un sourd entende, qu'un muet parle, qu' aveugle voie, et si elles opèrent ces miracles, elles sont de Dieu... ; si elles n'opèrent pas c miracles, qu'on ne les reçoive pas »[70]. Cette condition fut remplie, bien que partiellemer A la veille des cérémonies de 1072, on eut connaissance de trois miracles qui avaient eu li à l'époque de Jaroslav et du métropolite Jean Ier : la guérison de deux boiteux et d'un aveug Le métropolite Georges, qui de par sa fonction était tenu de veiller à l'observance des exigenc de la procédure de canonisation, pouvait ressentir quelques doutes, ne serait-ce que pour simple raison qu'il ressortait des témoignages qui lui étaient présentés que les saints avaie révélé leur don de thaumaturges cinquante ans plus tôt, sous son lointain prédécesseu Aussi présenta-t-on au métropolite des preuves concernant trois autres miracles plus récent la guérison d'un boiteux et d'un muet, d'une manchote et d'un aveugle. La description dernier miracle contient une allusion significative, provoquée apparemment par le rigorisr du métropolite Georges : saint Georges, le patron du métropolite enjoignit à l'aveugle qui

69. *Ibid.*, p. 21, 40-42, 261 et ss, 282, 286, 294-296 ; E. Temnikovskij, *K voprosu o kanonizacii svjatych*, « Vremen Demidovskogo Juridičeskogo Liceja », LXXXVIII, 1904, p. 14-41 ; H. Delehaye, *Sanctus*, Bruxelles, 1927, p. 162 et H.-G. Beck, *Kirche und theologische Literatur im byzantinischen Reich*, Munich, 1959, p. 274-275.
70. A. V. Gorskij et K. I. Nevostruev, *Opisanie slavjanskich rukopisej Moskovskoj Sinodal'noj biblioteki*, II Moscou, 1857, p. 283 ; E. E. Golubinskij, *Istorija kanonizacii*, p. 44 et ss, 265.

ait de s'adresser à Boris et Gleb, car « Dieu leur a donné la grâce dans cette contrée, le pays
se, de pardonner et de guérir toute souffrance et toute maladie »[71].

ccomplissement des exigences canoniques formelles permit au métropolite de procéder
personne au rite de canonisation, qui coïncida avec la translation des reliques dans l'église
vellement construite par Izjaslav. La description de la translation révèle un détail signi-
tif : les restes de Boris se trouvaient en 1072 dans un cercueil en bois, et ce n'est que lors
la translation dans la nouvelle église que « ses reliques furent déposées dans une châsse
pierre », alors que la dépouille de Gleb reposait déjà dans l'ancienne église dans une châsse
pierre. Ce renseignement montre que les destinées mortuaires des deux frères avant 1072
taient pas identiques[72]. Si la glorification des princes-martyrs avait eu lieu à l'époque de
oslav, on comprendrait difficilement la position particulièrement privilégiée de Gleb,
utant plus que les *Vies* prêtent plus d'attention et de place à l'aîné, Boris. Les restes de
b avaient été déposés dans un sarcophage en pierre (de schiste?) lors de la translation de
jadyn' à Vyšgorod, qui avait eu lieu — comme on l'a indiqué plus haut — selon toute
isemblance dans les années quarante du XIe s. et avait précédé la naissance du culte[73].
dans ce cas aussi la description de la translation des saints par Jean Ier et de leur tombe
mmune en terre révèle un emprunt littéraire de l'auteur. Les cercueils en bois étaient mis
terre sous le sol d'une église, tandis que les sarcophages en pierre étaient placés dans des
pelles latérales et dans des enfeux. Si la dépouille de Boris se trouvait dans un cercueil
bois avant 1072, cela signifie qu'aucune tentative concrète pour obtenir une reconnaissance
cielle du culte n'avait été faite jusqu'alors. La comparaison des descriptions des deux
émonies de Vyšgorod, en 1075 et 1115, fait clairement ressortir en quoi l'admission au
nbre des saints se différenciait d'une simple translation des reliques. Lors des cérémonies
1115 le moment culminant fut la translation ou plus précisément le transfert des châsses
c les reliques des saints dans la nouvelle église. En 1072, c'est l'ouverture des châsses et
découverte des reliques : « et toute l'église fut remplie merveilleusement de parfum et
rômes ». Les fidèles furent admis à baiser les reliques. En 1115, en revanche, les châsses
Boris et Gleb ne furent pas ouvertes.

---

1. *Die altrussischen hagiographischen Erzählungen*, p. 59-69. On ne peut pas accepter la tentative d'attribuer au culte
tien de Boris et Gleb des traits païens et scandinaves (E. S. REISMAN, *The Cult of Boris and Gleb : Remnant of a*
ingian Tradition ?, « Russian Rev. », XXXVII, 1978, p. 141-157). L'auteur, en donnant une réponse positive à la
tion posée en tête de son article, voit dans la vénération des saints princes des traces du culte du dieu scandinave
n. On lit avec intérêt ses considérations, inspirées par les hypothèses fécondes de G. Dumézil dans le domaine de
ythologie comparée, sur la manifestation dans le culte de Boris et Gleb de la « sainte royauté ». Cependant Reisman
preuve d'un mépris total pour les problèmes philologiques que soulèvent les témoignages sur la première inhumation
leb apportés par les œuvres consacrées aux deux princes martyrs, et utilise les sources sans aucun esprit critique.
r prouver que le corps de Gleb avait été suspendu sur un arbre à l'instar des victimes immolées à Odinn, il transforme
ot *bereg* (« bord », « rivage ») en *bereza* (« bouleau »), en interprétant le locatif *na brezě* comme *na berezě*, et la *koloda*
luit en anglais par le générique « trunc » au lieu de « log » plus précis) en tronc d'un arbre vivant, alors que ce terme
e désigne toujours une partie du tronc d'un arbre *abattu* : il peut s'agir d'une grosse bûche en position horizontale ou
objet fabriqué par l'excavation d'une partie d'un tronc, tels que, par exemple, un canot, un cercueil, une ruche,
onneau, etc. Notons que le peintre qui illustra le *Dit* au milieu du XIVe s. a compris l'ensevelissement du corps de
» « entre deux *kolody* » *(mežju dvema kolodoma)* comme entre deux troncs horizontaux (miniatures du recueil de
estre, fo 135, 135 vo et 141, dans D. A. AJNALOV, *Miniatury...*, p. 22). Cependant, dans son sens initial, cette expression
it sans conteste désigner un cercueil fait de deux troncs creux ou de deux embarcations. La coutume d'enterrer les
ts dans une *koloda*, c'est-à-dire dans une souche d'arbre creusée, s'est maintenue en Russie jusqu'au XVIIIe s. inclus.
2. L'article 1072 dans la copie synodale de *Novg. 1 let.*, p. 17, qui dit : « Boris et Gleb furent transférés de la L'ta à
gorod », n'est qu'une interprétation embrouillée et abrégée par le chroniqueur novgorodien du XIIe s. de l'information
ée par la *PVL*. Voir de même la description de la translation de 1115 dans *Novg. 1 let.*, p. 20, et A. A. ŠACHMATOV,
jskanija, p. 201-202, 205, 378-380, 628-629 ; M. Ch. ALEŠKOVSKIJ, *Povest' vremennych let*, p. 85-86.
3. Au XIe s. on enterrait dans des sarcophages en schiste non seulement les princes, mais aussi des nobles,
. KARGER, *Drevnij Kiev I*, Moscou/Léningrad, 1958, p. 472.

Nous trouvons un nouveau témoignage de ce que la canonisation eut lieu seulement sou$ métropolite Georges dans la même description des cérémonies de 1072 : quand le métropo$ fut persuadé, en ouvrant leurs châsses, de la sainteté de Boris et Gleb, « il fut saisi de fraye car il n'avait pas grande foi dans les saints, il se prosterna et les pria de lui pardonner ». $ telle conduite ne traduisait pas, comme certains l'ont proposé, une renonciation, de la p d'un hiérarque byzantin, au doute en la sainteté des princes russes et à un préjugé con leur culte, elle était dictée par le rôle qui lui revenait puisqu'il constituait l'instance qui a$ à prendre la décision finale. De même, le métropolite Jean émit des doutes, *ex officio*, env les apparitions miraculeuses sur les tombes des saints russes : « la crainte et le doute le saisir$ ainsi que la confiance et la joie en Dieu »[74]. En l'occurrence il importe peu que la descript du comportement du métropolite Georges soit moins dépendante, pour la description du $ de la canonisation, que celle qui dépeint l'attitude de Jean Ier des *topoi* hagiographiqu dont les deux textes sont directement inspirés. L'essentiel est que, si Boris et Gleb avai été avant 1072 reconnus par l'Église comme des saints et si les cérémonies de Vyšgorod cette année n'avaient été qu'une simple translation de reliques, comme le propose L. Mül le métropolite Georges n'aurait pas été tenu de remplir successivement le rôle d'*advoca diaboli* et d'*advocatus Dei*, trait caractéristique d'une cérémonie de canonisation[75].

Dans le récit hagiographique de la canonisation de Boris et Gleb sous Jaroslav le Sage, t n'est pas invention littéraire. Il existait une église à cinq coupoles bâtie par Jaroslav d laquelle reposaient les restes de ses frères. La dédicace de cette église demeure toutefois problème. Le *Dit des miracles* ne mentionne pas son appellation dans le passage corresponda et plus loin l'auteur remarque : « Izjaslav décida d'édifier une nouvelle église pour les d$ saints martyrs »[76]. On peut supposer que, tout comme l'édifice antérieur, l'église à cinq coup$ pouvait avoir été dédiée à saint Basile, le patron du prince Vladimir Ier, ou bien, ce qui plus plausible, que tout comme l'église à coupole unique bâtie par Izjaslav, elle avait placée sous le vocable des saints Romain et David, sous réserve toutefois que l'église éri par Jaroslav fût consacrée non point à Boris et Gleb eux-mêmes sous leurs noms de baptê$ mais aux saints patrons de ces princes. Le culte qui se développa ultérieurement effaça c$ distinction.

La consécration de la fondation de Jaroslav eut lieu selon les indications du *Dit des mirac* le 24 juillet, date anniversaire du meurtre de Boris. Le problème de l'origine et du ch$ précisément de ce jour pour la célébration de la mémoire des saints princes a suscité différe$ remarques[77]. Nous n'y reviendrons pas ici, puisque cette question concerne les sources de tou les œuvres consacrées à Boris et Gleb. Mais, quoi qu'il en soit, la date est liée à la naissance culte et elle fut reconnue dès l'époque de la glorification officielle des saints par l'Égl A l'encontre de l'affirmation de l'auteur du *Dit des miracles* et de Nestor, selon laquelle la $ du 24 juillet fut instaurée par Jaroslav et Jean Ier, une glose digne de foi du chroniqu$

74. *Die altrussischen hagiographischen Erzählungen*, p. 53, 56.
75. Voir les remarques pertinentes sur le rite de la canonisation faites par L. MÜLLER, *Studien zur altrussischen Leg$ der Heiligen Boris und Gleb*, « Zeitschr. f. Slav. Philol. », XXX, 1962, p. 20, 43 ; le même, *Neuere Forschungen*, p. ainsi que l'explication — qui contredit ces remarques — du caractère des cérémonies de 1072 dans : le même, $ *Problem ...*, p. 39-40. En l'occurrence il convient d'accepter le point de vue bien étayé selon lequel le comportemen$ métropolite Georges faisait partie du rite de la canonisation, A. M. AMMANN, *Untersuchungen zur Geschichte der kirchl$ Kultur und des religiösen Lebens bei den Ostslaven*, Wurzbourg, 1955, p. 37.
76. *Die altrussischen hagiographischen Erzählungen*, p. 55. Selon Nestor c'était déjà une église « dédiée ... à Bor Gleb » (*ibid.*, p. 18).
77. Cf. A. A. ŠACHMATOV, *Razyskanija*, p. 84, 475-476 ; N. N. IL'IN, *Letopisnaja stat'ja*, p. 152-155 ; L. MÜLLER, N$ *Forschungen*, p. 312-314.

cise explicitement à propos des événements de 1093 : « fête de Boris et Gleb qui est une
e nouvelle du pays russe »[78]. Ainsi à la lumière des faits qui viennent d'être exposés, il
paraît que la mémoire de Boris et Gleb n'était pas célébrée par l'Église avant 1072.

us en trouvons une confirmation supplémentaire dans l'absence d'une fête de Boris et Gleb
ɔmain et David) dans le calendrier de l'Évangéliaire d'Ostromir (1056-1057). Certes il ne
ıt pas chercher une mention de cette fête dans tous les calendriers ecclésiastiques qui furent
usage en Russie aux xiᵉ-xiiᵉ s., puisque le culte de Boris et Gleb resta limité socialement
géographiquement. Mais dans un évangéliaire copié pour un dignitaire civil de haut rang,
gouverneur de Novgorod, Ostromir-Joseph, apparenté à la maison princière d'Izjaslav
roslavič, l'omission d'une fête en l'honneur des patrons de la dynastie serait improbable,
utant plus que le calendrier qui fut ajouté en appendice ne fut pas simplement recopié,
is composé sur la base de différentes sources, entre autres des prologues et des menées.
fête de Boris et Gleb apparaît pour la première fois le 24 juillet dans le calendrier de
vangéliaire copié en 1117 à la requête du prince Mstislav, fils de Vladimir Monomaque[79].

analysant le sort de ces noms, nous avons essayé de dévoiler la « préhistoire » du culte de
ris et Gleb, ce qui nous conduit au milieu du xiᵉ s. Le *Dit des miracles* jette, semble-t-il,
elque clarté sur cette période. Après le récit de la guérison du boiteux pendant la consé-
tion de l'église et la translation des reliques le 24 juillet en présence de Jaroslav et du
tropolite Jean, l'auteur passe immédiatement à un autre sujet : « Après ces jours, Jaroslav
teignit après avoir vécu dans l'honneur trente-huit ans après la mort de son père. » Puis,
rès avoir mentionné le partage des territoires entre les fils de Jaroslav, il continue : « Vingt
s plus tard. comme l'église était devenue vétuste, Izjaslav eut l'idée d'édifier une nouvelle
ise avec une coupole pour les deux saints martyrs »[80]. Il ressort de ce récit que Jaroslav
ɔurut après la consécration de l'église à cinq coupoles. Mais à partir de quel événement
ıt-il compter les vingt ans? Si l'auteur les a comptés à partir de la mort de Jaroslav, il
st trompé : Jaroslav mourut la nuit du 19 au 20 février 1054[81]. En 6579-6580 (1071-1072),
ınd Izjaslav conçut le projet et édifia l'église en bois, il n'y avait pas tout à fait dix-huit
s que Jaroslav le Sage était mort. L'auteur ne se trompait pas en affirmant que Jaroslav
ıit mort trente-huit ans après la mort de son père Vladimir (15 juillet 1015-29 février 1054 =

---

78. *PVL*, I, p. 145. Vladimir Monomaque, comme le montre son *Instruction (Poučenie)*, *ibid.*, p. 160-161, en décrivant
événements de 1094, considérait le 24 juillet comme le jour de la Saint-Boris, c'est-à-dire le jour commémoratif de la
rt de Boris.
79. P. S. Biljarskij, *Sostav i mesjaceslov Mstislavova spiska evangelija. Izvlečenija iz sočinenija prof.
K. Nevostrueva*, « Izvestija Imp. Akad. Nauk po russk. jaz. i slov. », X, 1861, p. 110-137. La fête de Boris et Gleb n'est
davantage mentionnée dans le calendrier de l'évangéliaire d'Archangel'sk, mais il s'agit d'un manuscrit modeste, bien
érent des splendides évangéliaires d'Ostromir et de Mstislav; de plus sa provenance territoriale n'est pas claire,
B. Tichomirov, *Katalog russkich i slavjanskich pergamennych rukopisej XI-XII vv.*, 1ʳᵉ partie, « Zapiski otdela
opisej G. P. Biblioteki im Lenina », XXV, 1962, p. 149-152, 166-175. Au xiiᵉ s. on note la fête de Boris et Gleb dans
majorité des livres liturgiques, archimandrite Sergij, *Polnyj mesjaceslov vostoka I-II*, Moscou, 1875-76 (index) ;
. Sreznevskij, *Drevnij russkij kalendar' po mesjačnym minejam XI-XIII v.*, « Christianskie Drevnosti i Archeologija »,
862, p. 7. On remarquera toutefois avec intérêt qu'elle manque dans des monuments dont l'origine galicienne est
aine : trois évangéliaires, de 1144, de la fin du xiiᵉ s. et du xiiiᵉ s., G. Voskresenskij, *Charakternye čerty četyrech
akcij slavjanskogo perevoda evangelija ot Marka po 120 rukopisjam evangelij XI-XVI vv.*, Moscou, 1896, p. 11, 34, 41.
'on ajoute à cette constatation qu'il n'y a pas de trace d'églises dédiées à Boris et Gleb sur le territoire de la Russie
icienne ni de leurs prénoms parmi les princes du bassin du Dnestr au xiᵉ-xiiᵉ s., il est légitime de conclure que les
cendants de Rostislav « bannis » *(izgoi)* qui conquéraient leurs droits dans les batailles et non pas en pratiquant « la
mission de l'aîné », ne portaient pas une vénération particulière à leurs princes-martyrs. Dans la discussion
cernant le lieu où l'évangéliaire de Dobrilo de 1164 a été copié (N. B. Tichomirov, *Katalog*, 2ᵉ partie, *ibid.*, XXVII,
5, p. 123-125), le fait que ce manuscrit mentionne dans son calendrier les deux saints sous le 24 juillet pourrait constituer
argument supplémentaire contre son origine galicienne.
80. *Die altrussischen hagiographischen Erzählungen*, p. 55.
81. B. A. Rykabov, *Zapis' o smerti Jaroslava Mudrogo*, « Sovetskaja Archeologija », 1959, nᵒ 4, p. 245-249 ;
. Vysockij, *Drevnerusskie nadpisi*, nᵒ 8, p. 39-41.

38 ans 7 mois) ; aussi n'y a-t-il plus de raison de douter de la véracité de son information d₃
le second cas : il est par conséquent licite de considérer que cette période de vingt ans sépar
la construction de l'église à cinq coupoles de Jaroslav de celle de l'édifice à coupole uni
d'Izjaslav. Le fait d'avancer les années 1051-1052 comme date de fondation, sous Jarosl
d'une église très vraisemblablement dédiée aux saints patrons de Boris et Gleb, Rom
et David, fait écho aux considérations exposées plus haut selon lesquelles le début du cu
des frères défunts du « pieux » Jaroslav se situe dans les dernières années de son règne.
en 1044, il ordonna dans son zèle de néophyte de baptiser, à l'encontre des canons, les os
ments de ses oncles Jaropolk et Oleg, fils de Svjatoslav, eux aussi victimes de meurt
fratricides, il est d'autant plus naturel qu'il prît soin de trouver un lieu de sépulture déce
à Vyšgorod, pour ses frères assassinés, et cela surtout s'il était, de quelque manière que ce f
coupable de leur meurtre. Le fils rebelle, qui avait refusé de se soumettre à son père, une f
devenu « l'héritier de son royaume » et alors qu'il approchait de la rive opposée de la « n
de la vie », glorifiait son père, en cherchant partout « à ne pas amoindrir les fondements de
piété ».

Quand, en 1051, grâce à l'appui de Jaroslav, Hilarion fut intronisé métropolite, celui-ci av₃
ainsi qu'il ressort du *Discours sur la loi et la grâce*, un programme clair et précis visant à rele
l'Église russe[82]. En 1049-1051, stimulé par Jaroslav, Hilarion établissait les droits de Vladi
à l'auréole de sainteté, en ayant ainsi conscience de l'importance du culte des saints loca
pour le développement et l'affermissement du christianisme dans le pays. A plus forte rais
pouvait-il comme métropolite contribuer à préparer le terrain pour un culte de Boris et Gl
Le développement du culte des princes, martyrs pour des idéaux politiques, ne fut pas entra
par le trépas inopiné de Jaroslav et l'écartement d'Hilarion du siège métropolitain, même
ces événements différèrent peut-être quelque peu la date de l'acte ecclésiastique officiel. C
à l'inverse du culte de Vladimir dénué de tout contenu vivant, le culte de Boris et Gleb revêt
une signification immédiate pour la dynastie dont les membres se trouvaient chaque f
devant le dilemme : « qui aura qui »? En analysant le sens politique et social du culte de Bc
et Gleb, D. S. Lichačev a relevé, à juste titre, l'idée, inhérente à ce culte, de l'harmonie en
les droits et les obligations qui définissaient les principes moraux des rapports réciproqu
entre les princes, entre le souverain et les vassaux[83]. Le double langage du culte de Boris
Gleb fut déterminé par l'idée politique et religieuse de la paix publique dans un contexte
pointaient les forces centrifuges.

La période initiale ou préparatoire, la plus dynamique de toutes, dans le développem
du culte de Boris et Gleb se situe entre les années cinquante et le début des années soixante-
du XIᵉ s. Elle trouve son achèvement dans l'acte de canonisation le 20 mai 1072. Quelq
observations permettent à ce propos de supposer que Boris et Gleb furent admis d₃
l'assemblée des saints sous les noms qu'ils avaient reçus lors de leur baptême. A cet éga
le fait suivant mérite de retenir l'attention : à l'inverse du *Dit des martyrs*, le *Dit des mirac*
met en avant de façon expresse, tant dans le titre que dans le corps du récit, les noms chrétie
des nouveaux saints. Le plus ancien office s'adresse aux martyrs du Christ, Romain et Dav
On remarque que le synaxaire grec de Sugdaia en Crimée ainsi que la traduction arménien

---

82. Sur les circonstances de l'intronisation d'Hilarion voir A. POPPE, *La tentative de la réforme ecclésiastique en Ru*
au milieu du XIᵉ s., « Acta Poloniae Historica », XXV, 1972, p. 5-31.
83. D. S. LICHAČEV, *Nekotorye voprosy ideologii feodalov v literature XI-XIII vekov*, « TODRL », X, 1954, p. 87-9

Dit connaissaient les saints sous ces noms chrétiens[84]. La détermination du cadre chrono-
gique des œuvres citées apportera plus de lumière sur cette question mais, dès à présent,
peut énoncer quelques considérations. La vénération de Boris et Gleb a pris naissance sous
urs noms princiers, mais quand se posa la question de la reconnaissance du culte par l'Église,
parurent, semble-t-il, des divergences sur la dénomination à donner aux nouveaux thauma-
rges. Elles n'étaient probablement pas dues à une dissension entre Russes et Grecs, mais
ıtôt à des prémisses théologico-canoniques, car il y avait là un dilemme peu commun pour
clergé qui se passionnait pour les disputes théologiques et canoniques. Le 20 mai 1072,
fut l'opinion du métropolite — gardien de l'orthodoxie —, qui prit incontestablement
dessus. Mais, en fin de compte, ce fut la vie qui l'emporta : on vénéra les nouveaux saints
us leurs noms princiers séculiers[85]. Nestor, qui écrivit sa *Lectio* quelque dix ans après la
nonisation, en imitateur zélé de l'hagiographie byzantine ne mentionne qu'une fois Boris
Gleb sous leurs noms chrétiens Romain et David, en conservant leurs noms princiers même
ns la description des miracles[86]. A l'opposé de l'église bâtie en 1072 en l'honneur des saints
uvellement canonisés Romain et David, l'église de pierre de Vyšgorod fut dédiée en 1115
x saints Boris et Gleb. Cette mutation des noms des saints princes-martyrs est également
e confirmation du caractère national de la jeune Église russe et de la souplesse interne du
ristianisme russe dans ses débuts.

s recherches sur les origines du culte de Boris et Gleb nous amènent à la conclusion qu'aucune
s œuvres hagiographiques, et plus encore liturgiques, qui leur ont été consacrées, aussi bien
lles qui nous sont conservées que celles dont l'existence est postulée, n'a pu avoir été
mposée avant les années cinquante du XIe s. Dans les recherches futures, il faudra tenir
mpte de cette limite chronologique ou bien montrer qu'elle n'est pas soutenable. Cette
estion est essentielle pour une étude ultérieure de la pensée politico-sociale et religieuse de
Russie kiévienne, de l'idéologie de sa dynastie, ainsi que du développement de la littérature
ux-russe, tout particulièrement des annales au XIe s.

84. *Die altrussischen hagiographischen Erzählungen*, p. 52 et ss, 136 et ss. En marge d'un synaxaire grec de Sugdaia
ıposé au XIIe s. (avant 1186 si l'on en croit la notice datée la plus ancienne), on trouve sous le 24 juillet écrit d'une
ın contemporaine du texte principal : « mémoire des nouveaux saints martyrs dans les contrées russes, David et
main », *Zametki XII-XV vv.* (cf. *supra*, n. 48), p. 620, no 170. Dans les deux recensions du synaxaire arménien (*Patrologia
entalis*, V, 1910, p. 397-403 ; XXI, 1930, p. 772-779, *supra* n. 34), les saints russes apparaissent toujours sous leurs
noms chrétiens ; ce n'est que dans le titre du plus ancien manuscrit de 1316 que sont mentionnés leurs prénoms
nciers : « Histoire des saints et glorieux martyrs du Christ Romain et David ... qui s'appelaient Boris et Hleb » (*ibid.*,
p. 397). Le milieu arménien (à Kiev ou en Crimée ?), pour lequel la traduction fut effectuée, était certainement informé
culte des saints russes Romain et David, aussi le traducteur unifia-t-il de façon consciente et conséquente l'emploi
leurs prénoms dans tout le texte. L'explication selon laquelle ce choix fut dicté simplement par le désir « d'éviter aux
teurs arméniens la confusion » (Ya. DACHKÉVYTCH, *Les Arméniens à Kiev*, p. 361-362) n'est pas convaincante. Par
eurs ce choix incite à admettre que le *Dit* a été traduit le plus probablement dans le milieu arméno-grec de Crimée et
ı à Kiev, où la colonie arménienne aurait dû être davantage familiarisée avec le culte des saints frères Boris et Gleb
ıs leurs prénoms princiers, qui y dominait depuis le XIIe s.
85. Peut-être la période des hésitations est-elle reflétée par une petite icône en pierre avec la représentation du saint
ıce et l'inscription de ses deux prénoms de Gleb et David de chaque côté. Elle a été trouvée à Tmutorokan' et
ionterait, d'après des traits stylistiques et paléographiques, à la seconde moitié du XIe ou au début du XIIe s. Cependant
ien entre cette petite icône et le prince Gleb Svjatoslavič, de même que la date ainsi obtenue de 1067-1068, se fondent
des présuppositions trop fragiles, B. A. RYBAKOV, *Russkie datirovannye nadpisi XI-XIV vv.*, Moscou, 1964, p. 18,
5 ; T. V. NIKOLAEVA, *Drevnerusskaja melkaja plastika XI-XVI vekov*, Moscou, 1968, p. 9, no 11. On ne peut pas davantage
uver l'attribution de cette icône à David Igorevič, qui séjourna à Tmutorokan' de 1081 à 1083.
86. Relevons que, même chez les savants qui considèrent la *Lectio* de Nestor comme antérieure au *Dit*, on trouve
ıramment la conviction que le *Dit des miracles* rend mieux et plus fidèlement la source hypothétique commune des
ıx œuvres que constitueraient les notices de Vyšgorod.

LE TRAITÉ DES AZYMES
ΛΕΟΝΤΟΣ ΜΗΤΡΟΠΟΛΙΤΟΥ
ΤΗΣ ΕΝ ῬΩΣΙΑΙ ΠΡΕΣΘΛΑΒΑΣ :
QUAND, OÙ ET PAR QUI A-T-IL ÉTÉ ÉCRIT?

Un traité polémique d'un Léon métropolite contre l'emploi du pain azyme pour l'Eucharistie dans le rite latin, nous a été transmis par une quinzaine de manuscrits, dont les plus anciens sont du XIIIᵉ siècle ([1]). Bien qu'il soit depuis longtemps connu, sa datation et l'identification de son auteur fournissent encore matière à discussion. Une partie des chercheurs voit dans l'auteur du traité le premier ou le deuxième métropolite de Russie : fin du Xᵉ ou premières années du XIᵉ siècle. Cette thèse, qui a été formulée par E. E. Golubinskij et a trouvé un accueil très favorable grâce à l'autorité bien méritée de ce savant, a été récemment soutenue sur la base d'une argumentation détaillée par V. Mošin ([2]). D'autres chercheurs, comme par exemple B. Leib, M. Jugie, J. Ledit, A. Michel, H.-G. Beck, partant de l'idée que l'objet de la controverse (les azymes) exclut toute date antérieure à 1053-1054, ont supposé que l'auteur du traité était métropolite de Preslav para-danubien, en Bulgarie, à la fin du XIᵉ

---

(1) Texte édité par V. N. BENEŠEVIČ dans *Pamjatniki drevnerusskogo kanoničeskogo prava*, (Monuments vieux-russes de droit canonique), II, 1, Petrograd, 1920, pp. 73-101 ; et par A. S. PAVLOV, *Kritičeskie opyty po istorii drevnejšej greko-russkoj polemiki protiv latinian*, (Essais critiques sur l'histoire de l'ancienne polémique gréco-russe contre les Latins), SPb, 1878, pp. 115-132.

(2) Cf. E. E. GOLUBINSKIJ, *Istorija russkoj Cerkvi*, (Histoire de l'Église russe), I², 1, Moskva, 1901, p. 274 sq., 853 ; V. MOŠIN, *Le traité du métropolite russe Léon sur les azymes dans un manuscrit d'Achrida*, (en russe), dans *Byzantinoslavica*, XXIV, 1, 1963, pp. 87-105.

ou au XIIe siècle ([1]). Cette opinion, fondée sur un texte du patriarche de Jérusalem Dosithée (1669-1707), a été formulée d'une façon particulièrement exhaustive par D. Cukhlev ([2]).

Le traité de Léon, métropolite τῆς ἐν ʿΡωσίᾳ Πρεσθλάβας, est de toute façon lié à la question de l'organisation de l'Église en Russie aux Xe-XIe siècles, au sujet de laquelle H. Grégoire et P. Orgels ont eu raison d'écrire : « On sait qu'il n'est guère de question plus obscure, ni qui ait été plus obscurcie par les partis pris et les idées préconçues, que celle des origines de cette Église » ([3]). Bien que l'étude de ces origines ait fait de grands progrès grâce aux travaux de V. Laurent, E. Honigmann et L. Müller, et qu'il ait été, en particulier, établi que la plus ancienne hiérarchie de l'Église russe a été une hiérarchie byzantine ([4]), il reste encore en ce domaine bien des questions ouvertes, qui exigent de nouvelles recherches.

En entreprenant d'étudier le traité du métropolite Léon, nous nous proposons de chercher dans les sources une réponse nette à la question de savoir s'il faut rattacher ce texte à l'Église russe. Si la réponse est affirmative, nous pourrons établir la valeur de ce texte en tant que source pour l'histoire

(1) Cf. B. Leib, *Kiev et Byzance à la fin du XIe siècle*, Paris, 1924-p. 34 ; J. Ledit, « *Russie* », dans le *Dictionnaire de Théologie catholique*, XIV, 1, 1939, p. 217 sq. ; A. Michel, *Humbert und Kerullarios*. II, Paderborn, 1930, p. 129 ; H.-G. Beck, *Kirche und theologische Literatur im Byzantinischen Reich*, München, 1959, pp. 312, 610.

(2) D. Cukhlev, *Istoria na bolgarskata Cerkva*, (Histoire de l'Église bulgare), vol. I (864-1186), Sofia, 1910, pp. 865, 919-921.

(3) H. Grégoire et P. Orgels, *La chronologie des Patriarches de Constantinople et la « question romaine » à la fin du Xe siècle*, dans *Byzantion*, XXIV, 1954, p. 169.

(4) Cf. V. Laurent, *Aux origines de l'Église russe. L'établissement de la hiérarchie byzantine*, dans *Échos d'Orient*, XXXVIII, 1939, pp. 279-295 ; E. Honigmann, *Studies in Slavic Church History*, dans *Byzantion*, XVII, Amer. Ser. III, 1944-1945, pp. 128-182 ; L. Müller, *Zum Problem des hierarchischen Status und der jurisdiktionellen Abhängigkeit der russischen Kirche vor 1039*, Köln-Braunsfeld, 1959. Cf. aussi P. Devos, *Chronique d'hagiographie slave*, II, dans *Analecta Bollandiana*, LXXIII, fasc. 1-2, 1955, pp. 220-226.

de cette Église. Il faudra d'abord fixer le cadre chronologique de la composition de notre traité des azymes, pour affronter ensuite la question de l'attribution.

I. La question chronologique

Notre examen de la première question — de la question chronologique — consistera surtout en une discussion avec V. Mošin. Ce savant a réuni les arguments qui, à son avis, nous imposeraient de situer le traité entre la fin du Xe siècle et le début du XIe.

V. Mošin, qui s'appuie dans une grande mesure sur certains auteurs dont il partage l'opinion ([1]), n'a pas tenu compte de la littérature critique de base, entre autres du travail de M. Čelcov. Les conclusions de ce dernier travail ont été confirmées par des études récentes, dont rend compte l'excellent manuel de H.-G. Beck, qui cite aussi abondamment la littérature concernant les controverses entre Rome et Constantinople ([2]). En suivant A. Popov et A. Pavlov, Mošin soutient que le traité du métropolite Léon constitue un chaînon intermédiaire entre les œuvres de Photius et de son contemporain Nicétas Paphlagon, d'un côté, et, de l'autre côté, les écrivains qui, à partir de 1053, traitent de la question des azymes : Léon d'Achrida, Michel Cérulaire, Pierre d'Antioche, Nicétas Stéthatos et Nicon de la Montagne Noire. Le traité de Léon de Πρεσθλάβα serait particulièrement proche des œuvres de Nicétas de Nicée. Ces deux écrivains, d'après Mošin, seraient à cheval entre deux époques, l'époque de Photius et celle de Michel Cérulaire ; en effet, à la différence des controversistes de la deuxième époque, qui s'occu-

---

(1) Spécialement A. Popov, *Istoriko-literaturnyj obzor drevnerusskikh polemičeskikh sočinenij protiv latinian (XI-XV v.)*, (Aperçu historique et littéraire des ouvrages polémiques vieux-russes contre les Latins (xie-xve siècles), Moskva, 1875, pp. 1-46 ; et A. Pavlov, *op. cit.*, pp. 26-39.

(2) M. Čelcov, *Polemika meždu grekami i latinianami po voprosu ob opresnokakh v XI-XII v.* (La polémique entre les Grecs et les Latins au sujet des azymes aux xie-xiie siècles), SPb., 1879 ; H.-G. Beck, *op. cit.*, particulièrement pp. 306-322.

peraient exclusivement de la question des azymes, Léon de
Πρεσθλάβα et Nicétas de Nicée n'oublieraient pas de mentionner le point crucial de la controverse, la question du *Filioque* (1).

Ces arguments seraient décisifs, s'il n'était un fait dont Mošin ne tient pas compte. Il est vrai qu'en 1053-1054 la question des azymes est au centre de la controverse ; mais c'est
à peu près à ce moment-là qu'apparaît la question dogma-
tique de base. Le patriarche de Constantinople Michel Cérulaire, dans sa première lettre au patriarche d'Antioche
Pierre, en énumérant les « erreurs » des Latins, mentionnait
aussi la question du *Filioque*. Prenant une position modérée
et conciliante, Pierre d'Antioche, dans ses réponses (1054)
à l'archevêque de Grado Dominique et au patriarche Michel
Cérulaire, affirme que les différences dans la pratique eucharistique n'ont pas, au fond, une importance essentielle, souligne par contre l'importance du dogme de la Trinité et con-
damne la doctrine des Latins sur la procession du Saint-Esprit. Le légat du pape, le cardinal Humbert de Silva Candida, souleva lui aussi, dans un memorandum écrit à Constantinople (juin 1054), la question du *Filioque*. C'est au problème de la procession du Saint-Esprit, que Nicétas Stéthatos
consacra son deuxième ouvrage polémique (2). Au début de
la polémique des années 1053-54, la question de la nature de
la Trinité, qui était depuis le temps de Photius le point cardinal de la divergence entre les Églises, ne constituait pas
l'objet principal de la controverse, bien qu'on ne l'oubliât
pas. A partir du moment (16 juillet 1054) où les légats du
pape déposèrent sur l'autel de Hagia Sophia la bulle qui ex-
communiait Michel Cérulaire et ses partisans, en leur repro-
chant entre autres le fait que *absciderunt a symbolo Spiritus
Sancti processionem a Filio*, la question du *Filioque* ne pou-

---

(1) Mošin, *op. cit.*, pp. 97-98 ; cf. Pavlov, *op. cit.*, pp. 38-39.
(2) *Acta et scripta, quae de controversiis ecclesiae graecae et latinae
saeculo undecimo composita extant*, ed. C. Will, Lipsiae et Marburgi,
1861, pp. 181-182, 201-202 ; *PG*, vol. 120, coll. 777 sq., 803 sq. ; A.
Michel, *op. cit.*, I, pp. 97-111, II, pp. 159-167, 343-409 ; cf. H.-G.
Beck, *op. cit.*, pp. 312, 317, 533-548.

508

vait plus être évitée (¹). Vers la fin du xiᵉ siècle, la controverse sur le *Filioque* s'intensifie. Chaque traité polémique
byzantin parle de cette question. Au xiiᵉ siècle, la question
domine, sinon par le volume des pages qui lui sont consacrées, du moins par son importance. Les disputes des théo-
logiens grecs et latins au synode de Bari en 1098 et à celui
de Constantinople en 1112, concernaient principalement la
procession du Saint-Esprit (²).

Dans le traité de Léon de *Πρεσθλάβα*, les azymes occupent
une place centrale ; 12 parmi les 19 questions concernent la
forme de l'Eucharistie. Un seul point du traité est consacré
au *Filioque* ; écrit dans un ton très modéré, il manifeste la
tendance qui apparaît dans la lettre déjà citée de Pierre d'Antioche aussi bien que dans la lettre du métropolite de Russie,
Jean II Prodromos, à l'anti-pape Clément III (vers 1085),
et dans le traité des azymes du patriarche de Jérusalem Si-
méon (1084-1099) (³). Remarquons que Jean II Prodromos,
dénonçant les « erreurs » de l'Église romaine, en met en relief deux comme étant les plus graves : l'emploi des azymes
et l'addition au *Credo*. C'est par la considération de cette
dernière question qu'il clôt la liste des « erreurs » latines, ainsi
que le fait Léon (⁴).

En rapprochant Léon de *Πρεσθλάβα* de Nicétas de Nicée,
qui serait son contemporain et traiterait des sujets semblables, Mošin ne fait que nous montrer la faiblesse de sa construction chronologique. En effet, Nicétas de Nicée n'a pas vécu
à cheval entre le xᵉ et le xiᵉ siècle, comme Mošin l'affirme en
suivant Pavlov ; il a vécu dans la deuxième moitié du xiᵉ
et au début du xiiᵉ siècle (avant 1117, il est chartophylax
du patriarche de Constantinople, après cette année, il est

(1) *Excommunicatio* dans *PL*, vol. 143, col. 1003 ; Will, *op. cit.*,
p. 153 ; voir aussi l'*Edictum Synodale* du patriarche, *PG*, vol. 120,
coll. 739 sq. ; Will, *op. cit.*, p. 158 sq. ; Michel, *op. cit.*, II, pp. 42,
44, 96.
(2) Cf. Čelcov, *op. cit.*, pp. 72-73 ; B. Leib, *op. cit.*, pp. 290-295,
312, 331-334 ; H.-G. Beck, *op. cit.*, p. 616.
(3) Cf. S. Runcimann, *The Eastern Schism*, Oxford, 1955, pp. 75-
76 ; Beck, *op. cit.*, pp. 610, 611.
(4) Texte grec et traduction vieux-russe chez Pavlov, *op. cit.*,
pp. 169-186 ; voir spécialement pp. 173-174, 184-185.

métropolite de Nicée) ; ce fait a été établi il y a presque cent
ans et a été confirmé par des recherches récentes (¹). L'affi-
nité du contenu des traités de Léon et de Nicétas de Nicée
s'explique entièrement par des sources communes : celles-ci
sont des ouvrages des années 1053-1054, écrits par Pierre
d'Antioche, Léon d'Achrida, Nicétas Stéthatos, et Michel
Cérulaire. Les deux traités sont tout à fait indépendants
l'un de l'autre, ce qui se manifeste par leur façon d'utiliser
les sources communes et par le choix indépendant de l'argumentation. Par exemple, dans la question de l'Eucharistie
du Christ, Nicétas de Nicée développe la thèse de Léon d'Achrida sur les deux Pâques, tandis que le métropolite Léon de
Πρεσθλάβα, en suivant Nicétas Stéthatos et Pierre d'Antioche,
place la Cène au troisième jour de la lune, un jour avant la
Pâque proprement dite. Nicétas de Nicée développe davantage que Léon de *Πρεσθλάβα* (et les sources communes)
le thème de la nature eucharistique du pain (²).

Lorsqu'il mentionne Nicétas Paphlagon comme un contemporain de Photius, Mošin le confond avec le Nicétas qui est
appelé par les chercheurs Nicétas de Byzance, controversis-
te connu, qui s'occupait de la question du *Filioque*. Mais ni
celui-ci, ni Nicétas Paphlagon du Xᵉ siècle, ni Nicétas David —
ces trois Nicétas sont souvent confondus par les chercheurs
— n'ont écrit sur les azymes (³). Cependant, sans nous en-
foncer dans les subtilités des attributions, il faut remarquer
que le traité polémique attribué par les titres des manuscrits à Nicétas David Paphlagon le Philosophe, et même à
Jean Damascène, mérite notre attention d'autant plus que,
d'après A. Pavlov et V. Mošin, il serait la source principale
du métropolite Léon de *Πρεσθλάβα* (⁴).

(1) J. HERGENRÖTHER, *Photius, Patriarch von Konstantinopel*, III,
Regensburg, 1869, pp. 802, 869 ; ČELCOV, *op. cit.*, pp. 8-9, 121 ; BECK,
op. cit., p. 619.

(2) Pour des informations plus détaillées, voir ČELCOV, *op. cit.*,
pp. 54-55, 110, 179, 269, 294. Le texte grec et slave de Nicétas de
Nicée se trouve chez PAVLOV, *op. cit.*, pp. 135-145 ; le texte grec se
trouve aussi chez MICHEL, *op. cit.*, II, p. 20 sqq.

(3) Cf. BECK, *op. cit.*, pp. 311, 530, 548, 565.

(4) Cf. PAVLOV, *op. cit.*, pp. 36-37 ; MOŠIN, *op. cit.*, p. 98 ; en ce qui
concerne l'attribution du traité à Jean Damascène, voir *PG*, vol. 94,
col. 413.

510

L'auteur de cet ouvrage est probablement un anonyme qui se présente sous le nom d'un écrivain plus ancien et connu ; en effet, il ressort du contenu de l'ouvrage que celui-ci a été écrit à l'époque où la controverse sur les azymes était déjà ouverte. Dans la lutte contre les « erreurs » des Latins, les controversistes byzantins faisaient souvent passer leurs écrits pour des œuvres non seulement de Photius et de Michel le Syncelle, mais aussi d'autorités plus anciennes, telles qu'Athanase le Grand et Jean Damascène, à qui ils attribuaient aussi des traités sur les azymes (¹). L'habitude, répandue dans les luttes confessionnelles, de se réclamer des autorités en leur attribuant des déclarations tendancieuses et des ouvrages polémiques, avait pour but d'impressionner les fidèles ; les chercheurs ne devraient pas s'y laisser prendre.

Le traité qui porte le nom de Nicétas David Paphlagon se distingue par le fait qu'il traite d'une seule question, celle du jour et de la forme de la Cène pascale (²). Déclarant que la dernière Cène eut lieu le treizième jour du premier mois, l'auteur non seulement abandonne la thèse de Léon d'Achrida sur les deux Pâques, mais ne s'accorde pas non plus avec Pierre d'Antioche et propose une interprétation plus subtile du « premier jour des azymes » des Évangiles : celui-ci serait le jour qui précède la « fête des azymes ». Par contre, Léon de Πρεσθλάβα répète la thèse de Pierre d'Antioche, d'après laquelle il faudrait interpréter « le premier jour

---

(1) Voir *PG*, vol. 26, coll. 1327 sq. ; vol. 95, coll. 388 sqq. Cf. HERGENRÖTHER, *op. cit.*, III, p. 172 s. ; ČELCOV, *op. cit.*, pp. 4 sq., 25, 41 sq. ; H.-G. BECK, *op. cit.*, p. 522 sqq.

(2) Cet ouvrage se trouve dans trois manuscrits (les mêmes qui contiennent aussi le traité de Léon de Πρεσθλάβα) de la Bibliothèque Synodale de Moscou, nos. 366 (239), ff. 106v.-110 ; 368 (240), ff. 110-115 ; 207 (250), ff. 351v.-356 ; son titre est le même dans les trois manuscrits : Νικήτα Παφλαγόνος τοῦ φιλοσόφου τοῦ καὶ Δαβίδ. Ὅτι τῇ ιγ τῆς σελήνης πρὸ μιᾶς τοῦ νομικοῦ πάσχα, τὸ μυστικὸν τοῦ Κυρίου γέγονε δεῖπνον καὶ οὐ τὸν ἀμνὸν τότε μετὰ τῶν μαθητῶν ἔφαγεν ὁ Χριστός. Cf. VLADIMIR ARKHIMANDRIT, *Sistematičeskoe opisanie rukopisej Moskovskoj Sinodalnoj (patriaršej) Biblioteki*, (Description systématique des manuscrits de la Bibliothèque Synodale (du patriarcat) de Moscou), vol. I, Manuscrits grecs, Moskva, 1894, pp. 313, 316, 340. La traduction en vieux-russe est publiée par ČELCOV, *op. cit.*, pp. 379-388.

des azymes » chez les trois premiers Évangélistes comme le dixième du premier mois, qui ouvrirait l'avant-fête de Pâques (¹).

Donc, si l'on acceptait le point de vue d'A. Pavlov et de V. Mošin, il faudrait admettre que Léon de *Πρεσθλάβα*, tout en ayant à sa disposition l'argumentation plus développée et plus convaincante d'un traité spécial sur la fête de Pâques, lui a préféré l'interprétation, non exempte de contradictions, de Pierre d'Antioche. Nous pensons que le traité sur la chronologie pascale n'était pas connu de Léon de *Πρεσθλάβα*, quoiqu'il ait été écrit dans la deuxième moitié du XIᵉ siècle. Il est mentionné par l'archevêque bulgare Théophylacte dans l'*Entretien avec l'un de ses disciples sur les griefs contre les Latins*, écrit en 1089-1091 (²).

Mošin, pour prouver que le traité de Léon de *Πρεσθλάβα* est né sous l'influence de la rupture les rapports entre Rome et Byzance en 996-998 ou, au plus tard, en 1009-1012 (cette dernière date serait moins probable), fait état du renouvellement de l'encyclique de Photius par les patriarches Sisinnius II et Sergius II (³). Ce sont là des témoignages extrêmement douteux (⁴) et même si l'on réussissait à les défendre, ils ne contribueraient en rien à établir la date du début de la controverse contre les azymites latins. Un auteur de la pre-

---

(1) BENEŠEVIČ, *op. cit.*, pp. 78-82. *Epistola Petri Ant. ad Dominicum Gradensem*, PG, vol. 120, coll. 733 sq. (chap. 20). Des renseignements détaillés dans ELCOV, *op. cit.*, pp. 54-55, 87-88, 109-110, 174-178, 180-181, 335.

(2) *PG*, vol. 126, col. 233 (chap. 8) : ῞Οθεν καί τις τῶν παρ' ἡμῖν θείων διδασκάλων ἐξηγούμενος τὴν παρὰ τῷ εὐαγγελιστῇ λεγομένην πρώτην τῶν ἀζύμων, πρώτην φησὶ τῶν ἀζύμων τῷ Ματθαίῳ τὴν πρὸ τὴν ἀζύμων ἡμέραν λέγεσθαι : cf. WILL, *op. cit.*, p. 239 (chap. IX). Sur la datation, voir V. VASILEVSKIJ, *Trudy* (Œuvres), I, SPb., 1908, pp. 147-149 ; LEIB, *op. cit.*, p. 41 sq. ; P. GAUTIER, *L'épiscopat de Théophylacte Héphaistos, archevêque de Bulgarie*, dans *Revue des Études Byzantines*, XXI, 1963, pp. 162-163. Cf. ČELCOV, *op. cit.*, pp. 180-185.

(3) Cf. MOŠIN, *op. cit.*, pp. 101, 104-105.

(4) Cf. V. GRUMEL, *L'encyclique de Photius aux Orientaux et les patriarches de Constantinople Sisinnius II et Sergius II*, dans *Échos d'Orient*, XXXIV, 1935, pp. 129-138 ; ID., *Les Regestes des Actes du Patriarcat de Constantinople*, I,2, Chalcédoine, 1936, nos. 814. 820 ; BECK, *op. cit.*, pp. 554, 599.

512

mière moitié du xiie siècle (probablement Nicétas de Nicée
ou Nicétas de Maronée), mentionnant le schisme entre « les
deux Sergii », ajoute : « je ne sais pas ce qui l'a fait naître » (¹).
V. Mošin ne dispose donc d'aucune preuve. En outre, il ne
s'est pas posé la question de savoir comment à Rome on réa-
git, entre la fin du xe et le début du xie siècle, à l'accusation
relative à l'emploi des azymes pour l'Eucharistie et à d'au-
tres accusations. S'il l'avait posée, il aurait dû constater que
la littérature latine, à l'opposé de ce qui s'est passé dans
les années 1053-1054, n'a pas conservé de traces d'une polémique pareille (²). Léon IX, au début de 1054, écrivait à
Michel Cérulaire : *illud autem quis non stupeat, quod post
tot sanctos et orthodoxos Patres, per mille et viginti a passione
Salvatoris annos*, novus *calumniator Ecclesiae Latinorum
emersisti, anathematizans omnes et publicam persecutioneu
excitans, quicumque participarentur sacramentorum ex azy-
mis?* Le cardinal Humbert, dans son *Dialogue*, qualifia la
prise de position de Léon d'Achrida contre les azymes de
hactenus inaudita audacia (³). La question des azymes n'a-
vait donc pas fait auparavant l'objet d'une controverse. Il
faut tenir compte aussi d'un autre fait essentiel : le traité de
Léon de *Πρεσθλάβα*, conçu sous la forme d'un dialogue, paraphrase les arguments contraires contenus dans le *Dialogue*
du cardinal Humbert de Silva Candida, comme Čelcov l'a
déjà fait remarquer (⁴). Mošin, en soutenant que Léon d'Achrida dépend de Léon de *Πρεσθλάβα*, ne tient pas compte de
la forme littéraire des deux ouvrages. Le fait même que
Léon d'Achrida ne polémique avec personne, mais rappelle et
enseigne, témoigne de la priorité de son écrit. L'opuscule
de Léon de *Πρεσθλάβα*, par contre, est un dialogue : chaque
λύσις est précédée d'une *ἀντίθεσις*.

---

(1) Cf. S. RUNCIMAN, *op. cit.*, pp. 32-34.

(2) La polémique officielle, ouverte par la lettre de Léon d'Achrida entre la fin de 1052 et le début de 1053, a été précédée, dans les
années 1046-1052, par des interdictions de pratiquer le rite grec en
Italie et le rite latin à Byzance. Cf. MICHEL, *op. cit.*, p. 112 sq. ;
S. RUNCIMAN, *op. cit.*, p. 38 sq. ;

(3) Cf. WILL, *op. cit.*, pp. 91, 94 ; *PL*, vol. 143, col. 775, 933 ; cf.
ČELCOV, *op. cit.*, p. 44.

(4) ČELCOV, *op. cit.*, pp. 56-57.

Le contenu et la construction, ainsi qu'il ressort d'une confrontation des textes, témoignent de la dépendance de Léon de *Πρεσθλάβα* par rapport à Léon d'Achrida, à Nicétas Stéthatos et à Pierre d'Antioche. En même temps, comme Čelcov l'a remarqué, Léon de *Πρεσθλάβα*, tout en empruntant à ses prédécesseurs les arguments les plus importants, les expose d'une façon tout à fait libre, dans une langue plus précise et plus concise. Le traité de Léon de *Πρεσθλάβα* discute, outre 1) la question de la forme de l'Eucharistie, aussi les questions 2) du jeûne du Sabbat ; 3) de la liturgie pendant le carême ; 4) du célibat des prêtres ; 5) de la consommation de la viande de bêtes étouffées (*πνικτά*) ; 6) de la procession du Saint-Esprit. Les points 1, 2, 5 et partiellement le point 3 étaient discutés par Léon d'Achrida ; les autres se trouvent chez Nicétas Stéthatos. Dans la question du *Filioque*, Léon de *Πρεσθλάβα* soutenait la thèse de l'addition au Credo de Nicée qui était la thèse dominante dans l'Église orientale depuis l'époque de Photius. Il est instructif de constater que vers 1085, dans une lettre à Clément III (Guibert de Ravenne), le métropolite de Russie Jean II Prodromos formule essentiellement les mêmes accusations, ajoutant seulement la question de la confirmation séparée du baptême et faisant allusion aux « moines qui mangent de la viande et des choses semblables » (²). Il faut aussi remarquer que, tout en suivant en général ses prédécesseurs, Léon donne une nouvelle interprétation de la parabole du levain. On a supposé (³) avec raison que cette nouvelle interprétation a été mise en avant pour remplacer celle de Léon d'Achrida, puisque celle-ci avait été réfutée par le cardinal Humbert. Sur la base de cette remarque et de celles qui ont été faites auparavant, on peut supposer que le *Dialogue* du cardinal Humbert (traduit en grec en 1054, à Constantinople) était connu de Léon de *Πρεσθλάβα*.

Il faut en outre souligner que, tandis que Léon développe l'argument philologique, emprunté à Nicétas Stéthatos, de

---

(1) ČELCOV, *op. cit.*, pp. 128-131, 239-240 ; cf. MICHEL, *op. cit.*, II, pp. 129, 132, 218, 237.

(2) Cf. le texte chez PAVLOV, *op. cit.*, pp. 178, 185.

(3) ČELCOV, *op. cit.*, pp. 266-268, 308-309.

514

l'emploi que le Christ aurait fait du pain fermenté, en analysant la signification de ἄρτος et de ἄζυμος dans les textes évangéliques, le métropolite Jean Prodromos se contente d'une brève allusion, considérant cet argument comme indiscutable. L'argument fut développé largement par les controversistes du début du xIIᵉ siècle : Nicétas Séidès et Jean Oxite, patriarche d'Antioche (¹). Ains donc, la comparaison entre le traité de Léon de Πρεσθλάβα et les controversistes byzantins des xiᵉ-xiIᵉ siècles, donne les résultats suivants : le premier dépend des principaux controversistes grecs qui ouvrirent la querelle en 1053-1054, et qui, à la différence de Léon de Πρεσθλάβα, étaient bien connus à Rome ; en outre, le traité qui nous intéresse manifeste, dans une série de questions, un degré d'élaboration inférieur par rapport aux controversistes grecs de la fin du xiᵉ et du début du xiIᵉ siècle. (²)

II. Qui était Léon de Πρεσθλάβα ?

Le fait d'avoir établi que le traité des azymes de Léon, métropolite τῆς ἐν Ῥωσίᾳ Πρεσθλάβας, n'est pas un document de la fin du xᵉ siècle, ni de la première moitié du xiᵉ, et qu'il ne témoigne donc pas de l'existence, à cette époque, d'une métropole de Πρεσθλάβα, ne résout pas d'autres problèmes : quand précisément et où cet ouvrage a-t-il été écrit ? qui était le métropolite Léon, son auteur ?

Parmi les candidats éventuels, nous pouvons déjà éliminer Léon, métropolite de Russie entre la fin du xᵉ et le début du xiᵉ siècle. Même si un métropolite portant ce nom avait été à cette époque le chef de l'Église russe, avec pour siège Perejaslav, il n'aurait pas pu être l'auteur de l'ouvrage en question. En confrontant celui-ci avec d'autres documents de la littérature polémique, nous avons vu qu'il appartient à la deuxième moitié du xiᵉ siècle et qu'il est peut-être plus ancien que la lettre du métropolite de Kiev Jean Prodromos

---

(1) Cf. les textes chez Beneševič, *op. cit.*, pp. 82-84, et chez Pavlov, *op. cit.*, pp. 180-181. Čelcov, *op. cit.*, p. 203 sq.
(2) Čelcov, *op. cit.*, pp. 119-128, 173-174, 203, 239, 306-307 ; cf. Beck, *op. cit.*, pp. 318, 534 sqq.

écrite dans les années 1084-1089, le plus probablement en 1085. Mais, en établissant l'année 1054 comme *terminus ante quem non*, il faut remarquer que le traité de Léon de *Πρεσθλάβα*, par le ton équilibré de sa polémique, est éloigné de l'année où l'irritation personnelle des principaux et ardents antagonistes — du patriarche Michel Cérulaire et du cardinal Humbert — donnait aux prises de position un caractère violent, accusateur et outrageant. Des recherches philologiques plus détaillées, conduites sur la base de tout ce qui s'est conservé de la controverse byzantino-latine de cette époque, nous permettront d'obtenir des précisions chronologiques ultérieures.

Si pour établir le cadre chronologique de la composition du traité du métropolite Léon, c'est son contenu qu'il faut surtout interroger, en ce qui concerne la question de savoir où il a été écrit et qui était son auteur, nous en sommes réduits aux informations contenues dans son titre. Examinons donc attentivement les titres des manuscrits connus (¹). Neuf parmi ceux-ci donnent à Léon le titre de métropolite, deux celui d'archevêque, un celui d'évêque ʽΡωσίας ou τῆς ἐν ʽΡωσίᾳ Πρεσθλάβας. Cette dernière indication se trouve dans cinq manuscrits : 1) Dans le Codex Ambrosianus 534, du xiiie siècle ; 2) dans le Codex Synodalis 368 (240) du Musée Historique de Moscou, du xive siècle ; 3) dans le Codex Synodalis 207 (250), du xviie siècle, très probablement copie du précédent ; 4) dans le Codex Vaticanus 706, du xive siècle. C'est probablement sur la base de ce manuscrit qu'Allatius inséra dans la liste des controversistes *Leo, item Prestlavae, quae in Russia est, metropolita* (²) ; 5) dans le Codex Marcianus 154, du xvie-xviie siècle, d'une façon légèrement déformée (*Λέοντος ἐπισκόπου ʽΡωσίας Πελτζάβας*). Quoique des trois manuscrits les

---

(1) Onze manuscrits et deux fragments sans titre sont énumérés par V. Beneševič, *op. cit.*, p. 73 sq. V. Mošin a indiqué dernièrement un vestige du traité de Léon qui s'est conservé dans la liste de titres dans le manuscrit 69 (85) du Musée National d'Achrida (xiiie siècle) : voir Mošin, *op. cit.*, p. 87 sq.

(2) L. Allatius, *De ecclesiae occidentalis atque orientalis perpetua consensione libri tres*, Coloniae Agrippinae, 1648, p. 872 ; cf. *Codices Vaticani Graeci*, III, 1950, p. 170.

516

plus anciens, du XIIIe siècle, seul l'Ambrosianus donne à Léon le titre de μητροπολίτου τῆς ἐν ῾Ρωσίᾳ Πρεσθλάβας, tandis que les deux autres (le Vallicellus B 53 et l'Achridianus 69 (85), maintenant perdu) l'appellent tout simplement μητροπολίτου ῾Ρωσίας, cette deuxième détermination de la position de l'auteur doit étre considérée comme une forme raccourcie. Cela ressort clairement de la comparaison des deux titres :

Τοῦ θεοφιλεστάτου Λέοντος μητροπολίτου τῆς ἐν ῾Ρωσίᾳ Πρεσθλάβας περὶ τοῦ ὅτι οὐ δεῖ τελεῖσθαι τὰ ἄζυμα ([1]).	Λέοντος μητροπολίτου ῾Ρωσίας πρὸς ῾Ρωμαίους ἤτοι Λατίνους περὶ τῶν ἀζύμων ([2]).

Il est significatif qu'aucun titre, dans aucun manuscrit, n'omette de mentionner la Russie, bien que, dans le titre original, l'expression ἐν ῾Ρωσίᾳ constitue une détermination secondaire. Manifestement, déjà au XIIIe siècle, le titre original n'était plus assez clair pour un copiste grec, qui ne connaissait qu'une métropole de Russie. Mais le titre original du traité des azymes attribuait cet ouvrage à Léon, métropolite de Perejaslav en Russie.

Cette attribution, à la lumière des données dont nous disposons, apparaît très probable. Lorsqu'il s'agit d'ouvrages polémiques, il est parfois difficile d'en établir l'auteur, car ces ouvrages étaient souvent attribués à des personnages historiques éminents, de préférence à des personnages que les deux parties reconnaissaient comme des autorités. Mais Léon de Perejaslav en Russie, connu exclusivement par le titre du traité qui lui est attribué, n'était pas un de ces personnages dont l'autorité aurait pu servir à un écrivain anonyme pour donner du lustre à son dialogue. Il est donc raisonnable

---

(1) Cité d'après le manuscrit de la Bibliothèque Synodale 368 (240), f. 243 (écrit en 1387). Ce titre se trouve aussi dans le Codex Synod. 207 (250), f. 413, et dans l'Ambrosianus 534, f. 226 v. Cf. BENEŠEVIČ, op. cit., p. 74 ; VLADIMIR, op. cit., pp. 317, 341 ; E. MARTINI et D. BASSI, Catalogus codicum graecorum Bibliothecae Ambrosianae, II, Mediolani, 1906, p. 648.

(2) Cité d'après le Codex Synod. 366 (239), f. 95 v. Cf. BENEŠEVIČ, loc. cit. ; VLADIMIR, op. cit., p. 312. Dans ce groupe, chaque manuscrit présente un titre partiellement différent.

d'admettre que Léon, métropolite de Perejaslav en Russie, a été réellement l'auteur d'un ouvrage polémique, qui, s'il n'est pas original par son sujet, est cependant indépendant dans la façon de le traiter. L'information contenue dans le titre de ce traité des azymes susciterait des doutes légitimes si elle était le seul témoignage de l'existence d'une métropole à Perejaslav en Russie. Mais nous disposons d'autres indices qui montrent que le traité en question a pu être écrit en Russie après 1054 et être l'œuvre du métropolite de Perejaslav.

Pendant longtemps, les savants ont pensé que le siège primitif du chef de l'Église en Russie, jusqu'en 1037, était Perejaslav ([1]). Des recherches récentes ont réfuté cette thèse et ont montré que le siège de la métropole de Russie, non seulement avant 1037, mais aussi avant 1017, était la cathédrale en bois de Sophie à Kiev, et que la métropole de Perejaslav appartient à la deuxième moitié du xie siècle ([2]). Deux témoignages dignes de foi prouvent l'existence, dans les années '80 et '90 du xie siècle, d'une métropole à Perejaslav. Nestor, moine du monastère des Cryptes, dans sa *Vie de Théodose du monastère des Cryptes* (Pečerskij), écrit au sujet d'un moine provenant du même monastère : « après cela, Éphrem l'eunuque s'en alla à Constantinople et y demeura dans un monastère, ensuite il fut appelé en ce pays et installé en qualité de métropolite à Perejaslav » ([3]). Cela a été écrit entre 1079 et 1088 ([4]). Éphrem, qui alla à Constantinople dans les années '60, y était encore vers 1072 ; il fut nommé métropolite

(1) Cf. E. E. GOLUBINSKIJ, *op. cit.*, I, 1, p. 328 sqq., et dernièrement A. D. STOKES, *The Status of the Russian Church 988-1037*, dans *The Slavonic and East European Review*, XXXVII, 1959, pp. 430-442.

(2) Cf. L. MÜLLER, *op. cit.*, pp. 22-26 ; A. POPPE, *Remarques sur la période la plus ancienne de l'histoire de l'Église en Russie*, I-II, (en polonais), dans *Przegląd Historyczny*, LV, Varsovie, 1964, pp. 369-384 et 557-560.

(3) *Sbornik XII veka moskovskogo Uspenskogo sobora*, (Recueil du xiie siècle de la cathédrale moscovite de la Dormition), ed. A. SAKHMATOV et P. LAVROV, Moskva, 1899. Photomechan. Nachdruck mit einer Einführung von D. ČIŽEVSKIJ, 's-Gravenhage, 1957, (*Apophoreta Slavica*, 2), p. 54 (f. 35 du manuscrit).

(4) Cf. A. POPPE, *Chronologie des œuvres de l'hagiographe Nestor*, (en polonais), dans *Slavia Orientalis*, XIV, Varsovie, 1965, pp. 287-305.

de Perejaslav probablement après le 15 juillet 1077 et avant octobre 1078 ; il mourut vers 1100. L'autre témoignage, indépendant du précédent, est un passage du *Récit des années*, sous l'année 1089/1090 ; il nous renseigne sur la consécration de l'église de St. Michel à Perejaslav par son fondateur « Éphrem, métropolite de cette église ». Une interpolation insérée dans ce texte au cours des années '20-'40 du XIIᵉ siècle, explique : « en effet, il existait à Perejaslav une métropole » [1]. Il s'agit maintenant de savoir quand l'évêché de Perejaslav fut élevé au rang de métropole et si Éphrem fut son unique métropolite. Le fait qu'en 1072 le diocèse de Perejaslav était régi par l'évêque Pierre, ne préjuge pas la question. Il faut, en effet, prendre en considération les circonstances qui, dans la deuxième moitié du XIᵉ siècle, firent naître, à côté de la métropole de Kiev, non seulement une métropole de Perejaslav, mais aussi une métropole de Černigov. Après la mort de Jaroslav le Sage (1054), il se constitua en Russie une sorte de triumvirat, formé par ses fils les plus âgés : le princeps Izjaslav à Kiev, Sviatoslav à Černigov et Vsevolod à Perejaslav. Cette situation ne pouvait pas échapper à l'attention de la cour byzantine, qui, face au manque de stabilité intérieure et à la pression extérieure sur les frontières, avait tout intérêt à entretenir des rapports amicaux avec la triarchie des fils de Jaroslav le Sage. A cette époque où la nomination de nouveaux métropolites faisait partie des compétences de l'empereur et, par une suite naturelle des choses, servait à ses plans politiques, la promotion des évêchés de Černigov et de Perejaslav au rang de métropoles apparaît tout à fait compréhensible. Jouant le rôle, en quelque sorte, d'ambassades byzantines, elles facilitaient le contact direct avec des princes qui participaient, en égale mesure, à la direction politique de la Russie. La métropole de Černigov, attestée par un texte russe de l'année 1072 et par l'*Ordo thronorum* du Codex Coislinianus 211, où elle est enregistrée à la 72ᵉ place comme ὁ Μαυροκάστρου ἤτοι νέας ῾Ρωσίας, fut fon-

---

[1] Voir le texte dans les chroniques *lavrentevskaja* et *ipatevskaja* publiées dans *Polnoe Sobranie Russkikh Letopisej*, (Recueil complet des chroniques russes), vol. I, 1926, p. 208, vol. II, 1908, p. 200. Cf. A. POPPE, *Remarques...* (cité), II, pp. 558-559.

dée au cours de la période 1059-1071, peut-être après 1060, c'est-à-dire après que le triumvirat des princes russes eut infligé une défaite écrasante aux Turcs-Ouzes, dangereux pour Byzance aussi bien que pour la Russie ; mais il n'est pas exclu qu'elle ait été fondée à l'époque de la rupture du triumvirat, dans les années 1068-1069. Les métropoles de Perejaslav et de Černigov avaient certainement un caractère titulaire ; aussi s'éteignirent-elles, à la mort de leurs chefs, dans les années '80-'90 du XIᵉ siècle, lorsque les circonstances politiques qui les avaient fait naître cessèrent d'exister (¹).

La fondation de la métropole de Perejaslav n'a pas dû être très éloignée dans le temps de celle de la métropole de Černigov. D'autant plus que le prince de Perejaslav, Vsevolod, était étroitement lié à la cour byzantine par des rapports de parenté (²). L'évêque de Perejaslav Pierre, étant donné le caractère titulaire de la métropole, ou bien n'a pas obtenu le titre de son prédécesseur, ou bien ne le possédait pas encore au moment où il participa à la translation des reliques des princes Boris et Gleb, le 20 mai 1072. Le métropolite Léon a pu donc être ou bien le successeur de Pierre et le prédécesseur d'Éphrem sur le siège de Perejaslav (après 1072, avant 1078), ou bien le prédécesseur de Pierre. Cette deuxième hypothèse nous paraît la plus probable pour deux raisons. D'abord, si l'on considère les rapports entre les princes en Russie, on ne voit pas pourquoi Byzance aurait accordé sa préférence au prince de Černigov et négligé celui de Perejaslav. Ensuite, la période du règne de Michel VII Doucas (1071-1078), qui était en correspondance avec Grégoire VII et lui promettait, en échange d'une aide de l'Occident contre les Seldjouks et les Petchénègues, l'unification des Églises (³), ne favorisait pas une polémique, qui, si elle était modérée dans le ton, soulignait cependant les différences, sans aucun esprit de compromis.

---

(1) Pour plus de détails, voir A. POPPE, *Remarques...*, III, dans *Przegląd Historyczny*, LVI, 1965, pp. 558-572.

(2) Cf. A. V. SOLOVIEV, *Marie, fille de Constantin IV Monomaque*, dans *Byzantion*, XXXIII, 1963, pp. 241-248.

(3) Cf. JAFFE, *Bibliotheca rerum germanicarum*, II, Roma, 1865, pp. 31-32, 64-65, 68-70, 144-146, 150-151.

520

En résumé : dans les années '60 ou, moins probablement, dans les années '70 du xie siècle, la métropole de Perejaslav a pu avoir pour chef Léon, qui, à cette époque, a écrit son traité des azymes.

En Russie, toutes les conditions étaient réunies pour qu'un traité pareil pût naître. Cela ressort des textes polémiques qui y ont été écrits ou traduits. Même si nous laissons de côté l'ouvrage polémique attribué à Georges, métropolite de Russie (vers 1072) — ouvrage dont la rédaction originale ne peut être datée avec certitude et dont la rédaction conservée est certainement tardive —, nous avons la lettre, déjà citée, du métropolite Jean Prodromos à l'antipape Clément III, au sujet des azymes, écrite vers 1085. Nous avons aussi deux lettres de Nicéphore, métropolite de Russie (1104-1121), aux princes russes, au sujet des « hérésies latines » ([1]).

Contre l'hypothèse de l'origine russe du traité des azymes, on pourrait invoquer le fait qu'il n'existe pas de traduction de cet ouvrage, bien que, dans la littérature vieux-russe conservée par les manuscrits des xive-xviie siècles, on trouve de nombreuses traductions d'ouvrages anti-latins, en particulier les traductions de presque tous les principaux polémistes byzantins. La lettre de Jean Prodromos adressée à Clément III, écrite en grec, fut immédiatement traduite. On pourrait répondre en invoquant un autre fait : les dévastations des bibliothèques russes. Mais peut-être le traité de Léon n'a-t-il vraiment pas été traduit, de même que l'écrit, déjà mentionné, de Théophylacte d'Achrida, archevêque bulgare, sur « les accusations contre les Latins ». Écrit en forme de dialogue, modéré dans le ton, adressant les réponses à la deuxième persone du pluriel, commençant par la phrase Ἄνδρες Ῥωμαῖοι, ἀκούσατε, il a pu être un ouvrage rhétorique destiné à être récité dans une dispute ([2]). Léon a pu participer à une dispute théologique pendant l'un de ses séjours périodiques à Con-

---

(1) N. Nikolskij, *Materialy dlja povremennogo spiska russkikh pisatelej i ikh sočinenij. X-XI v.* (Matériaux pour une liste chronologique des écrivains russes et de leurs œuvres. x[e]-xie siècles), SPb., 1906, pp. 197 sq., 211 sq. ; Popov, *op. cit.*, pp. 99-118 ; Pavlov, *op. cit.*, pp. 48-65, 157.

(2) Cela a été remarqué par V. Mošin, *op. cit.*, p. 101.

stantinople, qui faisaient partie de ses devoirs de métropolite. Les contacts avec Rome n'avaient pas cessé après 1054. A Constantinople arrivaient les légats du pape ; dans les années '60-'70, la route des nombreux pèlerins de l'Occident se rendant en Palestine passait par la capitale de l'empire. Les pèlerins étaient souvent guidés par des évêques ; avec ceux-ci on menait certainement des disputes ([1]).

III. Les sources de l'hypothèse
sur l'origine bulgare du traité

Il conviendra maintenant d'examiner de près une autre solution qui a été donnée au problème de l'attribution de notre traité des azymes, et à laquelle nous avons fait allusion au début du présent article. On a supposé que le métropolite Léon, auteur du traité des azymes, était métropolite de Preslav para-danubien, en Bulgarie, aux xiᵉ-xiiᵉ siècles ([2]). Cette hypothèse est née d'une constatation exacte : on a vu que le traité n'a pu être écrit avant 1053-1054 et que, par conséquent, il ne peut pas être l'œuvre du métropolite Léon, chef de l'Église russe entre la fin du xᵉ et le début du xiᵉ siècle, dont l'existence est attestée — c'est là l'opinion courante, que nous critiquerons tout à l'heure — par des textes tardifs. Mais on n'a pas pris en considération les témoignages de l'existence de la métropole de Perejaslav dans la deuxième moitié du xiᵉ siècle.

Le premier qui ait fait cette hypothèse, c'est l'historien de l'Église Dosithée, patriarche de Jérusalem (1669-1707), qui a consacré beaucoup d'attention aux controverses ecclésiastiques gréco-latines. Dans la liste alphabétique par lui dressée des « Grecs qui ont écrit contre les innovations des Latins »,

---

(1) Cf. V. Vasilevskij, *Trudy*, (Œuvres), I, p. 58 sqq. ; S. Runciman, *op. cit.*, p. 55 sqq. ; Id., *The Pilgrimages to Palestine before 1095*, dans *A History of the Crusades*, I, Philadelphia, 1958, pp. 68-78.

(2) Outre les auteurs cités plus haut, p. 505, notes 1 et 2, voir aussi Čelcov, *op. cit.*, pp. 50-53 et A. Demetracopoulos, *Graecia orthodoxa sive de Graecis qui contra Latinos scripserunt et de eorum scriptis*, Lipsiae, 1872, p. 93, qui a rangé Léon parmi les polémistes des xivᵉ-xvᵉ siècles.

522

figure, entre autres, *Λέων Πρεσλάβας ἤτοι Μαρκιανουπόλεως* (¹).
Remarquons que Dosithée place ce Léon entre Léon *Βουλγαρίας*
et Léon *Ἀχρίδινος*, sans se rendre compte que ces deux derniers Léon ne sont en réalité qu'un seul, l'archevêque bulgare Léon d'Achrida, qui ouvrit la controverse sur les azymes par sa lettre à Jean, évêque de Trani dans les Pouilles.
Dans les titres de ses ouvrages, cet archevêque est appelé
tantôt Léon de Bulgarie, tantôt Léon d'Achrida, puisque le
siège du chef de l'Église bulgare se trouvait à cette époque
à Achrida. Ce fait nous donne une indication précieuse sur
la façon dont Dosithée a dressé la liste des controversistes
byzantins : il puisait ses renseignements dans les titres des
ouvrages qu'il connaissait. Ceci établi, il apparaît surpre-
nant que, dans cette liste, il n'y ait pas Léon *τῆς ἐν Ῥωσίᾳ Πρεσθλάβας*, ou simplement Léon *Ῥωσίας* — d'autant plus que
notre traité des azymes était bien connu de Dosithée. C'est
justement Dosithée qui, en 1693, donna à la Bibliothèque Synodale de Moscou, avec d'autres manuscrits, les manuscrits
nos. 366 (239), 368 (240) et 207 (250), à présent au Musée
Historique de Moscou, qui contiennent le traité des azymes
de Léon ; ce qui plus est, dans ces manuscrits, se trouvent des
notes de la main de Dosithée (²). Puisque, d'autre part, on
ne connaît aucun ouvrage de Léon *Πρεσλάβας ἤτοι Μαρκιανουπόλεως*, il est — nous paraît-il — évident que Dosithée a
introduit ce Léon dans sa liste à la suite d'une interprétation
critique de l'expression *τῆς ἐν Ῥωσίᾳ Πρεσθλάβας* dans le titre
de notre traité des azymes — expression qui se trouve dans
les manuscrits de la Bibliothèque Synodale 368 et 207. Comme nous l'avons remarqué ci-dessus, dès le XIIIe siècle on
tend à simplifier ce titre, en gardant cependant la mention
de la Russie. Déjà à cette époque on avait oublié cet épisode
éphémère qu'avait été la métropole de Perejaslav. L'inter-

---

(1) DOSITHEOS, *Ἱστορία περὶ τῶν ἐν Ἱεροσολύμοις πατριαρχευσάντων
συγγραφεῖσα ... παρὰ — τοῦ ... πατριάρχου τῶν Ἱεροσολύμων...*, Bucarest, 1715, livre X, chap. 3, pp. 1143-1144.
(2) Cf. VLADIMIR, *op. cit.*, pp. 310, 489, 738, 786. C'est M. B. L.
FONKIČ qui a bien voulu attirer mon attention sur les notes autogra-
phes de Dosithée.

prétation de Dosithée alla dans un sens différent. La métropole de Perejaslav lui sembla une monstruosité ; par contre, il connaissait bien la métropole médiévale de Preslav ; il supposa donc qu'il s'agissait de cette ville. Pour mieux préciser, il ajouta au nom de Preslav ἤτοι Μαρκιανουπόλεως : cela était conforme à la tradition ecclésiastique, qui voyait dans la ville épiscopale de Preslav, fondée au moment de la christianisation de la Bulgarie, la continuatrice de l'ancienne métropole balkanique Marcianopolis (¹). Donc, le renseignement que nous donne Dosithée n'est pas la reproduction d'un témoignage plus ancien, mais une hypothèse d'un historien de l'Église du xviie siècle.

Ce renseignement de Dosithée a été accepté sans aucune réserve par D. Cukhlev, qui le considérait comme un « témoignage indiscutable d'un témoin presque contemporain ». Il pensait ainsi parce qu'il confondait le Dosithée, auteur de l'*Histoire du patriarcat de Jérusalem*, avec le Dosithée du xiie siècle qui fut, lui aussi, patriarche de Jérusalem (1187-1189). Par conséquent, il était prêt à voir dans l'expression ἐν Ῥωσίᾳ du titre du traité de Léon ou bien une interprétation tardive, ou bien une déformation du nom de la ville balkanique Ῥούσιον, d'où, à son avis, Léon provenait, ou bien dont il était le métropolite avant d'être déplacé à Preslav (²). La tradition manuscrite du traité ne justifie pas du tout ces conjectures. On ne peut pas non plus être d'accord avec M. Čelcov lorsqu'il soutient qu'au xie siècle, le nom Ῥωσία n'avait pas une signification nettement définie et que le manque de connaissances géographiques précises permit de situer Preslav bulgare en Russie (³).

(1) Probablement pour cette raison, d'après l'exemple de Dosithée, on situe parfois Preslav sur l'emplacement de Marcianopolis, qui, en réalité, se trouve à l'Est de Preslav, plus près de Varna (voir S. Stancev, *Pliska und Preslav*, dans *Antike und Mittelalter in Bulgarien*, Berlin, 1960, pp. 219 sqq.) : Pauly et Wissowa, *Real-Encyklopädie*, XIV, col. 1510 ; H.-G. Beck, *op. cit.*, p. 610.

(2) D. Cukhlev, *op. cit.*, pp. 919-920.

(3) Cf. Čelcov, *op. cit.*, pp. 52-53 ; pour plus de détails, cf. A. Poppe, *Remarques...*, II, pp. 566-567 ; sur le sens politique et géographique de Ῥωσία, voir A. Soloviev, *Le nom byzantin de la Russie*, 's-Gravenhage, 1957, p. 9 sqq. ; Id., Ἄρχων Ῥωσίας, dans *Byzantion*, XXXI, 1961, p. 237 sqq.

524

Il faut remarquer que, dans les textes byzantins des xiie-xiiie siècles, chez Michel Cédrénus, Anne Comnène, Michel Attaliate, Georges Acropolite, dans les sceaux des stratèges Léon Pégonitès et Andronic Doucas, la ville de Preslav en Bulgarie est toujours appelée μεγάλη Πρεσθλάβα (¹). C'est là encore un argument contre l'hypothèse d'après laquelle le traité des azymes aurait été écrit à Preslav de Bulgarie. En outre, il n'existe aucun témoignage qui prouve qu'aux xie-xiie siècles, Preslav — qui, à cette époque, n'appartenait pas à l'Église bulgare — ait été une métropole ; l'existence de la métropole de Preslav n'est attestée qu'à partir du début du xiiie siècle (²).

Donc le seul fait qui pourrait faire penser à Preslav paradanubien, c'est la coïncidence des noms des deux villes de Russie et de Bulgarie. Mais, face à l'indication explicite contenue dans le titre du traité des azymes et confirmée par l'existence d'une métropole titulaire à Perejaslav en Russie dans la deuxième moitié du xie siècle, la coïncidence des noms ne constitue pas une alternative.

IV. A-T-IL EXISTÉ UN LÉON, PREMIER MÉTROPOLITE DE RUSSIE ?

Nos considérations sur le traité de Léon, métropolite de Perejaslav en Russie, nous donnent l'occasion de faire une digression sur le premier métropolite, ou l'un des premiers métropolites de Russie — question qui n'est pas dépourvue d'intérêt pour les byzantinistes.

Récemment, V. Grumel, dans ses fines considérations sur la date de l'ordination du patriarche Nicolas II Chrysobergès,

---

(1) V. N. ZLATARSKI, *Istorija na Blgarskata država* (Histoire de l'État bulgare), II, Sofia, 1934, p. 480 ; N. BANESCU, P. PAPANAGI, *Plombs byzantins découverts à Silistrie*, dans *Byzantion*, X, 1935, p. 602 sq. ; G. G. LITAVRIN, *Bolgaria i Vizantija v XI-XII vv.*, (Bulgarie et Byzance aux xie-xiie siècles), Moskva, 1960, p. 282.

(2) Cf. H. GELZER, *Ungedruckte und wenig bekannte Bistümerverzeichnisse der orientalischen Kirche*, dans *Byzantinische Zeitschrift*, II, 1893, p. 61 ; V. N. ZLATARSKI, *op. cit.*, III, Sofia, 1940, pp. 155, 183, 195-196, 203.

a employé pour son argumentation des données de chroniques russes tardives (des xvie-xviie siècles), relatives au métropolite Léon [1]. Sans vouloir mettre en cause la thèse de cet excellent connaisseur des sources byzantines, il faut observer que les informations des chroniques russes sur Léon, métropolite de Russie, découlent toutes d'une source commune : du Statut ecclésiastique attribué à Vladimir I [2]. Ce texte, qui établit le statut juridique de l'Église en Russie, a été écrit entre la fin du xiie siècle et le début du xiiie ; le plus ancien parmi les manuscrits qui nous l'ont transmis, date des années 1282-1291 (Nomokanon de Novgorod). On lit dans ce manuscrit que le prince de Russie Vladimir reçut « le saint baptême de l'empereur grec et prit de Photius, patriarche de Constantinople, le premier métropolite Léon à Kiev ». Dans une autre rédaction, au lieu de Léon, figure le métropolite Michel. Sans entrer dans le détail, il suffira de dire qu'à notre avis, les rédacteurs du Statut ecclésiastique ne disposaient d'aucun renseignement immédiatement utilisable sur la question de savoir qui a été le premier métropolite de Russie. Ils ont dû faire des recherches savantes — les premières recherches qui aient été faites pour répondre à cette question, qui est encore ouverte aujourd'hui.

Lorsqu'on décida de codifier tous les privilèges jusqu'alors obtenus par l'Église russe sous la forme d'un document représentatif, l'exigence s'imposa de lier la genèse de ces privilèges à la fondation de la hiérarchie ecclésiastique en Russie. On dut alors constater avec consternation qu'il n'y avait aucun texte où ce fait, dont on commençait à comprendre l'importance, eût été enregistré. Les érudits russes eurent recours à des conjectures. Dans l'encyclique du patriarche Photius de l'année 867 — qui était certainement connue aussi dans la traduction slave — on lisait que le peuple des Ῥώς avait

----

(1) Cf. V. GRUMEL, *Chronologie patriarcale au Xe siècle*, dans *Revue des Études Byzantines*, XXII, 1964, pp. 51, 54-56, 70.

(2) L'édition la plus complète des nombreuses versions du Statut est celle de V. BENEŠEVIČ, *op. cit.*, pp. 1-72 ; voir aussi *Pamjatniki russkogo prava*, (Monuments du droit russe), I, Moskva, 1952, pp. 235-256. L'étude la plus approfondie de ce Statut est celle de S. JUŠKOV, *Issledovania po istorii russkogo prava*. I, *Ustav knjazja Vladimira*, (Recherches sur l'histoire du droit russe. I, Le Statut du prince Vladimir), Novousensk, 1925.

526

été converti et avait reçu un évêque ([1]). On se demanda comment cet évêque s'appelait. On proposa deux réponses : Michel et Léon. La première réponse était suggérée par l'instruction sur la profession de foi, contenue dans le *Récit des années* sous l'année 988 et qui aurait été adressée spécialement au prince de Russie Vladimir I à l'occasion du baptême. Ce texte est une traduction, adaptée à la situation, du *Credo* de Michel le Syncelle. La recherche de l'auteur de ce texte était facilitée par le fait qu'on connaissait en Russie ce *Credo* également sous la forme d'un ouvrage autonome avec le nom de l'auteur ([2]). En ce qui concerne la deuxième réponse, la source d'information a été probablement le traité des azymes de Léon. Même si cet ouvrage n'avait pas été traduit, il y avait assez de chances pour que l'information contenue dans son titre, et notée déjà dans certains manuscrits du XIIIe siècle sous la forme simplifiée *Λέοντος μητροπολίτου 'Ρωσίας*, fût connue en Russie. Le sujet même du traité invitait aussi à placer le métropolite de Russie Léon à côté de Photius, à qui, à partir du XIe siècle, on attribuait plusieurs écrits polémiques, entre autres des écrits sur les azymes ([3]). C'était là les premières tentatives de solution : des tentatives que nous pourrions prendre pour des témoignages dignes de foi, sans les asynchronismes qui nous révèlent leur nature ([4]).

Pour des raisons analogues, les recherches visant à établir la date du déplacement de Théophylacte de la métropole de Sébaste à celle de Russie ([5]) — question essentielle aussi

---

(1) Cf. GRUMEL, *Reg.*, no. 481 ; E. GOLUBINSKIJ, *op. cit.*, I, 1, p. 279.

(2) Sur la tradition manuscrite vieux-russe du *Credo*, voir N. NIKOLSKIJ, *op. cit.*, p. 16 sq.

(3) Cf. H.-G. BECK, *op. cit.*, pp. 522, 526 sqq., 538.

(4) Plus de détails dans A. POPPE, *Remarques...*, II, pp. 567-569 ; ID., articles *Léon-métropolite russe* et *Michel-métropolite russe*, dans le *Słownik Starożytności Słowiańskich* (*Lexicon Antiquitatum Slavicarum*), vol. III, sous presse. L'auteur se propose de consacrer une étude spéciale à la chronologie des métropolites russes des Xe-XIIe siècles.

(5) Les recherches sur ce sujet, commencées par V. LAURENT, et E. HONIGMANN, ont été développées par H. GRÉGOIRE et P. ORGELS, *op. cit.*, pp. 162-164, 169-172, et par V. GRUMEL, *Chronologie...*, pp. 51 sqq.

bien pour l'histoire de l'Église byzantine que pour celle de l'Église russe, — ne doivent pas s'appuyer sur les données des textes russes. Ceux-ci, en effet, dans ce cas particulier, n'ont pas conservé la trace d'un témoignage authentique, mais nous offrent seulement le fruit de l'ingéniosité d'un érudit médiéval.

Varsovie.

VIII

L'ORGANISATION DIOCÉSAINE DE LA RUSSIE AUX XIᵉ-XIIᵉ SIÈCLES

En vertu d'un accord byzantino-russe de 987/989, une nouvelle métropole fut créée — la soixantième province ecclésiastique du patriarcat de Constantinople — dans le but de christianiser la Russie, conformément à la décision du prince Vladimir 1ᵉʳ. Afin de remplir sa mission, l'église transporta en Russie la structure hiérarchique qui était propre à son organisation, en premier lieu la division en évêchés administrés par les suffragants de l'évêque supérieur, le métropolite. Mais la façon concrète dont s'est formé le plus ancien réseau de diocèses en Russie nous est mal connue à cause des lacunes des sources ou de leur défaut. La présente étude tente de reconstituer la géographie ecclésiastique de la Russie aux xiᵉ-xiiᵉ siècles, c'est-à-dire pendant la période où s'est formée la charpente de l'ancienne Église russe.

Déjà l'auteur de la chronique nikonienne du milieu du xviᵉ siècle (¹) s'interrogeait sur le nombre de diocèses dont se composait, à l'aube de son histoire, la province ecclésiastique russe. Son énumération de six diocèses, complétée par une assertion générale sur la constitution d'évêchés « dans beaucoup d'autres villes », a longtemps été considérée comme un témoignage digne de foi (²). Aujourd'hui nous y discernons aisément le résultat des recherches

---

(1) *Polnoe sobranie russkih letopiseï* (Recueil complet des chroniques russes, ici *PSRL*), vol. IX, SPb., 1862, pp. 84-85.

(2) Cf. N. Davidov, *Les éparchies de l'Église de toute la Russie dans leur ordre d'érection*, (en russe), dans *Christianskoje Čtenie*, 1875, IIᵉ partie, pp. 265-270 ; V. Kalinnikov, *Les métropolites et les évêques du temps de saint Vladimir*, (en russe), dans : *Trudy Kievskoï Duhovnoï Akademii*, 1888, t. 2, pp. 569-593. Makarij l'archimandrite, *Istoria russkoï Cerkvi* (Histoire de l'Église russe), t. I, 3ᵉ édition, SPb., 1889, pp. 36-40 ; E. E. Golubinskij, *Istoria russkoï Cerkvi* (Histoire de l'Église russe), Moscou, 1901, t. I-1, p. 334.

166

du chroniqueur du xviᵉ siècle, qui transfère à l'époque de Vladimir
Iᵉʳ le patriarche Photius (858-886), reprenant à son compte l'erreur
de ses savants prédécesseurs, et, cette fois de sa propre initiative,
les évêques de la seconde moitié du xiᵉ siècle dont les noms et les
sièges lui étaient connus. La seule certitude que nous ayons, c'est
que, dès la fondation de la province métropolitaine russe, celle-ci
ne pouvait se passer de suffragants. Leur présence à l'époque de
Vladimir Iᵉʳ est confirmée par le *Récit des temps passés*, dans une
notice qui est cependant postérieure au règne de ce souverain
d'environ 100 ans, et par le témoignage, encore plus important,
d'Hilarion, du milieu du xiᵉ siècle, qui pouvait encore se souvenir
au moins de la seconde moitié du règne de Vladimir Iᵉʳ (¹). E.
Golubinskij s'est efforcé de reconstituer d'une manière approfondie
le réseau diocésain de la Russie aux xᵉ-xiiiᵉ siècles. Mais cet auteur,
pourtant si sceptique envers les sources, a trop fait confiance à
des témoignages tardifs concernant l'organisation de l'Église russe.
D'après Golubinskij, faisaient partie des diocèses fondés sous
Vladimir Iᵉʳ, en dehors du diocèse métropolitain de Kiev, les évêchés
de Novgorod, Černigov, Rostov, Vladimir-Volhynsk, Bielgorod,
Tmoutarakan', Polotsk et Tourov. Deux autres évêchés, ceux de
Perejaslav et de Juriev, auraient été créés sous Jaroslav le Sage,
et finalement sept évêchés auraient été érigés aux xiiᵉ et xiiiᵉ
siècles. Au milieu du xiᵉ siècle, la métropole de Russie se serait
composée de 11 diocèses (²). Les données présentées chronologique-

---

(1) *Povest' vremennyh let* (Le Récit des temps passés, autrefois
appelé Chronique de Nestor) dans : *PSRL*, vol. I, coll. 126-127 ;
L. Müller, *Des Metropoliten Ilarion Lobrede auf Vladimir den Hei-*
ligen und Glaubensbekenntis, nach der Erstausgabe von 1844 neu
herausgegeben, eingeleitet und erläutert, Wiesbaden, 1962, (*Sla-*
wistische Studienbücher, II), pp. 117-118.
(2) Golubinskij, *op. cit.*, I-1, pp. 333-334, 664-703, repris par
L. K. Götz, *Staat u. Kirche in Altrussland. Kiever Periode 988-1240.*
Berlin, 1908, p. 20 ; A. V. Kartašev, *Očerki po istorii russkoï Cerkvi*
(Essais sur l'histoire de l'Église russe), t. I. Paris, 1959, pp. 182-
183, et d'autres. M. D. Priselkov est d'un avis différent : il considère
qu'il y avait trois évêchés à l'époque de Vladimir Iᵉʳ, à Kiev, à
Novgorod et peut-être à Bielgorod (cf. M. D. Priselkov, *Očerki*
po cerkevno-političeskoï istorii Kijevskoï Rusi (Essai sur l'histoire
ecclésiastique et politique de la Russie de Kiev), S Pb., 1913, pp.
48-49.

ment par N. Baumgarten pour servir à l'histoire de l'Église russe avant l'invasion mongole, ne permettent de se faire qu'une faible idée du développement du réseau diocésain (¹). Ce recueil de données incomplètes, prises au hasard, d'une valeur très inégale, non soumises à un examen critique, ne peut fournir un point de départ pour de nouvelles recherches. Les *Notitiae episcopatuum* grecques du xɪɪᵉ et du xɪɪɪᵉ siècles publiées par H. Gelzer, mal connues et encore insuffisamment exploitées, constituent une source complémentaire précieuse (²).

En examinant tous les témoignages utilisables pour la reconstitution du réseau diocésain au xɪᵉ siècle, on constate l'absence de données sphragistiques. Ceci est d'autant plus étonnant que nous possédons des sceaux des métropolites russes du xɪᵉ siècle. Or nous ne trouvons dans les collections sphragistiques aucun sceau d'évêque du xɪᵉ siècle ni des trois premières décennies du xɪɪᵉ. Ils apparaissent seulement au xɪɪᵉ siècle, mais il est curieux de constater que, pour la période précédant les invasions mongoles, nous disposons de 20 sceaux qui sont indiscutablement épiscopaux — des inscriptions le prouvent — mais qui ne proviennent que de 4 évêchés. Il s'agit des évêchés de Novgorod, de Smolensk, de Galič, de Polotsk. Ajoutons que nous n'avons de bulles de plusieurs hiérarques que pour Novgorod (³). On trouve également des sceaux épiscopaux parmi les 19 sceaux anonymes représentant la Vierge à l'avers et un saint au revers, datés de la période allant du xɪᵉ au début du xɪɪɪᵉ siècle. Mais, tout porte à croire que les

---

(1) N. Baumgarten, *Chronologie ecclésiastique des terres russes du Xᵉ au XIIIᵉ siècle.* Rome, 1930 ; cf. la liste des hiérarques des différents diocèses, établie sans esprit critique, pp. 160-166.

(2) H. Gelzer, *Ungedruckte und ungenügend veröffentlichte Texte der Notitiae episcopatuum. Ein Beitrag zur byzantinischen Kirchen- und Verwaltungsgeschichte — Abhandlungen der philosophisch- philologischen Classe der königl. Bayerischen Akademie der Wissenschaften,* B. XXI, Munich, 1901, pp. 585-589, 632 ; du même auteur, *Beiträge zur russischen Kirchengeschichte aus griechischen Quellen, Zeitschrift für Kirchengeschichte,* t. XIII, 1892, 241-281.

(3) V. L. Yanin, *Les bulles nominatives des évêques russes au XIIᵉ et au début du XIIIᵉ siècle* (en russe) dans : *Sovietskaja arheologia,* 1966, nᵒ 3, pp. 197-207. Cf. A. Poppe, *Les sceaux en Russie (jusqu'au milieu du XIIIᵉ siècle),* dans *Lexicon antiquitatum slavicarum,* t. IV, 1970.

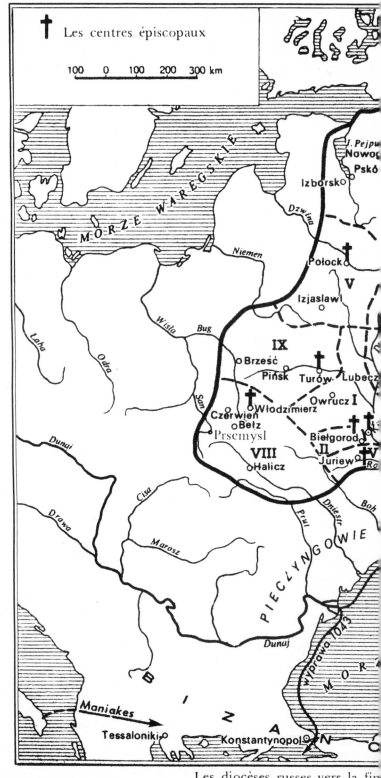

† Les centres épiscopaux

100 0 100 200 300 km

POLSKA

MORZE WAREGSKIE

J. Pejpu
Nowog
Pskó
Izborsko
Dzwina
Połock †
V
Izjasław
Niemen
Wisła   Bug
Laba
Odra
IX
Brześć
Pińsk   Turów † Lubecz
San
Owrucz I †
Włodzimierz †
Czerwien
Bełz
Prsemysl
Biełgorod †
II †
VIII
Haliczo   Juriew
Dunaj
Cisa
Marosz
Drawa
Prut   Dniestr   Boh
PIECZYNGOWIE
Dunaj
wyprawa 1043
MOR
B
I
Z
A
Maniakes
Tessaloniki   Konstantynopol   N
MOR

Les diocèses russes vers la fin

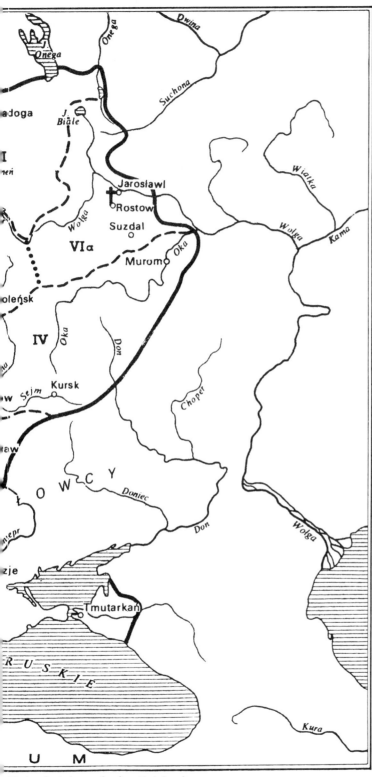

siècle (schéma de la division).

168

plus anciens, qui remontent à la seconde moitié du xie siècle, sont des sceaux princiers. On peut cependant considérer comme étant épiscopal un sceau représentant la Vierge à l'avers et l'archange Michel, patron de la cathédrale, au revers, qui a été trouvé, il y a quelques années, dans la curie épiscopale de Perejaslav à un niveau archéologique daté de la période allant du xie au début du xiiie siècle. Il faut également considérer comme étant épiscopal, et non pas princier, comme on l'a cru jusqu'à présent, le sceau trouvé sur l'ancien site de Riazan', portant l'image de la Vierge et des SS. Boris et Gleb, patrons de la cathédrale, et le situer entre l'érection de l'évêché, vers l'an 1200, et la destruction de la ville par les Mongols, en 1237.

Cet état de la documentation ne permet cependant pas d'affirmer que les sceaux épiscopaux étaient inconnus en Russie avant la quatrième décennie du xiie siècle.

1. La *Notitia episcopatuum, Cod. Athen.*, n° 1371,
ET LES ÉVÊCHÉS RUSSES ÉRIGÉS AU XIIe SIÈCLE.

Les recherches n'ayant pas donné jusqu'à présent de réponses satisfaisantes, nous essaierons d'éclaircir le problème de la création des plus anciens évêchés russes en prenant pour point de départ la situation au xiie siècle, qui est mieux connue grâce à la *Notitia espicopatuum* conservée dans le *codex* d'Athènes, n° 1371, f°s 389-391 v., que la paléographie situe à la fin du xiie ou au début du xiiie siècle. Publiée par H. Gelzer, qui la date à juste titre des années 1170-1179, elle reflète les changements intervenus dans la liste des suffragants des différentes métropoles, entre l'an 980 et 1170. D'après Gelzer, la rédaction de la *notitia* provient de la dernière période du règne de Manuel Ier Comnène et ne mentionne pas les innovations dues, en matière de géographie ecclésiastique byzantine, à Isaac II Ange (1185-1195) (¹). A la soixante-deuxième place, elle mentionne la métropole de Russie avec 11 suffragants.

(1) GELZER, *Ungedruckte* ..., pp. 585, 587, 588. Cf. H. G. BECK, *Kirche und theologische Literatur im Byzantinischen Reich*, Munich, 1959, p. 152.

ΞΒ. Τῇ μεγάλῃ ʽΡωσίᾳ	62. (Évêques soumis) à la (métropole de) grande Russie :
α. ὁ Πελογράδων	1. de Bielgorod
β. ὁ Νευογράδων	2. de Novgorod
γ. ὁ Τζερνιγόβων	3. de Černigov
δ. ὁ Πολοτζίκων	4. de Polotsk
ε. ὁ τοῦ Βλαδιμοίρου	5. de Vladimir
ϛ. ὁ Περισθλάβου	6. de Perejaslav
ζ. ὁ τοῦ Σουσδάλι	7. de Souzdal
η. ὁ Τουρόβου	8. de Tourov
θ. τὸ Κάνεβε	9. de Kaniev
ι. τὸ Σμολίσκον	10. de Smolensk
ια. ἡ Γάλιτζα	11. de Galič

La lecture du nom des localités russes donnée ici ne suscite en principe aucun doute. Il faut seulement remarquer que nous revenons au texte du manuscrit pour le nom ὁ Τουρόβου, qui avait été corrigé par Gelzer en ὁ τοῦ ʽΡο<στό>βου. Comme nous allons le démontrer plus loin, une émendation est ici superflue, car il s'agit bien en réalité de l'évêché de Tourov, et non de celui de Rostov.

Le *terminus ad quem* de la rédaction de la *Notitia* est confirmé par l'absence, parmi les suffragants de la métropole de Russie, de l'évêché de Riazan', fondé entre 1187 et 1207, probablement dans la dernière décennie du xiie siècle ([1]).

Les *Notitiae* observent en général le principe du classement des métropoles et des évêchés dans l'ordre de leur fondation, mais on note de nombreuses exceptions à cette règle dans le cas de jeunes sièges qui, avec le temps, prenaient le pas sur les plus anciens. C'est pourquoi la liste citée plus haut, indiquant avant tout le rang de dignité (τὸ αἰδέσιμον), admis à l'époque, des sièges épiscopaux, ne peut sans vérification préalable être considérée comme rendant compte de l'ordre de fondation des différents évêchés russes.

Quant au dixième et avant-dernier évêché, celui de Smolensk, nous savons, grâce au témoignage authentique du privilège de fondation établi par Rostislav, prince de Smolensk, qu'il a été

---

(1) GOLUBINSKIJ, *op. cit.*, I-1, pp. 695-696 ; A.L. MONGAJT, *Riazanskaja zemla* (La terre de Riazan'), Moscou, 1961, pp. 352-353.

170

créé en 1136 et qu'il englobait un territoire soustrait à la juridiction de l'évêché de Perejaslav, ce territoire constituant, du point de vue politique, un district autonome : la principauté de Smolensk. Grâce à une copie du xvɪᵉ siècle de l'acte de fondation et de donation (le seul acte de ce genre qui nous soit parvenu), il nous est possible de reconstituer les circonstances politiques et ecclésiastiques qui entraînèrent la fondation de cet évêché et établirent les bases juridiques et matérielles de son existence. Ce document permet en même temps de procéder à des observations susceptibles de mieux faire comprendre l'ensemble du processus de formation du réseau diocésain aux xɪᵉ-xɪɪɪᵉ siècles (¹).

L'origine de l'évêché de Galič, placé en fin de liste, remonte au milieu du xɪɪᵉ siècle. Son existence à cette époque est confirmée par trois sceaux épiscopaux ($K\acute{o}\sigma\mu\alpha\nu$ $\Gamma\alpha\lambda\acute{\iota}\tau\zeta\eta\varsigma$) et, pour l'année 1164/5, par une mention de la chronique hypatienne qui précise que Jaroslav, prince de Galič, a choisi « son évêque » Cosmas pour faire partie de la suite du neveu de l'empereur Andronic qui rentrait à Byzance (²). Cosmas fut probablement le premier évêque de Galič, car l'histoire politique de Galič, qui ne devint capitale princière qu'en 1141, prouve que la fondation du nouvel évêché, soustrait cette fois à la juridiction de l'évêque de Vladimir-Volhynsk, n'a pu se faire avant la cinquième décennie du xɪɪᵉ siècle. Ce n'est qu'en 1144 que la région du Dniestr, partagée entre les descendants de Rostislav, fut réunifiée par Vladimirko de Galič. Les relations compliquées entre les différents princes, et notamment l'hostilité existant entre Vladimirko et Vsevolod Olgovitch, grand prince de Kiev, excluent la possibilité que le nouvel évêché ait été institué avant 1146. Par la suite, lorsque le prince de Vladimir-Volhynsk, Iziaslav Mstislavovitch, fut maître de Kiev et que, soutenu par une partie des évêques, il nomma métropolite le moine russe Clément Smolatitch, Vladimirko de Galič appartenait à la coalition hostile à Iziaslav et opposée à ses plans ecclésiastiques. Dans ces conditions, l'évêque de Vladimir-Volhynsk, soutenant Iziaslav et Clément Smolatitch, ne pouvait exercer sa juridiction sur la principauté de Galič. C'est sans doute durant cette période que fut prise la décision de créer

---

(1) Cf. A. Poppe, *L'acte de fondation de l'évêché de Smolensk* (en russe), dans *Arheologičeskiï Ežegodnik za 1965*, Moscou, 1966, pp. 59-71.

(2) *PSRL*, vol. II, col. 524 ; Yanin, *Les bulles* ..., p. 206.

un évêché séparé à Galič. Prenant en considération l'alliance entre Vladimirko, puis, après 1152, entre son fils Jaroslav et Byzance, on peut penser que cette idée fut soutenue et acceptée par le patriarche. L'investiture laïque du chef du nouvel évêché à dû lui être conférée sans doute entre 1147 et 1155, et sa consécration a dû avoir lieu après l'arrivée à Kiev du métropolite Constantin Iᵉʳ, nommé par le patriarche après la période de désordres dans la vie ecclésiastique en Russie. Celui-ci arrive à Kiev après le 21 avril 1156 (¹).

En excluant deux sièges épiscopaux, celui de Smolensk et celui de Galič, datant sans aucun doute du xiiᵉ siècle, il en reste 9 qui ont été créés à la fin du xᵉ siècle et au xiᵉ siècle. Pour être plus exact, il y a 10 diocèses qui entrent en ligne de compte, car celui de Kiev, placé directement sous la juridiction du métropolite, est contenu dans le titre de la 62ᵉ métropole : τῇ μεγάλῃ Ῥωσίᾳ. L'expression « de grande Russie » signifie ici l'ensemble de la terre russe (πάσῃ Ῥωσίᾳ) et souligne l'unité de la juridiction ecclésiastique sur toute l'étendue de l'ancien État russe, politiquement démembré (²).

Il est curieux de constater que, dans la *Notitia* que nous examinons, le suffragant de Bielgorod est placé en premier lieu, avant Novgorod, alors que dans la *Notitia* de la seconde moitié du xiiiᵉ siècle, τὸ μέγα Νοβογράδι figure en premier lieu et Bielgorod, traduit en grec cette fois, est à la sixième place, τὸ Ἀσπρόκαστρον τὸ μέγα πλησίον τοῦ Κυέβου (³). Étant donné qu'il était d'usage dans une *Notitia* de citer en premier lieu le prôtothrone, on peut en conclure que la *Notitia* du *codex Atheniensis* nᵒ 1371 reflète encore un état de choses dans lequel le suffragant de Bielgorod occupe le poste de πρωτόθρονος de la métropole de Kiev.

<hr />

(1) Cf. M. Hruševskyj, *Istoria Ukrainy-Rusi* (Histoire de l'Ukraine-Russie), Lvov, 1905, t. II, p. 417 sqq, 465 sqq ; S. Soloviev, *Istoria Rossii* (Histoire de Russie), t. I, Moscou, 1959, p. 434 sq ; Pl. Sokolov, *Russkiï arhiereï iz Vizantii* (L'archevêque russe de Byzance), Kiev, 1913, p. 57 sqq, 88 sqq : A. Poppe, *Państwo i kościół na Rusi w XI wieku* (L'État et l'Église dans la Russie du xiᵉ siècle), Varsovie, 1969, pp. 155-157.

(2) Cf. A. Soloviev, *Le nom byzantin de la Russie*, La Haye, 1957, p. 15 ; Poppe, *Państwo ...*, p. 157, note 17.

(3) Gelzer, *Ungedruckte ...*, pp. 589-632 ; du même auteur, *Beiträge*, p. 252. Cf. G. Parthey, *Hieroclis Synecdemus et notitiae graecae episcopatuum*, Berolini, 1866, p. 130.

172

A partir de 1165, les évêques de Novgorod la Grande se firent appeler archevêques ; ce n'était cependant qu'une dignité titulaire, car ils continuaient à être les suffragants du métropolite de Kiev. Le rôle politique des évêques de la République de Novgorod et leur position dans l'Église, renforcée par l'évêque Niphon au cours des querelles de 1147-1155, firent que la première place parmi les suffragants de Kiev revint au hiérarque de Novgorod, avec le titre d'archevêque. Ainsi donc la liste des évêchés russes de la *Notitia* de l'*Atheniensis* n⁰ 1371 n'a pu être rédigée après 1165, date à laquelle l'évêque de Novgorod fut élevé au rang de prôtothrone ([1]).

2. L'ÉVÊCHÉ DE BIELGOROD

La plus ancienne mention confirmant l'existence de l'évêché de Bielgorod est contenue dans la note sur le transfert des reliques· de Boris et de Gleb dans une nouvelle église, le 20 mai 1072 ; ce document a été rédigé peu de temps après, entre 1073 et 1076, et cite l'évêque de Bielgorod, Nicétas ([2]). En 1088 et 1089, c'est Lucas qui occupe le siège de Bielgorod. Dans la liste des hiérarques participant à la dédicace de l'église de l'archange Michel, puis de l'église des Cryptes de la Dormition de la Vierge, il est cité juste après

---

(1) GOLUBINSKIJ, *op. cit.*, I-1, pp. 443-444. Il se trompe cependant en pensant que ce genre d'archevêché titulaire était inconnu dans l'église byzantine. L'évêché de Rhizaion en est un exemple. Le chrysobulle de Romain Lécapène (921-924) confirme le décret synodal selon lequel Rhizaion obtenait le rang d'archevêché, mais demeurait évêché suffragant du métropolite de Néocésarée. Les droits de Néocésarée ont été également confirmés, au XIᵉ siècle, par les patriarches Michel Cérulaire et Nicolas III, visiblement à la suite du litige. Cf. F. DÖLGER, *Regesten der Kaiserurkunden des oströmischen Reiches*, n⁰ 594 ; V. GRUMEL, *Les Regestes des Actes du Patriarcat de Constantinople*, n⁰ 333, 687, 879c. Cf. E. HERMAN, *Appunti sul diritto metropolitano nella Chiesa bizantina*, Orientalia Christiana Periodica, t. XIII, 1937, p. 539 ; A. MICHEL, *Die Kaisermacht in der Ostkirche* (843-1204), Darmstadt, 1959, pp. 18, 25.
(2) D. I. ABRAMOVIČ, *Žitia sviatyh mučenikov Borisa i Gleba* (La vie des saints martyrs Boris et Gleb), Petrograd, 1916, p. 56. Cf. POPPE, *Remarques sur la période la plus ancienne de l'histoire de l'Église en Russie*, III, (en polonais), dans *Przegląd Historyczny*, LVI, 1965, pp. 560-564.

Jean, le métropolite de Kiev, ce qui semble confirmer ses fonctions de prôtothrone de la métropole.

C'est peut-être la raison pour laquelle sa nécrologie a été gravée (en *graffito*) à Sainte-Sophie de Kiev. Le fait que ce *graffito* se trouve dans la galerie sud de la chapelle des saints Apôtres apparaîtra significatif, si l'on considère que le cathédrale de Bielgorod est placée sous le même vocable (¹). Les témoignages directs nous permettent simplement de déduire que l'évêché de Bielgorod a été fondé avant 1072. Les données indirectes nous incitent à faire remonter cette fondation plus haut et à considérer comme judicieuse l'idée du chroniqueur du xvie siècle (chronique nikonienne). L'évêché de Bielgorod est l'un des plus anciens qui aient été fondés sous le règne de Vladimir, et ceci peut être prouvé notamment par le fait que l'évêque de la ville était jusqu'en 1165 prôtothrone de la métropole. Bielgorod, situé sur le fleuve Irpen, à 25 km au sud-ouest de Kiev, l'une des résidences du souverain, forteresse aux portes de la capitale, était l'une des grandes villes de la Russie. La ville fortifiée — le *castrum* — s'étendait sur plus de 70 hectares, ce qui faisait d'elle un grand centre défensif de l'importance de Kiev (100 ha), de Perejaslav (plus de 60 ha), de Vladimir-Volhynsk (66 ha), de Riazan' (48 ha), et des capitales d'autres principautés. La datation archéologique des remparts — du xe et du xie siècle — concorde avec les données fournies par le *Récit des temps passés* : « En 6499, Vladimir fonda le *castrum* de Bielgorod, y installa des gens d'autres *castra*, et il en fit venir beaucoup, car il aimait cette ville » (²). On peut déduire de son étude que Bielgorod comptait de sept à dix mille habitants. L'extension impressionnante de ce centre s'explique en partie par les fonctions militaires qu'il remplissait aux portes de la capitale. En étroite association avec Kiev, la capitale, il ne joua aucun rôle politique indépendant jusqu'au xiie

(1) *PSRL*, vol. II, col. 199 ; S.A. Vysockij, *Drevnerusskie nadpisi Sofii Kievskoï* XI-XV vv., Kiev, 1966, pp. 45-46, tab. XIII-XIV. Cf. Poppe, *Państwo* ..., pp. 159-160.

(2) *PSRL*, vol. I, p. 122. Cf. P. A. Rappoport, *Očerki po istorii russkogo vojennogo zodčestva XI-XIII vv.* (Études sur l'histoire de la construction militaire russe aux xie-xiiie siècles), Moscou-Leningrad, 1956, pp. 54, 73-82 ; du même auteur, *Vojennoje zodčestvo zapadnoï Rusi* (La construction militaire de la Russie occidentale), Leningrad, 1967, pp. 187-190.

174

siècle. Vladimir Ier en fit, en quelque sorte, sa seconde capitale et c'est ainsi qu'on le considérait au tournant du xie et du xiie siècle. C'est donc parce qu'il était résidence princière que Bielgorod devint résidence épiscopale. L'évêque de Bielgorod, par conséquent, était, en quelque sorte, un *episcopus curialis*, comme l'a si justement fait remarquer E. Golubinskij, et c'est sans aucun doute la raison pour laquelle il devint prôtothrone de la métropole.

3. L'ÉVÊCHÉ DE NOVGOROD

Par contre, le centre le plus important après Kiev dut se contenter, du point de vue ecclésiastique, de la modeste position de second évêché-suffragant de la métropole. Pour le xie siècle, nous avons, concernant le siège épiscopal de Novgorod, des renseignements qui sont relativement moins incomplets, grâce aux annales que la curie du lieu tenait depuis la cinquième décennie du xie siècle. Bien qu'elles aient été conservées dans des recueils de chroniques postérieures qui ont parfois été interpolées, leur authenticité et, en particulier, la liste des évêques de Novgorod ne suscitent pas, en principe, de réserves ([1]). La notice du *Récit des temps passés* pour l'année 1036 évoquant la nomination de Lucas Jidiata à la dignité d'évêque de Novgorod, même si elle ne provient pas d'annales contemporaines, est due à la plume de Nikon, son contemporain, qui fut, dans les années 1078-1088, higoumène du monastère des Cryptes. Lucas Jidiata est connu également par le conflit qui l'opposa au métropolite Ephrem, vers 1055, et par un sermon qui nous est parvenu. Il est mort de 15 octobre 1060 (1059?) ([2]). Au xie siècle lui ont succédé tour à tour au siège épiscopal : Étienne

---

(1) En ce qui concerne les annales de Novgorod du xie siècle, voir A. A. ŠAHMATOV, *Razykanija o drevnejših russkih letopisnyh svodah* (Recherches sur les compilations d'annales russes les plus anciennes), S Pb., 1908, pp. 495 sqq, et A. POPPE, en polonais, dans *Lexicon Antiquitatum Slavicarum*, III-1, 1967, pp. 27-28.

(2) *PSRL*, I, col. 150, *Novgorodskaja pervaja letopis' mladšego i staršego izvodov* (Première chronique de Novgorod dans les rédactions récente et ancienne), éd. par A. Nasonov, Moscou, 1950, p. 181, *PSRL*, vol. IV-1-1, p. 114, vol. V-1, p. 131. Cf. ŠAHMATOV, *Razyskanija ...*, pp. 623-627.

(1061-1068), Théodore (décédé en 1077), Germain, élu en 1078, et Nicétas, élu avant 1096 et mort le 31 janvier 1109. La détermination de la durée de leur épiscopat est le résultat de calculs faits à une époque postérieure.

Les annales du XIe siècle de la curie de Novgorod ont permis par la suite à un érudit vivant au plus tôt à la fin du XIIe siècle, à l'époque où l'on avait tendance à conférer rétrospectivement le titre d'archevêque aux prélats novgorodiens d'avant 1165, de calculer d'une manière assez précise la durée du sacerdoce épiscopal de Lucas-24 ans, d'Étienne-8 ans, de Théodore-9 ans. Quoi qu'il en soit, les données concernant les évêques de Novgorod sont, à partir de Lucas Jidiata, relativement complètes et en principe exactes, bien qu'on ne puisse pas toujours faire la distinction entre le témoignage des sources et la juste déduction du chroniqueur qui, par exemple, partant de la date de la mort d'un évêque, en déduisait celle de l'élection de son successeur, la fixant en général à l'année suivante. Cependant la vacance du siège durait parfois plus longtemps que ne le prévoyaient les canons. Ainsi, après la mort de Nicétas, le 30 janvier 1109, l'évêque Jean, qui lui succéda, arriva à Novgorod le 20 décembre 1110. Après la mort de Niphon, survenue le 21 avril 1156, le diocèse de Novgorod fut administré par Arcadius, élu par l'assemblée des habitants de la ville, et il ne fut sacré évêque qu'à la fin de l'année 1158 [1].

Lucas Jidiata, nommé évêque de Novgorod en 1036, avait eu comme prédécesseurs Joachim et Ephrem, mais les renseignements qui nous sont parvenus à leur sujet ne peuvent être acceptés que sous réserve. Une analyse minutieuse des informations qui nous ont été transmises aboutit à la conclusion qu'Ephrem a pu être le successeur de Joachim, mort en l'an 1030. Du texte, dans lequel le mot « évêque » n'est pas employé à propos d'Ephrem, le compilateur du XVIIe siècle déduisait que celui-ci n'avait pas été sacré évêque, mais qu'il avait seulement administré le diocèse. Il rapprochait ce fait de la pratique bien connue à Novgorod selon laquelle le chef de l'église de cette ville ayant obtenu l'investiture, pouvait administrer le diocèse pendant des années sans avoir été sacré par le métropolite [2].

---

(1) *Novgorodskaja pervaja letopis'* ..., p. 203, 216-217, cf. POPPE, *L'acte de fondation* ..., p. 69.

(2) Cf. POPPE, *Państwo* ..., pp. 161-163. L'essai par Priselkov

176

La durée de l'épiscopat de Joachim a été fixée à 42 ans, dans la liste de 1423, à la suite d'un calcul simple qui prend pour point de départ la date de la christianisation de la Russie, en 988/9, et de la conversion de Novgorod d'après les indications de la chronique novgorodienne, rédigée d'ailleurs à une époque postérieure [1]. Remarquons également que, dans des témoignages plus dignes de foi, cet évêque est simplement désigné sous le nom de Joachim. Ce n'est que dans les rédactions ultérieures que lui est attribuée la qualité de Chersonésien. Visiblement, on déduisait l'origine de Joachim du *Récit des temps passés* qui parle de la venue en Russie de « prêtres chersonésiens », sur l'invitation de Vladimir.

Si nous refusons de croire à l'instauration d'un évêché à Novgorod dans l'année du baptême du monarque de Kiev, nous n'avons aucune raison de mettre en doute la version selon laquelle cette cité, le second centre politique de la Russie, aurait reçu un évêque dès le règne de Vladimir Ier, probablement au cours des années qui suivirent l'adoption officielle du christianisme. Nous savons que Novgorod avait un évêque avant 1030, en la personne de Joachim, mais nous n'avons pas la certitude qu'il fut réellement le premier, comme le suggère la tradition novgorodienne. En effet, à Kiev, à la fin du xiie et au xiiie siècle, on ne savait plus très bien qui avait été à la tête de la métropole à l'aube de son existence. La cathédrale novgorodienne de Sainte-Sophie, en bois, aux treize coupoles, détruite par un incendie en 1049, qui était une réplique de l'archicathédrale de la Sagesse Divine construite en bois sous le règne de Vladimir Ier, prouve également que l'évêché de Novgorod a été fondé très tôt [2].

(*Očerki* ..., pp. 111-114) d'identifier Ephrem de Novgorod au protoproèdre Ephrem, métropolite de Russie dans les années cinquante du xie siècle, est fantaisiste.

(1) *Novgorodskaja pervaja letopis'* ..., pp. 159, 163, 473. Cf. *PSRL*, vol. IV-1-1, pp. 90, 113. Pour la datation des listes d'évêques de Novgorod, seules sont valables les indications fournies par V. L. Yanin, *Novgorodskije posadniki* (Les gouverneurs de Novgorod), Moscou, 1962, pp. 14-49.

(2) Cf. Poppe, *Państwo* ..., pp. 44-46.

4. LES ÉVÊCHÉS ET LES MÉTROPOLES DE ČERNIGOV ET DE PEREJASLAV.

Les évêchés de Černigov et de Perejaslav semblent remonter à la même date que ceux de Bielgorod et de Novgorod, mais les témoignages directs sont exceptionnellement pauvres. Des renseignements sur l'existence de sièges épiscopaux dans ces cités princières ne proviennent que de la septième et de la huitième décennie du XIᵉ siècle. M. D. Priselkov est enclin à fixer aux années 1066-1070 la fondation des deux évêchés, la reliant à des événements d'ordre intérieur (¹). C'est cependant aux années soixante qu'il faut fixer la date de la promotion de ces évêchés, qui passent de simples provinces de la métropole de Kiev au rang de métropoles titulaires ; il devait donc y avoir des sièges épiscopaux auparavant.

La construction de la monumentale cathédrale du Sauveur, entamée avant 1036 par Mstislav, prince de Černigov, prouve indirectement l'existence d'un évêché à Černigov dans la quatrième décennie du XIᵉ siècle (²). Il n'y a pas de raison de lier la construction d'une cathédrale en maçonnerie à l'érection d'un évêché à Černigov, qui était à ce moment politiquement indépendant. Vu la situation existant à l'époque dans le domaine ecclésiastique, la division politique de la Russie le long de la ligne du Dniepr entre les fils de Vladimir Iᵉʳ, Jaroslav et Mstislav, aurait eu pour conséquence la fondation d'une nouvelle métropole, si Mstislav n'était pas mort trop tôt sans laisser d'héritier, ce qui fit de Jaroslav le seul maître. Avant la construction de l'église du Sauveur, en maçonnerie, il devait probablement y avoir, comme dans de nombreuses autres cités — y compris Kiev et Novgorod —, une cathédrale en bois. Le fait que Černigov était l'un des grands centres de la Russie, connu à Byzance au Xᵉ siècle (à preuve les traités byzantino-russes et le témoignage de Constantin Porphyrogénète), renforce la thèse selon laquelle on y aurait créé un siège épiscopal sous le règne de Vladimir Iᵉʳ, peu de temps après la fondation d'une organisation ecclésiastique. Il devait y avoir là une importante communauté chrétienne, tout

---

(1) PRISELKOV, *Očerki* ..., p. 116 sqq.
(2) *PSRL*, vol. I, col. 150. K. N. AFANASJEV, *Postrojenie arhitekturnoĭ formy drevnerusskimi zodčimi* (La construction des formes architecturales par les architectes vieux-russes), Moscou, 1961, pp. 52-56, 250-251.

comme à Kiev, bien avant l'adoption officielle de la religion chrétienne.

La situation était semblable à Perejaslav dès le xe siècle, mais les débuts de l'organisation ecclésiastique de la cité sont encore moins bien connus : la confusion est d'autant plus grande qu les idées de certains historiens sur l'existence du premier siège de la métropole russe dans cette cité, de la fin du xe siècle à 1037, se sont avérées dénuées de fondements (1). Le rôle ecclésiastique de Perejaslav dans les dernières décennies du xie siècle est considérable : la juridiction de l'évêque s'étend sur d'immenses territoires englobant, outre la province de Perejaslav, celles de Smolensk et de Souzdal. Mais dès la première moitié du xiie siècle, le territoire du diocèse se rétrécit notablement. Dans la *Notitia* du manuscrit d'Athènes n° 1371, approximativement de l'année 1170, Perejaslav ne figure qu'à la sixième place, après l'évêché de Vladimir-Volhynsk érigé bien plus tard. Ce recul doit être mis en relation, à notre avis, avec le déclin de l'influence politique de Perejaslav, qui est sensible dès la cinquième décennie du xiie siècle (2).

La cathédrale, en maçonnerie, de l'archange Michel, consacrée en 1089/90, fut bâtie à Perejaslav aux frais d'Ephrem, métropolite de la ville. Elle avait été précédée par une église (en bois?) placée sous le même vocable. C'est la conclusion que l'on tire de la fondation en 1070, à Kiev, par le prince Vsevolod de Perejaslav, de l'église Saint-Michel dans son couvent à Vydoubitchi. Le lien de ce monastère avec le siège épiscopal de Perejaslav est nettement discernable dans la coutume, attestée sous Vladimir Monomaque, fils de Vsevolod, de placer sur ce siège les higoumènes de Vydoubitchi (3). Étant donné que Vsevolod portait le prénom chrétien d'André, on peut expliquer le vocable sous lequel était placée

(1) Voir L. Müller, *Zum Problem des hierarchischen Status u. der jurisdiktionellen Abhängigkeit der russischen Kirche vor 1039*, Köln-Braunsfeld, 1959, p. 22 sqq. ; Poppe, *Les métropoles russes du patriarcat de Constantinople au XIe siècle* (en russe), dans *Vizantijskij Vremennik*, 28, 1968, p. 97 sqq.

(2) V. G. Laskoronskij, *Istoria perejaslavskoï zemli s drevnejšyh vremen do poloviny XIII stoletia* (Histoire de la terre de Perejaslav depuis les temps les plus reculés jusqu'au milieu du xiiie siècle), Kiev, 1897, p. 111 sqq. Hruševskyj, *op. cit.*, t. II, p. 340 sqq.

(3) *PSRL*, vol. I, coll. 174, 207, 281, 291.

la fondation de Vydoubitchi par le fait que l'Archange Michel était déjà le patron de la principauté de Perejaslav, c'est-à-dire que la principale église de Perejaslav était placée dès avant l'année 1070 sous l'invocation du prince des archanges combattants. La chapelle et la série de fresques de Sainte-Sophie de Kiev qui lui sont dédiées témoignent du culte de Saint-Michel en Russie sous le règne de Jaroslav le Sage. L'archicathédrale, comme on le sait, fut construite sur le lieu où une bataille victorieuse avait été livrée, en 1036, contre les Petchénègues. Le culte de Saint Michel, patron des chevaliers luttant contre les infidèles, particulièrement répandu à cette époque à Byzance, avait été également introduit de bonne heure en Russie (¹).

Le choix d'un patron valeureux pour la marche de Perejaslav qui, au sud et à l'est, s'étendait dans les steppes et qui était constamment exposée aux incursions des nomades dont elle protégeait la Russie, s'imposait de lui-même. Perejaslav avait sûrement son propre évêque à l'époque de Jaroslav ; il l'avait obtenu au plus tard au début de la sixième décennie du XIᵉ siècle, lorsque la ville devint la capitale du domaine du prince Vsevolod, marié à une fille de Constantin IX Monomaque. Rien n'interdit de penser que l'évêché avait déjà été érigé par Vladimir Iᵉʳ. La légende que rapporte le *Récit des temps passés* à propos de la fondation de Perejaslav sur le théâtre même de la bataille victorieuse de 992 contre les Petchénègues, tire son origine des luttes contre les nomades, qui se sont réellement déroulées dans cette région. Pour affirmer son succès, Vladimir construisit un puissant *castrum*, constituant l'un des éléments d'un système défensif bien organisé. Le monarque fraîchement converti se devait d'y édifier une église à laquelle, dans cette marche avancée, convenait tout particulière-

---

(1) Cf. *PSRL*, vol. II, col. 269. V. Lazarev, *Mozaiki Sofii Kijevskoï* (Les mosaïques de Sainte-Sophie de Kiev), Moscou, 1960, pp. 52-54. Laskoronskij, *op. cit.*, p. 86 sq. Hruševskyj, *op. cit.*, t. II, p. 339 sq, 526 sq. M. N. Tihomirov, *Drevnerusskie goroda* (Les anciennes villes russes), Moscou, 1956, pp. 308 sqq., Rappoport, *Očerki ...*, pp. 82-87, 167 sqq. Ainsi, par exemple, à Vasilev, où, comme le déclare le *Récit des temps passés* pour l'année 996, il eut à en découdre avec les Petchénègues le jour de la Transfiguration ; il fit ensuite construire une église placée sous cette invocation. Cf. *PSRL*, vol. I, col. 125.

ment le nom de l'archistratège des forces célestes, victorieuses dans le combat contre les infidèles.

La fondation des métropoles titulaires de Černigov et de Perejaslav constitue dans l'histoire de ces deux évêchés un épisode particulier, de courte durée, déterminé par une conjoncture politique (1). L'existence d'une métropole à Perejaslav dans les années soixante-dix et quatre-vingt du xiᵉ siècle est attestée par les témoignages dignes de foi de Nestor l'hagiographe dans la *Vie de Théodose des Cryptes*, écrite entre 1079 et 1088, et par le *Récit des temps passés* pour l'année 1089/90, ainsi que par le traité grec sur les azymes de « Léon, métropolite de Perejaslav en Russie », de la seconde moitié du xiᵉ siècle. Ephrem, le dernier évêque de Perejaslav à porter le titre de métropolite, sacré en 1077/1078, exerçait encore ses fonctions en 1096, mais en 1101 le diocèse était dirigé par l'évêque Simon. Le métropolite Léon a pu être le prédécesseur d'Ephrem et le successeur de Pierre qui dirigeait l'évêché de Perejaslav en 1072. Il a pu être aussi le prédécesseur de l'évêque Pierre, comme le prouveraient les données concernant la métropole de Černigov.

L'existence de la métropole de Černigov est attestée par deux témoignages. La *Notitia episcopatuum* (*Ordo thronorum*) du patriarcat de Constantinople, dans le *Codex Coislinianus* nᵒ 211, rédigée vers 1084, énumère à la 72ᵉ place la métropole ὁ Μαυροκάστρου ἤτοι νέας Ῥωσίας. Si l'on prend en considération la date d'érection des métropoles de Basilaion et de Dristra, énumérées à la 70ᵉ et à la 71ᵉ place, et de Nazianze, à la 73ᵉ place, la fondation de la métropole de Maurokastron daterait de la période 1059-1071. Le fait que la *Notitia episcopatuum* ait placé géographiquement Maurokastron en Russie prouve que le nom grec n'est pas le toponyme original, mais sa traduction. Cette cité devait avoir un rôle politique et administratif qui justifiait sa promotion ecclésiastique. Tous ces éléments mènent à la conclusion que la cité qui se cache sous le nom de Maurokastron dans la source byzantine, ne peut être que Černigov, dont l'étymologie vient de *čern*, « noir ». Dès lors, l'addi-

---

(1) Pour plus de détails, voir A. POPPE, *Les métropoles russes...*, dans *Vizantijskij Vremennik*, vol. 28, 1968, pp. 85-108, vol. 29, 1968, pp. 95-104, et du même auteur, *Le traité des azymes Λέοντος μητροπολίτου τῆς ἐν Ῥωσίᾳ Πρεσθλάβας : quand, où et par qui a-t-il été écrit*, dans *Byzantion*, t. XXXV, 1965, pp. 504-527.

tion ἤτοι νέας ʿΡωσίας prend toute sa signification. Pour l'auteur
de la *Notitia*, qui avait placé plus haut, à la 60ᵉ place, la métropole
ʿΡωσίας, celle qui avait été fondée à Maurokastron, c'est-à-dire à
Černigov, était la métropole, non pas de la Russie tout court, mais
de la « nouvelle Russie ».

Un deuxième témoignage est fourni par la description de la
translation solennelle des cendres de Boris et Gleb, le 20 mai 1072,
qui constitue une partie intégrante de l'ouvrage hagiographique
intitulé *Récit du martyre et des miracles des SS. Boris et Gleb*, écrit
avant 1076, probablement en 1073. Parmi les personnes assistant
à la translation, le *Récit* nomme deux métropolites : « Et se réuni-
rent ... le métropolite Georges de Kiev, le second, Néophyte de
Černigov, et les évêques ... ». Dans la suite de la description du
cortège apparaît le mot МИТΡОПОЛИТА au duel («les deux métropolites ») (¹), ce qui prouve une fois de plus que pour l'auteur de
la description des événements de 1072, la dignité ecclésiastique
de Néophyte de Černigov était évidente. Ainsi donc, en 1072, Černigov
possédait sa propre métropole dont la fondation, d'après le témoignage de la *Notitia Coislin*. 211, remonte aux années soixante du
XIᵉ siècle.

C'est probablement à la même époque que l'évêque de Perejaslav obtint son titre honorifique. Ce qui n'est pas en contradiction
avec le fait qu'en 1072, Pierre, évêque de Perejaslav, ne le possédait
pas encore. Vu le caractère titulaire de la métropole, l'évêque
Pierre a pu ne pas obtenir le titre de son prédécesseur, ou bien
il ne l'avait pas encore lorsqu'il participa aux cérémonies de Vychgorod, le 20 mai 1072. Si l'on tient compte des rapports entre
les fils de Jaroslav, il est difficile de comprendre pourquoi, à Constantinople, on aurait eu des égards particuliers pour Sviatoslav, en
accréditant un métropolite à sa cour de Černigov, tout en ignorant
Vsevolod de Perejaslav, qui, beau-fils de l'empereur Constantin IX
Monomaque, était apparenté aux grandes familles aristocratiques
byzantines. L'absence de Perejaslav dans l'*Ordo thronorum* ne
prouve rien. On connaît des cas de diocèses qui ont existé très
peu de temps et qui ne figurent dans aucune des *Notitiae*.

Les métropoles de Černigov et de Perejaslav étaient titulaires,

(1) ABRAMOVIČ, *Žitia* ..., pp. 55-56, cf. POPPE, *Remarques* ...,
III, pp. 560-563.

donc provisoires. L'institution de la métropole titulaire consistait en ceci : un évêque était élevé à la dignité de métropolite à titre personnel, à vie ou pour une période déterminée, puis cette métropole, qui ne disposait pas de suffragants, redevenait un évêché suffragant de la métropole à laquelle il était soumis auparavant. La position d'une métropole titulaire était proche du statut juridique des archevêchés autocéphales. Ceux-ci non plus ne possédaient pas de suffragants et étaient soumis au patriarche. L'élévation, par l'empereur byzantin, des évêques au rang honorifique de métropolites — élévation qui les libérait, à vie ou pour une période donnée, de la juridiction du métropolite de la province-mère — se produisit assez souvent dans l'Empire au, XIe siècle, et, en particulier, précisément dans les années cinquante — soixante-dix.

La promotion ecclésiastique de Černigov et de Perejaslav avait sans conteste un caractère politique. Après la mort de Jaroslav le Sage, en 1054, un accord s'était institué en Russie, qui incluait d'une part le prince de Kiev, Iziaslav, fils aîné de Jaroslav, et d'autre part ses deux frères, Sviatoslav, prince de Černigov, et Vsevolod, prince de Perejaslav. Les décisions prises par eux en commun, concernant la guerre, la législation, les nominations aux autres trônes princiers, permettent de parler à juste titre d'un accord entre les trois fils de Jaroslav, accord que l'historiographie a qualifié à juste titre de triumvirat. Cet équilibre des forces appelait un équivalent dans le domaine de l'organisation ecclésiastique. La cour de Byzance tenait à avoir des relations amicales avec les princes russes, dans une période difficile, où il fallait faire face, à la fois, à l'absence de stabilité intérieure et aux poussées extérieures venant notamment des Petchénègues et des Turcs-Ouzes. La création de nouvelles métropoles remplissant du point de vue politique le rôle, en quelque sorte, d'ambassades byzantines, facilitait le contact direct avec des princes dont dépendait, dans une mesure égale, la politique de l'État russe.

La fondation de nouvelles métropoles a pu avoir lieu, par exemple, après les événements de 1060, lorsque les trois fils de Jaroslav infligèrent une défaite écrasante aux Turcs-Ouzes qui menaçaient également Byzance. A cette même époque, les Coumans commencèrent à menacer les possessions byzantines en Crimée. A Byzance, les succès de la Russie durent faire comprendre l'importance qu'avait l'action militaire russe pour affaiblir la pression des nomades sur les frontières nord ed l'Empire. C'est pourquoi il faut inscrire au compte de Byzance l'initiative diplomatique visant à promouvoir les évêchés de Černigov et de Perejaslav.

Les deux métropoles étaient nées d'une situation politique déterminée, et elles cessèrent d'exister lorsque celle-ci fut modifiée. La mort d'Ephrem vers 1100 entraîna la disparition du titre même de la métropole de Perejaslav. On ne peut pas non plus exclure qu'Ephrem perdit son titre de son vivant, puisque les titres étaient décernés soit à vie, soit pour une période déterminée. Mais en se basant uniquement sur le fait que le *Récit des temps passés*, pour l'année 1089, donne à Ephrem le titre de métropolite, et que, pour l'année 1091, il ne l'appelle plus qu'évêque, il serait difficile de conclure qu'entre-temps le maître du siège de Perejaslav avait perdu le droit de porter son titre honorifique. La mort du métropolite Néophyte amena la suppression de la métropole de Černigov. Son successeur, l'évêque Jean, fut intronisé avant 1088.

Le retour des sièges au statut de simples évêchés était conforme à la résolution du Synode permanent, demandant le respect de l'ancien principe de suppression des métropoles titulaires dès la mort des titulaires — résolution soumise, en 1084, à l'empereur Alexis Comnène par le patriarche Nicolas III Grammaticos. Une solution de compromis prévoyait que seuls demeureraient métropoles les diocèses qui possédaient ce privilège depuis plus de trente ans (¹).

Après 1078, Vsevolod étant devenu autocrate de la Russie, le maintien des deux métropoles titulaires n'avait plus de raison d'être. La position du prince, qui n'était pas intéressé au maintien de métropoles reflétant un rapport de forces qui avait cessé d'exister à la suite de la mort de ses frères, était partagée, pour d'autres motifs, par le métropolite de Kiev. La querelle qui se déroulait entre le métropolite d'Ancyre et son ancien suffragant de Basilaion prouvait quelle dangereuse concurrente pouvait être une métropole titulaire qui n'avait pas été supprimée à temps. Fort de l'appui

---

(1) Cf. GRUMEL, *Les Regestes* ..., nᵒˢ 934, 938, 943 ; DÖLGER, *Regesten* ..., nᵒˢ 1014, 1108, 1117, 1135, 1140. SOKOLOV, *op. cit.*, pp. 26-30 ; MICHEL, *op. cit.*, p. 24 sqq. ; BECK, *op. cit.*, p. 162. J. DARROUZÈS, *Documents inédits d'ecclésiologie byzantine*, Paris, 1966, pp. 37-53 ; et pp. 176-265 cf. le traité du métropolite d'Ancyre Nicétas défendant ses droits hiérarchiques à l'égard de son ancien suffragant, le métropolite titulaire de Basilaion.

184

du maître de la Russie tout entière, le métropolite Jean II, sur la base des décisions du synode des années 1084-1087, put prendre des mesures sauvegardant ses droits. La nomination à Černigov, à la place du métropolite Néophyte, d'un simple évêque souligna le caractère provisoire d'un titre attaché à une personne et non au siège épiscopal. Ce précédent fixa en même temps le sort de la métropole de Perejaslav. Après l'extinction de ces deux métropoles titulaires éphémères, la juridiction de la métropole de Kiev s'étendit de nouveau, à la fin du xie siècle, à l'ensemble de la Russie.

5. L'ÉVÊCHÉ DE POLOTSK

Le plus ancien témoignage de l'existence de l'évêché de Polotsk, est une notice attestant que Mina fut sacré évêque de cette ville le 13 décembre 1105. Nous possédons également une notice sur sa mort, survenue le 20 juin 1116, et une autre du début du xiiie siècle, mais fondée sur une tradition digne de foi et qui nous apprend qu'il était sorti du monastère des Cryptes de Kiev [1]. D. Priselkov serait d'avis que l'année 1105 est celle de la fondation de l'évêché, estimant que c'est à ce moment que furent couronnés de succès les efforts des princes de Polotsk tendant à avoir leur propre évêché [2]. Bien que l'on ne puisse pas admettre comme authentique la tradition postérieure liant la fondation de l'évêché de Polotsk à l'activité de christianisation de Vladimir Ier, l'opinion de Priselkov suscite des doutes, car il veut tirer trop d'un témoignage fortuit.

La mention du sacre de Mina, évêque de Polotsk, fait partie, dans le *Récit des temps passés*, d'une notice qui mentionne également le sacre d'Amphiloque, évêque de Vladimir, le 27 août 1105, et de Lazare, évêque de Perejaslav, le 12 novembre 1105. Dans ces deux cités, les sièges épiscopaux existaient déjà, ce qui explique la concision de l'information également dans le troisième cas : « le métropolite ... a consacré Mina évêque de Polotsk », qui manifestement ne se différenciait pas des deux autres. Le fait qu'en trois mois et demi, on ait procédé au sacre de trois évêques s'explique

(1) *PSRL*, vol. I, coll. 281, 291, *Das Paterikon des Kiever Höhlenklosters*, Munich, 1964, (rééd. 1930), p. 103.
(2) PRISELKOV, *Očerki* ..., pp. 118-119, 315-316.

facilement à la lumière d'une notice concernant l'arrivée à Kiev, en décembre 1104, du métropolite Nicéphore. Il est compréhensible que le nouveau chef de l'Église russe ait cherché en premier lieu, en accord avec les princes, à mettre un terme à la vacance des sièges épiscopaux. Celle-ci n'a pas dû être bien longue, puisque son prédécesseur, le métropolite Nicolas, exerçait encore ses fonctions en 1101 et qu'il est mort probablement en 1103 ou, au plus tard, au début de l'année 1104. A Perejaslav, Simon était évêque après Ephrem, qui vivait encore en 1096, et avant Lazare, consacré en 1105. Nous ne savons pas ce qui se passe au siège épiscopal de Vladimir-Volhynsk après la mort de l'évêque Étienne, le 26 août 1094, mais il n'y a aucune raison de croire que le siège fut vacant pendant 11 ans. Les indications données à ce propos par le *Récit des temps passés* ne sont pas complètes, et c'est l'intérêt que manifestait le chroniqueur, non pour les sièges épiscopaux, mais pour la personne des évêques attachés au monastère des Cryptes et de Vydoubitchi, qui lui a fait insérer les indications qui s'y trouvent. Les données annalistiques sur l'évêché de Polotsk au xiie siècle sont également prises au hasard et fragmentaires ([1]).

L'érection de l'évêché de Polotsk dans la situation créée par la mort de Vseslav, prince de Polotsk, en avril 1101, semble peu probable. La principauté de Polotsk, partagée entre ses 7 (?) fils qui ne s'accordaient pas entre eux, ne constituait plus une entité politique. Le prince de Minsk, Gleb Vseslavitch, était en conflit avec les princes du sud de la Russie, et, en particulier, avec le prince Sviatopolk II, prince de Kiev, et avec Vladimir Monomaque, prince de Perejaslav. La tension des relations amena une expédition contre Minsk en 1104, à laquelle participa également David Vseslavitch, s'opposant à son frère ([2]). Il est difficile de

---

(1) Cf. Golubinskij, *op. cit.*, I-1, pp. 287, 682. Il y a aussi un malentendu dans les ouvrages plus récents, qui, reprennent l'indication erronée de V. N. Tatiščev, l'historien du xviiie siècle (*Istoria rossijskaja* (Histoire russe), t. II, Moscou-Léningrad, 1963, p. 109) : celui-ci prétendait qu'en 1097, l'évêque de Polotsk fut nommé métropolite.

(2) Cf. V. E. Danilevič, *Očerki istorii Polotskoĭ zemli* (Essai sur l'histoire de la terre de Polotsk), Kiev, 1896, pp. 70-75. L. V. Aleksejev, *Polotskaĭa zemla* (La terre de Polotsk), Moscou, 1966, pp. 251-257.

186

supposer que le prince de Kiev ait voulu, dans cette période précisément, appuyer la réalisation de plans ecclésiastiques pour lesquels, auparavant, lui et ses prédécesseurs auraient refusé leur accord à Vseslav. Enfin, dans cette situation, ce genre d'initiative soulignant l'unité de la terre de Polotsk n'aurait pu convenir aux fils de Vseslav, occupés justement à la partager. Gleb, prince de Minsk, particulièrement actif, jouissant du soutien du clergé, aurait pu demander à avoir son propre évêché. Étant donné que le diocèse de Polotsk englobait, comme nous le savons grâce aux données des XIIᵉ-XIVᵉ siècles, toutes les terres appartenant, au XIᵉ siècle, à la principauté de Polotsk, il faut en déduire que l'évêché de Polotsk a été érigé à une époque où la principauté constituait un organisme politique unifié, vivant en harmonie avec Kiev.

Polotsk occupait une position politique toute particulière parmi les autres terres russes. Vladimir Iᵉʳ y avait établi Iziaslav, son fils aîné, ou peut-être le second de ses fils, qui mourut en 1001 du vivant de son père, privant ainsi ses autres descendants de leurs droits au trône de Kiev. Après 1036, deux lignées princières : le fils de Vladimir Iᵉʳ, Jaroslav, prince de Kiev, et le petit-fils de Vladimir, Briatcheslav Iziaslavovitch, à Polotsk, détenaient le pouvoir en Russie. Alors que toutes les terres russes passent, après 1054, aux mains des descendants de Jaroslav, Polotsk est toujours le domaine de la même dynastie princière. En 1044, Briatcheslav meurt et le trône de Polotsk échoit pour plusieurs dizaines d'années à son fils Vseslav. Ce que nous savons de lui, nous le devons à l'intérêt amical que lui portait le monastère des Cryptes. En 1060, Vseslav participa avec les trois fils de Jaroslav à une expédition contre les Turcs-Ouzes, mais, dès 1065, il déclenchait une action militaire visant à s'emparer de Novgorod, but qu'au début des années vingt s'était déjà fixé son père, qui fut vaincu par Jaroslav. Au cours de la sanglante bataille de la Nemiga, le 3 mars 1067, les fils de Jaroslav réussirent à répéter le succès de leur père, bien que les querelles et les combats se soient poursuivis jusqu'aux années soixante-dix et quatre-vingts (¹). Au cours de ces

---

(1) *PSRL*, vol. I, coll. 146, 155, 163-167, 171-174, 182, 248, 274. D. Leopardov, *Le prince Vseslav de Polotsk et son temps* (en russe), dans *Polotsko-Vitebskaïa Starina*, t. II-III, Vitebsk, 1911-1912, pp. 121-216, 85-180. Aleksejev, *Polotskaïa zemla ...*, p. 240 sqq.

nombreuses années d'inimitié, on assista également à des tentatives de rapprochement, comme, par exemple, lors de l'accord entre Vseslav et Iziaslav, prince de Kiev, accord qui, en 1073, coûta son trône à ce dernier. Les deux familles princières s'allièrent un peu plus tard ; en effet, le fils de Vseslav, Gleb, prince de Minsk, épousa Anastasie, la fille de Jaropolk Iziaslavovitch. Ce mariage pouvait favoriser l'établissement de rapports plus pacifiques entre Vseslav et le frère de Jaropolk, Sviatopolk II, prince de Kiev depuis 1093.

La situation qui vient d'être esquissée, bien qu'elle n'éclaire pas les débuts de l'évêché de Polotsk, permet de comprendre pourquoi l'évêque de cette cité, nommé en 1105, sortait du couvent des Cryptes. La nomination d'un évêque à Polotsk, même au cours du démembrement politique de la principauté, dépendait de l'acceptation de sa candidature par les forces locales, non seulement par les princes, mais aussi par les grands et le clergé. Cette coutume devait exister, à plus forte raison, à l'époque de Vseslav ; c'est pourquoi la dépendance de son évêque, du point de vue de la juridiction, du métropolite de Kiev, pouvait, pour lui, être acceptable. Un candidat venant d'un monastère étroitement lié à la famille princière de Polotsk donnait sans conteste des garanties d'impartialité. Les bons rapports avec le couvent des Cryptes ne datent pas de la nomination de Mina, en 1105, et ne résultent pas de la générosité de Gleb Vseslavitch pour le couvent, où il construisit un réfectoire en 1108 ; ils remontent à l'époque où vivait Vseslav, comme l'atteste nettement le portrait très favorable qu'a tracé de ce prince, avant 1101, un chroniqueur du couvent des Cryptes. L'adoption du culte des frères de son grand-père, alors canonisés, les princes Boris-Romain et Gleb-David, témoigne des rapports étroits de Vseslav avec le clergé et de la dévotion de ce prince. Ce n'est pas par hasard que les quatre fils de Vseslav portaient les prénoms princiers et chrétiens de leurs saints ancêtres. A cette époque et au XIIe siècle encore, les princes n'utilisaient que rarement les prénoms chrétiens dans la vie quotidienne. Les prénoms des fils de Vseslav éclairent d'une part le degré de christianisation de la cour du prince de Polotsk et, d'autre part, les contacts étroits avec les milieux ecclésiastiques de Kiev qui avaient lancé le culte de Boris et de Gleb ([1]).

(1) Cf. A. Poppe, *Le Récit sur le martyre et les miracles des SS. Boris et Gleb* (le problème de l'attribution), en polonais, dans *Slavia Orientalis*, XVIII, 1969, pp. 367-376.

L'église en maçonnerie de la Sagesse Divine, construite à Polotsk, témoigne encore mieux que sa dévotion du fait que Vseslav menait une politique ecclésiastique bien déterminée. L'église Sainte-Sophie de Polotsk, par sa technique et son architecture, est à ranger parmi les édifices du XIe siècle proches des cathédrales Sainte-Sophie de Kiev et de Novgorod. L'analyse des relations de modules a permis d'établir que c'est l'église Sainte-Sophie de Novgorod qui a servi de modèle aux architectes de Sainte-Sophie de Polotsk (1). Étant donné que la construction de Sainte-Sophie de Novgorod commença en 1045 et qu'elle fut achevée en 1050, il convient de dater la construction de l'église de la Sagesse Divine de Polotsk de la seconde moitié au XIe siècle, c'est-à-dire du règne de Vseslav, prince de Polotsk, mort en 1101. Une notice annalistique permet aussi indirectement de fixer une date approximative pour la construction de Sainte-Sophie de Polotsk : « en l'an 1066, Vseslav vint et s'empara de Novgorod ... et il prit les cloches de Sainte-Sophie. Oh ! cette heure fut un bien grand malheur, et il prit aussi les chandeliers à plusieurs branches qui étaient suspendus » (2). Ce pillage qui indigna tant les habitants de Novgorod était nécessaire à Vseslav pour décorer sa propre église de Sainte-Sophie. Le fondateur utilisa un procédé assez particulier, mais qui, à cette époque, n'avait rien d'extraordinaire. Plus de cent ans après, les princes archi-chrétiens de Vladimir et de Souzdal pillaient les églises de Kiev afin de pouvoir embellir aux moindres frais leurs propres fondations.

Le vocable sous lequel était placée l'église de la Sagesse Divine de Polotsk prend toute sa valeur si l'on considère que dans la Russie prémongole, en dehors d'elle, seules les cathédrales de Kiev et de Novgorod étaient ainsi dénommées. Ce fait révèle l'ambition de Polotsk d'être l'égal des deux principaux centres politiques de la Russie. Étant donné que les cathédrales en maçonnerie de Kiev et de Novgorod avaient succédé à des églises en bois placées sous le même vocable, il se peut que le cas fût identique pour la Sainte-Sophie en maçonnerie de Polotsk. Le fait même de la fondation

(1) AFANASJEV, *Postrojenie* ..., pp. 66-68, 197, 250-251. ALEK-SEJEV, *Polotskaïa zemla* ..., pp. 193-199.

(2) Cf. *Novgorodskaïa pervaïa letopis* ..., p. 17. Cf. ŠAHMATOV, *Razyskania* ..., pp. 627-628.

d'une cathédrale en maçonnerie par Vseslav prouve qu'un évêque résidait déjà à Polotsk au milieu du xiᵉ siècle. En était-il de même à l'époque du père de Vseslav, Briatcheslav, et de son grand-père Iziaslav ?

Dans la seconde moitié du xᵉ siècle, Polotsk n'était pas seulement l'une des principales cités des Slaves de l'Est ; elle représentait aussi, tout comme Kiev et Novgorod, une structure étatique autonome (¹). Ceci s'exprima à la fin du xᵉ siècle et au xiᵉ siècle par l'affermissement à Polotsk d'une lignée dynastique particulière, issue de Iziaslav, fils de Vladimir Iᵉʳ, et de Rogneda, fille de Rogwold, prince de Polotsk. Nos renseignements sur Sainte-Sophie de Polotsk nous ont permis de prouver l'existence d'un évêché dans cette cité dans les années cinquante-soixante du xiᵉ siècle, mais, vu le rôle de Polotsk, il nous semble qu'il faut approuver l'idée de E. Golubinskij qui attribue à Vladimir Iᵉʳ la fondation de l'évêché (²).

6. L'ÉVÊCHÉ DE VLADIMIR-VOLHYNSK

L'opinion générale des chercheurs est que Vladimir sur le Loug, en Volhynie, est devenu siège épiscopal dès la fin du xᵉ siècle, peu de temps après le baptême de Vladimir Iᵉʳ. Cette théorie basée sur la chronique nikonienne du xviᵉ siècle cherchait une confirmation indirecte dans le fait que la cité sur le Loug, édifiée ou agrandie par le seigneur qui lui avait donné son nom, devint de bonne heure la capitale d'un grand territoire entre le Horyn' et le Wieprz et celle de l'apanage de l'un des fils du prince (³). M. Priselkov était d'un autre avis : il a soutenu que l'évêché de Volhynie fut créé entre 1089 et 1091, à la suite d'efforts, qui durèrent plusieurs années, des princes de Vladimir-Volhynsk, Jaropolk Iziaslavovitch et, après sa mort en 1086, David Igorevitch (⁴).

La donnée de la chronique nikonienne ne saurait être considérée

---

(1) Cf. H. LOWMIANSKI, *La genèse de la terre de Polotsk* (en polonais), dans *Z polskich studiów slawistycznych*, III, Varsovie, 1968, pp. 7-24.

(2) GOLUBINSKIJ, *op. cit.*, I-1, pp. 334-335.

(3) Cf. V.S. IKONNIKOV, *Opyt russkoĭ istoriografii* (Essai sur l'historiographie russe), t. II, Kiev, 1908, p. 564 ; GOLUBINSKIJ, *op. cit.*, I-1, pp. 669-671.

(4) PRISELKOV, *Očerki ...*, pp. 154-156.

comme véridique ; elle ne constitue qu'un témoignage de la façon
dont on imaginait, au XVIe siècle, les débuts de l'organisation diocésaine de la Russie. Le fait même que le rôle de résidence du prince-
junior, exerçant son pouvoir de par la volonté du souverain de
Kiev, ait été dévolu à Vladimir-Volhynsk, ne signifie pas que
l'on y ait alors établi un siège épiscopal. Tourov, Rostov, Mourom,
qui étaient également des centres des apanages princiers, ne furent
pas non plus érigés dès le début en sièges épiscopaux. Vers la fin du
règne de Jaroslav le Sage, Vladimir-Volhynsk échut à l'un de ses fils
cadets, Igor, qui, après la mort de son frère Viatcheslav, en 1057, fut
transféré à Smolensk par décision de ses frères aînés. Cette cité reçut
un évêque quelques dizaines d'années plus tard. Ce n'est qu'à partir
de la fin du XIe siècle et surtout au XIIe siècle, au fur et à mesure
que progresse le démembrement du pays, que l'on voit régulière-
ment apparaître la résidence d'un prince de l'Église à côté d'une
cour princière.

L'opinion de Priselkov semble mieux étayée, bien que sa datation
demande à être vérifiée. Le plus ancien témoignage de l'existence
de l'évêché de Vladimir-Volhynsk n'est pas, comme le pensait
cet érudit, une information du *Récit des temps passés* sur la participation de l'évêque de Vladimir, Étienne, à la translation solennelle
des reliques de saint Théodose dans l'église des Cryptes, le 14 août
1091, mais bien la mention de la nomination d'Étienne au poste
d'évêque de Vladimir, contenue dans la *Vie de Théodose des Cryptes*,
écrite par Nestor, un peu avant 1088 ([1]). Il devient dès lors évident
qu'on ne peut dater *ex silentio* : l'absence parmi les hiérarques
participant, le 14 août 1089, à la consécration de l'église des Cryptes
de la Vierge, de l'évêque de Vladimir, n'autorise pas à conclure que
le diocèse de Volhynie a été fondé après cette date. Il n'est pas
non plus entièrement sûr qu'Étienne, sacré évêque de Vladimir
au plus tard en 1086-1087, ait été le premier pasteur du diocèse.
Seules des données indirectes semblent prouver que l'évêché avait
été fondé à une date récente.

(1) *Sbornik XII veka Moskovskogo Uspenskogo Sobora* (Recueil
du XIIe siècle de la cathédrale moscovite de la Dormition), éd. A.
Šahmatov et P. Lavrov, Moscou, 1899. Photomechan. Nachdruck
mit einer Einführung von D. Čiževskij, s'Gravenhage, 1957 (*Apophoreta Slavica*, 2), p. 63 ; A. POPPE, *Chronologie des œuvres de
l'hagiographe Nestor*, (en polonais), dans *Slavia Orientalis*, XIV,
Varsovie, 1965, pp. 292-297, 305.

La situation intérieure de la terre de Volhynie au milieu du xie siècle était indécise, les tendances centrifuges encore peu développées, les liens avec Kiev durables. C'est ce que prouvent, entre autres, la suppression par la triarchie des aînés de Jaroslavovitch, en 1057, du rôle autonome du centre princier de Vladimir sur le Loug et son incorporation au territoire soumis directement à Kiev et administré par le gouverneur du prince kiévien. Ce n'est qu'après la mort de son frère Iziaslav, survenue en octobre 1078, que Vsevolod, « s'étant emparé du pouvoir sur toute la Russie », décida d'installer son neveu Jaropolk à Vladimir, « en lui donnant en plus Tourov ». Cette union, artificielle, et d'ailleurs de brève durée, de deux terres distinctes, de Tourov-Pinsk et de Volhynie, répondait, comme on l'a fait remarquer judicieusement, aux intérêts centralisateurs du monarque kiévien. Par sa volonté, Jaropolk devint prince-gouverneur, bien qu'il ait eu l'ambition, comme l'ont prouvé les événements de 1085-1086, d'être un prince indépendant (¹). D'après le témoignage du moine des Cryptes, il était extrêmement pieux, sensible aux besoins de l'Église ; il prenait donc certainement au sérieux sa mission de prince chrétien. Le processus de christianisation des marches occidentales de la Russie de Kiev n'avait pas tellement de retard par rapport à la région du Dniepr, comme le prouve l'existence, dans les années soixante, du couvent de « la Montagne Sainte », fondé auparavant près de Vladimir-Volhynsk (²). Son nom même indique des liens génériques avec la congrégation du Mont Athos, *"Αγιον "Ορος*. Jaropolk, soucieux de la poursuite fructueuse de l'évangélisation des terres qui lui avaient été confiées, a pu, à Kiev, solliciter de Vsevolod et du métropolite Jean II Prodromos un évêque pour ses apanages situés jusqu'alors dans les limites du diocèse métropolitain. Jaropolk a pu voir encore ses efforts couronnés de succès. Étienne, sacré évêque de Vladimir, venait du couvent des Cryptes : après la mort de Théodose, en 1074, il était devenu higoumène ; chassé de son office après le 15 juillet

---

(1) *PSRL*, vol. I, coll. 204-207. Cf. A. N. Nasonov, *Russkaja zemla i obrazovane territorii drevnerusskogo gosudarstva*, (La terre russe et la formation du territoire de l'ancien État russe), Moscou, 1951, pp. 134-135. Poppe, *Państwo* ... pp. 176-178.

(2) V. la *Vie de Théodose des Cryptes*, dans : *Sbornik XII veka* ..., p. 62.

1077, au plus tard en 1078, il avait fondé le couvent de Notre-Dame des Blachernes sur le Klov, près de Kiev, d'où il fut élevé à la dignité d'évêque de Vladimir, probablement du vivant de Jaropolk, soit avant le 22 novembre 1086. Il est peu probable, en effet, que David Igorevitch, installé peu de temps après à Vladimir par Vsevolod de Kiev, également en tant que prince-gouverneur, ait pu obtenir d'emblée un évêque pour son domaine. Lorsque Nestor écrivait la *Vie de Théodose*, Étienne était déjà évêque : c'était au plus tard en 1087, car Nestor cite comme étant vivant Sophrone, higoumène de Vydoubitchi, et en 1088, c'est Lazare qui exerçait cette fonction (¹). Le fait que l'évêque Étienne, décédé le 27 avril 1094, fut enterré dans son couvent de Kiev semble également témoigner en faveur de l'érection à une date récente de l'évêché de Vladimir. Étienne n'était visiblement pas très attaché à son siège sur le Loug, mais considérait presque comme une mission les devoirs pastoraux qui lui avaient été confiés. Vladimir-Volhynsk ne disposait pas à l'époque d'une cathédrale en maçonnerie ; elle ne fut construite qu'au milieu du XIIᵉ siècle, sur l'emplacement d'une cathédrale en bois. Il convient de remarquer que la cathédrale des évêques de Vladimir était placée sous l'invocation de la Dormition de la Sainte Vierge, tout comme l'église du couvent des Cryptes. N'était-ce pas dû à l'ancien moine higoumène des Cryptes, qui aurait été alors le premier pasteur du siège nouvellement fondé? Dans la *Notitia episcopatuum* du début du XIVᵉ siècle, parmi les évêchés-suffragants de la métropole nouvellement érigée de Galič, Vladimir-Volhynsk est cité en premier lieu. Dès lors également l'évêque de Vladimir prenait le titre de prôtothrone (²). Le siège épiscopal de Vladimir-Volhynsk obtint le premier rang, comme étant le plus ancien des évêchés-suffragants, avant Peremyšl, Loutsk, Tourov, Cholm, de la nouvelle métropole de Galič.

---

(1) *Sbornik XII veka* ..., pp. 95-96. Cf. A. Poppe, *Chronologie* ..., pp. 294-297.

(2) Gelzer, *Ungedruckte* ..., p. 632 ; J. Fijalek, *Les évêchés du Moyen Âge de l'Église orientale en Russie et en Lithuanie* (en polonais), dans *Kwartalnik Historyczny*, X, 1896, p. 494 ; XI, 1897, pp. 59, 61.

7. L'ÉVÊCHÉ DE ROSTOV

Rostov était d'habitude classée dans l'historiographie parmi les cités qui obtinrent leur évêque dès l'époque de Vladimir Ier (¹). Cependant Priselkov et, en particulier, N. N. Voronin démontrèrent que les données contenues dans la *Vie de Saint Léonce de Rostov* sur les « premiers » évêques de la ville ont été inventées de toutes pièces au cours des années soixante du xiie siècle, lorsque le prince de Vladimir-Souzdal, André Bogolioubski, s'efforçait de créer une métropole indépendante de Kiev. A leur avis, le siège épiscopal de Rostov a été fondé dans les années soixante du xie siècle, puisque son premier pasteur, Léonce, aurait péri en 1071, durant l'insurrection des paysans et la réaction païenne dans la terre de Rostov (²). Cependant les circonstances qui entraînèrent la création d'un nouveau siège épiscopal, ainsi que son histoire jusqu'au milieu du xiie siècle, ne sont pas encore élucidées.

C'est dans la *Vie de Théodose des Cryptes*, de Nestor, que nous trouvons la plus ancienne information qui soit sûre concernant l'évêché de Rostov. Nous apprenons que le prince de Kiev, Iziaslav, nomma higoumène de son couvent de Saint-Démétrius à Kiev le moine Isaïe, du monastère des Cryptes, qui fut ensuite sacré évêque de Rostov. L'évêque Isaïe participa par la suite aux cérémonies de la dédicace des églises de Vydoubitchi et des Cryptes, en 1088 et 1089. Il devint higoumène, comme on peut le déduire de la *Vie de Théodose*, vers 1066 ; son sacre épiscopal a donc eu lieu après 1066 et avant 1088 (³). La date de 1077-1078 pour la consécration d'Isaïe, que nous donne sa *Vie* écrite au xve siècle, trouve une confirmation indirecte dans le fait qu'étant higoumène du couvent princier, Isaïe jouissait d'égards particuliers de la part

---

(1) GOLUBINSKIJ, *op. cit.*, I-1, pp. 199-205, 677-679 ; IKONNIKOV, *op. cit.*, II, p. 864.

(2) PRISELKOV, *Očerki* ..., pp. 135-140 ; N. N. VORONIN, *La « Vie de saint Léonce de Rostov » et les relations russo-byzantines dans la seconde moitié du XIIe siècle* (en russe), dans *Vizantijskij Vremennik*, XXIII, 1963, pp. 23-46. ID., *Sur les débuts des chroniques de Rostov-Souzdal* (en russe), dans *Arheologičeskiï Ežegodnik za 1964 g.*, Moscou, 1965, pp. 21-24.

(3) *Sbornik XII veka* ... pp. 62-63 ; cf. POPPE, *Chronologie* ..., pp. 292-297, 299-300 ; *PSRL*, vol. II, col. 199.

d'Iziaslav. Celui-ci ayant recouvré le trône de Kiev le 15 juillet 1077, a eu la possibilité, avant de périr le 3 octobre 1078, de présenter son candidat à l'évêché de Rostov.

Après 1054, année où se fit le partage des terres russes entre les fils de Jaroslav le Sage, celles de Perejaslav et de Rostov revinrent à Vsevolod. Des *Préceptes* de Vladimir Monomaque à ses enfants et de sa lettre à Oleg Sviatoslavovitch, il résulte que jusqu'en 1070, Rostov appartenait au domaine de Vsevolod et que plus tard encore il fut considéré comme une propriété héréditaire des descendants de Vsevolod ([1]). Cependant, la terre de Rostov ne fut pas de façon permanente un bien de Vsevolod. Après le 22 mars 1073, date où s'est dissout le triumvirat des fils de Jaroslav, Iziaslav dut s'enfuir de Kiev, et ses frères se partagèrent à nouveau la terre russe. Sviatoslav prit Kiev, Vsevolod passa de Perejaslav à Černigov, tout en conservant la terre de Perejaslav. C'est à cette époque sans doute qu'il obtint également Smolensk, mais il remit à Sviatoslav la terre de Rostov, ou, en tout cas, sa partie septentrionale ([2]). Après la mort de Sviatoslav, le 27 décembre 1076, et le retour de Iziaslav, le 15 juillet 1077, les fils de Sviatoslav furent déshérités, le partage de 1073 fut cependant, en principe, maintenu, mais le domaine de Sviatoslav passait à Iziaslav avec la terre de Rostov. C'est ce qui explique qu'un prêtre qui lui était proche devint évêque de Rostov ([3]). La situation évolua après la mort de Iziaslav, le 3 octobre 1078, lorsque Vsevolod devint le seul maître de la Russie, et après sa mort, en 1093, la terre de Rostov-Souzdal, ainsi que celle de Perejaslav, passèrent aux mains de son fils Vladimir Monomaque.

Jusqu'en 1073, la terre de Rostov, constituant une partie de la principauté de Perejaslav, relevait de la juridiction de l'évêque

---

(1) *PSRL*, vol. I, coll. 237, 247, 250, 254 ; *PSRL*, vol. II, coll. 226-227 ; V. A. Kučkin, *La terre de Rostov-Souzdal du Xe siècle au début du XIIIe siècle* (en russe), dans *Istoria SSSR*, 1969, n° 2, pp. 66-67, 70-76.

(2) Poppe, *Państwo ...*, pp. 180-181. Id., *Récit sur le martyre ...*, p. 363, note 119 ; Kučkin, *La terre ...*, pp. 67-70.

(3) Cette thèse est renforcée par l'érection, avant 1096, de l'église Saint-Démétrius (patron du prince Iziaslav) à Souzdal. N. Voronin relie ce fait, avec raison, à l'activité d'Isaïe au siège de Rostov. Cf. Voronin, *Sur les débuts ...*, p. 23.

de Perejaslav, et ni le prince, ni l'évêque n'avaient intérêt à fonder un nouvel évêché. Ce fut la séparation de cette terre de la principauté de Perejaslav qui posa la question de l'organisation ecclésiastique d'un territoire qui jusqu'alors, avait été faiblement évangélisé. Le passage de Rostov sous la tutelle directe, politique et ecclésiastique, de Kiev, favorisait la fondation d'un nouvel évêché dans cette cité.

Une tradition postérieure de cent ans, rapportée dans la plus ancienne rédaction de la *Vie de Léonce*, évêque de Rostov, voyait en Isaïe son successeur sur le siège épiscopal. D'après le témoignage digne de foi de Simon, évêque de Vladimir-Souzdal du début du xiie siècle, martyrisé par les païens, Léonce fut le premier pasteur de l'évêché de Rostov ([1]). A la lumière des données sur l'histoire de la terre de Rostov, on peut admettre que Léonce fut sacré évêque du siège nouvellement créé, entre 1073 et 1076, et que peu de temps après son arrivée à Rostov, il périt en s'évertuant à convertir les païens rostoviens. D'où la nécessité de nommer un nouvel évêque ; ce fut Isaïe, après le 15 juillet 1077. Léonce et Isaïe venaient tous deux du couvent des Cryptes, ce qui permet de comprendre l'origine du vocable de la cathédrale de Rostov. L'église en maçonnerie de Souzdal, élevée peu après 1096 avec la participation d'Ephrem, évêque-métropolite de Perejaslav et ancien moine des Cryptes, fut également placée sous le vocable de la Dormition de la Sainte Vierge.

Les circonstances politiques qui virent naître l'évêché de Rostov expliquent pourquoi ensuite celui-ci cessa *de facto* d'exister. Il ne fut rétabli qu'après 1136, lorsque Georges Dolgorouki, prince de Rostov-Souzdal, perdit tout espoir d'obtenir Perejaslav ([2]). Lorsqu'en 1094, la terre de Rostov revint de nouveau à la principauté de Perejaslav, ni son prince Vladimir Monomaque, ni l'évêque Ephrem n'avaient plus de raison de maintenir l'existence de l'évêché de Rostov. Ainsi donc, après la mort de Isaïe (probablement vers 1093), l'évêché de Rostov ne fut pas pourvu d'un nouveau titulaire, mais placé sous l'administration du hiérarque de Pere-

---

(1) *Das Paterikon* ..., p. 102. *PSRL*, vol. I, col. 458. VORONIN, *Vie de Saint Léonce* ..., pp. 29 sqq ; ID., *Sur les débuts* ..., p. 22.

(2) PRISELKOV, *Očerki* ..., pp. 291-293. VORONIN, *Sur les débuts* ..., pp. 24 sqq. Cf. A. POPPE, *L'acte de fondation* ..., pp. 64-70. KUČKIN, *La terre* ..., pp. 76-80.

jaslav. En fait, il fut de nouveau incorporé au diocèse de Pereja-slav (¹). La construction de l'église en maçonnerie de la Vierge à Souzdal et le rôle ecclésiastique joué plus tard par cette cité, au XIIᵉ siècle, permettent de penser que le territoire du diocèse de Rostov fut divisé en deux vicariats de l'évêché de Perejaslav.

La fondation de l'évêché de Rostov, bien qu'elle eût indiscutablement pour but le renforcement de l'organisation ecclésiastique des terres du nord-est de la Russie et l'accélération de l'évangélisation de la population locale, était, en réalité, la conséquence des rapports existant entre les princes au cours de la huitième décennie du XIᵉ siècle. Lorsqu'à la fin du XIᵉ siècle, on en revint au *statu quo* politique d'avant 1073, l'évêché de Rostov ne survécut pas à son pasteur. Le rétablissement de l'évêché de Rostov, après 1136, fut, encore une fois, une conséquence de la situation politique.

Il reste encore à expliquer le fait que le diocèse de Rostov, dans la *Notitia episcopatuum cod. Athen.* nᵒ 1371, figure sous le nom ὁ τοῦ Σουσδάλι. H. Gelzer, ne trouvant pas dans la liste l'évêché de Rostov, était enclin à supprimer en sa faveur celui de Tourov, et à fixer une date plus ancienne pour l'émancipation de l'évêché de Vladimir-Souzdal par rapport au diocèse de Rostov (²). Cependant l'année 1214, date du partage du diocèse de Rostov entre deux évêchés, ne peut être rejetée (³). Si, dans la seconde moitié du XIIᵉ siècle, l'évêché de Rostov a pu être appelé évêché de Souzdal, c'est que souvent on employait indifféremment ces deux noms pour désigner le territoire de la principauté dans laquelle la vieille capitale, Rostov, le cédait de plus en plus en importance aux nouveaux centres, Souzdal et Vladimir-sur-Kliazma. Les évêques également étaient appelés tantôt rostoviens, tantôt souzdaliens. Ainsi, par exemple, dans la chronique hypatienne, nous lisors pour l'année 1183 que « Léonce, évêque de Rostov, est mort » et que l'on a nommé, pour lui succéder, « Lucas évêque pour la terre de Souzdal ». Cette dernière information est présentée de la façon

---

(1) On a pensé visiblement à cet événement lors de l'érection de l'évêché de Smolensk en 1136, et c'est pourquoi le prince et l'évêque de Smolensk insérèrent dans l'acte de fondation une réserve qui devait empêcher le retour de Smolensk au diocèse de Perejaslav. Cf. POPPE, *L'acte de fondation* ..., p. 62.

(2) GELZER, *Ungedruckte* ..., pp. 585, 588.

(3) *PSRL*, vol. I, col. 438. GOLUBINSKIJ, *op. cit.*, I-1, pp. 697-698.

suivante dans la chronique laurentienne : « Lucas fut désigné évêque de Rostov et de Vladimir et de Souzdal et de toute la terre de Rostov » (¹). La présence dans la *Notitia*, datée d'environ 1170, de l'évêché *τοῦ Σουσδάλι* peut s'expliquer non seulement par l'emploi de notions équivalentes : rostovien, souzdalien, mais aussi par des événements chronologiquement proches les uns des autres. En 1160, la cathédrale épiscopale de Rostov est détruite dans un incendie, et la résidence de l'évêque de la ville est transférée à Souzdal. En 1158, Léonce est intronisé « évêque à Rostov », mais, en 1162, il est chassé de Souzdal. En 1174, l'église de la Dormition de Souzdal remplit encore le rôle de cathédrale épiscopale, bien que la capitale princière, Vladimir-sur-Kliazma, devienne, elle aussi, une résidence épiscopale (²). De tout cela résulte la conclusion suivante : la liste des évêchés russes, dans la *Notitia Athen.* nº 1371, a été rédigée après 1160.

8. L'ÉVÊCHÉ DE TOUROV

La légende de la fondation de l'évêché de Tourov par Vladimir Iᵉʳ remonte au xivᵉ siècle, époque à laquelle fut fabriqué un privilège de fondation daté de l'an 1005, afin de justifier les limites territoriales du diocèse (³). Le *Récit des temps passés* a également contribué à répandre l'idée de la fondation de l'évêché de Tourov par « l'apôtre de la Russie (⁴) » : en effet, lorsqu'il évoque, pour l'an

(1) *PSRL*, vol. II, col. 629-630 ; vol. I, col. 391 ; cf. également les coll. 348, 349, 352. Cf. GOLUBINSKIJ, *op. cit.*, I-1, p. 678. SOKOLOV, *op. cit.*, pp. 96-103. NASONOV, *op. cit.*, pp. 176-177, 181.

(2) *PSRL*, vol. I, coll. 351, 355, vol. II, 512, 580, 491, 520. Cf. N.N. VORONIN, *Zodčestvo severo-vostočnoj Rusi*, t. I, *XII stoletie* (L'architecture de la Russie du nord-est au xiiᵉ siècle), Moscou, 1961, p. 113 sqq ; ID., *Vie de Léonce ...*, pp. 25, 28 ; ID., *Sur les débuts ...* p. 22.

(3) Cf. Y.N. ŠČAPOV, *La charte de Tourov du XIV siècle sur la dîme* (en russe), dans *Arheologičeskiï Ežegodnik za 1964 g.*, Moscou, 1965, pp. 255-256, 258, 271-273.

(4) Cf. A. S. GRUŠEVSKIJ, *Essai sur l'histoire de la principauté de Tourov-Pinsk aux XIᵉ-XIIIᵉ siècles* (en russe), dans *Kievskie Universitetskie Izvestia*, 1901, nº 6, p. 73. GOLUBINSKIJ, *op. cit.*, I-1, p. 324. HRUŠEVSKYJ, *op. cit.*, III, pp. 304-305. IKONNIKOV, *op. cit.*, t. II, p. 569.

198

988, les apanages des fils de Vladimir, il mentionne Tourov, en tant que cité-résidence de Sviatopolk Ier, à la troisième place, après Novgorod et Polotsk. Cependant, le témoignage du *Récit des temps passés* sur le rôle de Tourov à l'époque de Sviatopolk Ier date de la fin du xie siècle ou du début du siècle suivant, et doit être mis en relation avec la position de cette cité sous Sviatopolk II. A l'époque de Sviatopolk Ier, la principale cité dans la région du bassin du Pripet était plutôt Pinsk ([1]). Que la capitale de l'apanage de Sviatopolk Ier, qu'elle fût Pinsk ou Tourov, n'eût pas son évêché, est attesté indirectement par le fait que vers l'an 1009 y arriva l'évêque Rheinbern, appartenant à la suite de la fille du prince polonais Boleslas le Vaillant, que le fils de Vladimir avait épousée. Après son échec à Colobreg (Kołobrzeg), Rheinbern tentait d'évangéliser de nouvelles régions ([2]).

Si rien ne vient étayer la thèse de la fondation de l'évêché à une époque reculée, on ne peut, d'autre part, admettre la conclusion de H. Gelzer, résultant d'une connaissance incomplète des sources et d'un excès d'esprit critique, selon laquelle l'évêché de Tourov n'existait pas encore au xiie siècle ([3]). Les premiers renseignements bien datés attestant l'existence de l'évêché de Tourov, remontent aux années quarante du xiie siècle ; on y évoque, entre autres, le sacre, en 1144, de Joachim, évêque de Tourov ([4]). La méconnaissance de ces données a poussé H. Gelzer à une émendation superflue de ὁ Τουϱόβου, dans la *Notitia episcopatuum* du *Cod. Athen.* nᵒ 1371, en ὁ τοῦ ῾Ρο(στό)βου, évêché qui, comme nous l'avons démontré, se cache dans cette liste sous le nom de Souzdal.

Nous possédons un témoignage important et véridique pour l'histoire du diocèse de Tourov, dans le *Dit du moine Martin*, qui, contrairement à ce que pensait H. Gelzer, n'appartient pas au xviie siècle. Cet ouvrage, dont le plus ancien manuscrit est un codex en parchemin de 1406 ([5]), vu ses caractéristiques linguistiques, en particulier l'emploi fréquent du duel (29 fois), doit dater du xiie siècle, car c'est seulement au début du xiiie siècle que ce nombre, en tant

---

(1) Cf. Poppe, *Państwo* ..., p. 184.
(2) Cf. Thietmar, *lib.* VII, cap. 72-73.
(3) Gelzer, *Ungedruckte* ..., pp. 588-589.
(4) *PSRL*, vol. I, col. 314, vol. II, coll. 314, 330.
(5) Publié par Abramovič, *Žitia* ..., p. 199.

que catégorie grammaticale vivante, commence à disparaître dans tous les ouvrages. Le récit sans prétention du *Dit*, concernant la guérison miraculeuse par les SS. Boris et Gleb du moine Martin, atteint d'une hernie, contient des indications permettant de dater ce texte des années cinquante ou soixante du xiie siècle, lorsque Georges était évêque de Tourov ([1]). Martin fut le cuisinier de trois évêques de Tourov, Simon, Ignace et Joachim, et sous le quatrième, Georges, vu son âge avancé, il cessa d'exercer ses fonctions et fut admis au couvent des SS. Boris et Gleb, situé près de la ville. Ce témoignage permet de constater que le siège épiscopal de Tourov existait déjà avant 1144, lorsqu'il était dirigé par les prédécesseurs de Joachim, les évêques Simon et Ignace. Ceci ne veut pas dire qu'ils furent les premiers évêques de Tourov, comme le prétend M.D. Priselkov, qui cherche en outre à identifier Simon avec l'évêque Simon de Vladimir-Volhynsk, consacré en 1123 et mort en 1136. En conséquence, cet érudit voit en Ignace le premier véritable évêque de Tourov, et pense que cette cité, soumise jusque là à Vladimir-Volhynsk, a obtenu son évêché en même temps que Smolensk ([2]). Tout cet échafaudage repose uniquement sur une tendance à identifier sans fondement des personnes et des situations différentes — tendance que certains ont, à juste titre, qualifiée de « monoprosopomanie ».

Il ne découle pas du *Dit du moine Martin* que Simon a été le premier pasteur de l'évêché, mais on peut se faire une idée de la période durant laquelle il a exercé ses fonctions. Lorsque le moine Martin, du fait de son âge, fut relevé de ses fonctions de cuisinier de l'évêque, vers 1160, il devait avoir plus de 60 ans, peut-être même près de 70 ; il a donc pu devenir cuisinier de l'évêque vers 1120.

Un autre indice semble confirmer l'existence de l'évêché de Tourov avant 1114. La chronique laurentienne nous apprend que l'évêque Cyrille fut sacré le 6 novembre 1114 (6622). M. D. Priselkov rejette une hypothèse qui a été proposée par certains savants et selon laquelle Cyrille aurait été évêque de Tourov ; et il identifie ce Cyrille à l'évêque de Bielgorod, Nicétas, consacré, d'après la chronique hypatienne, l'année précédente (6621-style

(1) Cf. POPPE, *Państwo* ..., pp. 185-186.
(2) PRISELKOV, *Očerki* ..., pp. 332-334, 348-350.

de mars), en compagnie de l'évêque de Jourev, Daniel. Cependant, la supposition que le prêtre Nicétas, recevant les ordres monastiques et le sacre épiscopal, aurait choisi le prénom de Cyrille n'est pas recevable. Elle est contredite en premier lieu par le fait que cette même chronique cite encore Nicétas de Bielgorod parmi les évêques participant aux cérémonies de Vychgorod, le 1er et le 2 mai 1115 (6623) (1). Étant donné que, pour cette période justement, nous possédons les noms de tous les évêques des sièges dont l'existence est attestée, deux possibilités sont à envisager : Cyrille a pu être sacré soit évêque du diocèse de Rostov, soit de celui de Tourov. La première est peu probable, si l'on considère que le siège de Rostov avait cessé d'exister à la fin du xi\ :sup:`e` siècle, ou, plus exactement était vacant et administré par l'évêque de Perejaslav. Cyrille aurait donc été le prédécesseur de Simon à Tourov. Des données ultérieures, de nature politique, nous permettent de penser que lui non plus n'a pu être le premier évêque de cette ville.

Ni sous le règne de Vladimir Monomaque à Kiev (1113-1125), ni sous celui de son prédécesseur Sviatopolk II (1093-1113), les circonstances ne favorisaient l'érection d'un évêché à Tourov. Par contre, le règne de Vsevolod (1078-1093) a pu être propice à cette innovation. car Tourov était alors la capitale du domaine princier de Sviatopolk II. Les événements de 1078 témoignent encore de la position secondaire de Tourov : Vsevolod, montant sur le trône de Kiev, installa son neveu Jaropolk Iziaslavovitch à Vladimir-Volhynsk, lui « donnant en plus » Tourov. Après la mort de Jaropolk en 1086, le droit de succéder à Vsevolod sur le trône de Kiev revenait à son neveu Sviatopolk, le seul fils en vie de Iziaslav. De ce fait, Vsevolod procéda à des modifications dans le partage et la répartition des apanages des princes juniors. Nous ne connaissons pas l'étendue du nouveau domaine de Sviatopolk, mais nous savons que Tourov en était la capitale, où ce prince vint s'installer, venant de Novgorod, en 1088. Le fait de prendre le pouvoir sur un territoire constituant une partie du domaine proprement dit de Kiev soulignait nettement les droits du fils de Iziaslav à la succession de Vsevolod, et promouvait Tourov dans la hiérarchie des centres des apanages princiers. Au cours des négociations

---

(1) *PSRL*, vol. II, coll. 277, 280, vol. I, col. 290 ; cf. Priselkov, *Očerki* ..., pp. 324-325.

entre Vsevolod et Sviatopolk, en 1086-1088, le projet de créer un évêché, dont Tourov était dépourvu jusque là, dut se faire jour. Sviatopolk, ayant été prince de Novgorod, était en mesure d'apprécier pleinement l'importance de la présence d'un évêque pour relever le rang politique d'une principauté. Pour des raisons de prestige, il ne devait pas lui être indifférent que Tourov demeurât sous la juridiction de l'évêque de Vladimir-Volhynsk. Dès lors que Tourov avait conquis son autonomie politique, la tendance à s'émanciper également du point de vue ecclésiastique est compréhensible. Comme nous savons que, du temps du métropolite Jean II, se posait la question de la création de nouveaux évêchés, on peut fixer à 1088 la date de la fondation de l'évêché de Tourov.

Aux xiv\ :sup:-xvi° siècles, la cathédrale épiscopale de Tourov était placée sous l'invocation de la Dormition de la Vierge ([1]). C'était sans doute sa dédicace primitive, témoignant de l'influence du couvent des Cryptes, d'où était peut-être aussi sorti le premier évêque de Tourov.

9. L'ÉVÊCHÉ DE JURIEV

L'année 1072 comme *terminus ante quem* de la fondation de l'évêché de Juriev résulte de la description, datant des années 1073-1076, de la translation des reliques des SS. Boris et Gleb à Vychgorod, et du *Récit des temps passés* pour l'année 1073 ([2]). Le nom de cette ville, qui provient du nom chrétien slavisé de Georges (Gurgij, Jurij), le vocable de la cathédrale consacrée à Saint Georges et la situation de la ville sur la rivière Ros', affluent du Dniepr, constituent les arguments sur lesquels repose la conviction générale que la fondation de la ville et du siège épiscopal se rattache à la colonisation des territoires sur la Ros', entamée, en 1031-1032, par Jaroslav le Sage, dont le patron était Saint Georges ([3]). L'année 1032, lorsque « Jaroslav commença à construire des *castra* sur la Ros' », est le *terminus post quem* de la fondation de l'évêché ; quant au *terminus ante quem*, on peut le fixer à l'année

---

(1) GOLUBINSKIJ, *op. cit.*, I-1, p. 681 ; ŠČAPOV, *op. cit.*, p. 257.
(2) ABRAMOVIČ, *Žitia* ..., p. 56, *PSRL*, vol. I, col. 183.
(3) Cf. GOLUBINSKIJ, *op. cit.*, I-1, pp. 688-689, HRUŠEVSKYJ, *op. cit.*, II, p. 283, PRISELKOV, *Očerki* ..., pp. 79-80.

1054, date de la mort de Jaroslav-Georges. La fondation de l'évêché de Juriev a dû avoir lieu problablement peu après 1036. Les événements de cette année, qui, après la mort de son frère Mstislav de Černigov, firent de Jaroslav le seul maître de la Russie, ainsi que la grande victoire sur les Petchénègues remportée sous les remparts de Kiev, créaient des conditions favorables à différentes entreprises du monarque kiévien. La victoire remportée sur les Petchénègues permettait de déclencher une grande action de colonisation dans les marches méridionales du pays. Un réseau serré de *castra* sur la Ros' devait constituer un barrage contre les incursions des nomades pillards. Ce n'est pas par hasard que Jaroslav donna au principal centre de cette zone frontalière, dont la colonisation avait un caractère essentiellement militaire, le nom de son patron, qui était aussi celui de toute la milice chrétienne combattant et convertissant les païens. Les buts de la fondation d'un évêché à Jourev allaient au-delà de l'organisation de l'activité pastor* le au sein d'une population exposée au danger. A l'époque de Jaroslav, le souvenir de la mission de Bruno de Querfurt chez les Petchénègues, « les plus cruels de tous les païens », était encore vivace : si l'archevêque missionnaire n'avait pas remporté de succès notables et durables en cherchant à gagner de nouveaux adeptes au Christ, il avait eu du moins la vie sauve, en dépit des craintes que l'on pouvait avoir, et il s'était également acquitté d'une manière remarquable de la mission diplomatique que lui avait confiée Vladimir, en concluant la paix. L'évêché sur la Ros' renouait probablement, dans une certaine mesure, avec l'éphémère évêché *in partibus*, dont l'évêque avait été sacré à Kiev en août 1008 (¹). On espérait que la mission d'évangélisation des nomades indociles de la steppe arrêterait plus efficacement leur pression que des troupes constamment en état d'alerte. Dans la pratique, le missionnaire était aussi un excellent éclaireur et un diplomate : en Russie, on avait appris très tôt à apprécier le rôle du clergé, en particulier du haut clergé, dans des actions diplomatiques de tous genres. La création d'un évêché aux marches sud du pays était liée à la politique de la Russie à l'égard de la steppe : elle s'accordait d'ailleurs avec la politique de Byzance, et, de ce fait, était appuyée par un Grec, le métro-

---

(1) Voir *Epistola Brunonis ad Henricum regem, Monumenta Poloniae Historica*, t. I, pp. 224-225.

polite de Kiev. L'action de la Russie, visant à se concilier les différentes tribus nomades turques, consistait à les installer dans les
régions limitrophes, entre autres sur la Ros', et à les utiliser contre
leurs « sauvages » parents des steppes, en particulier contre les
Coumans. Cette politique, qui remporta de remarquables succès
dans la première moitié du xiie siècle, s'était révélée efficace dès
le xie siècle. Le clergé a également contribué à attirer et à « ama-
douer » les différentes tribus nomades, même si le bilan de l'évangélisation des nomades fédérés fut beaucoup plus modeste que dans
le cas de la population finno-ougrienne des terres de Novgorod
et de Rostov-Souzdal.

Pour une part de son activité, l'évêché de Juriev était un évêché
in partibus infidelium. Son caractère de pont est parfaitement
visible à la fin du xie siècle, au temps d'une pression croissante
venant cette fois des Coumans, lorsque les habitants du *castrum*
s'enfuirent de Juriev avec leur évêque Marin et furent établis
plus près de Kiev, sur le Dniepr. Mais dès l'été 1103, Juriev fut
reconstruit et devint à nouveau une résidence épiscopale ([1]).

A la lumière de ces faits, nous ne sommes pas convaincus par
l'hypothèse que Jaroslav aurait érigé un nouvel évêché pour donner
au métropolite un second vicaire (le premier étant celui de Bielgorod), afin qu'il puisse sacrer des évêques sans faire appel à d'autres
suffragants ([2]). Une situation dans laquelle la présence de deux
suffragants, celui de Juriev et celui de Bielgorod, dans le domaine
du grand prince kiévien, acquérait de l'importance, naquit au
xiie siècle, avec le démembrement du pays en principautés indépendantes, ce qui favorisait une plus grande autonomie des évêques
des différentes principautés par rapport à la métropole kiévienne.
L'évêque de Juriev, pas plus d'ailleurs que celui de Bielgorod,
ne pouvait être, au sens strict du mot, vicaire du métropolite ;
il était, en effet, évêque résidentiel, administrant son propre diocèse.
Celui-ci, englobant le bassin de la Ros' (environ 12.580 km²), pouvait
sembler très petit par rapport aux autres diocèses russes, mais il
aurait pu néanmoins contenir plusieurs diocèses byzantins. La
limite méridionale du diocèse de Juriev n'était pas déterminée ;

(1) *PSRL*, vol. I, coll. 229-280, vol. II, coll. 219, 256.
(2) GOLUBINSKIJ, *op. cit.*, I-1, p. 689. L'institution des évêques-
vicaires n'a été créée dans l'Église russe qu'au xviiie siècle.

l'activité missionnaire devait s'étendre profondément, dans la steppe, *in partes infidelium*.

L'évêque de Juriev, bien qu'il ne pût être vicaire *de iure*, remplissait parfois les fonctions d'aide du métropolite de Kiev. En 1073, l'évêque de Juriev, Michel, en l'absence du métropolite Georges séjournant à Constantinople, posa la première pierre de l'église des Cryptes. En 1184, seul l'évêque de Juriev Nicéphore assista le métropolite lors de la consécration de l'église Saint-Basile, à Kiev, bien que d'autres évêques fussent venus assister aux cérémonies. Les listes des hiérarques présents aux cérémonies ecclésiastiques de 1072, 1089, 1091 et 1115 semblent indiquer que l'évêque de Juriev, cité en dernier lieu, était le dernier dans l'ordre de préséance (¹).

Juriev ne figure pas dans la *Notitia* d'environ 1170. De cela H. Gelzer a tiré hâtivement la conclusion que cet évêché n'existait plus à l'époque. Cependant, l'évêché de Juriev figure sur cette liste sous le nom de τὸ Κάνεβε. qui, en dépit de ce que pensait ce savant, n'est pas énigmatique et ne constitue pas une notation erronée du nom de Kiev (Κύεβε) (²). Tout simplement, Kanev, l'un des grands centres urbains de la région de la Ros', situé au confluent de la Ros' et du Dniepr, fut pendant un certain temps la résidence des évêques de Juriev. La date du transfert du siège de l'évêché de Juriev à Kanev peut être établie avec assez de précision. L'évêque de Juriev, Damien, participa au synode de Kiev de 1147. Ce même Damien, appelé évêque de Kanev, au tournant de 1154-1155, fut envoyé en ambassade auprès du prince Iziaslav Davidovitch au nom des Kiéviens (³). Le transfert du siège épiscopal s'est donc produit entre 1147 et 1154. La région du bassin de la Ros' n'avait pas de prince propre, elle appartenait directement au domaine du grand prince. Ce n'est qu'en 1149 que Georges Dolgorouki, après s'être emparé du trône de Kiev, installa son fils Gleb à Kanev ; en 1155, il donna la région de la Ros' à son fils Vasilko. La situation de Kanev, près d'un gué du Dniepr, fit de cette forteresse, lors des fréquentes querelles entre les princes et

---

(1) *PSRL*, vol. II, coll. 173, 199, 202, 280, 634 ; Abramovič, *Žitia* ..., pp. 56, 64 ; cf. Poppe, *Państwo* ..., pp. 189-191.

(2) Gelzer, *Ungedruckte* ..., p. 588. L'erreur de cet érudit a déjà été corrigée par A.V. Soloviev, *Le nom byzantin* ..., p. 15.

(3) *PSRL*, vol. II, coll. 341, 476 ; vol. I. col. 344.

des invasions des Coumans, l'un des principaux centres sur la Ros',
et la résidence du prince-gouverneur du grand prince de Kiev.
En 1144, le prince kiévien Vsevolod Olgovitch fit construire à
Kanev l'église Saint-Georges, qui, peu de temps après, devint la
cathédrale des évêques de Juriev. Mais ce n'est pas seulement
l'accroissement de l'importance de Kanev qui explique le transfert
de la résidence des évêques, mais plutôt la destruction de Juriev,
qui fut incendié, probablement à la fin des années quarante, au
cours des combats violents que se livraient les princes dans cette
région avec la participation des Coumans. Dans des témoignages
de 1159 et de 1162, Juriev est de nouveau mentionné à propos de
combats se déroulant sur la Ros'. Il devient de nouveau résidence
épiscopale avant 1183, et il l'est également au xiiie siècle, comme
le prouvent les *Notitiae* de cette époque mentionnant parmi les
évêchés russes ὁ Ἅγιος Γεώργιος εἰς τὸν Ῥῶσιν ποταμόν (¹).
La présence de Kanev dans la *Notitia* du *Codex Athen.* no 1371,
dont l'auteur disposait d'une liste des évêchés russes établie entre
1160 et 1165, prouve qu'à cette époque la cité était encore le lieu
de résidence des évêques de Juriev.

10. Les évêchés russes aux xi-xiie siècles

Les résultats des recherches que nous venons d'effectuer, permettent de reconstituer la géographie ecclésiastique de la Russie aux
xie-xiie siècles. L'analyse détaillée de la liste des évêchés de la
métropole russe contenue dans la *Notitia episcopatuum* du patriarcat de Constantinople du *Codex Athen.* no 1371, faite à la lumière
des sources russes que nous possédons, a fourni plusieurs indications
indépendantes les unes des autres, permettant de dater cette liste
de la période 1160-1165. Les données obtenues ont également
confirmé que H. Gelzer avait raison lorsqu'il datait la rédaction
de la *Notitia* elle-même des années 1170-1179. Dans les années
soixante du xiie siècle, la province ecclésiastique russe se compo-

_____

(1) *PSRL*, vol. I, coll. 312, 321, 320-322, 345, 346 ; vol. II, coll.
317, 372 sqq., 502, 521, 634. Hruševskyj, *op. cit.*, II, pp. 285-
286. Parthey ..., p. 130 (*notitia* III). Gelzer, *Ungedruckte* ...,
p. 632. Id., *Beiträge* ..., p. 247. Dans la liste des évêchés russes,
tout comme Juriev, Bielgorod a été traduit en grec (Ἀσπρόκαστρον).

sait donc de 12 diocèses : celui de la métropole de Kiev et 11 évêchés-suffragants. Parmi ces derniers, les évêchés de Smolensk (1136) et de Galič (1147-1157) furent érigés au xiie siècle. Le siège épiscopal de Rostov fut recréé peu après 1136. La chronologie de la genèse des différents évêchés qui a été établie ici prouve que la liste des sièges épiscopaux de 1160-1165 maintient, à quelques exceptions près, l'ordre de leur fondation. Perejaslav se trouve en sixième position, sa place ayant été prise par Vladimir-Volhynsk. L'importance politique croissante de la capitale de la Volhynie à partir des années quarante du xiie siècle, allant de pair avec le déclin politique de Perejaslav et la réduction brutale de la superficie du diocèse de Perejaslav à la suite de la formation d'évêchés dans les nouvelles principautés de Smolensk et de Rostov-Souzdal, expliquent suffisamment ce changement du rang de préséance. Une autre exception est constituée par l'évêché de Juriev, qui s'est trouvé à la 9e place et qui clôt la liste des diocèses créés au xie siècle, sans doute parce qu'il changea de nom à la suite du transfert, vers l'an 1150, de la résidence épiscopale à Kanev. A la première place, que devait prendre, peu de temps après, Novgorod la Grande (en 1165), figure encore Bielgorod, comme prôtothronie de la métropole. La liste des évêchés russes de 1160-1165 se rattache donc génétiquement à l'*Ordo thronorum* des débuts de l'organisation ecclésiastique de la Russie.

Les bases de l'organisation de la province ecclésiastique furent posées après que Vladimir Ier eut fait du christianisme la religion d'État, lors de l'arrivée en Russie, vers l'an 990, d'un métropolite et d'évêques. Au cours des années suivantes, et certainement sous le règne de « l'apôtre de la Russie », leurs résidences furent fixées : le métropolite à Kiev, et ses 4 ou 5 suffragants à Bielgorod, Novgorod, Polotsk, Černigov et, probablement, Perejaslav. Polotsk, bien qu'on n'ait pas pu établir l'existence d'un siège épiscopal dans cette ville avant le milieu du xie siècle, a dû, vu sa position politique, obtenir son propre évêché dès l'époque de Vladimir ou, au plus tard, entre 1015 et 1024, lorsque Jaroslav le Sage, hostile aux princes de Polotsk, n'était pas encore assez puissant pour qu'il pût s'opposer à l'érection de cet évêché. Pour ce qui est de la fondation de l'évêché de Perejaslav, nous inclinons, non sans hésitation, à la dater du règne de Vladimir Ier, car celui-ci, ayant construit le *castrum* et entrepris énergiquement de coloniser les pays riverains de la Troubež et de la Soula, avait édifié une forte barrière dans les marches du sud-ouest de son État contre les Petchénègues. Ce n'est pas un hasard si le vainqueur des païens, l'archistratège et archange Michel, devint le patron de la terre et de la cathédrale de Perejaslav. Cette politique fut poursuivie par Jaroslav le Sage ; on ne peut donc exclure que l'évêché de l'archange Michel à Perejaslav ait été érigé à la même époque que celui de Saint Georges à Juriev, soit au cours de la quatrième ou de la cinquième décennie du xie siècle. Saint Georges, le vaillant patron de la chevalerie, devait veiller aux frontières méridionales du pays, sur la rive droite du Dniepr.

Le chiffre de 3 à 6 suffragants était habituel pour une métropole byzantine moyenne ; les plus anciennes et les plus importantes n'acquéraient un plus grand nombre d'évêchés suffragants qu'avec le temps ([1]). La localisation des centres épiscopaux : trois à Bielgorod, Černigov et Perejaslav, à proximité immédiate de Kiev, et deux au nord, à Novgorod et à Polotsk — prouve nettement que l'idée première et réaliste du « baptiseur de la Russie » n'était pas de couvrir d'un réseau diocésain l'ensemble de l'immense territoire de l'État kiévien. Le choix se porta sur des centres importants du point de vue politique et économique, où, d'une part, existaient déjà des communautés chrétiennes par suite des longs rapports commerciaux entretenus avec Byzance, et où, d'autre part, se concentrait une classe sociale supérieure dont la christianisation devait favoriser la diffusion de la religion chrétienne parmi la population des agglomérations urbaines. Bien que les évêques nouveau-venus aient possédé des résidences fixes et l'appui des autorités, ils furent en fait, pendant des dizaines d'années, des évêques missionnaires, et le champ de leur activité se restreignait aux villes où ils résidaient. Car même là, la nouvelle foi, menacée ouvertement par des retours au paganisme, ne se sentait pas encore très à l'abri, plusieurs dizaines d'années après le « baptême ». A cet égard, à Kiev, la situation, dans les années soixante-dix du xie siècle, n'était pas trop mauvaise : si une partie des Kiéviens suivaient encore les devins, les autres se moquaient déjà d'eux. Par contre, à Novgorod, à la même époque à peu près, les devins avaient réussi « à entortiller bien des gens,

---

(1) Par exemple, la métropole de Sébaste, dont le pasteur (Théophylacte) fut le premier métropolite de Russie, avait cinq suffragants. Cf. PARTHEY ..., p. 108 (*notitia* III).

presque toute la ville». Et sans l'intervention armée du prince et
de ses féaux, membres de la classe supérieure de Novgorod, l'évêque
de la ville, Théodore, aurait rejoint la légion des martyrs de la
foi, comme ce fut le cas pour Léonce, son contemporain, évêque de
Rostov (¹). La pratique des rites chrétiens était encore assez peu
répandue dans la population à la fin du xɪᵉ siècle ; à preuve les
paroles que le moine Jacob adressait au métropolite Jean II Prodromos (vers 1078-1089) et selon lesquelles princes et boyards
seulement recevaient le sacrement du mariage, et non les gens
du peuple (²). Le fait même que la question ait été évoquée par le
moine Jacob, ainsi que les recommandations du métropolite demandant que « ceux qui se marient en ignorant l'Église de Dieu et
sa bénédiction » se voient infliger une pénitence ecclésiastique
comme pour la débauche, prouvent que l'Église était déjà assez
puissante pour entreprendre de répandre les pratiques religieuses
parmi les couches populaires des centres urbains.

Les premiers évêques, peu nombreux, d'origine grecque, ignorant
en général la langue slave, perdus au milieu des immenses étendues
de la terre russe, ne pouvaient d'eux-mêmes entreprendre grand
chose pour la christianisation. Nécessairement, le poids principal
en retomba sur le clergé slave, nombreux dès la première moitié
du xɪᵉ siècle, et qu'animait une foi ardente, et sur les princes et
les grands qui dirigeaient, du fait de leur fonction, les missions et
qui faisaient construire à leurs frais de nombreuses églises dans
les villes et les *castra* de régions toujours plus éloignées de la Russie.
Le rôle des évêques, plutôt consultatif au début et purement canonique (consécration des prêtres, etc.), augmente au fur et à mesure
qu'apparaissent des évêques d'origine russe qui, dans la seconde
moitié du xɪᵉ siècle, deviennent de véritables pasteurs de l'Église

---

(1) Cf. *PSRL*, vol. I, coll. 180-181, *Das Paterikon* ..., p. 102,
Voronin, *Vie de Léonce* ..., p. 29 sqq. ; sur les retours au paganisme
en Russie au xɪᵉ siècle, voir A. Gieysztor, *Mouvements para-hérétiques en Europe centrale et orientale du IXᵉ au XIᵉ siècle : apostasies*, dans : *Hérésies et sociétés dans l'Europe pré-industrielle, XIᵉ-
XVIIIᵉ siècle*, Paris, 1968, pp. 163-164.

(2) *Pamiatniki drevnerusskogo kanoničeskogo prava* (Monuments
vieux-russes de droit canonique) publiés par A.S. Pavlov, t. I, S Pb.,
1880, nº 1, § 30, p. 18 ; L. K. Götz, *Kirchengeschichtliche und Kulturgeschichtliche Denkmäler Altrusslands nebst Geschichte des russischen Kirchenrechts*, Stuttgart, 1905, pp. 163-165.

et les artisans d'un programme visant à attirer les plus larges couches de la population à la nouvelle foi. L'étendue de la plaine de l'Europe orientale rendait illimitées les tâches que les évêques avaient à remplir. La nécessité de fixer les bornes de la juridiction des évêchés n'apparut donc pas tout de suite. Les limites des diocèses ne commencèrent à s'esquisser que dans la seconde moitié du xɪᵉ siècle, à la suite des partages politiques et du développement des centres locaux. La promotion des évêchés de Černigov et de Perejaslav au rang de métropoles titulaires au temps du triumvirat des fils de Jaroslav, dans la septième décennie du xɪᵉ siècle, fut sans doute un stimulant qui accéléra la formation des territoires diocésains. Le partage politique du pays après 1054 fit que, dans les terres placées sous l'autorité du prince de Perejaslav, Vsevolod (terre de Perejaslav, terre de Rostov-Souzdal), il n'existait aucun autre siège épiscopal que celui de Perejaslav. Ce fait détermina *eo ipso* l'étendue de sa juridiction. Il en fut de même du domaine du prince de Černigov, Sviatoslav, englobant les terres de Černigov et de Mourom-Riazan'. L'appartenance ecclésiastique de la terre de Smolensk, relevant de 1060 à 1073, probablement en entier, de Sviatoslav et reprise plus tard avec Černigov par Vsevolod, n'est pas claire. Ce n'est qu'à la suite des partages politiques de 1093-1096 qu'elle se trouva placée indiscutablement sous la juridiction de l'évêque de Perejaslav.

Le statut ecclésiastique de Tmoutorokan' (Matracha), soumis au prince de Černigov et disposant dès le xᵉ siècle d'un archevêché autocéphale (ὁ Ματράχων ἤτοι Ζιχχίας) relevant directement du patriarche de Constantinople, était tout particulier. Contrairement à certaines opinions, cette colonie russe des xᵉ-xɪᵉ siècles n'a jamais appartenu à la province ecclésiastique russe. Par contre, le pouvoir politique permettait aux princes russes d'influencer le choix des pasteurs du siège archiépiscopal de Tmoutorokan' (¹).

En dehors de celui de Polotsk, tous les évêchés suffragants (de Bielgorod, de Juriev et de Novgorod) se trouvèrent compris dans le domaine du maître de Kiev, Iziaslav, et c'est à eux que

---

(1) Pour plus de détails, voir Poppe, *Państwo* ..., pp. 192-196. Cf. G. G. Litavrin, *A propos de Tmutorokan'*, dans *Byzantion*, XXXV, 1965, pp. 221-234.

se limita l'autorité du métropolite de Kiev. L'unité ecclésiastique de la Russie, qui jusqu'alors n'avait pas fait l'objet d'une prise de conscience, se trouva menacée. Il est vrai que les métropoles de Černigov et de Perejaslav possédaient un caractère titulaire, mais il était également évident que le maintien du partage de la Russie entre les trois fils de Jaroslav devait aboutir à leur transformation en métropoles ordinaires, disposant d'évêchés suffragants. Leur étendue le cédait de peu à celle de l'archidiocèse de Kiev. Seules les querelles des princes en 1068-1069 et en 1073, amenant un nouveau partage du pays, puis la mort de Sviatoslav en 1076 et d'Iziaslav en 1078 mirent un terme à cette tendance. Les métropoles de Černigov et de Perejaslav cessèrent d'exister à la mort de leur titulaire. Le sentiment du danger qui avait menacé la métropole de Kiev et qui, à l'avenir, pouvait menacer l'unité de la province ecclésiastique russe, a dû créer à la curie de Sainte-Sophie un climat favorable à l'accroissement du nombre des évêchés suffragants. Si, à Byzance, l'augmentation du nombre des évêchés suffragants menaçait l'unité de la métropole, en Russie les conditions concrètes des années soixante et soixante-dix du xie siècle étaient tout autres. De toute évidence, si, dans les terres soumises à l'autorité de Sviatoslav et de Vsevolod, il avait existé plus d'un diocèse, on aurait évité, même dans le cas de la promotion des sièges des capitales Černigov et Perejaslav, la limitation sensible de l'autorité ecclésiastique du métropolite de Kiev qui se produisit. Ce n'est donc pas par hasard que le nouvel évêché de Rostov fut érigé peu de temps après les événements de 1073, alors qu'Iziaslav avait été éliminé, et qu'à l'issue du nouveau partage de la Russie entre les deux autres fils de Jaroslav, la terre de Rostov-Souzdal passait sous l'autorité de Sviatoslav, qui devenait prince de Kiev. Cet acte réduisait de près de trois fois l'étendue de la juridiction de l'évêque de Perejaslav, exercée d'ailleurs au nord dans une mesure très faible, puisque la terre de Rostov était toujours païenne.

L'attitude de la curie de Sainte-Sophie dans la question de l'érection de nouveaux évêchés est exprimée dans *Les Réponses* du métropolite Jean II Prodromos: «Si quelqu'un dans ce pays partage son diocèse, en particulier là où il y a force peuple, hommes et villes, poussé par le zèle et le souci à l'égard du peuple, cela nous plaît, à nous aussi, pourvu que cela se fasse dans la crainte (du Seigneur) : alors ceci seulement ne sera pas interdit, lorsque le premier évêque russe et le synode du pays tout entier le permettront ([1]) ». Le raisonnement contenu dans cette réponse est clair : l'autorité séculière, c'est-à-dire les princes, peuvent proposer un accroissement du nombre des diocèses « dans leurs terres », mais la décision définitive revient à l'autorité spirituelle, c'est-à-dire au métropolite et au synode des évêques. La réponse ainsi formulée est une invitation nette à accroître le nombre des diocèses et reflète sans aucun doute la position de la curie métropolitaine, car, s'il y avait été opposé, le γῆς Ῥωσικῆς πρόεδρος aurait pu invoquer les nombreuses résolutions des conciles interdisant le partage des diocèses.

La conséquence pratique de la position adoptée par Jean II fut la création, après celui de Rostov (1073-1076), des évêchés de Vladimir-Volhynsk (1078-1086) et de Tourov (vers 1088). La fondation, dans les années soixante-dix et quatre-vingts du xie siècle, de trois nouveaux évêchés découlait en même temps de la tendance à étendre l'organisation de l'Église, afin de rendre plus efficace l'œuvre de christianisation du pays. Les solutions pratiques et l'étendue des nouveaux diocèses furent déterminées par de nouveaux partages politiques, se dessinant toujours plus nettement sous la pression de tendances centrifuges. Dans l'esprit des princes des différentes terres, les sièges épiscopaux devaient conférer pérennité et autorité à leur pouvoir politique ; pour la curie métropolitaine, l'augmentation du nombre des suffragants, par la réduction de l'étendue des territoires soumis à la juridiction des évêchés existant alors, et donc aussi de la position politique de ceux-ci, devait couper court à tout danger de voir se former en Russie plus d'une province ecclésiastique. L'idée de l'unité de l'organisation ecclésiastique fut naturellement appuyée par le prince Vsevolod, lorsqu'il devint autocrate de la Russie (1078-1093), et trouva un chaleureux défenseur dans le monastère des Cryptes. Les évêchés de Rostov et de Vladimir-Volhynsk, et probablement celui de Tourov, ont été créés avec la participation active de ce monastère.

On peut lire en partie l'histoire de la création des évêchés dans les vocables de leurs cathédrales. Trois des cathédrales fondées

---

(1) *Pamiatniki* ..., n° 1, § 32, p. 19. Götz, *Kirchengeschichtliche* ..., pp. 166-167. Cf. Poppe, *Państwo* ..., pp. 200-201. Le premier évêque, dans le texte : первыи стольник, est un calque du grec πρόεδρος (et non pas πρωτόθρονος, comme le suggéraient les éditeurs du texte). C'est ce titre qu'utilisaient alors les métropolites byzantins.

sous Vladimir Ier, à Kiev, Novgorod et Polotsk, sont placées sous l'invocation de la Sagesse Divine. Novgorod et Polotsk étaient, à partir du xe siècle, des centres qui tranchaient sur les autres par leur position politique et les ambitions de leurs grands, qui se considéraient comme les égaux de ceux de Kiev et qui revendiquaient le droit de participer au choix de celui qui monterait sur le trône kiévien. Les cathédrales des deux centres épiscopaux les plus proches de Kiev, se trouvant dans sa zone d'influence politique directe, furent placées sous l'invocation des Douze Apôtres (à Bielgorod) et du Sauveur (à Černigov), choix qui n'était pas dénué d'un sens symbolique. Hilarion, dans sa fameuse oraison, salue Vladimir Ier, dans lequel il personnifie la Russie entière, du nom d'« élu du Sauveur » et d'« apôtre parmi les monarques » ([1]). Dans les marches méridionales de l'État, sur les deux rives du Dniepr, où de nombreux *castra* veillaient à la sécurité de la terre russe face aux incursions dévastatrices des nomades de la steppe, on édifia deux cathédrales, celle de l'archange Michel, à Perejaslav, et celle de Saint-Georges, à Juriev. Dès lors, les patrons des chevaliers chrétiens luttant contre les païens devaient veiller sur les défenseurs de la terre menacée. Les cathédrales de Rostov, de Vladimir et de Tourov ont été placées sous l'invocation de la Dormition de la Vierge, expression du culte en plein essor de la Theotokos, répandu surtout par le monastère des Cryptes. Les cathédrales de Smolensk et de Galič étaient également placées sous le vocable de la Dormition de la Sainte Vierge.

C'est au cours des dernières décennies du xie siècle que s'est constituée, dans sa première forme, l'organisation diocésaine englobant, en principe, l'ensemble du territoire de l'État vieux-russe. Au diocèse métropolitain, dont le siège était à Kiev, appartenait le territoire du cours moyen du Dniepr, relativement peu étendu mais très peuplé. Avec le diocèse de Bielgorod s'enfonçant vers le sud-ouest dans le bassin du Boh supérieur, et celui de Juriev sur la Ros', ce territoire englobait le domaine proprement dit du suzerain kiévien. Le diocèse de Černigov couvrait le domaine de Sviatoslav et de ses fils : la principauté de Černigov, s'étendant à l'est jusqu'au cours supérieur du Don et au cours moyen de l'Oka, avec les villes de Mourom et de Riazan'. L'apanage de Riazan'-

---

(1) Cf. MÜLLER, *Des Metropoliten Ilarion Lobrede ...*, pp. 168, 126.

Murom s'était émancipé politiquement dès les années vingt du
xiie siècle, mais son partage rapide en plusieurs principautés et,
à partir du milieu du xiie siècle, l'affrontement permanent avec
la principauté voisine de Rostov-Souzdal, lui firent chercher
une aide à Černigov, en maintenant d'utiles liens ecclésiastiques.
La défaite complète des princes de Riazan', en 1186/1187, établit
définitivement l'hégémonie de Souzdal, mit un terme à celle de
Černigov et provoqua la séparation ecclésiastique. Le nouvel
évêché de Riazan' fut fondé vers 1200, moins à l'initiative des
autorités locales (princes, boyards, clergé), dont la souveraineté
était restreinte, qu'à la suite d'un accord réalisé entre les deux
rivaux, Černigov et Souzdal, avec la participation du métropolite
et du prince kiévien, intéressés tous deux à cette solution.

Le diocèse de Perejaslav qui, dans les années 1073-1076, avait
perdu la terre de Rostov-Souzdal au profit de l'évêché de Rostov,
la recouvra vers 1094, et étendit également sa juridiction à la terre
de Smolensk sous l'autorité politique du prince de Perejaslav,
Vladimir Monomaque, héritier de la totalité des domaines pater-
nels. La marque distinctive de cette région, tant du point de vue
politique qu'ecclésiastique, était son émiettement. La principauté
de Perejaslav proprement dite, au sud, dans le triangle formé
par le Dniepr et la Vorskla, était coupée de la terre de Smolensk
et de celle de Rostov-Souzdal par la principauté de Černigov.
Cette situation favorisa l'émancipation politique des terres de
Smolensk et de Rostov-Souzdal, puis leur émancipation ecclésiastique dans les années trente du xiie siècle. Alors que les limites
de l'évêché de Smolensk demeuraient inchangées même au xiii^e
siècle, le diocèse de Rostov-Souzdal, après les efforts infructueux
du prince André Bogoloubski dans les années soixante du xii^e
siècle, visant à son partage et à l'érection d'une métropole dans
la nouvelle capitale de la principauté de Vladimir-sur-Kliazma [1],
ne fut partagé entre deux sièges épiscopaux qu'en 1214, par suite
de la séparation de la principauté de Rostov. Le siège que l'on

(1) Le patriarcat consentit seulement à transférer la résidence
de l'évêque dans la capitale de la principauté. Pour l'ensemble de
la question, voir GOLUBINSKIJ, *op. cit.*, I-1, pp. 330-332, 439-442,
SOKOLOV, *op. cit.*, p. 128-158. N.N. VORONIN, *André Bogoloubski
et Lukas Chrysoberges* (en russe), dans *Vizantijskij Vremennik*, XXi,
1962, pp. 29-50.

214

établit à Vladimir-sur-Kliazma devint, à la fin du xiiie siècle, la résidence de fait des métropolites de Kiev (transférée à Moscou en 1325) (¹).

Les limites du diocèse de Polotsk furent déterminées par celles du pouvoir politique des princes de cette terre. Sainte-Sophie sur le Volkhov exerçait sa suprématie ecclésiastique sur la terre de Novgorod, qui disposait de larges possibilités d'expansion territoriale vers le nord et le nord-est — expansion qui, plus tard (au xiiie siècle), s'accompagna d'une action de christianisation de la population finno-ougrienne —. Le diocèse de Vladimir comprit tout d'abord les territoires étendus de Volhynie, de Polésie et du Dniestr supérieur, confiés, en 1078, par Vsevolod à son neveu Jaropolk. Après sa mort, en 1086, l'apanage, qui réunissait des terres à fortes tendances centrifuges, fut partagé. Vladimir, c'est-à-dire la terre de Volhynie proprement dite, alla à David Igorevitch, Peremyšl et Terebovl aux fils de Rostislav. La Polésie, avec son centre Tourov, échut à Sviatopolk, frère du défunt Jaropolk, qui s'attendait à hériter aussi du trône de Kiev après la mort de son oncle Vsevolod. Ce partage politique entraîna, à Tourov, l'érection d'un évêché, qui s'étendit sur toute la Polésie jusqu'à Brest sur le Boug. En 1093, lorsque Sviatopolk II monta sur le trône de Kiev, son apanage fut incorporé au domaine du suzerain. La région du Dniestr supérieur demeura sous la juridiction des évêques de Vladimir-Volhynsk. D'une part, les fils de Rostislav nourrissaient encore, dans les années quatre-vingt-dix, l'espoir de régner sur Vladimir et, par conséquent, n'avaient pas intérêt à avoir leur propre évêque ; d'autre part, il faut tenir compte du fait qu'ils étaient considérés, non pas comme des princes *pleno jure*, mais comme des princes-*izgoï*, c'est-à-dire privés du droit d'héritage. L'intention de Vsevolod était de les réduire au rôle de gouverneurs des centres qu'il leur avait confiés, d'en faire donc des *posadniki* du prince-suzerain. Ce n'est que par une lutte armée qu'ils acquirent, à la fin du xie siècle, des droits héréditaires sur les terres qui leur avaient été confiées par Vsevolod, et c'est alors que put se manifester leur désir de posséder un évêché à part, aspiration réalisée par Galič au milieu du xiie siècle. Le diocèse de Galič fut partagé au début du

---

(1) Nous comptons consacrer une étude particulière à la géographie ecclésiastique de la Russie du xiiie au xve siècle.

xiiie siècle, lorsque se détacha de lui l'évêché de Peremyšl ([1]).

Du territoire soumis à la juridiction de l'évêché de Vladi-mir-Volhynsk se détachèrent, dans la période allant des années vingt à quarante du xiiie siècle, deux nouveaux diocèses dont les sièges épiscopaux se trouvaient respectivement à Ougrovsk (bientôt transféré à Cholm) et à Loutsk. L'existence de ces nouveaux évêchés au xiiie siècle, à une époque où s'accentuait le clivage entre la Russie du sud-ouest et celle du nord-est (ce qui se refléta dans la nomenclature byzantine: μεγάλη ῾Ρωσία, μικρὰ ῾Ρωσία) créa les prémisses d'où devait naître, au début du xive siècle, une nouvelle union métropolitaine. La métropole de « petite Russie » à Galič était aussi une réponse au déplacement du centre de la vie ecclé-siastique de la « grande Russie » de Kiev à Vladimir-sur-Kliazma.

Les progrès de la christianisation et la nécessité, pour l'Église, d'administrer des territoires très étendus, alors que le nombre de sièges épiscopaux était réduit, ont dû entraîner le besoin de diviser les diocèses en zones administratives. Telles sont certainement les causes de la genèse de l'institution des vicaires épiscopaux ([2]). Dans une certaine mesure, on peut la comparer à l'archidiaconat de l'Europe occidentale, les deux institutions résultant du processus de perfectionnement de l'administration du diocèse et visant à éviter de nouveaux partages. Mais le vicariat vieux-russe possède un caractère original : il se rattache probablement au système d'administration princière fondé sur les *posadniki*, c'est-à-dire les gouverneurs du prince régissant les différentes terres de la princi-pauté. Si le schéma de l'organisation du vicariat a été élaboré en Russie conformément aux besoins du pays, la justification canonique a été peut-être fournie par les institutions paléo-chrétiennes de l'organisation ecclésiastique, notamment par celle du χωρεπίσ-

---

(1) Le siège de Peremyšl a été érigé après 1187, mais avant 1220, date de sa première mention. Les suppositions selon lesquelles l'évê-ché aurait été fondé à la fin du xie siècle, au début du xiie ou même sous le règne de Vladimir Ier sont dénuées de fondements. Cf. GOLUBINSKIJ, *op. cit.*, I-1, pp. 698-99, POPPE, *Państwo ...*, p. 156, note 15.
(2) Par ce terme d'origine latine, qui lui correspond sémantique-ment, je traduis le terme vieux-russe « namestnik » (remplaçant) Il ne faut pas confondre cette institution avec celle, bien connue, de l'évêque-vicaire.

216

κοπος et celle du *περιοδευτής* (¹). L'Église de Byzance ignorait l'institution de vicaire de l'évêque. Cela est si vrai que, au xive s., le vicaire du métropolite moscovite à Vladimir-sur-Kliazma, le moine grec Malachias, dans une note écrite sur son psautier, se donne le titre de *ἱερομονάχου καὶ ναμεστνίκου τοῦ Βολοδιμίρου* (²). S'il a conservé à l'office ecclésiastique son nom russe, c'est qu'il ne pouvait trouver de mot correspondant dans la nomenclature ecclésiastique byzantine.

Administrant la zone qui lui avait été confiée par le mandat de son évêque, le vicaire avait pour l'aider une corporation de prêtres, le *kliros* (³), organe collectif administratif et judiciaire. Le *kliros* du vicaire correspond, mais avec des compétences plus réduites, au *kliros* de l'évêque, gérant les affaires de l'ensemble du diocèse. A la fin du xie siècle, on constate la présence de vicaires épiscopaux à Souzdal et à Smolensk. C'est peut-être dans le diocèse de Perejaslav, si étendu et si dispersé, que l'on a pour la première fois amélioré de la sorte le système de l'administration ecclésiastique. La question a pu se poser à la suite de l'incorporation du diocèse de Rostov. Rattaché de nouveau à Perejaslav, celui-ci a pu être aussitôt divisé en deux vicariats : Rostov et Souzdal. Indépendamment de l'intention des fondateurs, les vicariats se transformaient, lorsque les circonstances politiques étaient favorables, en évêchés (ce fut le cas à Smolensk).

Le trait particulier de l'organisation ecclésiastique en Russie, qui s'accusa dès le xie siècle et qui devait la caractériser constamment par la suite, c'est le petit nombre de diocèses sur un grand

---

(1) Cf. Golubinskij, *op. cit.*, I-1, pp. 383-388 ; Poppe, *L'acte de fondation* ..., pp. 70-71, et du même auteur (en polonais) dans *Przegląd Historyczny*, LVII, 1966, pp. 552-554.

(2) E. E. Granstrem, *Le moine Malachias le Philosophe* (en russe) dans *Arheologičeskiĭ Ežegodnik za 1962 g.*, Moscou, 1963, pp. 69-70.

(3) Le grec *κλῆρος*, clergé ; calque russe utilisé surtout dans un sens restreint, désigne le clergé de la cathédrale, le collège des prêtres et des diacres auprès de l'évêque (correspond à *πρεσβυτέριον* -presbyterium). Cette institution, qui exige encore des recherches approfondies, a disparu en Moscovie aux xive-xve siècles, mais s'est maintenue jusqu'au xviiie siècle dans l'église orthodoxe sur les terres qui firent partie du Grand Duché de Lithuanie et de la Pologne. Cf. Golubinskij, *op. cit.*, t. I-1, pp. 376-383, 387-388, Hruševskyj, *op. cit.*, III, p. 284.

territoire. Bien que les grandes dimensions des évêchés de Russie
sautent au yeux, ce pays ne constitue pas une exception à cet
égard. Ceci semble être la caractéristique des organisations ecclésiastiques de toute l'Europe barbare, aussi bien à l'est qu'à l'ouest,
où le christianisme introduit d'en haut devint d'emblée la doctrine
officielle de l'État et réalisa sa mission en usant de l'appareil de
l'État. La diversité de la géographie ecclésiastique de la zone
méditerranéenne semble découler non seulement de la structure
de l'habitat (la cité antique), mais aussi du fait que le christianisme
remporta ici des succès sans disposer au début de moyens de coër-
cition administrative. Toute la Russie, avec environ 6 à 7 millions
d'habitants vivant sur un territoire d'une superficie d'environ
1.400.000 km² à la fin du xɪᵉ siècle, se contentait de 9 diocèses,
et, au seuil du xɪɪɪᵉ siècle, de 13, alors qu'à Byzance, pour une superficie à peu près égale, au milieu du xɪᵉ siècle, avec à peu près 20
millions d'habitants, le nombre d'évêchés était d'environ 750.
Ce caractère des évêchés russes devait déterminer la position sociale
de leurs pasteurs. Ceux-ci devenaient de plus en plus de véritables
princes de l'Église. A la fin du xɪᵉ et au xɪɪᵉ siècle s'établit le
principe de la division en diocèses en fonction des partages politiques, aussi bien que de la loi non écrite selon laquelle le siège
épiscopal devient un attribut indispensable d'une principauté
reconnue. Ce facteur politique déterminera le développement ultérieur de l'organisation du réseau diocésain aux xɪɪɪᵉ-xvᵉ siècles.
Les princes tendant à l'autonomie et à la stabilisation politique
de leur domaine seront favorables à la création de nouveaux évêchés.
Une fois leur but atteint, ils s'opposeront à de nouveaux partages
ecclésiastiques.

Varsovie.

IX

LE PRINCE ET L'ÉGLISE EN RUSSIE DE KIEV DEPUIS LA FIN DU Xᵉ SIÈCLE JUSQU'AU DÉBUT DU XIIᵉ SIÈCLE *

A partir du IXᵉ siècle, l'idéologie chrétienne, surtout sous sa forme byzantine et formulée en langue slave, a commencé à s'infiltrer dans les couches dominantes de la société des Slaves orientaux et, vers la fin du Xᵉ siècle, elle a été définitivement acceptée par le souverain. Hilarion, en glorifiant, soixante ans après le baptême, cet acte apostolique de Vladimir, a constaté «qu'on ne se baptisait pas tant parce qu'on était épris de la nouvelle religion, mais plutôt parce qu'on craignait le souverain dont la piété allait de pair avec son pouvoir» [1]. Par la volonté du monarque russe le christianisme était devenue une norme légale. Vladimir Iᵉʳ avait en effet renoncé à tout essai d'élargir et de renforcer le culte païen et s'était décidé de choisir le système des croyances et des idées chrétiennes, dont l'influence et l'attrait étaient incomparablement plus grands.

L'adhésion de la Kiévie à la communauté chrétienne au moment même où

---

* Cet article résume un ouvrage plus vaste que l'auteur a consacré aux relations entre l'État russe et l'Église nouvellement établie dans cet État. Il présente donc en bref certaines solutions qui sont basées sur une argumentation plus détaillée dans d'autres de ses ouvrages, surtout dans son livre *Państwo i Kościół na Rusi w XI w.* [*L'État et l'Église en Russie au XIᵉ s.*]. Le titre slave du souverain de la Russie kiévienne *kniaz* est traduit dans cet article par *prince* dans le sens historique du terme : seigneur souverain. Sa sémantique politique et constitutionnelle répond plus exactement au titre de *rex* que l'on donnait aux souverains de la Russie dans les pays de culture latine. Cf. A. V. Soloviev, «*Reges*» et «*Regnum Russiae*» au Moyen Age, «*Byzantion*» vol. XXXVI, 1966, pp. 144 - 173. Le titre de *kniaz*-prince s'était déprécié au cours des siècles. Les titres de *dux* et de *princeps* que l'on donnait dans les sources latines aux souverains des Slaves occidentaux (polonais et tchèques) découlaient de la politique de l'empereur et du pape qui s'attribuaient le droit exclusif de couronner les rois. Cela fait que seul un *rex coronatus* avait droit au titre de roi. Cf. J. Baszkiewicz, *Państwo suwerenne w feudalnej doktrynie* [*L'État souverain dans la doctrine féodale*], Warszawa 1964, pp. 59 et suiv. et 439 et suiv.

[1] *Des Metropoliten Ilarion Lobrede auf Vladimir den Heiligen und Glaubensbekenntnis*, éd. L. Müller, Wiesbaden 1962, p. 105. En ce qui concerne la société des Slaves orientaux à la veille de leur conversion au christianisme, cf. A. Gieysztor, *La strutturazione culturale dei paesi slavi nell'alto medioevo*, dans: *Settimane di studio del Centro italiano di studi sull'alto medioevo*, vol. XI, Spoleto 1964, pp. 371 - 392.

le prince russe — appelé par une des parties — intervenait dans les luttes internes pour le pouvoir de l'Empire byzantin, prouve que cet acte avait nettement un caractère politique. C'était une mesure mûrement réfléchie et dictée par le besoin croissant de moderniser l'État et la société. Il s'agissait de consolider la couche dominante et d'acquérir les instruments idéologiques permettant d'exercer une influence sur toute la société. Dans l'ancien État russe, qui comptait diverses ethnies, mais où le substrat slave l'emportait de beaucoup, le pouvoir désireux de trouver des stimulants d'intégration, devait forcément remarquer que, malgré un grand nombre de nationalités, l'État byzantin (oikoumenē Romaiōn) conservait aussi son unité grâce à une religion commune.

A partir du moment où l'Église s'établit en Russie, elle fut une partie intégrante de l'organisation de l'État. Il ne pouvait en être autrement. Grâce à l'État, à sa couche dominante et surtout grâce au souverain, l'Église disposait d'un vaste champ d'action où seule l'aide active de l'appareil d'État pouvait lui assurer des progrès. Les liens canoniques et juridiques qui la liaient à Constantinople, ne l'empêchaient pas d'être une Église nationale, bien qu'il soit évident que les contacts religieux et politiques, soigneusement cultivés par les deux parties, avaient un sens spécifique et durable. Dans l'Église russe, nous retrouvons les traits caractéristiques non seulement de l'Église byzantine, étroitement liée à l'État, mais aussi des organisations ecclésiastiques d'État de l'Europe latine avant la réforme grégorienne [2].

La prééminence du facteur politique, incarné dans la personne du souverain russe, sur l'organisation de l'Église ne signifiait pas que celle-ci ne servait qu'à consolider l'État et la société. La religion chrétienne, avant qu'elle ne se soit fait connaître comme élément stabilisant la hiérarchie des valeurs sociales, a ouvert aux couches supérieures des possibilités de   réception idéologique et culturelle inconnues jusqu'alors et   a enrichi leur vie spirituelle et intellectuelle. Lorsque Vladimir décida d'admettre le christianisme comme religion d'État,   la couche dominante, dont une partie avait déjà été christianisée,   aida efficacement l'Église à s'enraciner dans les territoires nouvellement conquis. L'alliance organique de ces deux institutions et des couches sociales qu'elles représentaient, se basait sur les principes apostoliques connus depuis le IXe siècle dans leur traduction en langue slave et rappelés aux fidèles durant les services divins. Le premier principe faisait ressortir « que toute personne soit soumise aux autorités supé-

---

[2] Les rapports entre le souverain et l'Église en Russie semblent avoir beaucoup d'analogie avec la situation dans l'État des Mérovingiens et des Carolingiens. En puisant dans les exemples byzantins il convient de ne pas oublier le rôle exceptionnel que le pouvoir impérial a joué dans l'Église orientale, où ce pouvoir personnifiait non seulement l'État, mais constituait aussi un élément durable de l'enseignement de l'Église et de ses traditions. Cf. G. A. Ostrogorskij, *Otnošenije cerkvi i gosudarstva v Vizantii*, «Seminarium Kondakovianum», vol. IV, 1931, pp. 121 - 134; A. Michel, *Die Kaisermacht in der Ostkirche*, Darmstadt 1959, p. 121 et suiv.; H. G. Beck, *Kirche und theologische Literatur im byzantinischen Reich*, München 1959, pp. 36 - 37.

rieures, car il n'y a point d'autorité qui ne vienne de Dieu [...]» (cf. épître de
Paul aux Romains 13, 1 - 8) et le second indiquait les limites de cette soumission:
«Il faut obéir à Dieu plutôt qu'aux hommes» (*Actes des apôtres* 5, 29, cf. 4, 19).
Lucas Jydiata, évêque de Novgorod, a résumé ces principes dans son sermon
en disant: «Craignez Dieu et honorez le prince, car vous êtes avant tout les serviteurs de Dieu et ce n'est qu'ensuite que vous êtes les serviteurs des souverains».
Il en résultait le droit de ne pas obéir aux autorités si leurs ordres étaient en contradiction avec les recommandations religieuses [3]. Le chrétien russe n'envisageait
pas en général ce dilemme. Une orthodoxie que rien ne venait contaminer valait
en effet aux princes russes — à quelques exceptions près — d'être qualifiés
par les écrivains contemporains de «princes épris du Christ» et de «princes orthodoxes».

La christianisation, évidemment la christianisation formelle, de la société
russe était impensable sans l'application de la terreur quand il fallait déraciner
le paganisme et étouffer toute velléité païenne . Là, où il y avait une confrontation drastique des deux structures religieuses, la hache du prince ou de
l'un de ses fonctionnaires ou la potence avaient le dernier mot [4]. Tant qu'une
évangélisation plus vaste que la simple formalité du baptême n'avait pas dépassé
les milieux de la classe dominante et que des mesures repressives veillaient sur
la mise en pratique des coutumes chrétiennes, seule une forte administration de
l'État pouvait garantir à l'Église le monopole dans le domaine idéologique. L'Église
comprenait parfaitement qu'elle avait intérêt à être étroitement liée à l'organisation
de l'État et elle s'efforçait de persuader la classe dominante, surtout le souverain,
que, l'Église et l'État ne faisant qu'un, l'État était responsable du succès de
la mission chrétienne et d'une vie de ses sujets conforme aux «lois divines». La
métropole de Kiev était une filiale de l'Église de Byzance, mais ce fait n'a pas
exercé une influence négative sur l'intégration de l'État et de l'Église en Kiévie.
Grâce au développement intensif du mouvement monastique, alimenté surtout
par les couches supérieures de la société, dans les monastères et près des cathédrales
épiscopales de la Russie se sont formés, au cours du XIe siècle déjà, des centres
nevralgiques qui devaient décider du dynamisme de la christianisation. Le métropolite — d'origine grecque, nommé à Constantinople, n'était pas toujours capable
de diriger la nef de l'Église en Kiévie et de prendre l'initiative de mesures pouvant
transformer la «Russie païenne» en «sainte Russie». Il s'efforçait plutôt de servir
cette Église de son érudition théologique et de ses conseils et, plus d'une fois,

---

[3] Cf. G. Voskresenskij, *Drevnij slovianskij perevod Apostola i jego sud'by do XV v.* Moskva 1879, pp. 211, 219; *Russkie dostopamiatnosti*, vol. I, Moskva 1815, p. 10; V. Valdenberg,
*Drevnerusskie učenia o predelah carskoj vlasti. Očerki russkoj političeskoj literatury ot Vla-
dimira Sviatogo do konca XVII veka*, Petrograd 1916, pp. 28 - 40.

[4] Cf. *Povest vremennyh let* (dans la suite PVL) vol. I. Moskva 1950, pp. 117 - 121. Cf. A. Gieysztor, *Mouvements para-hérétiques en Europe centrale et orientale du IXe au Xe siècle : apostasies*,
dans: *Hérésies et sociétés dans l'Europe pré-industrielle 11e - 18e siècles*, Paris 1968, pp. 163 - 164.

l'envergure de cette entreprise devait l'épouvanter, d'autant plus que 'en tant que représentant de l'Empire, il déployait à la cour du prince une activité politique et diplomatique tendant avant tout à obtenir son aide pour repousser les nomades qui attaquaient l' *Oikoumene Romaion*. Sans amoindrir le rôle que les métropolites grecs ont joué durant le premier siècle du christianisme en Russie — la personnalité de certains d'entre eux mérite de retenir l'attention — c'est cependant le clergé russe qui a contribué le plus efficacement à édifier l'Église russe et qui a réussi d'ores et déjà à former une pléiade d'évêques et d'higoumènes connaissant leur propre pays.

Le prince et le synode des évêques à Kiev élevèrent, en 1051, un moine russe, Hilarion, à la dignité de métropolite de Kiev sans la participation de Constantinople, ce qui représentait, avant l'époque mongole, un événement exceptionnel dans la procédure habituelle des nominations à ce poste. Les recherches effectuées pour connaître les circonstances qui ont accompagné la nomination d'Hilarion permettent de rejeter l'opinion généralement admise par les historiens selon laquelle Iaroslav le Sage aurait décidé de prendre cette mesure pour rendre l'Église russe indépendante de Byzance. Ce point de vue implique que, avant 1051 et peu de temps après cette année, la Russie kiévienne devait tolérer la juridiction byzantine, c'est-à-dire qu'elle était *de facto* et *de jure* un État dépendant de l'Empire, obligé d'obéir en dépit de ses propres ambitions et de son programme politique. Partant de ce point de vue, le retour après 1051 de l'Église russe sous la juridiction de Constantinople aurait signifié une défaite politique, réduisant la Kiévie au rang de vassal de Byzance. La situation politique et la position internationale de la Russie à cette époque excluent cette éventualité [5].

Les liens unissant la province ecclésiastique russe au patriarcat de Constantinople avaient été acceptés de bon gré. Les contacts, établis par ordre du souverain, s'étaient resserrés au cours de quelques dizaines d'années et avaient contribué à former une couche sociale peu nombreuse, mais saturée d'idéaux chrétiens, consciente de sa vocation et prête à évangéliser sa propre société. Sous l'influence des principes du monachisme byzantin, surtout des monastères de l'Athos, se forma en Kiévie, au cours de près d'un demi siècle, un mouvement monastique particulièrement sensible aux courants réformateurs qui étaient dirigés contre les erreurs de plus en plus nombreuses dans l'Église, contre les déviations et les abus, et contre toute infidélité envers les idéaux.

La nomination d'Hilarion à la dignité de métropolite de Kiev doit être considérée comme une manifestation du courant de rénovation propre au milieu monastique byzantin, qui s'efforçait de restituer à la hiérarchie ecclésiastique son

---

[5] Pour plus de détails cf. A. Poppe, *Państwo i kościół* [*L'État et l'Église*], Warszawa 1968, chapitre IV; dans le chapitre III de cet ouvrage, l'auteur traite du conflit russo-byzantin (1043 - 1046) et démontre que ce conflit n'avait pas été causé par les affaires de l'Église, comme le suggère la littérature de l'objet, mais que l'expédition contre Constantinople en 1043 avait été provoquée par le souverain de Kiev qui avait pris le parti du prétendant au trône, Georges Maniakes.

autorité morale, et exigeait que le synode des évêques de la province ecclésiastique disposât de ses anciens droits. La participation de Iaroslav le Sage à la nomination du métropolite était due au fait que les évêques et le clergé de la Russie kiévienne reconnaissaient à leur prince les mêmes droits que ceux qui, selon l'opinion du clergé byzantin, revenaient à l'empereur. L'acte de 1051 n'a été engendré ni par l'opposition contre le byzantinisme, ni par l'intention d'édifier une Église russe indépendante, mais par le besoin de rénover la vie de l'Église en général, un besoin ressenti avec le plus d'acuité dans les monastères et mis en pratique là où le monachisme orthodoxe exerçait une grande influence sur le pouvoir de l'État et sur la hiérarchie de l'Église, comme c'était le cas en Georgie (cf. *Vie de St. Georges l'Hagiorite*) et probablement aussi en Russie kiévienne. Si le synode des évêques et le prince avaient élevé Hilarion à la dignité de métropolite de Kiev, cette nomination ne pouvait être considérée, ni en principe, ni du point de vue canonique, comme une rupture des liens juridiques avec Byzance, ou comme leur mise en question. Cette nomination tendait uniquement à réformer l'Église, dont l'organisation était trop centralisée, et à rendre au synode des évêques le rang que lui avaient attribué les Pères de l'Église. Ceux qui avaient pris l'initiative de cette rénovation obtinrent d'abord l'appui du souverain, mais pas pour longtemps. Iaroslav était avant tout un homme politique, et l'organisation de l'Église avait encore trop peu d'importance et elle était trop étroitement liée à l'État pour que le droit de proposer un candidat au poste de métropolite pût être pour lui une prérogative particulièrement désirable. Il avait, en effet, toute possibilité d'exprimer sa volonté en accréditant près de sa cour le métropolite envoyé de Byzance. La procédure relative à la nomination du métropolite, qui avait déjà été acceptée par Vladimir, garantissait la durabilité des contacts avec l'Empire et ouvrait de vastes perspectives.

Les transformations survenant dans la structure de l'État devaient évidemment exercer leur influence sur l'Église russe. Le XIe siècle était non seulement le premier siècle du fonctionnement de l'Église en Russie, mais aussi — ce qui est particulièrement important — de son fonctionnement dans un État uni en principe sous le sceptre du monarque kiévien. Malgré certaines tendances à la décentralisation, cette unité fut maintenue par le triumvirat des fils de Iaroslav dans le troisième quart du XIe siècle. En 1093, mourut le dernier autocrate de la Russie de Kiev, le prince Vsievolod, et bien que la suprématie du prince de Kiev ne faiblêt pas immédiatement et semblât même retrouver son ancien éclat au temps de Vladimir Monomaque (1113 - 1125), la fin de la monarchie russe approchait inéxorablement. L'idée de l'unité de l'État ne quittait pas les princes prétendant au trône de Kiev, mais, au XIIe siècle, la Russie kiévienne se transforma en une fédération de principautés indépendantes. L'Église russe fut alors le véritable continuateur des traditions, le porte-parole de l'unité de l'État russe. Ce nouveau rôle politique semble définir le plus exactement l'étape suivante de l'histoire de l'Église russe.

L'Église s'était établie en Kiévie en tant qu'institution riche en traditions et en expériences dans les domaines les plus divers. Ces traditions définissaient les influences de l'Église et la place privilégiée qu'elle devait occuper dans la structure sociale, économique et politique de l'État chrétien. Pour l'organisation ecclésiastique russe, cet héritage n'était cependant qu'un modèle idéal et, malgré le zèle du souverain et de la couche dominante nouvellement convertie, sa mise en pratique dans un pays jusqu'alors païen exigeait non seulement du temps, mais aussi le travail de nombreuses générations. Ce n'est donc pas le fait du hasard si les bâtisseurs de la nouvelle organisation ecclésiastique avaient recours à l'expérience du paléochristianisme. Mais une activité déployée dans des conditions nouvelles ne pouvait évidemment reconstituer fidèlement la structure servant de modèle. Même en respectant avec soin ce modèle et en donnant aux formes de l'organisation un caractère traditionnel, les domaines et les degrés de cette activité dépendaient du rapport des forces locales. Les princes russes prirent soin des conditions, tant juridiques qu'économiques, de l'existence de l'Eglise, en accordant au clergé le privilège (élargi ensuite) d'une institution autonome et en la dotant de revenus stables et puis de biens immobiliers.

La juridiction ecclésiastique en Russie kiévienne n'avait pas encore atteint le niveau qui est reflété dans ce qu'on appelle les statuts ecclésiastiques de Vladimir Ier et de Iaroslav le Sage, ces statuts ne datant en réalité que du XIIIe et du XIVe siècle. Il ne fait cependant pas de doute que certaines normes des deux statuts remontent au XIe siècle [6]. Le privilège accordé à la fondation de l'évêché de Smolensk, en 1136, est particulièrement utile pour une reconstruction rétrospective de la situation juridique du clergé à cette époque, de la portée de la juridiction ecclésiastique et des sources des dotations [7]. Les transgressions des normes de la vie de famille et de la morale chrétienne, qui ne devinrent des délits qu'à la lumière des nouvelles conceptions religieuses, étaient déjà au XIe siècle subordonnées à la juridiction ecclésiastique. Par contre, la juridiction des princes fut réduite quand on accorda à l'Église une immunité juridique qui s'étendait au clergé,

---

[6] Éd. dans: *Pamjatniki russkogo prava*, vol. I, Moskva 1952, pp. 235 - 285, avec un commentaire de A. A. Zimin, trad. franç.: M. Szeftel, *Documents de droit public relatifs à la Russie médiévale*, Bruxelles 1963, pp. 234 - 238, 251 - 262. Cf. E. E. Golubinskij, *Istorija russkoj cerkvi*, vol. I, 1, Moskva 1904, pp. 399 - 409; M. Gruševskij, *Istorija Ukraini-Rusi*, vol. III, Lvov 1905, pp. 284 - 290; S. V. Juškov, *Obščestvenno-političeskij stroj i pravo Kijevskogo gosudarstwa*, Moskva 1949, pp. 190 - 216; J. N. Ščapov, *Cerkov v sisteme gosudarstvennoj vlasti drevnej Rusi*, dans: *Drevnerusskoje gosudarstvo i jego meždunarodnoje značenie*, Moskva 1965, pp. 279 - 296, 338-354. Sans tenir compte de l'argumentation présentée par la critique des statuts, M. Hellman (*Staat u. Recht in Altrussland*, «Saeculum», vol. V, 1954, pp. 58 - 59) est prêt à les traiter comme des privilèges réels de Vladimir Ier et de Iaroslav le Sage.

[7] Éd. *Pamjatniki...*, vol. II, Moskva 1953, pp. 39 - 44, trad. franç. M. Szeftel, *Documents...*, pp. 289 - 294. Cf. E. Golubinskij, *Istorija...*, vol. I, 1, pp. 411 - 415, 640 - 641; A. Poppe, *Učreditelnaja gramota smolenskoj episkopii*, dans: *Arheografičeskij Ežegodnik za 1965 g.*, Moskva 1966, pp. 59 - 71.

aux moines, aux familles des prêtres séculiers et aux personnes se trouvant sous la protection de l'Église, par exemple aux divers *homines miserabiles*. L'indépendance juridique du clergé n'était cependant pas complète, le clergé ayant été obligé de comparaître également devant le tribunal du prince.

Durant cette première période, l'Église basait son existence matérielle sur la générosité de la classe au pouvoir. Les dotations accordées aux différentes institutions ecclésiastiques étaient en général prélevées, sous forme de dîmes, sur certains revenus du prince. Malgré les opinions généralement admises, il convient de constater que cette dîme ne constituait pas la dixième partie de tous les revenus du prince. En effet, non seulement au XI⁰ siècle, mais aussi au XII⁰, l'Église était encore une organisation bien trop modeste pour pouvoir dépenser un dixième des revenus de l'État. En Russie, cette dîme n'était pas obligatoire, elle n'était qu'une coutume que Vladimir I⁰ʳ avait instituée pour doter les institutions ecclésiastiques de revenus. Cette coutume n'était pas empruntée à l'Europe occidentale, mais dérivait des préceptes moraux concernant «la dixième partie qui revient à Dieu», recommandation que l'Église avait apportée en Russie kiévienne [8]. À cette époque, l'Église ne disposait pas de biens fonciers plus importants, et ce n'est qu'à partir de la seconde moitié du XI⁰ siècle que sa fortune foncière commença à s'accroître au fur et à mesure que les représentants de la classe des grands propriétaires terriens affluaient dans les rangs du haut clergé ainsi qu'aux monastères. Au XII⁰ siècle, les propriétés foncières des monastères et des évêques étaient cependant encore modestes [9].

L'Église complétait de façon essentielle non seulement l'idéologie de l'État russe, mais aussi sa structure. L'identité des deux institutions était mise en relief aussi bien par la participation des princes à la direction des affaires de l'Église que par les liens étroits qui unissaient le clergé aux autorités supérieures de l'État. Les représentants de l'Église prenaient part à la vie politique et exerçaient leur influence sur différents domaines de l'activité de l'État, mais, au XI⁰ siècle, cette influence était beaucoup plus modeste que dans les siècles suivants. D'après les témoignages d'Hilarion, qui sont dignes de foi, Vladimir I⁰ʳ prenait souvent part aux délibérations du synode des évêques, réfléchissant avec eux sur les moyens qui permettraient de renforcer la «loi divine» parmi les néophytes. Au temps de ses successeurs, il n'en était pas autrement: les Pères de l'Église russe comprenaient parfaitement que la participation du souverain donnait une valeur juridique aux décrets promulgués par le synode et que l'appareil de l'État permettait de les mettre plus efficacement en pratique. La collaboration du monarque avec le synode s'est approfondie au fur et à mesure que les évêques de nationalité

---

[8] Cf. A. Poppe, *Państwo*... [*L'État*...], pp. 215 - 218. En prenant une attitude critique à l'égard de la littérature du sujet qui cherchait un modèle dans la pratique de l'Europe occidentale, J. N. Ščapov (*Cerkov*..., pp. 297 - 325), considère que la dîme destinée à l'Église, était accordée auparavant au culte païen.

[9] Cf. J. N. Ščapov, *Cerkov*..., pp. 326 - 338.

russe étaient de plus en plus nombreux, car ils servaient d'intermédiaires au souverain et lui permettaient d'avoir une meilleure connaissance des affaires se rapportant aux territoires administrés par les jeunes princes et par les *posadniki*. Dans le synode, le monarque mettait ses droits à profit en nommant ou en acceptant l'élection d'un candidat au siège épiscopal vacant ou nouvellement érigé.

Bien que dans les sources du XIe siècle il ne soit pas question de dignitaires de l'Église ayant fait partie du conseil princier, leur participation aux délibérations et aux missions importantes en qualité de délégués et d'intermédiaires est dûment attestée. En août 1018 — comme l'écrit Thietmar — c'est sur l'ordre du prince polonais Boleslas le Vaillant et du prince de Kiev Sviatopolk Ier que le métropolite de Kiev se rendit à Novgorod pour entamer des pourparlers avec Iaroslav. Vladimir Monomaque, dans la lettre qu'il adressa en février 1096 à Oleg de Tchernigov (Černihov) proposait des négociations et l'envoi dans ce but «d'un délégué ou d'un évêque». En novembre 1097, la population de Kiev, qui aspirait à la paix entre les princes brouillés, délégua auprès de Monomaque la femme de son père défunt et le métropolite Nicolas. En 1067, Nikon, le supérieur du monastère russe à Tmutarakan, était le porte-parole des habitants de cette ville auprès du prince Sviatoslav de Tchernigov dont ils avaient encouru la défaveur [10]. La cérémonie religieuse instituée dans les milieux princiers au XIe siècle et consistant à prêter serment en baisant la croix contribuait à accroître le rôle du clergé [11]. En recevant ce serment, le clergé devenait le confident des accords conclus entre les princes et, de ce fait, le gardien spirituel de leur inviolabilité. La cérémonie du serment avait un caractère solennel et se déroulait dans l'église. Le clergé accompagnait aussi les princes au cours de leurs expéditions. Par exemple, en 1067, après une bataille victorieuse, les trois fils de Iaroslav baisèrent la «sainte croix» et prêtèrent serment de ne faire aucun mal au prince Vsieslav de Polotsk, si celui-ci venait dans leur camp [12]. Les prêtres qui avaient assisté à la prestation de ce serment se rendirent ensuite chez Vsieslav pour lui garantir l'immunité. L'importance accordée aux serments a fait que l'on condamnait sévèrement tout parjure, considérant qu'il portait atteinte non seulement au

---

[10] *PVL*, vol. I, p. 165 et 174 - 175; *Sbornik XII v. Moskovskogo Uspenskogo Sobora*, éd. A. Šahmatov, P. Lavrov, Moskva 1899, f. 41 *v*. (p. 63).

[11] Première notice de 1059 se rapportant au serment prêté sur la croix: *PVL*, vol. I, p. 109. Cette cérémonie de la prestation du serment était connue des chrétiens russes déjà au Xe s. comme en témoignent les traités de 911 et de 944. Pour les XIIe et XIIIe siècles, cf. L. K. Götz, *Staat u. Kirche in Altrussland*, Berlin 1908, pp. 33 et suiv.

[12] *PVL*, vol. I, p. 143. Le clergé qui accompagnait les princes lors de leurs expéditions contre les païens avait pour tâche d'encourager les «armées du Christ»; cf. l'expédition en 1111 contre les Coumans (*PVL*, Vol. I, p. 191). Les aumôniers accompagnaient également les fonctionnaires des princes qui percevaient les redevances, comme en témoignent les événements de Beloozero (1073 - 1076) (cf. *PVL*, vol. I, p. 117). C'était probablement un des moyens qui permettaient à l'Église de se rendre compte de la situation aux confins de l'État et d'y procéder à l'évangélisation, lorsque les circonstances le permettaient.

système chrétien des valeurs morales, mais aussi à la confiance à l'égard des prêtres qui étaient les garants de ces serments. L'appui idéologique et moral de l'Église avait de l'importance dans les controverses et les luttes politiques. Après avoir pris Kiev, en mars 1073, Sviatoslav et Vsievolod s'efforcèrent d'obtenir du clergé qu'il les appuie contre Iziaslav, mais Théodose, higoumène du monastère des Grottes (Pečerskij), invité à prendre part à l'assemblée des princes, refusa «d'assister à cette délibération injuste» [13]. Il convient cependant de faire ressortir que, au XIe siècle et jusqu'au milieu du XIIe siècle, il n'y avait pas de conflits entre les princes et le clergé supérieur, le métropolite et les évêques. Seul le monastère des Grottes s'opposait à l'activité illégale des princes. Son opposition, inspirée d'ailleurs par des préceptes religieux et les traditions du mouvement monastique byzantin, découlait de la liaison étroite de la congrégation avec la couche dominante. En se servant de la nouvelle idéologie comme d'un instrument politique, les boïars en habits de moine exprimaient en principe le mieux les intérêts collectifs de leur propre classe. Le monastère fut en conflit avec Iziaslav en 1068, lorsque ce dernier ne réussit pas à défendre efficacement les terres russes contre les incursions des Coumans et provoqua une tension à l'intérieur du pays en jetant en prison Vsieslav de Polotsk, malgré le serment qu'il avait prêté sur la croix [14]. En mars 1073, le monastère des Grottes prit résolument la défense du même Iziaslav qui avait été chassé de Kiev et accusa Sviatoslav d'avoir «porté atteinte à la loi paternelle et encore davantage à la loi divine». Théodose accusa alors violemment Sviatoslav, et ce n'est qu'en cédant aux sollicitations pressantes des moines de son monastère et des boïars qu'il consentit à modérer ses accusations. Mais l'entente entre le nouveau prince de Kiev et l'higoumène ne tarda pas à intervenir, car en août 1073 Sviatoslav prit déjà part à la pose de la première pierre de l'église du monastère et fit don d'une grande somme pour sa construction [15]. L'attitude que le monastère avait prise dans les années 1093 - 1095, en s'opposant au prince de Kiev Sviatopolk II, entraîna la déportation de l'higoumène Jean. Les causes de ce malentendu ne sont pas claires, mais il est permis de présumer qu'il était dû au mécontentement de l'aristocratie de Kiev qui en voulait au prince d'avoir pris des décisions sans avoir demandé l'avis du conseil princier de son père et de son oncle. L'aveuglement du prince Vassilko ne fit qu'envenimer le conflit, mais peu de temps après, le monastère avait déjà gagné la faveur du prince de Kiev [16].

Le monastère des Grottes, qui était particulièrement privilégié, pouvait être le porte-parole d'un programme politique défini, mais l'Église russe, en tant qu'ensemble, et le clergé en tant qu'état et malgré les fonctions que ses mem-

---

[13] *Sbornik XII v.* ..., f. 58 (p. 85).

[14] Cf. *PVL*, vol. I, pp. 112 - 116, 128.

[15] *PVL*, vol. I, pp. 121 et 122; *Sbornik XII v.* ..., f. 58 - 60 v. (pp. 85 - 88); *Das Paterikon des Kiever Höhlenklosters*, «Slavische Propyläen», vol. II, München 1964, p. 8.

[16] *PVL*, vol. I, pp. 153, 186 - 187.

bres assumaient au service de l'État, n'avaient pas de représentants qui, à l'instar des boïars, auraient fait partie des assemblées et des conseils princiers. Très caractéristique de cet état de choses était, à la fin du XIe siècle, la tentative — qui a d'ailleurs échoué — d'introduire les dignitaires de l'Église dans l'assemblée des princes. En 1096, Sviatopolk II et Vladimir Monomaque proposèrent à Oleg de Tchernigov de se rencontrer à Kiev afin de s'entendre et de protéger ensemble les terres russes contre l'agression des Coumans. L'accord devait être conclu en présence «des évêques, des higoumènes, des grands de nos pères et des gens de ville». Oleg, qui profitait des renforts de Coumans, rejeta ces propositions, donnant comme motif de son refus «l'inconvenance d'être jugé par des évêques, des higoumènes et le bas peuple». Notons qu'Oleg ne s'opposait pas à la présence des représentants des grands qui siégeaient déjà traditionnellement dans le conseil des princes, mais qu'il protestait contre la présence — ce qui était sans précédent — du clergé et des habitants de Kiev. En 1097, lorsque les princes se rencontrèrent à Lioubetch (Lubeč), les représentants de la hiérarchie de l'Église n'y assistèrent pas,bien que les participants aient promis de respecter les conditions de la paix en prêtant serment sur la croix, probablement en présence des aumôniers qui accompagnaient les princes. De même, les dignitaires de l'Église n'ont pas pris part à l'assemblée des princes en 1100 à Uvietitche (Uvetyče) où ce sont les boïars des princes qui ont servi d'intermédiaires entre les parties [17].

L'Église ne participait pas à l'activité législative des princes lors de leurs assemblées, comme en témoignent la *Justice* (*Pravda*) des fils de Iaroslav de 1072 et le Statut de Vladimir Monomaque de 1113 (art. 2 et 53 réd. étendue de la *Justice russe* (*Pravda russkaja*) qui mentionnent dans leurs titres les principaux participants, c'est-à-dire les princes et les représentants des grands [18]. Dans le cas de la *Pravda* des fils de Iaroslav, c'est d'autant plus significatif que la codification avait eu lieu à Vychgorod (Vyšgorod) où les princes s'étaient rencontrés à l'occasion des cérémonies de la canonisation de leurs oncles Boris et Gleb, cérémonies auxquelles presque toute la hiérarchie supérieure de l'Église avait assisté, à savoir: 5 évêques et une quinzaine d'higoumènes.

L'analyse des normes de la *Justice russe*, normes profondement enracinées dans la tradition législative indigène, prouve, elle aussi, que les représentants de l'Église n'ont pas contribué à la rédaction de ce code d'origine princière dressé

---

[17] *PVL*, vol. I, pp. 150, 170, 181. Au sujet des institutions du pouvoir étatique en Russie et de leur structure cf. V. T. Pašuto, *Čerty političeskogo stroja drevnej Rusi*, dans: *Drevnerusskoje gosudarstvo...*, pp. 11 - 76.

[18] *Pamjatniki...*, vol. I, pp. 108, 113, 79; *Pravda russkaja*, vol. II, Moskva 1947, pp. 121 - 131, 244 - 254, 425 - 428, trad. franç. M. Szeftel, *Documents...*, pp. 34, 68, 79. Cf. L. V. Čerepnin, *Obščestvenno-političeskie otnošenia v drevnej Rusi i Russkaja Pravda*, dans: *Drevnerusskoje gosudarstvo...*, pp. 175 et suiv., 234 et suiv.

au cours des XIᵉ - XIIᵉ siècles [19]. Une certaine influence des coutumes chrétiennes ne se manifeste que dans les parties ultérieures de la *Justice russe* qui datent déjà du XIIᵉ siècle [20]. Dans les décisions du XIᵉ siècle, seule celle de Iaroslav au sujet du *Wehrgeld* (*vira* — amende imposée pour homicide et payée en général par versements) démontre qu'elle a été formulée par un chrétien: elle prévoyait, en effet, que le fonctionnaire du prince qui percevait le *Wehrgeld* aurait un supplément les jours maigres pour s'acheter du fromage et du poisson.

Au XIᵉ siècle, la pratique juridique, de même que la législation, échappait au contrôle de l'Église, bien que celle-ci eût la possibilité d'exercer une influence indirecte en prêchant que les jugements devaient être équitables et qu'il fallait pardonner les offenses. Dans certains cas, elle pouvait aussi s'efforcer d'atténuer la sévérité des jugements en se référant à la miséricorde chrétienne [21]. Mais cela ne signifie pas que le clergé supérieur, d'origine grecque, n'ait pas tenté d'influer sur la jurisprudence dans l'esprit des normes byzantines. L'échec de ces tentatives est attesté dans la *Chronique des temps passés* (*Povest' vremennyh let*) de 996: Vladimir s'était conformé aux conseils des évêques et avait commencé à appliquer des peines corporelles pour le brigandage, mais après quelque temps, ayant besoin «d'armes et de chevaux», il dut y renoncer et revenir aux «coutumes de son père et de son grand-père». Plus important que l'authenticité de ce témoignage nous paraît le fait qu'environ cent ans plus tard un moine du monastère des Grottes crut nécessaire de rappeler cet événement ou bien la légende seulement. Il prouvait ainsi qu'il convient de faire preuve de modération en puisant dans les coutumes étrangères et qu'il faut appliquer ses propres lois là où elles ne sont pas en contradiction avec l'éthique chrétienne. Ces conseils semblent refléter des polémiques suscitées par la fameuse affaire du prince Vassilko, fils de Rostislav, qui, accusé d'avoir voulu attenter à la vie de Sviatopolk II, fut aveuglé en novembre 1096, malgré l'intervention en sa faveur des higoumènes des monastères de Kiev. Ce moyen typiquement byzantin d'éliminer les adversaires politiques,

---

[19] Cf. S. V. Juškov, *Obščestvenno-političeskij stroj...*, pp. 145 et suiv.; A. Soloviev, *Der Einfluss des Byzantinischen Rechtes auf die Völker Osteuropas*, «Zeitschrift der Savigny-Stiftung», Roman. Abt., vol. LXXVI, 1959, pp. 432 et suiv.; L. V. Čerepnin, dans: *Drevnerusskoje gosudarstvo...*, pp. 128 et suiv.

[20] L'art. 92 permet de percevoir une partie de l'héritage pour dire «des prières pour le repos de l'âme», si le défunt n'a pas laissé de testament. Les sources de l'art. 98, qui traite des enfants nés d'une esclave, sont controversables. Ces enfants n'héritaient pas de leur père, mais ils étaient affranchis avec leur mère. Cf. *Pamjatniki...*, vol. I, pp. 117 - 118; M. Szeftel, *Documents...*, pp. 89 - 90 (§§ 83, 88). Au XIᵉ et XIIᵉ s., les fils nés d'une concubine-esclave, avaient les même droits que les fils légitimes. Cf. S. V. Juškov, *Obščestvenno-političeskij stroj...*, pp. 450 - 451. Cf. L. K. Götz, *Kirchenrechtliche u. Kulturgeschichtliche Denkmäler Altrusslands*, Stuttgart 1905, pp. 278 - 279. Au sujet de l'influence que l'Église russe a exercée sur l'esclavage cf. V. O. Klučevskij, *Sočinenija*, vol. VII, Moskva 1959, pp. 338 - 359.

[21] Cf. p. ex. *PVL*, vol. I, p. 182 et la lettre que le métropolite Nicéphore a adressée à Vladimir Monomaque, dans: *Russkije dostopamiatnosti*, vol. I, Moskva 1815, pp. 71 - 72.

qui fut alors appliqué pour la première fois en Russie kiévienne, a été jugé si sévèrement que Sviatopolk II, pour éviter d'être détrôné, a nié d'y avoir pris part et en a rejeté la faute sur David Igorevitch que l'on punit en lui enlevant sa principauté de Vladimir-Volhynie [22]. Il ne fait pas de doute que ceux qui avaient prononcé ce jugement s'étaient référés aux coutumes admises dans l'empire archi-chrétien, mais il est fort significatif que l'affaire de Vassilko ne devint pas un précédent en Kiévie qui, dès le XIe siècle emprunta à Byzance des formes plus modérées de répression à l'égard des adversaires politiques, les obligeant par exemple à entrer au monastère [23].

Les querelles violentes entre les princes, querelles qui vers la fin du XIe siècle accompagnaient le déclin de la monarchie, ouvraient un nouveau champ d'action non seulement aux représentants respectifs de la hiérarchie ecclésiastique, mais aussi à l'Église en tant qu'institution défendant l'ordre politique et social. Les princes qui se combattaient réciproquement devaient s'assurer l'appui des milieux influents de la société et faire appel à l'autorité morale de l'Église, qui de plus en plus souvent avait ses propres points de vue politique. Elle représentait avant tout les intérêts de la classe dominante, mais elle prenait aussi en considération les questions qui intéressaient les larges masses de la société (par exemple la protection des régions situées sur la frontière contre les attaques des nomades de la steppe).

Le monastère des Grottes était le précurseur de changements qui s'approchaient. La participation de l'Église à la vie politique s'accroissait au fur et à mesure que faiblissait le pouvoir des princes et que se poursuivait le morcellement territorial du pays. L'idée de l'unité des terres russes, incarnée jusqu'alors par la monarchie, trouvera un nouveau porte-parole lorsque cette monarchie lui fera défaut. Les princes qui avaient l'ambition de ne pas laisser perdre l'héritage de la monarchie russe des Xe et XIe siècles appréciaient de plus en plus le rôle constructif que l'Église avait joué en contribuant à maintenir l'unité de l'État. De la compréhension de ce fait découlait la collaboration étroite de Vladimir Monomaque avec l'Église. Ce prince, en tentant d'introduire les dignitaires de l'Église dans l'assemblée des princes, indiquait la place que l'Église devait occuper dans la structure de l'État russe. Cette tentative se heurta cependant à une opposition décidée et ce n'est qu'après bien des années que la place indépendante de l'Église dans l'État et dans la société russe fut généralement admise.

La religion chrétienne, après s'être imposée dans l'État russe, lui a apporté en échange des arguments servant à renforcer l'autorité du pouvoir princier. La littérature du XIe siècle traite souvent de l'origine divine de cette autorité, en s'adressant parfois directement au prince: «Toi, que Dieu a désigné...»

[22] Cf. *PVL*, vol. I, pp. 173 - 181; cf. M. Gruševskij, *Istoria...*, vol. II, pp. 91 - 99.
[23] *PVL*, vol. I, p. 109; cf. L. K. Götz, *Staat u. Kirche...*, p. 52.

La conviction que le «prince terrestre» exécutait la volonté de «l'empereur des cieux» était de plus en plus générale [24].

Le *Nomocanon en XIV titres* fit connaître à la Russie kiévienne la formule puisée dans la sixième Nouvelle de Justinien qui définit les rapports réciproques du pouvoir laïc et du pouvoir ecclésiastique: l'empire et la sacerdoce sont des dons divins découlant d'une même source, leur coopération n'est harmonieuse que si chacune des deux parties accomplit ses tâches, c'est-à-dire, si le sacerdoce sert les affaires divines et l'empire dirige les affaires humaines. Le souverain a le devoir de se soucier des dogmes de la foi, de l'honneur du clergé et de veiller à ce que les canons saints soient respectés [25]. Ce principe, complété par une connaissance approfondie des idées politiques byzantines, a servi de base à la déclaration d'Hilarion sur les rapports harmonieux entre l'État et l'Église en Russie et sur le droit et le devoir du prince de protéger l'ensemble de l'Église et sa pureté [26]. On pourrait exprimer la crainte qu'en qualifiant le monarque russe de protecteur de l'Église, Hilarion n'a exprimé que ses propres opinions qui reflètent tout au plus la politique ecclésiastique de Iaroslav le Sage. Un demi-siècle plus tard, le métropolite Nicéphore, un Grec, qui était le sujet aussi bien de l'empereur des Romains que du souverain de Kiévie, prétendait cependant, lui aussi, que le pouvoir monarchique avait la prééminence sur l'Église. Ce fait est significatif pour autant qu'il démontre que même le métropolite ne croyait pas que sa nomination par Constantinople lui permettait de revendiquer une position indépendante dans l'Église russe. Nicéphore, dans une lettre [27] (un *Speculum principis* en son genre) s'adresse à Monomaque «Vénérable chef de nous tous et de toute la terre éprise du Christ» et le compare à l'âme humaine qui dirige toutes les fonctions — sans en excepter une seule — du corps humain. Et du moment que le prince joue dans l'État le même rôle que l'âme dans le corps humain, il en résulte clairement qu'il doit aussi surveiller les questions religieuses qui

[24] Cf. *PVL*, vol. I, p. 86; *Izbornik 1076 g.*, Moskva 1965, pp. 242, 675. Plus en détail et tenant compte avant tout des matériaux ultérieurs: M. D i a k o n o v, *Vlast' moskovskih carei*, SPb, 1889, pp. 40 et suiv.; V. S e r g e j e v i č, *Drevnosti russkogo prava*, vol. II, 3e éd., SPb, 1908, pp. 541 et suiv.; V. V a l d e n b e r g, *Drevnerusskie učenia...*, pp. 82 et suiv.; F. D v o r n i k, *Byzantine Political Ideas in Kievan Russia*, «Dumbarton Oaks Papers», vol. IX/X, 1966, pp. 95 et suiv.; M. C z e r n i a v s k y, *Khan or Basileus: An Aspect of Russian Medieval Political Theory*, «Journal of the History of Ideas», vol. XX, 1959, n° 4, pp. 459 et suiv. Nous ne polémiquerons pas ici avec la littérature du sujet, qui ne consacre d'ailleurs que fort peu d'attention au XIe s. et tire ses conclusions surtout de matériaux ultérieurs, datant même du XVIIe s.

[25] *Syntagma XIV titulorum sine scholiis secundum versionem palaeo-slovenicum adjecto textu greco*, éd. V. B e n e š e v i č, vol. I, SPb, 1906, pp. 739 et suiv.; Cf. V. V a l d e n b e r g, *Drevnerusskie učenia...*, pp. 50 et suiv., 143 et suiv.

[26] Cela a déjà attiré l'attention de: V. V a l d e n b e r g, *Drevnerusskie učenia...*, pp. 93 - 98, et F. D v o r n i k, *Byzantine Political Ideas...*, p. 106 et suiv.

[27] Écrit peu de temps après 1113. Éd.: *Russkie dostopamjatnosti*, vol. I, pp. 61 - 75. Au sujet de Nicéphore, voir *Lexicon Antiquitatum Slavicarum*, vol. III, Warszawa 1968, pp. 369 - 370.

constituent l'un des domaines de la vie de l'État [28]. Nicéphore admet non seulement que le prince a le droit de protéger l'Église et son orthodoxie, mais il lui
apprend qu'en héritant le pouvoir, il hérite aussi le devoir suivant: «Je t'ai trouvé
orthodoxe grâce à Dieu et fidèle à ta première foi [...] et je demande à Dieu
qu'il te garde tel que tu es jusqu'à la fin de tes jours; tu conserveras ta foi et toi-
même si tu ne laisses pas pénétrer un loup dans la bergerie du Christ et si tu
ne permets pas de planter des épines dans la vigne plantée par Dieu, mais si
tu conserves les anciennes traditions de tes pères» [29]. Dans une autre lettre
adressée à Monomaque, il dit clairement que le souverain a le devoir de protéger
son pays contre le schisme occidental et que, fort des prérogatives que Dieu lui
a accordées, il doit instruire ses sujets: «Il sied aux princes, en tant qu'élus de Dieu
et fidèles à Sa foi, de comprendre exactement les paroles du Christ, car elles sont
le fondement de la sainte Église en servant à instruire les hommes que Dieu
a confiés à leur protection [c'est-à-dire à celle des princes — A. P.]. Un seul Dieu
règne dans les cieux et, avec son aide, vous les princes, vous devez régner ici-bàs,
d'une génération à l'autre» [30]. Nicéphore — remarquons-le — a reporté sur toute
la race des princes russes la thèse d' Hilarion, selon laquelle Vladimir Ier était
«notre maître et guide vers la vraie foi». Conformément à cette tradition, les princes
russes, au temps du morcellement en principautés, considéraient qu'ils étaient
les protecteurs de l'Église bien que leur pouvoir n'égalât pas celui des autocrates
du XIe siècle [31]. Le clergé rappelait d'ailleurs aux princes leurs devoirs envers
l'Église, comme, par exemple, le moine Akindin qui, vers 1312, exigeait du prince
Michel de Tver que celui-ci mît fin à la simonie pratiquée par le métropolite:
«Toi, mon Seigneur, tu es empereur sur ton territoire et tu devras répondre
au Jugement Dernier si tu passes maintenant sous silence l'injustice du métropolite» [32].

En admettant que le prince russe recevait son pouvoir de Dieu, le métropolite
— un Grec — tirait un trait d'égalité entre le pouvoir du prince et le pouvoir
de l'empereur, considérant que, tous les deux, ils étaient créés à l'image et à la
ressemblance de Dieu. Nicéphore a exprimé cette pensée d'une façon qui ne laisse
subsister le moindre doute en prétendant que Dieu est une vraie image anticipée

---

[28] *Russkie dostopamjatnosti*, vol. I, pp. 63 - 68. Cf. V. Valdenberg, *Drevnerusskie učenia...*
pp. 114 et suiv.

[29] *Russkie dostopamjatnosti*, vol. I, p. 70.

[30] K. Kalajdovič, *Pamjatniki russijskoj slovesnosti*, Moskva 1821, p. 163.

[31] Cf. L. K. Götz, *Staat u. Kirche...*, pp. 64 et suiv.; 74 et suiv. Ce qui fait que nous sommes prêts à reconnaître comme un *novum* la tentative des empereurs byzantins dans la seconde
moitié du XIIe s. de jouer le rôle de protecteurs de l'Église russe et d'arbitres dans les controverses ecclésiastiques et politiques.

[32] *Russkaja Istoričeskaja Biblioteka*, vol. VI, SPb, 1880, n° 16, p. 158. Cf. V. Valdenberg,
Drevnerusskie učenia..., pp. 137 et suiv. Cf. l'équivalent en Europe occidentale de la formule
d'Akidin *«rex in regno suo imperator»*. En ce qui concerne la notion de la souveraineté au Moyen
Age, cf. J. Baszkiewicz, *Państwo suwerenne...* [*L'État souverain...*], pp. 31 et suiv.

des images de l'empereur et du prince [33]. En reportant cet attribut au pouvoir du prince, Nicéphore s'écartait du système byzantin des notions d'après lesquelles le pouvoir absolu sur terre, que Dieu a confié à un seul souverain, au *basileus* des Romains, était un et indivisible, à la ressemblance du pouvoir céleste [34]. La conception du *rex imago dei* était déjà connue en Kiévie grâce à la *Schede basilike* que le diacre Agapet avait écrite pour Justinien vers 527. Ce traité (ou ses fragments) devait se trouver dans la bibliothèque des princes de Kiev, car un certain Jean en a profité en 1076 pour compléter sa collection de sentences portant sur le caractère divin du pouvoir des princes, sur le prince en tant que «gouverneur» de Dieu sur terre et sur le devoir d'obéir au prince (souverain visible) et de le respecter comme Dieu (souverain invisible). Ces sentences brossaient un tableau du prince à la ressemblance de Dieu [35].

Considérant que le pouvoir de l'empereur et celui du prince étaient égaux, la littérature russe du XIe siècle n'octroyait pas, cependant, au prince russe le titre du *basileus, cesar*. Bien qu' Hilarion tire un signe d'égalité entre Constantin le Grand et Vladimir Ier, et bien qu'il admette que le prince *(kagan, vladyka)* de la Russie kiévienne soit un souverain du même rang que l'empereur, il ne lui donne jamais le titre d'empereur [36]. L'auteur du code de 1076 en a adapté toutes les notions à la réalité russe et là où il était question du souverain, il a remplacé *basileus* du texte original et *cesar* de l'ancienne traduction slave, par prince *(kniaz)* en conservant le titre d'empereur pour désigner le souverain des cieux. Nicéphore ne qualifie pas non plus le prince d'empereur, bien qu'il dise que Dieu «règne dans les cieux», et le prince «règne sur la terre» [37]. Si, au XIe siècle, les princes russes n'employaient pas le titre d'empereur, cela résultait d'une part de la valeur qu'ils attribuaient au titre héréditaire de prince qu'ils avaient complété au Xe siècle par le titre de *kagan (chacanus)* après s'être emparés du royaume des Khazars, et d'autre part, de la signification historique du titre impérial qui évoquait *Orbis Romanus* et la succession romaine que les princes russes ne revendiquaient pas, comme le faisaient les souverains bulgares et les rois allemands.

---

[33] «*Gospod'* [. . .] *jest' istinnyj ikunnik carskoje i kniažeskoje ikuny*» (Russkie dostopamjatnosti. . .), vol. I, p. 75.

[34] Cf. F. Dölger, *Byzanz u. europeische Staatenwelt*, Ettal 1953, pp. 291 et suiv.; A. Michel, *Kaisermacht*..., pp. 127 - 132. Cf. J. Baszkiewicz, *Państwo suwerenne*... [*L'État souverain*...], pp. 139 et suiv.

[35] *Izbornik 1076*..., pp. 241 - 244, 675. Cf. I. Ševčenko, *On Some Sources of Prince Svjatoslav's Izbornik of the year 1076*, dans: *Orbis scriptus, Festschrift für O. Tschiževskij*, München 1966, pp. 724 - 730.

[36] Cf. *Des Metropoliten Ilarion Lobrede*..., pp. 110 et suiv., Dans *La vie des Saints Martyrs Boris et Gleb* (éd. D. Abramowič, Petrograd 1916, rééd. München 1967, p. 6) Nestor qualifie la décision de Vladimir Ier de «droit impérial».

[37] «*Régner*» est ici une traduction du verbe slave *carstvovati* — équivalent de l'orig. Βασιλεύω *(imperare)*. Cf. K. Kalajdovič, *Pamiatniki*..., p. 163; *Sbornik 1076 g.* ..., pp. 241 - 244, 263, 296, 335, 514, 670 et 675; cf. le texte grec pp. 715, 741, 766, 815, 816.

Bien que la littérature russe du XIᵉ siècle ne donne pas aux princes le titre d'empereur [38], elle met cependant en relief le caractère monarchique du pouvoir des princes de Kiev au XIᵉ siècle en empruntant à Byzance des titres tels que: *autarchos, autoctrator, monocrator, monarchos* et en les traduisant en langue slave: *samovlastec, samoderžec, jedynoderžec, jedynovlastec* [39]. Dans ce cas également, le clergé a servi d'intermédiaire.

Les liens juridiques qui unissaient l'Église russe à Constantinople ne garantissaient pas à l'Empire une suprématie politique en Russie, mais il est possible qu'on ait tenté de les utiliser pour classifier les souverains russes d'après la hiérarchie byzantine qui attribuait à l'empereur de Byzance la première place dans la famille des souverains. Au Xᵉ siècle s'est déjà manifestée la tendance — à peine perceptible dans les matériaux qui se sont conservés jusqu'à ce jour — à définir la parenté spirituelle entre l'empereur byzantin et le prince russe en donnant à ce dernier le titre de frère ou de fils spirituel (πνευματικὸς ἀδελφός, πνευματικὸν τέκνον). D'après F. Dölger, le fait d'avoir qualifié deux fois la princesse Olga de fille d'empereur dans la description de son baptême doit être compris comme définition de son degré dans la hiérarchie des souverains [40]. Selon nous, il convient de comprendre de la même façon la notice de Skylitzes concernant «Vladimir, frère de l'empereur» Βλαδιμηροῦ, τοῦ ἀδελφοῦ τοῦ βασιλέως. Dans ce cas, Skylitzes n'a pas commis d'erreur (comme l'a supposé un des copistes qui a remplacé ἀδελφοῦ par γαμβροῦ), parce qu'il connaissait parfaitement les liens de parenté qui unissaient Basile II au prince russe Vladimir (Anne, la femme de Vladimir était en effet la soeur de l'empereur Basile) [41]. Dans la correspondance diplomatique, Basile II pouvait donner le titre de frère à Vladimir Iᵉʳ, étant donné qu'il s'adressait à un membre de la famille des sou-

---

[38] Un graffito de la cathédrale Sagesse Divine à Kiev, qui porte la date de la mort de Iaroslav le Sage, qualifie ce dernier de «notre césar» (cf. S. A. Vysockij, *Drevnerusskie nadpisi Sofii Kievskoj*, Kiev 1966, n° 8, pp. 39 - 41). Ce serait cependant un malentendu que d'en conclure que Iaroslav lui-même avait pris le titre d'empereur. C'est plutôt une contribution intéressante qui met en lumière l'idée que la cour et les milieux ecclésiastiques se faisaient du pouvoir du prince. Un deuxième exemple nous fournit une notice dans *l'Évangile* du prince Mstislav, qui date d'environ 1115, et où un fonctionnaire du prince, Naslav, donne à son maître, le prince de Novgorod, le titre d'empereur. Cf. F. Buslajev, *Istoričeskaja hrestomatija*, Moskva 1861, p. 35. Le titre d'empereur est donné ensuite de plus en plus fréquemment à certains princes, mais toujours dans des circonstances particulières.

[39] Le titre «autocrate de toute la terre russe» n'était d'ailleurs pas en contradiction avec le titre *basileus kai autokrator Romaion*. Ce n'était pas le cas des souverains serbes et bulgares, qui prétendaient être «les autocrates» non seulement des Bulgares (Serbes), mais aussi des Grecs. Cf. F. Dölger, *Byzanz...*, pp. 140 et suiv.

[40] F. Dölger, *Byzanz...*, p. 170. Dölger écrit (p. 50) que le prince Rostislav (1254 - 1258) nommait l'empereur byzantin son père. Il n'est cependant pas possible de tirer des conclusions de cet exemple qui se rapporte à une situation complètement différente.

[41] *Skylitzes-Kedrenos*, vol. II, (Bonnae 1839), pp. 464, 444, 478; γαμβρός: mari de la fille où de la soeur.

verains. Les frères et les fils spirituels occupaient dans la famille des souverains la place la plus proche de son chef, l'empereur des Romains, et on donnait, par exemple, le titre de fils spirituel au tsar de Bulgarie, et celui de *nobilissimus frater* à l'empereur, le roi des Allemands [42]. Nous ne savons pas cependant comment les souverains de la Russie de Kiev acceptaient cet ordre hiérarchique très subtil. Il se peut qu'ils ne s'intéressaient guère aux aspirations idéologiques de l'empire, de même que les Normands d'Italie, qui avaient refusé au XIe siècle le titre honorifique de «fils» de l'empereur.

Dans la pratique byzantine, on donnait à partir du IXe siècle le titre d'archonte aux souverains russes, probablement pour éviter d'appliquer aux princes slaves (pour des raisons semblables on ne traduisait pas *reges* du monde latin) le titre plus adéquat de *basileus*, réservé exclusivement à l'empereur de Romains. Le terme grec ἄρχων qui répond à prince et englobe les notions de chef, dirigeant, roi, souverain, satisfaisait d'ailleurs pleinement les souverains russes, comme en témoigne la sphragistique [43]. Les Byzantins, en se rendant compte des larges possibilités sémantiques du terme que les hauts fonctionnaires de l'administration territoriale de l'empire employaient également à l'époque, complétaient le titre d'archonte donné aux princes russes par un prédicat honorifique. Dans la pratique de la chancellerie impériale, les prédicats avaient plus d'importance que les titres, comme G. Ostrogorsky l'a déjà fait remarquer [44]. Les métropolites russes qualifiaient le prince russe de *blagorodnyj kniaže* (prince noble). Les empereurs byzantins donnaient probablement aux princes russes les prédicats équivalents : de πανευγενέστατος et de εὐγενέστατος (*nobilissimus*) ἀδελφός (aux jeunes princes de τέκνον) [45]. La traduction faite vers 1085 de l'une des réponses du métropilite Jean II prouve que ce prédicat, qui complétait le titre de prince, avait été introduit en Russie de Kiev par les Grecs (dans la titulature russe ce prédicat n'était qu'une tautologie). Le traducteur russe a traduit le terme de τοῦ εὐγενεστάτου ἄρχοντος qui figure dans cette réponse, par *blagovernogo kniazia* (prince orthodoxe), considérant que le prédicat chrétien y était plus

---

[42] Cf. G. Ostrogorsky, *Die byzantinische Staatenhierarchie, Seminarium Kondakovianum,* vol. VIII, 1936, pp. 41 et suiv.; F. Dölger, *Byzanz...*, pp. 34 - 69, 159 - 182; J. Baszkiewicz, *Państwo...*, pp. 142 et suiv.

[43] Il ne fait pas de doute que c'est sous l'influence du *megas archon* byzantin (cf. dans les traités du Xe s.) que le titre de *velikj kniaz* (grand prince) a fait son apparition en Russie. Il n'a cependant été employé qu'à partir du XIIe siècle, au fur et à mesure du morcellement en principautés et du pouvoir de plus en plus restreint du prince aîné. Malgré l'ouvrage de L. K. Götz (1911), cette question exige des recherches approfondies. Au sujet du titre d'archonte, cf. A. V. Soloviev, *Archôn Rhôsias*, «Byzantion», vol. XXXI, 1961, pp. 237 - 244, et le même auteur, *Reges...*, p. 147 - 149.

[44] G. Ostrogorsky, *Die byzantinische Staatenhierarchie...*, p. 52.

[45] Cf. le sceau de Vladimir Monomaque: Σφραγ[ὶς] Βασιλείου τοῦ πανευγενεστάτου ἄρχοντος 'Ρωσίας τοῦ Μονομάχ[ου]

indiqué [46]. Il est d'ailleurs caractéristique de la littérature russe que, même dans les cas où les titres étaient nombreux, elle n'employait pas le prédicat *blagorodnyj*, mais ajoutait des définitions qui accentuaient le caractère chrétien du pouvoir des porteurs de ces titres.

Les nombreux prédicats auxquels les oints de Dieu (l'empereur et les évêques) avaient droit à Byzance et qui avaient été introduits également dans les titres des princes de Kiev, exprimaient la nature charismatique de la personne et de la dignité princière [47]. Nicéphore appelle le prince *expressis verbis* l'oint de Dieu [48]. Ce n'est pas seulement sa propre conception, mais une conséquence logique de l'idée qu'il se faisait de la source du pouvoir princier. Les souverains russes étaient également conscients du rôle qui leur incombait. En 1096, Monomaque engageait le prince Oleg de Tchernigov à s'humilier et à s'entendre «au nom de Dieu». Il lui citait l'exemple de «l'oint de Dieu» David pour lui prouver que le fait de s'humilier ne porterait pas atteinte à l'honneur de l'oint de Dieu, prince Oleg, comme il n'avait pas porté atteinte à l'honneur du roi biblique [49]. La conviction que le prince avait été oint par Dieu ne s'accompagnait pas en Russie kiévienne du rite de l'onction, et à Byzance la *chrisma basileias* n'avait qu'un sens métaphorique   ce n'est que sous l'influence de l'Occident que vers le début du XIIIe siècle elle devint un sacrement physique [50].

La cérémonie du couronnement et le port de la couronne comme attribut du pouvoir ne sont pas entrés dans les coutumes de la Russie kiévienne. Les princes, qui étaient des souverains héréditaires, ne ressentaient pas le besoin d'imiter l'empereur byzantin électif, qui n'était un oint qu'à partir du moment de son couronnement, alors qu'eux, ils étaient oints dès leur naissance. Par contre, il semble que, déjà au XIe siècle, l'intronisation avait le caractère d'une cérémonie religieuse. Les témoignages du XIIe siècle, relatifs aux intronisations qui se déroulaient dans la cathédrale où se trouvait le trône du prince, prouvent que ces cérémonies étaient coutumières [51]. Le caractère charismatique de la personne du prince se manifestait aussi dans l'habitude d'inscrire les noms des souverains

---

[46] L. K. Götz, *Kirchenrechtliche...*, pp. 138 - 139. Jean II confère au prince des prédicats qui ne sont pas traduits: Εὐσεβὴς γάρ ὢν Θεοῦ χάριτι καὶ ὀρθοδοξώτατος... .

[47] Cf. p. ex.: *bogolubivij, blagovernij, pravovernij, bogohranimij, hristolubivij* (en grec.: θεοφιλής, εὐσεβέστατος, πιστότατος, ὀρθόδοξος, θεοφρουρητός, χριστοφιλός).

[48] *Russkie dostopamjatnosti...*, vol. I, p. 63.

[49] Cf. *PVL*, vol. I, pp. 164 - 165.

[50] Cf. A. Michel, *Kaisermacht...*, pp. 10 - 13, 174 - 175. Le rite oriental ne connaissait pas l'onction physique, aussi dans le cas du sacre des évêques. Cette onction s'éffectuait symboliquement au cours des cérémonies du sacre, appelées aussi chrisme.

[51] Cf. *Polnoie Sobranie russkih letopisej*, vol. I², Leningrad 1926 - 1928, col. 306, 423; vol. II², SPb, 1908, col. 276, 327; L. K. Götz, *Staat u. Kirche...*, pp. 30 - 33. La tonsure des jeunes princes était également une cérémonie religieuse, comme en témoignent les documents de la fin du XIIe, et du début du XIIIe siècles. Nous n'avons cependant aucune donnée pour admettre que cette cérémonie se déroulait déjà au XIe siècle.

dans les diptyques et de les citer au cours des prières liturgiques (*ektene*). Nous en trouvons le témoignage le plus ancien dans la Vie de Théodose des Grottes où il est question des événements de 1073. Il est cependant permis de présumer qu'à l'instar de Byzance cette coutume a déjà été acceptée au temps de Vladimir [52]. La canonisation des fils de Vladimir Ier, les princes Boris et Gleb, qui a eu lieu le 20 mai 1072, a contribué incontestablement à sanctifier toute la dynastie, aussi bien dans l'Église que parmi le peuple chrétien [53].

Et, enfin, la coutume empruntée à Byzance de faire représenter le souverain et sa famille sur les murs des églises, créait aussi une ambiance mystique et sanctifiante autour de la dynastie. Les fragments d'une peinture à fresque, qui date des années quarante du XIe siècle, se sont conservés dans la cathédrale Sagesse Divine à Kiev. Cette peinture, qui peut être reconstituée grâce aux matériaux iconographiques des XVIIe et XIXe siècles, occupait environ 25 m² de l'aile occidentale de la nef centrale et representait le fondateur de la cathédrale — Iaroslav le Sage — qui, portant le modèle de cette église, se rendait en procession avec sa femme, ses fils et ses filles vers le trône du Christ [54]. Le choix de la place dans la nef centrale de l'église, dans l'entourage d'une série de peintures consacrées à des thèmes christologiques et en face d'une frise en mosaïque dans l'abside représentant l'Eucharistie, donne l'impression que la procession des douze personnes de la famille du monarque est une réplique de la procession des apôtres, symbole visible de la mission apostolique que la dynastie devait remplir auprès de ses sujets. Les regards sévères d'une pléiade d'ascètes et de martyrs, le visage grave de l'implacable Juge du monde, du Pantocrator, sur une mosaïque immense qui occupe toute la coupole, rendaient les fidèles conscients de leur propre insignifiance et renforçaient leur sentiment d'humilité et de piété. Celui qui venait prier, parce que le mystère angoissant de l'au-delà l'affligeait, voyait la famille princière qui avançait vers le Christ et, au-dessus de cette scène, sur les tribunes il pouvait également admirer le monarque lui-même et son entourage. Les multiples impressions visuelles et vocales (la liturgie) accroissaient les émotions spirituelles et affermissaient la conviction que le pouvoir temporel était l'intermédiaire du pouvoir céleste. Les portraits du souverain et de sa famille personi-

---

[52] *Sbornik XII v.* ..., f. 60 (p. 88). Au sujet du diptyque à Byzance, cf. A. Michel, *Kaisermacht*..., pp. 88 - 99.

[53] Cf. A. Poppe, *Legenda o Borysie i Glebie* [*La légende sur Boris et Gleb*], dans: *Lexicon Antiquitatum Slavicarum*, vol. III, 1, Warszawa 1967, pp. 33 - 34. Le culte de «l'apôtre de la Russie» Vladimir Ier, dont le métropolite Hilarion et Iaroslav.le Sage avaient pris l'initiative, n'a pas abouti à sa canonisation ni au XIe ni au XIIe s. L'ascète Théodose du monastère des Grottes ayant été porté sur les autels (1091 - 1108), les boïars russes eurent leur représentant parmi les saints.

[54] Pour plus de détail et documentation iconographique voir: A. Poppe, *Kompozycja fundacyjna Sofii Kijowskiej. W poszukiwaniu układu pierwotnego* [*La composition votive de l'église Sainte Sophie de Kiev. A la recherche de la disposition primitive*], «Biuletyn Historii Sztuki», vol. XXX, 1968, 1, pp. 1 - 29, reconstr. il. 10.

fiaient l'idée qu'en Russie kiévienne le pouvoir temporel avait été confié à Iaroslav et à sa famille. Cette composition votive devait démontrer la légitimité du pouvoir de la dynastie dont le fondateur aurait pu être accusé d'usurpation.

La pensée politique qui se formait dans le milieu ecclésiastique de la Russie kiévienne et s'inspirait des idées byzantines et de sa propre réalité, accordait au prince un grand pouvoir dans les affaires de l'Église, veillant toutefois à ne pas amoindrir la responsabilité et le rôle des dirigeants canoniques de la hiérarchie spirituelle. En accordant aux princes des droits étendus, devant servir à renforcer la foi chrétienne et les lois divines, l'Église se réservait le droit et le devoir de servir le pouvoir laïc de ses conseils et se chargeait de veiller sur l'ordre moral, social et politique, un ordre conforme aux traditions de l'État et de la société chrétienne et à celles des coutumes locales qui n'étaient pas opposées à ses traditions.

Nicéphore accomplissait ces devoirs avec beaucoup de tact, sachant que l'efficacité de son enseignement dépendait complètement de la volonté de celui auquel il s'adressait. En recommandant à Monomaque de penser à ceux qui étaient condamnés à être expulsés ou jetés en prison, le métropolite lui demandait de ne pas croire que son intervention portait sur un cas concret, mais qu'il ne faisait qu'observer la coutume qui exige qu'à la veille de Carême «on dise quelque chose d'utile également aux princes». Après avoir traité longuement du salut de l'âme et des avantages qui en découlent, il a rappelé sa recommandation: «[...] n'oublie pas ceux que tu as jugés, répare si un homme a calomnié un autre homme et statue toi-même»[55]. Le métropolite Jean II s'est trouvé dans une situation assez embarrassante lorsqu'il a dû répondre au moine Jacob, celui-ci lui ayant demandé si la fille du prince pouvait être donnée en mariage dans un pays où on professe le rite romain? Le métropolite, respectueux de l'attitude prise par l'Église byzantine, a admis l'inoportunité des mariages mixtes de ce genre et il a constaté que «le plus noble des princes et le plus pieux par la grâce de Dieu et aussi le plus orthodoxe» devrait expier ce mariage (ἐκκλησιαστικῶς παιδευθήσεται). Bien qu'à Byzance l'Église pût imposer des pénitences à l'empereur lui-même, le traducteur russe a préféré éviter cette question délicate et il a traduit la réponse de Jean II de façon très générale, disant qu'une action de ce genre «n'est pas digne et ne sied pas à un orthodoxe»[56]. Les mariages avec les membres des dynasties de l'Europe occidentale étaient en Russie à l'ordre du jour et la hiérarchie ecclésiastique, même dans les cas où des moines trop zélés voulaient l'obliger à faire des déclarations orthodoxes, ne se hâtait pas d'intervenir, désireuse qu'elle était d'éviter tout conflit avec le souverain. Le clergé russe, surtout le clergé régulier, pouvait faire preuve de plus de courage. En 1073, Théodose, l'higoumène du monastère des Grottes, qui aurait peut-être voulu jouer le rôle de «maître des souverains», joué jadis par Théodore Studite auquel il vouait

---

[55] *Russkie dostopamjatnosti...*, vol. I, pp. 72 - 74.
[56] L. K. G ö t z, *Kirchenrechtliche...*, pp. 138 - 140.

une admiration particulière, tonnait dans ses discours et ses écrits contre le prince Sviatoslav parce qu'il «était monté illégalement sur ce trône [de Kiev] en chassant son frère aîné, comme s'il avait chassé son père». Dans son entretien avec le prince, il a justifié son attitude en disant: «Que peut notre colère contre ta puissance, mon Seigneur, mais nous avons le devoir de vous indiquer vos erreurs et de vous en parler pour sauver vos âmes et vous, vous avez le devoir d'écouter» [57].

Notons que, durant la seconde moitié du XIe siècle (pour la première moitié les données nous manquent), les milieux ecclésiastiques critiquaient presque exclusivement l'activité politique des princes. L'Église, et plus exactement le clergé russe (la hiérarchie grecque se tenait à l'écart de ces questions) défendait les coutumes légitimes selon lesquelles le trône de Kiev revenait au prince aîné. A partir des années 70 du XIe siècle, le monastère des Grottes devint le défenseur de la conception monarchique du pouvoir et donc aussi de l'unité de l'État russe. Les idées et opinions politiques du milieu ecclésiastique russe, surtout du milieu monastique, sur la légitimité du pouvoir du prince, idées et opinions qui ont été formulées sous l'influence de la situation politique à cette époque et proclamées pour servir d'avertissement à la classe dominante, sont exprimées le plus pleinement dans les oeuvres hagiographiques consacrées à Boris et à Gleb et aussi dans la *Chronique des temps passé*, rédigée au monastère des Grottes.

La canonisation et le culte de Boris et de Gleb avaient avant tout un caractère politique. Les fils cadets de Vladimir Ier avaient été tués, en 1015, quand leur frère aîné Sviatopolk, après la mort de son père, «tendait à prendre tout le pouvoir en main». Boris et Gleb ont subi le martyre parce qu'ils étaient fidèles au droit d'aînesse et qu'ils avaient fait preuve d'une humilité sans bornes à l'égard de leur frère aîné qu'ils voulaient avoir «pour père et seigneur». Devant choisir entre l'opposition ou la mort, ils ont choisi cette dernière, et ils sont morts en martyrs, mais ce n'était pas pour attester leur foi, mais pour ne pas trahir leurs idéaux politiques [58].

Le culte des deux princes martyrs, que leur hagiographe compare à une épée à double tranchant, devait remplir une double fonction: protéger les terres russes contre les païens et les sauver des luttes entre les princes. Les teneurs idéologiques du culte devaient donc servir à consolider l'État, à l'intérieur et à l'extérieur. L'initiative et la propagation de ce culte revenaient au clergé russe, ce qui témoigne de sa maturité politique. L'Église ne pouvait encore se passer de l'aide de l'État, mais l'État, lui aussi, avait déjà la possibilité d'apprécier de mieux

---

[57] *Sbornik XII v.* ..., f. 58 - 59 *v.* (pp. 85- 88). En ce qui concerne le devoir moral de la hiérarchie de prévenir l'empereur, et de lui donner des conseils, voir A. Michel, *Kaisermacht...*, pp. 144 et suiv. et 185 et suiv.

[58] L'Église condamnait sévèrement toute action dirigée contre l'oint. Mais elle acceptait en général *post factum* les dérogations à ce principe. Cf. A. Michel, *Kaisermacht...*, pp. 135 - 138. Cf. F. Kern, *Gottesgnadentum und Widerstandsrecht im frühen Mittelalter*, 3 éd. Darmstadt 1962, pp. 175 et suiv., 350 - 354; S. Russocki, *Opór wladcom i prawo oporu u Słowian w wiekach średnich*, «Czasopismo Prawno-Historyczne», vol. XX, 1968, n° 1, pp. 17- 52.

en mieux l'appui idéologique de l'Église. Cet appui était d'ailleurs fort élastique et adaptait le choix des arguments aux besoins politiques du moment donné. Très instructive à ce propos nous paraît la comparaison de deux oeuvres hagiographiques consacrées à Boris et à Gleb.

La première version, intitulée *Récit du martyre et louange des saints martyrs Boris et Gleb* date des préparatifs de la canonisation des deux frères, donc d'avant le 20 mai 1072, c'est-à-dire de la période où Iziaslav revint à Kiev après un séjour en Pologne (1068/1069). Comme il était l'aîné, il occupa la première place, mais il était évident que tous les trois fils de Iaroslav étaient alors plus que jamais responsables de l'État russe. L'auteur anonyme de ce *Récit*, qui l'écrivait au moment où les trois princes établissaient les principes de leur coexistence politique et d'un pouvoir commun, cet auteur, fidèle au principe du droit d'aînesse, mais conscient des conséquences de l'attitude injuste que l'aîné avait prise à l'égard de Vsieslav de Polotsk, recommanda non seulement la subordination des cadets à l'aîné, mais aussi une attitude juste de l'aîné à l'égard de ses frères cadets. Boris et Gleb sont le symbole de l'obéissance, mais il y a des limites à l'injustice; Iaroslav avait le droit de s'opposer à la tyrannie de l'aîné. Lorsque Iziaslav exigeait que ses frères lui obéissent, il pouvait se référer à l'exemple de leurs oncles, et lorsque Sviatoslav, à son tour, chassa Iziaslav du trône de Kiev, en mars 1073, il put rappeler l'exemple de son père qui avait écarté Sviatopolk et restauré un gouvernement juste. C'est à cette double signification politique que le culte de Boris et de Gleb devait sa vitalité au temps du morcellement du pays.

Après que l'autocrate Vsievolod eut pris le pouvoir en 1078, il fallut apporter des retouches aux idées exprimées dans le *Récit*. Vers 1080, Nestor, un moine du monastère des Grottes, écrivit à nouveau la biographie des saints frères. Il avait l'intention de baser son oeuvre sur les modèles recommandés dans l' hagiographie byzantine, mais il visait aussi un autre but politique. Il dirigeait le tranchant des préceptes moraux contre les rébellions des princes cadets, exigeant qu'ils obéissent inconditionnellement à l'aîné. Bien qu'il connût le *Récit* et l'eût mis à profit, il n'attira l'attention que sur le droit d'aînesse, menaçant de mort les princes rebelles. En leur posant en exemple les saints princes, il faisait ressortir que Boris et Gleb n'auraient pu être canonisés s'ils s'étaient opposés à leur frère aîné. Nestor passe sous silence le droit des princes cadets de s'opposer à l'injustice du prince-seigneur, en interprétant très adroitement l'action de Iaroslav. D'après lui, ce dernier ne serait monté sur le trône de Kiev que lorsque Sviatopolk, chassé par la «révolte des gens», avait péri [59].

---

[59] Cf. les deux textes dans l'édition citée de D. Abramovič, pp. 1 - 51; cf. D. S. Lihačev, *Nekotoryje voprosy ideologii feodalov v literature XI - XIII vekov*, «Trudy otdela drevnerusskoj literatury», vol. X, 1954, pp. 87 - 91; A. Poppe, *Predanie o Borisie i Glebie v drevnerusskoj pis'mennosti XI-načala XII v.*, «Slavianskaja Filologia», vol. VIII, Literaturoznanie, Sofia 1966, pp. 55-57; le même auteur, *Chronologia utworów Nestora — hagiografa [La chronologie des oeuvres de Nestor — hagiographe]*, «Slavia Orientalis», vol. XIV, 1965, n° 3, pp. 291, 297 - 305.

La *Chronique des temps passés* montre que le monastère des Grottes a conti-
nué, durant les décennies suivantes, à recommander l'obéissance absolue au
souverain. Le moine-chroniqueur partait du principe providentiel d'après lequel
«Dieu donne le pouvoir à qui il veut» et qu'un pouvoir injuste est une pénitence
infligée pour les péchés. Il ne jugeait le souverain — qui n'était responsable
que devant Dieu — que du point de vue moral et, ce qui est essentiel, il élargis-
sait la notion du prince injuste. Le prince injuste est aussi un prince qui écoute
les conseils des «conseillers mauvais et insensés». Dans cette critique perce le
mécontentement de l'aristocratie aborigène de Kiev, dont la participation au
pouvoir était déjà bien limitée au déclin du règne de Vsievolod et qui n'exerça
aucune influence sur ce pouvoir à partir du moment où Sviatopolk II monta
sur le trône de Kiev en 1093. Une pensée énoncée ici mérite cependant, de notre
part, une attention particulière: les princes étaient personnellement responsables devant Dieu des conséquences nuisibles pour le pays que pouvaient avoir
les conseils donnés par de «mauvais conseillers» et l'activité injuste des fonctionnaires, car ils ne sont que les mandataires du souverain. A la lumière de ce qui précède, les paroles «Fais que les boïars soient des sages», paroles qui se trouvent
dans la prière d'Hilarion pour la prospérité des terres russes, acquièrent un
sens plus profond [60]. Sans parler plus longuement de la *Chronique des temps
passés* [61], il convient cependant de faire ressortir qu'elle reflète — de même que
d'autres oeuvres de la littérature russe de cette époque — une tendance conséquente à renforcer l'autorité du pouvoir laïc. Cette littérature, bien quelle soit
pauvre en détails, brosse cependant un tableau réel de l'activité de l'Église qui
lui valait l'autorité morale qui était la sienne. Cette autorité, elle en jouissait
avant tout dans le milieu dont elle dépendait et dont elle tenait particulièrement
à gagner la faveur.

*

*   *

L'orientation nationale de l'Église russe s'est cristalisée déjà au XIᵉ siècle.
La métropole, malgré son caractère grec, n'a pas empéché l'Église russe de devenir une partie intégrante d'un État souverain, mais l'a aidée de son expérience.
La connexité unissant l'Église russe à l'Église byzantine se renforça au cours
du siècle non seulement à cause des rapports entre les institutions, mais plutôt
grâce aux liens idéologiques de plus en plus étroits qui unissaient les mouvements

---

[60] *PVL*, vol. I, pp. 95, 98, 132 - 133, 142 - 143; *Des Metropoliten Ilarion Lobrede...*, p. 139·
Cf. *Russkie dostopamjatnosti...*, vol. I, pp. 67 - 68; V. E. Valdenberg, *Poniatije o tirane v drevnerusskoj literature v sravnenii s zapadnoj*, «Izvestia po russkomu jazyku i slovesnosti», vol. II, 1929,
pp. 214 - 236; du même auteur, *Drevnerusskie učenia...*, pp. 108 - 112; S. A. Korf, *Zametka
ob otnošeniah drevnerusskogo letopisca k monarhičeskomu principu*, «Žurnal Ministerstva Narodnogo Prosveščenia», nov. ser. vol. XXII, 1909, nᵒ 7, pp. 50 - 71.
[61] A ce sujet cf. récemment M. Hellmann, *Das Herscherbild in der ѕogenannten Nestorchronik*, dans: *Speculum historiale*, München 1967, pp. 224 - 236.

monastiques russes et byzantins. Ce sont précisément ces liens qui ont décidé de la fidélité de la Russie envers l'orthodoxie sous sa forme byzantine. La métropole de Kiev dépendait du point de vue canonique et juridique de Hagia Sofia. Cette dépendance, qui au début avait été définie par l'entente entre les deux souverains, acquit après cent ans un fondement idéologique, probablement par l'intermédiaire du monastère russe de la Mère de Dieu à Athos. La légende de l'apôtre André, enrichie de nouveaux épisodes, proclamait qu'après avoir fondé le siège épiscopal à Byzantion sur le Bosphore, l'apôtre, en suivant les bords de la mer Noire, arriva en Russie et planta une croix au lieu même sur lequel Kiev devait naître. On trouva donc une raison excellente pour justifier la prééminence du successeur de l'apôtre André, le patriarche de Constantinople, sur l'Église russe [62].

L'Église dépendait du patriarche de Constantinople mais cela n'amoindrissait nullement la souveraineté du prince russe, les rapports entre l'Empire et la Russie étant définis par la situation politique. Dans l'histoire de Byzance, il y avait en effet des périodes de paix avec le monde arabe où, forts de l'autorisation du calife, l'empereur, le patriarche et son synode exerçaient leur influence sur la nomination des patriarches de Jérusalem et d'Alexandrie [63]. Dans ces cas, la nomination de leurs propres candidats dépassait les compétences canoniques et témoignait, d'une part, de la bonne volonté des califes et, d'autre part, de l'autorité dont jouissait Constantinople en tant que centre de l'orthodoxie. A Byzance même, les Églises d'Antioche, de Chypre et de Bulgarie étaient en effet indépendantes du patriarche de Constantinople en ce qui concerne les questions canoniques et juridiques, mais elles dépendaient davantage de l'empereur lui-même. La subordination de la métropole de Kiev en tant que province ecclésiastique du siège patriarcal de Constantinople était le résultat d'une entente politique, mais elle n'existait que sur le plan religieux, sanctionnée qu'elle était par les canons et les traditions de l'Église. La liaison entre les Églises favorisait une collaboration étroite dans d'autres domaines. L'Empire, qui était continuellement attaqué par ses ennemis, avait intérêt à s'assurer l'aide militaire de la Kiévie et à établir des contacts commerciaux. L'intérêt que Byzance suscitait en Russie kiévienne était plus multiforme et consistait, avant tout, à s'assimiler sa culture et ses idées, dont la propagation n'était pas due à la force d'expansion immanente de la civilisation byzantine, mais à la recherche de stimulants pouvant faciliter aux bâtisseurs de l'État russe la solution des problèmes qu'ils devaient envisager.

---

[62] *PVL*, vol. I, p. 12. Il me semble que c'est un malentendu que d'attribuer une tendance antibyzantine à la version russe de la légende relative à l'apôtre André. Cf. A. Pogodin, *Povest' o hoždenii apostola Andreja v Rusi*, «Byzantino-Slavica», vol. VII, 1937/1938, pp. 128 - 148 où la littérature précédente est également indiquée; F. Dvornik (*The Idea of Apostolicity in Byzantium and the Legend of the Apostole Andrew*, Cambridge Mass 1958) n'a pas, hélas, porté attention à la version russe.

[63] Cf. Beck, *Kirche...*, pp. 93 - 94, 98; cf. p. ex. le traité de 1027 au sujet de Jérusalem, F. Dölger, *Regesten der Kaiserurkunden des oströmischen Reiches*, vol. II, München 1925, m n° 824.

En Kiévie, la couche dominante, d'origine ethnique diverse, mais rapidement assimilée dans le milieu slave dont la conscience nationale était clairement formulée, avait pris l'habitude de vastes contacts internationaux. Elle était libre de cette étroitesse de vues que les adeptes d'origine aborigène de la civilisation russe étaient disposés à lui attribuer. Entreprenants et persévérants, les bâtisseurs de cet État multinational, ne se sont pas cantonnés dans leur propre acquis, ce qui les aurait menacés de stagnation et d'obscurantisme. Ce n'est pas l'activité des Romains orgueilleux, mais l'initiative de la couche dominante, l'initiative des princes, des boïars, de la družina, du clergé et des marchands qui a entraîné la Russie dans le courant de la civilisation byzantine. Il convient donc de citer ici un principe rappelé récemment à l'attention des historiens: «[...]ce n'est pas celui qui exerce son influence qui est actif, mais celui qui subit cette influence [..] La réception — pour employer le langage des scolastiques — s'effectue toujours *modo recipientis*» [64].

Après cent ans d'activité en Russie kiévienne, l'Église n'était pas encore une force politique indépendante. Son aptitude à identifier ses propres intérêts avec les intérêts de l'État a fait de l'Église une partie inhérente de la structure de l'État. Les affaires de l'Église n'étaient qu'une des nombreuses tâches qui incombaient au prince. Ces affaires méritaient cependant son attention particulière. En tant que protecteur de l'Église, il exerçait le pouvoir en frayant la voie à un nouvel ordre idéologique. Malgré cela, au déclin de la période en question, la plus grande partie de la société ne subissait pas encore l'influence de l'Église. La nouvelle religion remportait des succès — mais pas encore la victoire — parmi la population des centres urbains. Ce sont les besoins de la christianisation de la classe dominante qui ont absorbé les principales forces de l'Église. C'est en formant l'attitude idéologique de cette classe et en la rendant consciente du bien-fondé de la mission de l'Église que l'on a établi les fondements des succès que l'Église devait remporter en Russie au cours des siècles suivants.

(Traduit par Janina Kasińska)

---

[64] Cf. A. Gieysztor, *Kasztelanowie flandryjscy i polscy* [*Les châtelains en Flandre et en Pologne*], dans: *Studia historyczne. Księga jubileuszowa z okazji 70 rocznicy urodzin prof. dr S. Arnolda* [*Mélanges S. Arnold*], Warszawa 1965, p. 107. Cf. L. Kołakowski, *Jednostka i nieskończoność. Wolność i antynomia wolności w filozofii Spinozy* [*L'individu et l'infinité. La liberté et l'antinomie de la liberté dans la philosophie de Spinoza*], Warszawa 1958, p. 612.

THE RULERS OF KIEVAN RUSSIA (PRINCES OF KIEV)
from the mid-10th century until 1132
(Christian names in brackets if known)

1. IGOR', son of half-legendary Rjurik	?	–	ca.945
2. OLGA (Helena), Igor's widow	ca.945	–	ca.960
3. SVJATOSLAV, son of Igor' and Olga	ca.960	–	spring 972
4. JAROPOLK, son of Svjatoslav	972	–	980
5. VLADIMIR (Basil), son of Svjatoslav	980	–	15 July 1015
6. SVJATOPOLK, son of Vladimir, and the struggle for the throne of Kiev	1015	–	1019
7. JAROSLAV (George), son of Vladimir	1019	–	24 Feb. 1054
8. IZJASLAV (Demetrios), son of Jaroslav	1054	–	15 Sep. 1068
9. VSESLAV, son of Brjačeslav, great-grandson of Vladimir, prince of Polotsk	15 Sep. 1068	–	April 1069
10. IZJASLAV (for the second time)	2 May 1069	–	March 1073
11. SVJATOSLAV (Nicolas), son of Jaroslav	22 Mar. 1073	–	27 Dec. 1076
12. VSEVOLOD (Andrew), son of Jaroslav	1 Jan. 1077	–	July 1077
13. IZJASLAV (for the third time)	15 July 1077	–	3 Oct. 1078
14. VSEVOLOD (for the second time)	Oct. 1078	–	13 Apr. 1093
15. SVJATOPOLK (Michael), son of Izjaslav	24 Apr. 1093	–	16 Apr. 1113
16. VLADIMIR (Basil) Monomach, son of Vsevolod	20 Apr. 1113	–	19 May 1125
17. MSTISLAV (Theodore), son of Vladimir	20 May 1125	–	15 Apr. 1132

THE METROPOLITANS OF KIEV

1. THEOPHYLACT	988	–	before 1018
2. JOHN I	before 1018	–	ca. 1030
3. THEOPEMPTOS	ca. 1035	–	till 1040's
4. HILARION	1051	–	ca.1053/54
5. EPHRAIM	1054/55	–	ca. 1065
6. GEORGE	ca. 1065	–	ca. 1076
7. JOHN II PRODROMOS	1076/77	–	after Aug 1089
8. JOHN III	summer 1090	–	before 14 Aug.1091
9. NICOLAS	ca. 1093	–	before 1104
10. NICEPHOROS	Dec. 1104	–	April 1121
11. NICETAS	autumn 1122	–	9 March 1126
12. MICHAEL	summer 1130	–	1145

THE ORGANISATION OF THE RUS'IAN CHURCH
as a province of the Constantinopolitan patriarchate, from
its foundation in 988 to 1134, under the metropolitanate of
Kiev with its Archcathedral of St. Sophia

SUFFRAGAN BISHOPRICS:

residence	founded	cathedral	remarks
1. BELGOROD	988	Holy Apostles	Prototronos of metropolitan
2. NOVGOROD	988/990	St. Sophia	
3. ČERNIGOV	988	Transfiguration of Saviour	After 1060 till ca.1085 titular metropolitanate
4. POLOTSK	988 or 1015-1024	St. Sophia	
5. PEREJASLAV	988 or after 1036	Archangel Michael	After 1072 till ca. 1100 titular metropolitanate
6. YUREV on the Ros'	after 1036	St.George	
7. ROSTOV	1073-1076	the Dormition of the Virgin	Vacant from ca. 1093, administered till ca. 1134 from Perejaslav
8. VLADIMIR in Volynia	1078-1085	the Dormition of the Virgin	
9. TUROV	ca.1088	the Dormition of the Virgin	
10. SMOLENSK	1134-1136	the Dormition of the Virgin	Previously part of the eparchy of Perejaslav

INDEX

VIII 181,182,194,209,210;
IX 102,103,116
-Izbornik 1073 of: VI 43;
IX 109 n.35
Svjatoslav,son of Oleg,
prince: VI 45 n.58
Svjatoslav,son of Vseslav
of Polotsk,prince: VI 44
symbolism of church domes:
IV 23,55 nn.45-46
Synaxarion,armenian: VI
36 n.34,53 n.84
-of Sugdaea: VI 53 n.84
synodos endemousa: III 44;
V 13

Tale of the beginnings of
Caves monastery: V 6
Tale of the Destruction of
the Russian Land: I 348 n.41
Tauroscythians: II 211,214,244
Terebovl': VIII 214
Thebes: III 22
Theoctistus,abbot of Caves
monastery: V 22
Theodora,empress: II 234
n.128; V 14
Theodore Balsamon: III 27
n.70,32; V 13
Theodore of Sebaste,
metropolitan: II 204; III
27,28,30,31
Theodore,bishop of Novgorod:
VIII 175,208
Theodore Prodromus: V 25
Theodore the Studite: V 15,
16,21
Theodosius,St.,abbot of Caves
monastery: I 343; II 209
n.50; IV 57 n.67,61 n.106;
V 18; VIII 191; IX 103,
113,114
-cult of: VIII 190
-relics of: VIII 190
-Life of: IV 20,21,61 n.107;
VI 31; IX 113
Theodosius the Greek,abbot:
II 209 n.50
Theopemptus,metropolitan of
Kiev: III 11,27 n.69,
43,44; V 5,18,30; VI 30
n.4,47
Theophano,empress: II 200
n.10,216,230 n.114,231,
233,234,235
Theophylact of Sebaste,
metropolitan of Kiev: I
345 n.34,351 n.47; II 204,

205,225,228; III 27-29,
30,31,33,34,35; VII 526
Theophylact,archbishop of
Ohrid: VII 511,520
Theotokos,patroness of Kiev:
IV 26
Thietmar of Merseburg: I 338
n.10; II 202,224 n.93, 230
n.114; III 9,13,17,39; IV
16,18,19,28,51,52 nn.10-11,
53 n.21; IX 102
-chronicle of: VI 29
Thrace: II 215
Tmutarakan': II 199,209; III
14,15,17,18,19 n.36; VI 43,
53 n.85; VIII 209; IX 102
-diocese of: VIII 166
Trajan's Gate,battle of:
II 205,224
Treaties,russo-byzantine
-of 911: I 339
-of 944: I 339; II 239
-of 971: II 222 n.87
Treatise on the metropolitan
prerogatives,anonymous: V 19
Turks,Uzes: VIII 182,186
Turov: IV 26; VI 42; VIII 190,
191,192,214
-diocese of: VIII 166,169,
197-201,211
-church of the Dormition:
VIII 201,212
Tyropoion (Jeros),fortress:
II 226

Ugrovsk: VIII 215
Uvetyče: IX 104

Vaclav,St.Life of: VI
32 nn.14 & 17
Varangians: II 229
Vasil'ev: II 208
Vasil'ko, son of George
Dolgoruky,prince: VIII 204
Vasil'ko, son of Rostislav,
prince: VI 44; IX 103,
105,106
Vjačeslav,son of Jaroslav I:
IV 41; VI 43 n.52; VIII 190
Vladimir I,prince: I 336,337,
339,340,354; II 197-202,
203 n.26,205,207-209,211,
212,215,217,221,224,227-231,
238,240,241-243; III 5-10,
15,18,35,37,38,39 n.96,41,
43; IV 16,18,19,22-29,52
n.10,54 n.36,55 nn.39,48
& 50; V 22; VI 29,38-40,